LABOR
IN A GROWING ECONOMY

LABOR

JOHN WILEY & SONS INC., NEW YORK

Chapman & Hall, Limited, London

IN A GROWING ECONOMY

MELVIN W. REDER

Professor of Economics
Stanford University

In Memory of Frank Reder,
my father,
and
Lloyd H. Fisher,
my colleague and friend.

Preface

This is a textbook designed for a one-semester undergraduate course in labor economics as given in an economics department or school of business administration. As such it is, in a sense, an amalgam of two books: one on unions and industrial relations and another on wages, income distribution, labor mobility, etc. Therefore, the reader will perceive a difference in emphasis in Part II, which deals with industrial relations, from that in Parts III and IV, which deals with "labor economics." Because of this, it is possible to proceed directly from Part I (which serves as a general introduction) to Parts III and IV, or to study the chapters in order. I have tried both procedures and found that each has its advantages, and correlative drawbacks.

However, the various parts of the book are not disconnected. Apart from rather numerous cross-references, they are unified by the fact that both the institutions and the economics of labor are studied as parts of a growing economy. The emphasis upon economic growth pervades not only the two introductory chapters, but also the discussion of union institutions and wage determination.

In keeping with this emphasis, I have devoted considerably more than the customary amount of space (Chapters 3 and 4) to the history of the labor movement. This has several advantages: it enables the instructor to describe various features of union organization in an historical context (i.e., as a response to certain concrete problems). By so doing, the merger of AFL-CIO can be seen as an integral, and understandable, development of American labor history. Furthermore, it makes it possible to discuss certain topics (e.g., unions in politics and Communists in unions) in relation to other material with which they are closely related, and not as separate subjects. Because of this method of treatment, it has not been necessary to include a separate chapter on the role of unions in politics.

In the course of writing this book, I have been asked by the publisher (and other interested parties) about the distribution of space between "institutional" and "theoretical" material. I am proud to say that I do not think the question can be answered. It has been my endeavor, in all chapters of the book, to interweave theoretical and descriptive materials so that they are inseparable. If the book could be said to have a motto, it would be: "No theories without facts, no descriptions without explanations."

This attitude can be most clearly observed in Part III. In the first three chapters of this section (Chapters 11, 12, and 13), I attempt to develop the theory of wage determination in the labor market and explain how unions enter into this process. However, the theory is deliberately kept at a low level of abstraction, and it is specifically designed to enable the reader to understand the discussions of wage structure (regional, industrial, and occupational) that follow in Chapters 14 and 15.

The chapters on wage theory were, by far, the most difficult to write. Indeed, Parts III and IV are a very substantially modified version of an earlier draft that I found, both from complaints of students and comments of professional colleagues, to be "too abstract." Part of the difficulty involved the role of marginal productivity. When developed thoroughly and carefully, this is a beautiful theory, but one that unfortunately is not *directly* applicable to labor-market phenomena. The difficulties lie mainly in connection with changes in employer hiring policy (discussed in Chapters 11, 12, and 13) that make it difficult to define and use the concept of a "factor of production" that marginal productivity analysis requires. These difficulties can, to a great extent, be overcome—or evaded—and, in the earlier draft, I endeavored to show how. But this involved a long analytical argument, not readily appreciated by an undergraduate, and not really necessary for a workable understanding of labor markets and wage structure. In rewriting these chapters, I have carefully eschewed any attempt at reconciling the analysis of labor-market phenomena with conventional economic theory.[1]

As things stand, the reader is given a brief introduction to marginal productivity theory (pp. 308–314), enough to understand what is it about, but not so much as to distract him from the main business of understanding the functioning of labor markets. The subsequent argument does not make explicit use of marginal analysis, and so there is no need for further development of the theory here. However, the instructor who wishes to use marginal analysis explicitly, can easily do so by supplementing the brief discussion in the text with lectures or reading assignments in any of a number of textbooks in economic theory.

[1] The reader who may happen to be interested in my views on these matters will find them set forth in "Wage Setting in Theory and Practice," to be published as part of *A Survey of Industrial Relations Research,* Vol. I. (Industrial Relations Research Association volume for 1957.)

Chapter 16, which deals with the general level of wages (as distinguished from wage structure) also presented some problems with regard to the role of "pure theory." Here, too, I have introduced only the minimum necessary for understanding the specific phenomena with which the chapter deals.

In writing this book, I have received the assistance of a number of persons. At one time or another most of my colleagues at Stanford have helped me by discussing difficult points, and many of my ideas on labor were formed in the intellectual melting-pot of the Institute of Industrial Relations at the University of California (Berkeley). Its former Director (now Chancellor) Clark Kerr gave me the benefit of a rare combination of friendship, inspiration, and instruction for which I shall ever be grateful. He also took the time to read and helpfully criticize a first draft of the manuscript. Professors Kenneth Boulding and Walter Galenson also read the first draft and made a great many careful—and painful—suggestions, many of which I have accepted. They have earned both my thanks and the reader's.

I am painfully reminded of the fact that books are long, but life is short, by the loss of two persons who—in different ways—contributed much to whatever merit this book possesses. Lloyd H. Fisher, who had kindly agreed to criticize the manuscript, died before a first draft was written. Nonetheless the book bears the stamp of his mind in more ways than I can possibly enumerate. My intellectual indebtedness to him, like any really heavy debt of this kind, cannot be specified; it can only be acknowledged. My father, who died last spring, made many contributions to my work, but they were of the personal sort that cannot even be indicated to others. It is to them that this book is dedicated.

To anyone who has written a book, and is married, it is hardly necessary to mention that the pain cost of composition is shared by wife and children. Mine have put up with more than their share of mental absence through preoccupation, and general paternal disinterest, because of what they have learned to call the "damn book." I hope they will one day feel that my preoccupation was not entirely fruitless.

Melvin W. Reder
Palo Alto, California

June, 1957

Contents

Part I   Introduction   1

    1   LABOR AND ITS PROBLEMS   3

    2   THE LABOR FORCE AND AMERICAN ECONOMIC
           DEVELOPMENT   15

Part II   Unions and Collective Bargaining   26

    3   THE GROWTH OF AMERICAN UNIONISM.
           I: ORGANIZATION   29

    4   THE GROWTH OF AMERICAN UNIONISM.
           II: PURPOSE, PHILOSOPHY, AND POLITICS   87

    5   THE STRUCTURE AND GOVERNMENT OF UNIONS   112

    6   THE PROCESS OF COLLECTIVE BARGAINING   143

    7   THE SUBJECT MATTER OF COLLECTIVE
           BARGAINING   174

    8   LABOR UNIONS AND THE LAW   203

    9   THE TAFT-HARTLEY (LABOR-MANAGEMENT
           RELATIONS) ACT OF 1947   227

   10   GOVERNMENT AND STRIKE CONTROL   259

Part III   Employment, Wages, and Income   279

   11   THE WAGE EARNER AND THE SUPPLY OF LABOR   283

   12   THE EMPLOYER AND THE DEMAND FOR LABOR   302

CONTENTS

13 THE LABOR MARKET AND THE UNION   320

14 WAGE DIFFERENTIALS: THE STRUCTURE OF WAGES
IN THE UNITED STATES   357

15 WAGE SETTING WITHIN THE FIRM: JOB
EVALUATION AND INCENTIVE SYSTEMS   377

16 WAGES, EMPLOYMENT AND LABOR'S SHARE   400

17 THE PROBLEM OF EMPLOYMENT   431

Part IV   The War on Poverty   446

18 THE CAUSES OF INCOME INEQUALITY   447

19 SOCIAL SECURITY   470

20 THE GOVERNMENT AS WAGE SETTER   496

Part V   The Role of the Union in Modern Society:
An Appraisal   517

Index   523

PART ONE

Introduction

1 Labor and Its Problems

Labor problems in a modern economy arise in connection with the employment of wage earners; the principal concern of this book is with the economic aspects of these problems. In this chapter we will survey, in a preliminary way, some of the more important labor problems. This survey will serve as an introduction to the more detailed discussions in later chapters.

LABOR: A DEFINITION

Definitions are both arbitrary and boring, but they are necessary to coherent discourse. Therefore, let us define the term "labor." By labor we mean (roughly) all persons working for wages or salaries who belong to a family whose income was derived primarily (80% or more) from wages or salaries and was in 1954, less than (say) $7000. That is, we would not include high salary earners in "labor"; nor would we include low earning women whose husbands received a large income; nor persons with large amounts of property income, irrespective of their wages.

Obviously our income limitation of $7000 per year is arbitrary; probably it will "trap" some persons in labor whom we would not want there, and vice versa. However, the above characteristics, taken together, do distinguish those persons we usually think of as "labor." They have relatively low incomes and are employed—and supervised—by others. They may be manual or white-collar workers; they may supervise (e.g., foremen) as well as be supervised, but they may not be "rich"; their income must derive mainly from their own work and/or that of some other family member, i.e., their income from capital (if any) must be small. They may be part-time or full-time earners, but they must earn wages or salaries; full-time housewives do not count in this definition.

The group of people designated as labor cannot be precisely measured, but it would include the great bulk of the nation's 50 odd million wage

3

and salary earners. For certain purposes we shall not want to include all of the above persons in "labor"; for others, we may wish to include some persons excluded by the above definition. However, the definition should serve to indicate to the reader who we mean by labor.

LABOR PROBLEMS: THE ECONOMIC ASPECT

Labor problems obviously have psychological, political, and sociological aspects (as well as economic), and, from time to time, we shall have occasion to consider them. However, our primary focus will be on the economic aspect of the subject matter. This focus is a matter of conscious choice, but the choice made does not imply a depreciation of other aspects of the subject; valuable studies of labor problems can and have been made from the viewpoints of other social sciences.

To a considerable extent, labor problems involve conflict between the employer and the wage earner. Conflict arises because, among other things, the employer and his employees jointly produce a product for sale, but each wants as much of the proceeds as he can get. The resulting conflict about the division of the dollar proceeds takes the form of bickering about the wages and other perquisites the employer is to pay the wage earner as a condition of the wage earner "working for" the employer; this conflict is popularly viewed as a conflict between "wages" and "profits."

Wages and Profits: the Conflict

From the point of view of the employer, wages are a share of the sale proceeds of the output of his business. He pays wages to his workers in exchange for their assistance in the firm's production. The employer owns the firm's product and has sole title to the proceeds derived from selling it. He assumes the risk of hiring and paying workers and of providing raw materials, capital equipment, etc., in advance of the emergence of the saleable product. The difference between the money the employer receives for selling a particular collection of articles and what he spends in the process of getting them produced and sold is, of course, the source of his profit or loss.

Despite a great many qualifications that we shall have to make, it is nonetheless true that virtually all employers want their profits to be "large"; many economists would say as large as possible. The obvious interest of employers in making profits "big" is in conflict with the equally obvious desire of the workers to get as large a wage as possible. What goes to wages *might* have otherwise gone to profits, and vice versa. Now it must not be supposed that the relations between workers and employers are simply one long battle over the division of the receipts from which wages, profits, and other income shares must come. As we shall see, wage earners and their employers have many interests in common. But, nevertheless, there is this basic difference of economic interest which conditions all worker-employer relations.

WAGES AND EFFORT. One important facet of the conflict between wages and profits relates to the issue of what a worker should do for his wages. Wages are often said to be a "payment for labor services," but how do we measure "labor services"? If a man is hired for (say) a week, his wage will be a perfectly definite amount (e.g., $75) determined in advance; usually, the employer is legally bound to pay this wage. But the employer is not (legally) entitled to anything in exchange for the wages other than a certain amount of the worker's time. The agreement between employer and employee (whether written or not) usually specifies the employee's compensation and the number of hours to be worked, but often it does not state how hard the employee is to work or how much he is to do. After hiring a worker, an employer must then "get the work out of him." To do this the employer or his representative (e.g., a foreman) must supervise workers to see that they perform satisfactorily.

This is the source of a whole host of "labor problems"; there is the question of how "hard" an employee should work and the related one of how much work he should turn out per hour or per day. There is the issue of how much authority to discipline unsatisfactory workers should be given to the foreman, what "work rules" should be promulgated, what provision should be made for the expression and adjustment of employee complaints concerning working conditions; etc.

The above remarks refer to those situations (which are the most common) where wages are paid on a "time basis," so much per hour, per day, etc. However, in order to give the worker an incentive to perform efficiently, employers quite frequently[1] pay wages on the basis of so much for each unit of output produced; this method of payment has been variously referred to as a "piece-rate" system, an "incentive" system, etc. The advantages of such systems to the employer are that they assure him a more or less definite amount of product in exchange for his wage dollar. By giving the worker an incentive to work efficiently (and by reducing the employer's concern with his efficiency), paying on the basis of output may serve to keep down the expenses of supervising workers. However, incentive systems are not always applicable, and even where they are they have disadvantages, both to employer and worker, that often outweigh their good features. As this subject is considered later (pp. 388–399) it need not be pursued here.

[1] According to a sample survey of the Bureau of Labor Statistics, approximately 30 per cent of all plant workers in manufacturing were on an incentive basis. U. S. Bureau of Labor Statistics, "Supplementary Wage Practices in American Industry, 1945–1946," *Bulletin* 939, Washington, 1948, p. 5. See below, pp. 388–399.

The power of discharge is probably the most powerful instrument for securing industry and efficiency in the employer's possession. Fear of discharge is a spur that keeps employees anxious to work sufficiently well to induce the employer to retain them. (The employment relation is, *legally,* a purely temporary one which may be terminated—by either party—at the expiration of the usually short "hiring period," typically a day or a week.[2]) However, fear of layoff is not the only reason why (most) workers try to do a "good job." Workers often take a sense of pride in their work and sometimes feel a genuine loyalty to the employer; and employers often feel paternal benevolence toward their employees (especially those of long tenure) and take pride in treating them well.

But although most workers would concede that they owe the employer a "fair day's work," and most employers would grant that they ought (and insist that they do) give their employees a "fair day's pay," it is inevitable that they should often disagree on the interpretation of these terms. The workmen's view of what constitutes a "fair day's work" will usually imply less output than an employer's; while an employer's concept of a "fair day's pay" is likely to be somewhat less than a workingman's. This should not occasion surprise; it reflects the very natural tendency for persons to espouse their own claims in the event of a conflict of interests and to justify those claims, both to the world at large and to themselves, as being "fair" and "just." It would be very difficult to understand the long and continuing history of disputes about wages and working conditions except on the hypothesis that workmen want to be paid more and/or work less than their employers think necessary.

The Employment Relation and Economic Security

The ability of the employer to discharge his workers implies, as a correlative, that the employees have no assurance of continued employment. The employer's freedom to discharge workers is an important disciplinary instrument, the threat of which can be used to spur workers to greater efforts and to punish those who fail to meet his minimum standards. But the freedom to discharge for any reason—or none—confers a great deal of power upon him that possesses it. This power is always feared and resented by workers, and they have made great efforts to curtail it.

The attempt of wage earners to protect themselves from arbitrary discharge is responsible for those provisions of collective agreements that make discharge a matter for adjudication by "grievance procedure" (see

[2] Collective bargaining introduces a number of limitations upon this legal freedom. See p. 159 et seq.

below, pp. 159–162). Such provisions occur quite frequently in present day union-management agreements. Indeed, the very existence of a grievance procedure is symptomatic of a modification of the traditional employer "freedom of arbitrary discharge." So long as an employer or foreman could say to a complaining workman, "if you don't like it here, you can find work elsewhere," there was no possibility of a worker getting a grievance redressed, except at the pleasure of the employer or his representatives. Indeed, the first order of business of a labor union in dealing with a newly unionized firm is to restrict the employer's freedom to discharge workers for belonging to the union.[3]

But fear either of arbitrary discharge or of discharge for "cause" (in either case someone is hired to replace the discharged worker) is not what the ordinary workingman has in mind when he worries about unemployment. What he fears is a reduction in the number of workers employed, a "layoff." Layoffs of large numbers of workers often occur simultaneously in whole industries, regions, and nations. When a large number of firms are all laying off workers at about the same time, it is obviously difficult for those who are laid off to find jobs with new employers. Consequently, large numbers of workers have, at times, been compelled either to live off their small savings and credit, or resort to the charity of relatives, private institutions, and government.

In other words the employment relation is such that, if adverse business conditions suggest to the employer that he might make a larger profit (or smaller loss) by reducing his work force and payroll expense, he is able to do so promptly and usually does.[4] But the wage earner's "costs of living" continue; he must provide for, at least, the minimum needs of himself and his family for food, shelter, and clothing. If he should have any outstanding debts, he may lose hard-won assets to satisfy his creditors.[5] To a wage earner, wages are income, and their cessation implies hardship to himself and his family. To his employer, wages are a cost which can be born only if the resulting output can be sold at a profit. We shall find many instances of social conflict rooted in this basic difference of viewpoint regarding wages.

[3] Such discharges were outlawed by the National Labor Relations Act of 1935 (commonly known as the "Wagner Act"); this provision of the Act has not been amended by subsequent legislation.

[4] This is not to depict employers as typically heartless or unconcerned with the well-being of their employees. However, the extent to which most employers can keep workers on the payroll (when they are unable to sell the output of these workers) is very limited. In certain foreign countries (e.g., Italy and Mexico) the freedom of layoff is appreciably less than in the United States.

[5] For example, if he has bought an automobile or furniture on the installment plan, he may lose his purchase and what he has already paid if he is unable to continue the payments.

Wage earners have attempted, in a number of ways, to gain security against unemployment caused by unfavorable business conditions. For example, at an early stage of their development, many trade unions were intimately connected with "mutual benefit associations" which sometimes paid unemployment benefits; some of the older unions are still affiliated with a mutual benefit society. Workmen have also sought a measure of security by demanding from their employers (through their unions) such things as severance pay, guaranteed annual wages, etc. In addition, they have attempted to restrict their employers' freedom to lay off men on the basis of ability (or other criteria they might choose to apply) and to compel them to lay off (and rehire) in reverse order of seniority, etc.

Wage earners may lose employment and income not only because of declines in business activity but also through personal misfortune. Accidents or illness can make a worker unemployable for a long period of time while simultaneously saddling him with heavy medical expenses. Consequently, employees (and their unions) have been greatly concerned with securing accident and health insurance and having it paid for (at least partly) by the employer and/or the government; they have also made efforts to secure similar provision for the retirement of elderly workers.

In short, as it developed in the 19th century, the "wage system" made the individual wage earner entirely responsible for maintaining himself and his family at all times. But wage earners have not been able to assume this burden when, for any reason, they were unemployed for an appreciable span of time. In consequence, they have sought to shift all or part of this burden to their employers, the government, or both. The story of their partially successful attempt to shift this burden, and their continuing efforts to achieve still greater provision for the unemployed or disabled wage earner, constitutes the subject matter of Chapter 19.

SOCIOLOGICAL ASPECTS

Labor Problems in Business and Family Producing Units: a Contrast

Most of the labor problems we have discussed would exist, to some extent, in any economic system. But the legal and customary relationships (i.e., the institutions) that guide the conduct of individuals toward one another greatly affect the form in which these problems present themselves. For example, in the "frontier economy" of the United States a century ago, most families had their own farms and lived off them. They did most of their own "manufacturing" and bought a bare minimum from others. On such a farm the labor was performed by the members of the family, with the father (usually) acting as director as well as helping with the chores. The problem of dividing up the product of the farm existed, but to a considerable extent the distribution was traditional and not subject to question. If issues arose they were family quarrels which, however bitter they might become, were very different from wage disputes. Questions of work-discipline, loafing on the job, etc., also existed, but they took the form of complaints against parental tyranny, or of protests that one brother was not doing his fair share of the family chores, or the like. They were not employee grievances against management.

The essential difference between "labor-management" relations on a family farm and those in a modern business enterprise employing wage labor arises from the fact that each member of the farm family has a fairly definite share in the common product of the farm depending upon his age, marital status, need, etc., and not upon what his services are worth in a market sense. He will not be cut off from the family, and his livelihood, because "business is bad," or because he is ill or incompetent, or for any other (economic) reason. On the other hand, the family member recognizes that he shares in the family's economic fate; if the family prospers, so will he; if it suffers adversity, he will partake of that. Consequently, the identification of group with self-interest reinforces the ties of family loyalty and parental discipline.

In a business enterprise, on the other hand, the employment relation is, as we have seen, typically dominated by the self-seeking of both parties. Wages and other perquisites are paid in *exchange* for work performed; they are not given because of concern for the worker's well-being or out of a feeling of paternal responsibility. And the worker's efforts are made not out of a sense of loyalty to the firm but in order to avoid being fired, or to earn more money under an incentive system, etc.

The above contrasts between the relationships among family members and those between employer and employee in a business enterprise is somewhat exaggerated, although it is not misleading. As we have already pointed out, there are many enterprises in which the employer takes a personal interest in the welfare of his workers. In such firms, pay raises and bonuses may be granted upon the arrival of a new child; the "boss" may pay the hospital bills of a sick or injured employee; he may refuse to discharge workers in the event of a decline in business activity; etc. In short, the boss may behave more like a father than an employer. In such situations workers sometimes, but not always (see below, pp. 313–314), respond by making extra effort when needed and, in general, striving to do their jobs as well as they can.

But unfortunately, there are severe limitations to the ability of the employer to play the generous parent. He must make at least some profit and, therefore, must consider the relationship between his (unit) costs of production and those of his competitors. If he is, for one reason or another, partially protected from the rigors of product market competition, he will be correspondingly able to pass on to his customers the cost of his generosity to his employees. Or if he is unusually adept or fortunate at keeping his unit costs below those of his competitors, he may use the profits resulting from his comparative advantage for the benefit of his workers. But, where there is keen competition in the product markets and an employer has no advantage in productive technique, what he can pay to (or do for) his employees is narrowly circumscribed by the behavior of his competitors.

The fact that an employer's beneficence is restricted by his means does not, of course, distinguish him from a father; a father can give only what he has. The distinction between a generous employer and a "good" father becomes apparent when business conditions become adverse and losses must be taken. It is then that most employers, no matter how good their intentions, will discharge unneeded workers in order to reduce expenses. The employer's first responsibility is to his business (and his own family or stockholders who depend upon it). But "layoffs" do not happen in a family enterprise; what there is, is shared.[6]

Personal relations in a small business have many characteristics in common with a family enterprise. In both types of enterprise all persons are well known to one another and dealings have personal connotations, sometimes amicable, sometimes hostile. Situations of this kind are qualitatively different from those in a modern large corporation employing many thousands of workers (sometimes in plants hundreds or thousands of miles apart) in which it is manifestly impossible for the chief executives of the firm to know many of the workers personally. The ordinary worker comes into personal contact with management representatives only at the lower fringes of the "managerial hierarchy," e.g., foremen and subforemen. The amount of discretion in the hands of these representatives in dealing with "rank and file" employees is necessarily limited, and the ordinary workman rightly feels that his pay, working conditions, and the like are largely governed by an impersonal set of rules which do not take any account of his individual needs, abilities, and peculiarities. These rules may be harsh or mild, generous or grasping, but they are (and must be) impersonal.

Status and Contract

To a considerable extent, the employment relation may be conceived of as simply a purchase and sale of labor services. But a full understanding of worker-employer relations cannot be achieved if the employment relation is thought of simply as a matter of contract; it must be recognized

---

[6] Of course, individual members of the family may leave a farm (because of poverty) to seek their own livelihood. Such a course of action is often encouraged by other members, but a family member is rarely compelled to leave in the manner of a discharged worker.

that the employment relation also has status implications. Historically, the employer has been the social, and often the legal, superior of his workers.

There is much truth in Sir Henry Maine's dictum, "the progress of man is from status to contract"; but it must be added that this progress has been by no means completed. The relation between employer and employee in contemporary western societies is one of contract in that the relationship is entered into voluntarily by both parties (legally, neither party is compelled to enter into an employment relationship and either party, especially the employee, is free to terminate the relationship if he is dissatisfied). Freedom to terminate the employment relation sharply distinguishes a contractual employment relation from a status relation, such as serfdom or slavery, where such freedom is absent. "Freedom to quit," is obviously an important protection against abuse by an *individual* employer; if he is too harsh a "master" an employee can always quit, an alternative open neither to serf nor slave.

But "contract" and "status" are not mutually exclusive. Although it is no longer so frequently the case as formerly, it is still generally true that employers are property holders and that employees typically are, more or less, propertyless. The employment relation thus parallels a distinction which has historically been an important determinant of status. A few illustrations should make this point clear; universal manhood suffrage (i.e., the right of all men to vote irrespective of whether they own property) was attained in most of the United States in the first quarter of the 19th century, well after the adoption of the Constitution. In England, manhood suffrage was attained (substantially) only with the Reform Bill of 1884, and, in many countries of continental Europe, voting equality for all men was attained only in the first part of the 20th century.

Another example to the same point is the "Master and Servant" Act (of Great Britain) which, as recently as 1867, provided (among other things) that in the event of a breach of a labor contract (1) an employer (master) could be sued only for damages while an employee's (servant's) breach was a criminal offense for which he might be imprisoned; (2) a single magistrate could order a workingman imprisoned, without hearing, on the basis of an employer's assertions; and (3) an employer might testify in his own behalf in the event of a law suit, but a workingman could not give such testimony.[7]

Clearly, in the United States (and in Western European countries) at the present time, there is no such difference in political or legal status between employer and worker; however, significant social and economic

[7] Cf. S. and B. Webb, *The History of Trade Unions,* Longmans, Green & Co., London, Toronto, and New York, 2nd edition, 1920, pp. 249–253; also G. D. H. Cole, *A Short History of the British Working Class Movement, 1789–1947,* Allen & Unwin, London, Revised Edition, 1948, pp. 197–198.

distinctions still exist. The implications of the word "boss," as applied to an employer, suggest both the existence and the function of these distinctions. A "boss" is more than just the buyer of labor service; few persons would think of being their doctor's boss or their lawyer's boss. One's boss is essentially someone from whom one takes direction in the course of work, to whom one is responsible for the performance of one's job, and who can reward satisfactory performance and punish failure. In any complex enterprise requiring coordination of the efforts of many different persons, the existence of "bosses" and "bossed" is more or less inevitable. In the nature of the case, in a business enterprise, it is the employer (or someone representing him) who is going "to boss" the employee (within limits), and not vice versa.

As a further indication of the status distinction between workers and employers, it is usually assumed that workers are comparatively "poor" and employers "rich." This assumption is generally true if we think of employers as the owners or managers of "middle-sized" or large businesses, and of workers as "labor" (as we have defined it on p. 3). But there is a very large number of employers who hire only one or two workers (as well as many one-man firms with no employees), and whose incomes are as low (or lower) than those of most manual workers. (These employers are most likely to be found in retail trade, service, clothing manufacture and building construction.) A similar statement applies to small farmers who hire hands "to help with the harvesting." As there are a large number of these small employers (see p. 461), their attitudes and prejudices are of considerable political importance. As we shall see, they are often very unsympathetic to unions. However, in terms of income they are often not much better, and sometimes worse, off than the workers they employ.

Most employees receive relatively low incomes. There are exceptions to this; executives, managers, and professional persons who frequently earn high incomes are often employees of a firm. Thus "wage (or salary) earner" cannot be automatically identified with low income receiver, and "employer" with high income recipient. Nevertheless, the owner or manager of a firm employing more than 100 workers (such firms employ most nonagricultural wage earners in the United States) is much better off than virtually any of the workers in his employ. It is this fact that is responsible for the impression that "labor" wears overalls, and "capital," a top hat.

Social Stratification and Social Mobility

The significance of status or "class" differences between workers and employers obviously depends upon how easily one may cross from one category to the other. If everyone began his economic life as a laborer but eventually became an employer or at least self-employed, the distinction between worker and employer would become almost identical with that between youth and age. Clearly, this is quite different from a situation in which most people are, all their lives, on the same side of the fence.

In the United States, we pride ourselves that the avenues of social and economic ascent are "open to talent." That is, there are substantial opportunities for advancement within the managerial hierarchies of large corporations (and governments), which are open to people with one or more of the various technical skills needed. Widespread and growing opportunities for education at the college level, and beyond, are putting these skills within the reach of an appreciable and growing percentage of the total workforce. Furthermore, there is the traditional American route of self-improvement; accumulating some capital and going into business or farming on your own.

Because of these opportunities, status in American society is to a considerable extent the correlative of age; i.e., older people have already climbed in the "status hierarchy" while younger ones are just entering at the bottom. Unlike societies in which status is predetermined by birth, there is considerable uncertainty as to how high (on the status ladder) any given individual will climb (and how fast) which produces rivalry for place, position, and the corresponding income. The substantial opportunities for social and economic ascent keeps status lines from becoming hard and fast lines of demarcation between distinct hereditary social classes, and is part of what is meant when the United States is referred to as the "land of opportunity."

The opportunity for social and economic advance, of which the United States is justly proud, is open mainly to youths, because it arises principally from the availability of free education and other training opportunities. Its practical consequence is a relatively high degree of rise of sons above the occupational levels of their fathers (see pp. 20–24). However, despite the opportunities for training that do exist, many youths are unable, for various reasons, to take advantage of them, with the result that there is an observable tendency for sons to inherit the occupational grade of their fathers.

Of course, opportunities for occupational advance exist for older persons as well as for youths. However, these arise primarily in connection with starting one's own business. As we shall see, the opportunity for starting one's own business, or farm, has always been, and still is, a major avenue of social and economic ascent for ambitious Americans. However, it is a road that has been travelled successfully by only a small minority of wage earners. Most members of "labor," over 25 years of age, are going to remain laborers to the end of their productive lives, and know it.   The phenomena with which we are to deal are strongly conditioned by this fact.

DISCUSSION QUESTIONS

1. To what extent is the employer's freedom to discharge essential to the maintenance of worker efficiency?   What does your answer suggest as to the possible effect of full employment on worker efficiency?

2. Compare the principal techniques for maintaining discipline in the Armed Forces with those used in an office or workshop.   Give the main reasons for the differences.

3. Is is ever possible to raise wages without lowering profits?   Indicate two ways in which this might be done.

4. Is it merely "hard-heartedness" that leads employers to lay off workers when business becomes worse, or are other factors involved?   Under what conditions might profit-seeking employers retain workers despite the fact that they might not be needed currently?

2 | The Labor Force and American Economic Development

Laborers have, for the past 100 years or so, continuously strived to better their condition. They have tried to do this by raising their wages, reducing their hours of work, increasing the safety and healthfulness of their work environment, improving the provision made for them when they were made idle by business conditions, accident, illness or old age, increasing the number of years of schooling received by their children, etc.   They have sought these objectives both as individuals (by attempting to find better jobs) and, collectively, through their unions and government.

The details of how labor has worked to attain these objectives will be discussed later.   In this chapter, we shall be concerned with describing the ways in which the condition of wage earners has improved and indicating the economic developments that have made this improvement possible.   It is essential to remember that the gains that labor has made during the last century have been the result of an enormous increase in output per worker.   There has been no appreciable tendency for labor's share of the national output to grow at the expense of capital's share; rather the joint output of labor and capital has grown so that both labor and capital have been able to get more.   This growth in output is what we call "economic progress."

ECONOMIC PROGRESS AND WORKER PRODUCTIVITY

Column 1 of Table 2.1 gives per capita national income per annum (and, for later years, gross national product) valued at constant prices; these figures indicate the value of the goods and services produced per capita, after allowing for changes in the general price level.[1]   The marked

---

[1] National income, roughly speaking, measures the output of goods and services of a given nation in a given time period (usually per year) net of the depreciation and depletion of the instruments of production (including mineral deposits) used up

15

increase in per capita annual national income between the decades of 1869–1878 and 1919–1928 gives a rough indication of the increase in the volume of goods and services[2] (including those furnished by government) available (per annum) to the "average person" between these two decades.   The increase in annual per capita national income and gross national product is reflected in the increased per capita physical production (and consumption) of goods and services of all kinds, e.g., foodstuffs, clothing, housing, education, etc.[3]   This increase in annual real production per capita is the most widely used indicator of economic progress.

However, there are other indicators of economic progress; column 2 of Table 2.1 shows the steady increase in the quantity (i.e., value at constant prices) of capital goods available to assist private producers in the process of production.   Accumulation of (inanimate) instruments of production (capital goods) is, of itself, an indicator of economic progress; in addition it is of causal significance in explaining the figures set out in column 1.   Certainly one of the major reasons for the increase in annual real national income per capita is the enormous increase (as compared with 50 years ago) in the quantity and quality of the instruments that are available to assist most laborers; these instruments are embodied in numerous and commonplace mechanized "labor saving" devices.

The effect of mechanizing productive processes has been to generate a long-term rise in output per hour of the "average" American worker. This increase in output of a man-hour of labor (valued at constant—1948 —prices) is indicated by column 3 of Table 2.1; these figures imply an average annual rate of increase (compounded) of a little over 2 per cent. This does *not* mean that American workers, *by themselves,* have increased their hourly output by an average of about 2 per cent per year.   This result is attributable not only to the increased efficiency of laborers but also to the use of more numerous and improved tools, to improved management, to a more helpful government, etc.   Output per man-hour is a measure of the productivity of the whole economic system; identifying the

---

in production during the specified time period.   Thus per capita national income National Income/Total Population is a measure of physical output per person. But if changes in per capita national income (which is a dollar magnitude) are to serve as an indicator of changes in per capita physical volume of output, it is necessary that the dollar magnitudes in the various years be adjusted so that they mirror only changes in output and not changes in prices; this is accomplished by expressing per capita national income in terms of the prices of some one year; e.g., 1929.

[2] Including the capital goods which they purchase (directly or indirectly) with their savings.

[3] For details, see *Monthly Labor Review,* (35th Anniversary Issue) July 1950, especially pp. 23–31 and 38–39.

Table 2.1

(1) Per Capita National Income (Net National Product) at 1929 Prices (in Dollars)		(2) Capital (Except Land and Improvements), Total and per Labor Force Member, Valued at 1929 Prices	(in Billions of Dollars) Total	(in Thousands of Dollars) Per Member of Labor Force
1869–78	216	1879	38.8	2.32
1879–88	326	1889	62.6	2.77
1889–98	358	1899	101	3.56
1899–1908	461	1909	152	4.17
1909–18	515	1919	215	5.19
1919–28	612	1929	283	5.87
1929–38	572	1939	288	5.12
1939–48	790	1944	347	5.70

(3) Index of Output per Man-hour 1910 = 100		(4) Average Weekly Hours Worked by Wage Earners in the U. S.
1850	43.1	69.8
1900	87.0	60.2
1910	100.0	55.1
1915	104.9	
1920	113.3	49.7
1925	135.5	
1930	135.6	45.9
1935	152.3	
1940	179.0	44.0
1945	210.7	44.5
1950	232.5	40.0
1955	264.9	(1953) 40.1

Sources: Column 1. Decade averages from S. S. Kuznets, *Long-Term Changes in the National Income of the United States of America Since 1870. Income and Wealth of the United States; Trends and Structure*, Income and Wealth, Series II, edited by Simon Kuznets, Bowes and Bowes, Cambridge, England, 1952, Table 4, column 4, p. 55. Column 2. S. S. Kuznets, *op. cit.*, Table 11, columns 1 and 4, p. 78. Column 3. 1850 and 1900 from J. F. Dewhurst and Associates, *America's Needs and Resources*, Twentieth Century Fund, New York, 1948, Table 3, column 7, p. 23. Later years from *Potential Economic Growth of the United States During the Next Decade*, Congressional Joint Economic Committee, Washington, D.C., 1954. 1955 is an estimated figure. 1850 and 1900 refer to National Income per Manhour; 1910 and later date refer to Real Private Product per Manhour. Column 4. J. F. Dewhurst and associates, *America's Needs and Resources: A New Survey*, Twentieth Century Fund, New York, 1955, Appendix 20-4, column 5, p. 1073.

contribution of any one productive agent (e.g., labor) to the net result is a different, and far more difficult, matter.

The significance of the increase in man-hour productivity is that it suggests one important source of the increase in annual output per capita indicated in column 1 (of Table 2.1). That is, it indicates that part of the increase was due to greater output per hour of work. This impression is heightened by column 4 which shows that the increase (in column 1) cannot be explained as the result of workers doing more hours of work per week. For, as column 4 shows, the increase in per capita output has accompanied a steady decline in the number of hours worked per week by an "average" worker; this table also shows that the rate of decline in weekly hours has accelerated since 1920.

Column 1 of Table 2.2 suggests that not all of the increase in per capita national income is attributable to the increase in man-hour productivity. That is, this column shows that there has been a steady rise in the percentage of the adult population that is enrolled in the nation's work force.[4] This suggests a further reason why per capita national income has grown; i.e., the nation has a larger annual income (per capita) because more of its members are working. Although no one would deny that this factor has helped to increase per capita national income, all serious students would agree that it is of far less importance than the increase in man-hour productivity.

THE CHANGING EMPLOYMENT STATUS
OF THE AMERICAN POPULATION

Columns 2 and 3 of Table 2.2 show that in the last 80 years the percentage of gainfully employed women has grown far more than that of men. However, the increase of women in the labor force is greater than the increase in their contribution to the nation's output. To a considerable extent what has happened is that production formerly done in the home (e.g., the baking of bread, the making of clothes, etc.) is now done in factories, and some women have used the time "freed" to earn cash income. Nevertheless, it would not be seriously denied that the increased tendency of women to obtain gainful employment has made some contribution to the growth of per capita national income.

Examination of Table 2.2, shows that in April 1950 over 90 per cent of the males between 20 and 64 years of age were in the labor force, but

---

[4] Members of the "labor force" are those persons gainfully employed plus those without a job but who are looking for work. The gainfully employed include wage and salary earners; the self-employed and the owner-managers of businesses employing others. For a more detailed definition, see A. J. Jaffe and C. D. Stewart, *Manpower Resources and Utilization*, John Wiley & Co., Inc., New York, 1951, especially Chapters 2, 4, and 7.

less than 40 per cent of the females (in the same age group).[5]   Of persons under 15, only 5.3 per cent were working or looking for work; and of the older people (above 65 years), about three-fourths were unavailable for gainful employment.   In short, in 1950 (and at present) the American worker is, with few exceptions, an adult; he is far more likely to be male than female and, of those who live to be 65, only about one-quarter continue to work or look for work.

Table 2.2.   Percentage of Persons of Working Force Age in Working Force (Including Armed Forces) for the United States, 1870–1950; Median School Year Completed by Age Group and Sex, 1950.

	(1)	(2)	(3)	(4)	(5)	(6)		
				Workers as Percentage of Population Aged 10–15 years	Workers as Percentage of Population 65 years and over	Median School Year Completed by Age Groups (in 1950)		
	Both Sexes	Male	Female				Male	Female
1870	44.4	74.9	13.3	13.2		20–21	12.1	12.2
1880	47.3	78.7	14.7	16.8		22–24	11.9	12.2
1890	49.2	79.3	17.4	18.1	38.7	25–29	12.0	12.1
1900	50.2	80.0	18.8	18.2	not available	30–34	11.5	11.8
1910	52.2	80.8	21.5	15.0	not available	35–44	9.9	10.5
1920	51.3 } 54.3*	79.7 } 84.4*	21.4 } 22.7	11.3	31.7	45–54	8.7	8.9
1930	54.5	84.1	24.3	4.7	30.7	55–64	8.4	8.5
1940	55.2	82.6	27.9	1.8†	24.6	65–74	8.1	8.3
1950	57.5	83.7	32.1	5.3†	26.8	75 and over	7.9	8.2

Sources: Columns 1, 2 and 3, A. J. Jaffe and C. D. Stewart, *Manpower Resources and Utilization,* John Wiley & Sons, Inc., 1951, Table 14, p. 164.   Column 4, *ibid,* Table 16, p. 168.   Column 5, *ibid,* Table 17, p. 169.   Column 6, *U. S. Census of Population, 1950,* Education, Special Report P. E. No. 5B, Table 5, pp. 42–5.

* Age 10 and over for 1870-1910 and first entry in 1920; age 14 and over for subsequent entries.

† Age 14 and 15.   Only a negligible number of children in the 10–13 age group were employed in 1940 or thereafter.

But this has not always been so.   Column 4 in Table 2.2 indicates that, not long ago, it was fairly common for children between the ages of 10 and 15 to go to work (in 1900, 26.1 per cent of all males between 10 and 15 were gainfully occupied).   The fact that in recent decades child labor has been drastically reduced has tended to keep the "overall labor force ratio" (i.e., column 1) from rising even faster than it has.   The decline in child labor has been accompanied by an increase in the percentage of children and young people attending school.   This is indicated

[5] See Jaffe and Stewart, *op. cit.,* Table 1, p. 123.

by the steady rise in the median number of school years completed; this rise is reflected in column 6 of Table 2.2, which shows that (in 1950) older persons had a lower number of median years of schooling than younger ones.

At the other end of the age scale, the percentage of gainfully employed males (over 65) has also declined steadily. This last development has been partially due to the increasing number of people with pensions, annuities, etc., and, in the last 15 years, to the federal government's old age pension system (see below, pp. 484–491). However, the steady relative decline of agriculture as a source of employment (see below, Table 2.3) has also worked in the same direction.[6]

In short, the development of the American economy has increased the percentage of mature adults (especially women) in the labor force, but has decreased the percentage of the very young and the aged. As mature workers are (presumably) more productive than those at either end of the life span, it is reasonable to suppose that the change in the age composition of the labor force has made some contribution to the growth of per capita national product.

The major trends in Table 2.3 show a movement of workers from industries where the value of output per worker (per year) is low, as in Agriculture, to those where it is relatively high. Obviously, this has tended to raise per capita national income. Indeed, it would be generally agreed that the shift of workers from agriculture to other industries where the value of their services is greater, e.g., manufacturing, has been a major factor in the economic development of the United States.

ECONOMIC DEVELOPMENT AND THE CHANGING NATURE OF THE JOB

The mechanization that has produced enormous increases in man-hour productivity has, at the same time, transformed the worker's job. The mechanization process has changed the worker from a supplier of muscle power to the director of a machine. It has also tended to make him less of a machine *operator* and more of a machine *supervisor*. Consequently, for most American wage earners, the nature of work has undergone substantial change during the last century. The back-breaking toil characteristic of labor in unmechanized economies has been greatly diminished; "manual labor" in the modern American economy is, typically,

---

[6] Older persons living primarily on family farms never really retired; their duties "just faded away," i.e., retirement was gradual and never quite total. "Grandpa" would work less hard than he used to and rest more, but would always put in some work. In industry, however, when an oldster is no longer able to accept a job with more or less definitely defined duties he becomes either unemployed or retired, as the case may be.

Table 2.3.   Estimated Industrial Composition of the Working Force, for the United States: 1870–1950

Percentage Distribution

Industry Group	1950	1940	1930	1920	1910	1900	1890	1880	1870
Total	100.0	100.0	100.0	100.0	100.0	100.0	100.0	100.0	100.0
Agriculture, forestry, and fishing	11.8	18.4	21.9	27.6	31.6	38.2	43.4	50.0	53.5
Extraction of minerals	1.5	2.2	2.0	2.6	2.6	2.4	1.9	1.7	1.4
Manufacturing and mechanical industry and construction	31.1	29.6	28.9	30.3	28.5	24.8	23.7	22.1	20.5
Manufacturing and mechanical industry	25.7	23.8							
Construction	5.4	5.7							
Transportation, communication, and other public utilities	7.8	6.9	7.9	7.3	7.1	6.7	6.0	4.8	4.2
Professional and related services	8.6	7.1	6.7	5.1	4.6	4.1	3.8	3.2	2.6
All other services and white-collar industries	39.4	35.8	32.6	27.0	25.6	23.8	21.3	18.4	17.8
Trade			12.5	10.0	9.7	10.6	8.8	7.9	6.8
Public service (not elsewhere classified)			1.8	1.7	1.2	1.0	0.9	0.8	0.7
Domestic and personal service			10.1	8.0	10.1	9.7	9.6	8.8	9.7
Clerical occupations			8.2	7.3	4.6	2.5	2.0	0.9	0.6
Wholesale and retail trade	20.4	16.9							
Finance, insurance, and real estate	3.5	3.2							
Business and repair services	2.1	2.0							
Amusement, recreation, and related services	0.9	1.0							
Personal and domestic services	7.4	9.1							
Government	5.1	3.8							

Source: 1870–1940, Jaffe and Stewart, op. cit., Table 23, p. 192.   Data for 1950 from U. S. Bureau of the Census, Income of Families and Persons in the United States: 1949, Series P-60, No. 7, p. 24.

the rendering of careful attention to the control and operation of a machine.

This change in the nature of manual labor is reflected in Table 2.4 by the steady decline (since 1910) in the percentage of the labor force employed as unskilled workers (largely "muscle suppliers") and the rise in the percentage of semiskilled workers (essentially machine tenders).   But technical progress has made possible, and caused, further and more fundamental changes in the occupational distribution of the American labor force.   For example, there has been, in recent decades, a marked increase of clerical, sales, professional, and other "white-collar" workers relative to "manual laborers."   This increase reflects the fact that business firms have become more complicated organizations and have, therefore, found it necessary to employ a growing number of white-collar workers.   Looked at in a different way, this trend implies that the reduction in man-hours of *manual* labor per unit of output has been partially offset by the necessity for increasing man-hours of administrative and similar work (per unit of output).[7]

[7] Thus it has been estimated that the ratio of "administrative" to "production" workers in American manufacturing industries rose steadily from 1899, when it was 9.9 per cent, through 1947 when it was 22.2 per cent.   Cf. S. Melman, *The Rise of Administrative Overhead in the Manufacturing Industries of the United States, 1899–1947,* Oxford Economic Papers, February 1951, pp. 52–112, especially Tables II, p. 66.   Table 1 (p. 63) of this reference indicates that this tendency has occurred in other countries as well as the United States.

Table 2.4.   Socioeconomic Composition of the American Labor Force

	1910	1920	1930	1940	1950
Total	*100.0*	*100.0*	*100.0*	*100.0*	*100.0*
Professional persons	4.4	5.0	6.1	6.5	8.9
Proprietors, managers, and officials	23.0	22.3	19.9	17.8	17.0
Farmers and farm managers	16.5	15.5	12.4	10.1	8.0
Others	6.5	6.8	7.5	7.6	9.0
Clerks and kindred workers					
(including sales workers)	10.2	13.8	16.3	17.2	18.8
Skilled workers and foremen	11.7	13.5	12.9	11.7	13.7*
Semiskilled workers	14.7	16.1	16.4	21.0	19.8*
Unskilled workers	36.0	29.4	28.4	25.9	20.5
Farm laborers	14.5	9.4	8.6	7.1	4.5
Other laborers	14.7	14.6	12.9⎱	18.7	16.0
Servants	6.8	5.4	6.9⎰		

Source: For 1910–1940, A. M. Edwards, *Comparative Occupation Statistics for the United States, 1870–1940*, U. S. Bureau of the Census, Washington, 1943, Table XXVII, p. 187. For 1950, *1950 Census of Population, Preliminary Reports*, Series PC-7, No. 2, Table 6, p. 28. The data for 1950 are not precisely comparable with those for earlier years but are believed roughly to indicate the major trends.

* We have assumed that "Operatives and kindred workers" were analogous to "Semi-skilled workers"; and have included in "Other Laborers and Servants," "Service workers, except private household," "Private household workers," and "Laborers, except farm and miscellaneous."   The listed percentages will not total 100 per cent because of the omission of 1.4 per cent of persons not reporting their occupation.   1950 data refer only to *employed* persons.

In general, white-collar jobs require a much higher level of education than manual jobs; consequently, continued improvement in the general level of educational attainment (indicated by column 6 of Table 2.2) has been necessary to provide a sufficient number of trained persons to operate an increasingly complicated economic system.   As a result, economic progress has accompanied a general occupational "up-grading" of the labor force.

Consequently, Table 2.4 shows that in each succeeding decade a larger percentage of employed persons is to be found in occupational classifications (such as professional, nonfarm managers and officials, etc.) that require a relatively high level of educational attainment, pay high wages and have a high "socioeconomic" status.[8]   Conversely, there has been a

[8] The socioeconomic status of a worker depends partly on his social and partly on his economic status.   As the Census Bureau puts it, "The workers in each group have been included partly because of their social and partly because of their economic status."   The standard if it be a standard, is thus a hybrid—partly social and partly economic.   And the weight of the social factor varies from one group to another and from one occupation to another, as does, also, the weight of the economic factor." A. M. Edwards, *Comparative Occupation Statistics for the United States, 1870–1940,* p. 180, U. S. Bureau of the Census, Washington, 1943.

steady (percentage-wise) decline of unskilled workers who are, notoriously, low wage receivers. This suggests that one aspect of the rise in per capita national income has been a relative shift of workers from low to higher wage occupations.

OCCUPATIONAL MOBILITY AND ECONOMIC GROWTH

The facts so drily summarized in Table 2.4 are, in a nutshell, the story of America as a land of opportunity. American economic development has not been such that a constant percentage of the labor force has been compelled to work at humble, low wage occupations. Instead, it has made it possible each decade for a part of the labor force to climb the occupational ladder.

This climb has been largely an ascent of each generation over the occupational level of its parents. To a considerable extent this is but a reflection of the occupational differences between immigrants and their children. These immigrants, to a considerable extent, were rural in their native countries, and their migration to the United States was part of the process of urbanization that has characterized the economic development of the past two centuries. In the United States they provided a disproportionately large part of the unskilled urban labor force;[9] in 1910, 32 per cent of all employed foreign born males were employed as nonfarm unskilled laborers while only 16 per cent of the native born workers were so employed. Thus the children of each generation of immigrants climbed the occupational ladder, but their places were taken at the bottom by a new crop of immigrants.

During World War I, the tide of European immigration (temporarily) halted while there was a sharp increase in the demand for labor of all kinds in the war industries. The consequence of this was a great impetus to the cityward migration of rural native workers, especially southern youths (including many negroes). For a few years after 1920, immigration began to climb toward its prewar levels, but restrictive legislation in 1924 curbed this trend and ended the "immigrant phase" of American history.

The full effect of the restriction of immigration on the American labor force was not felt immediately. This was largely due to the fact that the urban demand for unskilled and semiskilled labor could be easily filled (in the 1920's) by the natural increase of the native population and by farm migrants. In the 1930's the prevailing unemployment guaranteed that the immigrant contribution to the labor force would not be missed.

[9] Not all immigrant workers were unskilled. Indeed, many types of skilled workers had to be "imported" throughout much of the 19th century. However, in the 20th century, immigrants (especially from southern and southeastern Europe) have entered the American labor market largely as unskilled workers.

But since 1940 the steadily increasing demand for workers in occupations above the unskilled level has tended to denude the ranks of the unskilled. Perhaps this would have occurred even had unrestricted immigration continued; however, the curbing of immigration certainly eliminated one major source of replenishment of our supply of unskilled workers.

WAGES AND ECONOMIC DEVELOPMENT

The economic progress of the past century has benefited all classes of the population, including wage earners. Average real hourly wages for the economy as a whole (i.e., average hourly wages corrected for changes in living costs) rose by 132 per cent between 1890 and 1947.[10] The growth in hourly earnings was, in percentage terms, greater than that in weekly earnings because of the decline in average hours worked per week; e.g. between 1890 and 1947, average weekly earnings in Manufacturing (corrected for changes in living costs) rose only 100%.[11]

This increase in hourly wages does not reflect entirely the effect of changes in the earnings on particular jobs. As we have already seen, the labor force has been "promoted," over time, to better paying jobs; and, to some (unknown but appreciable) extent, the increase in average hourly earnings is the reflection of this. In other words, average hourly earnings on the "average" job did not rise by 132 per cent (from 1890 to 1947) but by appreciably less; the earnings of the "average" worker showed a greater rise because (during this period) he improved his job.

To summarize: the economic development of the past century has raised the wages—hourly, weekly, and yearly—of the average worker; it has educated him, given him a better paying job, mechanized his work, shortened his hours, made his work safer, given him a longer life, and given him some protection against economic adversity. It has also urbanized him, naturalized him, and—unionized him. This last phenomenon we shall study in some detail in Part II.

DISCUSSION QUESTIONS

1. Do you think per capita national income would have grown more during the past century if the average length of the work week had not been reduced? In your discussion, consider the possibility that had the work week been longer fewer wage earners would have been hired and (perhaps) more would have been unemployed.

[10] See W. S. Woytinsky and Associates, *Employment and Wages in the United States,* Twentieth Century Fund, 1953, Table 21, p. 51. The correction for changes in living costs is a procedure that enables us to treat the corrected wage data as though they measured (roughly) changes in the purchasing power of the worker's time; i.e., as though an hour of an "average" worker's time would enable him to buy 132 per cent more goods and services in 1947 than in 1890.

[11] *Ibid.*

2. Can you conceive of circumstances under which it might be socially desirable for all children over 10 years of age to work 40 hours per week? Hint: consider the case of a country with a very low per capita national income.

3. What occupational groups do you think gained most by restricting immigration into the United States? Were there any groups (and, if so, which) that were harmed by such restriction?

Suggested Readings

Kuznets, Simon, *Long Term Changes in the National Income of the United States of America since 1870*, pp. 29–241; *Income and Wealth of the United States, Trends and Structure,* Income and Wealth Series II, edited by Simon Kuznets, Bowes and Bowes, Cambridge, England, 1952.

Rogoff, Natalie, *Recent Trends in Occupational Mobility,* Free Press, Glencoe, Ill., 1953.

Thomas, Brinley, *Migration and Economic Growth,* National Institute of Economic and Social Research, Economic and Social Studies XII, Cambridge University Press, 1954, Chapter IX.

Woytinsky, W. S., and Associates, *Employment and Wages in the United States,* Twentieth Century Fund, New York, 1953,, Chapters 3–5.

"50 Years' Progress of American Labor" in *Monthly Labor Review,* Vol. 71, No. 1, 35th Anniversary Issue (July 1950), pp. 5–40.

PART TWO

Unions
and Collective Bargaining

3 | The Growth of American Unionism
I: Organization

This chapter and the next deal with unionism in historical context. Because the history of American unionism is so complex, it is convenient to divide it topically into two parts: organization and objectives. However, no one should suppose that the organizational aspects of unions can be intelligently understood apart from their objectives, or vice versa. The separation of these two aspects of labor history is a divorce of convenience only.

A BIRD'S-EYE VIEW OF UNION GROWTH

Unionism is a world-wide phenomenon. In one form or another, every country with an industrial labor force has unions. Indeed, through cultural imitation, many "backward" areas of Asia and Africa have already acquired sizeable union movements although their industrialization has hardly begun. However, in Europe, the United States, Australia, and Canada, the rise of unions has been a concomitant of the twin processes of urbanization and industrialization. The casual connections among unionism, industrialism, and capitalism are none too well understood, and students of the subject are far from agreement. However, it is agreed that there is some intimate relation, at least between unionism and industrialism. This means that unionism, as an important phenomenon, is no more than a century and a half old. Indeed, its importance in most countries (including the United States) is confined to this century and, perhaps, the final quarter of the last.

As we shall see it was only in the 1890's, after a half-century of failures, that American labor first managed to form enduring union organizations. These organizations were confined largely to the skilled workers and covered no more than 3 to 5 per cent of the civilian labor force. From 1900 to 1914 union membership grew from 868,000 to 2,687,000; but as the labor force also grew rapidly, the percentage of the labor force enrolled in unions increased only from 3.0 per cent to 6.8 per cent.   From 1914 to 1920, union membership rose from 2,687,000 to 5,048,000; or from 6.8 per cent to 12.0 per cent of the labor force.   A sharp decline then ensued; union membership fell to 4,027,000 in 1922 and continued a steady decline thereafter until 1933, when the 2,973,000 union members comprised only 5.8 per cent of the labor force, less than in 1914.[1]

However, since 1933 union membership has climbed steadily, both in absolute numbers and relatively to the labor force.   By 1941, unions had 8,614,000, a little over 15 per cent of the labor force.   By 1945 there were 14,500,000 unionists, about 22 per cent of the labor force.   From 1945 to 1950, union membership was roughly constant, but from 1950 to Jan. 1, 1955, it climbed to 17,757,000, about 25 per cent of the labor force.[2]   The 1933-1941 growth represented an extension of unionism into the theretofore nonunionized manufacturing industries and an extension to other areas previously untouched.   The war-time increase reflected both an increased degree of unionization in manufacturing and a growth of manufacturing employment relative to (essentially nonunion) agriculture.   The post-war increase in membership is due largely to the relative growth in employment within the unionized sector of the economy.

It can be readily seen that the course of union growth has not been smooth.   Before the 1890's union organizations tended to collapse during depressions, and even in recent times union membership has shown a tendency to fluctuate with business activity.   (For example, the worldwide depression of 1920–1921 played havoc with union membership in a number of countries, as well as in the United States.)   In addition, political developments have at times encouraged the growth of unionism, and at other times retarded it.

However, despite the complexity of the forces that have affected the course of unionization, for the long run it may be said that the growth of unions is one of the customary by-products of industrialization.   Now let us examine the evolution of American unions in more detail.

UNIONS BEFORE THE CIVIL WAR

Before 1827

There is ample evidence of union activity before 1850; indeed, union activity is reported as early as 1792!   However, the unions flowering

---

[1] The data cited are from Irving Bernstein, "The Growth of American Trade Unions," *American Economic Review*, June 1954, pp. 301–318, especially Table 1, pp. 303–304.

[2] The data for 1945 and subsequent years are from William Paschell, "Structure and Membership of the Labor Movement," *Monthly Labor Review*, November, 1955, pp. 1231–1239.

before 1850 were delicate blooms, expanding in the warmth of prosperity but withering before the chill blasts of depression and unemployment.[3]

The early development of unions in the United States occurred entirely in the cities of the eastern seaboard, Boston, New York, and Philadelphia. The workers involved were mainly skilled journeymen, such as tailors, shoemakers, shipwrights, carpenters, etc. As manufacturing was embryonic before (say) 1815, most union members (or unionists, for short) worked for rather small employers and primarily by hand.

The unions of this period were, like their descendants, greatly interested in securing wage increases and resisting reductions, and they went on strike to enforce their demands. To make their strikes effective, they sought to dissuade customers from dealing with employers who had been struck and had hard words, and blows, for strike-breakers.

All this sounds very modern, but it must not lead us to see the world of the early 19th century as an archaic replica of the mid-20th. In this (early) period, producing units were small and it was comparatively easy for ambitious workers to go into business for themselves; i.e., it was not so difficult as later for a worker to raise enough capital to start his own business. Furthermore, in the first quarter of the 19th century, the eastern cities were not so far from cheap land that there were serious obstacles to the many workers who wanted to settle on farms of their own. These circumstances created a relatively high degree of mobility between worker and employer status, which tended to prevent individuals from permanently identifying themselves with the "working class" and its viewpoint.

Most of what little we know of these early unions is obtained from occasional newspaper stories concerning their more eventful activities, e.g., strikes. From what can be inferred about their day-to-day existence, it would seem that these unions had little, if any, formal organization and were, to a high degree, evanescent. Indeed, it is quite possible that many of the strikes occurring in this period were fought by unions that were formed in the heat of battle and disintegrated soon after.

For reasons that will later become apparent, if they are not already, an embryonic union is more likely to survive a strike if victorious than if defeated. Consequently unions were more likely to be found in prosperous times, when strikes were more frequently successful, than in periods of depression. This gave rise to a cyclical pattern of unionism (growth in prosperity, decline in depression) which appeared early in American history (as well as in other countries) and persisted until the late 1930's.

We know nothing of the number of workers involved in union activity during this early period. But they could not have been a very large part

[3] J. R. Commons and Associates, *History of Labor in the United States,* The Macmillan Co., New York, 1918, Volume I, Part I, Chapter IV.

of the work force, for at this time the American population was over-whelmingly rural and townsmen were but a small minority. For this, if no other, reason union activity in this period was of no great historical significance.

However, political developments in the first part of the 19th century exercised a major influence on the future of the American wage earner. In particular, this period saw the extension of the electoral suffrage so as to include virtually all adult males.

We had emerged from the Revolutionary War with a large number of British (18th century) institutions. Among these was the reservation of the right to vote to those possessing (in some cases, substantial) property. Voting eligibility was determined separately in each state by its own consti-tution, and in the 35-year period, 1790–1825, a prolonged battle was waged in the various states between the friends and enemies of broader suffrage. The victory of the democratic forces gave the ballot to the American workingman long before he had organizations to demand it on his own behalf. In European countries, on the other hand, labor unions had to fight (in the later 19th and early 20th centuries) not only for the economic interests of their members but also for their right to vote. This difference is of considerable importance in explaining the relatively low degree of political concern of the American, as compared with Euro-pean, labor movement.

The various state governments inherited from Britain not only many of their political institutions and ideas but also their legal system, includ-ing the institutions of the Common Law.[4] Under the Common Law, labor union efforts to raise wages were illegal conspiracies, and in the first part of the 19th century the Common Law was applied in the various city and state courts to restrain the activities of embryonic unions. Most of these unions were found in the seaboard towns in the "old" states where the judiciary was dominated by Federalists, who not only felt the Com-mon Law to be applicable but were entirely satisfied with its consequences. From 1806 through 1815 and later in the 1830's, there was a number of law suits (against unions) growing out of strikes. Although the precise legal grounds for the decisions varied from one case to the other, their general effect was severely to hamper union activities such as strikes, attempts to secure a closed shop, boycott the products of nonunion em-ployers, etc., by making such actions of doubtful legality.[5] The indig-nation of the unions and of their plebian supporters was directed not only against the decisions, and the judges who made them, but also against the

---

[4] C. O. Gregory, *Labor and the Law*, New York, W. W. Norton & Co., Revised Edition, 1949, Chapter I.

[5] Gregory, *loc. cit.*, Chapter I and Commons, *op. cit.*, Vol. I, pp. 162–165 and 401–412.

"tyrannical" legal concepts that inspired them. These expressions of indignation were part of the general political agitation of the "common people" which became especially vehement during the early 1830's.

From 1827 to 1837

In the decade following 1827 unions flourished, achieving far greater prominence than before. However, the specific economic demands for which unions contended were not very different from those of the earlier period. During the decade, 1827–1837, labor unions struck (in prosperity) for higher wages and the ten hour day; in depressions, they fought to prevent wage cuts. The stronger unions of skilled workers also tried to control apprenticeship, to restrict employment of female and child labor, and to govern the allocation of work.

The activity of unions increased in intensity as the decade wore on. From 1833 to 1837 there were 173 distinct strikes recorded,[6] this strike wave was related to the boom, and sharp consumer price increases, of 1835–1837. Strikes for wage increases to offset rising living costs were often successful, and each successful strike stimulated further union activity. The ten hour day was also demanded frequently and sometimes was obtained, though only temporarily.

The formation of employers' associations suggests that the growing unions were able, at first, to play off employers against one another. The employer associations attempted to blacklist union workmen and to hold employers "in line" during strikes. Employers also continued to fight unions in the courts, achieving considerable success in having union practices, especially the "closed shop," declared unlawful.

The unions operating in this period were primarily local in character; i.e., they were confined to a single city and not coordinated with similar unions elsewhere. To be sure, there were a few attempts to form national unions, but these attempts were feeble and abortive.[7]

Of more importance were the "City Trades' Unions"; these were essentially local federations of trade unions similar in purpose to present-day City Central Federations of Labor. City Trades' Unions were formed (in the 1830's) in New York, Baltimore, Philadelphia, and Boston as well as a number of smaller cities. Their purposes were (1) mutual support and aid in the event of strikes or lockouts and (2) the securing of favorable publicity for "labor's causes." Usually these central unions put out a newspaper that espoused labor's views on current affairs. In addition, the City Trades' Unions assisted the affiliated unions by endorsing their boycotts of "unfair" employers.[8]

---

[6] Commons, *op. cit.,* Vol. I, p. 381.

[7] *Ibid.,* pp. 438–453.

[8] The revenue of these organizations came from a per capita tax paid by affiliated

It is not possible to say how much control these City Trades' Unions exercised over the behavior of the affiliated unions, but it is certain that they exercised far more influence than the feeble national unions. The various City Trades' Unions, themselves, attempted to federate and form a National Trades' Union. There were three conventions of this ambitious organization, but it never performed any real function in the labor movement and disappeared in the "great depression" of 1837, along with virtually all the other labor organizations formed during the decade, 1827–1837.

The depression of the late 1830's and early 1840's so completely obliterated the unions then existing, that the next period of union development, in the 1850's, had to begin almost from scratch. The unions of the 1830's, like their predecessors, disintegrated under the impact of lost strikes and employer refusal to hire union members during a period of job scarcity. In retrospect, the flurry of unionization in the 1830's must be judged as belonging to the "preindustrial" period of American history. Most of the striking workmen were craftsmen in construction or ship building, printing, cigar-making, etc. (Factory workers were still a relatively small portion of the labor force and were not so able, or willing, as the others to fight for their interests.)

From 1837 to 1860

The 1840's were a period of great difficulty for unions. At both the beginning and the end of the decade, money wages were kept under heavy downward pressure from declining product prices and a greatly intensified rate of immigration.[9] Further improvements in transportation and the beginnings of mechanization (especially in New England textile mills) frequently pushed down product prices, and the immigrant-swollen labor force could not resist the resulting pressure for wage cuts. Given these generally adverse conditions, the few union embryos that did appear in the 1840's were impotent on wage issues.

The 1840's saw the beginning of "ethnic tension" in the American labor force. The availability of immigrant laborers who would accept hours and conditions that native workers would not, led (e.g., in New England textile mills) to "ethnic substitution,"[10] a process that engendered much bitterness. Job competition, between native and immigrant workers or immigrants of different national origins, appeared even in the 1830's, but it became much intensified during the depressed 1840's. In

---

unions. On occasion, they collected extraordinary taxes because of unusually severe conflicts. However, financial aid was usually contingent upon the strike being approved by a committee of the City Trades Unions.

[9] Norman Ware, *The Industrial Worker: 1840–1860,* Houghton, Mifflin & Co., 1924, Chapters II and IV.

[10] *Ibid.,* Chapter IX.

this period, native hostility was directed primarily against the Irish. Irish immigration was, in the 1840's, largely a result of famine conditions in Ireland, and the Irish immigrants came in greater numbers than the labor market could absorb. These immigrants tended to congregate in the larger cities where they formed pools of low wage labor. Often hunger or ignorance led them to accept jobs as strike-breakers which intensified the general animosity toward them.

The early 1850's saw a resurgence of union activity, which was fostered by the general prosperity of the time. Once again it was the organizations of the skilled workers that were most effective; where their strength warranted, these unions sought a closed shop and control of apprentices. Skilled unions of this period also provided for strike benefits and collected initiation fees and regular dues.

One problem that the unions of the 1850's confronted, that had not faced those of the 1830's, was that of unifying workers of different languages and national backgrounds. From the 1850's until well into the 20th century, union locals would often be organized on a language basis, and building an effective union involved securing the cooperation of linguistically diverse groups. In the 1850's the principal foreign language group among wage earners was German; as they were highly skilled and quite prone to unionize, they were very important in union affairs.

Like their predecessors, the unions of the 1850's were very sensitive to business conditions. A mild business downturn in the winter of 1854–1855 brought wage cuts and the collapse of a number of unions. Many of them recovered with the revival of business in the following year, but the whole movement was almost completely obliterated in the depression that followed the crash of 1857. The use Norman Ware's (slightly exaggerated) description, "The labor movement in America finished the period 1840–1860 as it has begun, practically in nothingness.[11]

FROM THE CIVIL WAR TO THE FOUNDING OF THE AFL

From 1861 to 1873

The initial impact of the Civil War upon the American economy was depressive, and it was not until 1862 that the typical wartime situation (of labor shortage and rising wages and prices) began to appear. There were not many union *organizations* functioning in 1860–1862, but the union activity of the preceding decade had given a large number of workers an experience of union activity, and the idea of acting collectively to redress their grievances. This fact greatly assisted in the union building that began in 1863. At the end of 1863, an informal survey found only 79 union locals in the entire country; more than two-thirds of these were in either the Iron Molders' or the Machinists' and Blacksmiths' union;

[11] *Ibid.,* p. 240.

about 60 per cent of all union members were located in New York, Pennsylvania, and Massachusetts. One year later there were 270 locals.[12]

The union movement of 1860–1873, like its predecessors, vibrated in sympathy with business conditions. It expanded rapidly in the prosperity of 1863–1866, grew slowly, if at all, during the business setback of 1866–1868, resumed growth in the moderate prosperity of 1868–1870, and spurted forward rapidly in the boom of 1870–1873. In 1869 it was guessed that there were about 170,000 union members, about 50,000 of whom were in the Knights of St. Crispin (Shoemakers), 30,000 in Coal Miners' unions; 17,000 in Typographical Unions, etc.[13] In the years 1870–1873, when the union movement was at a (temporary) peak, total membership was estimated at 300,000.[14]

To understand American unions of the 1860's, and those of earlier periods, it is necessary to recognize that their leaders (and probably members) were not committed to the proposition that the major function of unions is to improve wages and working conditions through collective bargaining with employers. Enthusiasm for collective bargaining varied with business conditions, and the ease with which strikes could be won. In prosperity, demands for wage increases backed, when necessary, by strikes were in vogue. But in depressed conditions, union leaders looked more to politics and producers' cooperatives. It is fairly clear that many, perhaps most, union leaders were, in this period, skeptical of the long-run possibilities of improving wages, hours, and working conditions by the tactics of collective bargaining. They felt that the wage depressive forces of product market competition and technological progress were too strong to be controlled by unions. They believed that collective bargaining was in the nature of a temporary palliative, more useful in prosperity than in depression, and that labor's ultimate "salvation" was to be found through other channels. For example, after 1866 the Iron Molders Union started and largest union of the period, sought to have its locals establish cooperative self-employment to the membership.[15] The Knights of St. Crispin, the largest union of the period, sought to have its locals establish cooperatives for, as the Grand Scribe of the order said, "The present demand of the Crispin is steady employment and fair wages, but his future is self-employment."[16] The Coopers established a number of cooperatives, those in Minneapolis being quite successful.[17]

[12] Commons, *op. cit.,* Vol. II, p. 19.

[13] *Ibid.,* p. 47.

[14] *Ibid.*

[15] Jonathan Grossman, *William Sylvis, Pioneer of American Labor,* Columbia University Press, 1945, Chapter IX.

[16] Commons, *op. cit.,* Vol. II, p. 79.

[17] *Ibid.,* p. 76.

However, cooperation was only one of the panaceas that attracted attention in labor circles during this period. It was during the Civil War that Ira Steward (a member of the Blacksmiths' Union) began his campaign for the eight hour day; this demand was to have a prominent place in labor's objectives during the following half century.[18]

During this period labor unions also agitated for various institutional reforms affecting labor supply. Their spokesmen inveighed against convict labor, demanding either that it be paid the same wages as free labor or prohibited altogether. They also demanded (and secured) cessation of the importation of indentured laborers (recommenced temporarily during the Civil War) and began agitating for restriction of the immigration of Chinese coolie labor.

But more important than these, in labor's list of political demands, was the "money question." In the twenty years following the Civil War, fluctuations in the money supply were greatly influenced by Congressional legislation. This legislation was condemned by currency reformers as being the cause of panics, depressions, and falling prices. These reformers sought to attract the support of labor organizations for their panaceas, and often succeeded.

In the late 1860's and early 1870's, the political activities and general interests of labor unions were pursued, at the local level, through Trades Assemblies. These were similar to the City Centrals of the 1830's, both in structure and in function. Arising in most of the larger cities during the later years of the Civil War, they actively promoted labor newspapers, workers' libraries, cooperative stores, and, most of all, the organization of the unorganized trades.

These Trades Assemblies, together with the aforementioned national unions, combined to form the National Labor Union. This union, like its predecessor in the 1830's, was concerned mainly with legislative issues of the type already mentioned. This union's conventions were attended by many important labor leaders during the years 1866–1870; for the last two years of his life (1868–1869) William Sylvis (president of the Iron Molders) was its president. However, most of the persons attending its conventions could not effectively commit the organizations they represented, or claimed to represent, and many of those attending represented only themselves.

By and large, the National Labor Union was controlled by middle-class

[18] In response to this agitation, in the late 1850's several states (California, Illinois, Connecticut, New York, Missouri) passed eight hour legislation of one kind or another, but the laws were easily avoided and generally unenforced. The federal government, in 1868, also adopted eight hour legislation for federal employees in public works which, after some pressure from labor sources, was enforced—and without wage cuts proportional to the reduction in hours.

reformers. But many of the major union leaders of the time were, in outlook, as much social reformer as labor leader. The National Labor Union has been harshly, but not inaccurately, described by Norman Ware as a "typical American politico-reform organization, led by labor leaders without organizations, politicians without parties, women without husbands, and cranks, visionaries and agitators without jobs."[19]

Chief among the short-run economic problems of this period was, once again, that of boosting wage rates to keep pace with living costs. However, the consequences of technological progress became increasingly serious during the 1860's. The unions of this period were, almost entirely, unions of skilled workmen whose jobs were jeopardized by the rapid pace of mechanization. Mechanization divorced manual skill from the worker and placed it in the machine, making it possible to substitute completely unskilled, or partially trained, workers for skilled craftsmen on a great many jobs. This process greatly reduced the demand for skilled workmen, with the result that skilled jobs became difficult to find and the tendency to compete for work by violating union standards became wellnigh irresistible. These problems plagued the Coopers, Iron Molders, Cigar Makers, Shoemakers, Machinists, and probably other unions of the time.

The unions' reaction to this problem was to seek control of entry to the trades; this implied control of apprentice training. Often, the twin processes of mechanizing production and specializing labor were accomplished by training apprentices in only part of their tasks, leaving them proficient in one or a few operations but ignorant of the rest of the trade's skill. By means of such specialized training, apprentices could learn certain limited operations in a few months and then offer themselves as cut-price, partly skilled journeymen. A manufacturer could easily assemble a force of such semiskilled workers, each capable of doing (or learning) only a limited job, and (given suitable mechanization) substantially reduce cost (per unit of output) although the (quality of the) product was often worsened as a result. To halt this development, unions tried to compel employers to hire only properly trained journeymen, to limit the number of apprentices, to prescribe a full course of training for apprentices, to regulate their pay, to get (state) legislation revising the system of indenturing apprentices.[20] Except in the printing trades, where it was important to maintain quality, these attempts to control apprenticeship and the conditions of entry to the trade were generally unsuccessful, as employers evaded and/or resisted them.

The control of apprenticeship was intimately connected with the

[19] See N. J. Ware, *The Labor Movement in the United States: 1860–95,* D. Appleton & Co., New York, 1929, pp. 11–12.

[20] Commons, *op. cit.,* Vol. II, p. 83.

closed shop and entrance to the union. In the 1860's, as later, unions sought to keep nonmembers from employment. But this objective ran counter to the desire to exclude "improperly trained" apprentices. If a union was to include all workers in its trade, it would be obliged to drop its insistence that less skilled workmen be excluded from employment. If the union held firmly to its skill requirements, it would exclude an increasingly large part of its potential members, forcing them to work as nonunion men. Many a craft union was wrecked on the horns of this dilemma. Although this problem became more acute later, it was already a serious issue (for some unions) in the 1860's and 1870's.

From 1873 to 1886

The great depression that began in 1873 almost totally wrecked the unions formed in the preceding period. Union membership fell from approximately 300,000 in 1872 to about 50,000 six years later. Of the 33 national trade unions in existence in 1873, less than one-half were left in 1877, and these were in poor shape. However, these survivors[21] had developed a corps of leaders who were convinced that the future of the American labor movement lay in strong, well-financed, and disciplined unions of skilled workmen. They were uninterested in cooperativism and their interest in politics was confined to obtaining specific favors for their unions; they were not concerned with political ideology.

Among these union leaders were Adolph Strasser and Samuel Gompers of the Cigar Makers. These two men had, in the midst of the 1870's, built a strong union local in New York City and, in 1877, Strasser had been elected president of what remained of the national organization. The national organization of the Cigar Makers, like that of most unions of the 1860's (except the Iron Molders) was very weak, with power being concentrated at the local level. The depression of the 1870's strengthened the tendency toward local autonomy in that the union locals that survived did so on their own without help from the national organization.

But local unions were insecure in an economy like the American in the 1880's. Cheap, nonunion goods produced in one locality could destroy the markets for union-made goods in others. Consequently, Gompers and Strasser tried successfully to build a strong national organization among the Cigar Makers. They did this, in the early 1880's, by installing a system of benefits; they introduced the principle of "equalization of funds" (copied from British unions) which gave the national organization the right to take funds from one local and transfer them to another.[22]

[21] E.g., Typographers, Locomotive Engineers, Iron Molders, Hat Finishers, Cigar Makers, Bricklayers and Masons, Railway Conductors, and Coopers.

[22] Commons, *op. cit.*, Vol. II, pp. 307–308.

The "equalization of funds" gave the national organization effective control over the locals, a matter of great significance for the future of American unions, as the structure of the Cigar Makers union was widely copied by the other trade unions formed (or rebuilt) during the last two decades of the 19th century.

The early 1880's were generally prosperous and unionism flourished. From a low of 50,000 members in 1878, trade union membership (exclusive of the Knights of Labor) climbed to between 200,000 and 225,000 in 1883 and about 300,000 in 1885.[23]   To a considerable extent the trade unions found their new recruits among recent immigrants, as a large part of the skilled labor force had to be recruited from Europe.[24]

Although these trade unions were destined to become the dominant organizations of the American labor movement, this was not apparent in the early 1880's.   In most unions, the national organizations were by no means dominant over the locals, and the revival of union activity brought with it a resurgence of the City Centrals that had disintegrated in the 1870's.   It was not clear whether the "center of gravity" of the labor movement was to lie with the City Centrals or with the nascent national unions.

The Knights of Labor

The 1880's had yet a third contender for control of the destinies of American labor, the Knights of Labor.   This organization was founded at Philadelphia in 1869 as a secret society.   The initial reason for secrecy was its founders' desire to imitate conventional fraternal societies. The "Noble and Holy Order of the Knights of Labor," to use its full name, had secret passwords, grips, meeting places, etc.   Indeed, until 1878 the very name of the order was not public, it being referred to as *****.   In the 1870's there was yet a further reason for secrecy; it served to protect members from employer blacklists at a time when refusal to hire known unionists was common practice in many areas.

However, secrecy seriously impeded recruiting, especially among Catholics.   The Catholic Church was opposed to any secret society whose ritual could not be disclosed in the Confessional.   To facilitate recruiting among Catholics, and for other reasons, secrecy was abandoned toward the end of the 1870's.

Membership grew slowly at first; in 1878 there were 9,287 members, in 1881 there were only 19,422.   Thereafter the organization grew more rapidly, attaining over 50,000 members in 1883, 100,000 in 1885, and reaching a peak of over 700,000 in 1886.[25]   However, the extent of the

[23] *Ibid.*, p. 314.
[24] *Ibid.*, p. 315.
[25] *Ibid.*, pp. 342–343, 381 *et seq.*

Knights' influence is understated by the number of members on its rolls at any one moment. For it had an extremely high membership turnover and influenced a far larger number of persons (who passed through the organization) than its membership, on any given day, would indicate.

The Knights were easy to join; they accepted anyone not a "professional gambler, stockbroker, lawyer, banker, liquor dealer, or scab." There were no barriers of race, color, creed, or citizenship; dues and initiation fees were low; and there were no skill requirements to meet. It is not surprising that the Knights should have had a considerable attraction for the nonskilled worker who was not sought after, and even rebuffed, by the trade unions of skilled workmen.

But the Knights' membership rolls were by no means confined to unskilled workers. For the Knights were not "merely" an organization of wage earners. They admitted small tradesmen, farmers, etc., and their locals in small towns, especially in the western and southern states, consisted largely of these lower middle class elements.

The willingness of the Knights to accept nonwage earners reflected the ambiguity of its objectives. Its program was very similar to the earlier labor-reform associations that reached back from the National Labor Union of the 1860's to the organizations of the Jacksonian period; they were for uplifting the "common man." Large sections of the Knights espoused adult education, producers' cooperatives, currency reform, etc. Indeed, the 1880 General Assembly (i.e., convention) set aside 10 per cent of the Order's "defense fund" for purposes of adult education.[26] The major officers of the national organization, especially T. V. Powderly (chief officer from 1879 to 1893), were much more interested in worker education and similar matters than in union activity as such.

But the Knights were also a labor organization. Many national unions that later became part of the AFL were nurtured as district assemblies of the Knights, e.g., the Brewery Workers, an important part of the United Mine Workers, the Window Glass Workers, Boot and Shoe Workers, etc. The Knights acquired members in the early 1880's in two ways: (1) as individuals and (2) by absorbing locals of defunct national unions and even whole unions. To struggling union organizations, the Knights could offer the assistance of their organizers and even (limited) financial help. In addition, many workers in a union's trade might already be members of the Knights, and these would be transferred to the union in question as soon as it affiliated with the Knights. The Knights could also render effective assistance in boycotting unfair employers.

The attractions of the Knights were frequently enhanced by their organizers' practice of approaching groups of workers on strike, or about to go on strike, with offers of assistance (if they joined the Knights). This

[26] Ware, *op. cit.*, p. 120.

practice kept steady pressure on the organization's treasury and led to frequent crises and charges of bad faith when promises could not be honored. However, a token of financial aid was often given which, together with the practical assistance of the organizer, frequently secured the adherence and gratitude of the workers involved.

The Knights' staff of organizers was quite large for the time. The national organization had only four organizers, but the various district assemblies appointed many more. In a number of cases, the district organizers were compensated with a portion of the charter fees of newly formed locals. This added to their zeal and willingness to promise whatever was necessary to sell a Knights' charter.

Superficially, it seemed that the Knights' organization was controlled by its national conventions and officers. But, in practice, each district assembly managed its own affairs and controlled its own strike funds. The district assemblies were of two kinds: mixed and trade. The mixed assemblies consisted of locals which included workers in a variety of occupations. The locals of the trade districts included only members of a given trade and were, to all intents and purposes, trade unions.[27] The mixed assemblies made it possible to organize workers in small towns where there were too few in any one trade to maintain an organization. However, in the larger cities, the mixed assemblies tended to become hotbeds of political radicalism and engaged in factional struggles with the trade districts for control of the organization.

The growth of the Knights, especially in the hectic year 1885–1886, was largely an historical accident, or series of accidents. The Knights had won several well-publicized strikes culminating in (partial) victories over, first, the Wabash and then the Missouri, Kansas and Texas Railroads in 1885. These roads were controlled by Jay Gould who, for reasons of temporary expediency, chose to negotiate on friendly terms with the Knights, rather than fight them. The effect of these victories, exaggerated by the press and eager Knight organizers, inspired thousands of unskilled wage earners to join the Knights. The organizational structure of the Knights was peculiarly well adapted to absorbing such an amorphous mass of workers and, as a result, membership climbed from 104,000 in July 1885 to over 700,000 one year later.

This flood of recruits was received by the national leadership with mixed feelings. Naturally they were pleased with the growth of their organization, but the attitudes and expectations of the new recruits were

---

[27] As the districts were organized on a geographical basis, there were seeds of jurisdictional conflict between mixed and trade assemblies. However, these were, for the most part, adjusted satisfactorily (Commons, *op. cit.,* Vol. II, pp. 482 et seq.) until 1887 when, in the declining phase of the Order's career, the struggle between the two types of assembly became quite bitter.

alarming. Workers joined on the eve, or in the midst, of a strike, expecting immediate aid. To them, and to a credulous public, the Knights were strike winners, par excellence. The irony of this is that the national leadership opposed strikes and favored compulsory arbitration.[28] But, despite their feelings, the national leaders could not control the strike actions of their district organizations, nor could they repudiate them, especially as the right of workers to join the Knights was frequently a major strike issue.

Captive of their victories, the national leadership of the Knights was, in 1886, shoved forward by a surge of labor militancy. Confident of their strength, the rank and file and many district leaders prepared for a general strike for the eight hour day, to commence on May 1, 1886. The eight hour day agitation dated back to the 1860's, but it had been revived by some of the trade unions who talked of an eight hour day strike for May 1, 1886. The Knights had been invited to join the movement and many of their organizers made glowing promises about the coming reduction in the work day. It is not altogether clear why this particular issue should have assumed such importance at this particular time, but there is no doubt that it was an important demand of the Knights' recruits.

Despite the attempt of the Knights' national leadership to discourage the strike, on May 1, 1886 over 300,000 workers throughout the nation laid down their tools in an attempt to secure the eight hour day. This strike had a few temporary successes, but by the beginning of 1887 these had been largely obliterated by employer counteroffensives. The famous Haymarket bombing occurred in Chicago as an aftermath of this strike;[29] the Knights were (unjustly) associated with this affair and thereby acquired a reputation for violence which contributed to their rapid decline.

THE AFL'S FIRST PHASE: 1886 TO 1914

From 1886 to 1893: The Knights and the Trade Unions

The year 1886 is famous in American labor history as the year in which the American Federation of Labor was founded.[30] The AFL was created

---

[28] Commons, op. cit., Vol. II, p. 416. The sympathy of the Knights' leadership for compulsory arbitration was not unusual among labor leaders of the 1880's. The strike history of the 1870's was a prolonged series of union defeats, and the strike instrument was greatly discredited among unionists. Not surprisingly, employers were bitterly opposed to compulsory arbitration.

[29] On May 3, 1886, at a night meeting in Haymarket Square, Chicago, a number of anarchists addressed a rather small group. As the meeting was about to break up, the police appeared and attempted to disperse those congregated; as the police charged the gathering, a bomb was thrown killing or wounding several of the policemen. For this act, by unknown parties, four of the anarchists were hanged and three others imprisoned.

[30] The nascent trade unions had formed, in 1881, the Federation of Organized

during a struggle of the trade unions with the Knights of Labor; its features still reflect the circumstances of its birth.

For a number of years, the trade unions and the Knights had coexisted peacefully; many workers belonged both to a trade union and to the Knights.   However, during the rapid growth of the Knights in 1885–1886, locals of skilled workers, disgruntled over one matter or another, began to leave their union and join the Knights.   In some cases, the Knights had also accepted individuals and groups expelled by other unions.   Furthermore, the unskilled workers within the Knights began to compete with the higher wage, more highly skilled workers in the trade unions.

As a result, struggles between Knights and trade union locals arose in a number of places in 1886.   The battle reached its height in New York City where it involved the Cigar Makers headed by Gompers. There, the struggle reached the point where the Knights and trade union locals were attempting to break one another's strikes.   The trade unionists attempted to come to terms with the Knights, but the latter refused to accept the conditions offered by the unionists.   To the trade unionists, the issue was (or seemed) a matter of life or death.   The rapid growth and expansionist tendencies of the Knights threatened to swallow the entire labor movement, and they demanded assurances that the Knights would cease to raid their membership.   Within the Knights, the trade union element was anxious to make peace with the trade unions (outside), but the other factions (especially the New York District Assembly) were indifferent and rather contemptuous of the trade unions.   At this juncture, July 1886, the Knights were under the control of the anti-trade union faction, and the die was cast.

The trade unions and the AFL opened war to the hilt upon the Knights. And it was not only the AFL with whom the Knights had to contend. The strike wave of 1886 thoroughly alarmed employers, and they redoubled their efforts to destroy the Knights.   Dismissals for membership in the Knights were frequent, and rather than deal with Knight locals, employers would lock out[31] their workers, accepting them back, if at all, only upon assurances that they had left the Order and would not rejoin.

Coupled with intensified employer discrimination was the loss of self-confidence attendant upon a series of strike defeats.   The eight hour day

---

Trades and Labor Unions of which Samuel Gompers was secretary.   This organization was concerned almost exclusively with legislative matters and is noteworthy only because the AFL was founded as its successor organization.   Sometimes the AFL dates its birth year as 1881, claiming to be merely a continuation of the aforementioned Federation.

[31] A lockout occurs when the employer refuses to employ his workers further (i.e., "locks them out") until they agree to certain terms.   See pp. 163–164.

strikes were largely defeated; a major railroad strike was lost in the spring of 1886 and, in the fall, a big strike in the Chicago packing-houses was lost. The fact that the defeat in the packing-house strike was at least partially due to the incompetent intervention of Powderly further discouraged the Knights, and the membership, especially among unskilled workers, began to melt away.

There were other examples of incompetent strike leadership which disgusted the trade union element within the Knights.[32]   To this was added resentment over the interference by the nonunion elements in the activities of the trade districts and a growing feeling that employers were more ready to deal with other unions than with Knights.   This dis-satisfaction gave Gompers (president of the AFL) the opportunity to separate the various trade districts from the Knights and secure their adherence to the AFL.

Gompers assiduously wooed the trade districts of the Knights throughout the decade 1886–1896; by 1890 he had gathered most of them into the AFL.   As more and more of the trade union elements left the Knights, the relative strength of the other factions grew, further weakening the influence of the remaining unionists.   By 1890, the Knights (reduced to a membership of 100,000) were dominated by their rural midwestern locals who converted the organization into an ally of the Populist movement.

The trade unions within the AFL grew slowly, at first.   The organizations that formed the AFL in 1886 had about 138,000 members.   Their growth, the adherence of other trade unions, and transfers from the Knights brought the AFL's membership to 225,000 by 1890.[33]   In total, union membership had declined sharply from its peak of 1886, but what remained were in organizations of far greater permanence than the Knights.   These organizations were strong enough to weather the sharp depression of 1893–1894 and enter (in 1897) a period of sustained growth.

The AFL: 1894 to 1904

The AFL, in this period, consisted mostly of craft unions of skilled workers.   These unions had shown their survival value by continuing to grow during the 1880's and 1890's when the organizations of the unskilled collapsed.   There is no great mystery as to why it was mainly (skilled) craft unions that survived this period.   The strength of a (craft) union of skilled workmen lies in its ability to secure a virtual monopoly of workers having a particular skill essential to certain employers.   So long as their

[32] See Commons, *op. cit.*, Vol. II, pp. 413–423 and 482–488.
[33] Leo Wolman, *Growth of American Trade Unions, 1880–1923,* National Bureau of Economic Research, New York, 1924, p. 31.

monopoly holds, the employer must come to terms with them if he is to engage in production.[34] This does not give the skilled union "absolute power," but it makes it a redoubtable opponent whose good-will is worthy of cultivation; in short, its strikes are not easily defeated because it is hard to get adequate substitutes, even during depressions. The reverse is true of unskilled workers; during a temporary labor shortage they may be able to contend successfully with an employer, but, as soon as business worsens and (unskilled) workers become plentiful, their members can easily be replaced and their power to win strikes is correspondingly reduced.[35] Furthermore, the skilled unions charged higher dues and could therefore afford larger strike (and other) benefits.

An additional advantage of skilled unions lay in the relatively small numbers of their members, which made concessions to them far less costly to an employer, than concessions to the "great mass" of unskilled workers. Indeed, it was far easier for skilled workers to gain concessions for themselves if they did not insist upon them for the unskilled also. And, in the period before World War I, skilled workers took full advantage of this fact. In fact, in order to "honor their trade agreements,"[36] it frequently happened that skilled workers would cross the picket lines of other workers. The Railway Brotherhoods (Locomotive Engineers, Firemen, Conductors, etc.) were especially noted for this policy of honoring agreements with employers, but they were by no means unique. This policy was the antithesis of the slogan (and policy) of the Knights of Labor, "An injury to one is the concern of all," and it provoked bitter criticism of craft unions by the Knights and (later) by others (see pp. 52–55). However, the defenders of the craft unions have argued, and with reason, that maintaining the sanctity of contracts was necessary for the survival and development of any union in this period.

As a result of these circumstances, in a number of industries there developed small groups of unionized and relatively well-paid skilled workers whose status contrasted sharply with much larger numbers of workers without unions or distinctive skill. This contrast gave rise to the saying that the AFL comprised the aristocrats of American labor. In addition to the scattering of craft workers throughout the economy, the AFL contained concentrations of workers in certain industries where economic conditions favored union organization, e.g., newspaper printing

[34] This point is well stated by J. T. Dunlop, "The Development of Labor Organizations: A Theoretical Framework," in *Insights Into Labor Issues*, edited by R. A. Lester and J. Shister, Macmillan and Co., New York, 1948, pp. 181–183.

[35] In this period it was virtually impossible to bar entry to a struck plant by picketing.

[36] A "trade agreement" is an agreement between a union and one or more employers governing the terms of employment of its members for some specified period of time. (For further discussion, see pp. 174 et seq.).

and building construction. As the output of these industries was sold locally,[37] the unions involved had no need to fear that their achievements in one city would be endangered by nonunion production elsewhere. This made it possible for these unions to progress slowly and steadily; a possibility denied to unions whose members' output was sold in a national market.

Unionization is also facilitated by the necessity for continuous production or operation. Thus the skilled workers in transportation, especially railroads, were unionized to a considerable degree by the early 1900's. Where the sale of the employer's product was helped by a union label,[38] or harmed by a union boycott, unionization was also facilitated. The union label was especially valuable on goods sold primarily to wage earners; thus the Brewery Workers, Cigar Makers, Cap Makers, Overall Makers, Printers, etc. were able to unionize many firms through customer pressure. The "union label" also helped to unionize the employees of service establishments such as restaurants, bars, taverns, etc. that catered to a working class clientele.

In short, where workers were skilled, especially if the product had to be produced locally, the AFL (and the Railway Brotherhoods) made substantial gains in membership between 1890 and 1904, especially after 1897. However, unskilled workers, particularly in manufacturing, remained unorganized. Indeed, the rise of the giant manufacturing corporation, in the 1890's, brought a new and powerful type of antiunion employer upon the scene. In 1892, the Carnegie Steel Company (the predecessor of the U. S. Steel Corporation) broke the powerful Amalgamated Association of Iron and Steel Workers in the famous Homestead strike. This presaged the expulsion of the union from all plants of the U. S. Steel Corporation in the 1900's. As this corporation was then the largest in the country and had a widely respected management, its behavior set a pattern for other firms in heavy industry.

One major exception must be noted to the general failure of the AFL to organize the unskilled, the coal miners. The United Mine Workers was formed in 1890, by uniting (Miners') Trade District 135 of the Knights of Labor with an independent miners' union; it was issued one of the few industrial union charters issued by the AFL.

An industrial union charter was necessary because craft unionism among coal miners was impossible. The cohesion of skilled and unskilled

---

[37] This statement did (and does) not apply to book and job printing which has (as a result) been unionized much more slowly than newspaper printing.

[38] A union label is placed on merchandise certifying it was produced under union conditions by workers of the union named on the label. Signs in bars, restaurants, etc. stating that the establishment employs only members of a specific union serve the same purpose.

miners is very strong and is rooted in their conditions of work and life. Coal miners lived in isolated small towns or camps which, of itself, develops a strong group feeling. Before the 1930's it frequently happened that all the men in a family worked in the local mine, the less skilled work being performed by the younger members, often boys. Furthermore, the hazardous work conditions make the safety of every miner dependent upon the other members of his work group while the physical circumstances of mining make for close personal contact among all the members of a work group. These considerations are generally believed responsible for the fact that, in most western countries, miners are among the first groups of workers to unionize and that they almost always form industrial unions. However, with the exception of the Miners, the Brewery Workers, and a few other cases of lesser importance, the AFL (circa 1900) consisted of craft or semicraft unions.

The first years of the AFL saw the (national) trade union displace the City Central as the dominant force within the American labor movement. The control of the trade unions over the AFL was assured by a constitutional provision that (in practice) gave overwhelming voting power to the affiliated trade unions as compared with the City and State Federations of Labor. The predominance of the trade unions was confirmed by the 1890 convention which refused to seat the New York City Federation because it had accepted the affiliation of a political organization, the Socialist-Labor party.[39] This act not only testified to the impotence of the City Centrals within the AFL but also assured their "depolitization."

The emasculation of the City Centrals marked a change in the center of gravity of the American labor movement. Before the 1880's it was primarily to these organizations that embattled local unions had looked for assistance. It was these organizations that took the lead in unionizing discontented workers, demanding legislative reforms, issuing pronouncements, publishing labor newspapers, etc. Because these organizations were largely propagandistic in nature, they had great need of the literary and agitational skills of middle-class intellectuals and frequently came under their control. Gompers and other trade unionists distrusted the influence of intellectual reformers upon labor unions. They feared that, as in the past, these reformers would embroil the City Centrals in political struggles to the detriment of union activity. Moreover they (rightly) felt that the reformers' interest in politics was not "practical" but educational; i.e., the reformers were not so much interested in immediate victories or gains in influence as in educating the electorate in "ultimate aims." What was, to Gompers, even worse was the failure of the intellectuals to appreciate the value of organization and discipline; i.e., he deplored their tendency to call recklessly for sympathetic strikes without considering the effect of

[39] Commons, *op. cit.*, Vol. II, p. 517.

such strikes upon the organizations to be involved or upon the employers with whom these organizations dealt. Finally, the City Centrals had been (and to some extent continued to be, see pp. 58–59) sources of aid for union locals rebelling against their national organizations. For all of these reasons, Gompers and the other trade union leaders were determined to minimize the power of the city organizations within the AFL.[40]

The AFL from 1905 to 1914

From its inception in 1886, Gompers' strategic objective was to make unionism respectable. He sought to sell his kind of trade unions to employers as bulwarks against political radicalism, irresponsible strikes, and as helpful associates in securing government contracts, markets for union label merchandise, etc. In pursuit of this end, he encouraged the signing and fulfilling of trade agreements, even at the cost of ignoring the picket lines of other unions. He also cultivated the society of business leaders and "respectable" political figures through organizations such as the National Civic Federation.

This tactic was imitated by other union leaders and met with some success, as evidenced by Federation membership which reached the one million mark in 1902, and climbed to 1,676,000 two years later. However, beginning with 1905, the AFL's organizing activities met with such resistance that its membership did not again reach the 1904 level until 1911; this, despite the fact that the labor force was growing rapidly due to the high rate of immigration.

The stiffening of employer resistance to unionism was especially noticeable in smaller cities in the middle west. Gompers' program of selling unionism to employers had succeeded with some of them, but by no means with a majority. And the antiunion employers, in the early 1900's, inaugurated a campaign of propaganda against unionism and the closed shop. This campaign was carried on by a number of local "Citizens Industrial Associations," coordinated by the National Association of Manufacturers. Its objective was to build up antiunion sentiment among employers and other middle-class groups in order to make unionization more difficult; i.e., the objective was to prevent unionism from becoming socially acceptable. To a considerable extent this antiunion campaign succeeded, especially in the small towns into which unionism (in the early 1900's) had been spreading from its sources in the big cities.[41]

In addition to this campaign, the cause of unionism had to face the unrelenting opposition of large manufacturers. Yet a third source of

---

[40] The determination to minimize the influence of the City Centrals had ideological implications; they were centers of Socialist influence.

[41] See Perlman and Taft, *History of Labor in the United States, 1896–1932*, Macmillan & Co., New York, 1935, Chapters II and XIII.

difficulty for unionism was the attitude of the courts which began to issue strike-halting injunctions in increasing numbers and to hamper union boycotts and other "self-help" activities by means of the Sherman Antitrust Law (see pp. 214–215).

Defeat intensified the opposition within the AFL to "Gompersism." The advocates of greater militancy had never been sold on Gompers' methods and had always been vociferously critical of them.   And after 1905, it was no longer possible for Gompers to answer his critics with a record of organizing success.   On the level of union organization (politics and ideology are discussed on pp. 91–98) the principal complaint of the anti-Gompers forces was that the craft union leaders were uninterested in organizing the unskilled workers, that they did not wish to spend money for organizers, that they were prejudiced against the unskilled because they were new immigrants.   These accusations were garnished with accusations of corruption, "narrow craft unionism," political conservatism, and organizational inertia.   Unfortunately, these criticisms were not without foundation, even though they were exaggerated.

To simplify a long and complicated story, the situation within the AFL, about 1910, was as follows: the advance of unionism had (by the early 1900's) made it possible for union leaders to obtain comfortable salaries and expense accounts.   Many of these leaders had grown old in service and had become discouraged by the failure of their attempts to extend further the boundaries of unionism.   As a result, they were resigned to leading small groups of well-entrenched skilled workers.   They knew the hazards and costs of organizing drives to gain new members and were disinclined to risk the treasuries of their compact little organizations in such attempts.

An even more serious objection (from the craft unionists' viewpoint) to organizing the unskilled was that once in a union the unskilled would dominate it by force of numbers.   This would endanger the jobs of present office-holders, undermine craft standards of workmanship and associated wage differentials, disturb good relations with employers, and so on.   To the fuel of vested interest was added the match of ethnic prejudice. The skilled workers, and their leaders, were either native born or immigrants of long standing from northwestern Europe.   The unskilled workers who were to be unionized were recent immigrants, largely Slavs, Italians, and East European Jews.   It was easy to excuse organizational inertia or failure by assertions that these "foreigners" were not good union material, and craft union leaders made many statements to this effect.

In a certain narrow sense, the statements were true.   The unskilled workers could not afford the relatively high dues of the craft unions; indeed, many would pay dues only immediately before a strike.   In brief, they were not "organization-minded."   But they could (and did) wage bitter strike battles and, when properly handled, could be made into "all weather" unionists.

However, proper handling meant using organizers who spoke to immigrant workers in their native tongue, publishing newspapers in their native language, etc. Union representatives had to manifest a genuine interest in the problems of these workers and display a respect for their customs, if they were to gain their confidence; i.e., the successful union organizer had to be half social worker. But this type of organizer was precisely what the old-line AFL unions lacked; the few men they did send out were usually contemptuous of the immigrants and betrayed it. The result was a long series of organizational failures and lost strikes.[42]

These remarks certainly do not apply to all AFL unions of this period and, perhaps, not even to the majority. But there were enough unions with these general characteristics to give substance to the widely-publicized charges (of Socialists and IWWs) that the AFL unions were led by reactionary bureaucrats who were uninterested in unionizing unskilled workers and disliked immigrants and negroes.

The AFL leadership found it difficult either to refute these accusations or remove their basis. The AFL had no control over the internal policies of its affiliates, including those regarding admission. Indeed, had it tried to assume such powers, the stronger unions would probably have left it forthwith. As Gompers well knew, the price of unity in the American labor movement was tolerance of the practices of individual unions. But this often implied that the entire AFL had to suffer loss of esteem because of the practices and policies of certain affiliates. For example, it was neither easy nor convincing for Gompers to argue that the AFL, as such, was in favor of racial equality but had no control over the admission policies of the various affiliates which excluded negroes.[43] Such protestations clearly (and correctly) implied that Gompers thought it more important to advance the interests of America's unionized wage earners, even though this meant harming the unorganized, than to risk a battle on the issue of making it easier for the nonorganized (particularly immigrants and negroes) to join unions. In short, Gompers defended the American union member and leader as he was, irrespective of what he ought to have been. This was, perhaps, necessary for the continued unity of the AFL, but it earned the AFL the hatred of those who were excluded from its membership, and of their sympathizers.

[42] On this point see the interesting discussion of W. M. Leiserson, *Adjusting Immigrant and Industry,* Harpers, 1924, pp. 201–206.

[43] On the question of AFL policy toward negroes see F. E. Wolfe, *Admission to American Trade Unions,* Johns Hopkins Press, Baltimore, 1912, Chapter VI; also Spero and Harris, *The Black Worker,* Columbia University Press, New York, 1930, Chapters IV and V.

One bright spot in the AFL's organizing record during this period should be noted, the garment workers. The predominantly Jewish garment workers generated from their ranks a large number of excellent leaders and won two major strikes in New York City, in 1909 and 1910, that established the International Ladies Garment Workers (ILGWU)[44] as a major union with over 65,000 members in 1911.

In men's clothing manufacture the road to organization was somewhat slower because production was scattered in a number of cities and not concentrated in New York (as is ladies' clothing). However, a major strike of immigrant tailors in Chicago in 1910 gained the union a bridgehead in the huge Hart, Schaffner and Marx plant; this was developed until, within a few years, a preferential union shop had been obtained. In 1912 a major strike of the New York tailors was won, and many semiskilled and unskilled workers were unionized as a result.

But these strike victories (in men's clothing) had been obtained despite the attempts of the national leaders of the United Garment Workers (the national union with jurisdiction) to settle the strikes behind the backs of the local strike leaders. The agreements obtained by the national leaders were repudiated by the strikers, who thereafter obtained better terms. As a result there was much bitterness between the national officers of the United Garment Workers and the New York and Chicago tailor locals, accusations and insults were freely exchanged. (The behavior of the national leaders of the United Garment Workers provides a classic example of an AFL union's failure to cope with the problems of leading unskilled immigrant workers.)

When it seemed likely that the membership would oust the national officers at the 1914 convention, the officers sought, by trickery, to disenfranchise a large part of the opposition. This led to a rebellion by the locals involved who proceeded to form the Amalgamated Clothing Workers, which soon became the dominant union in men's clothing manufacturing. The success of the Amalgamated in unionizing unskilled immigrants provided a striking contrast to the failures of the United Garment Workers.[45]

The Industrial Workers of the World

Criticism of the AFL's failure to organize the unskilled came from a number of sources within and without the Federation. But the most

---

[44] An interesting, though opinionated, history of the ILGWU is Benjamin Stolberg, *Tailor's Progress,* Doubleday, Doran and Co., New York, 1944. A less controversial account is in Joel Seidman, *The Needle Trades,* Farrar and Rinehart Co., New York, 1942.

[45] A good account of these struggles is in Matthew Josephson, *Sidney Hillman: Statesman of American Labor,* Doubleday and Co., Inc., Garden City, New York, 1952, Chapter Four.

vituperative source, by far, was the group of labor militants associated with the Industrial Workers of the World, the IWW, or "Wobblies," as they were sometimes called. The IWW was founded in 1905 by a number of discordant elements whose common denominator was disapproval of craft unionism and AFL policies and a correlative faith in the virtues of the industrial form of union organization. Most of the founders were "radicals"; they included Debs,[46] Haywood, DeLeon, and other prominent left-wingers of the period. Many of the founders represented no one but themselves. Several left-wing leaders of AFL locals were in attendance at the birth of the IWW, but they were not able to commit their organizations.

In its early years (1905–1907) the bulk of the IWW's membership and revenue came from the Western Federation of Miners (WFM).[47] However, the WFM left in 1907 as the result of the first of two splits within the first three years of the IWW's existence. The second split created two organizations, the Detroit IWW (dominated by DeLeonists)[48] and the

---

[46] Eugene Debs was, before World War I, the perennial nominee for President by the Socialist party. In his youth Debs had been one of the founders of the Brotherhood of Locomotive Firemen, and had served for many years as its secretary and treasurer. He resigned this position in 1893 to become president of the American Railway Union (ARU), an industrial union designed to include all railway workers and replace the existing (skilled) Brotherhoods.

This organization had a meteoric career. After winning a big strike against the Great Northern Railroad, its membership jumped to 150,000 and it seemed that it would engulf the Brotherhoods. However, the organization was drawn into a strike of the Pullman Company and, in the course of refusing to handle Pullman cars on the railroads, became the object of a Federal Court injunction which troops were used to enforce. As a result the strike was lost, and the railroads, by refusing to hire ARU members, destroyed the organization within a year. Debs was sentenced to six months in prison for violating the federal injunction. A few years later he joined the Socialist party. Although present at the formation of IWW, Debs never played any active role in it. An excellent account of Debs' career is Ray Ginger's biography, *The Bending Cross*, Rutgers University Press, New Brunswick, N.J.

[47] The Western Federation of Miners was the union of metal (silver, copper, lead, and zinc) miners in the Rocky Mountain region. It had a history of militancy and violence (dealt and received) unmatched in American labor history. In 1897, it withdrew from the AFL in protest against its conservatism and its failure to support WFM strikes. In later years the organization became more conservative, and it returned to the AFL in 1911; in 1916 it changed its name to the International Union of Mine, Mill, and Smelter Workers. In 1935 it joined the CIO and has recently attracted considerable attention as being (allegedly) Communist dominated. A full account of the history of this union prior to 1930 is V. H. Jensen, *Heritage of Conflict*, Cornell University Press, Ithaca, N.Y., 1950; a briefer account is Perlman and Taft, *op. cit.*, Chapters XVII to XIX and XXII.

[48] Daniel DeLeon was the head of the Socialist Labor Party (which still functions in the United States). A Marxist of rigid views and sharp tongue, he was a cause

Chicago IWW, which is the organization known to history and the one to which the following brief account refers.

The (Chicago) IWW was an extremely decentralized organization if, indeed, it could be called an organization at all. It had a small staff of paid organizers attached to the central office and a much larger number of amateur sympathizers. The paid organizers served as a kind of flying squadron; one or more of them would be dispatched to situations where trouble was brewing, or a strike had already broken out, and offer leadership, publicity, and a campaign to secure outside aid. As these "situations" usually resulted from a more or less spontaneous revolt of unskilled workers badly in need of guidance, the IWW organizers were welcomed with open arms. And the IWW organizers built good will for their "organization." Unlike many AFL organizers, the IWW representatives accepted the objectives of the strikers and fought to attain them. Furthermore, the IWW organizers were usually more adept than AFL men at strike tactics, more skillful at dramatizing issues, and (above all) more willing to risk violence and jail.

The IWW was unable to build permanent organizations and really did not try. Its purpose was to imbue workers with the feeling of working class solidarity and power through strike action. Although it never had more than 30,000 members at any one time, the IWW influenced a much larger number of workers who passed through its ranks.

In this respect, as in its stress upon "working class solidarity," the IWW resembled the Knights of Labor. But, unlike the Knights, the Wobblies had a clear-cut concept of the working class (i.e., they excluded all nonwage earners), and its idea of class solidarity implied relentless hostility to the rival (employer) class. Any strike was viewed as a battle in the class struggle, and all members of the working class were urged to lend assistance. The IWW opposed written contracts specifying a definite date of expiration because they might interfere with the necessity for sympathetic action; and it advocated the abrogation of such contracts where they existed. To the IWW, industrial peace was simply an interval of truce between battles in the unending class war.

That sympathetic strike action might destroy a union that had taken years to build did not bother the Wobblies. What was needed, according to the IWW, was not organization but working class solidarity. Given the appropriate attitude, whatever organization was needed for strike action could be built overnight and, for any other purpose, organization was pernicious.[49] The ultimate "aims" of the IWW were never very

---

of intensive warfare (ending in expulsion of one side or the other) in every organization he was permitted to enter. See Perlman and Taft, *op. cit.,* pp. 217–224 and 235–236.

[49] The Wobblies were very critical of the salaries and perquisites of AFL officials. The salaries of their own (few) paid officials were extremely low.

clear; they were against "capitalism" and in favor of attacking it by strike action, but they had no specific plans for replacing it. For a time, some of the IWW leaders (including Haywood) were members of the Socialist party, but after 1910 they found themselves increasingly out of sympathy (and vice versa) with the "respectable" and increasingly conservative eastern right-wing of the party.

The Wobblies have been called Syndicalists (see pp. 97–98) and certainly their behavior suggested such a doctrine. Some spokesmen of the movement did have contact with French Syndicalists and mouthed some syndicalist doctrines, but the Wobblies were not much influenced by theory; they stressed practice, i.e., strikes.

Between the years 1906 and 1920, the IWW was active all over the United States. In a real sense, it moved into the void left by the lethargic behavior of many AFL unions. (Where an AFL affiliate vigorously organized the unskilled, as in coal mining and clothing manufacture, the IWW rarely made headway.) In the east the IWW worked with unskilled immigrant strikers, using foreign language organizers. Their greatest success came in textile manufacturing where, in 1912, they led 25,000 strikers (at Lawrence, Mass.) to victory and wage increases. They also led big strikes at McKees Rocks, Pa. (1909) and at Patterson, N.J. (1913). In the west, the Wobblies organized in mining camps, logging and construction camps, among itinerant harvest workers, and among longshoremen and sailors.

The western IWW was typically an itinerant and proudly accepted the designation of "bum"; one of the IWW's most famous songs was "Hallelujah, I'm a Bum." The western Wobblies have contributed greatly to the folklore of the American labor movement; their intransigeance, their combats with the forces of law and order, and their martyrs such as Joe Hill are famed in song and story.

But since 1920, the IWW has been a negligible part of the American labor movement. Its decline began with its active opposition to American participation in World War I. This opposition caused the jailing of most of its leaders for several years (1918–1922), which were critical in the development of American unionism. The resulting lack of experienced leadership, together with a split among the remaining leaders on the issue of whether to affiliate with the Communist International, permanently weakened the IWW. In addition the stigma of being "unpatriotic," which the Wobblies gained during the war, and the violence directed against its members tended to frighten workers away from it.[50]

---

[50] The standard history of the IWW (prior to 1917) is P. F. Brissenden, *The IWW*, Columbia University Press, New York, 1919; also see Perlman and Taft, *op. cit.*, Chapters XXI to XXIV. For interesting personal accounts of IWW leaders, see *Bill Haywood's Book—an Autobiography*, International Publishers, New York, 1929 and Ralph Chaplin, *Wobbly*, University of Chicago Press, Chicago, 1948.

THE AFL FROM 1914 TO 1935

From 1914 to 1920

From 1913 through 1915, union membership declined slightly, being 2,716,300 in the former year and 2,582,000 in the latter. However, the economic consequences of World War I began, in 1916, to swell union membership; and from then until 1920 workers enrolled in unions at an ever increasing rate. In 1920, 5,047,800 workers were enrolled in unions, a number not reached again until 1937. The major part of the influx occurred between 1918 and 1920 when over 1,500,000 additional members were acquired.

During World War I almost all unions gained members, but the big increases were concentrated in a small number of war-stimulated industries such as metal working, machinery, construction, shipbuilding, transportation, and men's clothing manufacture. Unions in these industries accounted for about two-thirds of the total increase in union membership.[51]

The causes of the rapid growth of unionism in this period are not far to seek:

1. After 1915 the boom in war production created a genuine labor shortage which could not, because of the European war, be relieved by a flood of new immigrants. This greatly reduced the power of antiunion employers to frighten their employees away from unions by the threat of discharge. At the same time the labor shortage made it difficult to secure strike-breakers, and the almost limitless demand for output made work stoppages very costly to employers. In short, employers lost much of their customary power to resist unionization.

2. A second factor that (temporarily) encouraged unionization was the government boards (especially the War Labor Board) that attempted to prevent work stoppages. These boards acted, formally, as conciliators, but great moral pressure was placed upon both unions and employers to submit disputes to the appropriate board for adjudication and to accept the resulting awards. The principles of dispute settlement followed by the boards generally forbade both compulsory unionization and discrimination against union members by management. This meant that antiunion employers could not, under the awards, continue their policy of refusing to hire union men. In addition, the War Labor Board and certain other government agencies actively encouraged collective bargaining.

3. To some extent, the increase in unionism during World War I was due simply to a lessening of employers' power to resist it. However,

---

[51] Leo Wolman, *Ebb and Flow in Trade Unionism*, New York, National Bureau of Economic Research, 1936, Table 10, p. 30.

soaring living costs must also be given credit, especially during 1919–1920, for impelling unionization. From 1917 through 1920, wage earners were forced repeatedly to demand wage increases to forestall reductions in real income resulting from rising prices. The discontented workers, whose wages did not keep pace with price increases, were highly receptive to the promises of union organizers.

During this period, gains in membership accrued to many old-line AFL unions. But important gains were also made by the Amalgamated Clothing Workers which was born (in December 1914) out of the aforementioned revolt against the United Garment Workers and, therefore, not permitted to affiliate with the AFL. The Amalgamated rose from 38,000 members in 1915 to 177,000 in 1920; these statistics reflect the unionization of a major part of men's clothing manufacturing.[52] (The growth of the Amalgamated was aided, during the war years, by its success in getting the government to insist upon the maintenance of minimal standards of wages and conditions in factories manufacturing uniforms for the Armed Forces.)

Flushed with victory in men's clothing manufacture, the Amalgamated's organizers moved on, in 1919, to assist the unskilled textile workers of New England who were dissatisfied with the policies and methods of the United Textile Workers.[53] They established the Amalgamated Textile Workers which, for a short time, was a formidable competitor to the United Textile Workers. However, after 1920, unionism among the unskilled textile workers of New England was virtually destroyed, and with it the Amalgamated Textile Workers.

Important organizing work was done by yet another organization dissatisfied with the AFL craft union leadership, the Chicago Federation of Labor. Its leader, John Fitzpatrick, commissioned William Z. Foster (then an organizer for the Brotherhood of Railway Carmen)[54] to unionize the packinghouse workers of Chicago on an industrial basis. Foster and Fitzpatrick managed to get the various craft unions to cede jurisdictional rights to a Stockyards Labor Council which established a set of uniform dues and managed to circumvent various obstacles to organiza-

---

[52] The organizing activity of the Amalgamated was not unimpeded. Prodded by Gompers, who was anxious lest the revolt against the United Garment Workers (UGW) succeed and inspire imitation, the theretofore sedentary leadership of UGW set about organizing unskilled tailors in competition with the Amalgamated. However, despite the active intervention of Gompers, the skill of the Amalgamated's organizers—and the bad reputation of the United Garment Workers—prevailed. See Josephson, *op. cit.*, pp. 100–148.

[53] Budish and Soule, *The New Unionism*, Harcourt, Brace & Co., New York, 1920, Chapter X and M. D. Savage, *Industrial Unionism in America*, Ronald Press Co., New York, 1922, Chapter VIII.

[54] Foster later became head of the Communist Party.

tion embedded in the constitutions of the craft unions (such as barring negroes from membership). By threatening a strike, federal mediation was secured and a large part of the Council's demands were achieved. As a result, a sizeable part of the Chicago packinghouse workers were unionized and remained so until the Stockyards Labor Council was smashed during the depression of 1920–1921.

Fitzpatrick and Foster went from meat packing to steel. At their insistence, a committee (National Committee for the Organizing of the Iron and Steel Industries) of 24 unions (claiming jurisdiction over various crafts in steel manufacture) was established; each union was supposed to furnish money and organizers to aid an organizing campaign. The unions involved agreed to accept a small standard initiation fee in lieu of their regular fees and to parcel out the recruits to the appropriate unions after the organization drive had been completed. The organizing campaign met with a great deal of success in recruiting members. However, the various unions involved showed little enthusiasm for a struggle with the big steel corporations and were very sparing of organizers and cash contributions. (The biggest single cash contribution, $100,000, came from the Amalgamated Clothing Workers!)

When the aforementioned committee demanded recognition as the bargaining representative of the various steel companies' employees, the companies responded by discharging union members, thereby compelling a strike. When the strike call was issued in September 1919 over 360,-000 workers responded, but the steel companies, led by U. S. Steel, were adamant in refusing to deal with the unions. By the first of 1920 the strike was broken and the Committee dissolved amidst mutual recriminations.[55]

Discontent with the leadership of the AFL had still other manifestations and causes. In 1919 and 1920 there was a veritable wave of strikes resulting from the rapid rise of living costs. Price rises made union members impatient for contracts to expire (in order to negotiate wage increases) and intolerant of leaders who urged caution. The labor shortage made workers confident of their strength, while the rising cost of living made them desperate. The leaders of established unions were frequently insensitive to the attitude of the rank and file and, too often, attempted to substitute descipline for leadership. As a result, there were strikes in defiance of the national leaders of various unions;[56] these provoked disciplinary action which generated further bitterness. These "outlaw" strikes were occasionally supported by City Centrals, which caused the AFL conventions (in 1920 and 1922) to reaffirm the

---

[55] Perlman and Taft, *op. cit.,* Chapter XXXV; also Interchurch World Movement, *Report on the Steel Strike of 1919,* Harcourt, Brace & Co., New York, 1920.

[56] See Perlman and Taft, *op. cit.,* Chapter XXXIV.

subordinate positions of the City Centrals and further to reduce their limited power.[57]

The strikes of 1919–1920 were highly contagious; "sympathetic" strikes were frequent. However, it usually developed that the "sympathizers" had similar demands of their own, i.e., cost of living adjustments and, frequently, a 44 hour week. In 1919, these sympathetic strikes reached the level of short-lived general strikes in Seattle and Winnipeg.

The effect of this strike wave upon middle-class opinion can be judged properly only if it is remembered that these strikes were seen against the background of the year old Russian revolution and the presence of (short-lived) communist regimes in Central Europe. The inability of "responsible" labor leaders to control their followers, a nation-wide coal strike (in 1919) against a government order, a Policeman's strike in Boston (in 1920), the general strikes in Seattle and Winnipeg, hopeful manifestoes from radicals and warnings from alarmed conservatives disturbed many solid citizens and helped set the stage for an employer counterattack upon the exuberant union movement. The opportunity for this counterattack came with the depression that began in the fall of 1920.

From 1920 to 1933

The depression of 1920–1921 involved sharp price declines which put great pressure upon employers to reduce costs; hence, they demanded large wage reductions. In addition, employers had been experiencing, during 1917–1920, the indiscipline and poor workmanship that is the inevitable accompaniment of a labor shortage (see pp. 292–295). The unions, anxious to serve their new members, often supported them in disputes over working conditions which led employers to blame their labor troubles upon unionism. (Many employers who had, during the war, accepted unions under government duress felt that their initially unfavorable opinion had been confirmed by their experience.) Consequently, they were anxious not only to cut wages but to rid themselves of unions.

The antiunion feelings of individual employers were organized and reinforced by the propaganda of a number of employer organizations. In 1920, both the U. S. Chamber of Commerce (following a referendum of its membership) and the National Association of Manufacturers came out strongly for the right of employers to run an "open shop." They were joined in this by the National Grange and the American Bankers Asso-

---

[57] The conventions defeated motions to compel local unions to join their City Centrals; they also refused to grant the City Centrals any autonomy on the question of admitting or expelling locals. The City Centrals were compelled to expel locals expelled by their national unions, to accept whatever delegates the locals chose to send, etc.

ciation. These general declarations of philosophy were implemented by the organization of a nationwide network of open shop or "American plan"[58] associations. In many cases, these organizations were merely revivals or continuations of those that had arisen in the early 1900's in response to the initial growth of AFL.

Thus inspired, employers attacked not only high wage rates and a shortened work week but also contractual provisions giving union members employment preference. Employer demands, accompanied by discharges of active unionists, led to a shipping strike at all Gulf and Atlantic ports. The strike was defeated after 52 days; as a result, the Seamen's union which had 103,000 members in 1921 (before the strike) was reduced to 18,000 in 1923.[59] Similar aggressive tactics by the meat packers forced a desperation strike by the Amalgamated Butchers (in December 1921) which was completely defeated within two months. There was a similar pattern of events in textiles.

The workers in railroad repair shops who had been unionized during the war (when the roads were run by the government) struck, in July 1922, against repeated wage cuts. Although they were beaten within two months and 175,000 members lost to AFL unions, the number of shop craft workers remaining in AFL unions (after the strike) was considerably greater than before the war.[60] "Open shop" drives were also launched in clothing manufacture, printing, and construction; however, in these fields the unions were sufficiently well established to defeat the attacks without serious damage.

By 1924, unions had 3,536,000 members (8.3 per cent of the civilian labor force) as compared with prewar highs (in 1913) of 2,716,300 and 6.9 per cent respectively. Permanent gains had been made in men's clothing manufacture, building construction, railway shopcrafts, railway clerks, and public service. There had also been losses, e.g., in brewing (because of prohibition) and cigar manufacture.

With the business recovery from the depression of 1921, it might have been expected that unionism would continue its prewar growth. But it failed to do so; indeed, in every year of the prosperous 20's (except 1927) unions (in total) experienced a net loss of members. The year-to-year losses were not great after 1923, but by 1930 they had reduced union members to 6.8 per cent of the civilian labor force, the same percentage as in 1914. The causes and implications of this cessation of

---

[58] "American plan" was a term used by antiunion spokesmen to describe the "open shop." An open shop is supposed to be one open both to union and nonunion members; however, union spokesmen have always insisted that, in practice, open shops have not hired union members, i.e., have been "closed" to union men.

[59] Perlman and Taft, *op. cit.*, pp. 494–496.

[60] *Ibid.*, Chapter XXXVIII.

growth have provoked much speculation among students of the labor movement, and it is still an interesting and significant problem.

Unions in the 1920's: Why They Failed to Grow

THE CHANGING INDUSTRIAL STRUCTURE. The rapid changes in products, locations, and methods of production that are characteristic of the American economy make the task of recruiting union members an unending one. An American union cannot for long rest comfortably upon control of a specific set of jobs; if it tries, it will find its members have been replaced by a whole new set of workers, perhaps 1000 miles away working with different tools on a physically different product. This erosion of "job territory" by economic progress has been occurring since 1865. However, it acquired an unprecedented speed in the 1920's, and it caught a number of important unions in an immobile position.

Consider the United Mine Workers: in 1923 it was the largest union in the United States, claiming 515,700 members. By 1929 it claimed only 262,200 members, and many of these were not paying dues. What had happened was that low wages in the nonunion mines of West Virginia and states further south had caused a steady invasion of the nation's soft coal markets by nonunion output.[61] This, of course, tended to displace the unionized miners of Pennsylvania, Illinois, Ohio, etc. A further factor undermining the employment opportunities of all coal miners was the growing tendency to substitute oil for coal as heating fuel.

Until 1927, the United Mine Workers refused to accept wage cuts that might have ameliorated (but probably would not have been great enough to cure) its members' growing unemployment.[62] When the wage cuts came, after a major strike defeat, it was too late to prevent a virtual collapse of unionism in bituminous coal.

The "real solution," from the union's viewpoint, was to organize the nonunion coal fields. But sheriffs and court injunctions made organization of the mines of West Virginia, Kentucky, Tennessee, etc. impossible in the 1920's. The resulting inability of the United Mine Workers to expand the area of unionization seemed, in the 1920's, to doom their union to an early grave.

The plight of the clothing workers' unions was not so serious as that of the miners, but they too lost ground in the 1920's. As with the miners, a major cause was the shift of production from high to low wage areas, i.e., from large cities, especially New York, to smaller towns. In the large cities the labor force was already unionized, but in the small towns it had to be organized afresh. Although the garment unions (especially

[61] A geographical shift of coal-using firms also contributed to this result.

[62] It should be noted that the internal struggle for control of the union made a different wage policy "politically impossible."

the Amalgamated Clothing Workers) kept organizing new workers, during the 1920's the percentage of unionized workers in the garment industries probably diminished.   The geographical movement of industry coupled with technical progress also undermined unionization in textiles. Prohibition all but destroyed the Brewery Workers, while technical progress coupled with short-sighted (but long-followed) policies virtually wiped out the Cigar Makers.   Generally, throughout American industry, mechanization tended to replace skilled craftsmen (often union members) with semiskilled machine tenders who were unorganized to start with and whom the unions were (in the 1920's) unable to recruit.

EMPLOYER TACTICS.   The major obstacle to union organization after, as before, World War I was employer resistance.   This was particularly true with regard to large manufacturers in heavy industry, and it was precisely in this part of the economy that employment was growing most rapidly, e.g., automobiles, rubber, radio, electrical appliances, etc.

The power of employers to resist unionization was probably greater in the 1920's than it had been before World War I.   Discharges and blacklists continued to deter the union-minded worker, while antiunion injunctions (see pp. 209–213) reached a new peak of efficiency in hampering union organizers.   But employers not only resisted unionism upon appearance, they commenced attempts to dry up its principal source, employee discontent.

The 1920's saw the first flowering of "scientific management" in the field of personnel relations.   This took the form of attempts to build up loyalty to the firm among workers.   These attempts were by no means universal and frequently they were made in so clumsy a manner as to inspire distrust rather than loyalty.   However, the attempts did mark a significant change in employer attitudes.

It would be unfair and inaccurate to say that the "welfare capitalism" of the 1920's was merely an antiunion device; there was a change in social attitudes toward manual laborers by employers (see above, pp. 20–24). However, most of the firms that adopted one aspect or another of employee welfare programs did oppose unions (except company unions), and considered membership as evidence of disloyalty.   And the proponets of welfare programs certainly stressed their union discouraging effects.

The spread of employee welfare programs was associated with the development of company unions.[63]   Company unions blossomed during

[63] A company union is one whose membership is confined to the employees of a single company.   Prior to 1935 these unions were, as a rule, under the complete control of the company.   This statement does not hold for the present day *independent* unions of the workers in a single company, see p. 78.

A company union involves a formal organization with dues, officers, etc.   The

World War I under the auspices of the War Labor Board. By 1919 there were 403,765 workers in company unions or "employee representation plans" (12 per cent of the number in AFL unions).[64] In the 1920's membership in AFL unions declined, but the rolls of company unions grew; by 1928 there were 1,547,766 members of company unions, (53 per cent of the number in AFL unions).[65] As can well be imagined, the AFL denounced employee representation plans and company unions as counterfeits for genuine unions, arguing that company employees could never adequately represent their fellow workers for fear of being punished "if they bargained too hard."

Frequently, the charges of counterfeit unionism were well founded. Employers would sponsor employee organization without any very clear idea of what degree of opposition (to management policy) they were prepared to tolerate, and what issues they were prepared to discuss. For example, some employers expected employee representatives to discuss such things as lavatory facilities, and were annoyed when the representatives raised questions about wages, output standards, etc., about which they did not intend to (and did not) negotiate. As management did not, as a rule, propose to share authority, on important labor issues, with the company unions, the accomplishments of such unions were slight. But, for a time, they did serve as a partial substitute for "genuine" unionism.

Many large employers, in the 1920's, established programs to benefit their workers; for example, there were pension plans, subsidized sales of company stock to employees, health and safety programs, training programs, etc. However, employers looked upon these benefits as gifts, to be dispensed only when they could be afforded. Consequently, when losses replaced profits after 1929, many of the benefit plans were scrapped, creating much disappointment and resentment.

THE AFL IN THE 1920's. The failure of unions to make headway in the 1920's cannot be attributed solely to external circumstances. The lack of ambition to grow, noticeable in many AFL unions before World War I, became even more acute after 1920. The rebellions of local unions in 1919 and 1920 increased the craft union leaders' fear of rapid member expansion. And the open shop offensive, the hostility of the courts, and the generally unsympathetic attitude of a conservative govern-

---

members and *officers* of a company union must be employees of the company. An employee representation plan does not involve a formal organization but simply the election of (usually unpaid) representatives to speak for workers concerning grievances, etc.

[64] Perlman and Taft, *op. cit.*, Chapters XXXVI and XLI.

[65] H. A. Millis and R. E. Montgomery, *Organized Labor*, McGraw-Hill Book Co., New York, Table 16, p. 837.

ment made the AFL leaders extremely pessimistic about the prospects for further unionization.

In the 1920's, the AFL's attempts at organizing were confined to a weak and futile gesture at organizing steel (in 1923),[66] an equally ineffective effort in automobiles in 1926–1927,[67] and an abortive, poorly financed drive to unionize the southern textile mills in 1929–1930.[68] These gestures at organizing were feeble because the craft unions involved were unwilling to support them with sufficient money and organizers.

The Federation itself became, in the 1920's, a weaker and less vital organization than it had been previously. Samuel Gompers, president for 37 of the Federation's first 38 years, died in 1924 and was succeeded by William Green. Green, Secretary of the United Mine Workers, was a compromise candidate chosen because of a stalemate between John L. Lewis (president of the United Mine Workers) and Matthew Woll (president of the Photo-Engravers).

Because of his stature as longtime spokesman for American labor, his prestige as founder of AFL, and his many claims to personal loyalty from the various union chieftains, Gompers had an influence within the Federation that far exceeded his authority under its constitution. Gompers made the office of President of the American Federation of Labor an important one. His successor had no such influence and was clearly dominated by the stronger members of the executive board (of the AFL) who were both vice-presidents of the AFL and chieftains of the various national unions. These men were predominantly old craft union leaders, anxious above all to protect their own unions and not greatly concerned with the "labor movement" as a whole. Bold leadership was not to be expected of them.

The pre-World War I opposition to "craft unionism" largely disappeared after 1923, as erstwhile spokesmen for "industrial unionism" (primarily the Brewers, Miners, and Garment Workers) had troubles enough of their own. The Brewery Workers had been obliterated by prohibition. The internal battles of the United Mine Workers had erupted into a life-and-death struggle for control of the union. (This struggle continued throughout the decade and was ended only by John L. Lewis' complete victory and emergence as virtual dictator.)

The ILGWU became the battleground of a struggle between Communist and anti-Communist factions (see pp. 100–101). At the peak of the struggle in 1926, the New York City locals under Communist control embarked upon a disastrous strike which ended, after five months, in com-

---

[66] L. L. Lorwin, *The American Federation of Labor,* Brookings Institution, Washington, D.C., 1933, pp. 218–220.

[67] *Ibid.,* pp. 244–248.

[68] *Ibid.,* pp. 248–258.

plete defeat.[69] This strike made a major contribution to the union's decline from 78,000 members in 1926 to 32,000 three years later; the ILGWU did not really recover from this debacle until 1933–1934.

Unions in the Great Depression

The violent decline in employment in 1929–1933 did not reduce union membership (statistically) so much as one might have expected; union membership fell from 3,625,000 in 1929 to 2,857,000 in 1933. However, membership statistics (never entirely reliable) are particularly questionable in a period of sharp union decline. Many unemployed unionists were carried on the books despite their failure to pay dues and even possible employment as nonunion workers. There can be little doubt but that the great depression (1929–1932) dealt unions a grievous blow.

The United Mine Workers virtually fell to pieces after the strike defeat of 1927; in 1932 it still claimed 150,000 members, but it is doubtful that it had more than 90,000 dues payers and these were confined largely to the anthracite fields of northeastern Pennsylvania. The Building Trades (whose membership had been increased by the building boom of the 1920's) lost heavily through unemployment, as did the Railway unions. The garment unions were plagued with "run-away shops,"[70] and so on. At the beginning of 1933, American unions were not in a healthy condition.

THE EMERGENCE OF THE CIO: 1933 TO 1940

The Split in AFL

The year of 1933 saw a pronounced improvement in the condition and prospects of a number of unions. The improvement was due both to legal and to economic events. In 1932 the Norris-LaGuardia Bill became law (see pp. 212–213); this law made "yellow-dog" contracts unenforceable as contrary to public policy and so circumscribed the conditions under which injunctions could be issued (by the federal courts) in labor disputes as to eliminate them as antiunion instruments. The Norris-La-Guardia Act gave union organizers a legal freedom they had not hitherto enjoyed.

The cause of unionization was further advanced by the National Industrial Recovery Act (NIRA) of 1933. Section 7a of this law stated (among other things) that "employees shall have the right to organize and bargain collectively through representatives of their own choosing."

---

[69] For an account of this struggle see Joel Seidman, *The Needle Trades, op. cit.*, Chapter 9; also Stolberg, *Tailor's Progress, op. cit.*, Chapter VII.

[70] "Run-away shops" are small employers that move out of areas of union control to nearby small towns where they can operate on a nonunion basis.

As it later developed, section 7a was quite ambiguous; however, this did not dampen the ardor with which unions welcomed it. Pointing to section 7a, in the summer of 1933 the United Mine Workers sent out their organizers to proclaim that "the President wants you to join a union." Aided by the short-lived business improvement of mid-1933, the organizing drive met with great success and re-established the United Mine Workers as a major union.

The unions that most benefited by the National Recovery Act were those that had previously been frustrated by the opposition of low wage, nonunion employers, e.g., the United Mine Workers and the unions in clothing manufacture. The codes of fair competition developed for these industries (under the National Recovery Administration with the active participation of the unions), curtailed the ability of nonunion employers to pay low wages and to undersell competitors by charging lower prices. This reduced employers' incentive to avoid unionization and many employers, weary of cut-throat price competition, welcomed a strong union as a police agent to prevent "chiseling." In this favorable environment, the ILGWU and the Amalgamated Clothing Workers, as well as the United Mine Workers prospered during 1933–1934.

But in heavy manufacturing (steel, automobiles, rubber, etc.) employer opposition to unionism continued unabated. However, effective resistance had become more difficult; section 7a (of NIRA) obviously required that some form of unionism be permitted. Hence employers turned to company unions or employee representation plans. Workers included in these plans increased from 1,263,194 to 2,500,000 between 1932 and 1935;[71] these unions were especially prominent in Iron and Steel firms.[72] As the company unions were established at the instigation of the employer, he expected to control them, and usually did.[73] In addition to sponsoring company unions, employers continued to discourage "outside" unions by the time-tested method of discharging their active supporters. (In a period of large-scale unemployment, this weapon has considerable potency.)

Despite these obstacles, the social discontent of the early 1930's was such that workers began to join AFL unions in sizeable numbers during

[71] Millis and Montgomery, *op. cit.,* Table 17, p. 841. The authors point out that this increase was about equal to the gain in AFL membership during the same period.

[72] In 1935, 34.0 per cent of all workers in durable manufacturing were in company unions as compared with 12.2 per cent in trade unions. Wolman, *op. cit.,* Table 32, p. 128.

[73] However, company unions have, on occasion, "backfired" on their employer originators by becoming independent and, on occasion, militant. An important example of this is the case of the company union started by U. S. Steel which was captured by the Steel Workers Organizing Committee in 1936–1937 (see below, pp. 69–70).

1933. The Amalgamated Association of Iron, Steel and Tin Workers (AA) experienced an influx during 1933, and membership in the federal locals[74] established in automobiles and rubber manufacturing grew noticeably during 1933–1935. However, the membership gains were not held; the AFL organizers came with membership cards and dues receipts, but no plans for action. The "quietism" of the AFL unions not only discouraged the angry men who demanded strikes but left them exposed to discharge for union activity. The unwillingness and inability of the AFL unions to protect their members caused thousands of recruits to leave the federal locals and frightened away many more. As a result of the failure of the AFL unions to capitalize on their opportunities, a number of independent unions sprang up (during 1933–1935), especially in automobiles and rubber; these were the building blocks of the United Auto Workers and United Rubber Workers. In steel, many union-minded workers joined the company unions as more promising, and safer, instruments for improving wages and working conditions than AA.

A further reason for the meager accomplishments of the AFL in 1933–1935 was the insistence upon the principle of craft jurisdiction. At the insistence of the craft union leaders, skilled workers in the "mass-production industries" were siphoned off into craft locals, with or without their consent. Frequently, this led to the craftsmen leaving both the federal local and the craft union.[75]

The problem of craft jurisdiction was as old as the Federation; the heads of the various craft unions believed their affiliation with the Federation gave them a contractual right to the dues of all workers exercising a given skill, irrespective of the workers' wishes.[76] And they were not

[74] Federal locals were local unions directly affiliated with the AFL, and not with any of its affiliated international unions. Federal locals are used to recruit members in fields where no affiliated international claims jurisdiction, or where it is agreed that unionization can proceed more effectively if done by the Federation itself. However, the federal locals were supposed to serve as vestibules for those members within the jurisdiction of affiliated unions, and it was Federation policy to apportion them to their "proper" unions as quickly as possible.

[75] See H. S. Roberts, *The Rubber Workers,* Harpers, New York, 1944, pp. 96–100 and 133–142; also Edward Levinson, *Labor on the March,* Harpers, New York, 1938, pp. 77–78 and 97–98.

[76] A classic statement of this attitude is found in a statement by the (then) president of the Teamsters' Union, Daniel Tobin, at the 1934 AFL convention. This statement was made during a debate concerning the union affiliation of the drivers of beer trucks; these drivers had been "awarded" by the Federation to the Teamsters, but they refused to leave the Brewery Workers causing Tobin to say, "We have to use force in our organizations. If we didn't use force, and enforce the decisions, we would not have an international union of 135,000 members—and they are not the rubbish that have lately come into other organizations." (Quoted by Levinson, *op. cit.,* p. 84.) It should be remarked that this attitude is far less prevalent, and important, than it was twenty years ago.

prepared either to relinquish these rights or to accept the correlative obligation of unionizing their claimed jurisdictions as vigorously as possible.[77]   Before 1937 the craft unions simply would not spend large amounts of money to organize factory workers.

In 1934 and 1935 the old pre-World War I battle between the adherents of craft versus industrial unionism was, once again, fought out on the floor of the Federation's annual conventions; the industrialists were, as in 1912, led by the Miners, Brewers, and Garment Workers.   At the 1934 convention, a compromise resolution (on the matter of craft jurisdiction) was adopted; however, it did not settle the issue.   Under the authority of this resolution, William Green presented an AFL charter (in August 1935) to the first convention of the United Auto Workers, which excluded jurisdiction over Tool and Die Makers and various other skilled workers. Exclusion of the craftsmen provoked a storm of protest from the assembled delegates.   This protest became even stronger when Green nominated an unpopular Federation organizer as president of the new union; when this nominee was rejected by the convention, Green proceeded to appoint him president.[78]   Two weeks later, a similar performance was enacted at the first convention of the United Rubber Workers.[79]

At the 1935 AFL convention in October, the floor battle of the preceding year was renewed; once again the craft unionists had the majority of the votes.   But this time the industrial unionists refused to accept the verdict of the convention.   Two weeks after the convention ended, John L. Lewis announced the formation of the Committee for Industrial Organization (CIO); the unions affiliated with CIO were the United Mine Workers, Amalgamated Clothing Workers, ILGWU, Mine, Mill and Smelter Workers, United Textile Workers, and the Oil, Gas and Refinery Workers.

The CIO

The avowed purpose of CIO was to work within the AFL, but the AFL executive council insisted that CIO dissolve upon pain of expulsion from the Federation; the expulsion occurred in August 1936.   During the course of 1936, the other industrial unions were forced to choose between AFL and CIO.   Almost all of them chose the latter, and by the end of the year CIO comprised virtually all the industrial unions in the country.

[77] Some of the craft union leaders feared the influx of a large number of undisciplined militant factory hands into their well-run organizations.   For example, the aged Michael Tighe, president of AA, was faced in 1933–1934 with a rank and file rebellion from his new recruits.   His response was to expel them.   (Levinson, *op. cit.,* pp. 67–73 and R. R. R. Brooks, *As Steel Goes,* Yale University Press, New Haven, 1940, pp. 69–70.)

[78] Levinson, *op. cit.,* p. 54.

[79] *Ibid.,* pp. 93–96; also Roberts, *op. cit.,* pp. 136–141.

In addition, it had absorbed, under duress, the Amalgamated Association of Iron, Steel and Tin Workers[80] which it merged with its newly formed Steel Workers Organizing Committee (SWOC).

The CIO was financed mainly by loans and contributions from the United Mine Workers, ILGWU, and Amalgamated Clothing Workers; the first mentioned making the heaviest donations. These unions also furnished officers and organizers to the newly formed unions and organizing committees. However, these unions did not have nearly enough trained organizers to man the huge drive upon which the CIO was embarked. Consequently, Lewis accepted the services of many experienced Communist organizers. Because of the recently changed "party line" the Communists were anxious to help the CIO, and they rendered important service in the years 1936–1939. However, they used the opportunity to entrench themselves in a number of CIO unions from which they were later dislodged with great difficulty (see pp. 80–82).

The CIO's first big victory came in February 1937 when, after a two month "sit-down" strike, General Motors capitulated and signed a contract with the United Auto Workers (UAW).[81] A "sit-down" strike is one in which the striking workers refuse to leave a plant, or permit others to enter, until the strike is settled. The advantage of the technique is fairly obvious; it eliminates the risk of the company attempting to operate the struck plant with nonunion workers. The illegality of sit-down strikes has been generally conceded since 1938, and they have not been used since that time. However, the sit-downs were an invaluable tactical weapon in the campaign to unionize automobile and rubber manufacturing.) Two weeks after General Motors signed a union contract Chrysler followed suit.

The second big CIO victory occurred in steel where (in March 1937) U. S. Steel, the arch-foe of unionism, signed a contract with the SWOC. This agreement climaxed a year of intensive, well-financed, and highly imaginative organizing work (directed by the organizing staff of the United

[80] Lewis accomplished this by donating $500,000 to the Steel Workers Organizing Committee to organize the basic steel industry. He offered to take the AA into the new organization (on condition that it waived all jurisdictional rights) or to proceed despite it. The AA had little alternative but to join. Brooks, *op. cit.*, pp. 72–74 and Levinson, *op. cit.*, pp. 122–125.

[81] The General Motors strike was certainly one of the most dramatic episodes in American labor history. The essence of the drama was the three-sided war of nerves among the General Motors management who wanted the sit-downers evicted but were afraid of damaging their plants, the Governor of Michigan (and behind him the President of the United States) whose heart was with the union but was being badgered to enforce the law, and the union leaders and men who gambled their lives on the belief that the Michigan National Guard wouldn't risk destroying the factories. An excellent account of the struggle can be found in Saul Alinsky, *John L. Lewis*, G. P. Putnam, New York, 1949, pp. 106–147.

Mine Workers) within the company unions established by U. S. Steel. By securing effective control of these unions, SWOC placed the company in an extremely awkward position from which it retreated by signing a union contract without the duress of a strike.[82]

The victories over General Motors and U. S. Steel were won without the aid of the Wagner Act. This Act (National Labor Relations Act of 1935) had been under heavy attack, on constitutional grounds, since its passage in June 1935 and had been largely ignored by employers, on advice of counsel.[83] But on April 12, 1937, the U. S. Supreme Court upheld the Act by a five to four majority, and employer resistance to unionization became illegal (see below). This decision of the U. S. Supreme Court, together with the CIO's victories in steel and automobiles, set in motion a CIO bandwagon. Hundreds of employers signed contracts with CIO unions so that, by the autumn of 1937, the CIO claimed 3,718,000 members as compared with AFL's claim of 2,861,000.

However, after the summer of 1937, the CIO's membership did not increase appreciably until 1941. One important reason for this was the sharp downturn in business activity in the fall of 1937; the CIO success in early 1937 had been materially aided by the prevailing business prosperity. Throughout much of 1938, unemployment kept down the number of dues paying members and made strike victories difficult.[84]

Another reason for the slackened rate of growth in CIO's membership was the unaltered opposition of many manufacturing employers to dealing with unions. Ford Motor Co. and most of the "little steel" companies, as well as many others, continued to resist unionization. This resistance, which led to considerable bloodshed in 1937 and 1938, was frequently in contravention of the Wagner Act and led to citations for "unfair labor practices" before the National Labor Relations Board (NLRB) which had been established to enforce the Wagner Act. Many

---

[82] The process of taking over the Company Unions is described in Brooks, *op. cit.,* pp. 85–109; also F. H. Harbison, *How Collective Bargaining Works,* Twentieth Century Fund, 1945, pp. 512–524. The top level of negotiations is described in Alinsky, *op. cit.,* pp. 148–149. (The accounts of Alinsky and Brooks are, to some extent, inconsistent.)

It is worth recognizing that, by signing with the union, U. S. Steel was enabled to take advantage of a very favorable market situation. It is also possible that U. S. Steel was afraid of provoking a "knock-down, drag-out" battle with the union so soon after President Roosevelt's landslide victory in November 1936.

[83] In 1936, the U. S. Circuit Court of Appeals had declared the act unconstitutional. See Elias Lieberman, *Unions Before the Bar,* Harpers, New York, 1950, Chapter 15, for a full account of the validation of the Wagner Act before the courts.

[84] One further reason for the CIO's failure to expand during this period was the defection of the ILGWU in 1938. The ILGWU left the CIO when, in 1938, it set itself up as a permanent organization, called the Congress of Industrial Organizations. After two years of independence, ILGWU returned to the AFL in 1940.

of these companies appealed the NLRB orders through the Federal Courts up to the U. S. Supreme Court. Although the orders were usually upheld, the process of appeal took several years during which employers continued their antiunion practices.

But, although the CIO did not grow during 1938–1940, the fact that it survived unimpaired was of historic significance. Industrial unions had achieved short-lived victories before 1937 (e.g., the Knights of Labor, the IWW, and various unions in 1918–1920); however (with the exception of the clothing unions), they had been destroyed by employer counterattacks during the first spell of serious unemployment, if not sooner. That this did not happen again, in the depression of 1937–1938, was a fact of historic significance.

The Revival of AFL

When the executive council of the AFL expelled the CIO, it started an outbreak of interunion disputes unparalleled in labor history. In 1937, the AFL launched an organizing drive of its own, financed by an increase in its per capita tax from one to two cents per member, per month. The success of the CIO demonstrated to the defeatist bureaucrats of the AFL what energy and money could accomplish, while the aggressiveness of the CIO unions alarmed[85] and angered them. As a result, the AFL unions soon became as aggressive and expansion-minded as their CIO rivals; in the late 1930's there were literally dozens of areas in which CIO and AFL affiliates were competing for members.[86]

The fratricidal struggles, which frequently involved strikes and boycotts of employers dealing with a rival union, damaged the cause of unionism before the public. By 1939 it was apparent that a reunification would bring many advantages to both CIO and AFL. However, the personal animosities engendered in the battles of the preceding five years, the rivalry for position and power involved in the jurisdictional fights, and the ideological differences (existing in the late 1930's) between AFL and (an important part of) CIO precluded an early reunification.

The first phase of CIO's history was ended in 1940 when, after a series of disagreements with President Roosevelt, John L. Lewis made a nation-wide address in support of the Republican nominee for President, Wendell Willkie. In the address he said that if Roosevelt were re-elected he (Lewis) would resign as head of the CIO. Accordingly, in December 1940, he resigned (as head of CIO) to be succeeded by his long-time lieutenant, Philip Murray, whom he had appointed head of SWOC,

[85] In the summer of 1937, locals from a number of AFL affiliates began to desert to the CIO in the desire to join a progressive, expanding organization.

[86] Walter Galenson, *Rival Unionism in the United States,* American Council of Public Affairs, 1940, pp. 21–24, has a full catalog of the areas of conflict.

and who had become head of the United Steel Workers (USW) when that organization was formed (from SWOC) in 1939. Murray, like most CIO leaders, had supported Roosevelt in the 1940 election.

THE WAR AND POST-WAR YEARS: 1941 TO 1953

Wartime Developments

During World War II, as in World War I, union membership expanded rapidly. The basic causes of the growth in the two wars were similar: (1) a labor shortage which reduced employer resistance to strikes and unionization, (2) a rapid expansion of employment in war industries, and (3) a governmental policy favorable to unionization. However, the political and economic environment and the state of union organization were very different in 1941–1945 from what they had been in 1917–1918; therefore, it is not surprising that the results were very different.

In 1941 the CIO unions, strong and well-financed, moved forward to complete the unionization of heavy manufacturing industry that had been sought since 1937. The high level of business activity, the orders from NLRB (to employers) to bargain collectively with the unions, and the support of a prounion administration, newly re-elected for a third time, all augured success. By the end of 1941, the "little steel" companies, Ford, and a number of other concerns that had effectively resisted unionization since 1937 had begun collective bargaining with CIO unions.

But the defense and war booms benefited AFL also. Once shaken from its lethargy by the CIO revolt, the AFL began to accumulate members avidly. From 1937 to 1940 its ranks grew from 2,861,000 to 4,247,000. During the war years it continued to grow, reaching (in 1945) a level of 6,936,000 members as compared with CIO's claimed 6,000,000. Jurisdictional conflicts with CIO unions continued, but the wartime ban on strikes prevented their being contested with prewar intensity; furthermore, for various reasons, the fundamental tension between the two organizations had begun to lessen.

The principal agency through which the government dealt with labor matters during World War II was the War Labor Board (WLB). This board was established by the President soon after Pearl Harbor; it contained representatives of labor, management and the "public." Spokesmen for both labor and management agreed to eschew strikes and lockouts for the duration of the war and to let all disputes be settled by the WLB. From the viewpoint of union organization, the most important decision made by WLB concerned the question of union security,[87]

[87] Union security clauses in labor-management agreements are those which protect the union's interests in the agreement (see pp. 175–180). They may include among other things, provisions for compulsory membership in the union as a condition of employment.

i.e., compulsory unionism.   Labor spokesmen argued that, in the absence of freedom to strike, unions should be protected from possible employer attacks and loss of member interest (because of inability to strike for higher wages) by being awarded either closed or union shops.[88]   Needless to say, management representatives vehemently disagreed.   As a compromise, the WLB adopted the "maintenance of membership" principle and ordered that clauses embodying it be inserted in union-management contracts where a dispute existed as to the form of union security (if any) to be adopted.[89]

"Maintenance of membership" means that workers who belong to the union at the time a union-employer contract is signed are compelled to continue membership, as a condition of employment, for the duration of the contract.[90]   As the vast majority of the employees of unionized firms[91] were already union members, maintenance of membership created, in many companies, something closely approximating compulsory membership.

The net effect of the wartime situation was to expand union membership greatly.   In 1940 there were about 8,500,000 union members, comprising about 16 per cent of the nation's labor force; by 1946, unions had about 15 million members, constituting 24 to 25 per cent of the labor force.   Much of this gain in membership occurred in war industry and might have been expected to evaporate with the coming of peace.   However, the nation did not experience a recurrence of the 1920–1921 depression.   The postwar boom caused a great expansion in durable manufacturing employment that cushioned the shock of reduced employment in military production.   First the Cold War, and then the struggle in Korea reinforced the high level of civilian activity, so that a readjustment of the 1920–1921 variety has not occurred since World War II.   (However, certain war industries, such as shipbuilding, have never, since 1945, approached their wartime employment peaks.)

Postwar Turmoil

But, although the labor movement has been spared a major depression, it has undergone a postwar inflation that caused, in 1946, a strike wave reminiscent of 1919.[92]   During World War II, price control and other

[88] For the distinction between a closed and a union shop see p. 178.

[89] Where a closed or union shop agreement had been in effect, previously, it was continued.   "Maintenance of membership" was applied only in situations where no provision for compulsory membership had previously been in effect.

[90] A fifteen or thirty day "escape period" was usually provided for workers who might wish to leave the union before "maintenance of membership" went into effect.

[91] By unionized firms we mean firms signing agreements with one or more unions governing the conditions of employment of their nonmanagerial employees.

[92] In man-days lost on account of strikes, 1946 was by far the worst year in American history.

measures had suppressed inflation "fairly well." As part of this program, labor had submitted to a wage freeze and a no-strike pledge which was, on the whole, well observed. However, at the end of hostilities in 1945, there was a general desire to be rid of controls on output and prices (consumer rationing was especially unpopular). Similarly, many workers were anxious to throw off the wartime restraint on strikes in order to combat grievances that had remained unadjusted for long periods. Furthermore, workers who had become accustomed to overtime pay were determined that they should get wage increases sufficient to maintain their weekly earnings, despite the loss of overtime.

Consumers were hungry for goods of all kinds, and their eagerness was backed with liquid assets accumulated during the war. The resulting level of effective demand was far too great for the stream of goods and services available at the price level of early 1946. And, as the dykes of price control were washed away, prices, especially those of foods, soared. The unions, pushed by an angry membership, set out to "keep up with the cost of living." The aforementioned strike wave was the result.

The combined effect of strikes, rising prices, and shortages of goods was infuriating to middle-class citizens and to many wage earners as well. The depression-born sympathy with unionism had already begun to wane in the late 1930's, and hostility toward unions mounted steadily during the war years; the events of 1946 brought it to open anger.

Antiunion feeling stemmed largely from the belief that strikes had materially impeded the war effort. The fact was that, during the war years, most unions adhered scrupulously to their no-strike pledge. This did not, however, prevent the occurrence of a large number of "quickie" strikes; these "quickies" as the name would suggest, were of short duration and resulted from dissatisfaction with the handling of grievances.[93] These strikes were unauthorized by the unions, and union officers usually assisted in terminating them promptly. Nonetheless, these strikes were widely publicized, and condemned, and they created an impression that unions were indifferent to the national safety.

The unfavorable impression created by the quickies was enormously increased by the systematic defiance of the WLB and the government by John L. Lewis and the United Mine Workers. Lewis had never accepted the proposition that collective bargaining should be curbed during wartime, and he pressed hard the tactical advantage given him by a war-born coal shortage. In 1943, and again in early 1945, the United Mine Workers embarked upon strike action to secure their economic demands; in both cases, concessions were made to the miners in order to obtain

[93] Frequently, the strikes resulted from impatience with prolonged delays, often greater than six months, in getting a specific complaint acted upon. The "quickies" were an effective means of getting attention.

production. The 1943 settlement was made "over the head" of the WLB and in violation of its general "wage freeze" policy.[94] Although it can be effectively argued that the miners' wage claims deserved special consideration, the consequences of the 1943 coal settlement were unfair to other union leaders and members who were making economic sacrifices in order to cooperate with the government's anti-inflation policy.

But, irrespective of the merits of the matter, in 1946 the "public" was angry with John L. Lewis, and it did not differentiate between Lewis and other labor leaders.[95] The fall elections of 1946 occurred in a tense atmosphere of mounting inflation, threats of yet another coal strike, and no little labor annoyance with President Truman.[96] As a result, the Republicans, many of whom were avowedly antiunion, gained control of both Houses of Congress. The following spring, Congress enacted the Taft-Hartley Bill, over a Presidential veto; this law is analyzed in detail in Chapter IX.

Since Taft-Hartley

With the enactment of the Taft-Hartley Bill, government sponsorship of unionization ceased. The Wagner Act declared it to be public policy to encourage collective bargaining through unions of the workers' own choosing; Taft-Hartley makes no such commitment. It is by no means clear that the Taft-Hartley Act is importantly responsible for the failure of unionism to expand beyond its 1945 limits (see pp. 84–85), but the object of the law is consistent with the failure of unionism to expand further.

As of early 1956, the only major attempt, in the postwar period, at organizing new job territory was a drive to organize the south, especially the textile mills, in 1946–1947. Employer resistance was extremely effective, and the drive failed. Since 1945 there has been some growth

---

[94] See pp. 412–413.

[95] Lewis was not the only labor leader who had made himself persona non grata with the public. Petrillo, the head of the Musicians' union, had acquired a very unfavorable press, and various local leaders, especially in the Building Service and Stagecraft unions, had been convicted of a variety of unsavory crimes. All these events were well publicized.

[96] This was due to his public attack on two of the Railway Brotherhoods and their leaders during a nationwide railway strike. On May 23, 1946, President Truman appeared before Congress on the second day of the strike to demand passage of an extremely drastic antistrike law; before his speech was finished, he received notice of the termination of the strike. The proposed legislation was never passed, but it helped to build support for the antiunion Case Bill which was defeated only by a Presidential veto. Truman's behavior in the rail strike infuriated many unionists, who may have abstained, or voted Republican, in the following election. These remarks refer only to 1946; within two years, relations between the Truman administration and labor had been thoroughly mended (in good part, because of his vigorous veto of Taft-Hartley) and labor supported him wholeheartedly in 1948.

in the number of union members (from about 14.5 to 17.8 million), but this has come about as a result of the expansion of employment in firms and industries where unionism was already well entrenched. For example, the building boom has appreciably expanded the membership of the Building Trades' unions. As a result, the unionized portion of the labor force has remained (roughly) constant since 1945.

Despite the failure to conquer new territory, the years since 1947 have not been void of union achievement. In these years, unions have not only made important economic gains for their members but have also established (what at present appears to be) firm and enduring bargaining relations with the principal manufacturing firms of the country.

These relations did not exist in 1945; at that time, many collective bargaining arrangements had functioned only under wartime conditions, and their peacetime future was obscure and ominous. In the early postwar period, many employers who had accepted unionism only under duress probably hoped soon to rid themselves of it. The antiunion agitation of 1945–1947 that culminated in the Taft-Hartley Act would certainly suggest this attitude. And had a major depression occurred in 1947–1949, it is by no means impossible that employers might have utilized the opportunities existing in Taft-Hartley[97] to launch an antiunion offensive similar to that of 1920–1921.

However, as demand continued strong and profits high, employers began to realize the advantages of living with the unions. This attitude was, no doubt, reinforced by President Truman's unexpected electoral victory in 1948, for which (rightly or wrongly) the CIO's Political Action Committee (see pp. 105–106) received much credit. After 1948, if not before, the major employers of the United States reconciled themselves to the proposition that there was no going back to the "good old preunion days," and began to adjust to permanent coexistence with unions.

This adjustment has been manifested in a number of ways. One of the more dramatic of these is the virtual absence, since 1945, of attempts by employers to operate struck plants. Before World War II, such attempts were almost a routine employer strike tactic, and they led frequently to violence and permanent ill-feeling. Since 1945, high level employment has made it difficult to recruit strike-breakers, but (apart from this) most employers now seem prepared to accept the fact that the union can close their plants in a "lawful strike,"[98] and the jobs of their workers are not part of the stakes of such a strike.[99] A further indication

[97] See pp. 238–239.

[98] See pp. 208–209. Employers, sometimes, still attempt to break unauthorized local strikes in violation of contract.

[99] This is quite different from the legal state of affairs, as defined in the Taft-Hartley Act (pp. 237–238).

of the same tendency is the increase in the percentage of workers employed under union conditions who are covered by a union-shop contract; this percentage increased from 49 per cent in 1949–1950 to 64 per cent in 1954.[100]

The fruit of more stable industrial relations has been a variety of benefits obtained through collective bargaining. Since 1949, employer-financed pension plans have become widespread, as have employer provisions for health insurance and, most recently, there has begun a movement toward a "guaranteed annual wage." These "qualitative" improvements are in addition to a substantial increase in both money and real hourly wage rates. As these phenomena are discussed in detail later, they are only mentioned here as evidence of the economic gains that have accrued to union members during the past decade.[101]

The Formation of AFL-CIO

The big event of the past decade in the field of labor organization was the creation of AFL-CIO at the end of 1955; this organization is the result of the merger of AFL and CIO. The unification does not imply that the original rupture has been unnecessary or had failed; the entire structure of the new organization implies that the CIO largely accomplished its "historic mission," the organization of the mass-production industries, and that because of this the need for a separate labor organization has ended. Indeed, the CIO "mission" had been largely accomplished by 1941, but more than another decade was required to reduce, to manageable size, the personal animosities and organizational frictions that had been created by the events of the middle and late 1930's.

The creation of AFL-CIO was presaged, in 1954, by a "no-raiding" past signed by CIO and AFL and most of their affiliated unions. This pact set up a board of arbitration to settle all disputes between AFL and CIO affiliates concerning union jurisdiction, and the signing unions agreed not to accept workers awarded to other unions. (A few unions, notably the Teamsters, refused to sign this pact, see pp. 112–113.) The very possibility of such a pact, which a few years earlier would have been considered utopian, indicated that the major organizational conflicts between AFL and CIO affiliates had become sufficiently settled so that the parties

---

[100] Rose Theodore, "Union-Security Provisions in Agreements, 1954," *Monthly Labor Review*, June 1955, Chart 1, p. 655. (These figures refer to workers employed under collective bargaining agreements analyzed in the Bureau of Labor Statistics studies of such agreements.) In 1954, 7,405,000 workers were covered by union-shop agreements.

[101] It is not asserted that union policy "caused" these gains; whether it did is a much debated question (see pp. 339–342). All that is stated here is that union members, among others, have obtained these benefits.

concerned were prepared to arbitrate the remaining issues, and whatever new ones might emerge.

There were five main reasons for the improvement in AFL-CIO relations.

THE END OF THE "CRAFT-INDUSTRIAL" UNION CONFLICT. The historic conflict between craft and industrial unionism that had led to the formation of CIO had been settled permanently by the acquisition of a large semiskilled factory membership by various important AFL affiliates. That is, these unions are now (to a considerable extent) industrial unions themselves. For example, the Butchers have acquired a large number of packinghouse workers; the Machinists have gained important membership in aircraft manufacturing; the Carpenters are now heavily involved in the growing pre-fabricated housing industry; the International Brotherhood of Electricians have a stake in electrical and electronic manufacturing; etc. There is no longer any practical issue of parcelling out factory workers to various craft unions.[102]

THE LESSENING OF JURISDICTIONAL CONFLICT. Obliteration of the craft versus industrial union problem did not, of itself, end jurisdictional problems. Throughout the 1940's there were frequent contests for members between rival unions of AFL and CIO, both acting (in the disputed area) as industrial unions. These contests were reflected by the frequent appearance of two competing unions on the ballot in an NLRB "representation election,"[103] with the unions campaigning against one another. Not infrequently the defeated union would later try to exploit member dissatisfaction in an attempt to "make a comeback."

It became increasingly clear that these CIO-AFL contests benefited neither and tended either to discourage interest in unionism altogether or (in some cases) to benefit a third (Communist-dominated or "independent"[104]) union. The latter possibility had been apparent even before World War II; the former became important in the postwar period when the anti-Communist CIO unions attacked, and later expelled (from the CIO), those unions that were Communist-dominated (see pp. 80–82). In the struggles between pro and anti-Communist CIO (or former

---

[102] There is, of course, the policy of NLRB, required by Taft-Hartley, of encouraging separate unions for craftsmen (see pp. 232–235). But this is no longer a seriously divisive issue in American labor.

[103] I.e., an election to determine (by voting preference) which union, if either, was to represent the workers involved. Also see below, pp. 236–237. J. Krislow, "Raiding among the 'Legitimate' Unions," *Industrial and Labor Relations Review*, October 1954, pp. 19–29, has a good summary of the history of these elections.

[104] These "independents" are unions that propose to remain independent of labor organizations that include employees of other firms. Historically, they are the successors of the "company union" (see p. 62 and 66) but are far stronger organizations than the former. Needless to say, they were not liked by either AFL or CIO unions.

CIO) unions, the intervention of an (anti-Communist) AFL union could only serve to divide the anti-Communist forces. To prevent this, a series of working agreements between AFL and (anti-Communist) CIO unions began to develop in the late 1940's; the no-raiding pact was the culmination of these separate (informal) agreements.

TAFT-HARTLEY AND PUBLIC OPINION. A third important force that impelled first the no-raiding pact and then the merger of CIO and AFL was the Taft-Hartley Act. Among other things, this law outlawed jurisdictional disputes. Moreover, it was clear that (at least) this part of the law had wide public support, even from union sympathizers, and would be difficult to repeal. One result of this has been that the unions in the building trades historically intransigeant on jurisdictional issues) established, in 1947, a set of boards to adjudicate jurisdictional disputes. These boards have been quite successful in curbing the once irrepressible jurisdictional conflicts in this industry.[105] The willingness of the Building Trades unions to accept these awards is a considerable testimonial to their fear of the consequences of challenging the Taft-Hartley law (and public opinion) on the issue of jurisdictional disputes.

The new-found desire of the building trades to avoid jurisdictional conflicts has been paralleled in most other unions, including many that had previously been heavily engaged in (jurisdictional) warfare with CIO rivals.[106] The urgency of avoiding such warfare began, of itself, to cause the development of informal jurisdictional boundary lines which were later given de facto ratification in the aforementioned no-raiding pact.

Taft-Hartley made a further contribution to labor unity in that it gave CIO and AFL a common political objective of paramount importance, i.e.. repeal of Taft-Hartley. The passage of Taft-Hartley and the continuing struggle with state "right-to-work" laws[107] made clear, to both labor organizations, the extent of their common interests and the importance of unified effort to protect them.

The antiunion climate of the postwar period taught many labor leaders yet another lesson; the fact that, in the sphere of public opinion, every union is its brother's keeper. Public resentment against John L. Lewis'

[105] The final board of appeals, in this administrative arrangement, is headed by Professor J. T. Dunlop of Harvard University; Dunlop is a well-known labor economist, many of whose works will be cited.

[106] It is necessary to note that a few unions, notably the Teamsters, have not abandoned the use of economic pressure (e.g., strikes) as an instrument of jurisdictional warfare. It should also be pointed out that most unions have felt that no holds were barred in competing with Communist-dominated unions.

[107] Taft-Hartley specifically permits state governments to forbid unions the right to demand that union membership be made a condition of employment (see pp. 177–180). Consequently, there has been a continuing drive by certain employer groups to enact such legislation, called "right-to-work" laws.

intransigence has been visited upon all unions and not upon the United Mine Workers alone. Disgust at corruption in certain local unions has lead to attacks upon all unions as "crooked," etc. The last presidents of AFL (George Meany) and CIO (Walter Reuther) both recognized that it was extremely dangerous to permit the national unions to exercise *complete* autonomy over their own affairs.

However, the AFL and CIO were not able effectively to implement their desires to "clean up" their affiliated national unions. The *large*[108] national unions have been, and still are, sufficiently strong to live with or without affiliation to a major labor federation; consequently, attempts to discipline a major union have been few and futile. For example, in 1953 the AFL's executive council suspended the International Longshoremen's Association (ILA) for its failure to clean up the racketeer-dominated locals on the New York waterfront. But in an NLRB representation election, the New York longshoremen rejected the AFL-backed Teamsters and retained the ILA as their representative. In the course of its struggle with the AFL, the ILA had the open support (moral and financial) of John L. Lewis. Lewis' defiance of the AFL on this and other occasions made no small contribution to lowering its prestige.[109]

THE EXPULSION OF THE COMMUNISTS FROM CIO. As we have already noted, the Communists did important work in the CIO organizing drives of 1936–1939. As a result, they acquired important positions in a number of unions, in state and local CIO organizations, and in the national CIO organization itself. When the Communist party "line" changed on August 22, 1939, as a result of the Nazi-Soviet pact, the Communist elements in these unions changed their position from support of the New Deal and alliance with anti-Fascist countries to one of isolationism. Accordingly, they attacked President Roosevelt as a war-monger and urged militant pursuit of collective bargaining advantages by strikes without consideration of the national emergency.

In this, their position paralleled that of John L. Lewis, and they gave him vociferous support in his struggle with the pro-Roosevelt elements in CIO. However, on June 22, 1941, when Nazi Germany invaded Russia,

---

[108] Smaller unions cannot be so independent, unless they have a virtual monopoly of a particular type of skilled labor. Failing this, a small union relies (not always successfully) upon its affiliation with a federation to protect it from the raids of larger unions.

[109] The United Mine Workers left CIO in 1943 and later returned to the AFL of which Lewis again became vice-president. In 1947, because of a dispute over AFL policy on signing non-Communist oaths, as required by Taft-Hartley, Lewis once again pulled the United Mine Workers from the AFL. His manner of withdrawal was especially contemptuous; he sent Green (president of AFL) the following message—"Green—We disaffiliate—Lewis."

their position changed abruptly. Lewis' intransigeance became treason, and Philip Murray became their hero because of his cooperation with the war effort.

During the war years, the Communists were the most zealous spokesmen of the no-strike, "all for the war effort" position in the labor movement. They even went so far as to advocate piece-work in auto factories, in order to stimulate production; this view lost them considerable support in the United Auto Workers. Until the "party line" changed once again, in late 1945, the Communists were urging an indefinite continuation of the wartime no-strike policy in order to facilitate production for war ravaged areas. But once the "line" changed, they returned to their old stance of militancy.

These shifts of position cost the Communists much of their following. Defence of the Nazi-Soviet pact lost them the sympathy of many anti-Fascist intellectuals, and their wartime no-strike position caused some labor militants to become disgusted. However, numerical support was never the Communists' strength. Their strength lay in the "political machines" (see pp. 102–104) they had built in various CIO unions. These "machines" could not win elections by themselves, but they were valuable allies to one or another of the non-Communist factions with whom they made deals, trading electoral support for union patronage and assistance in securing passage of resolutions desired by the Communist party.

To break Communist influence in the CIO, it was necessary to isolate them from their allies. Because of personal rivalry among the non-Communist leaders, this was not easy to accomplish. Fear that purging the Communists would destroy CIO stayed the hand of Philip Murray (a Catholic and ardent anti-Communist) for a number of years. However, the Communists, by their behavior in 1946–1948, made the task of purging them both easier and more necessary. By supporting Soviet Russia in its increasing hostility toward the United States, they alienated many of the unionists who had tolerated or supported them for ulterior motives. As a result, in 1946, Walter Reuther became president of the United Auto Workers on an avowedly anti-Communist platform; by 1949, he had virtually purged the union of Communist influence. In 1947, two erstwhile "fellow-travelers," Joe Curran (head of the National Maritime Union) and Michael Quill (head of the Transport Workers) broke with the Communists and expelled the pro-Communist factions in their unions.

Increasing friction produced by the Communist support of Henry Wallace in the 1948 presidential election and opposition to the Marshall Plan brought matters to a head. In 1949, two Communist-dominated unions, the United Electrical Workers (UE) and the Farm Equipment Workers, withdrew from CIO and merged. CIO thereupon chartered a rival union, International Union of Electrical, Radio, and Machine Workers (IUE), which has, ever since, fought a bitter jurisdictional war with UE. IUE has captured, perhaps, 70 per cent of the 400,000 members UE had at the time of its withdrawal. However, UE continues (as of early 1956) to be a factor in electrical, radio, and television manufacturing.

In 1950, nine other CIO unions were expelled as being Communist dominated. Of these the most important were the Fur Workers, the Mine, Mill, and Smelter Workers, and the International Longshoremen's and Warehousemen's Union, which controls water front employees on the Pacific Coast and Hawaii (where it has also organized plantation workers).

Of the eleven (allegedly) Communist-dominated unions in the CIO in 1949, only four (UE, Mine, Mill, and Smelter Workers, International Longshoremen and Warehousemen, and the small American Communications Association) were operating at the end of 1955. These unions retain perhaps a third of the 850,000 to 900,000 members they had in 1949–1950.

The purges of 1949–1950 ended the Communist party as an important factor in the CIO although a few scattered locals are still under Communist domination. Although the purges cost the CIO heavily in numbers and resources, they removed one important obstacle to unity with AFL, dislike of many AFL leaders of being associated, however distantly, with Communist organizations.

PERSONAL RIVALRY AMONG LABOR LEADERS. It is quite possible that fear of the machinations of Lewis and certain other leaders of large unions gave added motive for the merger of CIO and AFL. This can be seen more clearly if we note certain events of the years 1946–1953. One of these is the decline in membership of the CIO; this decline was due, in good part, to the "red purge." But, whatever the causes, the fact is clear that in 1950 CIO had substantially fewer members than in 1946. As the AFL continued to grow during the postwar period (the big gains being made by the Teamsters and the Building Trade unions), CIO ceased to be a serious rival for dominance in the American labor movement.

CIO was further weakened by the death of Philip Murray in 1952. Walter Reuther (president of UAW) won the battle for succession (as head of CIO) over the bitter opposition of David MacDonald, Murray's successor as head of the Steelworkers. Time did not improve relations between Reuther and MacDonald, and the latter made no secret of his hostility toward Reuther and his independence of CIO. As a result, the CIO became internally unstable and its presidency a rather empty honor. This eliminated one major obstacle to the unification of American labor; necessity for the head of one of the two merging organizations to accept second place in the combined setup. Reuther had little to lose by stepping down as head of CIO;[110] he traded what little prestige the office had for the "number two" position in AFL-CIO.

The president of AFL, George Meany, also had reasons to desire a merger. Like Reuther, Meany was relatively new to his job, having succeeded William Green upon the latter's death in 1952. Before then, he had been for a number of years secretary-treasurer of AFL and, still earlier, head of the Plumbers' union. In Green's declining years, Meany became to an ever-increasing degree the "real" head of AFL. But, like Reuther, he has been threatened by the possible "disaffiliation" of a major union, the Teamsters. There were rumors (in 1953–1954) of a possible coalition of the Teamsters, Steelworkers, and Miners; such a coalition would have constituted the basis of yet a third labor federation that might have attracted many independents and provided a haven for AFL and CIO dissidents that would have further reduced the authority of the older organizations. Whatever foundation these rumors may have had, the vulnerability of both AFL and CIO was real enough.

Ultimately, the formation of AFL-CIO may be to enhance the authority of the "peak" organization (i.e., AFL-CIO) over the component national unions. However, in the foreseeable future the large national unions will continue to determine their own policies on all important issues and are well able, if necessary, to dis-affiliate and "go it alone." The ultimate balance of power between AFL-CIO and its major affiliates is far from determined.

Indeed, as the constitution of AFL-CIO gives more power to the larger national unions than they had in the AFL, it has tended to encourage the amalgamation of smaller unions with one another, or with larger unions, to form more powerful units. These larger unions have virtues of efficiency and economy, but they reduce the number of small unions which have, in the past, been a source of political support for the administration of either CIO or AFL.[111] Consequently, the initial result of forming AFL-CIO may be to increase, rather than reduce, the influence of the (large) national unions relative to that of the peak federation itself.

THE FUTURE OF AMERICAN UNIONISM

The formation of AFL-CIO and the accompanying process of union mergers have made unaffiliated organizations anxious to join a large national union. In a number of instances, Communist-led unions have deposed their tainted officials in order to become acceptable to a non-

---

[110] As head of the United Auto Workers, Reuther continues to enjoy great influence within the labor movement.

[111] Because of their dependence upon the national organization for past and hoped for future assistance.

Communist union. The motive for this behavior has been the desire to avoid being trampled by the major organizing campaigns planned by the new organization.

Communist-controlled unions (not protected by merger with a large and respectable union) will be obvious targets for this drive. The drive may also capture many "independent" unions that have remained outside AFL and CIO only because of worker confusion, or disgust, resulting from past union rivalry.

However, students of labor problems disagree as to the likelihood that unions will be able to organize substantially more job territory than they now hold.[112]   Some economists contend that unions have now captured about as large a part of the American labor force as they can get, at least in the near future.[113]   They argue that the sectors of the economy that remain to be unionized are "tough nuts" to crack; i.e., they are firms whose employers are especially determined to resist unionization or whose workers are uninterested in what unionization promises. Geographically, the nonunionized firms tend to be concentrated in small towns and in the southern states, which are places where unionization has traditionally been difficult to achieve because of strong employer resistance. At present, Taft-Hartley and the various state "right-to-work" laws facilitate such resistance. Also, the nonunionized firms tend to be relatively small, especially the large number in retail trade and service. These firms can be unionized,[114] but the small town locals of such unions (which have few members) are expensive both to form and maintain[115] and, therefore, tend to be unattractive to national organizations.[116]

From a longer-run viewpoint, there are certain labor force trends that are likely to restrict the growth of unions. The white-collar and professional jobs are growing, relative to the labor force; workers in these jobs have, in the past, resisted unionization. A similar statement also applies to women workers, whose numbers are growing relative to the labor force.

[112] See Daniel Bell, "The Next American Labor Movement," *Fortune,* April 1953; Irving Bernstein, "The Growth of American Unions," *American Economic Review,* June 1954, pp. 319–338; and the comments upon Bernstein's article in the *American Economic Review,* June 1955, (pp. 386–392) by Fristoe; Davey, Jacobs, and Monroe and a reply by Bernstein.

[113] This does not mean that union membership will remain stationary, but that it will grow, or decline, with employment in the firms and industries already unionized.

[114] Bernstein, "Reply," *op. cit.,* pp. 390–392.

[115] On this point see Monroe Berkowitz, "The Economics of Trade Union Organization and Administration," *Industrial and Labor Relations Review,* July 1954, pp. 575–592.

[116] Especially since the absence of intercity competition in these industries relieves the unions of the necessity of further organization to protect the areas already unionized.

But, there are students of labor relations who believe that the adverse effects of these factors are exaggerated.[117] They argue that there has been an historical growth of unionism among workers once thought impervious to its appeals, and that there is no reason to suppose this development has ended. They would stress the fact that small towns are now less isolated than formerly and that, as a consequence, workers living in them are far more willing to "stand up for their rights," by joining a union, than formerly. They also point out that the number of farm workers (who are usually considered as "nonorganizable") has been steadily declining, relative to the size of the labor force.

Only the future can reveal which contention is correct. The significance of the dispute for us is that it serves to indicate that, despite its gains of the past two decades, unionism is not evenly distributed among the American labor force. It is confined, primarily, to manual occupations, to urban centers of 100,000 or more, to the nonsouthern parts of the United States, and to males. It may spread further, but to do so it will have to overcome considerable resistance from many of the workers to be organized and from their employers.

DISCUSSION QUESTIONS

1. "Prior to 1936, the AFL was dominated by men who believed it more important to secure benefits for the workers already enrolled in unions than to devote union funds and energies to increasing union membership by 'organizing the unorganized.' The Knights of Labor, IWW, and CIO all represented, in one way or another, the opposite point of view." Discuss.

2. "Union membership tends to grow in periods of business prosperity and decline in periods of depression." In what way does the experience of the 1920's and 1930's contradict this statement? Why did union membership fail to grow in the 1920's? What forces were responsible for the growth of union membership in the 1930's?

3. "Had it not been for the Wagner Act, manufacturing employers would have been able to defeat the CIO's organizing drives and the mass-production industries would still be nonunion." Discuss.

4. It is generally believed that, despite some concessions to CIO, the AFL exercised a controlling influence in the formation of AFL-CIO. What evidence is there for this belief?

Suggested Readings

Brissenden, P. F., *The IWW,* Columbia University Press, New York, 1919. The standard work on the IWW.

Commons, John R., and associates, *History of Labor in the United States,* Vols. I–IV, The Macmillan Co., New York, 1951. These are primarily reference volumes for the student interested in details.

Lorwin, Lewis L., *The American Federation of Labor,* Brookings Institution, Washington, D.C., 1933. The best and most comprehensive work on the AFL's

---

[117] Notably, Bernstein, *op. cit.*

history.   Unfortunately, it ends in 1932; there is, as yet, no comparable volume
for more recent developments.

Perlman, Selig, *The History of Trade Unionism in the United States,* Augustus
Kelly, New York, 1950.   A brief summary.

Ulman, Lloyd, *The Rise of the National Union,* Harvard University Press, Cambridge, Mass., 1955.   An important recent work on the history of union
structure.

Ware, N. J., *The Labor Movement in the United States, 1860–1895,* D. Appleton
& Co., 1929.   The best single reference on the Knights of Labor.

4

The Growth of American Unionism
II: Purpose, Philosophy, and Politics

The previous chapter described the growth in American union membership and the development of union organization over the past century. This chapter deals with the ideas, ideals, and politics of those who participated in that development.

THE FORMATIVE PERIOD: BEFORE THE AFL

Social Reform

To the "labor agitators" of the pre-Civil War period, the "wrongs" of the wage earner were only one example of the injustices heaped upon the weak and poor by the strong and rich. The injustice of low wages was seen as the kin of an unjust tax system, or an unfair system of credit, or an inequitable method of distributing western farm land, etc. The reformers of the period 1825–1850 battled to improve the world in a variety of ways, of which bettering the lot of the wage-earner was only one.

Indeed, it was not then clear that the wage earners' problems were especially important. Urban wage earners were but a small part of the population and their status was widely believed to be temporary; i.e., it was believed that they would, after suitable institutional reforms, become self-employed artisans or farmers. Accordingly, many reformers believed that the economic and social reforms most helpful to the wage earner would be those that facilitated his climb to self-employment. Thus many reformers wanted to help the wage earner by giving him improved educational facilities, cheap, or free, land, etc.[1] To be sure, the imme-

---

[1] For a discussion of these early reformers, see N. J. Ware, *The Industrial Worker, 1840–1860*, Houghton, Mifflin & Co., Boston, 1924, and Commons and Associates, *History of Labor in the United States*, Vol. I, Part II, Chapter III and Part IV. Also see Joseph Dorfman, *The Economic Mind in American Civilization*, Viking Press, New York, 1946, Vol. 2, Chapter XXIV.

diate problems of the wage earner were not ignored. Demands for shorter hours and higher wages were supported, but these demands were usually thought of as mere palliatives and not as basic remedies for the "workingman's problem."

Indeed, prior to the late 1850's, it is very difficult to distinguish proposals to benefit labor (i.e., wage earners) as such from a pot pourri of schemes for uplifting all of mankind. The social reformers who campaigned at various times for women's suffrage, free land for settlers, cheap money and easy credit, the abolition of slavery, the establishment of model socialist communities, etc.[2] were in frequent contact with those who fought for shorter hours and better wages. Indeed, the two groups had many common members.

These reformers were not the men who led the unions of the period in their struggles for immediate gains. The leaders of these unions were workers themselves and probably had more mundane ideas than those of the more famous reformers. However, the union leaders were not given to writing and their ideas, if any, have been lost to posterity. Whatever ideas of this period were handed to later generations of labor spokesmen, came from the "social reformers."

Among these reformers there was a fairly high rate of turnover, with new converts replacing those who became distracted or disillusioned. But despite this turnover, there began to emerge as early as the 1840's a program that, with minor amendments, was typical of labor ideology until the 1880's. It involved: (1) demands for improving the workingman's status before the law, e.g., mechanics' liens and abolition of imprisonment for debt; (2) control or abolition of convict labor in order to protect the living standards of wage earners; (3) currency reform (of one kind or another); (4) establishment of a shorter working day; and (5) creation of producers' cooperatives.

These demands were made, in one form or another, by most of the various associations, leagues, etc. formed from 1840 to 1880 that claimed to speak for the "laboring man." These various labor organizations were almost always controlled by social reformers, and interest or participation in them by actual workingmen was slight. Consequently, there is no way of knowing what wage earners thought of these various proposals; however, the fact that politicians who sought workers' votes frequently paid lipservice to some or all of them suggests that they had genuine popular appeal.

Support of these proposals was not antithetical to belief in trade unionism. In most cases friends of unionism supported "labor's cause" on all fronts, political as well as economic. However, the issue of producers' cooperatives had far more impact upon the nascent unions of 1850–1880 than all the others combined. Throughout the 1860's and well into the

[2] For details see the references in note 1.

1870's, important union leaders exhibited a strong interest in establishing producers' cooperatives. The interest was far more than academic for, as we have already seen (pp. 36–37) many unions actually tried to establish such co-ops. To be sure, these co-ops served more than an ideological function; they were usually started in depressions to provide work for unemployed members and, incidentally, to keep the union together. But there is abundant evidence that the union leaders of the time seriously hoped to supplement, or replace, capitalist enterprise with producers' cooperatives.[3]

The incompatibility between "cooperativism" and trade unionism was not so much ideological as practical. Financing co-ops drained union treasuries, thereby reducing their fighting power. In prosperity, when strikes could be won and wages raised, bargaining activities tended to absorb union funds and energies; but, in depression, when wage bargaining seemed hopeless and unemployment became a major problem, establishing a co-op or two appeared extremely attractive. However, financing the co-op made it necessary to avoid strikes; as a result membership tended to fall off, except among workers directly involved in the co-op activities, and the union would tend to become, for practical purposes, a cooperative organization.

As we have already noted, the producers' co-ops were, with few exceptions, total failures. But the idea of trying them died hard. An important segment of the Knights of Labor was very much interested in "cooperation" and fought hard against the Knights' tendency to develop into a trade union organization.[4] However, this was the last flicker of an expiring dream; by the 1880's it was clear that there was no resisting industrialization and large scale enterprise, which implied that America was to have a large and growing force of permanent wage earners. By the 1880's the question for the American labor movement had become "how to improve the economic condition of these urban wage earners."

Marxism

The Marxists had a ready answer to this question. The working class must capture the means of production and operate them for the benefit of "those who toil." That is, the working class must establish Socialism. The Socialism proposed by Marxists was very different from what they termed the "utopian socialism" of the reformers of 1840 vintage. These earlier reformers attempted to establish small model socialist communities, which they hoped would inspire other groups to emulation. Marx and his followers rejected such activities as utopian, and proposed to build Socialism by socializing the means of production within existing communities.

[3] Commons, *op. cit.*, Vol. II, pp. 53–55, 79, 430–438.
[4] *Ibid.*, pp. 430–438.

To the Marxists, capitalism was a necessary stage of economic development in the creation of an industrialized society. In the Marxian view, capitalism creates the means of production, factories, railroads, etc., which a modern industrial community requires. It also generates the labor force of wage earners, the proletariat, to operate these productive facilities. It is the historic mission of the wage earners to expropriate the capitalists and "own" the instruments of production in common, operating them for the benefit of "all"[5] and not for the profit of any individual.

According to Marx, it is the historic function of the proletariat to establish a socialist society based upon an industrial technology. To perform this task, the proletariat must be awakened to its destiny and given a realization of its power. Trade unions, as institutions of the working class, must be utilized as media for educating the proletariat to its historic role. It is illusory to expect that "significant" economic gains for the working class as a whole can be obtained through collective bargaining; whatever gain in wages or working conditions that unions obtain for their members would be either temporary or confined to only a small segment of the working class. In any event, pursuit of these immediate objectives must be subordinated to the ultimate objective of preparing the working class for its revolutionary mission.

For the Marxists, trade unions were but a vehicle for conducting class warfare on the "economic front"; they considered it equally important to wage political warfare as well.[6] To do this, they organized Socialist parties[7] which they attempted to affiliate with union organizations. As Marxian Socialists believed the primary function of union

[5] "All" is deliberately ambiguous. To a Marxist the wage earning class tends, through the process of economic development, eventually to become almost the whole population. The validity of this contention is, to put it mildly, not undisputed.

[6] This is, of course, an oversimplification. There were, and are, a wide variety of "Marxist" positions on this, as on other matters. At one extreme there were Marxists who wished to use strikes as revolutionary instruments; at the other there were moderate socialists who considered trade unions simply as instruments for collective bargaining, and who believed that socialism should be achieved only through the ballot. There were also a wide variety of intermediate positions, all claimed as "Marxist." The position described in the text is, more or less, "middle-road" Marxism.

[7] There have been several such parties. The interested reader may consult H. H. Quint, *The Forging of American Socialism: Origins of the Modern Movement,* University of South Carolina Press, 1953 and Ira Kipnis, *The American Socialist Movement: 1897–1912,* Columbia University Press, New York, 1952. The best brief account is Daniel Bell, "The Background and Development of Marxian Socialism in the United States," Chapter 6 in *Socialism and American Life,* edited by D. D. Egbert and Stow Persons, Vol. I, Princeton University Press, Princeton, N. J., 1952. See especially pp. 228–267.

activity was to "educate" the working class, their main concern was obtaining union support for the political demands of the (pertinent) Socialist party.

Marxian ideas never had many adherents in the United States inside the labor movement, or outside. However, from time to time, they have had a significance quite disproportionate to the number of their adherents. One of these periods was the 1870's and 1880's. During these years there were not many persons actively at work in attempting to build a "labor movement"; among this small group, the Marxists were a sizeable and important minority.[8] They were especially important among foreign born workers (e.g., Germans) and had considerable influence in union organizations (e.g., the Knights of Labor) in New York and Chicago.[9]

In the years before World War I, Marxism provided the only serious ideological challenge to the views of the dominant leadership of the AFL. The AFL was not equipped with a well-organized ideology, a fact in which Gompers took pride. He had no use for intellectuals and was suspicious of their "product." However, a type of doctrine did emerge as a rationalization of Federation attitudes and policies, and a brief discussion of it may serve to clarify certain basic trends in AFL policy, especially as regards the relation of unions and politics.

THE PHILOSOPHY AND POLITICS OF AMERICAN LABOR: 1886 TO 1914

There is no coherent statement of the AFL's "philosophy"; it must be inferred from the writings and speeches of Samuel Gompers and from its policy declarations on specific issues. Insofar as union structure is concerned, we have already considered AFL's philosophy (see pp. 43–50), but its "philosophy" had a number of facets other than a preference for the craft form of union organization. The tenets of this philosophy were not thought out in advance of practical applications but emerged as rationalizations of AFL policies in the face of attacks by Socialists from the left and antiunion spokesmen from the right.[10]

---

[8] Most Marxists are politically active and, when in unions, are active members. Because of this, Marxists often constitute an appreciable fraction of the active and articulate part of a union's membership, although constituting but a small fraction of the total.

[9] Marxism is, of course, a "foreign" ideology. Its appeal can be more easily understood if it is remembered that, in the last quarter of the 19th century, a considerable part of urban American wage earners were foreigners, i.e., recent immigrants.

[10] We treat the AFL's philosophy, in this period, as identical with that of its president, Samuel Gompers. This is proper, as Gompers' views were, on all major matters, identical with the AFL policy decisions.

Class Struggle and Socialism

Gompers, who had been a Socialist during the early 1870's, shared two important premises with Marx: both believed (1) that there was no reversing the course of economic progress that resulted in capitalism and large firms and (2) that wage earners had economic interests distinct from those of impecunious farmers and small businessmen. For both Gompers and Marxists, the task was to promote the interests of the wage earners. However, they differed enormously in their ideas of procedure.

Marxists were fundamentally optimistic about the actual and potential strength of the working class. To them, the principal obstacle to the overthrow of capitalism was the confusion and disunity of the workers; but this confusion could be eliminated by proper education (on Marxian lines), while further economic development would bring to workers a keener appreciation of "reality" and enhance their numbers by "proletarianizing" more and more small businessmen and farmers. The Marxist believed that "history was on his side."

Gompers' attitude was almost the reverse of this. He was a cautious pessimist about the strength of the wage earning "class," and felt that only its most educated and skilled portion was then (in the 1880's) capable of sustaining permanent organizations. Accordingly, he concentrated his attention upon the skilled craftsmen for whom he became spokesman and whose attitudes he fully shared. The craftsman felt, and to some extent still feels, that his training and the opportunity to use it are a kind of property and that it was the business of his union to protect this property.[11] The skilled unions, to be sure, had demands to make upon employers (for example, a shorter working day); but they were at least as interested in protecting the market for their skills from erosion through economic change as in obtaining "more."

Gompers' primary objective was to create durable unions of skilled workers. To do this he did not need to overthrow capitalism, and he (rightly) believed that durable unions could be more readily built with the cooperation, or at least the neutrality, of employers than in the face of their hostility. Consequently, he sought to placate employers in every way possible; for example, he joined the National Civic Federation[12] in the hope of persuading industrialists, like Senator Mark Hanna, of the

[11] This view of the skilled unions' philosophy has received its classic statement in Selig Perlman, *A Theory of the Labor Movement*, Augustus Kelley, New York, 1949, especially Chapter VII.

[12] The National Civic Federation was an organization that, among other things, tried to reduce industrial conflict by encouraging collective bargaining contracts and mediating labor disputes. It had the support, in the late 1890's and early 1900's, of a number of important capitalists and seemed to Gompers a useful channel for persuading the business community of the "respectability" of unions.

advantages of dealing with unions. Gompers also urged that unions should sign trade agreements (i.e., collective bargaining contracts) providing for no strikes (or lockouts) for a specified time period and live up to them even if it became necessary to cross another union's picket lines.

In short, Gompers' theory and practice was to sell AFL unionism to employers and the whole middle-class community as a respectable, law-abiding institution that stood as a bulwark against disorder, revolution, etc. In such a campaign there was, of course, no place for doctrines of class warfare. This is not to say that Gompers was insincere in rejecting Marxism; he rejected the idea of a class struggle because he thought it inconceivable that American wage earners could undertake such a struggle, let alone win it.

Gompers' rejection of the idea of class struggle went hand-in-hand with his rejection of socialism. In the early days of the AFL, he fought the Socialists because they desired to oust him from office[13] and because he feared that endorsement of their policies would alienate some conservative unions from the AFL and cause internal division within a number of others. Gompers' struggles with the Socialists intensified his opposition to their doctrines, and his antisocialism soon became ideological. It may also be that he found his anti-Socialist position helped his campaign to make unionism acceptable to employers.

Gompers fought not only to avoid an alliance with a Socialist party but to keep the AFL free of all *permanent* political alliances. As he put it, in politics we must "reward our friends and punish our enemies." This meant there was to be no permanent affiliation of the AFL with any political party; it was to be open to advantageous "deals" with all parties.

This policy, which has been subjected to the most severe criticism (see pp. 96–98), is yet another manifestation of Gompers' basic attitude of "cautious pessimism." He recognized that the Republicans frequently won elections and would continue to do so irrespective of what the AFL did. Accordingly, he tried to become as friendly as possible with their leaders and, in 1896–1905, was on good terms with McKinley, Hanna, Roosevelt, and other leading Republicans. This friendliness considerably offset the many ties to the big-city Democratic machines that AFL unions have always possessed. As a result, Gompers and the AFL tended (in this period) toward political neutrality.

But despite the friendliness of some of its important leaders, large elements of the Republican party were bitterly antiunion; these were the employer groups that engineered the open shop drive of the early 1900's (see pp. 49–50). This faction was sufficiently influential to block, after

[13] In one year, 1894, the Socialists combined with other dissenters and defeated Gompers' candidacy for re-election. This was the only year until his death (in 1924) that Gompers was not elected president of the AFL.

1902, almost all Congressional legislation sponsored by the AFL.   The failure to achieve their modest political objectives disturbed the AFL leaders, especially as the federal courts began to issue strike-hampering injunctions (pp. 209–211) in increasing numbers.   Congress would not curb the injunctive power of the courts, and the courts were imposing ever greater restrictions upon union economic activity.   As a result, in March 1906, the Federation drew up a "Bill of Grievances" which specified a set of legislative measures desired by labor; primary emphasis was placed upon the control of injunctions.

As the relevant legislation was bottled up in committee, Gompers and other AFL officials campaigned actively (in the Congressional elections of 1906) to defeat some of the more antilabor Congressmen (mainly Republicans).   Although Gompers claimed credit for the reduction of the Republican majority in the House of Representatives (from 112 to 50), the new House was even less friendly to AFL than its predecessor.

At their 1908 convention, the Republicans nominated William Howard Taft, a known sympathizer with labor injunctions who was called by Gompers the "injunction standard bearer."   The Republican platform, by implication, supported the use of injunctions while the Democratic platform included (at the request of the AFL) an anti-injunction plank. Accordingly Gompers, and most AFL leaders, supported Bryan.   Despite Bryan's defeat, the Federation had no choice but to continue fighting the Republicans on the national scene.   In the 1912 Presidential election they supported Wilson and the Democratic party in general.

From Wilson's victory, organized labor obtained the Clayton Act of 1914,[14] the Adamson Act of 1916, a friendly attitude toward unions by the federal government during World War I, and the appointment of labor leaders to a variety of governmental commissions.

Voluntarism; the Primacy of Economic Activity

The expression, "Reward your friends and punish your enemies," does not fully convey the peculiar character of Gompers' and, for many years the AFL's, attitude toward politics.   The AFL was prepared to deal with any party and have none of its own, because it asked, and expected, very little from government action.   What little it wanted in the way of *economic* legislation could be granted by one major party as easily as by the other.

Gompers believed that wage earners could make gains only through economic pressure[15] and desired only that the laws of the land permit

[14] The Clayton Act (especially Sections 6 and 20) was, for several years, thought to have ended union liability under the Sherman Anti-Trust Law (see pp. 215–216). At the time of its passage it was hailed as labor's Magna Carta.

[15] There were, however, exceptions; e.g., government employees (because they were not permitted to strike), women, and children.

them to organize and exert this pressure. Accordingly Gompers opposed legislation establishing maximum hours or minimum wages for men;[16] he also opposed federal or state unemployment insurance and old age pensions.

In reference to wages and hours legislation, Gompers argued (1) that governmentally established *minimum* standards for wages and hours would tend to become *maximum* standards and (2) that depending upon government action for economic betterment would weaken workers' loyalty to their unions.[17]   On the subject of compulsory social insurance, Gompers denounced the idea of compulsion, claiming it was inimical to the freedom of the worker.[18]   Consistent with his stand against wage and hour legislation and social insurance, Gompers also opposed governmental interference with business, e.g., he opposed the Sherman Act in toto and not merely as applied to unions.   He also opposed government ownership of coal mines, railroads, etc.

It should be realized that Gompers' attitude on these matters was that of the controlling group within the AFL, and was official Federation policy until the 1930's.   In this general outlook, the AFL leaders were (probably) far removed from the views of their own rank and file and not far from those of the most conservative section of American public opinion.

The AFL took an even less favorable view of governmental intervention in the affairs of unions than in those of business.   It opposed such intervention, even to protect union members from corrupt officers; for example, Gompers objected to proposals aimed at providing protection of the rights of union members, resolutely arguing that correction had to come from within the union and not from legislative enactments.[19]   In Gompers' view unions were voluntary associations; therefore, their internal affairs were not subject to governmental intervention.   Not surprisingly, the AFL also opposed all legislation aimed at restricting the right to strike.

Gompers' distrust of legislation as a supplement to (let alone a replacement for) union economic pressure on employers was rooted in a great deal of unpleasant experience.   State laws aimed at limiting hours were an old story; but these laws were usually not enforced effectively by government agencies, or were nullified by the courts.   Such enforcement as did occur was usually supplied by union strike action.   There was sub-

---

[16] This remained the Federation position until well into the 1930's.   Gompers did support wage and hour legislation for women and the abolition of child labor, but the AFL never campaigned for these reforms on an extensive basis.

[17] On this and related matters, see G. G. Higgins, *Voluntarism in Organized Labor in the United States,* Catholic University Press, Washington, D.C., 1944, pp. 30–31.

[18] Lorwin, *op. cit.,* pp. 284–285.

[19] Harold Seidman, *Labor Czars,* Liveright, 1938, pp. 240–241.

stance to Gompers' argument that legislation, as such, accomplished little and that diverting union funds and efforts to achieving it was a waste.

This general philosophy concerning the role of government in economic affairs is often called "voluntarism"[20] or "pure and simple trade unionism;" it has an obvious affinity to the laissez-faire position of many conservatives. Unfortunately for its proponents, most of the conservatives who might have sympathized with "voluntarism" also disliked unions intensely; on the other hand, most union sympathizers have never had much use for laissez-faire.[21] Consequently, the philosophy of voluntarism has never had many devotees, and its importance is due entirely to its acceptance by the leadership of the AFL.

Even AFL leaders could not, for long, accept the full implications of this philosophy. The necessity of freeing union economic activity from the incubus of judicial restraint forced the AFL into increased political activity after 1906. This activity compelled the Federation to enter into political alliance with reform groups who intended to use governmental authority to accomplish a wide variety of reforms, of which abolishing antiunion injunctions was only one. After 1906, the fortunes of the AFL campaign to free unions from injunctions fluctuated with those of the social reformers in both major parties. Thus the major part (but not all) of the AFL leadership became tied to the political coat-tails of middle-class social reformers, whose philosophy (of governmental intervention in economic affairs) they rejected.[22]

THE OPPOSITION TO VOLUNTARISM

SOCIALIST. The modern Socialist party was formed in 1901 by a fusion of parts of earlier parties.[23] These earlier parties, especially the Socialist-Labor party, were the "Socialists" against whom Gompers fought in the 1880's and 1890's. Many, but by no means all, of these

---

[20] For a discussion of "voluntarism," see Higgins, *op. cit.;* also by the same author, "Union Attitudes toward Economic and Social Roles of the Modern State" in *Interpreting the Labor Movement,* Industrial Relations Research Association, 1952, pp. 149–170.

[21] The paradoxical nature of Gompers' views is well indicated by Will Herberg's characterization of him as a "conservative Syndicalist." Will Herberg, "American Marxist Political Theory" in *Socialism and American Life,* 1952, pp. 491–492.

[22] To be sure, Gompers was not consistent in his opposition to legislation on economic matters. "Voluntarism" was the general tendency of his thinking, but he was above all a practical man not given to unnecessary struggle for the sake of ideological consistency. For example, he supported the Railway Brotherhoods' demands for a federal eight hour day law (granted by the Adamson Act of 1916); he also supported the Miners' demands for safety laws. Doctrines or no, Gompers did not offend powerful interests lightly.

[23] See Bell *op. cit.,* pp. 267–293.

earlier Socialists entered the Socialist party. The Socialist party was, formally, Marxist in philosophy and was affiliated with the Second International. However, before World War I it gained much of its strength from ex-Populists in the Middle West, and its level of doctrinal purity was always low.

The more conservative, right-wing Socialists were always concerned with specific economic reforms to be achieved by government action, under capitalism; e.g., public ownership of utilities, progressive income taxation, banking reform, slum clearance, improvement of wages and hours, abolition of child labor, etc. These "immediate" demands were supposed eventually to lead to the establishment of socialism, but to an increasing degree the right-wing Socialists focussed their primary attention upon the immediate reforms and the electoral victories that were their prerequisite. With regard to union activity, the right wing wished to work within the AFL and convert it to their viewpoint. Accordingly, they fought, year after year, at AFL conventions for endorsement of their party and its program. They always lost, but they constituted a vocal minority and their resolutions usually produced lively debate; most of the doctrine of "voluntarism" was developed in this (roughly) 24-year debate between the Socialists and Gompers.

To a considerable extent, the Socialists and the advocates of industrial unionism (within the AFL) overlapped. The Socialists were anxious to organize the unskilled workers; for this would (they believed) increase their strength within the Federation and also increase the Federation's political influence by expanding its size. They attributed the AFL's failure to unionize the unskilled to the insistence upon high dues, the craft form of organization, and the hostility of many union leaders to the unskilled immigrant workers. The Gompers faction, of course, argued that the failure was due entirely to employer opposition and the indifference of the unskilled immigrants to unionism.

The successful organization of unskilled immigrants in the garment trades in 1909–1912 (and the contemporaneous exploits of the IWW) considerably improved the Socialist case, and the huge increase of membership in the (largely Socialist) Garment unions greatly increased their voting power within the Federation. As a result in the years immediately prior to World War I, the Socialist minority in the AFL had become more powerful and vociferous, and more radical.

THE IWW. The left wing of the Socialist party stressed the revolutionary traditions of Marxism and deprecated the right wing's concern with electioneering, piecemeal reform, and legality. The left wing Socialists were not clear as to what they wanted, but they vibrated sympathetically to talk of "revolution," "militancy," etc.

There was a certain sympathy between the Socialist left and the IWW.

However, the IWW placed little value upon "dropping pieces of paper in a hole" (the ballot), which limited its concern with any political party. The IWW, like Gompers, believed that social decisions are made in the economic and not in the political sphere. The implication that the IWW drew from this premise was that a social revolution must come through strike action, ultimately a general strike.

The success of a general strike would result in the workers retaining the seized property and using it for the benefit of all; the government was assigned little or no role in the postrevolutionary commonwealth. This doctrine is usually referred to as syndicalism, and the IWW has often been said to have had a syndicalist ideology. However, the IWW leaders were even less given to written programs than those of the AFL; they were "practical men," in a negative way, and were concerned with organizing strikes to the virtual exclusion of thinking about "ultimate aims."[24] Furthermore, the "ideas" of the various leaders of IWW were by no means identical. Therefore, to identify the IWW as "syndicalist" is to simplify; however, if they could be said to have had a philosophy, "syndicalism" would describe it better than any other label.

THE IDEOLOGY OF AMERICAN LABOR SINCE 1914

With the possible exception of communism, American labor has seen nothing new in ideologies during the last forty years. The scant development that has occurred has been mainly a modification of the doctrines of "voluntarism" under the impact of the great depression of the 1930's and the New Deal.

Gompers held fast to the principles of voluntarism during and after World War I. For a time after his death in 1924, the AFL continued to adhere to these principles. However, the unemployment of the early 1930's, and later the opportunities for favorable legislation presented by the New Deal, more or less compelled the AFL to abandon its stand against government intervention in economic affairs.[25] The two most striking reversals of previous AFL positions were the abandonment of opposition to (1) unemployment insurance and (2) wage and hour legislation for men. By 1940, the laissez-faire implications of voluntarism were almost completely abandoned among the AFL leaders, and they never had currency in the CIO.

However, one important tenet of Gompers' philosophy was retained

---

[24] Syndicalism is, in its essence, an anti-intellectual doctrine which deprecates detailed plans, objectives, etc. A revolution's objectives are said to emerge from its activity. Careful articulation of objectives is considered a bourgeois-intellectual fetish. The classic statement of the syndicalist attitude is George Sorel, *Reflections on Violence,* George Allen and Uwin, London, 1915.

[25] Higgins, *op. cit.*

by the AFL and absorbed by the CIO, i.e., the doctrine of "no ultimate ends." Gompers' denial that the AFL had any ultimate ends was originally made to distinguish the position of "pure and simple" unionism from that of the Socialists (and others) who viewed collective bargaining as a temporary palliative pending some final "cure." He denied that the AFL had any ultimate "cure" for the wage earners' ills except amelioration through collective bargaining, i.e., by getting "more."

Gompers believed that government could not, and would not, aid unions in obtaining more; the most that labor could hope for was that government would remain neutral. For Gompers' day and age this was probably a sound judgment; but as applied to the era that began in the early 1930's, it is clearly erroneous and has been so recognized by the labor leaders of all ideologies, who have come to rely upon governmental assistance in one connection or another. However, increased reliance upon government has not diverted American unions from the path of economic self-help through collective bargaining; the government economic aid that present-day unions seek is primarily designed to improve the conditions under which they bargain with capitalist employers.

To be sure, the scope of governmental economic action that present-day unions demand is far broader than anything imagined possible, under capitalism, 25 years ago.[26] But it is still activity designed to improve the lot of workers, here and now, and in no way does it involve changing the economic system. As in the days of Gompers, labor continues to strive for "more" (under capitalism) without ultimate end. The difference is that nowadays labor, like other groups, finds that a favorably disposed government can be of great assistance.

The changed role of government in our economy has brought about most of the specific reforms that (right-wing) Socialists used to demand, and Gompers attack, before World War I. As a result, most of the right-wing of the Socialist party (especially the trade union elements) drifted away to become New Deal supporters during the 1930's; and they have not returned.[27] In some states, these erstwhile Socialists became Democrats; in others, notably New York, they have formed separate parties. But what is important is that they have ceased to have any distinguishing ideological characteristics; after 1936 the erstwhile right-

[26] For example, unions (and others) demand, with some success, increased government expenditure to relieve unemployment. Their collective bargaining contracts involve, intimately, the operation of the Federal Social Security System. A number of unions rely upon the Fair Labor Standards Act to protect them from the competition of low-wage employers and the unions affected are continually attempting to influence the administration of these laws and to amend them in various ways. The remarks apply, with even greater force, to state and federal laws governing the process of collective bargaining.

[27] See Bell, *op. cit.,* pp. 388–391.

wing Socialists became (at least on domestic issues) reformers, pure and simple.

At present, there are few American labor leaders who have any distinctive ideology. Most of them are more or less New Deal-Fair Deal Democrats; although some are more politically minded, and articulate, than others. It is no accident that labor leaders have a rather conventional set of political affiliations;[28] administering a large union and advancing its immediate objectives leaves little opportunity for pursuit of "ultimate ends." These ends must, therefore, be jettisoned outright or placed in cold storage for an indefinite period. This does not mean that union leaders may not make drastic and far reaching demands (see pp. 180 et seq.), but these demands are attempts to solve the problems confronting their organizations. These are to be distinguished from ideological demands which are made independently of union problems, and to which union tactics are forced to conform.

THE COMMUNISTS

The Communists provide a major exception to the generally non-ideological character of American unionism.[29] In its initial stages, the Communist party inherited the tradition of intransigeant radicalism from the pre-World War I. left-wing Socialists and IWW. The success of the Bolshevik Revolution in Russia fired the imagination of many native and newly immigrated radicals and made them anxious to identify themselves with the world's first successful socialist revolution. Most of the right-wing Socialists[30] did not (for long) share this desire and wanted to avoid becoming a tail to the Russian kite. The prewar tension between the right and left wings of the Socialist party quickly mounted to the breaking

[28] Some labor leaders, notably Walter Reuther, have a flair for suggesting new specific reforms. However, in terms of political action, Reuther is a Democrat (although many years ago he was a right-wing Socialist).

[29] A further, minor, exception may be noted; the case of Catholic unionism. In many continental European countries and in French Canada, there are well organized Catholic unions which compete for members with other unions (which often profess a Marxist ideology). However, in the United States, the Association of Catholic Trade Unionists (founded in 1937) has attempted to work solely within existing unions and has not sought to create rival organizations. Its purposes have been both to help in general organizational work and to fight Communist infiltration into unions; it has done very useful work in a number of cities. See Philip Taft, "The Association of Catholic Trade Unionists," *Industrial and Labor Relations Review,* January 1949, pp. 210–218.

[30] Most of the pre-1914 right wing left the party during World War I because of opposition to its anti-war position. This remark refers only to the minority of right-wingers who remained. And even among this group there was confusion and fluctuation of opinion; Bell, *op. cit.,* pp. 318–328.

point, and the party split into a number of pieces.   Several of these united to become the Communist party.

The Communist (Third) International was, from the beginning, dominated by the Russians who dictated the policies and selected the officers of the parties in other countries, including the United States.   As a result, the policies of these parties reflected the course of the struggles for power within the Kremlin.   The various purges of the Russian party and government had their repercussions within the U. S. Communist party, with the result that (in the late 20's and early 30's) there was a series of purges which created a number of ex-Communist sects; of these, the most famous were the Trotskyites.

Internal Communist party politics affected the American labor movement in that the party's success and failure in union activity were implements of intraparty factional struggle.   Communist doctrine (like most variants of Marxism) declared that capture of the trade unions was a necessary step in preparing a proletarian revolution.   Accordingly, success or failure in trade union work was a primary indicator of the effectiveness of the Communist party.   In the early 1920's, the Communists adopted Foster's tactic of "boring from within" AFL unions in the hope of capturing them.[31]   This policy led to the internal struggle within ILGWU (see pp. 64–65), and several other though less significant struggles within a number of other unions.

By 1928 the Communist attempts to capture AFL unions were completely defeated, and the Communist elements had been either expelled from, or isolated within, almost all of them.   This, and the vagaries of intraparty politics, lead to a new trade union program, the building of dual (rival) unions.   These unions were affiliated with the Trade Union Unity League (TUUL) created by the Communists in 1929, out of the earlier Trade Union Educational League (TUEL).   The TUUL unions never had a very large membership, and most of what they had was in the New York City area.   The only TUUL union which was a major factor in its industry was the Fur Workers, which the Communists captured during the middle 1920's.

Despite its small membership, TUUL built up a fairly sizeable staff of trained and energetic organizers from the ranks of the Communist party.   These organizers were sent wherever labor trouble threatened and became a familiar part of the labor scene in the turbulent period of the early 1930's.   Their historic importance, however, arises from their role in the organizing work of the CIO.

The participation of the Communists in the CIO stems from the change in the "party line" occurring in 1935.   Throughout the early 1930's, the

[31] That is, attempting to gain elective and appointive union offices for Communists and ultimately controlling the unions.

Communists resolutely refused to cooperate with other anti-Fascist groups in Germany or elsewhere. Their doctrine was that fascism was a temporary phase of capitalist development which would ultimately accelerate the triumph of socialism. But by 1935, Nazi Germany began to appear as a real menace to the Soviet Union, and the "line" was changed to the promotion of "popular fronts" of all anti-Fascist forces.

The objective of the popular-front policy was the establishment of a collective security alliance among Great Britain, France, the United States, and Russia against the German-Italian-Japanese Axis. Its implementation involved (temporary) abandonment of the revolutionary program, cooperation with all sympathetic groups, including "bourgeois" parties, and a serious attempt to pose as a respectable political organization. In the United States, the popular-front program caused the Communists to reverse their earlier hostility to the New Deal and to become its ardent supporters in the years 1936–1939. They also sought to infiltrate organizations of all kinds, in order to persuade them to adopt a "progressive, anti-Fascist" policy. Of major importance, in this connection, were labor unions.

The formation of CIO occurred at just about the same time as the Communists adopted the popular-front tactic. There were small but active Communist minorities in the various embryonic industrial unions that sprang up (in automobile, rubber, electrical manufacturing, etc.) in 1935–1936, and the TUUL had its crew of trained organizers. Lewis needed both and accepted the aid of Communist unionists, putting many of them on CIO payrolls.

During the years 1936–1939, the Communists made an important contribution to the CIO organizing drives. In the course of so doing, they installed themselves in key positions in a number of CIO unions; positions from which they were later dislodged only at a heavy cost. The influence of the Communist party during the period 1936–1939 was enormously enhanced by their ability to identify themselves with such popular causes as the New Deal and opposition to Fascism. Clothed in their mantle as "progressives," the Communists, inside of unions and out, made many converts and secured many more "fellow travelers." These provided the sizeable blocs of union votes which the Communists were able to control. Much of this Communist influence was destroyed during the Hitler-Stalin pact of 1939–1941; and most of what remained was lost after World War II.

Today, the Communists are an isolated minority in the American labor movement, and it is very unlikely that they will ever regain their former strength. However, it is necessary to explain the fact that they could ever have attained so much influence when their beliefs were never shared by more than a small fraction of the members of the unions they controlled. The explanation lies partly in the Communist appeal to racial minorities. Communists have consistently exploited the grievances of these groups; they have also tried wherever possible to nominate members of racial minorities for union office. Their opponents have often taken a weak stand on racial discrimination and even covertly supported it.[32] Furthermore anti-Communist resistance to racial discrimination is often less dramatic than that of the Communists who wish to exploit racial tension, rather than eliminate it. As a result, the Communists have had considerable success in unions where there are racial, or ethnic, minorities.

A second reason for Communist influence in unions is the indifference of most union members toward union activities (see pp. 121–123). Communists are under orders to "work" in the unions; hence, they go to meetings, accept unpaid or low paid jobs which others shun, and thereby insert themselves into the union organization. Once there, they try to bring in other Communists. Unless and until they make themselves a source of factional trouble, they are a convenient instrument for union organizations with small budgets and insufficient personnel.[33] This was an especially important factor in the early hectic days of CIO.

Communists are not interested in influencing a union's bargaining policies or tactics. There is no identifiable Communist wage or strike policy; Communist-dominated unions pursue highly aggressive policies in some industries but "realistically" accept wage cuts in others. (In the past, crude attempts by party "experts" to interfere with union policy have caused disasters for both the unions and their Communist fractions.[34]) What the Communists desire is to secure control of the union newspaper, to secure as many of the key offices as possible, and to have the union commit itself to the support of various aspects of the party program, especially on foreign policy. They are also anxious to divert union funds for party purposes and to give union jobs to party members or fellow-travelers in order to further party influence. To promote some or all of these objectives, Communists will make political bargains with other union elements; trading support on other issues (toward which they are indifferent) for support of (some of) their candidates and resolutions.

At bottom, the Communists' primary objective in a union is to utilize it as an instrument for attaining their political objectives. They do not and, by their own standards, should not scruple to sacrifice the interests of the members of a single union in order to promote the Communist

[32] This was much more true in the past than now; however, anti-Negro discrimination can still be found in some unions, despite the genuine opposition of CIO and AFL leaders.

[33] I.e., small union organizations.

[34] The disastrous strike in the garment industry in 1925–1926 is an outstanding example of this.

program which is assumed to be identical with the "true" interests of the entire working class.

THE ROLE OF AMERICAN LABOR IN POLITICS

The political behavior of American labor has been largely determined by its ideology, or lack of it.   Apart from the Socialists and Communists, it has eschewed pursuit of long-range objectives in order to achieve lesser goals more quickly.   It has sought these lesser goals by making "deals" with the two major political parties.

The Nature of Union Political Power

The essence of a political "deal" is a trade.   A political party or machine trades legislation, appointments to office, lucrative public contracts, etc. for political support.   This support may consist of endorsements and speeches or cash contributions for political expenses.   In seeking to deal with a political party, labor organizations can and have used all of the conventional media of political transactions.   Of these union endorsement is only one, and not always the most important, boon a union can offer a candidate for public office.

UNION ENDORSEMENTS.   To be sure most candidates for office, in urban areas with large union membership, are glad to accept the public support of labor organizations.   However, the precise value of these endorsements has been the subject of much debate.   If the vote of all or most union members could be "delivered" by their leaders, there is no question but what it would be of overwhelming importance in large cities.   But it is by no means clear that union members always vote as their leaders direct.   A union member has a number of other interests and affiliations: he may belong to a church or fraternal association, he may belong to an ethnically oriented organization (e.g., an Italian-American club), to a veterans' organization, an athletic organization, etc.   Any or all of these affiliations may outweigh his union membership in determining his vote; he is also highly responsive to candidates' personalities.

Furthermore, a candidate with a strong prolabor record cannot easily, or effectively, be repudiated by union leaders.   This was clearly shown when Roosevelt carried most mining districts in the Presidential election of 1940 despite John L. Lewis' support of his opponent, Wendell Willkie.   And, conversely, a well-known opponent of labor cannot be helped greatly by a union endorsement.[35]

In short, union members do not behave as a disciplined bloc of voters.   By and large, their voting behavior does reflect their status as wage earners, but their votes also depend upon a number of other factors.

[35] Where a candidate is not well-known, a labor (or other) endorsement is of more importance than otherwise.

CONTRIBUTIONS. The argument of the previous paragraph explains why candidates and parties who see union support are often more interested in cash contributions, or the aid of a union controlled political organization, than in an endorsement. Political warfare requires money, and unions have, in recent years, become an important source of funds. In the United States, financial support for political campaigns has traditionally come from a small number of wealthy individuals and/or from political organizations whose sources of revenue have been donations from office-holders and individuals seeking favors.

Union cash contributions were not of great importance until the 1930's when the Democrats lost many of their big contributors because of the business community's dislike of the New Deal. By the same token, in 1936, labor had a larger stake in the re-election of President Roosevelt than it had ever had in any one election. Consequently, a number of unions, especially the United Mine Workers,[36] contributed large sums to the Democratic campaign fund.

Labor's cash contributions to political campaign funds have received wide publicity and wide criticism. However, labor has merely followed the lead, after a long delay, of wealthy individuals and business firms that have long provided their political allies with the sinews of political warfare. The campaign contributions of both labor and business have often been criticized for being so large as to make candidates the prisoners of the contributors. However, campaigns, especially at the national level, are enormously expensive; radio and television time, campaign literature, office rent, etc. cost millions of dollars. And the party or candidate without these instruments of electioneering has virtually no chance of success.

Nevertheless, the feeling against large campaign contributions has been such as to prompt several attempts to regulate them by federal law. The Hatch Act of 1940 attempted to restrict the contributions of any individual or group, while the Smith-Connolly Act of 1943 and the Taft-Hartley Act of 1947 contained provisions aimed specifically at the campaign contributions of unions. None of these laws has been successful in its avowed purpose as all of them have contained loopholes of one sort or another. For example, the Taft-Hartley Act prohibited contributions by unions to elections, primaries, or conventions involving federal offices. However, it did not restrict the activities of independent organizations sponsored by prominent union members or leaders. Consequently, the CIO (operating through its Political Action Committee, PAC) and the AFL (using Labor's League for Political Education, LLPE) have been able to make cash contributions without great difficulty. Since the AFL-

---

[36] The United Mine Workers contributed $500,000 to the Democratic campaign fund. Saul Alinsky, *John L. Lewis*, 1949, pp. 172–178.

CIO merger, LLPE and PAC have been combined into the Committee On Political Education (COPE). COPE operates in a manner similar to its predecessors.

Attempts to impose legal restrictions upon union political activity are, in part, mere reprisals by legislators opposed by unions. However, they also reflect a belief that unions ought not to use funds collected (from workers with varying political opinions) for nonpolitical purposes to support the political views of the majority of the union. There is a nice question of individual rights involved here, but the difficulty is largely met by the voluntary nature of COPE.[37]

Individual rights aside, it must be recognized that effective restraint on union campaign contributions would give an enormous political advantage to the opponents of union objectives. It is only wealthy persons and business firms that can make large individual donations, and most of these are opposed to the political objectives of unions. To derive a large fund from a large number of small (individually solicited) contributions is both difficult and costly; furthermore, the desire of a large number of small contributors cannot be effectively expressed except through an organization, such as a labor union.

POLITICAL ACTIVITY OF UNIONS. To a considerable extent, cash contributions to a political campaign simply provide the means for hiring workers to distribute literature, get voters registered, escort people to the polls on election day, etc. Performance of these tasks has been traditionally the function of the Democratic and Republican organizations. However, in certain areas this task has been partially, or largely, taken over by the PAC and LLPE.[38] These organizations have also prepared, printed, and distributed campaign literature, sponsored radio and television programs on behalf of favored candidates, etc. These activities are, of course, tantamount to indirect cash contributions and are much sought after by candidates.

MISCELLANEOUS FAVORS. Politicians sometimes need favors that unions can grant. Unions hire lawyers, buy buildings and supplies, administer large amounts of cash, appoint trustees of pension funds, etc. The union officials who control these various activities can provide comfortable jobs and profitable business opportunities for displaced legislators or for the friends, relatives, etc., of those currently in office. In exchange, unions may frequently obtain favorable consideration of their political requests.

Another source of union beneficence arises in situations where a union acts as the local hiring office for the employers in a particular industry.

---

[37] That is individual union members are not compelled to contribute to these organizations if they do not wish to do so.

[38] An outstanding example is the major role played in the Michigan Democratic Party by the PAC.

In these cases, especially where a union official has more or less complete authority to send workers on jobs,[39] he may do a friend in City Hall a favor and give one of his proteges a job—and a union card. The dispensation of these favors can be a source of graft to the union officers involved; but it may also be a useful device for securing political advantage for the union.

UNIONS AND OTHER PRESSURE GROUPS. The above description of their political activities may seem to put unions in a bad light. However, union political tactics are in no way different from those of other "pressure groups" seeking to advance one "cause" or another. In a political democracy such as ours, there are a large number of "special interest groups" that seek governmental favors of various kinds; e.g., there are industry associations seeking tariffs, local business associations seeking federal government expenditures in their vicinity, veterans' associations seeking more benefits for ex-servicemen, organizations seeking to influence the conduct of foreign affairs for one reason or another, farm organizations seeking higher crop support prices, etc. This is to say nothing of various business firms and individuals that seek special privileges. Each of these tries to exert pressure upon those with the power to help or hinder its cause; they do this by promises of political aid, if helped, and threats of reprisal, if hindered.

When organized labor's full strength can be brought to bear on an issue, it is obviously a very powerful interest group. (After all, the 18 million union members, together with their families, constitute a very large section of the population.) However, the very number of union members makes it difficult to unify them; union members are drawn from a variety of religious, ethnic, and even economic groups, and they have, in consequence, a variety of interests and opinions. And when all, or most, union members do unite upon a particular issue, they are likely to encounter the vigorous opposition of employer pressure groups. Employers are not so numerous as union members, but their wealth gives them great political influence, and they are often able to gain support from farmers, white collar workers, etc. The political power of employers and their allies is indicated by their successful resistance (since 1947) to repeal of, or major change in, the Taft-Hartley Act despite the combined efforts of AFL and CIO. It is also indicated by the growing list of states enacting "right-to-work" laws (see p. 177). In short, the political power of organized labor is by no means so great as its mere numbers would suggest.

Labor has been more successful in securing desired governmental action when its demands have been on behalf of a small part of the labor force (and only a relatively small number of employers were opposed) than when its demands have affected employers at large. And it has been

[39] See below, pp. 187–189.

most successful when a particular union has joined with its employers to seek favors to the industry concerned. Thus unions together with associations of employers have had considerable success in getting local communities to impose building codes, health and safety regulations for barber shops, public conveyances, etc. Employer-Union coalitions have also had considerable success in getting state and local governments to adopt minimum price regulations. At the national level, such coalitions have had some influence on tariffs.

It is obvious that labor organizations are interested in legislation affecting them. They seek to influence legislation through their representatives, lobbyists, who work full time in Washington, and in many state capitals as well. However, the political objectives of labor do not end with legislation; the administration of laws is fully as important as their enactment. The actual effect of laws establishing standards for wages and hours, protecting workers from unfair labor practices, etc. depends, to a large extent, upon how they are interpreted and how vigorously violators are punished (see pp. 496–502). Consequently, unions seek to have the bureaus and commissions that deal with labor matters, manned by labor sympathizers. Appointments to these jobs are in the nature of political favors and are an important part of the "pay-off" for labor's political support.

Labor and the Two-Party System

The foregoing remarks about labor as a pressure group refer to its role in a political situation where, as in the United States, it does not have a party of its own. However, the American situation is atypical; in most countries of Western Europe and the British Commonwealth there is a Labor Party[40] which is affiliated with the peak federation of the nation's trade unions. Many theorists of the labor movement, inside the Socialist party and out, have believed that sooner or later American unions would be obliged to form their own party also. But thus far they have not done so, and it does not seem likely that, in the foreseeable future, they will.

One important reason why labor has not formed its own party is that, especially since the 1930's, the Democratic Party, in the northern states, has been highly sympathetic to union demands. A purely labor government might have been even more responsive to the wishes of unions, but it is highly unlikely that such a party could have elected a President or many Congressmen. Hence, by urging union members to vote for a third party instead of the Democrats, labor would have relinquished immediate political benefits in exchange for uncertain gains in the remote future.

[40] Usually called the Labor, or Socialist, or Social Democratic party.

Of course, not all Democrats are prolabor; there has always been a powerful group of wealthy northern conservative Democrats, and many Democratic Congressmen from the southern states have (especially in the last two decades) been extremely antiunion.   Nevertheless, even before the 1930's, the Democrats under Bryan and Wilson (i.e., from 1896 to 1920) generally promised organized labor substantially more than their Republican opponents.   And, as we have already seen (p. 94), they made good on some of these promises during Wilson's administration. To be sure, Socialists and others in the labor movement have often wanted more than the Democrats would give; however, the Republicans have usually seemed so much less sympathetic to labor's claims,[41] and the balance of political power so precarious, that most labor leaders have felt it prudent to support the Democrats.

On one occasion, 1924, when the Democrats nominated a conservative lawyer (John W. Davis), the AFL and the Railroad Brotherhoods supported the nominee of the Farmer-Labor party, Senator Robert M. LaFollette of Wisconsin.   LaFollette was highly popular with middle-western farmers; he also had the support of the major part of organized labor and of the Socialist party.   In November 1924, he polled 4,826,000 votes (the highest ever given a third party candidate) but carried only his home state of Wisconsin.   Despite the sizeable popular vote drawn by La-Follette, most of the labor leaders were discouraged by his failure to carry the eastern states and refused to participate in an attempt to build a permanent third party.   This attitude of impatience with long-range political aims has been no small factor in preventing the rise of a party representing American labor.

Most labor leaders and members are, and traditionally have been, Democrats,[42] but this is not true of all.   For example, John L. Lewis has supported the Republican nominee for President most of his life, and the late William L. Hutcheson (president of the Carpenters) was a consistent Republican.   Furthermore, at the local level, many union functionaries have intermittently supported Republican candidates.   Thus, in California, recent Republican governors have gained considerable AFL support; e.g., in 1954 Governor Knight gained the support of the (AFL) State Federation of Labor by promising to veto "right-to-work" laws if passed by the legislature.

---

[41] Especially with regard to relieving unions from judicial interference.

[42] C. W. Mills, *The New Men of Power*, Harcourt, Brace & Co., New York, 1948, p. 172, found in a survey made in the mid-1940's that 51 per cent of AFL officials and 65 per cent of CIO officials, among respondents, stated they were Democrats while only 19 per cent of the AFL and 7 per cent of the CIO identified themselves as Republican.   The remainder of the respondents were either bipartisan or supported a third party.

In recent years, the labor movement (both AFL and CIO) has supported the Democratic party at the national level, endorsing its nominee for President, Adlai Stevenson, both in 1952 and 1956. This resulted largely from the Democrats forthright opposition to the Taft-Hartley Act, the anti-union attitude of many Republican Congressmen and Senators; and, since 1953, dissatisfaction with President Eisenhower's administrative appointments, especially to the National Labor Relations Board. However, in 1956, a substantial minority of the AFL-CIO Executive Council opposed any endorsement for the presidency for fear that Eisenhower would win whatever they did, and in the hope that they might receive better treatment if their did not endorse his opponent.

The stand of this minority represents the views of a sizeable part of the American labor movement.   As a rule, where Republicans have competed actively for labor support, they have not been rejected.   Indeed, most labor leaders prefer, when possible, to back a winner.   The main reason why labor has usually been Democratic is that the Republican party has served as the spokesman of the nation's business interests and has usually reflected their opposition to unionism.   The Democratic party, on the other hand, has been the predominant party in the large cities where its principal basis of support has been among wage earners. Consequently, it has had at least to pretend concern for the wage earners' welfare and to support his unions.[43]   The Democrats have, therefore, tended to be more sensitive to the demands of labor, and lower income groups generally, than the Republican party.

DISCUSSION QUESTIONS

1. Suppose Samuel Gompers, in 1900, had become converted to Marxian socialism. What effect, if any, do you think this would have had upon the subsequent history of American unionism?

2. "The CIO and the AFL never had any ideological differences. Their disputes were entirely over matters of organizational tactics and personalities." Discuss.

3. Why has the American labor movement failed to develop its own political party?

4. "The secret of Communist infiltration of unions is the apathy of union members and the inability of unions to secure adequate personnel for the lower-ranking union jobs, especially in small unions." Comment and suggest possible remedies if they seem to be needed.

Suggested Readings

Bell, Daniel *The Background and Development of Marxian Socialism in the United States,* Chapter 6 of *Socialism and American Life,* edited by D. D. Egbert and Stow Persons, Princeton University Press, 1952.

[43] There are, of course, other factors that account for labor's tendency to vote Democratic; e.g., Catholics, who tend to vote Democratic, are more heavily represented among wage earners than among the population as a whole.

Common, J. R., and Associates, *History of Labor in the United States,* Vols. I and II, The Macmillan Co., 1918.

Higgins, Father, G. G., "Union Attitudes Toward Economic and Social Roles of the Modern State," *Interpreting the Labor Movement,* Industrial Relations Research Association, 1952, pp. 149–170.

Hoxie, R. F., *Trade Unionism in the United States,* 2nd edition, D. Appleton & Co., 1923.

Perlman, Selig, *A Theory of the Labor Movement,* Augustus Kelley, 1949.

Saposs, David, *Left-wing Unionism in the United States,* International Publishers, New York, 1926.

Taft, Philip, "Theories of the Labor Movement," *Interpreting the Labor Movement,* Industrial Relations Research Association, 1952, pp. 1–38.

5

The Structure
and Government of Unions

To the casual reader of newspapers, organized labor tends to be identified with large organizations such as AFL-CIO, United Auto Workers, United Mine Workers, etc., with a few outstanding personalities such as John L. Lewis or Walter Reuther, and with dramatic events such as union mergers and strikes. This is not surprising; these organizations, persons, and events are newsworthy. However, headlines are often misleading both as to the motives for and the consequences of the actions of unions and their leaders. To understand what is happening, it is essential that we know the more prosaic and fundamental characteristics of unions, their members, and their leaders.

THE FORMAL STRUCTURE OF UNIONS

AFL-CIO

The peak federation of American labor, AFL-CIO, had at its birth on December 1, 1955, about 16 million members. As we have seen, this organization was formed by merging the AFL and CIO, and it has substantially the same (limited) functions as its predecessors. It will probably assist national unions in their organizing drives, especially those to unionize the south. Like its predecessors it furnishes research, legal, and educational services for those affiliated unions that are too small to provide them for themselves; it also has a newspaper. AFL-CIO will represent labor's interests before Congressional committees and administrative agencies of the government, and make political recommendations (such as its endorsement of Adlai Stevenson for President) to its members and sympathizers.

AFL-CIO charters are supposed to define the jurisdiction of the affiliated unions; AFL and CIO charters, prior to merger, were also supposed to perform this function but frequently failed to do so (pp. 246–

247). AFL-CIO has inherited all of the jurisdictional problems of its predecessors, and, like them, must proceed slowly in settling these troublesome disputes. The machinery of the no-raiding pact has already solved some of the problems, but many more remain. The most troublesome jurisdictional questions involve the expansion-minded and powerful Teamsters, the biggest union in the federation and one that has refused to ratify the no-raiding pact.

AFL-CIO has somewhat greater power to expel an affiliate than the AFL possessed. AFL-CIO may suspend a union by a majority vote of its annual convention and revoke its charter by a two-thirds vote. However, the significance of this power should not be exaggerated. The large national unions can live outside AFL-CIO as well as inside; e.g., the United Mine Workers and three of the four Railroad Brotherhoods are presently unaffiliated with AFL-CIO. Recognizing that large unions can live outside the organization will make AFL-CIO, like its predecessors, careful not to attack vital concerns of their affiliates unless absolutely necessary.

The governing body of AFL-CIO is its national convention which meets every two years. Between conventions it is governed by its officers, a president, a secretary-treasurer, and 27 vice-presidents; these officers are elected annually. (However, it was agreed that at the first convention 17 of the vice-presidents were to come from AFL unions and 10 from CIO.) The officers taken together constitute the executive council; however, the actual control of the Federation between conventions is vested in the hands of an executive committee (which meets every two months) consisting of the president, secretary-treasurer, and six vice-presidents chosen by the executive council. (It was agreed that, initially, three of these should come from CIO unions and three from AFL.) There is also a general board, consisting of the executive council and the principal officer of each national or international union which meets once a year to decide "all policy questions referred to it by the executive officers or by the executive council." The organization is financed by a per capita tax of 4 cents per month per member of affiliated organizations and various additional fees from federal locals, state and local organizations, and (possible) special assessments.

The subordinate bodies of AFL-CIO include the state and local organizations which exist in most states and large cities. The locals of various unions in the relevant area may, but need not, affiliate with the appropriate body in their area. The AFL and CIO state and local organizations are required to merge within two years (after December 1, 1955).[1] The

_____

[1] In the first year of AFL-CIO's existence, the merging of these organizations made considerable headway, despite occasional frictions due mainly to jurisdictional squabbling between the building trades and the industrial unions over construction

merged bodies will continue the functions of their predecessors. These are, principally, to furnish political representation for unions at the state and local level, i.e., lobby for union interests, endorse candidates for office, secure appointment of officials friendly to unionism, etc. They also facilitate cooperation between unions in a given area, promote respect for union picket lines and the union label, represent organized labor at public functions, etc.

There are also the Departments of the AFL which continue under the new organizations. There are departments for employees of railways, maritime trades, metal trades, building trades, governments, and a union label department. The first five are organizations which coordinate the activities of the various craft or semicraft unions operating within a given industry (or industries).[2] The Railway Employees Department customarily bargains for all of its (six) affiliated unions; local organizations of the Building and Metal Trades Departments frequently bargain for locals of the affiliated unions. These departments also strive to settle jurisdictional disputes of their affiliates; in this task they have not always been successful. Before 1947, the carpenters and electricians frequently defied jurisdictional awards of the Building Trades Department, and the Metal Trades Department also had troubles with recalcitrant unions. In recent years, however, these difficulties have become less serious. The Union Label Department has about 60 affiliated unions, and its functions are concerned only with promoting the use of, and respect for, the union label. As all departments of AFL-CIO are open to all qualified unions, many CIO unions are joining relevant AFL departments.

The CIO had no departments as such, but the merger has produced two new departments; the Department of Organization and the Council of Industrial Organizations. The Department of Organization, headed by John W. Livingston (former official of United Auto Workers), has the task of leading organizing drives in nonunion industries and areas. Obviously its work will have to be coordinated with the organizing efforts of the various unions; presumably its role will be that of aiding small unions unable to finance their own organizing campaigns and doing costly "spade work" in nonunion territory which will ultimately attract workers to unions generally, though not to any one union in particular.

The Council of Industrial Organizations includes virtually the whole of the former CIO, and those AFL unions organized wholly or partly on

---

work in manufacturing establishments. The Teamsters have also sabotaged local merger agreements because of jurisdictional disputes.

[2] In principle, a union may belong to all three of these departments and the International Brotherhood of Electrical Workers does. A number of other unions belong to two departments.

an industrial basis.   At bottom, it is a device for enabling the former CIO to preserve something of its identity within the new organization.   Presumably, this department will look after the common interests of industrial unions and be especially concerned with the interests of the factory worker. However, its precise functions are not yet clear.   It is interesting to note that in the first months of AFL-CIO's existence, the Teamsters attempted to enter the Council of Industrial Organizations, en masse; had they succeeded, their 1,400,000 members would have given them a very powerful voice in its councils.[3]   However, the president (George Meany) ruled that a union could be represented in the Council only to the extent of its industrially organized membership, in the case of the Teamsters about 400,000 members.

A very significant institution of AFL-CIO, which had no counterpart in either of its predecessors, is the Ethical Practices Committee; the establishment of such a committee was provided for in the merger agreement.   This committee, whose first chairman is A. J. Hayes of the Machinists' Union, is to investigate charges of corruption or communism in affiliated unions.   This committee will have to invade the sacred ground of union autonomy in the event corruption or communism is charged against a local or other part of an affiliated union.   Probably it will seek informally to persuade the national unions to act, resorting to coercion only as a last resort.   The Committee's powers of coercion would be recommendation of suspension or charter revocation; as threat of such action is not likely to terrify a strong union, the ability of the Committee to do more than "persuade" is open to question.

In its first action, the Ethical Practices Committee ordered (in September 1956) the Distillery Workers Union (25,000 members) either to show cause why it should not be suspended, because of its mishandling of a Welfare Fund, or face suspension.   At the same time, the Committee notified two larger unions (about 75,000 members each), the Laundry Workers and the Allied Industrial Workers, that they were under formal investigation by the Committee.   All of these unions had been accused of mishandling welfare funds by a Congressional investigating committee.

The merger agreement has also provided for the establishment of a committee to investigate charges of racial discrimination and eliminate any discriminatory practices uncovered.   However, the stand of AFL-CIO against racial discrimination appears to have been somewhat compromised by its accepting (in September 1956) the affiliation of the Broth-

[3] Had the Teamsters been able to enter the council with representation based on their full membership, it is likely that Beck (head of the Teamsters) and MacDonald of the Steelworkers, both enemies of Reuther, would have combined forces and become formidable contenders for control.

erhood of Locomotive Firemen and Enginemen (96,000 members), which permits discrimination against Negroes by its locals.   President Meany declared he had assurances that the Firemen would "eventually" end discrimination, but A. Philip Randolph (President of the Sleeping Car Porters Union and the only negro on the AFL-CIO Executive Council) voted against their admission.   It would seem that the ability of strong labor organizations to live outside the Federation still limits the power of the labor movement to impose its ideals of good conduct on individual unions.

National (or International[4]) Unions and Their Characteristics

National unions are of various sizes from the gigantic Teamsters (1,449,000 members) to tiny organizations such as the (500 member) Diamond Workers Protective Union.   As of January 1955, there were 199 national or international unions; 109 of these were affiliated with the AFL, 32 with the CIO, and 58 were unaffiliated.   Three unions (Teamsters, Auto Workers, and Steelworkers) had over 1 million members; these three unions, together, had 3.7 million members, slightly more than one-fifth of all union members.   Three other unions had between 500,000 and 1 million each.   These six unions had (in total) 5,962,000 members, about one-third of all unionists.   The seven unions having between 300,000 and 500,000 members each, had a total of 2,809,000.   In other words the 13 largest national unions had about 8,771,000, or 49.3 per cent, of all union members.   In short, there are a few large national unions and a lot of small ones.   As we shall see, the size of a union has a lot to do with its characteristics.

In almost all cases a national union has a president, one or more vice-presidents, a secretary, and a treasurer.   Some unions also have other permanent officers.   The chief executive officer of a national union is usually the president, although in some cases another officer, an executive vice-president or secretary, may be formally designated, or become in fact, the principal executive officer.   The power of the principal officers is often shared with an executive board or committee of the union; this committee usually includes the permanent officers of the union together with certain additional persons.   The distribution of authority between the officers and the executive board varies from union to union.   Where the leadership of the union is essentially harmonious, officers and board work together and the exact allocation of power is unimportant.   But, in the event of dissension, the precise limits to the authority possessed by the various officers and by the executive board may become a matter of great importance.

The officers and the executive board have authority to formulate union policy between union conventions, subject to the provisions of the union

[4] International unions differ from "national" ones only in that they have members in Canada.

constitution and of its by-laws. But ultimately both the officers and the executive board are responsible to the representatives of the union's membership. A union's basic policy is determined at its national convention where delegates from the various union locals meet, both to frame policy and to elect officers and members of the executive board. These conventions are usually the supreme authority of the union with complete power to amend the constitution and by-laws. Consequently, struggles between rival factions over policies, offices, or both are usually settled by the decision of the convention. Most unions hold conventions at stated intervals, usually every one to five years;[5] however, a few unions hold their conventions at wider intervals than every five years.

The decisions of the convention are settled by majority vote of the delegates; the delegates are chosen by the locals with the number of (voting) delegates given to each local varying with the number of members.[6] (As can be well imagined, when a struggle seems imminent, rival delegations, allegedly representing the same local, may arrive at the convention, thereby creating struggles over credentials, the procedure for seating delegates, etc.) Although in the majority of unions the convention is the supreme authority, a large but diminishing minority of unions rely upon the referendum for some or all of the following decisions:[7] (1) amending the union constitution, (2) choosing officers, (3) altering various union policies. In some cases the referendum takes the place of convention decisions; in others it is a method of appeal from the decision of the convention.

Union constitutions vest control of the union in the membership. But, in point of fact, the union officers often have effective control over the union and its policies; how this comes about is explained below.

Intermediate Units of Government

Most national unions have a number of locals; the number and size of its locals has much to do with the structure of a union. But, between the locals and the national union, there is usually a layer of inter-

---

[5] In 1954, of 192 unions reporting, 42 held conventions every year or more frequently, 72 held them biennially (including one union that convened every 18 months), 19 convened once every three years, 29 every four years, 13 every five years, 12 had no conventions, and 5 unions held referenda to determine whether a convention should be held. William Paschell, "Structure and Membership of the Labor Movement," *Monthly Labor Review,* November 1955, Table 6, p. 1239.

[6] In a study made in the early 1940's (Joseph Shister, "Trade-Union Government: a Formal Analysis," *Quarterly Journal of Economics,* November 1945, pp. 91–92) it was found that among 116 national unions studied, in 54 per cent representation of locals at national conventions was proportional to membership. In 46 per cent the smaller locals were given (by various devices) greater than proportional representation.

[7] *Ibid.*

mediate organizations. These intermediate organizational units are usually established on a regional basis and are designated as district or regional organizations. In (national) unions where power is strongly centralized, such as the United Mine Workers or the United Steelworkers, the staffs of the intermediate organizational units are appointed and paid by the national organization. In these cases, the intermediate organization functions as an administrative arm of the national office and exercises a great deal of influence over local union behavior. In other unions, the regional organizations are dominated by the locals in their area. In still other unions, the influence of intermediate organizational units is slight, and they are not well developed.

Most of the larger national unions also have a number of departments or administrative divisions to facilitate the handling of their variegated activities. Where a union has substantial membership within two or more industries, it is likely to have (in one guise or another) an administrative division for each. Indeed, where many of a union's locals deal with a huge multiplant company, it may have a special division for that company; e.g., the United Auto Workers has a General Motors division, a Chrysler division, etc. Staff work within the national organization is, of course, divided upon the basis of professional competence; e.g., there is a legal section, a finance section, etc. In the larger unions, these staff employees (including stenographers, secretaries, etc.) number into the hundreds.[8]

Besides the district or regional organizations, there are often local "joint boards" or councils. These are usually found in large cities where a national union has more than one local.[9] The purpose of the joint boards or councils is to secure united action in collective bargaining, to control differences in wages and working conditions within a given industry in a given area, and to settle jurisdictional disputes among the various union locals in the area. In some cases, these organizations do most of the bargaining with employers on behalf of the affiliated locals; in other cases, they have little function or significance.

[8] J. B. S. Hardman, *The House of Labor,* Prentice-Hall, 1951, p. 62, estimates that there are "not less than 15,000" full-time employees of the various national unions and "many thousand more" employed by local unions and auxiliary organizations. He also estimates that there are, in addition, about a half million unpaid, or partially compensated, office-holders or other union functionaries.

[9] Where an "interlocal" organization has locals of only one national union affiliated with it, it is often called a joint board, joint council, or district council. These organizations are often found in the clothing and building and service trade unions. Where an "interlocal" organization contains locals of several national unions, typically of allied crafts, the organization is usually called a "trades council"; thus there are, in many cities, printing trades councils, building trades councils and metal trades councils.

Local Unions

The local is the organizational unit through which the individual member has contact with his union. It is to his local that he pays his dues, whose meetings he attends, etc.[10] There are about 75,000 local unions in the United States, ranging in size from a few members to mammoths of over 60,000.

In larger firms, locals are often organized on a plant basis, one local to a plant. However, not infrequently, it happens that workers with well-defined occupations (e.g., plumbers, carpenters, toolmakers, etc.) are organized separately from other (less skilled) workers. In such cases, there will be several locals, belonging to different unions, in a single plant. Where individual employers employ comparatively small numbers of workers, e.g., in printing, building, construction, trucking, and service, the local is likely to include employees of a number of firms; frequently it will be city-wide.

In most locals, there is a president, vice-president, secretary-treasurer and, perhaps, a sergeant-at-arms. In small locals these officers are usually paid on a part-time basis, their union pay being less than one-quarter of their monthly "job earnings"; in larger locals, there are likely to be full-time (salaried) officials. These officers are almost always chosen by majority vote of the members. Where there is only one full-time (salaried) official he will usually be the "business agent." The business agent is more typical in unions where a local deals with a number of small employers (printing, trucking, service, building construction, clothing manufacture) than where there is one large employer for each local.

The policies of a local are determined, and current problems and complaints discussed, at its monthly or semimonthly meetings. It is at these meetings that the membership has the opportunity of discussing policy and participating in its formulation, of electing officers, etc.

The local union (or joint board) almost always has the responsibility for administering the contracts with the employers of its members. In the event of an alleged violation of a contract or a dispute over its interpretation, it is the function of the local to uphold the rights of the union and its members. The local is also the place where member demands for contract changes (concerning wages, hours, pensions, etc.) originate. Officers of the local almost always participate in the presentation of contract demands to employers and in the subsequent bargaining. However, representatives of the national union may also participate in these

---

[10] A few national unions (such as the Diamond Workers) have no locals, all functions being performed by the nationals; these are usually small craft unions with a membership concentrated in one geographic area. Some of the maritime unions have no locals but have branch offices of the national in various ports.

negotiations, and the relative influence of local and national officers in determining the final settlement is a matter of some complexity, varying from one union to another.

The local union is subject to the various laws of the national union with which it is affiliated. These laws may govern the behavior of the local with regard to the number of its officers and their titles and compensation (if any); they may also control local policy concerning admission and/or expulsion of members, initiation fees and monthly dues, etc. However, the extent to which a national union actually exercises control over the behavior of its constituent locals differs greatly from one situation to another.

Union Finances

The local is the dues collecting agency of the union; it remits a fixed proportion of its dues receipts to the national organization, retaining the remainder. The division of union income between local and national union offices varies from one union to another; the most typical basis of division is 50-50, but a few national unions take less than 25 per cent and another small minority takes more than half of the dues dollar. The amount of union dues varies from $2 to $15 per month, but only in few cases are the monthly dues over $10 per member.

The question of excessive union dues and/or initiation fees has attracted much attention because of the very high levels reached in a few small unions, and by a few locals of larger ones. In some cases, the high dues result from the fact that all union members must belong to a pension or life insurance plan, payments for which are made in the form of union dues. In other cases, high initiation fees are simply devices to exclude new members and are rarely paid. However undesirable such practices may be, they affect (fortunately) but a small minority of union members.

THE UNION: ITS MEMBERS AND OFFICERS

Union strength is such that, in large sections of the economy, it is necessary to join a union in order to keep a job. To many workers, therefore, union membership is not a matter of free choice but of economic necessity. (We shall consider the "pros and cons" of compulsory unionism below, pp. 176–178.) Because of this, it is sometimes supposed that the principal reason for an individual to join a union is to get or keep a job. In some cases this may be true, but it is not very likely to be true of the majority of union members.

There are several reasons for doubting that most union members are reluctant captives of their organization. (1) In most cases a union is certified as bargaining agent for the workers in a "bargaining unit" (usually a firm or plant) after an election[11] supervised by the National Labor Relations Board (NLRB) and with secret balloting in which a majority of the eligible workers voted in its favor. Voting for "no union" is always possible in these elections. (2) Furthermore, if a substantial group of workers (in a bargaining unit) should become dissatisfied with their representation by a given union they can, within a reasonable period of time, secure a new election and dismiss the union if they are in the majority. The fact that the great majority of voters have chosen some union in preference to none indicates that they are not reluctant captives of their union organization.[12]

There is even stronger evidence that most members desire to belong to their union. Prior to its amendment in 1951, the Taft-Hartley Act forbade unions to demand the union shop (in which it is necessary to join the union in order to retain employment) without first holding an election in which the majority of the workers eligible to vote balloted in favor of such a demand. These elections were supervised by NLRB; their records show that over 90 per cent of the votes cast were in favor of permitting the union to demand a union shop.[13] In other words, the overwhelming majority of workers voted in favor of restricting their own, and their fellow workers', freedom to stay out of the union. Wisely or not, they gave a mandate to compulsory unionism.

On the basis of these facts, it would seem reasonable to suppose that most members are enrolled in unions because they want to be. But this does not mean that they are, typically, eager and enthusiastic participants in union activities; clearly, most of them are not. In fact, the "active" and "passive" members are so different as to merit separate description.

The Passive Member

It is impossible to know how large a fraction of all union members are passive, or the degree of their passivity. However, it would not be seriously denied that the overwhelming majority are passive. One recent guess implied that about six out of every seven union members were

[11] In many cases, the employer consents to certification of a union as bargaining agent when it is clear from a comparison of union membership cards with the employer's payroll, or in some other way, that the union is the bargaining choice of the majority of the firm's employees.

[12] The Annual Reports of the National Labor Relations Board reveal that in no year since 1935–1936 (when the Board commenced operations) did unions fail to receive less than 73 per cent of all votes cast in NLRB elections. See Philip Taft, *Economics and Problems of Labor*, 3rd edition, Stackpole, Harrisburg, Pa., 1955, Table LXXVII, p. 554.

[13] Because of the overwhelming majorities for the union shop and the time and money spent in conducting such elections, the Senate repealed the requirement for union shop elections as a precondition for bargaining about the union shop.

passive.[14]   This passivity is manifested in various ways: nonattendance at union meetings, nonparticipation in union activities, nonpayment of dues when there is no checkoff,[15] faiture to vote in union elections, etc.

Many union spokesmen feel that the existence of widespread passiveness is an implicit rebuke to unions and, therefore, try to minimize its importance and even to deny its existence.   However, given the nature of unions and their large membership, this passivity is not surprising.   The nonparticipation of union members is similar to the usual disinterestedness of most small stockholders toward "their" corporation and of most citizens toward their government.

The passivity of most union members stems from the same roots as that of stockholders and citizens.   The great majority of all these persons are passive toward their organizations because they have too many other interests that compete for their attention.   They have families, fraternal organizations, etc. as well as purely social relationships that make demands upon their time.   The manner in which an individual distributes his leisure time among these competing interests varies from one person to another, but not many persons give a high priority to the business of a union, corporation, or government.   There are several reasons for this: (1) the meetings of unions (and, to some extent, of governments and corporations) are largely concerned with the details of routine operations that are not of great importance to ordinary union members.   The meetings are lengthy and boring; as they occur at night, they conflict with more entertaining activities or with needed rest and relaxation.   (2) Even when the meetings are concerned with interesting matters, it is difficult for members to participate.   Most persons, especially manual workers, do not have the verbal skills requisite to effective participation in debate, and are afraid to speak for fear of appearing foolish.   Indeed, many important union issues cannot be understood without considerably more training and experience than most members possess.

This being the case, most union members feel that their officers are hired to run the union and that their own responsibility ends with dues paying, (perhaps) voting in union elections, and answering strike calls. This attitude is very similar to that of "John Q. Public" toward government.   He pays his taxes (with grumbling), votes in "interesting" elections, and serves in the armed forces; but he does not inform himself on

[14] J. B. S. Hardman, *The House of Labor,* edited by J. B. S. Hardman and M. F. Neufeld, Prentice-Hall, New York, 1951, pp. 62–63.

[15] A "checkoff" exists where the employer deducts the member's union dues from his paycheck and remits them to the union; the checkoff is a common practice in the United States.   In 1954, 74 per cent of all collective bargaining agreements and 78 per cent of all workers covered by such agreements had their dues "checked off."   Rose Theodore, "Union-Secretary Provisions in Agreements, 1954," *Monthly Labor Review,* June 1955, Table 1, p. 651.

public affairs, write to his congressmen, etc. However, his indifference toward politics does not mean that J. Q. Public does not care what happens to his country, and the passive members' disinterest in routine union affairs does not imply lack of union patriotism.

The passivity of union members is not perpetual; like citizens, they become very active on occasion. The question of whether a strike should be called, the election of officers (especially if there is an active contest), or a discussion of contract demands, etc. brings a sharp increase in attendance at union meetings.[16] And, if there is a conflict over union policy, the membership will tend to split into partisan factions and to root hard for their side; their behavior, in this respect, is not dissimilar to the intense partisanship that Americans, in general, display during Presidential elections.

Despite the fact that member interest in union affairs is sporadic and temporary, it plays an important role in union politics. When the interest of passive members is aroused, they may challenge the conduct of union affairs by the officers. Consequently, fear of "stirring up" the voters imposes a very real check upon the behavior of union office-holders.

The Nonmember

At the one extreme, the passive member approaches the "union activist," see pp. 125–26; at the other, he becomes akin to the nonmember. In a firm where the union has a contract some individuals may still prefer to remain outside it. This usually reflects mere lack of interest, and/or desire to avoid paying dues. However, in a minority of cases, nonunionism stems from a genuine hostility to unions in general or to the particular union in question. Whether an individual should be compelled to join a union (desired by a majority of his co-workers) as a condition of employment, irrespective of his own wishes, is a difficult question that we shall discuss later (pp. 176–178). But the question of why some workers do not wish to join unions is one that can be considered now.

A worker may have anti-union convictions because (right or wrong) he believes any or all of the following: that unions are controlled by racketeeers; that they cannot or do not bring their members economic benefits; that they are controlled by radicals bent on undermining American institutions; that his employer has his true interests at heart, and it would be ungrateful for him to join a union, etc. The validity of these various beliefs can be judged by the reader himself, when he finishes the book.

However, an individual's decision to join a union (or refrain from doing so) is rarely determined by intellectual considerations. In a given firm

---

[16] L. R. Sayles and G. Strauss, *The Local Union,* Harpers, New York, 1953, Chapter 12.

or shop, an individual's behavior, and even his views, are likely to be strongly influenced by the prevailing opinion.   It is a rare person who will stand up strongly for his position against an overwhelming majority. Undoubtedly, many union members are recruited via the "band-wagon" from among those who have no strong convictions.   However, in some occupations and industries, prounion majorities are difficult or impossible to achieve because an unusually large percentage of the workers are in-different or hostile to unions.   Let us identify those sectors of the economy in which workers are most likely to be sympathetic toward unionism, and those in which they are likely to be indifferent or hostile.

Factory workers are, in general, inclined to be prounion.   It is not hard to see why this should be so.   When men work together under similar conditions and face common problems, it is only natural that they should act together in attempting to solve these problems.   It is clear that in a shop, even when no union exists as such, there tends to be a kind of "informal organization" in which some men are accepted as leaders, others as their henchmen, etc.   These informal organizations develop customary ways of behaving, both as regards purely social matters and also as regards economic matters such as the "proper" rate of output (see below, pp. 198–200).   When common problems arise concerning wages or working conditions, the group as a whole takes a stand and its leaders become its spokesmen.   By so doing the group becomes, willy-nilly, a union.   Many union locals in mines and factories have arisen "spon-taneously" from informal organizations.

But although factories tend to generate unions, unionism arises also from another source: desire to control the standards of a trade or profes-sion.   Thus, persons who belong to well-defined crafts or professions have a strong tendency to affiliate with associations that uphold the "standards," and remuneration, of the trade.   Among the earliest and strongest trade unions are those of the skilled craftsmen (printers, carpenters, locomotive engineers, etc.)   The members of these unions often do not work together in the same shop for any appreciable length of time, but their common interests are so apparent that they can easily perceive the need for common action.

Similarly, professional men such as physicians, lawyers, etc., tend to form strong professional associations which have many of the char-acteristics of unions, even though most spokesmen for such organizations would vehemently deny that they are "unions."   And it is true that professional associations do not, as a rule, bargain collectively with em-ployers about wages, working conditions, etc.   However, such associations do exercise control over entrance to their trades; regulate the kind of service that can be rendered to the public and control competition within the trade (e.g., by forbidding a specified list of "unethical" practices).

In these respects, modern professional associations are like medieval guilds, which also bear a strong resemblance to modern unions. It is not necessary to contend that guilds, professional associations, and unions are "really" the same type of organization. It is enough that we note their similarities.

An essential condition for creating a viable union is that its members have an interest in the *permanent* conditions of employment (including wages) in their *present* occupation. The belief that he will soon be able to improve his job or occupation undermines an individual's concern with the conditions of his present employment and makes him reluctant to accept the temporary sacrifices (involved in striking, paying dues, rendering financial assistance to other workers, etc.) required by successful unions. Because of these sacrifices, temporary workers such as students, housewives, etc. tend to avoid joining unions. For the same reason, industries that use large numbers of temporary workers (e.g., agriculture) tend to be difficult to unionize.

The attitude of workers toward unions is strongly conditioned by their emotional identification with employers (or lack of it), and by their hope of rising out of the ranks of "mere" employees. Because of this, manual workers constitute the main source of union members; white collar workers, whatever the facts of their status and economic situation, have long identified themselves with their employers and have (with relatively few exceptions) resisted attempts to "proletarianize" them by getting them to join unions.

The Active Unionist

The consciously anti-union worker is atypical, but so is the active unionist. The active unionist is a worker who makes union business a large part of his recreation. He comes regularly to meetings, keeps up with the details of union affairs, does unpaid union chores, etc. In some cases he tries to make trouble for the officers.

The interest of the active unionists may spring from a variety of sources: he may be genuinely devoted to the union and anxious to help; he may be lonely and without much else to do; he may be ambitious for office in the union; he may be embittered and anxious to fight the union officers. But, whatever his motivation, he is part of a small minority of the membership.

Not all union locals have active minorities, but where they exist they are extremely important for the operation of the union. By their reports of what goes on at union meetings and by their criticism or support of officers, active unionists do much to mold the opinions of passive members and, at times, to rouse them from their passivity. They can, and often do, operate as a political machine supporting the officers, but they can function as a bitter and active opposition. Changes in the predominant opinion of active members have a major impact upon the union's political life or lack of it.

It is from the ranks of the active unionists that most union functionaries are recruited. The lowest rank of union functionary, and the most numerous, is the unpaid shop steward or grievance committeeman. These officials are found mainly in large factories; their principal function is to represent members in disputes with management over the application of the collective bargaining contract. Where necessary they may also collect union dues, but, due to the growth of the checkoff system, this is now less important than formerly. By virtue of their position, if for no other reason, the stewards become active unionists and important channels of communication between the union organization and the bulk of the membership. As the stewards receive no financial advantage from their jobs,[17] they are financially independent of the union bureaucracy and can therefore criticize it.

Although union officers frequently come from the ranks, many, perhaps most, shop stewards or grievance committeemen are not vitally concerned with union affairs. This differs from place to place; in some factories men have to be drafted to serve as stewards, but in others a steward's position is an honor actively sought. By and large, the voluntary turnover among stewards is high; men accept or seek a steward's job for a time, but lose interest, find other outlets for their energy, get transferred or promoted, etc.

The Local Union Officer

The lowest rank of paid union officers are those of the local. Many of the smaller locals cannot afford full-time paid officials and pay their officers only for the time spent on union business. In such cases, the officers are members who work for the union in their spare time or who are paid by the union for working time lost while on union business.

Not all of the locals that can afford to hire full-time paid officials do so. But it is likely that most locals that are financially able do hire at least one full-time official and frequently hire more.[18] The full-time local official is usually not well paid; he does not usually receive much more than the men he leads. His reward for his long and irregular hours, for

---

[17] They are paid only their regular wages, usually by the employer, for time spent on official duties. They may also have "super-seniority" with respect to layoffs, see pp. 189–192.

[18] See Philip Taft, "Understanding Union Administration," *Harvard Business Review*, Winter 1946, p. 254; also M. F. Neufeld in *"The House of Labor*, pp. 20–21. Full-time officials are especially common where the union operates as a source of labor supply to employers; important examples of such industries are counstruction, service trades, trucking, printing.

the nervous strain of soothing complainants, etc. must come from the prestige attached to his job and the pleasure of working at more interesting tasks than those of an ordinary manual labor job.

Many local union officials do not find their jobs sufficiently rewarding to compensate for the disadvantages. The more able among them sometimes get promoted to better paying jobs with the national union or secure white-collar jobs in business or government. Others cannot stand up to the pressure of the job and resign. However, a goodly number of them desire to be re-elected. Securing re-election implies satisfying members' demands for "service." The services members demand vary with the functions performed by the local union; often union officials are called upon to serve as a member's spokesman in dealing with an employer.[19]

In the event a local union official fails to meet these demands adequately, or otherwise offends an appreciable number of members, a rival may arise from the ranks to oust him from office. This is far more likely to occur at the local than at the national level, because the organizational problems of creating an effective opposition are so much less in a union local. In a small local (one of no more than, say, 500 members[20]), an opposition candidate is, or can easily make himself, personally acquainted with all or most of the members. In such a small constituency, word of mouth electioneering is as effective as printed material—or more so. Because of this the electioneering advantage possessed by incumbents in national union offices (or in large locals) does not exist in small locals. To a considerable degree, this accounts for the higher turnover rate among local (as compared with national) union officers. No doubt, the lesser financial attractiveness and greater job insecurity of local union office also contributes to the relatively high rate of local officer turnover. In fine, in the comparatively small local, union politics are much like lodge or school politics, where popularity among personal acquaintances plays a major role in determining political success.

It must be emphasized that our remarks have, so far, referred to "small" locals. In large locals, especially those with more than 5000 members, politics become similar to those in national unions; accordingly, the analysis of the following section applies to them also.

The Officers of National Unions

The officers of a national union are almost invariably full-time professionals who are making a career of union work. The principal officers

---

[19] These remarks refer, typically, to situations where there are no shop stewards or grievance committeemen and the enforcement of the contract falls on the local union officers.

[20] The number of members at which a local becomes "large" for the purpose of this discussion varies with the extent of communication among the members.

of a national union must "run" the union. That is, they must direct the work of organizing new locals and recruiting members, guide locals in collective bargaining with employers, participate directly in major contract negotiations, ascertain that locals are observing rules of the national, represent the union in its dealings with government agencies and other unions, manage the assets of the union, and a variety of other tasks. Above all, they must keep political fences mended within the union so as to insure their re-election. Doing all these things involves direction of a staff of "international representatives," organizers, district officials, lawyers, office workers, etc. whose numbers may vary from a handful, in small unions, to many hundreds in the large ones.

The actual distribution of functions among a union's top officers is largely a matter of their personal predilections and abilities. In some unions, a few important leaders work as a team without any one person being dominant. More frequently, one man is the undisputed chief; he may delegate authority to his subordinates, but he always retains the ultimate power.

The principal leaders of national unions are obviously men of great importance in the industries in which they operate. Indeed, the leaders of the very large unions are among the most powerful figures in the country. This fact gives them fame or, at least, notoriety; they have power and, because their jobs pay fairly well (see pp. 136–138), they are economically comfortable. It is not surprising that few national union leaders resign from their jobs voluntarily.

In most cases, the present generation of national union leaders are self-made men who have risen from the ranks of the unions they now lead. Theirs is a peculiar kind of American success story; its peculiarity is due to the fact that leading a union is a very unusual occupation whose social and economic functions are not well understood.

A successful union leader must have a number of talents not often found in one person. The talents most needed in a union leader vary with his union's situation. Because of this, the men who lead a union in its early stages must often be replaced, a difficult process, as the union matures. In its early stages of development, the attributes most needed in a union's leader are those of the organizer, i.e., agitational skill, the capacity to "stand up to employers" in negotiation, mastery of strike tactics, and, not least, physical courage. But once a union is well established, the value of these fighting skills depreciates, and the arts of negotiation, administration, and public relations become essential.[21]

At the present time, many top union leaders are men who have exhibited both types of skill. They have done this in the process of "working their way up" in the union. As of now, most major officers of na-

[21] Of course, at all times in a union's history, both types of talents are needed. However, their relative importance varies from one historical phase to another.

tional unions have previously been officers of local unions, or paid organizers. They "made their mark" during the great union building period of the decade 1935–1945 and, hence, have had to demonstrate at least some of the talents needed to organize a union. However, these skills were sufficient only to get them started on a union career. To climb very far in a union hierarchy, it is necessary for an aspirant to impress his peers in the organization with his fitness for leadership. In the early days of a union's existence, or in a period of rapid growth, it has often happened that a number of apparently capable leaders emerge. In some cases, the potential struggle for power was, for a time at least, averted by various compromises. But in others, the struggle for power was soon fought to a finish; in the course of this struggle, one or a small clique of leaders emerged on top. The skills needed for success in such a struggle are those needed in any political contest; the crucial skill is that of persuading rivals that their wisest course is to abandon their own hopes for "supreme power" and accept good, but subordinate, positions.

In short, most successful union leaders have demonstrated the ability to survive in political "rough and tumble." This statement refers to the typical present-day union leader. However, there is an important and growing group of union leaders to whom it does not apply. These are "second-generation" leaders who have climbed to office through the bureaucracy of an already established union. These leaders have often climbed to the position of chief assistant and alter ego to the union leader by rendering efficient service within the union organization and inheriting the top position upon the demise of the previous leader. Important illustrations of this statement are provided by David MacDonald, president of the United Steel Workers (who had originally been Philip Murray's Secretary), Jacob Potofsky of the Amalgamated Clothing Workers, and Maurice Hutcheson of the Carpenters who succeeded to his father's position as president of that union just before the latter's demise. Obviously, it requires a certain type of ability to climb within a bureaucracy, but it is not the same as that needed to climb to leadership from the ranks. Because incumbents have, in union elections, a tremendous advantage, it is possible for persons to be re-elected to positions which they might never have reached in open competition. But no matter how union office is acquired, if the office-holder cannot perform its functions satisfactorily and keep his political fences mended, he will not remain there for long. Possession of office is a very great advantage in a union election, but it is not proof against repeated failure either to "deliver the goods" in bargaining with employers or to compose serious complaints of important sections of the membership. Failure, on either count, will be punished.

Most of the time, the affairs of union (like other) government proceed in routine, and dull, channels, attracting little attention except from those directly concerned. Its essential characteristics become apparent only in time of stress when part (or all) of the membership attempt to bend union policy to their will and find that the union is far less responsive to member wishes than its constitution would suggest.

THE MAJOR PROBLEMS OF UNION GOVERNMENT

Democracy versus Bureaucracy

Judging by their written constitutions, virtually all unions are governed in a completely democratic manner.   This is not surprising; in this country, we place great store by democratic forms of government and an openly undemocratic constitution would be considered improper by a union's members and officers, alike.   But, upon examination of its actual operation, it soon becomes apparent that few union governments are democratic in the same sense as the government of the United States.

Examination of union records reveals that at the national level, union officers, especially the president, are not ordinarily opposed for re-election. The most detailed study yet made found that, in thirty-four unions, between 1900 and 1948, the office of international president was contested in only 18.8 per cent of the elections where it was possible to do so; other international offices were contested in only 23.7 per cent of the possible opportunities.[22]   And most of the contests that did occur arose in the early "crisis-ridden" years of the various unions' lives.   Once a union settles down, it typically re-elects its major international officers (this statement does not apply to local officers) without opposition.

This tendency in labor unions has long been recognized and was baptized by the Swiss sociologist, Robert Michels, as the "iron law of oligarchy."[23]   One factor making for the operation of this "law," is the customary indifference of the great majority of union members that we have already noted.   But this cannot be the whole story, for the same apathy exists in public life toward political affairs.   The difference between union and public affairs is that, save for the famous exception of the Printers (International Typographical Union), there are no regular opposition parties within labor unions.   For long stretches of time, a union's leaders run its affairs without opposition.

[22] Philip Taft, *The Structure and Government of Labor Unions,* Harvard University Press, Cambridge, Mass., 1954, pp. 35–41, especially Table 1.
[23] Robert Michels, *Political Parties,* The Free Press, Glencoe, Ill., 1949; the book was originally published in 1915.   Michel's study referred to pre-1914 Germany, but it has wide applicability.   For a recent and penetrating discussion of the subject see S. M. Lipset, "The Political Process in Trade Unions: A Theoretical Statement," pp. 82–124, in *Freedom and Control in Modern Society,* edited by Berger, Abel, and Page, Van Nostrand, New York and Toronto, 1954; also see Will Herberg, "Bureaucracy and Democracy in Labor Unions," *Antioch Review,* Fall 1943, pp. 405–417.

The failure of political opposition to develop within labor unions is partly due to the concern of the union's leadership with removing the causes of opposition. That is, union leaders try hard to satisfy those demands of members that could, if left unsatisfied, lead to a rebellion. Much of the time, these efforts meet with success, as the tranquil internal political life of most unions testifies. However, it is not always possible to satisfy member demands, no matter how insistent; i.e., different sections of the membership may desire incompatible objectives, and/or employers may be unwilling or unable to meet the demands of the union as a whole.

But, even under the most favorable conditions (of widespread member discontent) an electoral rebellion against a union's national leadership is not easily organized. For such an uprising to succeed, it is necessary to find candidates for office who are known throughout the union and to run a campaign on their behalf. This means combating the union's staff of full-time professionals who, in the event of an electoral struggle, devote most of their time to defending the union administration. These professionals have contacts throughout the union through which they can spread the administration's propaganda. Furthermore, the incumbents have access to the union newspaper. This is to say nothing of the various devices for expelling disaffected locals, to which embattled administrations have sometimes resorted.

These facts make successful rebellion difficult, but they do not make it impossible. When member dissatisfaction reaches such a pitch that the possibility of ousting a union administration becomes apparent, ambitious or (secretly) embittered members of the ruling group, who have union-wide reputations, may accept leadership of the rebellion. Furthermore, enemies of the union's leaders, often leaders of other unions, may give the rebels moral and financial assistance.

Even if the rebels are unable to win a union-wide election, there is the possibility that the locals under their control may break away and join some other national union. (Member discontent with union government may take the form of secession, (ballot) revolution, or both.) It is therefore quite correct to say that there are strong pressures that serve to keep union policy consistent with the wishes of a majority of the members.

However, there is no denying that the imperfections of union democracy result in the concentration of a great deal of power in the hands of the union leadership. The apathy and ignorance of the membership as well as the effective monopoly of the channels of interlocal communication by the union's government[24] make it possible for the leaders to choose

[24] The lack of effective channels of interlocal communication about union affairs (outside the union's formal organization) is a crucial obstacle to the formation of an effective opposition. Any attempt to create such channels would probably be

among a wide range of policies, provided only that they take care not to flout the few strongly felt demands of large groups of members. The members always want "more"; but as to the form in which they obtain it (wage increases, fringe benefits, etc.) or the manner of its distribution among them, there is neither agreement nor clear ideas outside the leadership. If the union leaders take care to "sell" their program to the members in advance and if it is not manifestly unpalatable,[25] they can have almost a free hand in deciding its contents.[26]

This will not seem unfamiliar to anyone reasonably well acquainted with politics—national, state, or local. Such persons may well be tempted to comment that democracy in unions functions much as it does in public life. But the important difference between political life in unions and in public affairs is the absence of (a continuously organized) opposition to criticize the leadership's program, offer alternatives, and provide a rallying point for discontented groups. Even in the absence of an organized opposition within the union, the opinions of the membership do influence, and strongly, the actions and policies of the leaders. But the absence of organized opposition gives the leadership an enormous advantage in molding member opinion without having to overcome opposing views in public debate. As a result, national union leaders acquire a far greater degree of freedom in molding member attitudes and framing union policy than American public officials possess and have a correspondingly stronger hold upon their jobs.

However, surprising as it may seem, there is not broad agreement among students of collective bargaining that it would be desirable to have competing parties within unions. The drawbacks of more active de-

---

interpreted (rightly) by the union administration as an hostile act. See Lipset, *op. cit.*, pp. 87–89.

The most important channel of intraunion communication is the union newspaper or journal. Most national unions and many large locals have such a paper.

[25] For instance, if it does not require wage cuts or similar (obvious) worsening of contract terms.

[26] The one important exception to all this is the (printers) International Typographical Union (ITU), which has had a formal two-party political system for over half a century. However, students of the ITU are not optimistic about the chances for its example to be imitated. The explanation of the almost unique political behavior of the ITU would seem related to the following "peculiarities" in its situation: (1) printers are, to a considerable degree, a community in themselves and, hence, have channels of communication outside the union; (2) the high level of education among printers which produces an unusually high percentage of active members.

The political system of the ITU has been most recently studied by Philip Taft, *The Structure and Government of Labor Unions*, pp. 53–60 and in a truly pathbreaking study by Lipset, Trow, and Coleman, *Union Democracy: The ITU*, The Free Press, Glencoe, Ill., 1956.

mocracy within unions are well known: (1) when it is necessary to accept wage reductions or other unpalatable changes in contract terms, a political opposition may, and usually does, challenge the necessity of yielding to the employers' proposals. This makes it difficult to "sell" the wage cut to the membership, and attempting it may so endanger the political life of the leadership that they refuse to advocate such a policy.[27] That is, for fear of the political consequences of espousing an unpopular policy, union officers sometimes lead their organizations into what they know to be an untenable position, hoping that something will happen to avert the consequences of the policy they adopt. (In a number of cases, see pp. 343–344, the refusal of the members to accept the necessity of economic concessions, despite the appeals of the leaders, has led to the destruction of their unions.) (2) Also, an active political campaign within a union usually involves a fair amount of mud-slinging, accusations of dishonesty, etc. Whatever its outcome, many workers have their suspicions of the leadership aroused with the result that some locals may decide to leave the national organization and some individuals their locals, possibly in disgust with unions as such. Furthermore, the campaign may seriously interfere with the union's attempts to recruit new members.

These and similar arguments against union democracy have all been applied in attacking democracy in society at large. At bottom, such arguments rest on the premise that the electorate is indifferent, incompetent, or both. Unfortunately, in union affairs, there is a great deal of evidence to support such a contention. There are probably very few students of labor problems who could bring themselves to defend the suppression of political opposition within unions where it already existed. However, many of them do not regret, too greatly, that union democracy is such a fragile blossom.

If opposition to union administrations were more frequent and continuous, the student of labor affairs would have to contend seriously with an eternal problem of political theory—freedom versus organization. But, as things stand, the indifference of union members keeps the issue from becoming a serious one.

Union Discipline

One of the most important, and difficult, tasks of union government is to punish the violators of its laws. A union demands sacrifices of its members in the course of a strike: strikers must forego their wages, they may be asked to bear the rigors of picket line duty, and members not on strike may be asked to contribute part of their earnings to help strikers. In some cases, many members of a union have no direct interest in a

[27] Not infrequently, Communist elements in a union make political capital out of an unpopular contract.

given strike, or may even have opposed it; but if the union is to bring its full strength to bear in a given situation, it must be able to command the support of all its members.   Therefore it must be able to punish, by fine or expulsion, members not doing their duty.

Other situations in which unions must (and do) punish violations of their laws arise where members accept work at less than the union wage scale, or under other nonunion conditions.   Still other disciplinary situations arise when (some) members strike against, or in violation of, the terms of a collective bargaining agreement; in such cases, disciplining members is necessary in order to enable the union to live up to its agreements with employers.   In addition, each union has a number of other laws which it tries to enforce.

The technique of disciplining an individual member may be a fine, temporary suspension, or outright expulsion,[28] depending upon circumstances.   Discipline of individual members is almost always imposed by the local union after a trial of some sort.   However, most national union constitutions provide for appeal of punishments imposed by a local union to a tribunal established by the national organization; in some unions, it is even possible to carry appeal one step further, to the national convention.[29]

Despite these provisions, union judicial proceedings have been subjected to severe criticism, especially by C. W. Summers.[30]   Philip Taft, on the other hand, has argued that Summers' charges are greatly exaggerated and that union justice is, on the whole, quite satisfactory.[31]   There is no consensus on the issues under debate, and final judgement must be suspended. However, the following tentative conclusions seem to emerge from the argument: judicial proceedings in local unions vary greatly in the adequacy of procedural safeguards for the rights of the accused.   (E.g., in some cases, the accuser is also judge, judges and jurors are not impartial, procedure is frequently slow and expensive, punishment continues while the case is under appeal, etc.).   However, where a case is not connected with an interunion political dispute, union judicial procedures work fairly well, although there is much room for improvement.

[28] Under the Taft-Hartley law, unions may not compel employers to discharge an expelled worker unless said worker has refused to pay his dues.   Nonetheless, expulsion from his union is likely, in practice, to make a worker "wish" to resign his job.

[29] It is also possible to go outside the union and appeal to the courts.   In several such cases, the courts have upheld the appellants.

[30] See, for example, Clyde W. Summers, "Disciplinary Procedures of Unions," *Industrial and Labor Relations Review,* IV (October 1950), pp. 15–32; "Union Powers and Worker's Rights," *Michigan Law Review,* XLIX (April 1951), pp. 805–838; "Union Democracy and Union Discipline," *Proceedings of New York University Fifth Annual Conference on Labor,* 1952.

[31] Taft, *The Structure and Government of Labor Unions,* Chapter IV and Appendix, and pp. 243–246.

But, where the accused is part of an opposition to the union leadership, the situation may be quite different. In the course of contested elections, union administrations have suspended or expelled their opponents. Indeed, many unions actually prohibit the publication and distribution of campaign literature;[32] as this puts opponents of an existing administration at a hopeless disadvantage, it is very likely that they will tend to violate union law and thereby expose themselves to disciplinary action. Furthermore, attempting to induce a local to leave the national organization (and/or siding with another union in a jurisdictional dispute) is, in most unions, ground for immediate expulsion.

Union spokesmen sometimes defend such restrictions on freedom of speech as necessary for the preservation of the union. Such contentions are not always disingenuous or factually incorrect, but they do have a disturbing sound to those concerned with protecting the rights of individual members. And this concern is by no means based entirely upon a priori considerations; there is a long and unpleasant history of embattled union tyrants disciplining and expelling their opponents in order to retain power. Some of the worst examples of union tyranny have occurred in unions where the leaders were corrupt and determined to avoid facing the verdict of the membership.

Punishment of (union) law violators is not always a matter of dealing with individuals; in disciplinary situations, it frequently happens that a national union suspends the officers of a local union and governs it directly, not restoring self-government to the local until it has been "reorganized" to the national's satisfaction. Such proceedings always seem high-handed and undemocratic to outsiders, yet a case for them can be made.

For example, it sometimes happens that a local has come under the domination of racketeers or Communists who are exploiting it for their own purposes. To save said local from destruction and maintain the good name of the union, drastic action may be necessary. And union leaders, when they resort to such procedures, are inclined to speak of "saving the union from Communists" or "gangsters," as the case may be. Sometimes these protestations are the literal truth.[33] At other times they are downright lies, aimed at distracting attention from tyrannical behavior. Too often for intellectual comfort these statements have been partial truths; i.e., one or more union locals were "up in arms" over some policy of the national union and Communists tried to exploit the issue in order to gain control of the locals. It is often very difficult, even for those familiar with the situation, to decide whether the threat of Communist

---

[32] *Ibid.,* p. 119.

[33] For example, the United Auto Workers and the International Ladies' Garment Workers have both had occasion to lay firm hands on locals genuinely controlled by Communists.

domination is genuine or merely a convenient smoke screen for curbing a challenge to the authority of the union leadership.

In short, one's tolerance for disciplinary action by union government, towards individuals or locals, is likely to depend upon one's view of the purposes for which discipline is exercised. When used to curb Communists or racketeers, it is easy to be "realistic" and argue that the end justifies the means. But the procedures that have been used to curb Communists have also been used to protect the power of entrenched racketeers. There is no universally acceptable formula for deciding when the end in view (e.g., suppressing Communists or racketeers) is sufficiently important to justify undemocratic means for its achievement. This is a problem that has moral as well as political and economic implications, and each person must form his own judgements. The best advice is not to judge specific cases without careful investigation of the facts and to remember that any general rule of procedure is likely to have highly unpleasant consequences in some situations.

Compensation of Union Officers

Students and participants in union affairs often debate as to what union officers are paid and as to what proper compensation would be. Unfortunately the facts of officer compensation are not well known to anyone. The most thorough study of the matter yet made[34] found that, in 1950, the median salary paid to officers in 37 international unions was about $13,000 with less than 10 per cent receiving over $17,000.[35] If one were to include only chief officers the appropriate figures would probably be several thousand dollars higher.

Salaries are not the only source of officer compensation. There are also the very important "expenses," which are tax free; there is simply no basis for over-all statements as to their general magnitude.[36] One student concludes that "corporations are likely to pay a much more liberal amount per diem and higher allowances to their representatives than do the unions. The expense accounts allowed by unions compare much more closely with the modest payments of the government to its traveling employees than to those received by corporation personnel."[37] However, this view has not gone unchallenged.[38]

[34] Philip Taft, op. cit., pp. 97–116. The data, however, exclude many unions, some of which are very large and important ones.

[35] Ibid., Table 22, p. 103.

[36] Again our best source is Taft, op. cit., pp. 110–112. However, his data are very incomplete.

[37] Ibid., p. 112.

[38] In his foreword to Taft's book, Professor S. H. Slichter (p. x) questions whether the evidence concerning officer expenses was not confined (unavoidably) to "well-administered" unions.

But, whatever one thinks of the remuneration of international union officers, it far exceeds that of local officers whose compensation is rarely more than 50 per cent above that of their members. As of 1950, the median salary (exclusive of expenses) of full-time local officials would have been around $6000 per annum.[39]

So much for the facts. Now let us consider the proprieties of the matter: Are union officials overpaid? By one criterion most of them are; i.e., if a union officer is merely a workingman chosen to speak for his fellows, he should get no more than they do. This standard for judging officer compensation has had many articulate defenders. Not the least of the IWW accusations against AFL officials was that they received (for those days) high salaries and had ceased to live like workingmen. Charges of this type continue to be made by opponents of incumbent union officials with considerable effect upon member attitudes. Union members do not, as a rule, take kindly to high salaries for their officers and have often (via referenda) rejected proposed increases.

Sharp differences in living standards between union members and officers are clearly a source of friction, especially when the leaders are urging that the members forego benefits. When a union leader appeals for sacrifices in the name of "solidarity," it obviously does not help his cause if he arrives at the union hall in a new Cadillac. But, although member resentment of officer privileges and pay is understandable, it is not always wise or even fair.

The idea that the union leader should get no more than his members is a vestige of the early phase of unionism in which the leader was merely one of the workers chosen to serve as spokesman. In the large modern union, the leader is an executive in every sense of the word; he must match wits with highly paid corporate executives and, not unnaturally, often feels he is entitled to "something like" the same remuneration. In recent years, union assets have grown considerably so that, even by the standard of wealth administered, international union officers are entitled to salaries comparable with those of corporate officials. And for unions whose revenues run into millions of dollars per year, an extra few thousand dollars spent for salaries and perquisites is a trivial matter.

But despite the perfectly sound reasons for according a successful union leader the same financial treatment as the corporate executives with whom he bargains, he does not often demand or get it. At bottom, this reflects the ambivalent attitude that union members and officers themselves have toward the occupation of union leader. The union leader is, in fact, an executive of a large and wealthy organization. But the ideology of the labor movement retains a strongly equalitarian bias, not always avowed, according to which high incomes are antisocial. Labor leaders them-

[39] Taft, *op. cit.*, pp. 98–103.

selves, especially the more "idealistic," accept this ideology and resist taking the full salary that the "market might bear." And, where conscience does not restrain a union leader, fear of member reaction usually does.[40]

Corruption in Unions

Racketeering and corruption in labor unions have received an enormous amount of publicity at the hands of certain newspaper columnists. The effect of this publicity has been to convince some persons that all union leaders are corrupt, but it has also tended to lead some union sympathizers to deny, on principle, that corruption is a serious problem in American unions. Both positions are wrong; most union officials are honest, but corruption is a major problem in unions just as it is in business and government.

In any society that puts a high premium on acquiring wealth, those who possess power to benefit or injure others are subject to the temptations of bribery. Government officials are obviously subject to temptation; buyers for large firms with power to award lucrative contracts are also in a position to be bribed, and so are union officers. Union officers can, in certain cases, decide whether or not a firm is to be struck, whether it is to be forced rigidly to live up to union rules, which workers are to be sent out on jobs and which kept idle, etc. Most recently, the growth of union controlled health and welfare plans has given some union officials a chance to profiteer on their administration.

In unions, as elsewhere, there are various degrees of corruption. Toward the "harmless" extreme, there are the various presents, especially for Christmas, which employers give to union business agents as well as to the representatives of their customers. Such presents are designed to curry good-will; the exact expectation of the giver (and obligation of the recipient) is obscure, but it is obviously hoped to create an attitude in the recipient not entirely compatible with loyalty to his employer (the union).[41] "Padded" expense accounts, when done within reason, is an-

---

[40] There are some notorious exceptions to this statement. In 1955, the Teamster's union purchased the homes of its current president, Dave Beck, and its retired president, Dan Tobin, and then gave these officers the use of their former houses, free. (The price paid for Beck's house, $160,000, is said to represent a considerable inflation of its market value.) When asked, by the press, about possible member reaction to this display of union beneficence, Beck responded by citing the growth of union assets during his term of office, implying that he considered such a reward only proper compensation for his services.

[41] It has been reported that even in such a well-run union as the ILGWU the president (David Dubinsky) has expressed concern over the practice of business agents accepting gratuities from employers. See Benjamin Stolberg, *Tailor's Progress*, Doubleday, Doran and Co., New York, 1944, pp. 186–189.

other form of tolerated graft, in unions as well as elsewhere.   It is not easy to halt these and similar practices; they are part of the American way of doing business.

Gratuities accepted, or even expected, from employers *may* be harmless. This is not the case when union officials, who can decide which members are to secure the first chance at available jobs, accept or demand "tips" from *workers* as a condition of preference or to avoid discrimination. Such tips are essentially "kickbacks" from workers ill able to pay them and constitute a most unsavory source of revenue for corrupt local officials.   From time to time, these practices have been uncovered in the Building Trades and Building Service unions, Teamster locals, in Longshore unions, and in others.   Of course, foremen, private employment agencies, padrones, etc. have also sold jobs; but the practice is objectionable by whomever performed.

Getting into the still more reprehensible range of behavior, there is the acceptance (by union officers) of employer bribes not to enforce union rules rigidly or to accept a less favorable contract than the employers might be compelled to offer.   From accepting bribes, it is but a step to soliciting them and, finally, to extorting them by threatening a strike. The most famous type of union extortion was the sale of "strike insurance" to employers, i.e., employers who did not buy such insurance were sure to have strikes.   This type of practice, not much heard of in recent years, arose where a union official was given complete authority to call strikes "on the spot."   This type of authority is sometimes necessary, as in the construction industry, to enforce union conditions,[42] but the power conferred upon the official involved presents tempting opportunities for blackmailing employers; opportunities that have, in some cases, been exploited to the full.

Extortion has most frequently occurred in construction and in the service trades.   Since the 1890's, there have been intermittent scandals in a number of major cities, especially New York and Chicago, arising from the practices of unions in these trades; a number of union officers involved were imprisoned for their participation.   However, it must not be forgotten that employers have often cooperated heartily in these doings,

---

[42] In building construction, contractors often let out various jobs (e.g., painting, plumbing, etc.) to subcontractors.   The subcontractors complete a given job within a week or two.   As the award of subcontracts is usually to the lowest (responsible) bidder, competition is keen and pressure to cut costs severe.   The simplest way to cut costs is to violate union rules.   If the union local's business agent delays enforcing the rules, the job will be finished before anything can be done.   Hence, he must be able to deliver peremptory ultimatums to the contractors and subcontractors if union rules and pay scales are to be enforced.   But the power to enforce union rules, wink at violations, or pretend there are violations whatever the facts, implies the power to blackmail.

using the unions as instruments for throttling competition.   In many cases, local politicians also "got into the act."[43]   In short, union extortion has usually been part of a corrupt situation in which employers and government officials have also participated.

It has sometimes happened that a union's members cynically accepted the malfeasance of their leaders, "because they do well by the membership."[44]   Such cynicism is extremely short-sighted; where corruption creates large and illegal profits, gangsters are attracted.   Because the profits are illegal, the corrupt leaders cannot appeal to the law for protection. They must either share the loot with gangsters or hire rival gangsters to protect them.   In either event, the union is soon controlled by the gangsters who rarely leave much gravy for the rank and file.   The notorious situation on the New York waterfront is an extreme, but not unique, example of how far gangster control of unions can go.[45]

Another, but related, form of union corruption is the "sellout."   This occurs when a union leader agrees, for a consideration, to accept, or recommend acceptance, of a contract less favorable than what could be obtained.   It is easy to charge "sellout," but difficult to prove it.   Yet sellouts undoubtedly have occurred, although it is impossible even to guess at their number.

Finally, there is in unions, as elsewhere, opportunity for plain graft and misappropriation of funds.   In one famous case, the international president of the Printing Pressmen's union, George L. Berry, used union funds for personal investment in a number of enterprises.[46]   More recently, the growth of union administered "health and welfare funds" has given rise to

[43] See Harold Seidman, *Labor Czars,* New York, 1938 and William Haber, *Industrial Relations in the Building Industry,* Cambridge, Mass., 1930, especially pp. 318 *et. seq.*   The material presented in these sources is now "ancient history." For more recent material on extortion see the article by A. H. Raskin (*New York Times,* October 25, 1953, p. 10e) on Joe Fay (vice-president of the Operating Engineers Union) now in a New York State prison.   Daniel Bell, "The Scandal in Health and Welfare Funds," *Fortune,* April 1954, pp. 140 ff. cites a number of recent examples of union corruption.

[44] Haber, *op. cit.,* pp. 321–324.

[45] For a brief survey of the situation on the New York waterfront see C. P. Larrowe, *Shape-Up and Hiring Hall,* University of California Press, Berkeley and Los Angeles, 1955, Chapters 1–3.   The corrupt state of the New York locals of the International Longshoreman's Association had, in 1953, become so bad as to lead the AFL executive council, for the first time in its history, to expel a union because of internal corruption, see above, p. 80.

[46] These facts were disclosed by the union in reports to a Subcommittee of the House of Representatives' Committee on Education and Labor.   *Union Democracy.* Hearings before a Special Subcommittee of the Committee on Education and Labor, House of Representatives Eighty-First Congress, First and Second Session.   Pursuant to House Resolution 75, 1950, pp. 227 *et seq.*

a sizeable number of insurance agencies in which union officers have an important financial interest. These agencies earn their commissions by sale of accident and health insurance policies to the aforementioned funds of which the union leaders are, or are instrumental in appointing, trustees.[47] Both the CIO and the AFL (before their merger) expressed disapproval of such practices and have attempted to stop them. And, in 1956, the AFL-CIO's Ethical Practices Committee has begun investigating unions accused of such practices (see p. 115) and has taken steps to suspend one union found guilty. However, the union involved was a small one; whether the aforementioned committee will take steps against the misdeeds in larger unions remains to be seen.

One of the most disturbing aspects of union corruption was the prolonged reluctance of leading officials in the AFL to assume responsibility for curbing it. When confronted with indisputable evidence of corruption in the New York building trades, Samuel Gompers invoked the "principle of voluntarism," to argue that only the unions involved could (or should) attempt to remedy the situation.[48] In 1940, the AFL's executive council recognized that "men who have been influenced by criminal instincts have penetrated our movement" and urged that greater diligence be exercised in selecting officials. One important reason for the gingerly manner in which this whole issue was approached by AFL was that corrupt officials had substantial locals under their control and could threaten the national leadership of several unions with serious political opposition should they attempt a "clean-up" campaign.[49] Hence, the national unions insisted the AFL "keep its nose" out of their internal affairs; corrupt locals made similar demands of the national union and, for a long time, nothing was done.

However, the passage of the Taft-Hartley Act proved, beyond doubt, that unions are each other's keepers. The proved corruption of one union is a sin to be expiated, before the bar of public opinion, by all. Hence, the expulsion of the International Longshoremen's Association from the AFL in 1953 and the strong provisions in the AFL-CIO Constitution for expelling racketeer unions. The effectiveness of these provisions remains to be seen, but it is clear that the labor movement has decided to accept responsibility for "cleaning its own house."

To summarize: corruption, in unions as elsewhere, results from well-

---

[47] Bell, "The Scandal in Health and Welfare Funds," *op. cit.*

[48] Harold Seidman, *op. cit.*, Chapter XV.

[49] Matthew Woll, the influential president of the Photo-Engravers' union once told a city commissioner investigating a poultry racket, "We can't do anything about it. You see, we got (sic) to look to the votes of the boys down the line to hold our own jobs." Quoted in C. Wright Mills, *The New Men of Power*, Harcourt, Brace & Co., New York, 1948, pp. 129–130.

known human frailties.   However, one cannot achieve a very profound understanding of American government by attempting to deduce its main characteristics from the premise that some public officials are dishonest. Nor can one go far in studying unions by supposing that they are, typically, run as a racket for the benefit of their officers.   The fact of corruption and racketeering in unions must be recognized, and sound union and public policy must aim at curbing it.   However, at worst, racketeering is but an ugly excrescence upon the union body; it is not of its essence.

DISCUSSION QUESTIONS

1. "In order to get the union to live up to its agreements with employers, a union leader may have to compel the members to act contrary to the wishes of the majority." Discuss the implications of this statement for the possibility, and desirability, of retaining union democracy.

2. Discuss the pros and cons of paying union officials salaries as large as those paid business executives.

3. What are the factors that create apathy toward union affairs among the bulk of union members?

4. What connection, if any, is there between dictatorship and corruption in labor unions?

5. To what extent does the membership control national union policy?   To what extent is this policy decided upon by the leadership and then sold to the members?

Suggested Readings

Bell, Daniel, "The Scandals in Health and Welfare Funds," *Fortune*, April 1954, pp. 140 ff.

Hardman, J. B. S., *American Labor Dynamics,* Harcourt, Brace & Co., New York, 1928.

Hardman, J. B. S., and M. F. Neufeld, eds., *The House of Labor,* Prentice-Hall, New York, 1951.

Herberg, Will, "Bureaucracy and Democracy," *Antioch Review,* Fall 1943, pp. 405–417.

Lipset, S. M., "The Political Process in Trade Unions; a Theoretical Statement," in *Freedom and Control in Modern Society,* edited by Berger, Abel, and Page, Van Nostrand & Co., New York and Toronto, 1954, pp. 82–124.

Lipset, S. M., J. S. Coleman, and M. Trow, *Union Democracy in the International Typographical Union,* Free Press, Glencoe, Ill., 1956.

Michels, Robert, *Political Parties,* Free Press, Glencoe, Ill., 1949.

Mills, C. Wright, *The New Men of Power,* Harcourt, Brace & Co., New York, 1948.

Sayles, L. R., and G. Strauss, "The Local Union," Harper & Bros., New York, 1953.

Seidman, Harold, *Labor Czars,* Liveright, New York, 1938.

Seidman, Joel, "Democracy in Labor Unions," *Journal Political of Economy,* June 1953, pp. 221–231.

Shister, Joseph, "Trade-Union Government; a Formal Analysis," *Quarterly Journal of Economics,* November 1945, pp. 78–112.

Taft, Philip, *The Structure and Government of Labor Unions,* Harvard University Press, Cambridge, Mass., 1954.

6

The Process
of Collective Bargaining

We now have some general idea of the nature of union organization and its purposes. The most important of these purposes is to conduct collective bargaining with employers successfully. In the United States, the employers of most union members are private businesses, and it is the managers of these enterprises with whom unions bargain. (The government, as an employer, is discussed on pp. 513–515). As the attitudes and policies of the employers affect the entire bargaining process greatly we shall commence our analysis by studying in some detail.

THE ROLE OF THE EMPLOYER IN COLLECTIVE BARGAINING

Wages and Profits

As we mentioned in Chapter 1, the distribution of a firm's receipts are a more or less perpetual bone of contention between the worker and his employer. In a very important sense, a union is the agent of its members and, as such, attempts to serve their economic interest by making demands upon their employer. Not unnaturally, the employers tend to resist; partly for the obvious reason that the less they pay out in wages the more they can keep as profits for themselves or their stockholders.

It is not mere greed that leads an employer to refuse at least part of labor's demands. It also is "economic necessity"; if an employer cannot make some minimum return on the capital invested in the firm (see pp. 305–307), the owners of the capital will eventually remove it and invest elsewhere. Indeed, if there are consistent losses, the capital will eventually be dissipated and the enterprise disappear. The ability of a firm to earn the necessary minimum of profit is always restricted, more or less, by the operations of competing firms attempting to do the same thing. Competitors try to snatch buyers from one another by a number of well-known devices: offering lower prices, embarking on selling campaigns, attempting to improve or otherwise make their product more attractive, etc. All of these devices have one common result: they tend to limit profits per unit of product, and they curb the ability of any one employer to raise the price of his own product in order to pay more in wages (per unit of output). Consequently, an employer will often (correctly) respond to a given union demand: "I just can't pay this and stay in business."

Of course, the *successful* businessman is not likely to be driven to the wall by the *serious*[1] demands a union will make. In many lines of business, especially manufacturing, the employer is able to improve his methods of production. This improvement reduces the number of hours of labor required per unit of output and provides something of a "cushion" from which the employer may grant wage increases or other benefits to his workers without actually increasing the dollar amount he must pay for labor per unit of output. Furthermore, a firm's competitors are also likely to be under pressure to pay more for their labor. None the less, it is clear that there is a genuine limit to what an employer can, at any given time, pay for his labor, and he must take care that he is not driven to paying more. This fact is well understood by any experienced union negotiator, although there may be real disagreement between him and the employer as to what this limit is.

It is hardly necessary to point out that employers are well aware of the dangers of "paying too much," and that they do their best to keep wages down. This does not mean that a sensible modern employer is a "skinflint." Labor costs depend not only upon hourly wage rates but also upon quantity and quality of output per hour. Firms that pay very low wage rates frequently get inferior labor and sometimes have serious "morale" problems resulting in such low man-hour productivity as to make their labor costs (per unit of output) higher than those of neighboring firms paying higher hourly wages. Furthermore, most firms are anxious to appear to their workers and to their customers as "fair" employers; no one brags that he pays the lowest wages in town. Nevertheless, the typical employer wage policy is set with a weather-eye to cost control.

Employer Attitudes toward Collective Bargaining

Prior to unionization (or the threat thereof) the only thing that kept an employer from paying lower wages than he did was the necessity for

---

[1] Union negotiators sometimes, for bargaining purposes, open negotiations with a series of demands they do not expect to obtain; these are not "serious" demands. Roughly, serious demands are those for which a union is prepared to strike.

attracting and keeping the workers he desired.[2] When, and if, he discussed the terms of employment with an employee, said employee could speak only for himself; if dissatisfied with the terms offered by the employer, the employee's only recourse was to quit. Unless possessed of unusual talent, his quitting caused little inconvenience to the employer. But when a union speaks for all or a major part of the firm's employees, the situation is different; a strike of the union's members may well halt the firm's operations. To prevent this, the employer must either negotiate with the union or compel its workers to deal as individuals; i.e., destroy the union.

OPEN RESISTANCE. Because a union's demands cannot be disregarded so easily as those of a single employee, most employers who have operated their business in a nonunion environment have viewed the prospect of unionization with distaste. Prior to the passage of the Wagner Act in 1935, this dislike customarily led to active resistance to unionization. This resistance took the form of discharging known union members and refusing to recognize (i.e., bargain with) the union. This was frequently accompanied by a barrage of antiunion propaganda, threats to close down the plant if it were unionized, bribes to key workers to enlist their aid in fighting the union, etc. These tactics were, as we have seen,[3] successful in forestalling unionization, especially in manufacturing plants, prior to the late 1930's. But most of these tactics were outlawed by the Wagner Act and, although employer resistance to unionism has persisted, sometimes in defiance of the law, it has not been so common or so successful as before 1935.[4]

Many employers are still quite cool toward unions but, to an increasing degree, they have come to recognize that fighting them costs more than it is worth, especially when business is prospering. Consequently, the antiunion employer, nowadays, tries to convince his employees that the union will be harmful to them; but once the majority of his employees has become clearly prounion, he will usually accept the fact and negotiate, albeit reluctantly, with the union of their choice.

The typical process of unionization is now less stormy than two decades ago because so many employers have resigned themselves to its inevitability. Furthermore, the greater experience of unions with collective bargaining and their greater internal stability have greatly reduced the birth pangs of a new collective bargaining relationship. Thus "open resistance"

[2] It is necessary to point out that the difference between union and nonunion conditions is not so obvious, or so sharp, as this remark would suggest; see pp. 339–348. However, for the moment, this contrast will serve to focus the discussion.

[3] See above, pp. 49 et seq.

[4] The Taft-Hartley Act and subsequent rulings of the National Labor Relations Board have legalized a good many devices of employer resistance (to unionization) that had been illegal under the Wagner Act; see pp. 251–252.

is no longer the typical management attitude toward collective bargaining. However, it still exists, being found most frequently in small towns in the south, and it is more prevalent in the service and distribution industries than in others.

RELUCTANT ACCEPTANCE. The attitude termed "reluctant acceptance" is reflected by the following pattern of behavior: (1) refusal to concede anything that would tend to facilitate the operation of the union or to strengthen it in the company's plants. This is, typically, reflected in a determined effort to resist "union security" demands, such as the union shop. (2) Employers with this type of attitude are likely to be very anxious to preserve "managerial prerogatives." That is, they are inclined to insist that various matters are not subject to bargaining and must be decided solely by management. They are also likely to take a "legalistic" attitude toward disputes arising over the interpretation of a contract; i.e., they tend to be more concerned with their contractual rights than with finding the solution most likely to contribute to harmonious relations. (3) A further manifestation of "reluctant acceptance" is evidenced by attempts to undermine the position of the union. This may be done in a number of ways, e.g., appeals for a decertification election (see pp. 238–239), undertaking campaigns to promote company loyalty as opposed to union loyalty among the employees, deliberately favoring nonunion members in every way possible.[5]

"Reluctant acceptance" is frequently nothing more than petulance, which is outgrown once the employer perceives its costliness. However, it is, at times, part of a determined strategy to drive the union out of the company. Where the union is new and the workers not entirely "sold" on it a steady campaign of antiunion propaganda, plus some of the aforementioned tactics, may so discourage union members that they lose confidence in the union and abandon it at its first set-back. In the years between the first wave of CIO organizing (1936–1938) and the late 1940's, a great many of the major manufacturing companies followed policies that would seem to have been animated by this belief or hope.[6] However, since 1948–1949, there has been a gradual shift in attitude toward what we might term "genuine acceptance."

GENUINE ACCEPTANCE. The most important evidence of genuine acceptance is the absence of attempts to undermine the union's position with the workers. Where genuine acceptance prevails, union security is likely

[5] Many of the techniques of favoring nonunion workers were forbidden under the Wagner Act (as interpreted by NLRB), but Taft-Hartley permits the employer considerably more freedom in these matters. Hence, since 1947, an antiunion employer has had considerable scope for favoring nonunion members, provided he was reasonably discreet.

[6] Hope for repeal of the Wagner Act and for the election of a government less favorable to unionism, also contributed to this attitude (see pp. 76–77).

to be well-protected in collective bargaining agreements, and disputes under contracts are likely to be settled on their merits, and not treated as skirmishes with an enemy.   In short, genuine acceptance implies that the employer and the union have come to recognize the necessity for mutual survival and cease to make demands that threaten each other's vital interests.   This means (among other things) that the employer takes into account the union's internal political situation in formulating his demands.[7]   Consideration of the other party's "necessities" does not guarantee industrial peace, but it does eliminate a great many conflicts in which one of the parties must do or die, and the other cannot, therefore, hope to win its point without a long struggle.[8]

Genuine acceptance may arise simply because of employer good-will, but this is not the way in which it is usually achieved.   Usually, it emerges when the employer becomes convinced that the union is in his plant to stay and that it must be "lived with."   It takes time and often some hard struggles to inspire this conviction.

During the evolution of the employer's attitude, the union's demeanor also changes.   When first organized, a union local is likely to be belligerent and difficult in negotiation; this is especially so if the employer has fought hard against unionization.   Provided management hostility does not prevent it, the national organization usually presses the local, in various ways, to adopt a conciliatory attitude.[9]   Sometimes a local resists such pressure, but the sheer necessity of living with the employer eventually compels it to adopt a more conciliatory policy.   Where an experienced national union is guiding a new local in dealing with a recalcitrant employer, the union's attitude (if not the member's) is likely to be one of restraint while it attempts to convince the newly unionized employer that friendly relations will be mutually beneficial.   In short, it often happens that the attitude of a local union evolves from one of open hostility toward the employer, sometimes rationalized by an ideology of class struggle, to one of peaceful collaboration.

In the United States, as well as in Great Britain, Scandinavia, and Australia, there has been a gradual evolution of the typical employer attitude toward unionism from open resistance toward genuine acceptance. Terms like "open resistance," etc. are, of course, mere catch phrases designed to suggest attitudes (and related policies) rather than to describe

[7] That is, neither party makes demands, the satisfaction of which would threaten the survival of the other. "Survival" means economic survival to the firm and political survival to the union and its leadership.

[8] It sometimes happens that the survival needs of the two parties are incompatible. In such cases, strife is more or less unavoidable.

[9] When the national organization is itself new or faction-ridden, it will not be able to perform this role effectively. This was often the case with the CIO unions in the late 1930's.

them with any degree of precision. Each firm has its own history of collective bargaining, and some "genuine acceptors" of unionism are much more cordial than others; e.g., some firms are prepared to concede unions a share in managerial authority that others would bitterly resist even though they accept the union as a permanent fixture.

It should also be recognized that at no time are all firms in the same phase of development in their attitude toward collective bargaining. There is, at any one time, a more or less typical attitude, and this attitude tends to inspire imitation;[10] but there are important variations from one firm to another.

The reader may suspect from the tenor of these remarks a certain predilection for the attitude of "genuine acceptance." This suspicion would be correct, and it is a predilection which most students of collective bargaining share. Satisfactory bargaining relations can rarely be achieved unless both sides adopt this attitude. Failing this, perpetual warfare is inevitable unless the union can be destroyed beyond hope of resurrection. The reasons why this result would usually not be desirable will be discussed later (pp. 517–521); but desirable or not, in most cases it is impossible to achieve it. The preference for "genuine acceptance" is, therefore, a preference for industrial peace. Industrial peace does not mean absence of disagreement or even of an occasional strike; it does imply, however, that most causes for dispute are settled peaceably and that strikes are infrequent.

THE CONTRACT NEGOTIATORS

Collective bargaining, in its modern form, almost always involves a written contract between the union and the employer. This contract has an expiration date,[11] at which time a new agreement must be negotiated. The process of negotiating a contract is essentially a bargaining contest between the representatives of the union and of management.

Employer Representatives

The behavior of the employer at the bargaining table obviously reflects his attitude toward the union. If he is there under protest and does not accept the union, his attitude is likely to be unyielding; conversely, if he accepts the union as a permanent fixture, he is more likely to be conciliatory.[12] An employer's success in bargaining with the union will, to a

[10] That is, many employers absorb their attitudes on labor matters, as on other matters, from the climate of opinion among their fellow employers.

[11] Most contracts have a one year duration, but a substantial minority last for two years. Few contracts are for more than three years.

[12] Of course, employers (like others) vary greatly in their personal characteristics. Men who are disposed to compromise will tend to develop friendly relations with unions (under given objective conditions) more readily than belligerent ones.

considerable extent, depend upon his knowledge of his own situation and that of the union. As we shall see, a collective bargaining agreement is a complicated matter; an unwary employer may bind himself to certain policies of whose implications he is unaware. Conversely, a well-informed employer may be able to give a union what it wants without making undesirable concessions that the union may originally have thought essential to its objectives. Furthermore, an employer who is alert to the situation inside a union is sometimes able to surmise that there are certain demands the union representatives are prepared to sacrifice under pressure but for which they must (for political reasons) pretend to fight hard.

Conducting negotiations in the context of collective bargaining is a highly skilled task. As most employers do not possess the requisite skill and knowledge, there has developed a tendency for all employers who can afford it to obtain hired assistance for contract negotiation. Very small employers cannot afford such assistance and must haggle with union representatives as best they can. More affluent firms tend to hire labor relations specialists who are professionally skilled in negotiating with unions.

Small businesses often designate one of their principal executives to act as a labor or industrial relations specialist on either a part or a full-time basis. For special problems, such an official will hire outside consultants. Larger firms establish whole "industrial relations" sections, headed by a vice-president or director who is responsible for handling the firm's industrial (union) relations. However, contract negotiation usually involves several members of top management as well as the person responsible for industrial relations.

The presence of the industrial relations specialist in the management hierarchy reflects an important change in management attitude. Prior to unionization, the higher echelons of management tended to consider labor relations as a matter of secondary importance as compared with finance, sales, production, etc. Consequently, they tended to delegate a great deal of authority in hiring, disciplining, and wage setting to foremen and plant superintendents. This led, in large firms, to wide variations in company practice from one shop to another and, as a consequence, to considerable ignorance (by top management) of what went on in their own plants.

Their ignorance of the relevant facts and general inattention to labor problems caused many management officials to appear foolish during the early phases of collective bargaining. To remedy this, the industrial relations specialist was hired, either to brief other officials or to act as their spokesman. The hiring of this specialist usually accompanied a program of improvement and standardization of wage and personnel policies within the firm. As a result of these changes in labor policy, most management representatives have been, since World War II, well able to hold their own in negotiations. This has, of itself, improved personal relations at the bargaining table; in most cases there now is general agreement as to the facts, where not too long ago the "facts" were the subject of heated controversy.

The "employer" whom we are discussing is obviously not, except in very small firms, a single person. He is one or more individuals chosen to represent the firm in contract negotiations. He may have authority to enter into a binding agreement, but usually this authority is carefully circumscribed so that major changes in company policy or wage increases raising costs beyond a certain limit must be specifically authorized by the president, the board of directors, or both.

Multiemployer Bargaining

In our discussion thus far we have assumed that each firm bargained for itself. This is still the most frequent situation, but in recent years multiemployer bargaining has covered an increasingly large segment of the nation's workers. At the present time, perhaps a third of the nation's unionized wage earners are employed under contracts negotiated by an association of employers.

Multiemployer bargaining is much more prevalent in some industries than in others. It tends to occur where relatively small employers must deal with a union representing the employees of all of them and where differences in wage rates are of vital concern. Clothing manufacturing, textiles, coal mining, shoe manufacturing, printing, baking, service trades, and building construction are industries where employers tend to bargain (with unions) as a group.

In these industries, employers have found that unless they combined, the union could impose its terms on each of them separately. To bargain more effectively, the employers in these and similar industries have formed employer associations. In some cases, such associations are rather loose organizations whose members cooperate solely for purposes of contract negotiation, leaving contract administration to the individual firm. Such associations tend to leave substantial freedom to individual employers to modify contract terms to suit themselves (and the union). As Kerr and Fisher[13] point out, such associations are best adapted to a situation of rather peaceful union-management relations.

However, there are situations where a much higher degree of cooperation is required of employers if they are to bargain with the union on equal terms. In these situations, it is necessary to form veritable unions

[13] Clark Kerr and L. A. Fisher, "Multiple Employer Bargaining: the San Francisco Experience", in *Insights into Labor Issues,* edited by R. A. Lester and Joseph Shister, The Macmillan Co., New York, 1948, pp. 25–61.

of employers which not only negotiate but administer collective agreements with the union. It is necessary that these associations possess a great deal of disciplinary authority over the member firms in order to make them resist the temptation to break away during a strike. As a result, these associations have many of the internal problems of a union. That is, they must reconcile divergent interests of different firms; prevent weak or greedy employers from deserting the association during strikes, etc. To insure uniformity of contract terms and uniform enforcement of them, such associations absorb virtually all of the collective bargaining functions of their members. They employ staffs of legal, economic, and other experts to facilitate their bargaining activities. Employer associations of this type are more common in other countries, notably Britain and Scandinavia,[14] than in the United States. However, they are not unknown here[15] and may become more common in the future.

Employer associations are primarily designed to increase the strength of individual employers in dealing with unions. In their absence, an aggressive union can strike first one firm and then another. Each firm, seeing its customers taken by its rivals while it is struck, tends to yield in order to resume production. And the strikers can be supported by their fellow union members who remain at work. But where the employers are united, they can force the union to strike all firms or none. When all firms are shut down, the individual employer has less need to yield in order to protect himself from rivals and the union is less able to lend financial assistance to strikers as there are no working members from whom revenue may be secured.

But, although employer associations are instruments for strengthening the hand of employers, unions have not usually opposed their formation[16] provided they did not aim at destroying the union. Before 1935, there were many employer associations whose objective was to break unions. However, in recent years, employer associations have sought only to negotiate on favorable terms. As employer associations almost always

---

[14] See Walter Galenson, *Labor in Norway,* Harvard University Press, Cambridge, Mass., 1949, and *The Danish System of Labor Relations,* Harvard University Press, Cambridge, Mass., 1952. P. H. Norgren, *The Swedish Collective Bargaining System,* Harvard University Press, 1941, Cambridge, Mass. H. A. Clegg, "Employers," Chapter IV in *The System of Industrial Relations in Great Britain,* edited by Allan Flanders and H. A. Clegg, Oxford, 1954.

[15] The most famous American examples of this type of association have occurred in the San Francisco-Oakland area. These are fully described by Kerr and Fisher, *op. cit.*

[16] One of the few instances where a union has refused to permit employers, to combine occurred in the San Francisco construction industry during the first two decades of this century. See Perlman and Taft, *History of Labor in the United State, 1896–1932,* Macmillan & Co., New York, 1935, Chapter VII.

include the better paying firms in an industry, both the association and the union are anxious to force the nonassociation firms up to the association (and union) wage scale. Consequently, nonunion firms often find themselves pressed simultaneously by the union and the employers' association to bargain collectively through the latter.

There are several reasons why unions frequently encourage and even insist on firms joining an employers' association. (1) Frequently the national union prefers a multiemployer bargaining unit[17] in order to prevent disaffected locals from seceding. (2) Where the union is interested in helping the employer association to fix prices or promulgate other "rules" of competition, it is convenient to have all firms subject to the authority of the association. (3) On occasion, the union and a group of employers have combined to restrict employer entry to a particular line of business; this has happened in a number of cases in building construction. To accomplish this end, the union agrees to furnish labor only to association members, and the association refuses to admit new firms.

Employer associations may be conveniently divided into two categories: local and regional or national.

LOCAL ASSOCIATIONS. Where a product is sold locally and there is no intercity competition, as in hotels, restaurants, laundries, dry-cleaning, local trucking, newspaper printing, building construction, etc., the employer associations tend to be local in character. In these and similar fields, the agreements reached with the local unions are of concern only to the local employers. Hence there are local bargaining and local (i.e., city-wide) employer associations. In many industries that sell in a local market, wages are a large part of total cost; this is obvious in the case of services. Also many of the firms involved are very small and have very little opportunity to benefit from labor-saving devices. As a result, wage increases cannot be paid for long unless there are accompanying price increases. But this requires, in a closely competitive local market, that (virtually) all firms raise prices. And this is difficult to accomplish, as any one firm can profit by underselling the others.

Here is where the union can be extremely useful to the employers' association. The association admits only firms charging "fair" prices, and the union agrees to furnish labor only to association members. Hence, a price-cutting employer, even though he observes all union rules regarding wages and working conditions, will find his establishment struck if he attempts to cut the price of what he sells. In this way the union

---

[17] A multiemployer bargaining unit established by the National Labor Relations Board implies that only a union representing a majority of the workers in *all* firms in the bargaining unit can be recognized by one firm. For further discussion of the bargaining unit, see pp. 232–235.

renders valuable service to employers by the very actions that help enable employers to grant wage increases. There are a number of large cities where unions perform, or have performed, this function in retail trade, service, and building construction.[18]

Outside of the construction business, the union most involved in such practices is the Teamsters which has acquired an extensive membership in retail trade. The Teamsters are very effective in bringing recalcitrant employers to terms because of their power to halt deliveries. Their activities in this connection have brought them into conflict with many small businesses and have prompted considerable criticism, see pp. 147 et seq. (Unions generally have collected ill-will from the retail price-fixing activities of a few.) To some extent such criticism is merited, but unions, even those directly involved, are not alone in their guilt. Employer groups have long tried to control prices, with and without union assistance. Unions have, at worst, merely aided and abetted these practices.

REGIONAL AND NATIONAL ASSOCIATIONS. In general, employer bargaining associations tend to cover the same geographical area, within a given country, as that within which there is effective product price competition. Thus, there are regional or national organizations engaged in collective bargaining in garment manufacturing, hosiery, textiles, coal mining (bituminous and anthracite), furniture manufacturing, maritime trades, and others. Of course, some employers abstain from joining these associations, either because they prefer to bargain individually or because they operate on a nonunion basis. However, a large part of the unionized workers in all of these industries are subject to agreements made with employer associations.

In a few industries, such as men's clothing and bituminous coal, the union is quite large relative to any of the firms with which it deals. In consequence, unions in these industries have often become involved in developing and enforcing industry-wide plans for controlling output and prices. However, at the national or even regional level, union participation in such activities is exceptional.

At the present time in most industries, multiemployer bargaining at either the regional or national level is still at an early stage of evolution. The fact of nation-wide product market competition creates a need for such bargaining, but this need has been met, temporarily at least, by the institution of the "industry-wide" pattern. That is, most firms in the industry delay coming to terms with the union, if a new contract is to be negotiated that year, until the union has reached agreement with one or more "key" firms in the industry. Once the "key" bargains have been struck, then the other bargains are, by mutual consent, patterned

[18] See below, pp. 345–347.

upon them.   In some industries the "pattern" requires virtual imitation of
the key bargain; in others certain conventional variations are permitted; in still others the variations that may result from individual bargaining may be so large as almost to obscure the pattern.   However,
where product market competition is keen (and wages an important element in cost) an understood and closely followed bargaining pattern, or
an industry-wide bargain, is vital to collective bargaining.   In the absence of both, firms would be unwilling to conclude an agreement lasting
any length of time until they knew what other firms in the industry were
to pay for their labor.

In short, the institution of pattern bargaining serves as a kind of substitute for an employers' association.   Indeed, in several industries, pattern bargaining has lead to informal collaboration between key employers
and those whose wage policy is "pattern-dominated."   In time, such
collaboration may develop into a formal association.   However, even in
formal associations something like pattern bargaining remains.

For example, in bituminous coal mining, formal negotiations between
the union and the association of Mine Operators begins with policy
speeches to a large gathering of representatives of union district representatives and their opposite numbers from the Mine Operators Association.
However, the actual negotiations are between small negotiating committees from each side.   As the employers' committee usually includes
spokesmen from the large key firms, the agreement negotiated is really
a key bargain.   For the actual application of the industry agreement
to particular companies frequently involves considerable adjustment to
individual circumstances which involves further individual employer bargaining.

Union Representatives

The union representatives at the bargaining table include the heads
of the local unions concerned.   In some unions, where local control is
strong (e.g., building trades and services) representatives of locals and/or
joint boards may be the only officials involved in contract negotiation.
But, where the local union leaders are inexperienced and in need of
help or the bargain has repercussions beyond the local involved,[19] representatives of the national organization, in important cases the principal
officers, participate.   Where the union negotiates with a nation-wide employers' association, the national organization assumes full responsibility
for negotiating the contract.

It is always easier to reach agreement when the negotiators have full
authority.   A wise management negotiator will often hold out some concessions until he is reasonably sure that granting them will secure the con-

[19] That is, where the bargain may help to set a "pattern" for other contracts.

tract. Making all concessions before the union membership has ratified the contract will put the employer in a position where he has no room to maneuver in the event the members refuse ratification. Hence, he will often drag his feet on some points unitl the union negotiators pledge that an agreement conceding the disputed points will be accepted by the members.[20] This delays the whole bargaining process, and union leaders frequently desire to expedite matters by getting full authority to accept a contract.

However, negotiators empowered to sign agreements must bear the brunt of criticism in the event of member disapproval. Local leaders, fearful of electoral defeat, tend to avoid such responsibility, preferring that the members be compelled to ratify contracts. Consequently, where the local officers are responsible for negotiations, member ratification of the contract is usually required. It sometimes happens, however, that after negotiations have proceeded for a time, especially if they are dead-locked, the members will give their representatives full power to conclude an agreement.

Because national officers are in less danger of electoral defeat than local, they are more willing to assume the responsibility of concluding binding agreements in order to facilitate successful bargaining. As a result, where bargaining is on a regional or national basis, final authority is more likely to be vested in the negotiators than where it is done locally. However, this general statement is subject to important qualifications: in some cases, member dissatisfaction has caused national leaders to relinquish authority to conclude agreements that they had previously possessed; in other cases, the negotiators' power has gradually increased.

It should never be forgotten that, irrespective of the officers' formal authority to negotiate agreements, the wishes of the membership are always an important factor in negotiations. Ultimately, the members must ratify a contract by working under it; if they find it too obnoxious they will refuse to abide by it. This will necessitate either the imposition of discipline by the responsible union officers, with the danger of political reprisal by the offended members and their friends, or an attempt to re-negotiate the contract after having been repudiated by their members. As both alternatives are distasteful, union leaders will refuse to accept contracts that cannot be sold to the great majority of the members affected.

STRATEGIC CONSIDERATIONS IN CONTRACT NEGOTIATION

The actual procedure of bargaining is, in essence, an exchange of contract proposals (offers) by the respective parties. Each offer contains some concession which it is hoped will induce the other side to accept it,

[20] This, of course, implies that the employer has confidence in the willingness and ability of the union negotiators to make good on their pledge.

but which does not yield anything considered "vital." This process contains important elements of a poker game; each side tries to convince the other that, unless certain conditions are met, it will refuse to sign a contract and cause a work stoppage.[21] But it is understood that each side will bluff, i.e., will pretend it would refuse terms that it would, in fact, accept. The necessity for such bargaining tactics can be easily appreciated if we remember that, if either bargainer were to disclose what his minimum terms were, the other bargainer would never offer more. However, by pretending his minimum terms are higher than they really are, he may get somewhat more than his minimum and can always refuse to accept less (than his minimum).

Consequently, bargaining begins with each side demanding terms far more favorable (to itself) than it expects to obtain, and the bargaining process proceeds via a sequence of mutual concessions. As each side wishes to suggest that its minimum terms are relatively high, concessions tend to be offered cautiously, with both sides moving slowly toward a set of terms upon which a settlement can be reached.

Of course, it is not always possible for an agreement to be reached without a strike. Sometimes, the respective minimum terms of the union and the employer are simply incompatible. It also happens, on occasion, that one side feels a favorable moment is at hand for weakening the other and tries to force a fight. In such cases, it is difficult for the other party to avoid a struggle except upon onerous terms.

The role of a strike in collective bargaining varies with the attitude of the employer. If the employer is attempting to get rid of a union, and there is a real possibility of doing so,[22] a strike will be a life and death struggle for the union; if the strike is lost, the union will disappear. But where the union is expected to continue operating, a strike is merely a stage in negotiations. If either side comes to believe that the other is determined to be "tough," the most effective way of "softening it up" is to compel it to do without work, or output, for a time, until it becomes more anxious to negotiate. A strike is merely a maneuver in a continuing game, designed to impress upon the other player one's prowess and determination and the consequent need for being conciliatory. Sometimes a strike has to be endured, despite basic agreement among the bargaining representatives of both sides, in order to convince some group within the union or in management that more favorable terms could not be obtained.

Now it is only rarely that spokesmen, either for labor or management, will publicly discuss their bargaining strategy in these cold blooded, mat-

---

[21] Work stoppage" includes both strikes and lockouts; see pp. 163–164.
[22] Before the Wagner Act of 1935, it was entirely legal for an employer to work toward this end openly. Since that time an employer has been hampered (by both the Wagner and Taft-Hartley Acts) in ridding himself of a union.

ter of fact terms. Both union and management make public statements in order to justify their behavior, but not to explain it. Consequently, their statements abound with terms like "right," "fair," "just," etc. and avoid the jargon of power and strategy. There is good reason for this: in the event of a strike, the attitude of the general public, especially of government officials, may become crucial in deciding the terms of settlement. Consequently, both sides are anxious to appear peace-loving and to be seeking only their just due. Obviously, this inhibits frank avowal of a strategy based on calculated self-interest.

We have portrayed contract negotiation as a complex game of strategy in which both union and management representatives carefully plan each move in advance and make a series of offers and counteroffers. But this is descriptive only of negotiations between unions and the important firms that do the "key" bargaining. Most of the 100,000 or so union-management agreements signed every year in the United States involve relatively little negotiation. In many cases, the contracts between individual employers and unions are mere formal ratifications of agreements made by the union and an employers' association. In many others, the actual bargaining is greatly restricted by the fact that it is understood that the contract terms must follow closely a "pattern" already set by other bargains.

Perhaps, it is best to think of the few key bargains as located at one end of a spectrum and the completely pattern-determined contracts at the other. Most contract negotiations lie somewhere between the two extremes; the many small firms, employing a few workers each, tend to fall rather near the "pattern-dominated" limit, and the few large ones, each with many workers, are more likely to negotiate relatively independent or even key bargains.

COLLECTIVE BARGAINING AS MUTUAL PROBLEM-SOLVING

Throughout the book, we shall treat collective bargaining as a contest between parties concerning the terms upon which their *conflicting* interests shall be reconciled so as to permit continued operation of the employer's business. The interests that the workers and the employer share are assumed to be adjudicated without difficulty, as there is "nothing to fight about." This assumption would, however, be greatly disputed by many students of collective bargaining, especially those with a psychological orientation.

Such students contend that much of the conflict between workers and management stems from a failure to appreciate each other's needs and wishes, and not from a simple clash of economic interests. In this view, effective collective bargaining brings the complaints of each party to the attention of the other. In the bargaining process, they thresh out their mutual difficulties and mutually arrive at a solution which helps each side to solve its problems.   Collective bargaining thus involves joint problem-solving, a process which contributes to mutual understanding and good-will.

This view of collective bargaining has considerable relevance to situations involving small employers.   Where a union local must deal with many small employers, it cannot keep in close contact with the circumstances of each one, nor can small employers keep up to date on the union's affairs.   In such circumstances, collective bargaining involves a good deal of "fact-finding" and explanation of relevant circumstances concerning the state of the employer's costs and profits, the workers' living costs, the national union's stand on current contracts, etc.

However, where contract negotiation involves larger firms or employers' associations, its educative aspects are less important.   Even in these cases, it is quite likely that during the early stages of a collective bargaining relation both sides learn a good deal about each other's problems and sometimes about the operation of their own organization.   For example, top management has sometimes learned a good deal from union bargainers about the high-handed practices of their foremen.   However, after collective bargaining has proceeded for any length of time, both parties become fairly well aware of each other's situation.

We shall, throughout the book, treat collective bargaining as a method of settling conflicting interests in which each party seeks to advance its own.   This is the only way in which the *economic* aspects of collective bargaining can be understood.   However, there are circumstances in which collective bargaining involves mutual problem-solving as well as a conflict of interests.[23]   From time to time we shall refer to this fact, but for our purposes it is not of central importance.

ADMINISTRATION OF THE CONTRACT

Signing a contract is only the beginning of collective bargaining; the contract must be administered.   Administration of collective agreements is the main day-to-day business of a union local.   To understand the significance of contract administration, it is necessary to recognize that a labor contract, individual or collective, is not the same as an ordinary. purchase and sale agreement.[24]   The difference is due principally to the fact that a labor contract does not ordinarily specify exactly what the employee is to do in exchange for the wage stipulated in the contract.[25]

[23] This is especially true in connection with the interpretation of an existing contract (see p. 163 and p. 170.)

[24] This point is made by H. A. Simon, "A Formal Theory of the Employment Relationship," *Econometrica*, July 1951, pp. 293–305.

[25] Complete specification of the employee's duties would be possible only in the

To be sure, the physical presence of a worker may be required during specified times, on pain of not being paid. However, the employer is not interested in the worker's mere physical presence but in what he does. Usually, the employer wants his workers to follow the directions of a foreman or other supervisor in performing the various tasks that constitute his job. Depending upon what the supervisor orders him to do, a worker's job will be pleasant or unpleasant, hard or easy. And, as may well be imagined, directions which tend to increase output may also tend to require more effort by the worker; as a result there is ample opportunity for conflicts of interest.

Before unions became common in the 1930's, foremen usually possessed complete authority to command the workers under their supervision. Failure to obey orders was punishable by instant dismissal. The actual behavior of foremen under nonunion conditions was quite varied; some behaved like oriental despots, others like benevolent fathers and most of them were somewhere between the two extremes. However, the individual worker who resented his treatment had only one effective means of protest, to quit his job.

This mode of protest was not very effective as it was usually more painful to the worker (especially older ones and those with families) than to the employer. As a result, one of the most important things workers have demanded, and obtained, through collective bargaining is the right of protesting, without fear of discharge, the details of their day-to-day working conditions. This right is guaranteed by the grievance procedure.

The Nature of the Grievance Procedure

Most present day collective bargaining agreements contain elaborate provision for settling disputes arising while they are in effect. These provisions are the result of a long and frequently bitter experience with disputes over "interpretation of the contract." At the inception of collective bargaining, management often did not accept the union, and foremen tried to run their shops in the same manner as before. When the workers resisted orders they considered unjust, they would be discharged. Often the discharged workers were enthusiastic unionists, as it was such workers who most resented abuse of a foreman's authority and were most likely to get into trouble on this account. To protect its members, the union had to demand their reinstatement. If the union failed to achieve this, its members would lose heart and drop out while management would

---

rare case where he was paid entirely by results, so much per unit of output, with no guarantee of minimum earnings, and where he had no duties other than to produce output, e.g., no responsibility for the maintenance of a machine, etc.

become increasingly aggressive in its attempts to whittle away the concessions embodied in the contract.[26]

Obviously, where the management was bent upon undermining the union, trouble was inevitable. But, even where management was willing to "live with the union" it often did not recognize that coexistence implied sharing authority over working conditions and discharge. Fuller appreciation of the implications of collective bargaining came only after painful conflict.

The early stages of life under a collective agreement are likely to be stormy, even when management is prepared to share authority. For workers, newly released from arbitrary discipline, often feel that the employer ought to have no influence whatever over working conditions. As a result, even well-disposed employers often find newly established local unions to be a bit unreasonable.

For these reasons, the early phases of collective bargaining tend to be filled with disputes and work stoppages over issues of contract interpretation. However, as parties become more experienced in the ways of collective bargaining, they tend to develop procedures for the peaceful settlement of disputes arising under collective bargaining agreements. As most collective agreements leave management with the right to initiate changes in working conditions, subject to appeal through the grievance procedure, the typical dispute about contract interpretation is a protest (i.e., a grievance) by one or more workers over the acts of management representatives.

In most large and middle-sized firms, union stewards are chosen to present the grievances of men in their part of the shop; they deal directly with the foremen, or other supervisors, concerned.[27] An aggrieved worker usually has the right to be present at the discussion of his case and sometimes to participate actively in the negotiations. In most instances, the grievance is settled at this stage.

However, the worker, his steward, or both may be dissatisfied with the outcome of negotiations with the foreman, and appeal the case. The appeal is usually negotiated by a higher representative of management (e.g., plant superintendent) and a chief steward (on behalf of the union). Although most grievances are settled at the initial stage, the appeal machinery is necessary for the peaceful disposition of cases upon which agreement cannot be reached. In large firms there are usually several stages of appeal; at each successive stage the negotiations are conducted by higher echelons of union and management authority.

[26] Before the late 1930's, management counterattacked and destroyed many temporarily successful unions by seizing a favorable moment to tighten discipline and discharge active unionists, thereby forcing the union either to strike (at a time most convenient for management) or to accept death by slow disintegration.

[27] In small firms the employer usually deals directly with an official of the union local with which his employees are affiliated.

In most cases collective bargaining contracts provide for arbitration as the final step in the grievance procedure.[28]   That is, if agreement cannot be reached at the highest level of negotiations, the case is then determined by an arbitrator or arbitrators, chosen in some manner specified in the contract.   The most common practice is to appoint arbitrators each time they are needed.   Contracts frequently provide that in the event the parties cannot agree upon an arbitrator (or arbitrators) he will be chosen by some public official, often the head of the Federal Mediation and Conciliation Service, or by the head of a state Department of Labor, or by the American Arbitration Association.[29]   Where there is enough work for him, the parties often hire a permanent arbitrator on either a full- or part-time basis.   "Umpires" or "Impartial Chairmen," as these arbitrators are often called, are usually employed to service contracts between a union and a very large firm, such as General Motors or U. S. Steel, or between a union and an employer's association.

The significance of arbitration is that it provides a method of settling disputes arising under a contract other than by economic force, i.e., by strikes.   However, the mere agreement to arbitrate all disputes arising under a contract is no guarantee of industrial peace.   If the volume of grievances that cannot be settled at the initial stage (i.e., between shop steward and foreman) is very large, the appeals machinery becomes swamped and the processing of grievances becomes extremely slow. Delay in settling grievances causes great dissatisfaction among workers who must continue to live with the protested conditions while the grievance is being processed.   When workers feel strongly about an issue, they are not always willing to wait 6 to 18 months to get it settled.   Sometimes they take matters into their own hands, either by calling an unofficial strike[30] or by slowing down operations.   Such action has often been effective in getting prompt attention to grievances that have been in "the mill" too long.

Because of the trouble that results from dilatory handling of grievances, it is now stipulated in most contracts that grievances must be decided, even though they go to arbitration, within a specified period (usually 30 to 60 days).   Knowledge of such a contractual provision helps to make aggrieved workers more patient, but such a time limit can be observed

---

[28] As of 1952, 89 per cent of the contracts studied by the Bureau of Labor Statistics provided for arbitration of grievances (if needed) arising during the life time of a contract.   This reflected a substantial increase over the corresponding percentages in 1944, 73 per cent, and 1949, 83 per cent.   Cf, "Arbitration Provisions in Collective Agreements, 1952," *Monthly Labor Review,* LXXVI (March 1953), pp. 261–266.

[29] *Ibid.*

[30] That is, a strike called directly by workers, usually a small group without the union's authorization.

only if the number of grievances appealed beyond the initial stage is small.

One sure sign of unsatisfactory union-management relations is a tendency to carry a large percentage of grievances beyond the first stage and for the appeals machinery to become clogged as a result.

The Role of Grievance Procedure in Collective Bargaining

In the United States, formal grievance procedures were, in most firms, established only with the advent of collective bargaining, or even later. Before unionization, large employers were fond of asserting that their "door was open" to any workman with a complaint, and that a union was therefore unnecessary to secure justice to a worker who believed he had been mistreated. However honest such protestations may have been, there is little doubt but that most workers were (rightly) afraid to use such an avenue of protest. An employer's first reaction to a complaint would have been to call for information from the foreman concerned. Given the disciplinary power of the preunion foreman, the position of a complaining worker could not, thereafter, have been comfortable or secure, whatever the disposition of his grievance. Consequently, before they were protected by a union, most workers did not give vent to individual grievances.[31] Furthermore, prior to unionization an employer could reject a workman's complaint with relative impunity; at most, he risked the resignation of one or a small group of workers. But under collective bargaining a grievance must be settled to the union's satisfaction[32] or be arbitrated. The employer concedes this reduction in his authority in order to be free from strikes for the period of the collective bargaining contract.[33]

For the most part, agreements not to strike during the lifetime of a contract are observed;[34] however, if a group of workers feels very strongly about a particular grievance and cannot get satisfaction through the grievance machinery, they may strike irrespective of the contract, sometimes in defiance of the union. Most contracts provide some penalty for strikes

[31] The relation between collective bargaining and the establishment of formal grievance procedures is not one of logical necessity but simply of fact. For example, in Germany under the Weimar Republic, an aggrieved worker could appeal for redress to a labor court. See Frieda Wunderlich, *German Labor Courts,* Chapel Hill, 1946.

[32] This does not mean that the union always gets it way, but only that it is either sufficiently contented not to compel arbitration or that the issue is settled by arbitration. However, in no event, can the employer settle the dispute by fiat.

[33] In a minority of cases, employers and occasionally a union feel so strongly on certain issues that they will not permit them to be arbitrated. This usually means that, in the event of a disagreement, a strike may occur (during the lifetime of the contract) without the contract being breached.

[34] Violations of such agreements constitute an unfair labor practice under the Taft-Hartley Act, see pp. 255–256.

in violation of their terms although these penalties may vary considerably from one contract to another. In many cases, the *instigators* of unauthorized strikes may be discharged or suspended for fairly long periods. Mere participants are not usually punished very severely; short suspensions or small fines are the usual extent of disciplinary action. Furthermore, any disciplinary action the employer chooses to take may be appealed through the grievance machinery. (In only a few cases is provision made for punishing the *unions* for unauthorized strikes.[35]) Hence, management is likely to discuss disciplinary action with the union before embarking upon it; where relations with the union are good, management will usually not wish to endanger them by hasty action. As a result the punishment a worker may receive for engaging in an unauthorized strike is uncertain, and often depends upon the union's attitude and policy.

Although the terms of a collective bargaining contract apply, unless otherwise stated, throughout its life, sometimes unions successfully appeal for alterations because of changed circumstances. Many employers feel that such appeals are improper and insist that the letter of collective bargaining agreements be respected. However, some of the more sophisticated employers recognize that the objective of sound collective bargaining is continuous production with a high level of worker efficiency. Insistence upon the letter of the contract, even when successful, may defeat this objective either through lowering worker morale or by leading the union to adopt an obstructive attitude whenever possible. Therefore, some employers tend to interpret collective bargaining contracts as "living documents," and not as a rigid set of rules. This means that such employers sometimes make concessions to the union not required by the letter of their agreement, if they feel that it is equitable to do so and if they can afford it. However, such behavior is, at present, rather exceptional.

COLLECTIVE BARGAINING AND STRIKES

As we have already seen, strikes and the threat of them are an integral part of the collective bargaining process. By definition, a strike occurs where the union has initiated a work stoppage, and most stoppages are therefore termed strikes. This is rather unfortunate in that it puts the brand of aggressor upon the union, irrespective of the facts. Even when the employer offers outrageous terms, it is the union that must (as a rule) call the strike and appear to the naive observer as the disturber of the peace.

Employers can, of course, announce lockouts and refuse to reopen their plants unless the union accepts their terms. And, where collective bargaining is well-established, they sometimes scorn subterfuge and de-

[35] This is apart from the legal provisions of the Taft-Hartley Act and certain state laws.

clare lockouts; this frequently happens where members of an employers' association *lock out* their workers in pursuance of an agreement to bargain as a group. "Lockouts" are sometimes termed employer's strikes; however, the attempt to pigeon-hole disputes as strikes or lockouts is useless. Most work stoppages are termed "strikes," and we shall follow common usage. However, it is important that the reader remember that there is no presumption that the party declaring a strike is in the wrong. In fact, it is not usually worth while to determine the "aggressor" in a labor dispute, even in the relatively infrequent cases where it is possible to do so.

Strikes are, at bottom, trials of economic strength between employers and their unionized workers, the outcome of which sets the terms of a collective bargaining contract. In the absence of government intervention, the frequency with which strikes occur and their outcome depends primarily upon the relative strength of the bargaining parties. Let us, therefore, examine the factors that strengthen employers relative to the union and vice versa.

The Determinants of "Strike Power"

When an employer is unwilling to concede something that the union representatives believe important enough to justify a strike, they call, or take steps to call,[36] one. There is no simple formula which may be consulted to determine when a strike will or will not be called. In any strike, there is some risk of defeat and the certainty of some cost to the union and its members; these must be balanced against the chances of victory and the value of its fruits. Whatever circumstances increase the likelihood of strike victory, or reduce its cost, will increase the chance that a union will feel a given objective is worth a fight. Conversely, an employer will balance the costs of a strike (to himself) against the chances of victory and its importance to him.[37]

When a union feels that an issue is (given the prospects and costs of victory) worth a strike and the employer feels that accepting the strike is preferable to conceding the issue, a strike starts and continues until one or both parties alter their position. The course of a strike tends to alter the initial positions of the bargainers in two ways: (1) It forces them to bear economic losses. The strikers lose the wages they would have earned by working and the employers lose the profits they could have

---

[36] That is, ask the members to authorize a strike call where the union constitution requires such a step.

[37] The smaller the pecuniary cost of the union's demands to the employer the more likely (other things being equal) that he will yield. This implies, among other things, that when a union represents only a small fraction of a firm's workers or when wages are a small part of a firm's costs, an employer will be more likely to concede a given demand (on behalf of each union member) than if a large percentage increase in costs were implied.

made by continuing production. It often happens (but not always) that the greater the losses already borne the more anxious a party is to avoid further losses; this makes him more willing to compromise, or yield, than before. (2) It sometimes happens that one or both sides initially underestimated the strength and determination of the other (or overestimated its own) and was therefore overoptimistic about its chance of victory. In such cases the progress of the strike corrects misapprehensions and causes the mistaken party to offer more favorable "peace terms."[38] However, a strike has sometimes lasted for many months before the two parties could reach a settlement.

It is fairly obvious that the greater the ability of a union, or an employer, to impose economic loss by striking, and the greater its own ability to avoid or withstand such economic loss, the greater will be its chance of victory. Consequently, both unions and employers try to strengthen their own strike power as much as they can and, sometimes, to lessen that of their opponents.

Now let us consider the factors that determine the relative "fighting power" of unions and employers.

THE EMPLOYER'S FIGHTING POWER. The costs of a strike to an employer are primarily financial. However, they may include more than his out-of-pocket losses; an employer may also lose buyer good-will from a strike, either because of unfavorable publicity or because customers wish to deal with firms able to guarantee prompt delivery. The cost of a strike to an employer will be greater than otherwise if: (1) the demand conditions for his output are more than ordinarily favorable, (2) he produces a product that cannot be inventoried or of which inventories are temporarily low, (3) he is unable to replace his struck plants as a source of output, (4) he cannot get strike-breakers to man his struck plants, (5) his competitors are able and eager to fill orders he is temporarily unable to supply, (6) his financial position is such as to make a steady stream of receipts imperative to stave off his creditors. Let us discuss each of these factors briefly.

(1) In many lines of business, prospects for making sales at profitable prices vary greatly from one year to another. Consequently, when a firm's prospects are favorable, it is anxious to sell while it can and is ready to pay more than usual to secure continued production. This is an

---

[38] Further discussion of bargaining strength and strike behavior may be found in J. R. Hicks, *The Theory of Wages,* Macmillan Co., London, 1932, Chapter VIII. Also see A. C. Pigou, *Economics of Welfare,* 4th edition, The Macmillan Co., London, 1938, Part III, Chapter VI; *Principles and Methods of Industrial Peace,* Macmillian, London, 1906; J. Pen, "A General Theory of Bargaining," *American Economic Review,* March 1952, pp. 24–42 contains a good, but quite abstract, statement of the problem. Pen's article contains references to the modern contributions to the literature, especially those of Zeuthen, Lindblom, Denis, Shackle, and Nash.

important reason why unions have usually fared well in periods of prosperity and badly during depressions. (2) When an employer has larger inventories of his product than he desires, a strike does him no injury at all, provided he can make delivery. Consequently, employers who anticipate a strike try to build up their inventories; this is notably true in coal mining, but it is also a well-known phenomenon in other industries with a durable product. (3) If an employer owns plants not on strike or can purchase output from plants he does not own, a strike will cost him far less than if it rendered him completely unable to supply his customers. Consequently, a union will often strike all plants of a company, even though the dispute concerns only some of them. Furthermore, a union will, if it can, strike or picket other firms that are filling the orders of the one being struck. (Extending strikes in this manner may constitute a secondary boycott which is illegal under the Taft-Hartley Act)[39]. (4) If a struck firm can replace its workers with others (of satisfactory quality), the strike has obviously failed to put economic pressure upon the firm. Hence, the determination of striking unions to picket the premises of struck firms in order to deter strike-breakers from entering. As we shall see, the tactics that pickets may be permitted to use to accomplish this purpose have long provided a staple of controversy in the field of labor law. (5) If a firm has a virtual monopoly on its product so that its customers must wait for it to deliver or if all the firm's competitors are also on strike so that they cannot seize its customers, it will lose less by a strike than if the reverse is the case. Fear that its market may be invaded or, in seasonal trades, that it may lose the bulk of the year's profits has brought many an employer (small or middle-sized) to the union's terms. The success of unions in playing competing employers against one another has been a major factor in promoting employer associations and multiemployer bargaining. (6) Obviously a firm that greatly needs cash is at a disadvantage in any situation where someone threatens to interrupt its receipts. Firms in positions such as this sometimes bargain with unions by compelling the union to face the issue of whether it wants to put them out of business, and its employees out of jobs, or to cooperate in saving its life.

Where the union does not wish to destroy the firm and it rarely does, the conditions for the firm's survival impose a very real limit to what the union will demand (see pp. 338–339). But, where the firm's existence is not at stake, the more vulnerable a firm is to strike pressure, i.e., the more it loses as a result of a strike, the more will the union demand, and the more determinedly will it hold out for its terms. This is not so unpleasant for employers as it might seem, for the employer is most vulnerable to strike pressure when his current profits are highest. In other

[39] See pp. 249–251.

words, unions usually demand more from those employers who are better able to pay and tend to demand more at times when employers are unusually prosperous.

THE UNION'S FIGHTING POWER. The outcome of a strike, however, depends not only upon the employer's power of resistance, but also upon the union's. A union's fighting power is greater, the greater are: (1) the strike benefits it can pay each striker and the longer the period for it can pay them, (2) its members' liquid assets and ability to borrow, and (3) the ability of the members to secure outside income through odd jobs or, when possible, from unemployment compensation.

(1) The provision of strike benefits, payment to strikers in lieu of wages, varies from one union to the next. The unions of skilled craftsmen usually charge higher dues and make more adequate provision for strike (and other) benefits than unions charging lower dues. However, union strike pay rarely approaches ordinary earnings. Usually a union helps out as best it can in hardship cases but encourages its members to shift for themselves in order to conserve funds.

Contrary to common opinion, union treasuries are not adequate to pay substantial benefits in the event of a major strike. If 200,000 members, earnings an average of $75 per week, are on strike, it would take $7,500,-000 per week to pay them half of their weekly earnings. In the absence of income, this would exhaust a union treasury of $75 million (larger than any current union treasury) in ten weeks. Of course, if the union can secure additional income, benefits can be larger or paid for a longer period. Consequently, unions prefer to strike employers one at a time, the dues of the nonstrikers, sometimes raised temporarily for the duration of the strike, helping to support the strikers. To prevent this provides one important reason why employers sometimes insist on bargaining as a group.

(2) Since strike benefits are rarely adequate to meet the normal budget of a worker's family, a strike is the occasion for drawing upon savings when available, for borrowing when they are not and, in either case, for curtailing expenditure. The bigger a family's financial resources, the less discomfort a strike will impose upon it and the longer will its breadwinner be prepared to hold out. However, no family likes to eat up its savings, and the sight of a dwindling savings account can lead to a desire for compromise with the employer well before there is any real distress.

(3) When a striker, or some member of his family, can replace part of his sacrificed earnings by other employment, the financial burden of the strike is obviously reduced. Consequently, a union's powers of resistance are greatly enhanced by the availability of alternative employment for its striking members. This is another reason why unions are most likely to win strikes during periods of great prosperity and labor shortage.

In a few states, strikers may (under certain circumstances) draw unemployment compensation. Where this is possible, it obviously increases their staying power. Naturally, employers bitterly oppose making strikers eligible for unemployment compensation.

The Different Kinds of Strikes

SURVIVAL STRIKES. If the union and the employer have different opinions about their relative strike power, it is easy to see that they might be unable to reach an agreement without a strike. However, strikes are sometimes waged despite heavy odds against one side or the other; this happens when an issue of such vital importance is at stake that surrender is unthinkable. The most important example of this might be termed the "survival strikes" which occur when an employer is bent on destroying the union among his employees. To do this he might, before the Wagner Act of 1935, simply refuse to negotiate further with the union; in such cases, the union had to win or die. Since 1935 he could accomplish this same end by indirect means; he might offer the union such terms that its members would resign in disgust were they accepted, or he might refuse to rehire some (or all) strikers, thereby crippling the local union. Of course, the union cannot accept these terms and survive. (Employers bent on destroying a union will usually choose a time when their relative strength is greatest, e.g., as in 1921).

ORGANIZATION STRIKES. When a union first organizes an employer, it must frequently begin by waging an "organization strike." Such a strike is often prolonged and bitter because the existence of the union is at stake. As employers have not been free to refuse collective bargaining to a union (certified by the National Labor Relations Board) since 1935, one important reason for the organization strike has disappeared. And organization strikes have occurred far less frequently since 1945 than before.

However, some organization strikes still occur and, despite the Wagner Act, they were very numerous between 1935 and 1940. The reason is that a strike often plays a positive role in the establishment of collective bargaining. Not infrequently it has happened that the workers in a non-unionized factory were afraid to join a union for fear of displeasing the foreman. They did not believe that the union could or would protect them from discrimination or discharge in the event of their joining. Yet these workers would not want, or dare, to cross a picket line of their fellows. By calling a strike, the union forces such workers, who may be a majority, to "get off the fence" and side with the union. Such workers gain the confidence to express their grievances and to support the union openly only when they see the union is strong enough to win a strike.

In a very real sense, "a union is not strong because such workers support it, but such workers support it because it is strong." Because of this many union leaders believed, in the 1930's, that to command a majority in an NLRB election, it was necessary first to win a strike.[40]

"POLITICALLY-REQUIRED" STRIKES. At times, union and employer negotiators both recognize the equity or economic necessity of certain terms but cannot accept them without first "putting up a battle." Occasionally, it is a management faction that prevents the employer representatives from making necessary concessions. More frequently, the internal political problem arises within the union. The union is especially likely to have internal disagreement on a contract issue if the question involves accepting worse terms than the present ones. Union leaders are far more likely to appreciate the need for a wage cut, and to appreciate it sooner, than the members.

If the leaders anticipate bitter resistance to the terms upon which the employers insist, they frequently avoid an open fight (with the members) and issue a strike call. After the fighting edge of the members has been dulled by a few weeks of doing without paychecks, they seize a strategic moment to present a management offer they could have obtained before the strike but did not dare to present at that time.

An active political opposition within the union does much to compel strikes such as this; this is one reason why students of collective bargaining are rather cool to the idea of greater internal democracy in unions (see pp. 132–133). Furthermore, it should be noted that "politically-required" strikes do not always end happily. Before the leaders can convince the members of the necessity of accepting unfavorable contract terms, the union may be on the verge of destruction.

OUTLAW AND QUICKIE STRIKES: THE EMOTIONAL FACTORS. So far we have considered strikes solely as strategic moves in a continuing bargaining process. Of course, the bargaining discussion sometimes becomes heated, and rather harsh words are exchanged. Oratory at strike meetings is notoriously florid. However, the behavior of the bargainers can, without serious error, be interpreted as calculated. Major strikes are not undertaken by experienced bargainers in fits of anger.

However, small groups of workers in a factory, or sometimes a whole local, may become incensed by what they consider an injustice, and walk off the job without further notice. Such strikes are usually over in a matter of hours, for which reason they are called "quickies." Quickies do not usually arise from isolated instances of friction but result from a cumulation of unsatisfied grievances which are brought to a head by a single act.

[40] See, for example, R. R. R. Brooks, *As Steel Goes*, Chapter V, Yale University Press, New Haven, 1940.

An effective grievance machinery will greatly reduce the likelihood of quickie strikes and related behavior, but it cannot guarantee their absence. Workers may insist upon correction of certain working conditions, irrespective of what emerges from the grievance machinery. If a political faction exists, or arises, to exploit the issues involved, the workers may be kept in a state of discontent for months. Quickie strikes are only one possible manifestation of such discontent; sabotage and slowing down of work on various pretexts may also serve as vents for worker indignation.

Handling such situations presents a real challenge to management wisdom. Management may successfully insist upon adherence to the contract, but this will not get the cooperation of their workforce. Disciplinary action to punish recalcitrant workers is likely to produce quickies or intensified resistance on the job. To solve the problem, a sophisticated management may resort to the "living document" theory of collective agreements and yield part or all of what the workers want. However, yielding is not always wise; it may create unfortunate precedents or make the union feel the management is always ready to yield under pressure.

Where relations with the union are friendly, management frequently calls upon the union to assist it in straightening out the problem. In such cases, a national union representative will try to assist the local union and management in working out a settlement, at least for the duration of the contract. It sometimes happens, however, that the national union cannot induce the men to compromise; in this case management may have to take disciplinary steps. In such situations, the national union is placed in a very awkward position; it must choose between sanctioning a contract violation or acting as the ally of management against its own members. Which way the national organization will move depends upon the state of its relations with management, the political situation within the union, and the extent to which it fears a loss of members.

Of course, things are not always what they seem. The "spontaneous anger" of workers is sometimes carefully nurtured by the national organization, and "quickie" strikes may be part of its strategy. To make matters more involved, the resentment that the national union has encouraged may get out of control and boil over at inconvenient times and places. In short, quickie strikes involve emotional factors and cannot be understood merely as moves in a strategic campaign. However, the possibility of such strikes must be considered, by both unions and management.

Quickie strikes are only one variety of "outlaw" strikes. "Outlaw" strikes are those which are called in violation of the procedure specified by union law. Typically, an outlaw strike involves a revolution, real or feigned, against the union's leadership. We shall consider some of the legal issues involved in controlling such strikes on pp. 254–255.

Do Strikes Pay?

During strikes of sufficient importance to merit public attention, newspaper editors and columnists frequently demonstrate conclusively that the financial losses to either side resulting from the strike, far exceed the gain that could be obtained by getting their own terms rather than those offered by the other side. The inference drawn is that strikes are foolish, especially for the wage earners.

It may be conceded that, with rare exceptions, the pecuniary stake in a *single* strike is rarely worth the economic losses incurred by either party. Furthermore, when the bargainers achieve a modicum of sophistication they know this. Why, then, don't they settle without a strike? Mainly, because a collective bargaining relation has a permanent character and, if it is to be bearable, both parties must accept compatible standards of equity. To protect itself from imposition by its bargaining opponent, each party must impress the other with the fact that it can and will defend its interests and that unbridled aggressiveness will provoke costly stoppages. In other words, strikes serve to establish mutual respect; they also establish mutually acceptable standards of equity that can be used for settling future disputes. (These "standards of equity" often imply conforming to a mutually accepted industry or area pattern of contract terms.) Once mutual respect and standards of equity are established, strikes become rather infrequent.

Indeed, when bargainers are on very good terms and major issues are not at stake, it sometimes happens that contracts are negotiated on the basis of mutually accepted equitable considerations and without reference to immediate bargaining strength. That is, the bargainers refrain from exploiting temporary advantages they possess in order to continue a valued friendly relationship. However, neither party likes to be dependent, for long, upon the other's good-will nor is such dependence safe.

The Number and Cost of Strikes

The above remarks suggest what accords with general observation; newly established bargaining relationships are more likely to be strife-torn than older ones. It follows that periods when the area of collective bargaining is increasing rapidly will have a great many strikes, and

---

[41] There are a number of other "types" of strike: jurisdictional, sympathetic, general, political, etc. The more important of these are discussed in connection with the legal issues they create.

periods when the area of bargaining does not alter greatly will be relatively peaceful.

Thus, the number of strikes was far higher during the years of union expansion, 1916–1920, than in any year thereafter until 1937, also a year of rapid growth in union membership. The relatively high frequency of strikes in 1941–1946 also coincides with a period of rapid union growth. However, there are more variations in strike behavior than can be explained by reference to the growth rate in union membership or the number of firms engaged in collective bargaining. For example, the antistrike attitude of government and unions during World War II kept the average *duration* of strikes (in 1942–1945) well below their peacetime levels, although it did not reduce their *number*. That is, the typical wartime strike was short and frequently "outlaw."

The years 1919, 1945, and 1946 stand out as years when unusually large percentages of the labor force were involved in strikes. This suggests that years of rapid increase in living costs, coupled perhaps with much uncertainty about future business conditions, are conducive to strikes involving large numbers of workers. Major coal strikes in all of these years made a substantial contribution to the number of workers involved.[42]

Some writers claim to have found a cyclical pattern in strikes, but the evidence is unclear and the theoretical explanations are disputed and of uncertain validity.[43] There is clearer evidence of a consistent variation in the relative frequency with which strikes occur in different industries; e.g. coal miners, dock workers, and seamen seem, in most coutries, to be unusually prone to strike. Contrariwise, railroad workers and those in trade seem to be less strike prone than the "average" worker. However, it is not well understood why this is so; there are a variety of explantations of the facts, and study of the subject is still in its infancy.[44]

Strikes are an interesting phenomenon and deserving of serious study, but their importance can easily be exaggerated. In only one year, 1919,

[42] The data on strike statistics on which these statements are based are compiled and published regularly (in the *Monthly Labor Review*) by the Bureau of Labor Statistics.

[43] The best recent works in this field are Albert Rees, "Industrial Conflict and Business Fluctuations," *Journal of Political Economy*, October 1952, pp. 371–382 and K. G. J. C. Knowles, *Strikes—A Study in Industrial Conflict*, Oxford, 1954, Chapters IV and V. An earlier work is J. I. Griffen, *Strikes: A Study in Quantitative Economics*, Columbia University Press, New York, 1939.

[41] The best of the few studies directly bearing on this issue are: Clark Kerr and Abraham Siegel, "The Propensity to Strike—an International Comparison," in *Industrial Conflict*, edited by A. Kornhauser, R. Dubin, and A. M. Ross, McGraw-Hill Book Co., New York, 1954, pp. 189–212; A. M. Ross and Donald Irwin, "Strike Experience in Five Countries, 1929–1947: An Interpretation," *Industrial and Labor Relations Review*, April 1951; and Knowles, *op. cit.*

has there been as many as 15 per cent of the nation's employed workers[45] who went on strike; the usual figure is of the order of 5 to 8 per cent. And in only one year, 1946, was so much as 1 per cent of the estimated worktime of the labor force lost through strikes; in all years except 1946 and 1949, the percentage of worktime lost was well under ½ per cent.[46] Furthermore, much of this lost time was subsequently made up by overtime or by lower subsequent unemployment; this last factor is of substantial importance in industries (such as coal mining) which are subject to marked fluctuations in output and employment.   This is not to say that strikes are painless or costless; they are neither.   However, their economic significance can be, and often is, greatly exaggerated.

DISCUSSION QUESTIONS

1. What advantages may *employers* obtain through collective bargaining that would be unobtainable in its absence?

2. (a) What are the principal factors that have led to multiemployer bargaining?

(b) What are the economic characteristics of the industries in which multiemployer bargaining tends to flourish?

3. What are the principal advantages of granting full power to negotiate a contract to the union's bargaining representatives? What are the main disadvantages of such grants of power?

4. Appraise the validity of the contention that the existence of a grievance procedure prevents an employer from "running his own business."

5. Could collective bargaining, as we know it, exist without occasional strikes?

Suggested Readings

Chamberlain, N. W., *Collective Bargaining,* McGraw-Hill Book Co., New York, 1951; *Collective Bargaining Procedures,* American Council on Public Affairs, Washington, D.C., 1944.

Dunlop, J. T. and J. J. Healy, *Collective Bargaining: Principles and Cases,* Revised Edition, R. D. Irwin, Inc., Homewood, Ill., 1953.

Golden, C. S. and V. D. Parker, editors; *Causes of Industrial Peace under Collective Bargaining,* Harper and Brothers, New York, 1955.

Harbison, F. H. and Coleman, J. R., *Goals and Strategy in Collective Bargaining,* Harper and Brothers, New York, 1951.

Twentieth Century Fund, *How Collective Bargaining Works,* Twentieth Century Fund, New York, 1945.

[45] "Strikes in the United States, 1880–1936." *Bureau of Labor Statistics Bulletin 651,* Washington: Government Printing Office, 1937.

[46] For years prior to 1937, data are from *Strikes in the United States, 1880–1936,* op. cit.; data for subsequent years are from issues of *Monthly Labor Review.*

7 | The Subject Matter of Collective Bargaining

In the preceding chapter, we have discussed the procedures of collective bargaining. But we did not consider in any detail what was being bargained about. Obviously, wages are a very important part of the subject matter of collective bargaining, but they are not the whole of it. The issues of collective bargaining are never so simple as they appear at first glance. The idea that the employer and the union haggle about the division of a pie, of given size, is useful as a first approximation, but it greatly oversimplifies the problems of collective bargaining and can lead to serious misconceptions.

Collective bargaining agreements are complicated documents that often require dozens of finely printed pages. The reason for their complexity is that the agreement determines not only the wages and working conditions of union members as a group but also distributes various benefits among them. As we shall see, the various benefits granted by a collective bargaining agreement are not of equal concern to all union members, and what gets into the contract is often a compromise among the demands of various groups *within* the union, as well as between the union and the employer.

However, it is not only the internal conflicts of the union that complicate collective bargaining contracts. Further complications arise from the concern of the union organization with collection of dues, protection of its members against discrimination, repelling "raids" of rival unions, etc. These concerns of the union organization are reflected in certain contract clauses, called "union security" provisions, which do not *directly* benefit the membership. Management also demands, on occasion, clauses acknowledging certain "managerial prerogatives" (see pp. 180–183).

Nowadays it is taken for granted that collective bargaining should lead to a contract, signed by both union and management. However, this was not always the case. In the early days of collective bargaining, the "agreement" often consisted of nothing more than a posted list of "prices" to which the union and management agreed. Frequently, there was no written agreement at all, but merely an oral understanding.[1]   As recently as 1941, the U. S. Supreme Court, in support of a National Labor Relations Board ruling, was obliged to order a firm to sign a written contract.[2] (The legal status of collective bargaining contracts is discussed below, pp. 254–256.)

Most collective bargaining agreements specify a large number of procedural matters, e.g., the number of the employer's plants covered by the agreement, the identity of the employees covered, the length of the contract, provisions for "wage reopenings" before the expiration date, if any, the procedure for the termination of the agreement, and the details of the grievance procedure.   As these subjects either have been, or will be, discussed elsewhere in the book it is not necessary to cover them in this chapter.   Instead we shall concentrate our attention upon the substantive clauses governing union security, management prerogatives, wages, hours, fringe benefits, working conditions, and "job rationing."

UNION SECURITY

Union security clauses are those which assist the union in recruiting and retaining its membership and in collecting its revenue.   Clauses of this kind are usually demanded by the union from the inception of bargaining relations.   Indeed, such clauses are usually more important to the union during the early stages of a bargaining relation than later on when management is more inclined to grant them.   Employers frequently resist demands for "union security" because they hope to get rid of the union, and union security provisions make this more difficult.   This is, of course, precisely why the union desires such contract provisions. Therefore, the more anxious the employer is to avoid granting union security, the more the union feels a need for it.

Compulsory Membership

The provisions both of the Wagner and the Taft-Hartley Acts grant duly certified unions an important measure of union security.   They require that an employer negotiate and sign a contract with the duly certified union and deal with no other.[3]   This state of affairs is commonly designated by saying that the union has "sole bargaining" rights.   Sole bar-

---

[1] See N. W. Chamberlain, *Collective Bargaining*, McGraw-Hill, New York, 1951, pp. 144–147.

[2] H. J. Heinz Co. vs. NLRB, 311, U. S. 514 (1941).

[3] Some firms have employees in a number of different bargaining units.   In such cases they may be compelled to recognize different unions in each bargaining unit (see pp. 232–235).

gaining grants a measure of security to a union for which (prior to 1935) many unions had to fight bitterly and which is not automatically conceded to an uncertified union at the present time.

However, sole bargaining does not compel individual workers to join the union. They may remain outside, and the employer is able to negotiate the terms of their employment with them, individually. If the employer does not extend the union "genuine acceptance," the existence of such individuals is a constant threat to the union's survival and a cause of friction between union and management. The union is anxious that the employer should not discriminate in favor of the nonunion workers in the handling of grievances, layoffs, promotions, etc. If the employer should be able to favor the nonunion workers, union members would suffer and the less enthusiastic or more fearful ones would tend to drop out. Conversely, if the union can force the employer to favor its members, this will serve as a selling point to workers who have not yet joined. In short, when the union is not genuinely accepted, all management decisions affecting personnel become potential incidents in the struggle (between the union and the employer) for the allegiance of the workers.

But, even after the union has achieved "genuine acceptance," it has important reasons for desiring compulsory membership among all employees covered by the contract. (1) The union organization must be financed, but its cost is borne only by its members. Yet, unions argue, all the workers benefit from the union's bargaining activities and, therefore, all should contribute to its maintenance. (2) Where a union must fear the loss of dissatisfied members, it may be forced to acquiese in member acts of indiscipline or otherwise in violation of the contract. A union, secure in its hold over its members, can and often does cooperate with management in reducing labor unrest. The national organizations, and sometimes even the large local organizations, of such unions act almosts as mediators between small groups of aggrieved members and management.

Conversely, where the union must keep "selling itself" to its members, it has a continuing incentive to foster worker dissatisfaction. A union's best selling point is the real or imagined malevolence of the employer, and a union that must always be "selling itself," is likely to be always on the lookout for grievances to exploit.

These arguments indicate the advantages of compulsory union membership to employers, to union organizations, and to their members. Many of the careful students of collective bargaining feel that these considerations are of such importance as to make compulsory unionism desirable, where the majority of workers desire a union at all. Yet, it cannot be denied that compulsory unionism has drawbacks as well as advantages.

Compelling individuals to join an organization, of itself, diminishes their individual freedom.   The importance of this loss of freedom obviously depends upon what membership in the union implies.   If membership in a union were to involve financial or other support to certain political organizations or candidates, or to certain religious organizations, clearly it would be more objectionable than if the union sought only economic objectives.   (The issue singular of the proper range of union activities is discussed on pp. 180–184.)

American unions, unlike those in many other countries, usually confine their activities to economic matters.   In addition, the Taft-Hartley Act makes it unlawful for an employer to discharge a worker for backing union membership, provided the worker has paid (or offered to pay) his dues and initiation fees.   Thus, at present in the United States, compulsory union membership involves little more than compulsory payment of union dues. As these dues are usually very small, relative to worker income (see p. 120), the implied loss of liberty is not very great.   And most of the nonunion workers employed where a union contract is in force are indifferent to the union and/or disinclined to pay dues, rather than opposed to joining "on principle."

In the past, management officials often have made strong statements in support of the right of workers not to join a union.   But in recent years, these statements have become less frequent and less vehement as employers have come increasingly to accept compulsory union membership.   The decline in employer resistance to compulsory unionism is indicated by the fact that in 1949–1950 only 49 per cent of all workers surveyed were employed in either a closed or a union shop, but in 1954 the percentage was 64 per cent.[4]   Increased employer acceptance (of compulsory unionism) seems to have resulted from the growing realization that unions could not be dislodged and that satisfactory relations could be better obtained with secure, than with insecure, unions.

However, compulsory unionism is far from universal acceptance.   It is the large rather than the small employers who have become reconciled to the union shop, and many large firms continue to resist also.   The political strength of antiunion shop employers and their sympathizers is such that in 18 states[5] legislation has been enacted that forbids the adoption or renewal of collective bargaining agreements requiring workers to

[4] Rose Theodore, "Union-Security Provisions in Agreements, 1954" *Monthly Labor Review,* June 1955, pp. 649–658.

[5] Alabama, Arizona, Arkansas, Florida, Georgia, Iowa, Louisiana, Mississippi, Nebraska, Nevada, North Carolina, North Dakota, South Carolina, South Dakota, Tennessee, Texas, Utah, and Virginia.   It is obvious that the southern states are disproportionately represented in this list.   Consequently, in the southern states a far smaller percentage of union workers are employed in union shops.   (Cf. Theodore, *op. cit.,* Table 3).

join a union. Furthermore, the Taft-Hartley Act outlaws the closed, though not the union, shop.

Thus far we have spoken of compulsory union membership without further specification. However, there are different forms and degrees of compulsion. Let us distinguish among them briefly:

CLOSED SHOP. A closed shop is one in which only persons who are already members of the union may be hired. This type of shop is outlawed in establishments covered by the Taft-Hartley Act; however, in establishments not engaged in interstate commerce and not located where state laws forbid it, a closed shop is legal. Before the passage of Taft-Hartley in 1947, 33 per cent of all workers covered by collective bargaining agreements (about 4.8 million) were employed in closed shops.[6] But in 1954, only 7.4 per cent of such workers were employed in avowedly closed shops. However, it is very likely that in the industries where closed shops were prevalent prior to the Taft-Hartley Act (e.g., printing, building construction, service trades) they have continued despite the inability to prescribe them in contracts. Thus, in 1954, 12 per cent of the workers employed in union shops were employed where (1) the employer agreed to notify the union of the number and qualifications of the workers he desired (although not committing himself to hire the workers referred by the union) or (2) it was stipulated that workers with previous training or employment in the industry would be given hiring preference. It is likely that (1) is a thinly disguised cover for a closed shop arrangement and (2) has the effect of a closed shop in an industry with a long history of virtually complete unionization.

UNION SHOP. A union shop requires that all workers employed by the firm must join the union within some specified period of time after hiring, usually 30 days. The crucial distinction between a union and a closed shop is that the former gives the employer freedom to hire whomsoever he wishes, while the latter restricts his choice to persons already in the union. In 1954, 23.7 per cent of all workers employed in union shops were in "modified" union shops, i.e., shops where certain workers (usually employees already hired) were exempted from the requirement to join the union or where new employees were free to withdraw from the union after one year of employment.

THE PREFERENTIAL SHOP. This type of union security arrangement was formerly of considerable importance in clothing manufacture. This is, in essence, a union shop with the proviso that if the union cannot furnish workers within a short period (e.g., 24 hours) the employer may hire nonunion workers. The purpose of this proviso was to protect gar-

---

[6] Theodore, *op. cit.* All data cited in this section are taken from this article, and the statements made refer to the population of workers covered by the contracts studied in the Bureau of Labor Statistics survey on which the article is based.

ment manufacturers in the event that union workers were not available which sometimes happened at seasonal peaks in labor demand.

MAINTENANCE OF MEMBERSHIP.   Maintenance of membership provisions do not require employees to join a union.   However, they do require that workers in the union at the time the contract is signed must remain in it for the duration of the contract.   Usually an "escape period" of 15 to 30 days is provided for workers who wish to withdraw from the union.   One variant of membership maintenance (used in major steel agreements in 1952 and elsewhere) is to require new employees to sign a union membership application at the time of hiring but to permit cancellation of the application between the 15th and 30th day of employment. (The reader will not fail to notice the importance of worker inertia, in determining union affiliation, implied by this provision.)

In a few agreements the *agency shop* is combined with maintenance of membership.   The agency shop requires all employees to pay union dues and other assessments but does not require them to participate in any union activities.   (The agency shop is actually all that the Taft-Hartley Act permits; however, agency and union shops are not usually distinguished from one another.)

Maintenance of membership became prominent during World War II as a compromise between union demands for the union shop and management insistence upon no compulsory membership of any kind.   (Frequently the compromise involved the checkoff as well as membership maintenance.)   And it has retained its role as a kind of half-way house between the open and the union shop.   In 1946, 25 per cent of all workers covered by collective bargaining were under membership maintenance; this percentage declined to 17 per cent by 1954, as contracts switched from membership maintenance to union shop.   At present, this form of union security is of major importance only in the primary metal industries, notably steel.

Moving from the more to the less protective types of union security, we find *sole bargaining* which we have already discussed.   In 1954, 19 per cent of all workers under collective bargaining were employed under this type of arrangement.   Then, there is the *open shop,* where both union and nonunion employees are hired.   Employers have often stated a preference for the open shop which they claimed permitted them to hire the most qualified workers, regardless of union affiliation.   However, what is often termed on open shop is in fact a shop closed to union members. It has often happened that the most ardent employer advocates of the open shop have rigorously refused to hire union members and have discharged all known unionists among their employees.

CHECKOFF.   The dues checkoff is a device to ensure that workers pay their union dues.   It does this by having the employer deduct the dues from the paycheck and remit them to the union. In 1954, 77.7 per cent of all workers under collective bargaining contracts were subject to a dues checkoff; provisions for checking off initiation fees, special assessments, and other financial obligations to the union were less frequent.[7]

The case for the checkoff is similar to that for compulsory membership. It strengthens the union by assuring it of a steady income, thereby relieving it of the need for whipping up enthusiasm by attacking the employer. To keep the union member "shelling out" his monthly dues without complaint, his grievances must be pushed, whatever their merit. It can be easily imagined how a worker might respond to a shop steward's request for dues if a few hours previously the steward had told him that his grievance was without merit. Furthermore, a dues checkoff obviates the necessity for the "dues picket line" where union buttons are "sold" each month in exchange for dues. Such picket lines have created regular occasions for clashes between union and nonunion workers.

To an increasing degree, employers have accepted the checkoff. In 1946 only a little more than 40 per cent of the workers under collective bargaining were subject to it as compared with 77.7 per cent in 1954. The checking off of dues is legal under Taft-Hartley only if the worker gives his authorization in writing. This authorization may be irrevocable for no more than one year or the duration of the contract, whichever is less. There is some slight bookkeeping expense in checking off dues which the union sometimes defrays wholly or in part.

MANAGEMENT PREROGATIVES AND EMPLOYEE DISCIPLINE

Prior to collective bargaining, the employer or his representative, the foreman, had complete authority to enforce discipline through rewards and punishments. Infractions of factory rules or the foreman's orders could be punished by summary discharge, temporary suspension, or fines at the discretion of the foreman. The institution of collective bargaining changed all this; almost every collective bargaining agreement contains provisions governing the administration of punishment, especially discharge. (By discharge, we mean separation from the payroll for "cause," implying employer dissatisfaction, and not because of a reduction in the workforce. Separation from the payroll because of a reduction in the workforce is called *layoff*, which must be distinguished from discharge.)

---

[7] Theodore, *op. cit.* Checkoffs are less frequent in apparel, printing, construction, and hotel and restaurant industries than in unionized establishments elsewhere. This is probably due to the fact that, in these industries, workers move frequently from one employer to another which would complicate record-keeping. Also, the small size of such firms greatly increases the union's expense of collecting the dues checked off.

The power of summary discharge can be an extremely effective device for inducing maximum effort and enforcing discipline. It can also be a source of personal power to the individual exercising it which can be and has been used to intimidate subordinates. One of the first demands of any union is to curb the power of discharge, at least to the extent of preventing its use as a method of eliminating union sympathizers. But it is very easy to fire a man for belonging to a union while stating the reason to be "bad work," violation of safety regulations, etc. Hence the union must insist that any discharge be subject to negotiation in the event of a charge of antiunion discrimination; obviously this ends the power of arbitrary discharge. With the coming of the union, discharges become subject to appeal, and possible reversal, through the grievance procedure.

But restricting control over discharges is not worth much if the employer retains arbitrary power to punish workers through fines, suspensions, unfavorable work assignments, etc. Hence, the union must demand that all disciplinary acts be subject to protest through the grievance procedure. This serves the double purpose of protecting union members from persecution and of giving all workers the right of protesting (what they consider) unfair treatment without fear of employer reprisal.

Despite its unpleasant aspects, arbitrary power to enforce discipline did serve to induce effort. Many employers complain bitterly that unionization prevents the maintenance of proper discipline, causing marked reduction in worker productivity. There is no doubt but that this sometimes occurs, especially during the early stages of collective bargaining. Eventually, however, the union and the employer develop standards of worker performance which are mutually accepted, and the union consents to and even cooperates in their enforcement.

This implies that the union becomes involved, to some extent, in management decisions. Work assignments, speeds at which machinery is to be operated, and a wide variety of other matters bearing upon the efforts and rewards of employees become the concern of the union. Employers have frequently protested this tendency, claiming that the union is infringing "management's right to manage" or "management's prerogatives." In order to protect what they believe to be their prerogatives, employers have frequently insisted upon clauses that explicitly recognize certain decisions as being reserved exclusively to management and not subject to collective bargaining.

The reason for union "invasion" of management functions is not (usually) desire for power but because of member demands for job (and earning) protection. The efforts of management to reduce labor costs are often met by a union demand that desired changes in productive methods be abandoned or altered in order to protect the jobs or earnings of its members. Sometimes these union demands impede substantial savings in costs. Balked in one direction, management attempts to reduce costs through other channels. But most cost-saving decisions affect some workers adversely, and they demand that the union protect them. As a result, management finds its decisions challenged by the union in a number of areas; hence, the oft-heard protest: "the union won't let us run our business," and the demand for protection of management prerogatives.

However, most careful students of collective bargaining doubt that "management prerogative" clauses in union contracts are very helpful to management. For, if a particular managerial decision seriously injures a group of workers, they are likely to demand redress, whatever the contract says about managerial prerogatives. If they are sufficiently determined they may strike, with or without union permission, and management will then have to bargain, or discipline them. In either event, efficiency will suffer temporarily. The union organization may or may not cooperate with management, depending upon its internal political situation. But at best, all that management will have accomplished is to avoid bargaining on the issue for a year or two. For, at the next contract negotiation, the union will have to insist on bargaining about the disputed issue.

In essence, there is no subject that can be effectively excluded from collective bargaining (i.e., reserved as a managerial prerogative) if it seriously affects the welfare of an important group of union members. If management does not wish to make concessions on one issue, it must make greater concessions on others to get a contract the union will accept. If an acceptable contract cannot be found that does not involve a bargain on the disputed issue, a strike will occur until one side or the other changes its position. And experience indicates that lost issues neither die nor fade away but are put in cold storage till a time when the union is relatively stronger.

In short, refusal to bargain on a specific issue may involve heavy costs to the employer. The recent history of American collective bargaining suggests that the cost has often been heavier than most employers were willing to bear for, in the last ten years, employers have come to bargain on many issues that they had once claimed were the exclusive concern of management.

To minimize the friction attendant on decisions that affect the interests of union members, some firms discuss their plans with union representatives before embarking upon them. Sometimes they find that relatively small changes, or concessions on other matters, will lead to union acceptance of their plans and avoid trouble later on. Of course, many management officials resent this type of negotiation as "infringing upon their prerogatives" and try to avoid it.

The decisions with which unions insist upon "interfering" usually are those that greatly concern their members. It does not pay a union to sacrifice other gains in order to influence decisions about which it is not seriously concerned. However, the issues about which union members are concerned vary greatly from one situation to another; in the United Auto Workers, there is great concern about the speed of assembly lines but not about the selling prices of automobiles; however, the barber's union is very much concerned about the price of haircuts. The Railroad Brotherhoods are much concerned about work rules; the Amalgamated Clothing Workers (in men's clothing) attempt to control rigidly the quality of the garment that each firm produces and its choice of subcontractors; etc. Some unions have even become involved in the financial operations of business firms: for example, the Amalgamated Clothing Workers have loaned money to small firms in order to help them continue in business; the Teamsters have loaned money to the management of Fruehauf Trailer Co. to assist it in a "proxy fight" for control, and they also own enough shares of Montgomery Ward Stock to have been an important factor in the stockholder's fight within that company. The Steel Workers, Hosiery Workers, and other unions have all taken wage cuts from certain firms on condition that the firms used the money saved to buy improved equipment; unions in multiplant firms have sought to control the distribution of work among the various plants, and many unions, including the Auto Workers and the railroad shop-craft unions, have bargained about the amount of maintenance and repair work contracted out to other firms.

In short, it is impossible to designate any specific subject matter as beyond the scope of collective bargaining and subject only to the authority of management. In most cases some fields of decision-making will be left solely to management, but the identity of these fields will vary depending upon the way in which management decisions affect the interests of the union and its members. Most union leaders will insist, truthfully, that they do not wish to invade management's "proper" sphere of activities. However, this proper sphere has tended to vary with the needs and desires of the membership.[8] It is important to remember that an expansion of the union's sphere of influence in the firm's decision-making process is not always achieved over employer opposition. Where the union helps to finance the firm or where it helps to enforce selling price-agreements, etc., it usually does so with the employer's complete approval.

CONTROL OF EMPLOYMENT OPPORTUNITIES

In most collective bargaining contracts, some statement is made about job control. Control of employment opportunities has a number of facets: hiring, layoffs, discharges, promotion, transfer, etc. Control over

[8] See N. W. Chamberlain, *The Union Challenge to Management Control*, Harpers, New York and London, 1948, Chapter 6.

decisions on any of these matters confers power to benefit or injure the workers affected. Consequently, it is not surprising that workers should desire at least some degree of influence upon these decisions.

In the absence of union security, the union must exercise some control over decisions affecting personnel in order to prevent discrimination against its members. But unions usually have broader objectives than mere prevention of discrimination; they seek job control in order to make the distribution of earnings (and other benefits of employment) conform as nearly as possible to the wishes of the politically dominant section of their membership. The issues of job control involve, to some extent, a struggle between the union and the employers; but, to an even greater degree, they are bones of contention among different groups within the union itself.

Hiring

Some of the most crucial issues of job control are associated with control over hiring. In the absence of a closed shop, the employer designates new employees; union rules affect employees only after they are hired. Usually the employer retains absolute freedom to dismiss workers during a probationary period ranging from 30 to 90 days. In many cases, the employer agrees to rehire workers previously laid off (because of reduced work schedules) before hiring any new workers. However, under the union shop, maintenance of membership or lesser degrees of union security, the employer retains power to choose new personnel.

Under the closed shop, the situation *may* be different. One reason why some unions (e.g., those in construction, trucking, retail service, seafaring, etc.) have insisted on a closed, rather than on a union, shop is that the rapidity of job turnover would frequently render a union shop meaningless. For example where, as in longshoring, the typical job lasts no more than a day or two, it would be impossible for a union's business agents to get around to issuing membership cards and collecting dues before the job is completed; a similar statement would apply to any situation where jobs typically last for less than a month. Consequently, to insure that only union members are employed, it is necessary to insist that they be members in good standing at the time of hiring, i.e., that there be a closed shop.

However, this is not the only reason why some unions demand a closed shop. Highly skilled craft unions, notably in printing, construction, and skilled metal trades, are anxious to restrict the practice of their trade to persons who have undergone a prescribed apprenticeship which is made a prerequisite for membership. (Sometimes skill tests are used as a supplement to or substitute for apprentice requirements; e.g., some locals of the Musicians' Union pursue such policies.) Restricting employment to workers who have served an apprenticeship reduces the supply of potential job applicants and tends to increase the earnings of union members.

The significance of a closed shop for job control varies with the mechanics of the hiring process. Where union members must find their own jobs and the employer may choose freely among union workers, the requirement that only union members be hired usually imposes but a small restraint upon the employer's control of new hiring. But, where the hiring is done through the union office, a closed shop may imply that the union determines whom the employer shall hire.

LONGSHOREMEN AND PRINTERS: TWO INTERESTING CASES. Consider the case of the longshoremen on the Pacific Coast.[9] After many years of struggle, they achieved, in the mid-1930's, a system of job allocation under which (in each port) workers are dispatched in rotation (from a hiring hall) as jobs appear; i.e., members make application for work at the hiring hall and are assigned on a "first applied, first dispatched" basis. When a worker is sent out on a job, his name is removed from the dispatching board, and when he completes the job, he reapplies and the process is repeated.[10] The intention of this arrangement is to equalize earnings among "registered" longshoremen. The registration of longshoremen acts to reserve job opportunities for those who work regularly at the trade and depend upon it for a livelihood. It permits "occasionals," (who work at longshoring only when they cannot obtain some other type of employment), to secure jobs only when registered longshoremen are unavailable.[11] Consistent failure of a registered longshoreman to report for work without a valid excuse may cause his deregistration.

Prior to the establishment of hiring halls, most longshoremen in West Coast ports were, as in New York, hired through the "shape-up." This allowed the hiring foremen (the employers' representatives) complete freedom to choose workers. The consequences of this were the creation of certain "star gangs," who received steady work and relatively high incomes, and a large number of other workers who enjoyed much less employment. This latter group also competed for work with "occasionals," who sometimes obtained favored treatment. Competition for work under the shape-up gives hiring foremen enormous power which they sometimes exploit to collect kickbacks (bribes) from workers.

Substitution of a union controlled hiring hall with a rotation system

[9] C. P. Larrowe, "Shape-Up and Hiring Hall," University of California Press, Berkeley and Los Angeles, 1955, Chapters 4 and 5.

[10] This is an oversimplified version of the actual hiring process, but it is roughly accurate. For details see Larrowe, op. cit., Chapter 5.

[11] The hiring halls have had some difficulty under the Taft-Hartley Act, but are permitted to function providing they do not discriminate against nonunion workers.

transfers control over hiring from the employer's representative, the hiring foreman, to the union membership which establishes the rules under which jobs are allocated to workers.   The employer must accept the workers sent or complain via the grievance system.   The workers previously receiving steady work are (economically) injured to the benefit of the others.

It is worth noting that in West Coast hiring halls, the relatively easy jobs are not distributed either randomly or on the basis of favoritism; instead they are saved for the injured and the aged.[12]   This results in favoring the older at the expense of the younger and stronger workers; this is a very frequent consequence of the marked tendency for unions to use their power over job allocation to favor older as against younger workers via the "seniority principle."

Another interesting system of union job control is that of the Printers (International Typographical Union, ITU).   Under this system a job becomes virtually the property of the worker holding it.[13]   The ITU requires[14] that its members work only in union shops, that in such shops the foremen must be union members, and that only foremen have the right to hire and fire.   The union's position is that competency is a matter solely for the foreman to determine.   The employer can affect the hiring process only by his (unchallenged) right to select his foreman.

This state of affairs places great power in the hands of the foreman; and, at one time, the foreman had practically unlimited power to hire and fire.   However, as the result of a prolonged battle within the union,[15] the foremen have had their power greatly reduced until they can interfere with the mechanics of the seniority system only for "cause," and such interference may be challenged before a union tribunal which functions as a grievance-settling agency.[16]

In each establishment (of sufficient size) there is a list of permanent positions and their holders, as well as a list of substitutes.   The substitutes are ranked in order of "priority" (i.e., seniority) in the establishment; that is, the substitute on the list for the longest period has the

---

[12] Larrowe, *op. cit.,* pp. 141–142.

[13] A. R. Porter, Jr., *Job Property Rights,* Kings Crown Press, New York, 1954, has a fairly full description of ITU laws pertaining to job control.

[14] The national ITU, unlike most unions, imposes "laws," binding upon its locals, governing working conditions.   Locals may not arbitrate or negotiate about such laws; they must enforce them by strikes (backed by the national organization). The ability of the locals to enforce these laws is, of course, a reflection of their bargaining power; the laws are not adopted until most locals feel they can enforce them.

[15] See Porter, *op. cit.,* Chapter III.   This battle, as Porter shows (p. 28), is related to the origin of the two-party system in the ITU, mentioned on p. 132.

[16] Grievances thus become disputes between union members (the foremen and the worker) to be settled by a union tribunal.

most priority, etc.   When a permanent position becomes open, it is filled by the substitute with the most priority, and the others move up.   Any member of the union may get at the bottom of the substitute list in any shop unless the foreman objects for "cause," in which case the matter may be appealed to the local.

The priority system gives the man holding a permanent position a *property right* to that position.   If he wishes to absent himself for a union-approved reason, he may *choose* a substitute from the list of registered substitutes in the shop to fill in until he returns.   The printer's property rights in his job are subject to union laws.   Perhaps the most important of these is a ban on overtime work;[17] the purpose of the ban is, admittedly, to minimize the inequality in earnings between "regulars" and substitutes (who perform the overtime work).

HIRING CONTROL AND ITS CONSEQUENCES.   The printers and longshoremen are two rather extreme, though not unique, examples of situations where the employer has virtually no power to select his new employees.   However, in many closed shop situations, an employer may hire any union member he wishes.   But, even in these cases, employers often find it convenient to ask the union to send workmen.   Naturally the union office is always glad to have jobs at its disposal.

Union policy concerning hiring through the union office varies greatly from one case to another.   At one extreme, there are unions which are indifferent to the issue; there are intermediate cases where the union informally encourages hiring through its offices; then there are unions that insist upon complete control of hiring.[18]   Where an employer, whatever his reason, hires through the union, the process is somewhat as follows: An employer wishing to hire workmen telephones the local union and asks for a specific number of men for a certain type of job.   The business agent, or someone responsible to him, fills the order.   Depending upon local union policy and the employer's relations with the union, the employer may be able to reject unsatisfactory job candidates or even to specify the men he wants; in other cases, he may have to accept whomever he is sent.

Clearly the union functionary who decides which men are to be sent out on jobs may exercise a great deal of power over both union members and employers.   This power has sometimes been used to build a political machine within the union, to collect bribes from employers and kickbacks from workers, to practice nepotism, etc.   However, when jobs are scarce at the going terms of employment, *whoever* distributes them has power

[17] If overtime is performed, an equal amount of regular time must be taken off so that substitutes may have their fair share of employment.

[18] See S. H. Slichter, *Union Policies and Industrial Management,* Brookings Institution, Washington, D.C., 1941, pp. 83–90.

which may be exploited. For example, job selling by foremen was a well known phenomenon in the United States before the 1930's.

Arbitrary power to distribute employment is likely to be resented wherever it appears. Worker rebellion against the shape-up was a major factor in the big longshore strikes (on the West Coast) in 1934;[19] it was also an important stimulus to the development of an antiforeman's faction in ITU which later compelled the adoption of the present seniority system.[20]

Under an effective closed shop (i.e., where nonunion employees cannot be used) the labor supply of the given type of workers is controlled by the admission rules. Closed shop unions sometimes reserve employment opportunities for their old members by rigidly limiting the number of new members admitted. This has lead to situations where the demand exceeds the supply of union members. To accommodate employers and prevent them from looking for nonunion help, unions sometime issue "permit cards." These cards grant nonunion workers permission to work on union jobs. They are issued for a fee and only for short periods.[21]

The continuing use of permit cards raises an issue concerning the union's admission policies. It suggests that the union is deliberately excluding men competent to hold jobs in order to insure the employment and income of the present members.[22] This raises questions as to the fairness of the union's admission policy to outsiders (see pp. 348–356). It may also, in the long run, endanger the ability of the union to maintain job control, as the permit card holders often resent their exclusion from the union and accept nonunion employment, whenever they find it advantageous. In general, it is the local unions which are most inclined to restrict membership, sometimes (where national union law permits) even preventing transfers of members from other locals. National officers often point out the long-run dangers of such policies, but in local organizations member sentiment has often compelled exclusive admission policies, especially in the presence of unemployment.[23] In recent years, full em-

---

[19] Larrowe, *op. cit.,* Chapter 4.

[20] Porter, *op. cit.,* Chapter III.

[21] In principle, permit cards are issued only when there are not enough union members available to meet the current demand for labor. Probably this principle is adhered to in most cases. However, there have been a number of instances where union officers have issued permit cards despite member unemployment; in some cases this was due to bribery by the permit card holders, or to the desire of the officers to pocket the permit card fee (which should of course revert to the union treasury). See Slichter, *op. cit.,* pp. 68–71.

[22] It also suggests that the union wage scale is, at least for the moment, less than the maximum compatible with full employment of the members.

[23] Slichter, *op. cit.,* pp. 68–71.

ployment has considerably reduced the practice of exclusion, but its possibility remains.

Layoff Policy

Unionization is compatible with a wide variety of degrees of employer control of the selection of *new* employees.   However, the overwhelming majority of collective bargaining contracts provide that once an employee has served beyond the probationary period he must be laid off only in accordance with a specified procedure.   "Layoffs" occur when a reduction in a firm's rate of production reduces the number of workers it requires. Dismissal under these circumstances is presumed to be only temporary; frequently, the worker is told when to report back for work.

By far the most common procedure for regulating layoffs is *seniority*. Where layoffs are in order of seniority (or, more properly, in reverse order of seniority), the worker continuously employed for the shortest period of time, the worker with least seniority, must be laid off first.   The effect of seniority is to concentrate temporary unemployment and reduced earnings on the least senior workers, who are usually the youngest.   The older workers, of course, find such a procedure to their advantage.

The operation of seniority in layoffs is roughly as follows: When a worker is notified that he is to be laid off, he may "bump" any other worker in his seniority unit (job, department, plant, etc.) with less seniority; i.e., he may demand such person's job.   The "bumped" worker may, in turn, bump another worker with still less seniority, and so on. Where seniority is "broad," this may involve a number of shifts of workers from one department of a plant to another, as the bumping process works itself out.[24]

The idea of seniority, which favors long-service workers, seems to appeal to something fairly basic in our system of ethical beliefs.   Consequently, the *principle* of seniority is rarely challenged, even by those who suffer from its application.   However, its mode of application is sometimes debated with considerable vigor.

The application of the seniority principle is all-important in determining the degree of employment security a worker with a specific amount of seniority (i.e., length of continuous employment) actually has.   For example, there is the question of how "broad" seniority is to be.   Job-wide seniority protects a worker only against others holding the same job; a worker with ten years seniority may be laid off while another with only two years seniority, but on a different job, remains on the pay roll.   The

[24] A good description of the operation of the seniority system is G. W. Brooks and Sara Gamm, "The Practice of Seniority in Southern Pulp Mills," *Monthly Labor Review,* July 1955, pp. 757–765.

broader the application of seniority, the more employment security[25] possessed by senior workers; i.e., department-wide seniority gives more employment security than job-wide seniority, and plant-wide seniority gives still more.

The operation of seniority is obviously not aimed at maintaining productive efficiency. And, while seniority has not usually conflicted with efficiency to an intolerable degree, some rather desperate situations have arisen.[26] Employers rather naturally try to minimize the awkward consequences of seniority by striving to retain as much freedom as possible in its application. This is not because of opposition to the seniority principle as such, but because of a desire to exercise their discretion in the laying off process.

In the absence of reason to the contrary, employers will usually extend employment preference to senior workers. However, "reason to the contrary" is often a difference in ability, energy, adaptability to new processes, etc. Frequently younger employees are preferable, on these grounds, to older ones with greater seniority. Employers, or foremen, may also discriminate among workers by retaining personal favorites and/or consistently laying off those whom they dislike. Not infrequently, they have tried to discriminate against union members; this, of course, has given unions an important reason for insisting upon strict adherence to seniority in layoffs.

In bargaining about layoff policy, the employer's preferred position is usually "merit equal, seniority governs"; i.e., the more meritorious employee is retained irrespective of seniority which enters only when "merit" is equal. The union is likely to prefer "seniority equal, merit governs"; i.e., the senior worker is always kept, merit entering only where seniority is equal. Whichever formula concerning merit and seniority is adopted, its actual operation depends upon the grievance procedure. The factual question of the relative merits of the workers, where merit enters, is subject to negotiation and, in the event of disagreement, the grievance machinery. The tendency has been for seniority to become the dominant factor in layoff policy, with merit being secondary.

One reason why employers have acquiesced in this development is that it is frequently agreed (in the contract) that, in each department of the firm, 5 or 10 per cent of the workers may be selected by the employer for exemption from layoff. In this way, a firm is able to hold on to its most desirable employees, despite seniority factors. The union often obtains

---

[25] That is, the greater the number of workers who must be laid off before he can be separated from the payroll.

[26] Clark Kerr and L. H. Fisher, "Effect of Environment and Administration on Job Evaluation," *Harvard Business Review,* May 1950, pp. 77–96, give an excellent illustration of the operation of plant-wide seniority under unfavorable conditions.

"superseniority" for its shop steward, frequently with management approval, as experienced and efficient shop stewards greatly facilitate the operation of the grievance machinery.

Management generally desires to make the operation of seniority as narrow as possible, but the union is inclined to prefer broad seniority units. The result is a compromise, the terms of which vary from one contract to another. Where the seniority unit has very appreciable width (i.e., includes workers performing a variety of jobs), it is imperative that senior workers be able to handle the jobs of the juniors they "bump." Because of this it is usually specified that a senior worker must be competent at a new job. But whether he will be competent cannot be foretold; he must be given a "fair chance" to learn the job. Hence there is a trial period, frequently lasting 30 days. When a sizeable reduction in force occurs, a large number of workers may be learning new jobs simultaneously, with the result that operating efficiency may, for a time, suffer seriously.

By and large, seniority in layoffs has not created intolerable inefficiency in production. And it has the positive virtue, especially important where layoffs are for long periods, of protecting the older worker who is least likely to be able to secure another job (see pp. 294–295). Consequently, seniority in layoffs represents a kind of automatic job insurance for the older worker; in effect, his seniority is an asset that he has accumulated during his working life.[27]

Of course, the obverse side of seniority for the older worker is job insecurity for the younger; at times, this has been bitterly protested. Where its consequences are very strongly resented, or it is impractical, seniority in layoffs is supplemented or replaced by *work sharing*. Work sharing may be accomplished in a variety of ways, e.g., by requiring all workers to work short weeks (and take proportional wage cuts), by requiring all workers to skip work one or two weeks per month, etc. Work sharing is more or less automatic under a hiring hall arrangement such as the longshoremen's, but it has also occurred in garment making, printing, and elsewhere, especially in industries where seasonal fluctuations in demand are important.[28]

Work sharing and layoffs on the basis of seniority are not mutually exclusive. Sometimes work sharing occurs only until the work week is reduced to a specified number of hours; thereafter further reductions in

---

[27] When firms are merged, or plants combined, the seniority problems become acute and the controversies bitter. The problems posed to the ITU by the merger of newspapers are discussed by Porter, *op. cit.*, pp. 32–34.

[28] Slichter, *op. cit.* pp. 112 *et seq.* T. C. Fichandler in *Employment and Wages in the United States,* Twentieth Century Fund, New York, 1953, p. 280, states that as of 1947–1948, about 25 per cent of all union contracts analyzed by the BLS contained clauses implying some form of work sharing.

employment are met by layoffs in reverse order of seniority.[29] The idea seems to be that when weekly earnings fall to what a man might earn by odd jobs or obtain via unemployment insurance, no further reduction in earnings should be tolerated, and some workers should cease to claim part of the scarce job opportunities.   As might be expected, senior workers tend to oppose work sharing and junior ones to favor it.

Promotions, Shift-Preference, Etc.

An employer may discriminate among his workers not only by subjecting them to different risks of layoff but also by favoring them in promotion.   Obviously, workers usually wish to be promoted to better-paying jobs with more prestige.   The employer wishes to control this process; the union is anxious that it should not be used to discriminate against union members or to assist personal favorites of foremen.   Management argues for a free hand in promotion in order to reward merit and encourage effort; the union pushes for seniority to reward loyal service and prevent favoritism.   The issues and arguments are analogous to those concerning seniority in layoffs and need not be repeated.   (Promotion to supervisory positions is usually made solely on the basis of management selection).   In about three-quarters of all union-management agreements, seniority is a factor in determining promotions, but, in about half of these, it is applicable only when "merit is equal."   The union enters the promotion process only through grievance proceedings.[30]

Seniority may also play a role in the allocation of vacation times, choice of shifts (when more than one is worked), choice of overtime, work, etc. However, the seniority unit is not always the same for layoffs and the various other purposes for which seniority may be used.

WAGES, HOURS, AND FRINGE BENEFITS

The contract terms that govern the compensation of union members are usually quite complicated and are becoming more so with the passage of time.   In the early days of unionism, the wage terms of a contract were little more than a posted list of hourly or daily rates for specific jobs. Nowadays, however, all sorts of collateral or "fringe" benefits that employees receive are governed by contract terms.

It is important to remember that irrespective of the form in which the employer agrees to pay benefits to his workers, they represent a cost to him.   As there is always an upper limit to the cost per hour of labor that an employer can bear, what he pays his employers in one form (e.g., pre-paid medical care) reduces the compensation that can be paid in another

---

[29] Fichandler, *op. cit.* p. 280.
[30] *Ibid.*

form (e.g., hourly wages). In other words, to get more benefits in one form, a union must (usually) sacrifice benefits it could have obtained in some other. To be sure, employers are not entirely indifferent as to whether they pay a dollar in wage increases or (say) give it to a pension fund. However, employers are usually willing to trade concessions on one item of compensation for union concessions on others if the result would be to lower appreciably the cost of an hour of labor.

The most important economic issue to the employer in a contract is the size of the "package," i.e., the increase in dollar cost he must incur per man-hour of labor hired under the contract. The signing of major contracts usually touches off a great deal of discussion as to the size of the resulting "package," i.e., whether it represented a 15 or a 20 cent per hour increase, etc. Because collective bargaining contracts are complicated, it is not always easy to compute precisely the size of a given package. But, irrespective of this, the estimated size of the package is crucial to the employer.

The union, too, is concerned with the size of the package; but more than the employer it is concerned with its composition. In recent years, unions have tended to demand an increasing share of the contract package in the form of "fringe" benefits. Fringe benefits usually include paid holidays and vacations, health, welfare, and pension benefits, guaranteed annual wage plans, paid sick leave, call-in payments, etc. In short, "fringe benefits" include all those payments made by an employer on behalf of a worker other than those paid directly as wages. The growing importance of fringe benefits is indicated by the fact that in 1940–1954, supplementary wage payments[31] increased 36 per cent more than total wage payments; in 1954 such supplementary wage payments totalled over $11,700 million.

The growth of fringe benefits began during World War II, when the War Labor Board permitted various "fringes" to be introduced although it forbade direct wage increases. Because of this, fringe benefits became a popular device for attracting and keeping workers. A second factor that stimulated demands for fringe benefits was the fact that in the years 1943–1948, John L. Lewis obtained such benefits as "traveling time" and a "welfare and retirement fund," for the United Mine Workers. The wide publicity attendant upon Lewis' bargaining made all union members conscious of these benefits, while his determined attempts to regain a commanding position in American Labor made union leaders determined to "keep up with Lewis."

Yet a further factor that created interest in fringe benefits has been the growing awareness of perquisites given to executives. Unions argue that

[31] That is, employer payments to social security funds, private pension, health and welfare funds, etc.

if the stockholders provide pensions, paid vacations, etc. for officials, they should, in all fairness, provide them for hourly paid workers also. This contention is difficult to resist, especially before mediators, arbitrators, and ultimately, public opinion.

Employers have frequently resisted the introduction of specific benefits on grounds of "principle." That is, they have fought not only to limit the size of the package but also to control its contents. This attitude may have been inspired partly by the realization that executive benefits could not be distributed so lavishly as before if they were to serve as a basis for similar benefits for hourly paid workers. Also, it was feared that, once it was granted that pensions, employment guarantees, etc. were proper concerns of management, it would be difficult to avoid making adequate provision for each benefit with a resulting tendency toward increasing the whole package. Finally, it is likely that, in many cases, management simply felt that the "principle" of providing a particular benefit was (quite apart from the amount involved) of value to unions and shrewdly proceeded to barter the "principle" for a smaller package than would otherwise have been obtainable.

The economic factors that determine the size of the package have been partly discussed already (see pp. 164–168); they will be discussed further in Chapters 12 and 16. In this chapter we shall merely describe the more common ingredients of the various "packages" that emerge from collective bargaining.

Wages

All collective bargaining agreements cover wages. Wages are sometimes paid by time, so much per hour or per week, sometimes by result, so much per unit of output, and sometimes by a combination of both. That is, it is frequently specified (in effect) that workers on a particular job are to receive a certain hourly minimum, and in addition "incentive payments" (which depend on output) when output exceeds a certain minimum rate. Where wages vary with output, the exact relation between them is specified in great detail, both in the contract and in the interpretations made via the grievance machinery.

In collective bargaining agreements, the wage rate (or range of rates) is determined for each job covered by the contract. In some cases, one rate is prescribed for each job; in others, the wage rate may vary within a specified range, depending upon the merit and experience of the job holder. As can well be imagined, job holders frequently demand increases in the rates for their particular jobs. As a rule, it is impossible to satisfy all of these demands, and the union must select those it will support. This implies sacrificing one worker's demands in order to support another's.

In bargaining, unions always try, other things being equal, to raise wage rates. Employers tend to resist this demand. However, some unions are prepared to sacrifice other demands for wage rate increases whereas others place a different evaluation upon their various objectives. For example, unions whose members are subject to grave risks of unemployment are usually willing to trade wage rate gains for additional job security. However, any given union is likely, during a period of full employment coupled with inflation, to be more anxious than usual for wage increases. Conversely, during a depression with unemployment and falling consumer prices, a union is likely to be unusually preoccupied with maximizing employment opportunities and controlling their distribution.

Since 1950, it has been rather widely accepted that wages must rise more or less proportionately with the cost of living. Consequently, it has become quite common to "gear" wage rates to the cost of living via "escalator clauses"; this is discussed on pp. 413–415.

Hours

In the early days of the factory system, the work day was extremely long, twelve hours being typical; six day weeks were the rule, and seven day weeks not unknown (see Table 2.1). Consequently, workers were extremely anxious for shorter hours in order to have more time for rest and relaxation. However, they were unwilling to accept reductions in their daily wages proportional to the reduction in hours demanded. That is, they demanded (in effect) an increase in hourly wages coupled with a reduction in the working day. As employers resisted such demands the early struggles of trade unions frequently turned upon the ten hour day and, after the Civil War, the eight hour day.

Success in reducing the working day came slowly and gradually. It was not until 1915–1920 that the eight hour day became really common in American industry, while the half-holiday on Saturday came somewhat later (in the 1920's). Forty hours became the conventional work week only in the 1930's, as a combined result of the depression-born anxiety to spread employment and various New Deal measures, especially the National Industrial Recovery Act of 1933 and the Fair Labor Standards Act (FLSA) of 1938, see pp. 503 et seq.

In part, the demand for a shorter work week has been a demand for more leisure. However, in recent years it has been primarily an indirect method by which unions have sought to spread employment and to raise hourly earnings. Unions in various trades have long feared that technological progress or "automation," as it is now called, would reduce employment opportunities for their members by enabling each one to produce more per hour.[32] To prevent or reduce the (expected) un-

---

[32] The economic reasoning behind this contention is discussed on pp. 435–441.

employment, they have urged spreading the work among existing employees through a shorter work week, with no reduction in weekly wages. During the depression of the 1930's, these demands and contentions received support from a wide section of the community with the result that the "Codes of Fair Competition," established under the National Industrial Recovery Act (NIRA) of 1933, contained severe restrictions on the length of the work week; usually they limited the work week to five eight-hour days.   After NIRA was declared unconstitutional in 1935, agitation developed for a statute specifically regulating wages and hours.   This resulted in the Fair Labor Standards Act of 1938 which sought to spread employment by penalizing employers who hired individual workers for more than 40 hours per week, by compelling the payment of "time and a half for overtime."

In the depressed economy of the 1930's, the principal effect of the penalty rates on overtime would have been to spread available work among a larger number of workers.   But since 1941, its major result has been to make time and a half for overtime (i.e., hours in excess of the 40 hour week) automatic, instead of requiring unions to bargain for it. Whether weekly wages are higher because of the legal requirement of overtime pay is difficult to judge.   Possibly straight time rates might have been higher if overtime rates had begun at 44 instead of 40 hours or if the overtime rate was "time and a quarter" or "time and a third" instead of "time and a half."   However, this is obviously a debatable matter.

In the past few years workers in manufacturing, notably in automobiles, have become concerned about the possibility of "automation" reducing job opportunities.   To prevent this from causing unemployment, they have commenced agitation to spread employment by means of a 35 hour week, with no corresponding wage reduction.   To obtain a shorter work week they will have to forego (weekly) wage increases they might otherwise have obtained.   However, if they want a 35 hour week badly enough, they may be able to obtain it in exchange for other (foregone) benefits.

Employer opposition to a shorter work week has sometimes resulted from ignorance of the effect of fatigue on worker output.   One student has concluded that reducing the work day, in usual occupations, from twelve to ten hours has almost always increased *daily* output; reducing it from ten to eight hours so raises hourly output as to keep daily output constant; and further reductions, below eight hours, raise hourly output but insufficiently to keep daily output from falling.[33]   The relation between fatigue and worker productivity is very complicated and statements

[33] P. Sargent Florence, *The Economics of Fatigue and Unrest,* Henry Holt, New York, 1924, pp. 348–349.   See also "Hours of Work and Output," *Bureau of Labor Statistics Bulletin* 917, Government Printing Office, Washington, D.C., 1947.

such as this are subject to many qualifications. Nonetheless, there is good reason to believe that employers have sometimes injured themselves, as well as their workmen, by resisting reductions in the length of the work week. This statement applies more to the period before World War I, when the work week was very long, than to the period since 1935. Whatever the case for further reducing the work week, there is no general presumption that it will increase productivity per man-hour.

However, employer opposition to a reduced work week has not always resulted from mere ignorance. Often they feared that a decreased work week would, indirectly, cause an increase in hourly wage rates. Also, when they paid their workers *entirely* on the basis of output, they had no concern with increasing hourly productivity through a shorter work week; diminished output per man-hour called forth proportionately diminished hourly wage payments. The very real interest of *society* in the length of the work week is considered on pp. 502–505.

Work Rules

Almost all collective bargaining agreements impose a number of restrictions on employer practices governing working conditions. These "work rules" have different purposes; some of them have more than one end in view. One major objective of such rules is worker safety.

SAFETY. For industries where employment involves risk to life and limb, unions are understandably prone to demand that the employer make all possible provision against these hazards. In the 19th and early 20th centuries, employers were often ignorant and indifferent toward safety measures. Frequently, they opposed union pressure and legislation aimed at compelling the creation of safer working conditions.[34] In so doing, they were short-sighted; it has turned out that the cost reduction resulting from a lowered rate of accidents often far exceeds the cost of the necessary safety devices. As a result, most present-day employers are, in their own interest, as much concerned with safety as their workers.[35] The risk of industrial accident has been greatly reduced since the beginning of the 20th century as employers have become more concerned with safety measures.[36]

However, in some industries and occupations it is impossible, or very expensive, to reduce physical hazard to the bare minimum; in these cases

---

[34] Commons, *et. al., History of Labor in the United States,* Vol. III, Chapter XIX.

[35] For example, an employer's premium on the insurance policies required under Workmen's Compensation Laws (see pp. 491–492) varies with the accident rate of his employees.

[36] B. S. Sanders, "Protection Against Work Injuries," Chapter 16 in *Employment and Wages in the United States.*

(mining, longshoring, driving of dynamite trucks, heavy construction, etc.), the demands of union and employer continue to conflict over safety measures.

MAKE WORK.   The work rules that pertain to safety cannot be rigidly separated from those serving other purposes.   A requirement limiting the rate of speed of a machine may be demanded in the name of safety and may be relevant to it.   However, it will also tend to restrict output per worker and is often desired primarily for that reason.   It has sometimes happened that work rules originally intended as safety devices become obsolete for their original purpose but are retained, at the union's insistence, because they tend to make additional work for union members.

"Make work" rules are, in essence, rules which require the use of a greater number of man-hours of labor, for a given amount of output, than are actually "needed."   Such rules have several objectives, the most important of which is to create extra jobs.   It is in the industries and trades where employment opportunities are scarce, or declining, that one finds most of the serious attempts to "make work."   Another objective is to reduce the required work pace so that the slower workers (especially the older ones) can meet accepted work standards.   Here, considerations of health and safety merge with those of making work, i.e., what is a safe pace for a young worker may endanger the health of an older one.   Of course, some young workers like to limit work speeds in order to make their jobs "soft," and it is often alleged that this is the main reason for union work rules.   But, in fact, this particular reason for output restriction is probably less important than the others mentioned.

There are a number of ways in which work rules have created additional jobs.   During the 1930's, the Musicians' union required radio stations (in some cities) to hire stand-by orchestras when they rebroadcast music from a network.[37]   The Musicians' and Stagehands' unions have established rules concerning the minimum number of workers that must be used on specific jobs.   In order to make work, the Railroad Brotherhoods have succeeded in controlling the size of train crews and the length of freight trains.   They have achieved this result partly through collective bargaining and partly by "full crew" laws that they have successfully sponsored in a number of states.   The Building Trades unions, by controlling the methods and "quality" of work done have also restricted output per worker.[38]

Make-work rules frequently seem unreasonable to outsiders who are unfamiliar with their background.   No small amount of legislative hostility toward union practices comes from persons angered by apparent attempts to sabotage productive efficiency and subsidize lazy workers.

[37] Taft-Hartley declares such acts to be unfair labor practices, see p. 248.

[38] The best discussion of these practices is still Slichter, *op. cit.* Chapter VI.

However, it is often not appreciated that these practices are mainly devices to protect the jobs of union members in the face of a declining market for their services and that the workers who benefit most are the older ones who would find it most difficult to obtain new jobs. This is not to defend these policies but to explain why they have been adopted.

Make-work policies are analogous to crop-restriction devices of the Department of Agriculture on behalf of farmers, "fair trade" legislation to benefit small retailers, etc. All are attempts to protect the economic interests of certain producer groups at the expense of the users of their output. There are grave economic objections to any of these practices (see pp. 354–356); however, those of unions are not, a priori, any "worse" than the others mentioned.

Another common misconception on this subject is that output restriction is the policy of the union organization and is imposed on the members. Occasionally this may be true, but often it is just the reverse. Studies both of unionized and of nonunionized workers reveal that groups of workers tend to develop standards as to what constitutes an appropriate work rate; these standards are imposed, by social pressure, upon new members of the group.

These work rate standards usually imply a rate of output well below the maximum obtainable.[39] The rationale of these standards varies: sometimes it is a desire to avoid work, sometimes a desire to avoid reductions in incentive rates;[40] at other times it reflects a desire to make the job last for fear of unemployment when it is finished.

Union organizations accept and absorb these pre-existing attitudes toward output restriction. The contractual work rules unions demand are, to a considerable extent, attempts to codify these attitudes and make it possible to use union tribunals to punish workers who violate them. Unions also use work rules to increase employment opportunities and to control their distribution among the membership. However, the fact of output restriction by workers predates unionism, and is independent of it. Even in unionized establishments, it is likely that informal agreements among workers "in the shop" do more to control output than contractual clauses.

Output restriction, whatever its source, penalizes (at least) some of the workers engaging in it as well as their employers. For, by curbing out-

[39] The most famous studies of output restriction among unorganized workers are S. B. Mathewson, *Restriction of Output Among Unorganized Employees,* Viking Press, New York, 1931, and F. J. Roethlisberger and W. J. Dickson, *Management and the Worker,* Harvard University Press, 1939. An excellent recent case study of worker attitudes toward restriction is Donald Roy, "Quota Restriction and Goldbricking in a Machine Shop," *American Journal of Sociology,* March 1952, pp. 427–452.

[40] See pp. 394–396.

put per hour, they raise wage cost per unit of product. Had wage costs not been raised, all or part of the increase might have been captured in wage increases either through bargaining or higher incentive earnings.[41] The output restriction is intended to create more hours of employment and *may* do so, although this is not necessarily the result. But, in any case, restricting output involves redistributing earnings and employment from those who would have worked in any event to those who would have been (at least partially) unemployed had it not been for the restriction.

Holidays and Paid Vacations

In a growing number of contracts, provision is made for paid holidays. These usually number from six to eight per year, including Christmas, New Year's Day, Labor Day, Memorial Day, July 4th, etc. Paid holidays for manual workers have become common only since 1940. But, by 1952–1953, 83 per cent of all workers (covered in the Bureau of Labor Statistics survey of collective agreements) had some paid holidays, and 79 per cent had six or more. Where it is necessary to operate the plant on these holidays, the employees who work are usually paid bonus rates ranging from two to three times their normal rate of pay.[42] From the economic standpoint, the demand for paid holidays is simply a bargaining technique for obtaining more leisure without a reduction in wages. Much the same remarks can be made concerning paid vacations, premium pay for Saturday and Sunday work, etc., which are becoming increasingly common and generous.[43] Pay for time spent in washing up, cleanup, and changing clothes is also becoming more prevalent, as is paid leave for jury duty, sickness, military service, and death in the family. In 1954, 80 per cent of all workers studied were also guaranteed a minimum payment (usually four hours wages) for reporting for work (unless duly notified not to report), irrespective of whether there was any work available.[44]

Health, Insurance, and Benefit Plans

In 1945, only about half a million workers were covered by either a (private) health and insurance or a pension plan for which the employer paid wholly or in part. But by early 1954, "at least 11,290,000 workers were covered by some kind of health and insurance plan under collective bargaining agreements."[45] That is, about 70 per cent of all workers under

[41] See pp. 394–395.

[42] "Labor-Management Contract Provisions, 1953," *Bureau of Labor Statistics Bulletin* 1166, pp. 8–13.

[43] *Ibid.*, pp. 1–7.

[44] "Labor-Management Contract Provisions, 1954," *Bureau of Labor Statistics Bulletin,* 1181, 1955.

[45] E. K. Rowe, "Health, Insurance and Pension Plans in Union Contracts," *Monthly Labor Review,* September 1955, pp. 993–1000. This section is based on the material in this article.

collective bargaining agreements were under such programs. These plans are more common among manufacturing firms then elsewhere. Seven per cent of all workers under private pensions plans and 62.1 per cent of those under health and insurance plans made no contribution to their financing (i.e., they were financed entirely by the employer); the remaining plans were financed partly by the worker and partly by the employer. Since 1950, there has been a trend toward complete financing by the employer.

Almost all of the aforementioned 11,290,000 workers were covered by a health and insurance plan, but only 63 per cent of them were covered by a pension plan. This is due to the substantially greater cost involved in a pension plan which makes employers more reluctant to undertake them.

The most common benefit provided under health and insurance plans is life insurance; however, hospitalization, surgical, accident and sickness, accidental death and dismemberment, and medical benefits are often provided as well. It is becoming increasingly common to provide benefits (especially medical, surgical, and hospitalization) to a worker's dependents and to continue some benefits (typically life insurance, hospitalization, medical and surgical) for retired workers.

It is to be emphasized that the benefits discussed in this section are entirely paid for by the worker and/or his employer and do not involve government funds. However, pension plans have frequently been coordinated with Federal Social Security, and there are demands for a Federal health insurance program, see p. 493.

Guaranteed Annual Wage

The guaranteed annual wage made its first real progress as a common "fringe benefit" in 1955. It is not, as yet, very widespread, covering perhaps 1 to 1¼ million workers. Its pros and cons are considered on pp. 480–484.

Legislators, newspaper columnists, etc. frequently discuss the propriety of wage earners receiving one fringe benefit or another without considering the interrelation of all fringes, wages, work rules, etc., as part of a package. The reader should not make this mistake. Generally speaking, any fringe benefit a union obtains for its members it "purchases" by foregoing wage increases or improvements in other fringe benefits that it might otherwise have obtained.

DISCUSSION QUESTIONS

1. The Taft-Hartley Act [Section 8b(6)] declares it an unfair labor practice for a union "to cause or attempt to cause an employer" to pay for services that are not performed. This provision is aimed at the more obvious forms of make-work rules.

(a) Do you think such a provision can be enforced?

(b) Assuming it can be enforced, discuss whether it is desirable.

(c) If it were enforced, which workers would be most likely to suffer?

2. (a) Discuss the pros and cons of some form of compulsory union membership.

(b) If there is to be some form of compulsory membership, under what conditions is the closed shop most appropriate? Under what conditions is the union shop best?

3. "The power of arbitrary discharge reduces the worker to a sycophant." "Without the power of arbitrary discharge, it is impossible to maintain productive efficiency." Discuss the conflicting viewpoints implied by these statements and the practical problems that result from the element of truth in both of them.

4. (a) In your opinion is seniority in layoffs usually preferable to (equal) work sharing among current employees?

(b) Under what circumstances would you prefer (equal) work sharing to layoff according to seniority?

5. "The more reluctant an employer is to grant a union shop the more anxious the union is to obtain it and vice versa." Explain.

Suggested Readings

Bakke, E. W., *Mutual Survival,* Harper & Brothers, New York, 1946.

Chamberlain, N. W. *The Union Challenge to Management Control,* Harper & Brothers, New York, 1948.

Cooke, M. L. and Philip Murray, *Organized Labor and Production,* Harper & Brothers, New York, 1948.

Florence, P. S., *Economics of Fatigue and Unrest,* Henry Holt, New York, 1924.

Mathewson, S. B. *Restriction of Output Among Unorganized Workers,* Viking Press, New York, 1931.

Palmer, G. L., *Union Tactics and Economic Change,* University of Pennsylvania Press, Philadelphia, 1932.

Roethlisberger, F. J. and W. J. Dickson, *Management and the Worker,* Harvard University Press, Cambridge, Mass., 1939.

Slichter, S. H., *Union Policies and Industrial Management,* Brookings Institute, Washington, D.C., 1941.

Toner, Rev. J. T., *The Closed Shop,* American Council on Public Affairs, Washington, D.C., 1944.

8 | Labor Unions and the Law

From their beginning, labor unions have operated under the watchful eye of the law courts. The attempts of workingmen to advance their economic interest by collective action have frequently run afoul of Common Law, Statute Law, or both. In recent years, especially since 1935, the courts have shown far more sympathy with the objectives of unions and a more permissive attitude toward their tactics than theretofore. However, during the greater part of American history, the intervention of the courts in labor disputes almost always worked to the disadvantage of the union involved. As a result, there developed among labor leaders a tradition of distrust for lawyers and legal procedures. Although this attitude is gradually disappearing, its traces are still discernible.

The suspicion that legal processes favored the employer was not altogether unfounded. The judiciary has been recruited largely from the ranks of successful lawyers who had many ties of economic interest and social connection with employers. And, quite apart from considerations of personal interest, the concept of economic processes held by employers, lawyers, and the educated classes in general implied the desirability of individual contracts, freely undertaken. Given these preconceptions, labor unions seemed either futile or pernicious; in either case, their activities did not merit encouragement.

Furthermore, even for persons sympathetic with the purposes of unionism, there was difficulty in reconciling some of the activities necessary to its proper functioning with those preconceptions of English Common Law that lie at the base of our legal system. Effective picketing obviously conflicts with the rights of the owner of an establishment to the free use thereof. Boycotts clearly do economic injury to the boycotted firm, has it no right to recover damages? Generally acceptable solutions to these and other problems of conflicting rights and interests have not yet been found. However, it is *now* usually agreed that whatever solution is adopted must permit unions some opportunity of exerting economic pressure on employers. But this has not always been so; many judicial decisions, and some legislation, reflected the belief that the rights of individual workers and employers to contract mutually satisfactory terms of employment transcended any interest of third parties (i.e., unions) and ought to be protected irrespective of the injury such protection might inflict (upon such third parties).

CONSPIRACY AND UNLAWFUL BEHAVIOR

Conspiracy

Among America's English heirlooms are its institutions of law and jurisprudence. Since the founding of the Republic, these institutions have been greatly modified by statutory law, but, in the early part of the 19th century, the influence of English law upon American courts was very strong. In the early 19th century, American state and local courts, on a number of occasions, declared that unions were "unlawful conspiracies at common law," on the ground that combinations of individuals to raise wages were illegal per se.[1]   The most famous of these cases, that of the Philadelphia cordwainers (shoemakers), occurred in 1806; but judicial decisions continued to threaten the very existence of unions until 1842. Indeed, the antiunion attitude of certain judges provoked street demonstrations during the 1830's.

Unlawful Objectives

In 1842, Chief Justice Shaw of the Massachusetts State Supreme Court ruled, in the famous case of Commonwealth vs. Hunt, that unions as such were legal and that the legality of a strike depended upon the legality of its object.[2]   After this decision, there were few attempts to prosecute unions as conspiracies.   However, courts did enjoin union action or award damages (to be paid by the union) to nonunion workers, or employers, on the ground that they had been injured by "unlawful" acts of the union. Whether a particular act was adjudged unlawful frequently depended upon the legality of the objective (allegedly) sought by the union committing the act.

After the Civil War, improvement of wages and hours was usually accepted as a lawful objective; but a closed or union shop was frequently declared unlawful.   "Lawfulness" did not usually depend upon statutes specifically enacted by legislatures to govern union activities but upon ju-

[1] C. O. Gregory, *Labor and the Law,* Revised Edition, W. W. Norton & Co., New York, 1949, Chapter I; Elias Lieberman, *Unions Before the Bar,* Harpers, New York, 1950, Chapter 1; Commons, *et. al., History of Labor in the United States,* Macmillan, New York, 1935, Vol. I, Chapter V and pp. 162–165.

[2] Gregory, *op. cit.,* pp. 27–30; Lieberman, *op. cit.,* Chapter 2.

dicial interpretation of statute (and common) law enacted or developed to deal with very different types of problems. Because the proper application of such law to union activities was a speculative matter on which competent legal opinions differed, the decision tended to vary with the judge. What was an unlawful objective to one judge was quite lawful to another; furthermore, there were different patterns of interpretation of similar laws in different states.[3]

Until the 1930's, the courts (both federal and state) imposed rather serious restraints both upon the objectives that unions might pursue and the tactics they might employ. However, during the 1930's and 1940's, the trend of judicial interpretation was toward permitting unions broad latitude with regard both to ends and means. This led to a legislative reaction which has, since 1939, seen the enactment of a large number of statutes aimed at restricting union activities. This legislation has frequently proscribed union security arrangements, especially the closed shop, and there have also been attempts (as in the Taft-Hartley Act) to outlaw make-work rules and various other union objectives. Such legislation creates a class of "unlawful" objectives, and unions striking or boycotting to obtain such objectives may be open to damage suits or prosecution.

It is impossible to object to such statutes as "judge made" law; they were enacted by state legislatures or Congress for the specific purpose of controlling union behavior. However, it is by no means certain that such legislation can obtain its objectives—granting, for the moment, their desirability. There is an inherent difficulty in outlawing any specific objective of unions or employers if the party desiring the objective is able to bribe or coerce the other into accepting it.[4] Once agreement is reached, the two parties can usually cooperate in innumerable ways to evade the purpose of the law; the evasion of the ban on the closed shop imposed by the Taft-Hartley Act (see p. 178) is an excellent illustration of this.

However, the fact that it may be difficult to enforce a legal ban upon a particular objective of collective bargaining does not mean that such legislation is completely without effect. The legislation compels would-be evaders to take the trouble of disguising their activities, which may be so irksome as to lead them to desist altogether. For example, legislation forbidding racial discrimination in hiring is notoriously difficult to enforce if there is determined opposition; however, the mere fact that some states have placed such legislation on the statute books and appointed boards to "enforce" it has (apparently) caused many employers

[3] Gregory, op. cit., Chapter III.
[4] This is analogous to the difficulty encountered in attempting to exclude certain subjects from collective bargaining, see pp. 180–183.

to alter their hiring policies simply to avoid trouble.[5]   Another illustration is the success of the Wagner Act in helping to curb employer discrimination against unionists.   A third example is the Taft-Hartley ban upon jurisdictional strikes (see pp. 246–247); public opinion so strongly favored this part of the law that unions have (apparently) feared to challenge it by wholesale evasion.[6]   Even the Taft-Hartley prohibition of the closed shop, despite numerous evasions, has made it more difficult of attainment and, in borderline situations, has probably tipped the balance against it.

There can, of course, be no valid general statement about the desirability of legislative restriction on union objectives.   One's attitude toward making the closed shop, hiring of "unnecessary" workers, etc. unlawful objectives of collective bargaining depends largely upon his attitude toward the objectives themselves.   However, it is well to consider the cost, trouble, and probable futility of enforcing restrictions on collective bargaining objectives that neither party is anxious to observe.

Unlawful Means—the Status of Picketing

The courts have restricted union activity not only with regard to objectives but also by circumscribing the means they might use.   Of course, there are no lawful methods for achieving unlawful ends, but even lawful objectives may not be sought (lawfully) by illegal means.   The arm of the courts has struck, at one time or another, at almost all of the devices by which unions bring economic pressure to bear upon employers. Strikes for lawful objectives might be tolerated, but picketing in support of such strikes frequently was forbidden.   The boycott, especially the secondary boycott, has also led a precarious legal existence; the secondary boycott has been made illegal, an unfair labor practice, by Taft-Hartley (see pp. 249–251).

As we shall discuss the boycott later (pp. 249–251), let us now concentrate upon the issues involved in picketing.   Picketing is the act of patrolling (by one of more persons) of a business establishment engaged in a labor dispute.   The pickets usually carry placards or signs proclaiming the existence of a labor dispute and urging others not to accept employment or patronize (as the case may be) the picketed establishment.

The value of picketing to the union that sponsors it derives partly from the publicity given to the dispute.   Many union sympathizers will refuse to patronize a business while it is engaged in a labor dispute, and it is important (to the union) that they should be informed, or reminded, of the existence of such a dispute.   Also, before the 1930's,[7] strike-

---

[5] See p. 464.

[6] See p. 79.

[7] Since 1937, the transportation of strike-breakers across a state line has been forbidden by federal law, i.e., by the Byrnes' Act.

breakers were often brought from a distance, unaware of the existence of a strike; sometimes, when informed of the facts, they refused to work.

When picketing serves truthfully to advertise the facts of a dispute, i.e., is done without violence, fraud, or libel, it is termed "peaceful" picketing. In large part, the legal status of picketing has turned upon its peacefulness. In principle, a picket's placard may contain a polysyllabic disquisition upon the issues at stake in the dispute, but in practice the printed words are usually short, and the spoken accompaniment highly uncomplimentary. In theory, the pickets are merely informing the public about a dispute, which information may or may not be acted upon at the hearer's discretion. In fact, picketing involves moral suasion which, given the circumstances, often implies the threat of physical violence. It is too much to say, as a judge once did, "there is and can be no such thing as peaceful picketing, any more than there can be chaste vulgarity, or peaceful robbing, or lawful lynching."[8] Nevertheless, picketing is often more than the mere expression of opinion.

The courts have been well aware of the coercive potentialities of picketing. Indeed, some courts have occasionally proscribed all picketing. However, by the 1920's most judges permitted peaceful picketing by employees of the business picketed;[9] "stranger picketing" was another matter (see below). But, to ensure that the picketing was peaceful, they sometimes restricted it to the point of emasculation; for example, in one case the U. S. Supreme Court permitted only one picket at each entrance to a struck plant.[10] Under such restraints, picketing is not likely to be effective. It is not enough that pickets be allowed to announce (verbally or by placard) the existence of a dispute and their opinion of its merits, but they must, if they are to have a chance of dissuading strike-breakers, have the opportunity of discussing the matter with them individually. This requires that the number of pickets be more or less equal to the number of strike-breakers.

But, realistically, "discussion" between pickets and strike-breakers is not likely to be peaceful. It is questionable that even members of the effete occupations (e.g., schoolteaching, law, medicine) could discuss dispassionately the merits of strike-breaking when their own jobs were at stake, and manual laborers are likely to come to the boiling point quite rapidly. This is, of course, well understood, and it is expected that a picket line, in the face of strike-breakers, will frequently lead to violence.

Recognition of this fact led judges of an earlier day to forbid picketing in order to preserve public order. Such a course may have preserved

[8] Lieberman, *op. cit.*, p. 116.

[9] Gregory, *op. cit.*, p. 338.

[10] American Steel Foundries Company vs. Tri-City Central Trades Council, January 1919. See Lieberman, *op. cit.*, pp. 110–115.

"peace," but it also broke strikes and put striking unions (especially where members were unskilled, and potential strike-breakers numerous) at a great disadvantage.   As judges became aware of the handicap unions faced unless free to picket and as they grew more sympathetic with union objectives, they greatly broadened (in the late 1930's and 1940's) the circumstances under which picketing would be lawful.   However, the courts have never held that nonpeaceful picketing would be lawful.

Physical obstruction to the entrance of a struck plant continues to be unlawful.   Indeed, the National Labor Relations Board and the courts held (in 1948–1950) that mass picketing and threats of violence constitute "coercion" in the sense proscribed by [Sections 7 and 8b (1)] of the Taft-Hartley Act.[11]   Thus if an employer is determined to use, and can obtain, strike-breakers, it is illegal for the union to use force to prevent him from so doing.

Fortunately, the practical importance of this problem has been much less since the end of World War II than previously, as employer attempts to break strikes have become much less frequent than before (see p. 76.)   It may be that we are evolving toward the state of affairs existing in Great Britain, Scandinavia, and Australia, where employers rarely (if ever) attempt to break strikes and will therefore be able to by-pass the difficult legal and social issues presented by picketing that borders on physical violence.

By the 1920's most *courts* were, in the absence of legislation to the contrary, prepared to permit peaceful picketing by employees.   But they were not at all reluctant to permit *legislatures* to restrict picketing to any degree that they saw fit.   However, in the 1930's a new doctrine emerged; in 1937 Justice Brandeis remarked that picketing might be one means by which unions exercised their right of free speech in stating their view of a labor dispute.[12]   In 1940, the United States Supreme Court carried this view several steps further and ruled that picketing, as such, was a form of free speech and, therefore, protected by the 1st and 14th amendments; accordingly it held an Alabama statute (which banned picketing) to be unconstitutional.[13]   Since 1940, the Supreme Court has continued to uphold the position that outright prohibitions on picketing are unconstitutional restrictions upon freedom of speech.   However, it has acquiesced in judicial decisions and state legislation which prevented picketing because its objective was unlawful[14] or even because its ob-

---

[11] See Fred Witney, *Government and Collective Bargaining,* Lippincott, New York, 1951, pp. 447–451.

[12] Senn vs. Tile Layers' Protective Union.   See Lieberman, *op. cit.,* Chapter 14 and Gregory, *op. cit.,* pp. 337 et seq.

[13] Thornhill vs. Alabama; see Lieberman, *op. cit.,* Chapter 17, pp. 341 et seq.

[14] See Gregory, *op. cit.,* pp. 250 et seq.; also J. Tannenhaus, "Picketing—Free Speech: The Growth of the New Law of Picketing from 1940 to 1952," *Cornell Law Quarterly,* Vol. XXXVIII, Fall, 1952.

jective was contrary to (what the court believed to be) public policy. As a result, the present legal status of picketing is uncertain; clearly some restraints may be imposed by legislatures and courts, but outright prohibition under all circumstances is unconstitutional. The Supreme Court has not specified the precise boundaries within which picketing must be permitted as free speech, and the Justices seem to have differing ideas on the matter. In brief, the issue is unsettled and its current status unclear.

The courts have frequently distinguished between picketing by employees and by "strangers." In many cases, where employee picketing has been permitted, stranger picketing has not. Stranger picketing has often been ruled unlawful on the ground that the pickets had no legitimate economic interest of their own in the dispute. That is, it was argued that the economic damage inflicted upon an employer by picketing his place of business could be justified only by the economic advantage of the picketers and "strangers" had no such interest. However, such a view ignored the fact that a union has a very genuine interest in dissuading persons from patronizing nonunion establishments in competition with unionized employers, even though none of its members are employed in the establishments being picketed. In general, attitudes toward the propriety of stranger picketing are not dependent upon legal niceties but upon approval or disapproval of union objectives.

INJUNCTIONS AND YELLOW-DOG CONTRACTS: THE NORRIS-LA GUARDIA ACT

Injunctions

In the vocabulary of unionists, "injunction" is an obscenity. Injunctions are court orders forbidding a person or persons to commit certain specified acts. Their unpopularity with unionists results from the fact that they were frequently used to disrupt strikes and organizing campaigns.

The use of injunctions in strike situations began in the 1880's but became common only after 1895. The significance of this date is that, in 1895, the U. S. Supreme Court upheld the order of the federal court in Chicago that was crucial in breaking the great railroad strike of 1894. (For violation of this injunction, Eugene Debs and other leaders of the short-lived American Railway Union served short jail terms.) Thereafter, injunctions became a common feature of important strikes[15] with consequent court actions, threats of jail sentences, etc.[16] In the first three

---

[15] Witte, *The Government in Labor Disputes*, McGraw-Hill Book Co., New York, 1932, p. 84, lists 1845 labor injunctions prior to 1931. Of these 150 were issued before 1900, 328 in 1900–1909, 446 in 1910–1919, and 921 between January 1, 1920 and May 1, 1930.

[16] Use of criminal statutes against strikers and labor leaders for alleged riots, acts of violence, etc. is a quite different matter than that discussed here.

decades of this century, strike actions would often have to be waged on two fronts, the legal and the economic.

Typically, the antiunion injunction was issued on the ground that the union and its officers were, or might be, committing injuries to the employer's business far exceeding (in value) their ability to make restitution in the event of a successful damage suit.[17] Formally, its purpose was simply to prevent the commission of allegedly injurious acts until the court could determine whether the union was acting within its legal rights. But the delay between the imposition of the injunction and the court's final ruling was the essence of the matter; during this interval, the strike was (usually) won or lost. The injunction process (against a union) often began with a request by the employer's lawyer for a "temporary restraining order." This order could be issued by a judge without a hearing and, if obeyed, served to halt union action until the hearing took place. The judge was obliged to set a date for the hearing at the same time he issued the restraining order, but, despite the crucial significance of the time element, in more than 75 per cent of the cases where temporary restraining orders were issued, the hearing occurred more than ten days after the date of the order.[18]

The purpose of the hearing was to decide whether a temporary injunction should be issued. At the hearing, both parties were represented by legal counsel, but there was no opportunity for argument or refutation of allegations made by the other side. There was a mere filing of affidavits and counteraffidavits with the judge exercising discretion in deciding which affidavits to believe. Usually he decided in favor of the employer's allegations and issued the injunction. Months later, at the hearing for a permanent injunction, the union would have the opportunity to refute the employer's affidavits. However, this was cold comfort; by that time the strike was over. The party securing the temporary injunction was compelled to post a bond which might be forfeited in the event a permanent injunction was not granted and the enjoined could show damages. But the amount of the bond was small relative to the employer's stake in defeating the strike; besides, the damages to a union from a lost strike are immeasurable and, in practice, noncollectible. Consequently unions did not often trouble to resist making the injunction permanent. Nor were employers greatly concerned, as the issue at stake, the strike, had usually been terminated long before the trial could be held.

The effect of injunctions upon union activity can be seen from the manner of their enforcement; violation of an injunction is contempt of court and punishable as such (by fines, imprisonment, or both). And,

[17] For more details see Gregory, *op. cit.,* Chapter IV.
[18] E. E. Witte, *op. cit.,* p. 92, note 1.

it may be noted, the question of whether the injunction is eventually modified so as to permit the enjoined activity is no defense against a charge of contempt of court; i.e., it makes no difference whether the injunction improperly restrained the persons charged with contempt. Consequently, injunctions forbidding picketing, union meetings, attempts to urge workers to remain out on strike, etc. made union leaders and even ordinary strikers punishable for contempt of court, merely for attempting to carry on normal strike activities.

The effect of an injunction upon the morale of strikers often proved overwhelming. Workers newly introduced to the exigencies of industrial combat would find their leaders jailed and branded as law breakers. Worse still, in some cases, the injunctions issued were of a "blanket" character, i.e., directed at all persons whomsoever. The range of such injunctions was often difficult to determine (persons might be judged guilty of contempt without any knowledge of the court's order or of its applicability to them), and the actions enjoined often severely restricted freedom of speech and press. As a result, ordinary wage earners would sometimes find themselves jailed for contempt of court because they engaged in conventional strike activities. A few such arrests would terrorize the great body of strikers and lead them to feel that resistance was useless, as the government was allied with the employers.

"Yellow-Dog" Contracts[19]

The labor injunction's full significance was not disclosed until 1917 when the U. S. Supreme Court (in the Hitchman case) affirmed the legality of an injunction used to enforce a "yellow dog" contract. The Hitchman decision[20] declared, in effect, that an employer could require workmen, as a condition of employment, to sign an agreement not to join a union and then secure an injunction to prevent union organizers from seeking to recruit his employees on the ground that this was "inducing a breach of contract."

"Yellow-dog" contracts, under various names (e.g., "Ironclad Oath," the "Document") were well-known both in this country and in England during the 19th century. However, after the Hitchman decision, the yellow-dog contract came into a new popularity; the injunctions to which it gave rise have been judged a major factor in excluding the United Mine Workers from the West Virginia coal fields during the 1920's (see above, p. 61).

---

[19] A "yellow dog" contract is one in which a worker promises in writing not to join a union during his tenure of employment.

[20] This case is discussed in Lieberman, *op. cit.*, Chapter 7; also Gregory, *op. cit.*, pp. 174 et seq.

The Norris-La Guardia Act

Injunctions plagued union organizing efforts throughout the 1920's.[21] The AFL continued its efforts, begun in the early 1900's, to secure protection against injunctions, especially against those in support of yellow-dog contracts.   But, until the early 1930's, this campaign was of no avail.   However, the Congress elected in the fall of 1930 had a quite different attitude from its predecessors.   It mirrored the country's growing concern about the depression and resentment against the business community upon which, rightly or wrongly, the depression was blamed.   This change in sentiment redounded to the advantage of the labor movement which began to be thought of as a defender of the increasingly popular "underdog."

As a result, the labor sympathizers in Congress renewed their attempts to free unions from the intervention of the federal courts and, in 1932, they succeeded in passing the Norris-La Guardia Act.   In form, this Act was merely a law governing the conditions under which injunctions might be issued in labor disputes by the federal courts.   But, in substance, the law defined a broad area of economic conflict within which unions and employers might contend for economic advantage without interference from the courts.

The philosophy of the Act was stated in Section 2 which declared that "under prevailing economic conditions . . . the individual unorganized worker is commonly helpless to exercise actual liberty of contract . . . and thereby to obtain acceptable terms and conditions of employment, wherefore, though he should be free to decline to associate with his fellows, it is necessary that he have full freedom of association, self-organization and designation of representatives of his own choosing, to negotiate the terms and conditions of his employment and that he shall be free from the interference, restraint or coercion of employers of labor . . . in the designation of such representatives. . . . "

The main provisions of the Norris-La Guardia Act were as follows:

1. Yellow-dog contracts were made unenforceable in the federal courts, by injunction or otherwise.   In Section 3 such contracts were declared contrary to public policy; they were not made unlawful as such, but were merely declared unenforceable in the federal courts.   However, as employers demanded these contracts only to serve as the basis for injunctions, the Norris-La Guardia Act was sufficient to end their use.

2. Section 4 declared (in effect) that injunctions might not be issued to prevent union self-help in cases arising out of labor disputes.   This section protected, from intervention by the federal judiciary, the right to strike, pay strike benefits, picket, and peacefully assemble.

[21] Witte, *op. cit.,* p. 224.   It might be mentioned that on a few occasions a union secured an injuction against an employer.   However, this was a very infrequent occurrence and the injunction has always been considered as an employer's instrument.

3. Section 13, in effect, cancelled the narrow interpretation of economic interest which the courts had used to prevent unions form exerting economic pressure upon nonunion employers operating within the same industry or occupation.[22] This section states that, in an economic conflict concerned with employment conditions, not only the persons directly involved but also persons engaged in the same industry, trade, craft, or occupation, as employees or employers, and persons who have direct or indirect interests therein are to be considered legitimate participants. Clearly, this section legalized strikes and lockouts as part of the actions of a union or employers' association.[23]

4. Section 7 greatly limited the power of the courts to issue temporary restraining orders and/or injunctions. It specified that an injunction might be issued only if the damage to the injunction seeker would clearly exceed the loss to the enjoined party if the injunction were granted, that the injunction be issued only if substantial and irreparable damage would be done in its absence, etc. The Act further specified that an injunction might not be issued to a complainant who had not complied with all legal obligations touching upon any point involved in the dispute or who had failed to make every reasonable effort to settle such dispute. In addition, the act completely forbade "blanket" injunctions, directed at "all persons whomsoever," and circumscribed the manner in which contempt proceedings could be used to punish violators of labor injunctions.

Despite considerable fear that the courts would emasculate the Norris-La Guardia Act, as they had done to the Clayton Act (see below), the Supreme Court upheld it in 1937.[24] The Act applied only to the federal courts but, by 1950, 24 states had also enacted injunction control legislation of which 17 patterned their laws on the Norris-La Guardia Act.[25] Although the labor injunction has been, to a limited degree, revived by Taft-Hartley (see pp. 253–254), it has not been a major obstacle to union activities since the passage of the Norris-La Guardia Act.

THE SHERMAN ANTITRUST LAW AND THE CLAYTON ACT

The Sherman Act before 1914

The Sherman Act of 1890, or antitrust law, was primarily a measure aimed at halting the growth of monopoly in business. Its legal implications, even for the field of business enterprise, have not yet fully un-

[22] For example, in 1921, the U. S. Supreme Court held (Duplex vs. Deering, see pp. 215–216) the Clayton Act to be inapplicable to a dispute where the workers involved were not *directly* employed by the firm against whom the strike was directed. Lieberman, *op. cit.,* Chapter 8.

[23] Gregory, *op. cit.,* pp. 184–192.

[24] Senn vs. Tile Layers Protective Union, Gregory, *op. cit.,* pp. 198–199; also Fred Witney, *Government and Collective Bargaining,* Lippincott, 1951, pp. 134–141.

[25] Witney, *op. cit.,* p. 141.

folded, and legal experts debate them at length.   But its bearing upon the conduct of labor unions has been even more controversial.   It is not clear that Congress intended the Act to apply to unions at all (nor is the reverse clear), to say nothing of what actions it intended to forbid.

But despite the obscurity of Congressional intent, after 1894 the Act was a sword of Damocles to organized labor.   In 1894, the Federal District Court in Chicago issued an injunction against the striking American Railway Union on several grounds, including the allegation that it was violating the Sherman Act.   In the process of appeal the Supreme Court upheld the injunction on other grounds and did not comment on the question of the Sherman Act.

The Supreme Court did not have occasion to rule on whether unions were subject to the Sherman Act until 1908, when it ruled that they were subject.   This ruling was made in the case of Loewe vs. Lawlor, known to history as the Danbury Hatters' case.   The dispute arose out of the attempt of the United Hatters, in 1902–1903, to organize the firm of Loewe and Fuchs in Danbury, Connecticut.   Direct approach failing, the AFL placed the firm on its "we don't patronize list" and commenced a boycott. Apparently, the boycott had some success and the firm, backed by the newly formed American Anti-Boycott Association,[26] instituted a damage suit alleging violation of the Sherman Act; the union demurred,[27] and the argument wound up in the Supreme Court with the aforementioned result.

Once it was established that unions were subject to the Sherman Act, the damages had to be determined.   This involved two trials which, together with appeals, lasted another seven years; it was not until December 1914 that the Supreme Court made the final rulings.   It ruled that the union and *its members individually* were, under the provisions of the Sherman Act, liable to three times the assessed damages, a total of more than $250,000.

The AFL fought this case to the utmost, not only because of the Sherman Act but also because the courts had declared that the personal property of union members (specifically homes and bank accounts) might be seized to satisfy the judgement.   The union itself did not have the money to satisfy the judgment and so, to prevent the seizure of the union members' property, the AFL (in 1915) instituted two "Hatters' Days" on which union workers were asked to contribute one hour's pay to a fund to save the homes of the hat workers against which foreclosure proceedings had already begun; the funds raised were sufficient.[28]

---

[26] The activities of this association were part of the "employer's counteroffensive" of the early 1900's, to which reference is made on pp. 49–50.

[27] That is, it argued that the conduct for which it (or its officers) were being sued, was lawful.

[28] The case of the Danbury Hatters is discussed in Lieberman, *op. cit.,* Chapter 5.

The effect of this case on union organizing was extremely serious. Not only did it make use of the boycott dangerous for unions, but it threatened every worker who joined a union with loss of his personal property in the event the union was successfully sued for damages. The effect of the Hatters' case was reinforced by the Bucks Stove and Range Case, in which the AFL was enjoined (in 1906) from placing that company on its "we don't patronize" list. As a result of Gompers' alleged defiance of the injunction, he was held guilty of contempt of court and sentenced to 12 months in jail. He was saved from incarceration only by a statute of limitations, but the Supreme Court (in 1914) upheld the finding of contempt.

The Clayton Act

As a result of the Supreme Court's rulings in the Danbury Hatters and Bucks Range cases, union ability to engage in boycotts affecting interstate commerce was virtually destroyed. However, at the very time these cases were in process of final settlement, legislative relief appeared on the horizon. In his 1912 campaign, Woodrow Wilson had promised (to labor) relief from the Sherman Act. The redemption of this pledge was the Clayton Act of 1914. Section 6 of this act declared "that the labor of a human being is not a commodity, or article of commerce." It went on to declare that "nothing contained in the antitrust laws shall be construed to forbid the existence or operation of labor organizations from lawfully carrying out the *legitimate* objects thereof."

This section was hailed by Gompers as labor's Magna Carta, freeing unions from the Sherman Act. But the Supreme Court did not so interpret it. In the Duplex case of 1921,[29] the Court held that the Clayton Act did not authorize unions to commit any acts otherwise unlawful, or to enable unions to become a cloak for illegal combinations in restraint of trade. So interpreted, Section 6 was of little consequence.

Section 20 of the Clayton Act declared that the federal courts could not restrain or enjoin employees in a labor dispute from peacefully picketing, peacefully striking, peacefully boycotting, lawfully assembling, etc. and sought to limit and control the power of the federal courts to issue injunctions and restraining orders in labor disputes. But the benefits to organized labor from Section 20 were not very great. In the aforementioned Duplex case, the Supreme Court restricted application of the Clayton Act to disputes arising between workers and their own employers. It thus nullified the effect of the Clayton Act in cases where a union was attempting to organize nonunion firms. Only those sections of the act compelling a jury trial for contempt growing out of an injunction violation and re-

[29] Duplex Printing Press Co. vs. Deering; see Lieberman, *op. cit.*, Chapter 8 and Gregory, *op. cit.*, pp. 162–174.

quiring prompt hearings in cases of a temporary restraining order proved of any value to labor.[30]

The Sherman Act after Norris-La Guardia

As we have seen, the Norris-La Guardia Act accomplished much of what the Clayton Act tried, and failed, to do; but it said nothing explicit about the Sherman Act. However, the Supreme Court felt that it implied much. The implications that the Supreme Court drew virtually freed union activity from the Sherman Act altogether, except in cases where a union had combined with employers to accomplish objectives forbidden by that Act. And, as has been frequently pointed out,[31] unions can easily achieve the substance of a combination with employers while scrupulously eschewing its form.

The broad tolerance that Supreme Court decisions (in 1940 and later) granted to union activities reflected its changed attitude and membership. The new justices appointed by President Roosevelt in the late 1930's were men of liberal persuasion, especially as regards the allowable activities of unions, and their opinions contrasted sharply with those of the predominantly conservative courts that had preceded them. In the Apex Hosiery Case[32] the Supreme Court ruled (in 1940) that a union's actions did not violate the Sherman Act unless they *substantially* restricted competition and/or affected the prices of the product. It went even further to assert that the effect of successful union activity upon that part of price competition which is based on differences in labor standards is *not* proscribed by the Sherman Act.

The Apex decision was soon followed by the even more momentous ruling in the Hutcheson case.[33] The Hutcheson case arose from a jurisdictional dispute between the Carpenters and the Machinists over which union should have the jobs in an expansion of the facilities of the Anheuser-Busch Brewing Co. The company's contractor assigned the work to the machinists whereupon the carpenters struck Anheuser-Busch, refused to work for a contractor who was doing construction for a firm that had rented facilities from Anheuser-Busch, picketed both firms, and started a boycott of Anheuser-Busch beer.

The federal government secured an indictment against William L. Hutcheson, president of the Carpenters' union, and three of its other offi-

---

[30] Frankfurter and Greene, *The Labor Injunction,* The Macmillan Co., 1930, pp. 197–198.

[31] Gregory, *op. cit.,* Chapter X.

[32] Apex Hosiery Co. vs. Leader. This case is discussed in Lieberman, *op. cit.,* Chapter 18 and Gregory, *op. cit.,* pp. 255–269.

[33] United States vs. Hutcheson; see Lieberman, *op. cit.,* Chapter 19, and Gregory, *op. cit.,* pp. 269–274.

cers on the ground that the above acts constituted a conspiracy in restraint of interstate commerce. The district court ruled in favor of the defendants and the government appealed to the Supreme Court. In February 1941, the Supreme Court ruled that the Norris-La Guardia Act (by implication) made Section 20 of the Clayton Act applicable to the entire range of disputes declared nonenjoinable by Norris-La Guardia; i.e., made all union activities that were nonenjoinable under Norris-La Guardia also immune from prosecution under the Sherman Act (except when a union acts in combination with nonlabor groups). Chief Justice Hughes and Justice Roberts strongly dissented from this view.[34]

In any event the Hutcheson decision, for almost all purposes, freed unions from the Sherman Act. This has been borne out in a number of subsequent rulings by the Supreme Court and the lower courts as well.[35] However, the Taft-Hartley Act has reasserted some of the government's former power over union activities in its restraint upon "secondary boycotts"; this will be discussed in the next chapter.

GOVERNMENT ASSISTANCE TO UNION ORGANIZING: THE NATIONAL INDUSTRIAL RECOVERY ACT AND THE WAGNER ACT

Before 1933, the principal request that unions made of the law was to be let alone. Until then, their contact with the law had been almost uniformly unpleasant. The courts not only hamstrung their efforts to utilize the implements of collective bargaining but, as we shall see (pp. 497–502), they had also refused to enforce legislation aimed at improving wages and hours and preventing child labor. The most for which organized labor dared to hope was that the courts might cease to impede their exercise of economic pressure in the process of collective bargaining.

The National Industrial Recovery Act of 1933

The unions had never anticipated that the political climate could be so favorable to their aspirations as it was in 1933–1938, the New Deal era. The first New Deal measure that helped unionism directly was the National Industrial Recovery Act of 1933.[36] Section 7a of this Act provided that "employees shall have the right to organize and bargain collectively through representatives of their own choosing, and shall be free from . . . coercion of employers . . . in the designation of such representatives . . . and no one . . . shall be required as a condition of employment to

---

[34] As Gregory, *op. cit.,* pp. 269–278 makes clear, this decision was highly controversial from the legal viewpoint.

[35] Gregory, *op. cit.,* pp. 279–288.

[36] There was a prolabor clause in the Bankruptcy Act of March 3, 1933; but this was a minor matter. See Irving Bernstein, *The New Deal Collective Bargaining Policy,* University of California Press, Berkeley and Los Angeles, 1950, p. 22.

join any company union or to refrain from joining a labor organization of his own choosing." This language would seem to be clear enough; however, it contained important loopholes.

These loopholes became apparent in the framing of the individual industry codes of "fair competition" which the act prescribed. For example, the automobile employers succeeded in inserting in their code a "merit" clause, which implicitly preserved their right to hire, fire, promote, etc. on the basis of individual merit, as they determined it. As the AFL (rightly) protested, this gave employers complete freedom to discriminate against union sympathizers. Protest against the automobile "merit clause" was so great as to prevent its extension to other codes.[37] Nonetheless, the iron and steel industry made it clear that they did not intend to deal with AFL unions;[38] and it was only in the few industries where there were strong unions (e.g., in bituminous coal mining) that the codes conformed to the spirit of section 7a.[39]

The attempt to establish industrial codes for specific industries made it clear that Section 7a left unanswered the crucial questions of open versus closed shop, employer freedom to discriminate against union members, etc. Antiunion employers were determined not to abate their opposition, and a clash with the defenders of Section 7a was inevitable.

Preoccupied with other matters and, at first, a bit naive, the Roosevelt administration did not appreciate the irrepressible nature of the conflict. When faced with a wave of strikes in the latter part of 1933, about both economic issues and union recognition, it appointed the National Labor Board (NLB) to mediate them.[40] NLB was a tripartite body, with three employers, three employees, and three public representatives.

In its attempts to settle disputes, NLB began, of necessity, to develop an operational interpretation of Section 7a. This interpretation involved the holding of elections to determine collective bargaining representatives by majority choice.[41] Naturally, antiunion employers protested bitterly and resisted such an interpretation of Section 7a; they fought by openly supporting company unions and by defying the board's authority to hold elections or otherwise intervene in labor relations. Defiance of NLB immediately raised questions of compulsion, and here it foundered.[42] Its business representatives were usually opposed to exerting pressure upon recalcitrant employers; as a result NLB had to conciliate recalcitrants rather than punish them. Furthermore, NLB could not exert pressure

[37] Lewis L. Lorwin and Arthur Wubnig, *Labor Relations Boards,* The Brookings Institution, Washington, D.C., 1935, pp. 65–68; also Bernstein, *op. cit.,* Chapter III.
[38] *Ibid.,* pp. 60–65.
[39] *Ibid.,* pp. 69–73.
[40] *Ibid.,* pp. 88–91.
[41] This was known as the "Reading formula"; see Lorwin and Wubnig, *op. cit.,* pp. 95–99.
[42] Lorwin and Wubnig, *op. cit.,* pp. 266–272, 280–284, 335.

upon employers and unions directly but had to use the enforcement machinery of NRA. This led to considerable friction, as General Johnson (head of NRA) was much less sympathetic to union aspirations than the public members of NLB, of whom Senator Wagner was the leader. On several occasions, General Johnson made speeches and decisions that were clearly inconsistent with NLB policy.[43]

By the spring of 1934, it was clear that NLB could not enforce compliance with its interpretation of Section 7a and that new legislation was needed. Spurred by threat of a steel strike, President Roosevelt induced Congress, in June 1934, to pass Public Resolution No. 44.[44] This resolution empowered him to appoint a board (or boards) to conduct elections to determine collective bargaining representatives and to assure freedom from coercion of employees in all matters relevant to the election. However, the resolution did not touch upon the crucial question of enforcement. As a result, the boards established by the President, under authority of this resolution, were impotent to enforce their rulings. These boards ceased to function when the Supreme Court declared NIRA unconstitutional in May 1935.

The National Labor Relations (Wagner) Act of 1935

From the early part of 1934, Senator Wagner of New York had tried to secure passage of legislation that would spell out the implications of Section 7a (of NIRA) as he interpreted them and create a board with powers of enforcement. Public Resolution No. 44 represented a watered-down version of his proposals. When NIRA was declared unconstitutional, he and his allies seized the opportunity to push for new and stronger legislation; the result was the National Labor Relations Act of 1935, commonly, and justly, known as the Wagner Act.

The avowed purposes of the Wagner Act were to foster collective bargaining and to assure workers full freedom of choice in their bargaining representatives, without hindrance of any kind by employers. The Act provided that employees should choose their collective bargaining representatives in elections supervised by the National Labor Relations Board (NLRB) which it established, and that the choice of the majority was to be the exclusive representative of *all* workers in the bargaining unit. (However, individuals or groups of employees retained the right to present their *own* grievances.) The Act required that, irrespective of their wishes, employers must thereafter negotiate with the properly chosen representatives of their employees; failure to do so constituted an unfair labor practice under the terms of the Act. The Act forbade, as an unfair labor practice, discrimination against employees for union membership; it also forbade an employer to encourage or discourage member-

[43] *Ibid.,* pp. 109–110.
[44] *Ibid.,* pp. 258–259 and 335; also Bernstein, *op. cit.,* Chapter VI.

ship in any labor organization or to assist a labor organization in any way. NLRB was empowered to issue orders, whose enforcement was to be secured by orders of the U. S. Circuit Court of Appeals, violation of which would involve contempt of court. In short, the Wagner Act asserted (in effect) that henceforth an employer had no legitimate concern with his employees' choice of a bargaining representative; his duty was to bargain with the chosen representative in good faith.

The effectiveness of this legislation obviously depended upon the skill and determination with which it was administered by NLRB, and the extent to which the courts would enforce NLRB orders. There was good reason to fear that the Act would be emasculated or declared unconstitutional by the Supreme Court, and very many employers refused to obey NLRB orders until the Act had been tested in the courts. As a result, the Act did not begin to take serious effect until April 1937 when the Supreme Court upheld its constitutionality.

Once the Act's constitutionality was assured, the majority of employers complied with its provisions, albeit reluctantly. However, an important minority, including many large firms, continued a policy of evasion and resistance to the purposes of the Act. Here is where the NLRB entered the picture; to make the Act operative, it had to spell out in detail the behavior that was proscribed as "unfair labor practices." This involved issuing orders, most of which were tested in the courts, and most of which were upheld.

In accordance with Section 9b of the Act, NLRB determined the "bargaining units" within which election of employee representatives took place. (The important question of bargaining units is discussed on pp. 232–235.) To insure that the employee's choice was made without employer compulsion, NLRB supervised elections and required a secret ballot. It also scrutinized the pre-election campaign to determine whether the employer had attempted to influence or coerce his employees; in a number of cases where coercion was found, the election was set aside and a new one held.

In a considerable number of cases, employers attempted to influence their worker's choice of a union by supporting a company or "independent" union in opposition to an "outside" AFL or CIO organization. In such cases the Board (NLRB) ordered the company union "disestablished" on the grounds that it was company dominated. Orders of this type were very common in the early period of the Board's operation (1935–1938) when employers continued to back the company unions (see above, pp. 70–71) they had previously established. Since 1940, these cases have become less frequent, and the company unions that have survived are, on the whole, free of "employer domination."[45]

---

[45] The Board's criteria for deciding whether or not a union was company domi-

NLRB sought not only to insure that the employees would be represented by the union of their choice but also that the employer would bargain with said union "in good faith." This, of course, was difficult to insure, without specifying the result of the bargaining; the Wagner Act did not attempt this. However, the Board did attempt to lay down certain requirements that must be satisfied as conditions of "good faith" bargaining. The most important of these were: (1) that employers must put agreements into writing, if the union requested it, and (2) that employers must not merely reject union offers but must also make counter-proposals.[46]

In general, NLRB tried to induce compliance through persuasion rather than to compel it by orders. However, employer resistance was such that the Board's directives were, in an important minority of cases, ignored or resisted. This was particularly important in connection with securing "free elections" and preventing "employer coercion" in the choice of bargaining representatives. To secure these objectives, the Board found it necessary to proscribe some rather customary personnel practices. These involved the employers' freedom to discipline or discharge "insubordinate workers" who were, very often, active unionists. When the Board found employers guilty of discharging employees because of union activities, it ordered them reinstated with back pay from the time of discharge; between 1938 and 1947, 76,268 workers were reinstated because of discriminatory discharges, 40,691 of them receiving back pay totalling $12,418,800.[47] (Reinstatement with back pay was the only punitive action the Board was empowered to take.)

Both the Wagner Act itself and NLRB were subjected to bitter and unceasing attacks (from employers and their sympathizers) from 1935 until the Act was superseded by Taft-Hartley in 1947. The anger of employers with the Act is easy to understand. Within a period of less than five years, the antiunion employer found his legal position against unions almost completely reversed. Before the Norris-La Guardia Act he was able frequently to fight off a union with yellow-dog contracts and/or injunctions. Soon after Norris-La Guardia, Section 7a of NIRA, and, a little later, the Wagner Act, came to bind him hand and foot in the face of union organizing campaigns; not only did the courts refuse him succour, but they prohibited him from "self-defense" in the face of union "attack." And this occurred simultaneously with the CIO's big organizing campaign of the late 1930's. As it looked to the employer, the New Deal administration was using the Wagner Act to help its labor al-

---

nated were complex; see H. A. Millis and E. C. Brown, *From the Wagner Act to Taft-Hartley,* University of Chicago Press, Chicago, 1950, pp. 103–111.

[46] Brown and Millis, *op. cit.,* pp. 88–89.

[47] *Ibid.,* pp. 41–42.

lies fasten unionization upon American industry and make law breakers out of employers who resisted.

In point of fact, the avowed purpose of the Wagner Act was to promote unionization. The first section of the Act stated "It is hereby declared to be the policy of the United States to eliminate the causes of certain substantial obstructions to the free flow of commerce . . . by encouraging the practice and procedure of collective bargaining, and by protecting the exercise by workers of full freedom of association, self-organization, and designation of representatives of their own choosing, for the purpose of negotiating the terms of their employment or other material aid or protection." This was completely inconsistent with the practice of most large manufacturing employers. But, at the time of the Wagner Act's passage, these employers felt, and with reason, that laws are not always administered as they are written. For example, the administration of Section 7a of NIRA had prevented it from achieving its intended objective, and they hoped that the Supreme Court and/or "pressurable" administrators would save them from the jaws of the Wagner Act.

To their pained surprise, they were not rescued; the Supreme Court upheld the Wagner Act and the NLRB proved to be steadfast and completely dedicated to the purposes of the Act. The members of NLRB were criticized roundly, during the years 1937–1941, as being unfair, prounion, antiemployer, etc. Most of these charges were unfair and irrelevant; the Board was prounion and intentionally so. The purpose of the Act was to encourage unionization, and this implied that the Board should protect union organizing activity and prevent all employer attempts to counter it. That the Board did its job with enthusiasm was, no doubt, annoying to employers, but their criticisms, for the most part, should have been directed at the Act itself and not at the Board's orders that were merely the means for giving practical effect to the Act.

To be sure, it is likely that some of the Board's subordinate employees carried their support of unionization above and beyond the call of duty.[48] However, it was difficult for the Board (in the 1930's) to find experienced personnel who were willing to work for it, but who were not zealous supporters of unionism. The combination of enthusiasm and inexperience sometimes caused subordinate Board representatives to overlook the psychological problems of employers in adjusting to the Act and to treat (employer) violators as common law breakers instead of attempting to "sell" compliance. Despite the fact that the general policy of the Board was to induce, rather than compel, compliance, the zeal of a minority of the Board's agents was exploited by opponents of the Act to convey a misleading impression.

But not all criticism of NLRB originated with employers. The AFL craft unions strongly objected to Board policy on craft versus industrial

[48] *Ibid.*, pp. 35 et seq.

bargaining units (see pp. 232–234), arguing that it favored industrial units and the CIO.[49] (AFL demands, on this score, were largely satisfied by the provisions of Taft-Hartley.) AFL also protested strongly against several Board decisions in which elections won by AFL over CIO affiliates were set aside on the ground that the employer had favored the AFL union.[50] There can be little doubt but that, in the late 1930's, many employers felt (rightly or wrongly) AFL unions to be lesser evils than CIO and attempted to favor them accordingly. And the AFL encouraged such behavior,[51] despite the fact that it contravened the intent of the Wagner Act. For both of these reasons, AFL demanded, with some success, modification of the Act and removal of certain Board members as pro-CIO.

The precise contribution of the Wagner Act to the great increase of union membership during 1937–1941 is difficult to assay. The Act made organizing drives easier, in that employers could no longer simply refuse to deal with unions as they had done before 1935. But all that the Wagner Act required was that they bargain in "good faith" with duly certified unions. Nothing was said as to the terms upon which agreement was to be reached and, had employers wished, they could have offered absurdly poor terms (and haggled over them), thereby complying with all conceivable NLRB directives, which stopped short of prescribing actual contract terms. That employers did not follow this course reflects the economic power of the unions and, possibly, fear of even more drastic legislation. However, the protection from discriminatory discharge afforded by the Act no doubt encouraged many timid workers to join unions, and it also caused many employers, who did not like to "fight the government," to accept unionism for the first time. In short, the Wagner Act was one of several powerful forces that accomplished the substantial unionization of the American economy in the decade 1935–1945. The Wagner Act's other objective, the diminution of industrial strife, has been discussed on pp. 168–169.

THE COMING OF TAFT-HARTLEY

State Legislation

As we have already seen (pp. 74–75), the climate of opinion toward unions became hostile after 1938. This hostility was due partly to the unceasing campaign against unions, the Wagner Act, NLRB, etc. in the newspapers, but it was also due to union behavior. Jurisdictional strikes,

[49] See D. O. Bowman, *Public Control of Labor Relations,* The Macmillan Co.. New York, 1942, pp. 141–144.
[50] Joseph Rosenfarb, *The National Labor Policy,* Harper & Brothers, New York. 1940, pp. 256 et seq.
[51] See the frank statement on this point by Mr. Padway, counsel for AFL, quoted in Rosenfarb, *op. cit.,* p. 294, note 98.

criminal practices of certain union leaders, threats of war-time strikes, especially in coal, restrictive practices, such as those of the Musicians' union, changed the public image of labor unions from "protectors of the underdog" to "greedy trouble makers."

The changed attitude was manifested first in state legislation. In 1937, five states (Utah, Wisconsin, New York, Pennsylvania, and Massachusetts) adopted "Little Wagner" Acts which aimed at essentially the same objectives (for intrastate firms) as the Wagner Act sought to achieve in firms engaged in interstate commerce. (In 1941, Rhode Island and in 1945, Connecticut, also passed Little Wagner Acts.) But, from 1939 to 1947, eight states passed legislation restricting union activities; four of these states (Wisconsin, Pennsylvania, Massachusetts, and Utah) repealed or amended their Little Wagner Acts in order to enact these statutes. Several of these laws anticipated important parts of the Taft-Hartley Act. The aforementioned eight states were not the only ones to enact legislation imposing restraints upon union behavior; between 1939 and 1947, 37 states passed legislation aimed at curbing union activities in one way or another. This legislation was a reaction to the same forces that moved Congress during this period. Just as in Congress, antiunion feeling in state legislatures reached its crescendo in 1946–1947; the Taft-Hartley Act at the federal level was paralleled by a wave of state laws seeking some or all of Taft-Hartley's objectives.[52]

Since 1947, there have been moves to soften some of the restrictive laws passed by the states. In some states (Delaware, Louisiana, Missouri, Maine, and New Hampshire) restrictive statutes have been amended or repealed, but in 1952–1953, Alabama, Mississippi, Nevada, and South Carolina newly enacted or tightened antiunion laws already in existence.

At the beginning of 1954, 17 states had specifically outlawed force and violence, coercion, sit-down strikes, or mass picketing; these acts were unlawful anyway. A number of states had also banned jurisdictional strikes, sympathy strikes, strikes in violation of contract, and strikes to compel statute violations. Some states restricted picketing and, as we have seen (pp. 177–178), 18 states outlawed union security provisions.

Federal Legislation

Restrictive legislation by the federal government came more slowly than in the states, largely because President Roosevelt opposed it. How-

---

[52] The most complete discussion of this legislation is C. C. Killingsworth, *State Labor Relations Acts,* University of Chicago Press, Chicago, 1948. For a brief account see David Ziskind, "Countermarch in Labor Legislation," pp. 313–335, and 661–706 in *Labor in Postwar America,* Remsen Press, 1949; also Millis and Brown, op. cit., pp. 316–332.

ever, expression of Congressional resentment at unions could not be repressed indefinitely. In June 1943, during one of John L. Lewis' "on-again off-again" coal strikes, Congress passed the War Labor Disputes Act, commonly known as the Smith-Connally Act, over President Roosevelt's veto. This law gave the President power to seize essential war plants, mines, etc. that were threatened by a shutdown; it established penalties against instigators of a strike at a seized plant; it required that 30 days notice be given before commencement of a strike which might interrupt war production and that on the 30th day after such notice a secret ballot (supervised by NLRB) be taken to determine whether the workers involved desired the strike. This Act also prohibited political contributions by labor organizations in connection with a national election.

Supervision of the required strike votes seriously interfered with NLRB's other functions, and it failed completely to achieve its avowed purpose.[53] Unions desiring to threaten a strike would punctiliously give 30 days advance notice and would overwhelmingly vote in favor of the strike on the 30th day thereafter. After one such vote, John L. Lewis sarcastically thanked the government for providing him with such a handsome vote of confidence. The prohibition on union contributions to political campaigns was completely unrelated to the war effort and was simply a gratuitous insult to the labor movement. Incidentally, the prohibition was easily evaded. But however ineffective its provisions may have been, the Smith-Connally Act indicated the state of mind of Congress and of a large part of the public.

After V-J day, there was, as we have seen, an increase in the number of strikes. The strikes and subsequent wage increases were widely believed to be major causes of the postwar inflation, and the unions were blamed accordingly. In May 1946, a nation-wide railway strike was broken by President Truman, who excoriated the strikers (in a radio address broadcast nationally) and demanded drastic antiunion legislation.[54] Congress defeated President Truman's proposed legislation, but then proceeded to pass the Case Bill on which the President's veto was barely sustained.

Failing to pass the Case Bill in its entirety, Congress then enacted that part of it (the Hobbs Act), which removed exemption for unions from the federal Antiracketeering Act. This law was specifically aimed at the organizing tactics of the Teamsters' Union.[55] Earlier in 1946, Congress had also passed the Lea (anti-Petrillo) Act, which banned royalty pay-

[53] Millis and Brown, *op. cit.,* pp. 248–300. The expense and trouble of strike votes caused the repeal of this provision in 1945.
[54] See note 96 in Chapter 3, p. 75.
[55] Millis and Brown, *op. cit.,* pp. 288 and 332, note 51.

ments to the musicians' union from the sale of phonographic records.[56]

When an even more antiunion Congress was elected in the fall of 1946, some sort of antiunion legislation was inevitable; the Taft-Hartley Act was the law that resulted. Its most important characteristics and consequences are analyzed in the next chapter.

DISCUSSION QUESTIONS

1. Trace the changing judicial attitude toward unions from one that prohibited their existence in the early 19th century to one that permitted "very broad freedom of action" in the late 1930's and 1940's.

(a) List the important federal laws and cases in this development, and indicate the impact of each of them upon the effectiveness of union strike action.

(b) Discuss one of these laws or cases from the viewpoint of "sound public policy."

2. The Sherman Antitrust Law is not, at present, applicable to union behavior, except where unions combine with nonlabor groups.

(a) It is wise to protect unions, to this extent, from the Sherman Act?

(b) If the Sherman Act were to be amended so as to restrict certain union actions, which of the following actions would you feel it desirable to crub? (1) Sympathetic strikes, (2) secondary boycotts, (3) industry-wide bargaining, (4) strikes against (product) price cutting employers.

(c) In what types of industry would you expect to find unions exercising the greatest effect on the selling price of output?

3. (a) Debate the pros and cons of legislation aimed at making it illegal for an employer to operate his facilities during a lawful strike?

(b) What bearing would such legislation have on the social and legal problems related to the permission of picketing?

4. Why was the Wagner Act more successful than Section 7a of the National Industrial Recovery Act in promoting collective bargaining?

Reading Suggestions

Bernstein, Irving, *The New Deal Collective Bargaining Policy,* University of California Press, Berkeley and Los Angeles, 1950.

Frankfurter, Felix and Nathan Greene, *The Labor Injunction,* The Macmillan Co., New York, 1930.

Gregory, C. O., *Labor and the Law,* Revised Edition, W. W. Norton Co., New York, 1949.

Killingsworth, C. C., *State Labor Relations Acts, A Study of Public Policy,* University of Chicago Press, Chicago, 1948.

Lieberman, Elias, *Unions Before the Bar,* Harper & Bros., New York, 1950.

Millis, H. A., and E. C. Brown, *From the Wagner Act to Taft-Hartley,* University of Chicago Press, Chicago, 1950.

Sufrin, S. C. and R. C. Sedgwick, *Labor Law, T. Y. Crowell Co.,* New York, 1954.

Witney, Fred, *Government and Collective Bargaining,* Lippincott, New York, 1951.

Witte, E. E., *The Government in Labor Disputes,* McGraw-Hill Book Company, New York, 1932.

[56] *Ibid.*

9

The Taft-Hartley
(Labor Management Relations)
Act of 1947

The Taft-Hartley (T-H) Act merits close attention not only because it is the current law of the land in so many labor matters but also because it is the first federal statute that has attempted to control the behavior of unions over the whole range of their activities. The very comprehensiveness of the law makes it a convenient base from which to analyze the general problem of the public control of collective bargaining.

The issues involved in the public control of unions can be best understood if we recognize from the outset that a union is itself a species of government, i.e., a private government.[1] It is a government in the obvious sense that its officers are elected and that they must, to a greater or less degree, be politicians. But it is also a government in a number of other respects: (1) its decisions or laws are binding upon its member-citizens and violation of them must (sometimes) be punished; (2) like other governments, a union is greatly concerned with maintaining or extending its "boundaries," which means increasing the number of workers and/or jobs subject to its laws; (3) it must determine the conditions upon which new member-citizens are accepted; (4) it must levy and collect taxes, i.e., dues, assessments, and initiation fees; and (5) above all, it must wage war (strikes), negotiate terms of peace (contracts), and conduct continuing diplomatic relations with employers, other unions, and public authorities.

This list does not exhaust the similarities between unions and (public) governments, but it will suffice for our purpose. Unions are not, of course, the only example of private government in our society; cooperative societies, fraternal organizations, social clubs of all kinds, and business corporations are all, to some degree, governments. This fact is not

[1] I derived the idea of viewing the union as a private government from my late friend, Professor L. H. Fisher. My general indebtedness to him is especially heavy in this connection.

usually cause for concern, because the power of these organizations is so limited.[2] If these organizations are unfair to individual members, the members may leave with small injury to themselves; or even if such organizations exclude or expel individuals arbitrarily, the damage is not usually very large.[3] However, this is not true of the present-day union; where it has a union shop, it often exercises control of a wide range of employment opportunities and the dissatisfied member cannot withdraw without serious economic hardship. The individual refused membership or expelled is similarly injured. Furthermore, in the conduct of its relations with employers, a union may seriously affect the economic well-being of the community in that a major strike may injure a large number of persons not directly concerned with its outcome.

THE PHILOSOPHY OF TAFT-HARTLEY

The preamble to the Act states: "It is the purpose and policy of this Act, in order to promote the full flow of commerce, to prescribe the legitimate rights of both employees and employers in their relations affecting commerce, to provide orderly and peaceful procedures for preventing the interference by either with the legitimate rights of the other, to protect the rights of the individual employees in their relations with labor organizations whose activities affect commerce, to define and proscribe practices on the part of labor and management which affect commerce and are inimical to the general welfare, and to protect the rights of the public in connection with labor disputes affecting commerce."

The difference between the avowed purposes of this Act and those of the Wagner Act are clear. Wagner aimed at curbing the rights of employers in order to promote free collective bargaining and said nothing whatever about the rights of the public or of unions other than to specify [Section 8(3)] that the Act did not outlaw closed or union shop contracts for those unions certified as bargaining representatives. T-H, on the other hand, specifies a variety of rights of employers, of the public, and of union members against union governments. To give effect to these rights, union freedom of action is curtailed in a number of directions.

Section 7 of T-H indicates most succinctly the difference in philosophy between the Wagner and Taft-Hartley Acts. This section, "Rights of Employees," states that "Employees shall have the right to self-organiza-

---

[2] Exception to this statement should be made for large corporations able to exercise substantial degrees of control over the market for their output. The activities of such firms are regulated, though perhaps inadequately, by the Sherman and Clayton Acts and the various state incorporation acts.

[3] There are, of course, awkward borderline cases where this is not true; e.g., cases where membership in a social club confers enormous advantages in making business contacts. However, these are not situations where government can do very much; in any event, these are not pertinent to our discussion.

tion, to form, join, or assist labor organizations, . . . *and shall also have the right to refrain from any or all such activities . . .* " (italics are ours). Except for the clause in italics, the spirit of this section is similar to the Wagner Act; however, this clause, and the attempts of T-H to give it effect, are diametrically opposed to the policy of the Wagner Act.

In this chapter, the various restraints that T-H imposes upon unions will be individually appraised as methods for achieving specific objectives which may, themselves, be judged as desirable or otherwise. This is in sharp contrast to the enthusiasm of certain employer organizations for Taft-Hartley as such or the bitter condemnation of labor leaders for the "slave labor act." The strong emotions aroused by the name "Taft-Hartley" can be understood only if it is remembered that the law was enacted in the heat of political controversy by a Congress that was outspokenly antiunion. Many members of this Congress wanted a law that would have injured unions far more than T-H and accepted T-H only as the best that could be obtained, at that moment. T-H sought, in many ways, to injure unions; in no way did it attempt to enhance their power or status. Consequently, organized labor felt, and still feels, that enactment of T-H was a major political defeat as well as an insult, and therefore denounces it.

THE OVERALL EFFECT OF TAFT-HARTLEY UPON UNION STRENGTH

The attitude of AFL-CIO toward T-H is not without foundation. T-H was intended to weaken American unionism; that it has done so far less than its authors hoped, and its opponents feared, is due mainly to three more or less related developments: (1) the willingness of American workers to support the union shop in secret ballot elections.[4] Senator Taft and others apparently believed (in 1947) that, given the opportunity, many workers would vote to abolish compulsory union membership and leave their unions. (2) The fact that there has been no serious depression in the United States since World War II has lessened the significance of various curbs imposed by T-H upon union strike action. T-H makes it harder, in a number of ways, for unions to win strikes; in the event of a serious depression, this could put them at a serious disadvantage. But, in the prosperous economic climate we have experienced since 1945, employers have found it more profitable to get along with unions than to provoke them. (3) Employers have (see pp. 147–148) tended toward more amicable relations with unions. As many of T-H's provisions are devices to help the antiunion employer, they have simply not been operative in situations where unions were genuinely accepted. The change in employer attitudes is due in good part to the continued prosperity that has made "union busting" unprofitable or impossible and also

[4] See pp. 120–121.

to the realization (after the 1948 election) that there was no possibility of electing a government that would permit large-scale "union-busting."

In short, both the friends and foes of T-H envisioned its operation in a setting of postwar depression, like 1920–1922, in which it might well have enabled determined employers to destroy unions.[5] But, as it has functioned in an entirely different economic climate, its adverse consequences (for unions) have been far less serious than anticipated.

A further factor that worked to soften the effect of T-H upon unions was the composition of NLRB. T-H was enacted when the antiunion forces in Congress were confident that a President sympathetic to their views would be elected in 1948. The unanticipated re-election of President Truman meant that the members of the Board (NLRB) appointed from 1947 to the beginning of 1953 were not antiunion in sympathy. As Board members' terms are of five years duration, this meant that the Board was, until the mid-1950's, dominated by Truman appointees. Thus the interpretation of T-H was, during the early precedent-setting years, in the hands of men not nearly so hostile to unions as the 80th Congress (that enacted T-H). This fact is of some significance in connection with the conflict between the first General Counsel and the Board (see pp. 231–232).

The Eisenhower appointees to the Board have been generally less sympathetic to unionism than those of Truman. However, the collection of precedent-setting interpretations made in the early years of T-H together with the reluctance of many businessmen and moderate Republicans to "rock the boat" unnecessarily have thus far prevented any *wholesale* changes in general policy.

This is not to say that T-H has not injured unions at all; as we shall see, it has done so in a number of ways. However, it has not hurt unions sufficiently to keep their membership from continuing to grow (see pp. 75–77), and it has not kept them from achieving a fairly successful record of strikes won and economic gains registered. Of course, it is possible that, in the absence of T-H, union membership would have grown still more and the economic gains might have been even greater. However, it is impossible to test such an hypothesis, and the reader is free to form his own opinion on the matter.

TAFT-HARTLEY AND NATIONAL LABOR RELATIONS BOARD

One major criticism made of NLRB during the Wagner Act was that it combined the functions of prosecutor, judge, and jury. This criticism is, by implication, an attack upon the entire system of administrative agencies, all of which "combine" these functions. Whether such combination leads to improper behavior depends upon the way in which the agency conducts itself. Under the Wagner Act, there was much dis-

[5] See the discussion on representation elections, pp. 237–239.

agreement about the fairness of NLRB. Although much of the adverse criticism confused vigorous enforcement of the Wagner Act with unfairness towards employers, Congress decided that the organizational structure of the Board made for unfair treatment and proceeded to change it.

Under the Wagner Act, NLRB had three members appointed by the President with the advice and consent of the Senate. Taft-Hartley increased the Board from three to five members and created the office of General Counsel. The General Counsel is also appointed by the President (with the consent of the Senate) and is therefore independent of the Board.[6] The powers of the General Counsel are to some extent defined in the Taft-Hartley Act; they include the power to decide whether and which charges of unfair labor practices shall be prosecuted and to exercise "full and final authority and responsibility, on behalf of the Board" in any injunction proceedings.

As the precise division of power between the General Counsel and the Board was not specified completely by T-H, some negotiation between the two was required. In the early years of the Act (i.e., prior to 1950), to facilitate administration the Board delegated to the counsel "practically all the authority vested in the Board outside its judicial functions;"[7] this put the general counsel in control of some 80 per cent of the Board's staff and budget and of perhaps 85 per cent of the work of the agency.[8] However, the Board had the power to revoke its delegated powers at any time and did so early in 1950.

The Board's revocation of its delegated powers climaxed a prolonged struggle with the first General Counsel, Robert N. Denham. The struggle was due in part to differences in interpretation of T-H: (1) Denham believed that the ban on secondary boycotts (see pp. 249–251) required unions to handle "hot cargo," but the Board felt otherwise. (2) Denham wished to extend application of the Act as far as possible whereas the Board wanted to avoid adding cases to its already overcrowded docket that did not materially affect interstate commerce. These disagreements, coupled with personality clashes, led to a situation in which the General Counsel was sometimes refusing to prosecute employers found guilty of unfair labor practices by the Board. Although it was the duty of the General Counsel to defend Board orders when they were appealed to the courts, on a number of occasions Denham refused to do this because he disagreed with the Board's decisions.[9]

In short, the structure of the Act permitted, if it did not actually en-

---

[6] Under the Wagner Act, the General Counsel was appointed by NLRB and was responsible solely to it.

[7] H. A. Millis and E. C. Brown, *From the Wagner Act to Taft-Hartley*, University of Chicago Press, Chicago, 1950, p. 405.

[8] *Ibid.*

[9] Fred Witney, *op. cit.*, pp. 479–485.

courage, a struggle between the General Counsel and the Board.   In 1949 and 1950, this struggle came to a head with public attacks by the counsel and Board upon one another.   This struggle was further embittered by union demands that Denham be removed because he was biased against labor.   Furthermore, Denham's intimate cooperation with the Joint (Congressional) Committee on Labor-Management Relations (established under Title IX of T-H), of which Senator Taft was the leading member, gave rise to charges that the General Counsel was merely Taft's mouthpiece.   As a result Congressional supporters of T-H became Denham's backers, and the struggle between the Board and the counsel developed into a fight between prounion and antiunion forces in Congress and the Administration.[10]   To resolve the conflict, President Truman sought to have T-H amended so as to abolish the General Counsel's office.   Failing in this, he obtained Denham's resignation in September 1950.

Denham's successor, George J. Bott, has worked much more harmoniously with the Board than his predecessor.   However, although the distribution of powers within NLRB is not presently causing trouble, the events of T-H's first three years strongly suggest need for changes.

DEFINING UNION BOUNDARIES: BARGAINING UNITS AND ELECTIONS

Craft, Company, and Industry Bargaining Units

Section 9 of the Wagner Act stated that the choice of bargaining representatives was to be made by majority vote of the employees within a unit "appropriate for such purposes."   What constituted a bargaining unit was left to the determination of NLRB which was instructed to determine the unit in such a way as "to insure to employees the full benefit of their right to self-organization and to collective bargaining, and otherwise to effectuate the policies of this Act."

In very many cases, the choice of a bargaining unit presented no difficulty. All the manual workers employed by a firm were placed in a single bargaining unit and that ended the matter. However, a number of problems have arisen.   Under the Wagner Act, the most important bargaining unit question faced by NLRB was when to include all production workers in a plant or firm (as the case might be) in one unit and when to split off skilled craftsmen (such as carpenters, electricians, plumbers, etc.) and place them in separate units.   This issue generated a great deal of controversy because of the jurisdictional conflicts between AFL and CIO unions.   In many cases,[11] AFL unions sought to have the Board separate craftsmen (in given plants) into separate bargaining units; where this occurred, the CIO union frequently opposed it.   The members of

[10] *Ibid.,* Also Millis and Brown, *op. cit.,* pp. 626–629.
[11] But not in the majority of cases; see Millis and Brown, *op. cit.,* p. 143.

NLRB also disagreed with one another as to the conditions under which craft workers should be pulled out of larger groups of workers and placed in separate bargaining units.[12]   As a result of disagreement on this issue, individual Board members became known as pro-AFL or pro-CIO.

In general, the Board's policy was to consider the possibility of a craft bargaining unit whenever the craft workers involved had, in the past, usually bargained separately from other workers in the plant or firm. When the Board thought that a craft unit *might* be appropriate, it held a "Globe election."[13]   If the majority of the voters in the proposed craft unit voted in its favor, the craft unit was established; otherwise it was not. Of 260 "Globe elections" actually held, the craft unit won in 80 per cent of the instances.[14]

The "Globe election" principle was a tolerable compromise between conflicting pressures, but it must not be supposed that it was the only possible "democratic" procedure.   It gave to a minority of workers in a plant the right to "secede" from a plant bargaining unit irrespective of the wishes of the majority.   And such secession might well weaken the bargaining power of the majority.[15]   It has been remarked that by a "Globe election" the southern states could have seceded in peace; an appropriate reply might be "in a world-wide election unit the U.S. might be compelled to surrender its sovereignty to the U.N."

The question of craft versus broader bargaining units was not only a matter of minority rights; there was also the question of making collective bargaining effective.   For example, severing a craft from a plant unit might preserve the "rights" of the craftsmen, but it might destroy the possibility of the other workers waging successful strikes and hence bargaining effectively.   Some NLRB members felt that, as the avowed purpose of the Wagner Act was to promote collective bargaining, the unit chosen   should be the one most likely to facilitate the formation of a viable union.   This view tended to be associated with a general sympathy for larger "plant-wide" units; however, this view did not prevail.

Although the "Globe doctrine" might be thought to favor AFL, that organization (especially before 1940) was far from approving NLRB's interpretation of the "Globe doctrine."[16]   The AFL objected to the Board's freedom to decide whether or not a craft unit might be established; it demanded that whenever one or more craft workers wished to be placed

[12] D. O. Bowman, *Public Control of Labor Relations*, The Macmillan Co., New York, 1941, pp. 141–144; also Millis and Brown, *op. cit.*, pp. 133–136.

[13] So called after the initial election, in 1937, held in Globe Machine and Stamping Co.

[14] Bowman, *op. cit.*, p. 144.

[15] On this point see the views of board member, E. S. Smith, as cited in Bowman, *op. cit.*, pp. 189–192.

[16] Bowman, *op. cit.*, Chapter XI.

in a separate bargaining unit, the Board should be obliged to establish that unit.[17] The CIO, on the other hand, rejected the "Globe doctrine" except when there was an actual history of craft bargaining. Board policy gradually tended toward the AFL view and in 1946–1947, there was a noticeable tendency to establish craft units whenever possible. Section 9b of Taft-Hartley asserted that the Board should not "decide that any craft unit is inappropriate . . . on the ground that a different unit has been established by a prior board determination, unless a majority of the employees in the craft unit vote against separate representation." This does not make craft units mandatory, although it encourages attempts of unions to appeal for their establishment. However, like the Wagner Act, T-H has substantially left resolution of craft versus industrial bargaining units to the discretion of the Board.[18] In recent years, the Board has generally been sympathetic to craft units; however, in 1954, it ruled that craft units would not be established unless the members in the proposed unit were a "true craft" and the union seeking to represent them was one which "traditionally represents the craft."

Problems similar to the above also arose in connection with single plant versus (multiplant) employer bargaining units although these cases occurred infrequently. Such problems arose where (1) a union would have one of a firm's plants organized but would not have the adherence of a majority of a firm's workers, or (2) where the union had the majority of the workers in the firm as a whole but not in some of its individual plants. In the first case, the union would desire a plant unit and, in the second, an employer unit; an antiunion employer, or a rival union, would desire the reverse. In the 1930's, in order to promote collective bargaining, NLRB tended to favor the largest unit which the union appeared to have organized. In a number of cases, as unions gained majorities in an increasing number of a company's plants, the Board shifted from a single to a multiplant bargaining unit.[19] This policy may have served to promote collective bargaining, but it also led to violations of the rights of *majorities* within individual plants. In 1941, the Board abandoned this policy so that majorities in individual plants were not forced to accept a bargaining representative against their will. However, to make sure that the previous policy was not revived, Section 9c(5) of Taft-Hartley states that, in determining the appropriate bargaining unit, "the extent to which the employees have organized shall not be controlling."

Multiemployer units involve the same type of problems as multiplant units for single employer. There have been few of these, and such units

[17] *Ibid.*, pp. 165–174. Of course, the Board would still have had to decide when a group of workers actually constitutes a craft.

[18] Millis and Brown, *op. cit.*, pp. 521–525.

[19] *Ibid.*, pp. 148–149.

were created only when a substantial majority of the individual *employers* wanted them.[20]   The possibility of multiemployer units raises a number of important questions in regard to multi-employer bargaining which are discussed on pp. 150–154.

PROFESSIONAL WORKERS, PLANT GUARDS, AND SUPERVISORS

The definition of the bargaining unit has caused still other problems: 1. Should supervisory and professional workers be included in the same unit as production workers?   On these matters the Wagner Act was silent, leaving the problem to the discretion of NLRB.   T-H, however, prohibits inclusion of professional employees in a bargaining unit that also includes nonprofessionals, unless a majority of the professionals had voted in favor of such inclusion.   (This requirement is analogous to that made with regard to craft workers.)   This restriction did not alter Board practice greatly; it merely made the indicated elections mandatory instead of permissive at the Board's discretion.

2. T-H forbids inclusion of plant guards in the same bargaining unit as other workers and prevents certification of any union that permits membership of both guards and other workers.   This restriction was designed to prevent striking unions from being able to interfere with the control of management over plant guards.[21]

3. Section 14(a) of T-H states that employers are not required to bargain collectively with supervisors, including foremen, unless they so desire.   This section states that "no employer subject to this Act shall be compelled to deem individuals defined herein as supervisors as employees for any purpose of the law."   This means that employers are free to discriminate against (including discharge) supervisors who join unions. It is specifically stated, however, that it is *lawful* for supervisors to join any union they choose.   This provision was the outcome of a great deal of controversy in the 1940's about whether foremen were, or ought to be, covered by the Wagner Act.[22]   In March 1947, the Supreme Court, by a five to four decision, upheld an NLRB ruling that foremen were covered by the Wagner Act.[23]   Congress' response to this decision was Section 14(a) of T-H.

Bargaining Units and Union Jurisdiction

The power to determine the bargaining unit gives NLRB, indirectly, the power to affect the jurisdictional boundaries of unions.   For example, in

[20] *Ibid.,* pp. 150–155.

[21] This clause of Taft-Hartley was, apparently, a Congressional answer to a Supreme Court decision, announced May 19, 1947, which held the Wagner Act applicable to plant guards; Fred Witney, *op. cit.,* pp. 305–306.

[22] Witney, *op. cit.,* pp. 290–304.

[23] *Ibid.,* p. 301.

choosing a craft or a company unit within a given firm, the Board determines whether or not a craft union should gain some members.   It was this fact that so agitated the AFL on the "Globe doctrine."   Similar issues arise where different unions have organized the various plants of a given firm; i.e., if a company-wide bargaining unit is chosen, all but one union will lose members to the choice of the majority.[24]

If all jurisdictional disputes could be settled by the unions involved so that two unions never competed for the adherence of any group of workers, the influence of the Board on union jurisdiction could be greatly reduced.   For then, a union would never seek certification in a bargaining unit including workers awarded to the jurisdiction of another union, and all unions concerned would make a unanimous request as to the choice of the bargaining unit.[25]   However, even with the formation of AFL-CIO, we are still some distance from such a state of affairs.

Conflict between the jurisdictional claims of unions and the bargaining unit decisions of NLRB resulted, under the Wagner Act, in occasional "strikes against certification."   That is, the workers in a given bargaining unit would choose one union, but another union claiming jurisdiction would organize a boycott of the firm in question.   This put the employer in the unenviable position of violating the law if he negotiated with the boycotting union and possibly wrecking his business if he didn't.   A number of states outlawed such strikes and Taft-Hartley [Section 8b (4)] specifically declares strikes or boycotts to be an unfair labor practice if they are aimed at forcing an employer to negotiate with a noncertified union when another union has already been certified.

Majorities and Runoff Elections

The Wagner Act required that the bargaining agent certified as representative should be the choice of a majority of the workers in the designated bargaining unit.   This requirement was unambiguous, so long as the ballot contained only two choices (e.g., Union XYZ and no union).   This was the situation envisaged by the authors of the Wagner Act.   But it has frequently happened that two unions have demanded places on the ballot which, together with a no union option, creates three alternatives.   There is no problem so long as some one voting option gains an absolute majority of the votes, but, with more than two options, it is possible that no one of them will receive a majority.

[24] Recently, the Board virtually condemned the Marine Cooks and Stewards Union to extinction by redefining a bargaining unit so as to place cooks, stewards, and sailors in the same unit.   The sailors far outnumber the cooks and stewards and are affiliated with a union (Sailors Union of the Pacific) bitterly hostile to the Marine Cooks and Stewards.   See *Monthly Labor Review,* February 1955, p. 223 and April 1955 p. iii.

[25] Of course, employers might petition for a different bargaining unit.

The Wagner Act made no provision for handling such situations, and NLRB was forced to improvise; its policy was to conduct "runoff" elections.[26] This led to some disagreement among the Board members as to which option should be placed on the "runoff ballot," and the question was never settled in a completely satisfactory manner.[27] Taft-Hartley resolved the issue by prescribing that in the event no voting option receives a majority, a runoff election should be held with the two options receiving the greatest numbers of votes being placed on the (runoff) ballot.

Eligibility to Vote in Certification Elections

Under the Wagner Act, NLRB followed a policy of allowing all bona fide employees in the bargaining unit to vote. Complications arose when an election occurred during a strike in which replacements for the strikers were hired. Then it was necessary to decide whether strikers, replacements, or both should be given the right to vote. The procedure adopted was to permit both strikers eligible for reinstatement and *permanent* replacements hired during the strike to vote.[28] Sometimes this created more votes than jobs, but it proved a tolerable compromise between the union contention that only strikers should vote and the position of some employer groups that strikers, as such, have terminated their employment relation and only nonstrikers should be afforded the ballot.

Taft-Hartley altered NLRB procedure by specifying [Section 9c(3)] that "employees on strike who are not entitled to reinstatement are not eligible to vote.[29] Now under both Wagner and Taft-Hartley, employees striking against an unfair labor practice are entitled to reinstatement, and the employer will be compelled to reinstate them with back pay. But an "economic striker" (i.e., one striking to improve wages, hours, or conditions not specified by law) is not entitled to reinstatement; it is up to the employer to decide whether to replace him or rehire him.

So long as the employer must deal with the striking union, striker's

---

[26] Millis and Brown, *op. cit.*, pp. 134–135; also Bowman, *op. cit.*, pp. 142–155.

[27] The fundamental difficulty resides in the fact that, where there are more than two voting options, there may be no voting option which would not be opposed by a majority of the electorate. On this point see K. J. Arrow, *Social Choice and Individual Values*, Cowles Commission Monograph, No. 12, John Wiley & Sons, Inc., New York, 1951. The various Board members perceived various aspects of the difficulty but not the basic problem; see Bowman, *op. cit.*, pp. 142–155. The authors of Taft-Hartley do not seem to have understood the problem either.

[28] It is obviously not easy to determine whether a worker hired during a strike is a *permanent* replacement.

[29] In practice, NLRB under T-H, has permitted both strikers and replacements to vote, but segregates challenged ballots. If the challenged ballots could affect the outcome of the election, the Board rules, in each case, as to whether a striker has been permanently replaced and thereby determines whether he or his replacement is entitled to vote.

jobs are fairly safe as the union will not usually settle unless the employer takes back all workers without loss of seniority.   But this will not be true if the employer can avoid dealing with the union.   Both Wagner and T-H require an employer to bargain with a duly certified union, but if the employer can arrange to have a new election, the striking union may lose its certification.   And, if the nonstriking workers and newly hired replacements are allowed to vote but strikers are not, it is extremely likely that this is precisely what will happen.

This creates the following possibility: an antiunion employer wishing to rid himself of a union insists upon an absurdly large wage cut (which is not an unfair labor practice in the eyes of the law) thereby forcing a strike.   Once the strike is started, he replaces the strikers and asks for a new certification election in which the strikers are ineligible to vote. Presumably the replacements will vote against the striking union in order to keep their jobs, and the union will be driven from the plant.

This possibility has been much complained of by union spokesmen (and others)[30] who refer to the relevant clause in T-H as "union busting." It is this provision, as much as any in T-H, that has enraged and alarmed unionists—and justifiably.   In the event of serious unemployment, antiunion employers could exploit the aforementioned possibility to imperil the very existence of unions.

Elimination of this possibility was one of the changes in T-H proposed by President Eisenhower in a message to Congress in early 1954.   It was proposed that no certification elections could be held within a period of four months after the commencement of an economic strike.   However, the proposals made in this message have encountered strong opposition from both unions and employer groups, (the two groups objected to different proposals) and, as a result, they were not acted upon.

Petitions for Certification and Decertification Elections

In the previous section it was mentioned that the employer might petition for a certification election.   This is one of the changes instituted by T-H; under the Wagner Act, NLRB entertained employer petitions for certification elections only in the event two unions were demanding representation.   Now, an employer may seek an election even though there is no problem of union rivalry.   Also, as under the Wagner Act, one or more employees may petition for "decertification" of a union, and the Board may then order a decertification election held.   These election rules are subject to the condition that not more than one certification or decertification election may be held in any 12 month period; this proviso

---

[30] For example, *Business Week*, a conservative organ of business opinion, remarked (December 18, 1948) that this aspect of T-H, under the proper circumstances, "could wreck the labor movement."

is probably desirable in order to give unions a chance to stabilize bargaining relations without facing the political pressure of an imminent election.

The intent of the changes made by T-H in electoral procedure was to facilitate "revolution" by union members against their "government." Decertification elections are a channel of legal revolution[31] for the members of a union, additional to the possibility of voting out the officers. The importance of this channel lies in the possibility it creates for outvoted, but dissatisfied, minorities to change their union affiliation in order to secure more favorable treatment. Obviously, it is sometimes highly desirable that this channel should exist. However, this is not always so; the demands of minorities may be unfair and prejudicial to the interests and wishes of a majority.

T-H, in general, stresses the protection of minority rights. One consequence of this predilection is that the act tends to weaken the internal strength of union governments and their power of waging economic warfare. This consequence was neither unforseen nor unintended; T-H aimed at weakening unions in their "foreign relations" as well as internally. Many union spokesmen feel that T-H's concern with union minorities is merely a rationalization for measures whose real purpose is to reduce union fighting power. Although there is a good deal of evidence for this contention, the reader should not fall victim to the view that the interests of union minorities are unimportant or beyond hope of effective protection. However, extending such protection is a tricky business in which any measure taken has many, and often unforeseen, ramifications.

THE RIGHTS OF THE UNION MEMBER

Expulsion and Union Security

In our discussion of union security (pp. 175–180), it was indicated how Taft-Hartley sought to restrict compulsory unionism and the rather limited extent to which its provisions have accomplished this purpose. By seeking to permit workers to refrain from joining unions without sacrificing their jobs, T-H sought to reduce the control of union government over the "job territory" that comprises its zone of sovereignty. In the absence of compulsory membership, workers in a union's job territory need not submit to its ordinances, and may, if displeased by its actions, withdraw without loss of employment. But, as we have seen, T-H did not succeed in reducing the prevalence of compulsory unionism.

However, T-H has enhanced the rights of the union "citizen" in other ways. One protection given by T-H to the union citizen was to make it

---

[31] That is, a channel by which dissatisfied members of a union may secede from it.

an "unfair labor practice"[32] for a union to press an employer to discharge a worker for nonunion membership if said worker has offered to pay union dues and initiation fees.

This clause means that, if a union should expel a worker for violating a union rule but the worker continued to pay, or to offer, his dues, the union was debarred from seeking his discharge.   The desirability of such a prohibition obviously depends upon the types of offences against union "law" that it protects.   It can, of course, be used to protect strike-breaking, acting as the agent of an employer or rival union, working for wages below the union scale, or other behavior highly detrimental to the interest of the union.   Indeed, some defenders of unionism allege that this clause is merely a device for encouraging "sedition," and that it does not serve to protect any *legitimate* rights of union members.

There is no doubt but that this provision can serve to compel unions to keep enemies within their gates.   But (see pp. 133–136) the judicial proceedings against transgressors of union law are not above challenge on grounds of fairness.   Specifically, some union tribunals have shown a disturbing tendency to confuse political opposition with sedition.   This being the case, it may reasonably be contended that we cannot permit such tribunals the authority to exclude individuals from wide areas of employment by expelling them from the union.

In point of fact, where a union shop exists, few employers would dare continue to employ an expelled member—and fewer expelled unionists would dare to accept employment.   For this reason, the provision in T-H is probably not of much practical importance.   Far more protection could be given the rights of individual union citizens, and with less injury to the effectiveness of union government, if T-H (or some other law) specified a "bill of rights" for union members and a "penal code."   The bill of rights would designate, in broad terms, what acts of the individual member could not be restricted by union law,[33] while the "penal code" would specify the punishments for various infractions of union law.   Rules for the conduct of union tribunals, including an appeals mechanism, might also be specified.

Union Autonomy versus Public Control

Suggestions that a "bill of rights" and "penal code" (for union members) be prescribed by law are usually subjected to bitter opposition from organized labor. A long history of judicial hostility to unionism has imparted a strong "voluntaristic" flavor (see pp. 94–96) to union ideology on any issue of public control over union affairs.   Union spokesmen frequently

[32] See pp. 245 et seq.

[33] See, for example, Joel Seidman, *Union Rights and Union Duties*, Harcourt, Brace & Co., New York, 1943.

adopt the position that any needed reform of union practice must come by voluntary action of the unions concerned, and that it would be tyranny to impose it from without. In the course of such arguments, there often enters the unstated premise that unions are merely voluntary associations like social clubs. This premise is difficult to reconcile with demands for union security in collective bargaining contracts.

To a limited extent, T-H attempts to reconcile the conflict between compulsory unionism and complete freedom of unions to run their own affairs. However, instead of facing up to the problem directly, it begins by evading the issue, stating in Section 8b (paragraph 1) "That this paragraph shall not impair the right of a labor organization to prescribe its own rules with respect to the acquisition or retention of membership therein." Despite this disclaimer, in paragraph 5 (same section) it is declared an unfair labor practice for a union to require excessive or discriminatory initiation fees.[34] However, apart from this, T-H does not attempt to regulate union dues or entrance requirements.[35] Specifically, and significantly, it makes no attempt to compel unions to cease discriminating against negroes in admission requirements, it merely permits employers to use the fact of such discrimination as a basis for a charge of an unfair labor practice, if a union pressures them for a union shop.

T-H (Section 9f) attempts to regulate the internal affairs of unions via a second channel, i.e., by setting certain conditions that must be satisfied as a precondition to the use of the facilities of NLRB. These preconditions are: (1) that a union must publish (among other things) the names, titles, compensation, and allowances of its three principal officers and any others whose aggregate compensation and allowances exceed $5,000; (2) that the initiation fees and dues of the organization and its basic rules and laws be published; and (3) that it publish (annual) financial statements.

Obviously, it is difficult for unions to object to such requirements; in point of fact, either they already had been met voluntarily or easily could be met by *most* American unions. But the fact that the *majority* of American unions are "clean" and well-run does not justify a contention that legislative restraint upon the conduct of their internal affairs is unnecessary. After all, criminal statutes are not needed to change the behavior of the great *majority* of citizens. To be sure, AFL-CIO is earnestly trying to clean its own house; but it can do no more than expel recalcitrants, a measure of uncertain efficacy. Hence, it is likely that

[34] However, this provision has had but little effect on union practice.

[35] T-H does state in Section 8a, paragraph 3, that an employer may not justify discharge of a worker (under a union shop agreement) for nonmembership in the union if he has "reasonable grounds" for believing that the worker was not offered membership on the same terms as others. However, this provision at most helps an employer wishing to fight a discriminating union; it does not restrain the union and has been of little practical effect.

there will continue to be a role for public law in the regulation of union affairs.

The widespread existence of the union shop gives unions something of the status and responsibility of a public utility.   Accordingly, it is not unreasonable that they be required to conduct their affairs in accordance with the general ethical norms of the community.   And, for most unions, such requirements would not involve a change of their present (or pre-Taft-Hartley) practices.   (Most statutory law is but the imposition of the customary practice of the great majority upon a small and objectionable minority).

It is unfortunate that the first essay in public control of internal union affairs should have been part of a law aimed at weakening unions, relative to employers, and passed in a mood of hostility toward unions.   This circumstance has reawakened labor's fears that any such control is necessarily inimical to the cause of unionism.   However, for good or ill, it is unlikely that we shall ever again permit unions to go completely unregulated; it is to be hoped that one day AFL-CIO will help design a new and improved legislative code of union practice.

Union Political Activities

Title III of T-H contains an amendment to the Federal Corrupt Practices Act.   The amendment forbids any labor organization or corporation to make any contributions or expenditure in connection with an election or primary in which officials of the federal government (i.e., President, Vice-President, Congressmen, and Senators) are chosen.   This provision was obviously intended to hamper the political activity of unions; the officials and stockholders of corporations can (and do) make large contributions as individuals, but union members are not wealthy and funds cannot easily be raised from them by political subscription.[36]

Galling as this was, it has not seriously impaired union political activities, to the great disappointment of many supporters of T-H.   Unions have been able to carry on almost all of their customary political activities by means of affiliates (see pp. 105–107) to which individual union members are encouraged, and do, contribute.   Indeed, because of their indignation at Taft-Hartley, unions have engaged in political activity on a greater scale than ever before.

[36] This is not because workmen are peculiarly averse to contributing but because the cost of collecting a given sum increases rapidly with increase in the number of sources from which it must be collected.   Furthermore, individual contributions of (say) $1 from a million workmen, unless coordinated through a central agency, cannot command the same degree of political influence as $1,000,000 from one person.   No one worker's contribution is big enough to warrant a bargain by a candidate; it is only when workers pool their contributions and offer them as a quid pro quo (as business men do), that they can wield political influence.

Furthermore, almost as soon as T-H was passed, Philip Murray (then president of CIO) tested the implications of this section of the Act by causing the CIO News openly to support a candidate for Congress and circulating the relevant editions within the electoral district.   Murray was indicted, as he had intended, but the Supreme Court held by a five to four vote that T-H did not intend to prohibit unions from printing newspapers whose contents might influence political elections.   The minority contended vigorously that T-H had intended to prohibit precisely such behavior and that such prohibition was in conflict with the first amendment (which protects freedom of speech.)[37]

Because of its relative ineffectiveness, the debate over T-H's prohibition of political expenditures is somewhat less heated now than it was in 1947–1948.   However, an issue of principle does remain.   Supporters of T-H contend that it is unfair to compel a man to join a union in order to keep his job and then force him to submit to seeing part of his dues used to support a candidate of whom he may disapprove.   (It is undoubtedly true that such protestations often are, as opponents of T-H allege, mere rationalizations of a desire to weaken union political influence, but that is beside the point.)   This is an invasion of the rights of such individuals—and an unnecessary one.   It is not difficult for unions to allocate a specific part of their funds for political activity and permit individuals to withhold, or rebate to them upon application, a proportionate part of their dues.   (T-H requires separate contributions for political activity, which makes fundraising a bit harder.)   The principle of noncompulsion of individual members can here be applied without serious injury to the union.   However, the relevant section of T-H is subject to substantial improvement.

The Non-Communist Affidavit

Section 9h of T-H requires, as a condition of certification, that a union's officers submit non-Communist affidavits.   A number of important union leaders (notably Philip Murray and John L. Lewis) known for their anti-Communist views refused to sign such oaths on principle and eschewed the services of NLRB.   They felt that such an oath was insulting, and especially so since it was not required of employers.   The indignation of union leaders is easier to understand if it is realized that, at the time T-H was enacted, such affidavits were not so common as they became a few years later.

Whether one approves of anti-Communist affidavits in general, is a broad question which has no particular bearing upon the problems of collective bargaining.   But, at the time T-H was enacted, a number of CIO unions were dominated, or heavily infiltrated, by Communists, and Congress chose a rather clumsy method of ousting them.   It is doubtful that inability of

[37] See Witney, *op. cit.,* pp. 427–433.

Communist-led unions to avail themselves of NLRB services would have mattered much had not the labor movement itself (especially CIO) taken extreme measures to purge them from its ranks.   However, given the policy of the labor movement, the requirement of non-Communist affidavits proved to be a weapon of some utility.   Whether this requirement is any longer of value is a debatable matter.

UNION POWER TO WAGE ECONOMIC WARFARE: STRIKES

The Wagner Act attempted to curb only the unfair labor practices committed by employers.   Indeed, so far as the Wagner Act was concerned, unfair labor practices included only refusals to bargain in "good faith" and attempts to coerce employees in their choice of bargaining representatives. "Good faith" bargaining implied nothing as to the content of the agreement that emerged.   As of 1935, there were few problems about the willingness of unions to bargain; however, many employers (see p. 145) openly refused to deal with unions.   It was at this particular employer policy that the Wagner Act was directed.

However, by 1947, the situation had changed.   Their phenomenal growth, combined with court decisions that greatly widened the scope of permissible tactics and objectives in economic warfare, had bestowed great powers of economic coercion upon unions.   And there had been some (well-publicized) instances in which these powers were abused.   To prevent such abuses, T-H proscribed a whole list of "unfair" labor practices which it admonishes *unions* to avoid.   The intended effect of these admonitions is to restrict the power of unions to wage economic warfare.

Bargaining in Good Faith

There has never been a problem of getting unions to bargain that was at all comparable with the (pre-1937) refusal of employers to "deal with unions as such."   However, there have been a few cases where unions refused to bargain: For example, a Teamster's local in New York refused to deal with an employer who had been tried for, and acquitted of, killing a teamster during a previous labor dispute.[38]   Then there was the long-standing policy of the Typographers (and a few other unions) of refusing to permit their locals to bargain about national union "laws"; this policy has been held by NLRB to constitute a violation of T-H.[39]

T-H certainly makes it illegal for a union to refuse to bargain at all or even to refuse to discuss certain issues when NLRB has ruled that bargain-

[38] Hunt vs. Crumboch (1945).   The Supreme Court upheld the Teamsters legal right to behave as they did.   For a good discussion of this case see Gregory, *op. cit.* pp. 285–287.

[39] Brown and Millis, *op. cit.,* p. 642, note 74.

ing in "good faith" requires negotiation upon them. However, requiring that a union, or an employer, must bargain about a certain matter is of little effect if the party in question is determined to evade the requirement; i.e., the union or employer can always offer unacceptable terms on other matters unless this particular issue is settled to its satisfaction (see p. 182).

It would be too much to say that the requirement to bargain in good faith is of *no* effect. It can affect bargaining tactics; for example, in 1955, an employer who pleaded inability to pay a wage increase was ordered (by NLRB) to let the union see his books. Or, where public opinion is a factor, an NLRB order to bargain on a given issue may compel a party to take a "reasonable" stand on said issue. However, in most circumstances the requirement of "good faith" bargaining does not impose a serious restraint upon bargaining tactics.

Another instance where legislation to control the process of collective bargaining has failed in its purpose is the "cooling off" requirement of Section 8d of Taft-Hartley. This requirement was based on the misconception that *authorized* strikes frequently result from sudden outbursts of anger and that they could be reduced in number by requiring a delay to "cool off." Accordingly, it was required that (1) strikes shall not commence (at the termination of a contract) unless 60 days prior notice is given to the other party and (2) unless 30 days notice is given to federal and state conciliation agencies. Evasion of these requirements has been easy; unions have come to give strike notices as a matter of routine, in order to preserve maximum freedom of action and to convince employers that their demands are made in earnest.

Unfair Labor Practices by Unions

A far more serious restriction upon union activity is the list of union labor practices declared (in Section 8b) to be "unfair." These practices include attempts to gain a closed shop, to compel discharge of union members who have offered to pay dues, refusal to bargain in good faith with an employer, and charging excessive or discriminatory dues. These are matters that have already been discussed.

However, in addition to these practices, T-H also declares it to be an unfair labor practice to engage in secondary boycotts, jurisdictional strikes, strikes against NLRB certification, strikes to compel employers either to join unions or employers' associations, or strikes to enforce "featherbedding" rules. T-H also restricts the characteristics of the collectively bargained health, welfare, and pension funds. With the exception of the prohibition on secondary boycotts all of these are restrictions on the *objectives* of collective bargaining. Let us consider these in order, and reserve secondary boycotts for the last.

JURISDICTIONAL STRIKES. Jurisdictional strikes are those intended to compel an employer to award certain jobs to members of one union rather than to those of another. They represent attempts of a union to use economic force to set the boundaries of its jurisdiction.[40] Prior to 1947, the unions in the building trades were probably the most notorious jurisdictional strikers; since then the teamsters would probably merit this distinction. However, at one time or another most unions have been involved in jurisdictional disputes.

Although jurisdictional disputes are sometimes difficult to avoid, they are unfair and costly to employers who are often (though not always) innocent by-standers.[41] In any event, jurisdictional strikes are justly unpopular with the public, and there can be no doubt but that this part of T-H is here to stay, in one form or another.

However, it is one thing to outlaw jurisdictional strikes; it is another to adjudicate the disputes from which they arise. Section 10k of the Act gives the Board power to "hear and determine" such disputes if they have not been voluntarily settled within 10 days after notification of the Board. That is, NLRB is given authority to act as a court of compulsory arbitration to settle jurisdictional strikes, with violation of its awards being punished as an unfair labor practice.

The threat of compulsory arbitration of complicated jurisdictional issues has led the unions in the Building Trades Department of AFL, whose jurisdictional struggles were long famous, to establish (together with the Associated General Contractors of America) the National Joint Board for the Settlement of Jurisdictional Disputes.[42] This Board has succeeded in securing the compliance of the strong building trades unions (e.g., the Carpenters) whose intransigeance had frustrated earlier attempts at voluntary arbitration of jurisdictional disputes. Its procedure involves extensive mediation and uses local tribunals as much as possible; the National Joint Board operates solely as a court of last resort. Juris-

[40] The term "jurisdictional" dispute is not usually used to cover all struggles between unions. "Jurisdictional" disputes proper are those in which the contending unions wish to fill a given set of jobs with their present membership and do not attempt to acquire the members of another union who happen to be holding the jobs. Other union conflicts arise where two unions attempt to enroll a given group of workers; here, the objective is additional members rather than more employment for given members. In practice, the two types of conflict shade into each other.

[41] Not infrequently, employers provoke jurisdictional conflict by attempting to assign jobs ordinarily filled by (relatively) expensive workers to those receiving lower rates of pay.

[42] The National Joint Board, and its subordinate local boards, have the very considerable advantages of expertness and ability to act promptly, since settling these disputes is its sole business. The crowded NLRB calendar would surely prevent prompt adjudiction of disputes as well as expose the disputants to the risk of highly inexpert rulings.

dictional strikes are forbidden, and it is agreed that members of unions shall continue to work on the basis of original assignments, provided employers do not violate decisions or agreements previously recorded by the National Joint Board.

Undoubtedly T-H deserves credit for putting pressure upon the building trade unions to adjudicate their jurisdictional problems peacefully. It may also have made some contribution to the climate of opinion that led to the AFL-CIO no-raiding pact (pp. 77–78). However, the manner in which T-H proscribes jurisdictional strikes is open to criticism. T-H makes an unfair labor practice to strike against *any* allocation of work by an employer. This permits an employer to violate customary work allocations in order to favor the members of relatively low wage unions without permitting the injured unions to protect their interests.

STRIKES AGAINST CERTIFICATION. Strikes against certification are similar to jurisdictional strikes in that they involve coercive efforts by one union to force an employer to deal with it rather than with a rival union. They are, therefore, objectionable for the same reason as jurisdictional strikes. However, in these strikes there is the additional consideration that the rival union has obtained NLRB certification and is therefore (presumably) the choice of the majority of employees in the bargaining unit. Since strikes of this kind are attempts to use economic pressure to prevent the majority of the workers in a bargaining unit from choosing their own representatives, they are objectionable on this ground also.

Under the Wagner Act, strikes against certification occasionally took place, and the Board was unable to punish the striking union. Such a strike might completely halt a firm's activity and drive it to negotiate with the noncertified union. But NLRB would attempt to prevent such negotiation even to the extent of using its legal powers. The Board sympathized with the employer's plight, but it felt obliged to force the employer to comply with the Wagner Act, despite the economic damage he might suffer, and from which the Board could not protect him.[43] Fortunately, strikes against certification were not numerous, but those that did occur placed employers in an intolerable position, and the relief granted by T-H was certainly appropriate.

STRIKES TO COMPEL EMPLOYER AFFILIATION. Certain unions have attempted to compel self-employed persons, especially in retail trade and service, to join (see pp. 152–153). Their motive is not only to add to their dues receipts but also to control the work standards of self-employed competitors of unionized firms. One's attitude toward such union tactics depends upon his evaluation of the importance of encouraging small enterprise in these fields as compared with the desirability of preserving

[43] Brown and Millis, *op. cit.*, pp. 216–233.

minimum union standards for wages, hours, and working conditions. There is no general agreement upon the issue involved; this is an area in which the student must judge for himself.

Some unions have sought to cooperate with employer associations to promote various mutual objectives (see pp. 152–153). To assist these efforts, they have, at times, tried to compel nonassociation employers to join these associations. Use of economic pressure for such purposes is proscribed by Taft-Hartley and is also likely to run afoul of the Sherman Act (see pp. 216–217). In some cases, the cooperation of unions and employer associations may indicate no more than the existence of friendly, mature bargaining relations; in others, it signifies the union's participation in schemes to control product prices. Such schemes are not always indefensible, but they are subject to grave suspicion.

FEATHERBEDDING. "Featherbedding" arises when a collective bargaining contract requires that a specific number of workers be hired whenever a particular kind of job is to be performed, irrespective of the number "needed." Sometimes this results in some of the "workers" having literally no work to perform. The insistence of certain unions, e.g., the Musicians, on retaining these hiring requirements is usually due to their desire to maximize employment opportunities (at the union scale) in the face of declining demand rather than to get their members "something for nothing."

We have already discussed the pros and cons of union make-work rules (pp. 198–200). But, even if it be granted that it would be desirable to eliminate such rules, it is generally conceded that legislative prescription is either highly ineffective or destructive of "free collective bargaining." Taft-Hartley states, in effect, that it shall be an unfair labor practice for a union to require payment for services not performed; however, this prohibition could be (and has been) evaded by framing work rules so as to require excessive numbers of workers on whatever work is to be performed.[44] To prevent such evasion would require government control of union work rules and, if that control were not to be frustrated, of wage rates.

HEALTH, WELFARE, AND PENSION FUNDS. T-H imposes some minor restrictions upon the uses of pooled funds to which the employer has made a contribution. The customary use of such funds (medical, health and life insurance, pensions) are permitted; however, as T-H enumerates (in Title III, Section 302c) the permissible uses of such funds, those not mentioned are presumably outlawed. For example, use of such funds for vacation benefits would be illegal.

More important than the rather minor restriction upon uses of such

[44] For example, see S. C. Sufrin and R. C. Sedgwick, *Labor Law*, T. Y. Crowell and Co., New York, 1954, pp. 381–396.

funds is the requirement that they be administered jointly by employers and employee representatives. This provision conflicted with the long-established practice in the men's clothing manufacturing industry (and elsewhere) that such funds be administered solely by the union. The employers in men's clothing manufacturing protested that this section of Taft-Hartley was unnecessary and inconvenient to them, but their protestations were of no avail.

There can be little doubt but that careful regulation of health, welfare, and pension funds is desirable. However, it is doubtful that the provisions of T-H make much of a contribution to achieving this objective. The most that can be said for T-H, in this connection, is that it does little harm.

SECONDARY BOYCOTTS. All of the aforementioned restrictions upon union behavior have referred to the *objectives* of collective bargaining. The prohibition of secondary boycotts is a restriction upon the means of exerting economic pressure, *whatever* it's object.

The avowed purpose of limiting secondary boycotts is to protect neutrals in a war between an employer and a union. As in other types of warfare, it is difficult to protect neutrals without, at the same time, favoring one or the other of the belligerents.

As used here, the term "boycott" refers not only to refusals to purchase but also to refusals to perform work, i.e., to strikes. A "primary" boycott by a labor union is directed against the particular employer with whom it is engaged in a dispute; such a boycott usually involves exhortation by pickets and/or advertisements in newspapers not to patronize or accept employment from the employer (*A*) in question. A "secondary" boycott arises when the union attempts to induce the customers or employees of a second employer (*B*), not directly engaged in the dispute, to refrain from dealing with *B* in order to help the union win its struggle with the first employer, *A*.[45]

The traditional (Common Law) justification for permitting any person or combination of persons to inflict economic injury on others is that the "aggressors" are pursuing their own economic interest. This has been the rationalization the courts have used for permitting unions to engage in primary strikes or boycotts. For a long time, the courts refused to recognize any self-interest that would justify secondary boycotts. However, in the 1930's (see pp. 212 et seq.), they began to take an increasingly broad view of what constituted economic self-interest and (prior to Taft-Hartley) they had come, on various legal grounds, to permit a very wide

---

[45] The precise determination of whether any given boycott is of a primary or secondary nature is not so simple as this definition might suggest. For a more detailed discussion of the problem, see C. O. Gregory, *Labor and the Law,* pp. 105–157.

range of freedom for secondary boycotts. However, the courts have, in principle, always been free to insist that some (unspecified) degree of economic self-interest must be demonstrated to justify a boycott; the purely sympathetic strike has always had a doubtful status before the law.

Taft-Hartley outlaws secondary boycotts but permits primary ones. However, the boundary line between primary and secondary boycotts is not a sharp one; if firm A, which is struck, has its orders filled, on its behalf, by firm B, is the boycott called by the striking union against firm B primary or secondary? The NLRB ruled that boycott action in a case such as this would not be in contravention of Taft-Hartley, provided the contract between firm B and its employees stated that the workers might refuse to perform struck work or handle "hot cargo." The (then) general counsel, Mr. Denham, felt otherwise and protested vehemently.[46] In 1954 the Board (whose composition had changed in the meanwhile) partially abandoned its former position; in the McAllister Transfer case, the Board held that although an agreement providing that union members might refuse to handle "hot cargo" was legal, the union was forbidden to use economic pressure of any kind to enforce such a provision in the event that the employer refused to live up to it. This, of course, greatly weakens the value of such contract provisions.

The need to prevent at least some types of secondary boycotts is akin to the need for protecting persons going about their own business from being forced to choose a side and participate in a street fight. We permit economic warfare between bargaining partners; but most of us do not desire to permit the conversion of any given economic struggle into a nation-wide battle between employers and unions.[47] The practical problem is "how neutral must a noncombatant be to merit society's protection against 'conscription'?"

With but few exceptions, secondary boycotts are devices to help unions that are weak at the point of conflict.[48] A union that can compel an employer to shut down by striking (usually[49]) has little to gain by imposing a secondary boycott. It is the union that cannot prevent operation during a strike that needs outside assistance.

Secondary boycotts are also employed frequently during organizing campaigns. It often happens that a union attempts to organize firms (especially in southern textile mills, in retail trade, and service) in which the majority of the workers do not wish to join a union. However, as the

---

[46] See Witney, *op. cit.*, pp. 483–484.

[47] See pp. 259 et seq.

[48] An analogous statement applies to the employer; NLRB has held that T-H forbids the members of an employer's association to lock out their employees because of a struggle of one of their members with a union.

[49] Except where a firm can make deliveries from inventory (see p. 166).

output of these firms competes closely with that of unionized firms, the union has a strong interest in subjecting them to union conditions. Sometimes it can accomplish this only through a secondary boycott of distributive outlets.

In short, the neutrality of the "outsiders" against whom secondary boycotts are directed varies from one situation to another. Furthermore, in some cases a secondary boycott is the only effective device by which a union can bring economic pressure to bear upon an employer. T-H outlaws most secondary boycotts; "hot cargo" cases, where contractual arrangements specifically permit, are the only secondary boycotts allowed. The effect of so circumscribing this union weapon is to reduce union strength. Whether the added protection given third parties by such circumscription justifies the restraint imposed upon unions is an issue upon which opinions differ.

There is no general agreement as to just how to define the field of permissible secondary boycotts, and there are vocal minority opinions at both extremes; i.e., at one extreme, there are those who would permit any secondary boycott and, at the other, those who would forbid them all. Most expert opinion lies somewhere in the middle.

TAFT-HARTLEY AND EMPLOYER BARGAINING POWER

Reducing union power to conduct strikes obviously implies an increase in the relative bargaining strength of employers. However, T-H also contains certain provisions which increase employer bargaining power directly.

Coercion in Choice of Bargaining Representatives

Because of the long history of employer discrimination against unionists, in the early days of the Wagner Act NLRB sometimes used employer statements (made immediately prior to certification elections) as evidence of coercion. If, in such cases, the election was lost by the union, the NLRB sometimes declared it null and void because of employer coercion.[50] Where NLRB used employer statements as evidence of coercion, it was denounced for denying freedom of speech to employers. The Supeme Court ruled that, where employer statements were part of a pattern of coercive behavior, such orders did not constitute infringement of free speech. However, expression of employer opinion was never in itself considered proof of coercion. The Board was still in process of developing criteria for the limits of permissible employer statements when T-H was enacted in 1947.

Under T-H (Section 8c), it was specifically stated that "the expressing of any views, argument or opinion . . . shall not constitute or be evi-

[50] Millis and Brown, *op. cit.,* pp. 174–189.

dence of an unfair labor practice . . . if such expression contains no threat of reprisal or force or promise of benefit." This widened permissible employer campaign tactics, against unions seeking certification, considerably beyond what they had previously been.

The effect of enhancing employer campaign facilities may be to hamper the initial unionization of workers who are easily overawed by the employer's authority or impressed by his statements. Employees of this type are most likely to be found in small towns, especially in the south, where unions have complained that employer resistance is bolder and more effective than before the enactment of T-H. However, it seems unlikely that T-H has made any major change in the ability of employers to resist unionization, for the percentage of "no union" votes has not been appreciably higher since 1947 than in the four years preceding the passage of T-H.[51] It must, of course, be remembered that the high level of employment obtaining since 1947 may have restrained many employers from resisting unionization and prevented the full potentialities of this part of T-H from unfolding.

Since 1953, the Board has tended to permit a very wide degree of freedom to the employer in persuading his employees not to join a union. For example, an employer is now permitted (among other things) to make antiunion speeches on company time and company property without extending the union equal facilities; to state that if the union won a majority in an NLRB election, he would tie it up in prolonged litigation, meanwhile refusing to bargain; to "predict" that the plant would be closed if the union won an NLRB election; to question individual workers about their union activities and affiliations.[52]

All these things may be done without commission of an unfair labor practice, provided they are not accompanied by "threat of reprisal or promise of benefit." Failure to guard words carefully, in discussing unions with employees, may still cause citation for unfair labor practice, but, in the words of one authority, "I think it is an accurate statement that an employer may today, if he is legally advised, exert in one form or another through the medium of carefully moulded words his full economic power to affect an employee organizing effort.[53] This is a far cry from the days of the Wagner Act or even the policies of NLRB prior to 1953; obviously it facilitates employer resistance to unionization.

---

[51] S. H. Slichter, "Revision of the Taft-Hartley Act," *Quarterly Journal of Economics,* May 1953, pp. 154–155.

[52] C. A. Morgan, *Trends in NLRB Decisions During 1953–1954,* Research Series 10, Bureau of Labor and Management, College of Commerce, State University of Iowa, Iowa City, 1955, pp. 16–21.

[53] Remarks by W. W. Wirtz, before the Labor Law Section, American Bar Association, Philadelphia, Pa., August 22, 1955 (mimeographed), p. 8.

Unfair Labor Practices: Procedure

Even under the Wagner Act, the disposition of unfair labor practice cases was very slow. Workers found to have been discharged for union activities would be reinstated with back pay, but a year or two might elapse before this happened. As a result, the threat of discharge remained a potent weapon in the hands of antiunion employers, despite the intent of the Wagner Act. But under the Wagner Act, delays in handling employer unfair labor practices were unintended; T-H, however, deliberately encourages delay in such cases. It does this by requiring that investigation of alleged secondary boycotts must receive priority over all other charges of unfair labor practices. It is impossible to say how much this particular clause has actually delayed the processing of (employes) complaints about unfair labor practices by employers; however, the intent of the clause is clear.

The greater stress laid by T-H upon the suppression of the unfair labor practices of unions (rather than upon those of employers) is shown by the fact that, in the event of an allegation of a secondary boycott, a strike against certification, or a strike by a noncertified union, Section 10l *requires* the General Counsel to obtain a federal injunction against such action, provided he has "reasonable cause to believe such charge is true."[54] (The injunction may be effective for no more than five days.) No such requirement is made with regard to any unfair labor practice by an employer.

In addition to the mandatory injunctions the General Counsel *may,* at his discretion (under Section 10j), seek temporary injunctions against any person (i.e., union officer or employer) charged with engaging in an unfair labor practice. T-H does not completely undo the Norris-La Guardia Act in that it does not give private parties the power to seek injunctions. However, it bestows enormous power upon the General Counsel which organized labor, with its long memory of injunctions, greatly fears.

To be sure, discretionary injunctions may, and have, been used against employers as well as against unions. Nevertheless, unions feel that the possible gains from antiemployer injunctions are far outweighed by the risk of loss from those directed against themselves. Thus far, experience under T-H has not borne out the worst fears of unions concerning injunctions; they have been issued sparingly and have served more as a threat than as a weapon.

This fact reduces the urgency of reconsidering T-H's injunction provision, but it does not dispose of the problem. The alleged need for in-

---

[54] Usually referred to as "mandatory" injunctions as distinguished from the discretionary injunctions mentioned in the next paragraph. The practical distinction between the two types of injunction is not so great as the legal one.

junctions stems from the time consuming nature of the Board's processes. While its mill is grinding, the issues at stake in a dispute may be settled irrevocably by the operation of economic pressure. Although it is both desirable, and possible, to speed up the Board's machinery, it is unlikely that it can be accelerated sufficiently to preclude occasional instances where unimpeded economic force achieves results contrary to legal intent. This fact presents a difficult problem to the citizen who desires to protect all legitimate interests. Society must bear one of two risks; it may abolish injunctions in labor disputes and risk allowing a union or employer to "get away" with an unfair labor practice, or it may continue the present state of affairs and risk having improper injunctions materially affect the interests of bargainers.[55] Unfortunately, no fool-proof formula for resolving this dilemma has yet been, or is likely to be, discovered.

Damage Suits

In addition to injunctions, Taft-Hartley has brought the courts into the bargaining process in a second way; it has facilitated damage suits, both by unions and employers, to recover losses resulting from breach of collective bargaining contracts.[56] For the most part, when suits for breach of contract have been threatened (or even commenced) during labor disputes, they have been dropped as part of the settlement and have been carried to court only rarely.

One important reason for this lies in the very nature of industrial relations; most unions and employers desire to get along with a minimum of strife, and nothing is more likely to arouse hostility than a lawsuit in which charges and countercharges are hurled about a court room. It has been well said that the courts should treat industrial relations as they treat marital relations; i.e., they refuse to handle suits of spouses against one another, except for divorce. As Slichter puts it "One must not expect damage suits to be frequently used in industrial relations. They are not the sort of device that will be employed by parties who are seeking to get on with one another."[57]

There is a further reason why damage suits are not likely to be effective in curbing "misbehavior" by unions. That is because a union can easily

---

[55] The risk of "improper" injunctions being issued, i.e., injunctions against activities later found to be lawful, is by no means imaginary. Cases of this sort arose in the first year of T-H's operation. See Millis and Brown, *op. cit.*, pp. 617–618.

[56] By eliminating two preconditions for filing such suits in the federal courts: (1) before T-H, the parties to such suits had to be citizens of different states and (2) the damages had to be at least $3,000. T-H removed both of these preconditions and, in addition, eliminated some unclarity over the legal status of collective bargaining contracts by making them enforceable at law.

[57] Slichter, *op. cit.*, p. 174.

arrange to have those acts for which it might be sued performed by "unauthorized" members for whose behavior it disclaims responsibility. The framers of Taft-Hartley recognized this problem and tried to get around it by making the union responsible for the acts of its "agents," irrespective of whether these acts were authorized.[58]   But who is an "agent"? Senator Taft agreed that being a union member did not make an individual an agent of the union; but he did not specify what the definitive characteristics of an agent were. Is every shop steward an agent? Or are agents only paid officers? If so, may the funds of a national union be seized to remedy the misdeeds of local officers? These, and related questions, are by no means settled and are still in process of being answered in the courts.

To take a restrictive view of the identity of union "agents," makes it easy for a union to evade legal responsibility for its acts. But to take a broad view, opens wide the door for irresponsible persons or agents provocateurs, hired by antiunion employers or rival unions, to imperil a union's assets. Unfortunately, there is no formula that can guarantee union financial responsibility without exposing union funds to risk of seizure for actions not in keeping with union policy. However, T-H leaves union funds in a dangerously exposed position. This was recognized in President Eisenhower's suggested amendments to T-H (in 1954), in which it was proposed to specify that members were not "agents" unless specifically authorized to perform certain acts.

T-H also makes unions vulnerable to suit (in federal courts) by *anyone* injured by an illegal secondary boycott in which it participates. There is a better case for permitting damage suits by *neutrals* than by bargaining partners. But the loose definition of "agent" and the sweeping ban on secondary boycotts make the rights of neutrals to sue for damages a threat to the effective functioning of unions.[59]

Strikes in Violation of Contract

The possibility of suing unions for breach of contract is of importance mainly in connection with violations of no-strike clauses in collective bargaining agreements. However, strikes of this kind, usually "quickies," are rarely ordered by the national organization. They are usually the work of a particular group of workers or, at most, of a single local. Yet under

[58] Previous federal law on this matter was the Norris-La Guardia Act which stated (in effect) that a union could not be held responsible for the acts of its "officers, members, or agents, except upon clear proof of actual participation in, or actual authorization of, such acts, or of ratification of such acts after actual knowledge thereof."

[59] On the whole subject of damage suits against unions, see Millis and Brown, *op. cit.*, pp. 496–513.

T-H's concept of "agent," the local or even the national organization might be held responsible for their occurrence.

To avoid this possibility, some unions have simply refused to include no-strike agreements in their contracts, an ironical consequence of legislation designed to reduce strikes. However, more unions have adopted an alternative procedure;[60] they have insisted on including in their agreements, a clause in which management undertakes not to sue for damages on account of unauthorized strikes, provided that within a short time after their outbreak (e.g., 24 hours) the union posts a statement opposing the strike and ordering the workers to return to their jobs. Obviously a union interested in violating such an agreement could arrange to have its "back-to-work" order ignored. Thus, T-H provisions notwithstanding, the observance of bargaining agreements still depends upon the desire and willingness to observe them.

THE PRESENT STATUS OF TAFT-HARTLEY

Legislative

The Taft-Hartley Act has been, since its passage, a center of political controversy. President Truman vetoed the Act with a scathing message; this veto went far toward mending the bad state of his relations with the labor movement that had resulted from his behavior in the railway strike of 1946 (see p. 75). In the 1948 election, Truman promised to work for repeal of T-H and both AFL and CIO strongly supported him, and Congressmen taking a similar stand. That there were no major amendments to T-H during Truman's second term was not for lack of effort on his part.

By and large, urban Democrats of the northern states have supported repeal of T-H whereas the southern Democrats and the majority of Republicans have opposed it. As previously noted, President Eisenhower (in 1954) proposed some modifications in the Act. For reasons indicated above (p. 238), these modifications were rejected and no further attempts at modification have been made thus far.

The fact that T-H is a political symbol has made it very hard to get specific charges considered on their merits. To some extremely conservative Republicans and southern Democrats, the only trouble with T-H was that it didn't go far enough in curbing unions. More moderate members of both parties would probably want specific changes, whereas a few strong labor supporters want repeal of the whole Act. It is likely that the pressure of unions on the one side, and employer groups on the other, forces many politicians to pretend more intransigeance on the issue

---

[60] *Monthly Labor Review*, March 1952, p. 275.

than they feel, and that one day a compromise may be worked out. However, no one can say when that day will arrive.

Administrative

The effect of Taft-Hartley, or any statute governing labor-management relations, will depend upon how it is administered. Prior to 1953, the members of NLRB were appointees of President Truman and were generally sympathetic to the cause of unionism. Of course, they functioned within the letter of the (Taft-Hartley) law and, had they not done so, could have been overruled (on appeal) by the courts. But within the limits of the law there was room for interpretation, and this interpretation tended toward protection of union rights.

President Eisenhower's appointees have been animated by a somewhat different philosophy. It is not necessary to accept fully the charges emanating from some union circles that the "new board"[61] is antilabor. However, the "new board" has indicated that it believes American unions are now "big enough to take care of themselves" and has, therefore, given the employer as much freedom to combat union organizing as the T-H law permits. The board has also enhanced the employer's power to combat union economic pressure by ruling that employers may discharge union members engaged in exerting economic pressure short of strikes (e.g., collective refusal to work overtime, slow downs, etc.) without thereby committing an unfair labor practice.

Most important of all the policies instituted by the new board is the reduction of their jurisdiction. In July 1954, the Board established a set of criteria for the minimum dollar amount of annual (interstate) business that a firm must do before its activities come into the purview of NLRB. These minima are appreciably higher than those previously in effect. The Board stated the purpose of the new regulations was to reduce the case load and accelerate the handling of cases. This is undoubtedly true, but the regulations also withdraw the protection of federal law from organizing activities in the field of small business. The relevant state laws are usually much less protective (than Taft-Hartley) of employee rights to unionize.

The significance of withdrawing small firms from the jurisdiction of NLRB is that it is the small firms which are least unionized, and where current organizing activity is concentrated. Hence, what appears, at first glance, to be a purely administrative matter has serious consequences for future organizing work. Needless to say, organized labor has bitterly denounced this policy.

---

[61] The NLRB as constituted after President Eisenhower's 1953 appointments (i.e., as constituted at the beginning of 1954) is generally referred to (in 1955–1956) as the "new board" as distinguished from its predecessor, the "old board."

The precise impact of the attitude and policies of the new board are obviously difficult to measure, but their general tendency is obviously pleasing to employers and distasteful to unions. However, the present board has been bound, to a great extent, by the decisions of its predecessors, and it has overturned only a few of them; therefore, it has not, and will not, revolutionize the state of labor-management relations. The board's decisions, since the beginning of 1954, have tended to increase the employer's freedom both in dealing with existing unions and in resisting attempts to form new ones. But the consequences of such an attitude are not likely to be so disastrous for unions in 1957 as they might have been in 1947.

DISCUSSION QUESTIONS

1. Compare the concept of "unfair labor practice" in the Wagner and Taft-Hartley Acts.

2. It is sometimes said that, in the field of collective bargaining, Taft-Hartley "turned back the clock" to the 1920's.

(a) In your opinion, what provisions of T-H are most vulnerable to this accusation?

(b) Do you think that "turning back the clock" in these matters is bad public policy?

3. Draw up a "bill of rights" for union members, and consider how the government might best compel unions to accept it.

4. Under both Wagner and Taft-Hartley, an "economic striker" risks loss of his job if the employer can find a suitable replacement. Discuss the pros and cons of a federal law that required employers to rehire, without loss of seniority or other privileges, all strikers not guilty of any unlawful conduct.

5. (a) In what ways has Taft-Hartley attempted to regulate the *content* of collective bargaining agreements?

(b) Which of these regulations, if any, have succeeded in their purpose? Explain why at least some of them have failed to accomplish their ends.

Suggested Readings

See references at end of Chapter 8.

10 | Government and Strike Control

Like governments in all industrial countries, the government of the United States has used its authority to force the termination of strikes, as well as to prevent the disorder to which they sometimes give rise. State and local governments have acted similarly.

The intervention of an arm of the law in an industrial dispute is usually the occasion for heated controversy, as it is almost impossible to intervene without tipping the scales in one direction or another. If the soldiers or police do not permit the struck facilities to operate, they act as (very effective) picket lines to which the employers object; if they protect strikebreakers, they dishearten the strikers and undermine the strike, to which the union objects.

Historically, government intervention has tended to favor the employers; government has usually intervened to protect life and property or to insure that vital community services such as those furnished by the police, hospitals, the transportation system, etc. were not interrupted. The necessity for continuing these services uninterrupted, plus the public attitude toward strikes, picketing, etc. that prevailed prior to the 1930's, made it almost inevitable that the interests of the union should be neglected.

The change in the legal status of union activities that occurred in the 1930's forced legislatures and courts to reconsider the issues involved in guaranteeing essential services to the community during labor disputes. The result was a large body of legislation, both state and federal, aimed at controlling strikes in essential industries. In the latter part of this chapter, we shall discuss this legislation briefly. However, before doing this, it will be helpful if we consider the pros and cons of alternative methods of settling disputes.

COMPULSORY ARBITRATION

Few experts in the field of industrial relations consider compulsory arbitration a very promising road to industrial peace. Yet this method of settling disputes has an unending appeal to beginning students, legislators, and the "man in the street." And it is not surprising that this should be so; after all, arbitration is simply the submission of a dispute to a tribunal for settlement. This is the manner in which civilized people settle conflicts of interest or opinion on other matters; why should industrial relations be an exception? This question becomes especially insistent, when third parties, i.e., the public, are inconvenienced or injured by the struggle.

Back in the 1920's, the state of Kansas had a compulsory arbitration statute for a short time. Apart from its practical difficulties, the Supreme Court declared it unconstitutional. However, it is likely that if the community should decide it wanted compulsory arbitration of some, or all, industrial disputes, a constitutional method of achieving this end could be found. In any event, we shall assume that this is so for the purpose of our subsequent discussion which deals with the merits, but not the constitutionality, of compulsory dispute settlement.

Enforcement

To the man in the street and, too often, in the legislature, the problem of preventing work stoppages is merely a matter of passing a law and enforcing it. Unfortunately, it is never quite so simple. The first problem to be considered is "just how a law forbidding (some or all) strikes is to be enforced? A number of proposals have been made: draft strikers into the army and make them work under military discipline, fine or jail persons who participate in strikes forbidden either by statute or court order, require that illegal strikers be punished, at least to the extent of losing seniority advantages, etc. Unfortunately, none of these proposals comes to grips with the basic problem of getting people to work under compulsion.

One of these problems is "what happens if workers, believing strongly in the rightness of their cause, simply defy the law?" It is, of course, possible to fine or jail strikers, but how many and for how long? Jails have limited capacity, and jailed workers are hardly productive. Furthermore, after the stoppage is over, juries may be reluctant to impose heavy fines or jail sentences upon relatively poor workers with families, especially as the individual can always say that his fellow workers forced him to remain on strike against his will. This has severely inhibited punishment of illegal strikers in Australia where, from time to time, certain types of strikes have been declared illegal.[1]

This is not to say that antistrike legislation is unenforceable, as such; it is only to point out that enforcement is not a simple matter. Indeed,

[1] See, for example, K. F. Walker, "Australia," pp. 187–194 in *Comparative Labor Movements,* edited by Walter Galenson, Prentice-Hall, New York, 1952.

it is never easy to enforce a law if the law breaker has the support of a substantial part of the community. The poor enforcement record of prohibition ordinances and price control legislation will serve to illustrate this statement.

It should not be supposed that either the leaders or members of American unions casually flout laws or even Presidential requests. On the contrary, despite well-publicized exceptions, labor leaders have been extremely sensitive to public opinion. In fact, they have usually been willing to bow to its pressure without legal compulsion. But where, as in coal mining, members and leaders have been prepared to defy public opinion, legal pressure has been of doubtful value.

Further Problems of Compulsory Arbitration

Enforcement is not the only problem confronting the advocates of compulsory arbitration. For, if the terms of employment are not to be set by the process of "free" collective bargaining (including stoppages), they must be set in some other way. This means, in practice, the arbitrators, appointed by the government, will set wages and related terms of employment.

But, as is often asked, isn't this preferable to setting the terms of employment by the play of sheer economic power? There are strong reasons for answering this in the negative. Even if we grant that the arbitrators will be fair and competent, this is not enough to guarantee that their decisions will be acceptable to both sides. Suppose, for example, that the employer thinks, or pretends to think, that the arbitrators' terms are too expensive to permit profitable operation. If he refuses to accept these terms and keeps his plant closed, is the government to seize and operate it until he gives in?[2] Is the government to subsidize him so that he can earn a profit at the wages set by the arbitrators? Or, is the government to establish price regulations such that wage increases are passed on to consumers, the prices guaranteed (if necessary) by government price and output controls? Suppose the circumstances of a firm require that wages be set well below what ordinary considerations of equity would suggest; the union accepts this fact but argues that substandard wages should be matched by reduction in executive salaries and/or the installation of new and better equipment so as to raise productivity. Are the arbitrators to order these, or other, adjustments?

This is not to imply that any or all of these actions by arbitrators would be unbearable. It is only to indicate the ramifications of attempts to *impose* employment terms upon unions and managements. However, given the repugnance of a large segment of American opinion toward an extension of the role of government in economic life, it would seem that

[2] This is (nominally) what transpired during World War II; see pp. 266–268.

these consequences of compulsory arbitration would indicate that we should minimize its use.[3]

In recognition of the force of this argument, it has been occasionally suggested that we provide for compulsory arbitration only as a last resort, when all other techniques of dispute settlement fail.   But unfortunately, the very knowledge that arbitration *must* be used if all else fails, greatly increases the resistance of disputes to any method of settlement except arbitration.   This is because the weaker party often feels it has nothing to lose, and much to gain, by refusing to make concessions in order to force the dispute to arbitration (see pp. 273–274).

The Benefits of the Bargaining Process

A further consideration that militates against compulsory arbitration is its effect on worker attitudes and shop discipline.   Surprising as it may seem, a strike may have some beneficial effects.   Constant friction over work rules, policies of foremen, etc. can lead to an attitude of sullen resentment that requires expression.   A strike can serve as the occasion for release of this anger; when the workers return to work, either the cause for their anger will have been removed or they will have had to accept the fact that they must live with it.   Either situation is preferable to one in which workers are forbidden to strike and, therefore, manifest their anger in sabotage, unofficial strikes, etc.

To some extent, the figures on man-hours of labor lost through strikes (though small in themselves) are inflated because of inability to measure the extent to which strikes serve as a substitute for absenteeism.   That is, workers who, for one reason or another, need to take time off, do so while on strike instead of remaining away from work.[4]   For example, a strike gives workers an opportunity to see the dentist, go shopping, go fishing, or satisfy a psychological need to "play hookey."   In other words, the physical and psychological needs that cause absenteeism are partly satisfied by the time taken off during a strike, and the pay lost by striking renders additional payless holidays less desirable than otherwise.   This is not to urge "bigger and better strikes," but simply to indicate that they may cost less than is usually supposed.

EMERGENCY DISPUTES AND COMPULSION

The preceding section indicates the reasons why compulsion should be avoided in the settling of disputes.   But, despite these considerations,

---

[3] It is worth noting that the major employer organizations (e.g., the National Association of Manufacturers and the United States Chamber of Commerce) as well as the AFL and CIO have consistently opposed compulsory arbitration.

[4] K. G. J. C. Knowles, *Strikes,* Basil Blackwell, Oxford, 1952, pp. 225–228, points out the strong negative association (among British coal districts) between time lost because of strikes and absenteeism.

the community is simply unwilling to tolerate the interruption of certain services. Disputes which interrupt such services must, therefore, be settled by some method other than free collective bargaining; let us call this class of disputes "emergency creating." Let us define "emergency" strikes as those which create situations which a majority of the community, or a politically dominant minority, will not tolerate, irrespective of whether they create "emergencies" in any other sense.

One basic criticism for determining whether and how close a particular strike comes to creating an "emergency" is how well the community can find substitutes for the good or service whose production has been halted.[5] When a stoppage involves only a small part of the supply of a particular commodity, then the inconvenience will be very slight. The inconvenience grows with the percentage by which the supply is curtailed; it also grows with the "importance" of the commodity to consumers and the difficulty of finding substitutes. For example, even a nation-wide stoppage of cake production would be, at worst, a nuisance. But a nation-wide cessation of the production of all edibles would create the gravest of emergencies.

The geographical dimension of a commodity is also important; a cessation of food production in one small town would not be catastrophic, provided shipment of foodstuffs from elsewhere was unimpeded. But a region-wide stoppage would put such a strain on the nation's food supply and its transportation system as to create a crisis.[6]

The discomfort caused by a work stoppage also depends upon the durability of the commodity involved. If it is highly durable, a *temporary* cessation of even its entire output will not cause actual suffering to consumers; they can make their old units do until the strike is over, or can buy or borrow some of the existing units. For example, a nation-wide automobile stoppage, lasting no more than (say) three months, will not cause much inconvenience to the nation's auto riders who can make their old cars last a little longer. Of course, if the strike should last three years, the situation would be different.

In other words, the length of time that must elapse before a strike creates an "emergency" varies with the nature of the industry's product and the state of its existing stocks. In industry A, an emergency might be created after six months of complete stoppage; but in industry B the period might be three years, provided stocks were "normal."

[5] In economic terminology this may be translated as "a stoppage comes closer to creating an emergency, the greater the marginal utility of the good or service whose production has been halted."

[6] An elaboration of this criterion and its implications is contained in N. W. Chamberlain and J. M. Schilling, *The Impact of Strikes,* Chapters 2 and 3, Harpers, New York, 1954. Also see *Emergency Disputes and National Policy,* edited by Bernstein, Enarson, and Fleming, Harpers, New York, 1955, especially Chapter I ("An Economic Definition of the National Emergency Dispute") by G. H. Hildebrand.

If stocks should be less than "normal," emergencies will (other things equal) be created sooner than otherwise. The reason for this is that stocks of goods serve as buffers to protect the planned activities of one firm (or sector) of the economy from the effects of temporary fluctuations in the delivery rates of its suppliers, and purchase rates of its customers. When these stocks become abnormally low, as they were immediately after World War II, the partitions between the various sectors of the economy become thin, and interruptions to production in one sector affect the activity in others far more quickly than is ordinarily the case. For example, in 1946, a stoppage of coal production soon caused a "dimout" to be ordered in a number of East Coast cities in order to economize on coal consumption by electricity-generating plants; it also caused a sharp curtailment of steel production which, in turn, caused an output reduction by steel users, e.g., automobile manufacturers.[7] (Ordinarily, the repercussions would have been smaller and would have occurred only after a much longer interruption of production.)

The concept of "emergency" we have suggested above is incomplete in that it considers only the effect of a stoppage on the final users of a commodity. But stoppages, in the short-run, may raise far more havoc among business firms that supply or purchase from the struck firms, than among consumers. For example, as steel products are very durable, most household users would not be hurt much by a six months cessation of all steel production. But such a stoppage would cause widespread unemployment and loss of output in the steel-using industries, in coal and iron ore production, on the railroads transporting coal, etc. Just how large a loss of output and employment constitute an emergency cannot be specified in the abstract. But clearly, the "intolerable" point will frequently be reached well before consumers are injured.

Nonetheless, the effect of strikes upon consumers is what legislators are usually concerned with when they attempt to prevent emergency strikes. Such legislation is usually aimed at insuring the production of "essential" commodities. An "essential" commodity is not easily defined in a precise way; however, essential commodities usually include the services rendered by public utilities, medical and health facilities, police and fire departments, and the transportation system. The common characteristics of all these commodities are (1) they are services and (2) they are "essential." The fact that they are *services* means that they must be used when produced and cannot be stored; hence, a strike injures consumers almost immediately. That they are essential means that their absence affects adversely either public health and safety, or the employment opportunities of an appreciable number of persons.

---

[7] Chamberlain and Schilling, *op. cit.,* Chapters 4 to 6.

In time of war, military goods and a wide range of other commodities become "essential," for obvious reasons, and serious interruption of their production becomes intolerable. In recent years, the construction and operation of atomic energy plants has created a new industry in which work stoppages are intolerable.[8] Strikes "against the government" are also considered intolerable; they are specifically forbidden by Taft-Hartley and in many states as well; the state of public opinion on strikes of government workers is indicated by the fact that organized labor has not seriously objected to legislation forbidding strikes of government employees. In other countries, abhorrence of strikes by government workers is not nearly so great or so widespread as in the United States.

The essentiality of particular services depends upon the ease with which substitutes for them can be found. If all the hospitals in a city were closed by a strike, the situation would be calamitous; if one out of a hundred were shut down, the result would be little more than a minor nuisance. The reason why public utilities are often singled out as industries in which strikes are impermissible is not merely because their product is essential, but because all of it, in a given locality, is produced by one firm. Customers cannot buy elsewhere and, as the services are important, suffer severe inconvenience or worse.

Foodstuffs are surely no less essential than (say) telephone service, yet it is rarely urged that strikes in food processing should be outlawed as a menace to public health and safety. This is because food is processed by many different firms (bakers, butchers, canners, packers, etc.) and no appreciable share of a city's food supply is likely to be cut off by a strike of any one group of food workers. But, if all food workers struck simultaneously, a nation-wide crisis would develop in short order, and the responsible public authorities would have to take drastic action to prevent famine.

To summarize: there are situations in which stoppages of production cannot be tolerated, and compulsory methods for settling the terms of employment must be used despite their shortcomings. That these situations are not more frequent is due to the fact that a strike usually hurts (economically) those involved far more than it injures outsiders; this is the main reason why collective bargaining is compatible with a fair degree of industrial peace.

EMERGENCY DISPUTES AND THE LAW

American labor leaders have always been extremely hostile to legislation that restricts the right to strike. However, with but a few exceptions, they have all been extremely anxious to *cooperate* with public authorities

[8] On atomic energy see J. K. Mann, Chapter X in *Emergency Disputes and National Policy.*

in preventing or halting emergency-creating strikes. By and large, they have shared the attitude of the general community with regard to what kinds of strikes are intolerable, and have behaved accordingly.

The resentment of labor leaders at strike control legislation stems, to a considerable degree, from their feeling that such laws portray them as wanting in citizenship. In effect they wish to receive public praise for cooperating in curbing emergency strikes and not public threats as to what will happen if they fail to cooperate. In view of the continued defiance of the government by the coal miners (in the 1940's), it could hardly be argued that the voluntary cooperation of labor with government programs was 100 per cent. Nevertheless, labor leaders greatly resented being lumped together with Lewis in the public mind and (by implication) in the Taft-Hartley Act.

Strike Experience in World War II and Government Seizure

The sections of T-H that deal with emergency strikes can be best understood as the result of the nation's strike experience during World War II, and immediately thereafter. As we have seen, during World War II the unions gave the President a no-strike pledge and (with but few exceptions) observed it. Disputes were settled by the War Labor Board (WLB) which operated, unofficially as a board of arbitration for labor disputes. Its policies, so far as it could enforce them, set the terms of employment for virtually all wage earners in the United States.

In the event of non-compliance with a WLB award, the President would order the struck plant "seized" by the government; after being "seized" the plant was nominally operated by the government, and the workers were forbidden to strike. The seizure was almost entirely symbolic; except for the terms on which workers were employed, effective management and all profits remained with the owners. As a rule, after seizure, the government imposed the tems of employment ordered by the War Labor Board and "retained" the property until both parties agreed to accept these terms, whereupon the plants were restored to their owners.[9]

The great virtue of seizure, during the war, was that it usually worked. The unions would not strike against the government, and management was powerless to resist. To be sure, the effect of seizure was often to induce workers to accept terms of employment under the nominal management of the United States government that they had previously refused to accept from private business, although the profits went to their employer in either event. However, the union felt that the legal gesture of seizure, which was vocally resented by business, imposed sacrifices on both parties.

[9] The whole subject of seizure is well discussed by Archibald Cox, "Seizure in Emergency Disputes," in *Emergency Disputes and National Policy, op. cit.,* Chapter XII.

Hence, almost all union leaders cooperated in a whole-hearted manner that would not have been forthcoming had there been simple no-strike orders.

The cooperation of union leaders with wartime seizures represented a blend of naivete, patriotism, and an implicit recognition that their restive members could be far more easily controlled (i.e., prevented from striking) after government seizure than before. Also the seizure device had the advantage that it could be, and was, used to force recalcitrant employers to meet War Labor Board orders; this was especially desirable when the orders included maintenance of membership. Finally, labor leaders recognized that strikes had to be prevented during the war and, if seizure did not accomplish this, less pleasant methods would have to be introduced.

Business, although it did not suffer economic injury by seizure, resented its implication. It resented the idea that the government could seize their property at all, especially to settle a labor dispute. And employers feared that the government might negotiate union contracts while in possession of the plant (which it was legally empowered to do) that would be objectionable to them, but which they would have to accept "in order to get their property back."

However, even during the war, on two occasions seizure failed to halt strikes. In one of these, the 1943 coal strike, the government had to violate its wage stabilization standards (see pp. 412–413) in order to get continued production. And in the postwar period (especially in 1946–1947) defiance of seizure became much more frequent. This was because the wartime feeling that one ought not to strike against the government had disappeared and had been replaced by an awareness that, seizure or no, the profits were reaped by the private employer. Also, examples of successful defiance of seizure induced imitations.[10]

Despite its reduced effectiveness, seizure continued to be used during emergency disputes until 1952. The reason for this was that President Truman disliked using the injunction procedures of Taft-Hartley which were bitterly resented by his union supporters. However, when seizure failed, there was always the T-H injunction "in the closet." Awareness of this made unions treat seizure with an affectionate respect that would otherwise have been lacking.

Supporters of T-H bitterly critized the repeated evasions of its prescribed procedure and argued that, after the expiration of the Smith-Connally Act, the President had no power to order seizure, as Congress had not empowered him to do so. President Truman insisted that the President had this power inherent in his office. In May 1952, during a seizure of steel plants to halt a major strike, the companies appealed to the Supreme Court

[10] *Ibid.*

which ruled that the President had no power to "seize," at least when Congress had specifically provided (through Taft-Hartley) other means of coping with the problem which allegedly created the need for seizure. Whether, in the absence of legislation such as T-H, the President would have seizure power in time of peace is still open to question. In any event, for the time being seizure is not a usable technique.

Taft-Hartley and Emergency Injunctions

Quite apart from its legality, the effectiveness of seizure was due (after 1945) to fear of the more potent weapons at the government's disposal. Chief among these was the injunction. In November 1946, John L. Lewis led the coal miners on a nation-wide strike, despite the fact that the mines had been seized and were being operated by the government. The government proceeded to get an injunction against the continuation of the strike; when Lewis defied the injunction because of its (alleged) illegality, he and the United Mine Workers were found guilty of contempt of court. The union was fined $3,500,000 and Lewis $10,000 personally. In March 1946, the Supreme Court upheld the injunction on appeal, but reduced the union's fine to $700,000.

After Lewis and the union had been found in contempt, the strike was halted. This fact, and the large fines imposed for contempt, brought the injunction to the favorable attention of the authors of Taft-Hartley. By way of providing the President with adequate authority to cope with emergency disputes, T-H prescribes that wherever the President believes that a strike "affecting an entire industry or a substantial part thereof . . . will, if permitted to occur or to continue, imperil the national health or safety," he may appoint a "fact-finding" board to report on the issues but to make no recommendations. Upon receipt of the board's report the President may direct the Attorney General to secure an injunction halting the strike. The parties must then accept the aid of the U. S. Conciliation and Mediation Service (see p. 276) in continuing attempts to reach a settlement. If, sixty days after the injunction goes into effect, a settlement has not been reached, the fact-finding board must report to the President on the current state of the dispute, and the President must make this report public. Within the following 15 days, NLRB must take a secret ballot of the employees on their employer's final offer. If they reject this offer, the Attorney General within the following five days must have the injunction ended, leaving the workers free to strike. The President must then make a full report to Congress on the dispute and may make recommendations for appropriate legislation.

Emergency provisions of Taft-Hartley had been utilized twelve times (to the end of 1954); in nine of these injunctions were sought and obtained, and in all of these cases save one (bituminous coal strike of

1950) work was resumed after the injunction was issued. "Final offer" ballots were held in only five cases; in four of these the employer's offer was rejected, and in the other the union boycotted the election—not a vote being cast. In three cases, serious strikes followed upon the dissolution of the injunctions at the end of the 80-day period permitted by law, and in five others strikes occurred before injunctions could be used.[11]

The specific contribution of T-H to control of emergency strikes has not been great. The "fact-finding" boards are, in practice, primarily devices for mobilizing public opinion in support of some sort of compromise settlement and, in any event, could be used without any authorization by Congress. The period for which the injunction is effective, at most 80 days, cannot usually delay the action of a far-sighted bargainer. Anticipating the possibility of an injunction, he makes his threatening moves 80 days before he intends actually to strike. In some cases where a strike can be effective only during a seasonal peak in demand, an 80 day injunction may indeed reduce stoppages, but only at the cost of crippling the union's strike power and favoring the employer.

The polling of strikers on their employers' last offer was borrowed from the Smith-Connally Act, and is usually considered a futile gesture. It is based on the misconception that the employees are reluctant to strike and are being dragooned by their leaders. This infuriates union leaders quite unnecessarily; it would be extremely dangerous for a union leader to drag workers into a nation-wide strike if they were not "sold" on their demands. To do this would be to risk upheaval within the union, which union leaders are always anxious to avoid. Furthermore, the "final offer" ballot is not merely useless; it positively interferes with collective bargaining, as the parties tend to halt bargaining and take a stand for and against the "last" offer until the vote is completed. A shrewd employer, anticipating that the union will want a rejection of his "last" offer, will not make it his "best possible" offer in order to reserve some further concessions for later bargaining. It is worth noting that, in 1949, the late Senator Taft agreed that the "final offer" ballot should be abandoned.[12]

The ultimate answer to an emergency strike is, as Taft-Hartley implies, special legislation. But to enact a law forbidding a particular strike is, by the very nature of the case, to set the terms of employment in the industries affected.[13] (If nothing is said explicitly about the terms of employment but a strike is forbidden, then the terms are whatever the

[11] The record of Taft-Hartley on emergency disputes is summarized by C. M. Rehmus, in Appendix A to Emergency Disputes and National Policy, pp. 261–268.

[12] F. C. Pierson, "An Evaluation of the National Emergency Provision, "Chapter VIII, in Emergency Disputes and National Policy, op. cit. p. 142.

[13] Of course, labor market pressures (see pp. 319–324) and/or employers' beneficence may also affect the relevant rates, but union strike pressure cannot.

employer chooses to make them, in the light of labor market and other relevant considerations.)

In Denmark there has been, on occasion, special legislation enacted to set the terms on which nationwide strikes were to be settled. The consequences have not been catastrophic, but it is doubtful that we would be prepared to let Congress legislate about specific collective bargaining contracts, at least in peace time. To be sure, if strikes became big enough, often enough, we might be driven to such measures. However, the history and current outlook in American industrial relations does not suggest that the need for strike prevention has been so great as to warrant the adoption of such expedients.

The Ground between Mediation and Arbitration

A mediator is an intermediary between bargainers whose function it is to assist them in reaching an agreement. Sometimes a good mediator can do much to assist bargainers who are at loggerheads. Clearly, where strike prevention is desired, mediation should be facilitated. And, in emergency situations where a strike must be prevented, there is a temptation to do more than merely facilitate; there is a tendency to give the mediator additional power in order to strengthen his hand in negotiating with recalcitrant bargainers. Thus, during World War II the mediation efforts of the War Labor Board and its representatives were tantamount to orders; what was suggested could, in the last analysis, be ordered—and the bargainers knew it. A similar situation exists in Denmark on a more or less permanent basis.[14]

Mediation with a club in reserve is obviously very close to (compulsory) arbitration. To be sure there is something to be said for the "velvet glove" and for letting the bargainers take the credit for their statesmanship in reaching a contract without a strike. But, if the terms that are suggested are known to be those that will later be imposed (if necessary), the weaker bargainer need offer no concessions beyond what the government will require. This means that bargaining has ceased and that whoever appoints the mediator-arbitrator sets the terms of employment.

In practice, it is understood that "big" strikes cannot be tolerated for long. This means that, ultimately, opinion in the White House and Congress will set the terms of contracts in "emergency disputes." Awareness that creation of a favorable opinion depends upon having appeared "reasonable" usually exerts a very salutary restraint on bargainers. This fact does much to minimize the number and frequency of emergency disputes.

[14] Walter Galenson, *The Danish System of Labor Relations*, Harvard University Press, Cambridge, Mass., 1952, Chapter VII.

At bottom, there is no pat solution for the question of how to prevent emergency strikes without resorting to compulsory arbitration. In the final analysis, if strikes are forbidden, employment terms must be set by those forbidding them. But even legislation may fail to bring industrial peace. Workers may strike against their government or their own leaders; or, if they don't strike, they may deliberately loaf on the job. Against such tactics, there are no remedies except discharge and physical coercion.

The Railway Labor Act

Since 1888, the federal government has attempted to circumscribe collective bargaining on railroads with a number of procedural requirements designed to minimize stoppages.[15] The Railway Labor Act, first passed in 1926 and amended in 1934 and 1951, provides for what is virtually compulsory arbitration of disputes, over the interpretation of existing agreements, by the National Railroad Adjustment Board.[16] Disputes over the terms of new contracts are handled by the three man National Mediation Board. When mediative techniques fail to secure agreement, this Board requests that the parties submit the dispute to arbitration. If this is refused, the President is notified; he may appoint an emergency board to investigate the dispute. The emergency board has thirty days in which to file a report with recommendations. However, neither party is compelled to accept the recommendations. For thirty days thereafter neither party may make any change in the conditions giving rise to the dispute. After that (60 days from the date of appointment of the emergency board) a strike becomes legal. The similarity of this procedure to that prescribed by Taft-Hartley should be obvious.

Between 1926 and 1941, the procedures of the Railway Labor Act worked reasonably well; no major strikes occurred, and few were threatened. During this period, the Act was widely hailed as a model law. Since 1941, however, the Act has functioned quite poorly. Although there have been relatively few strikes, several have been averted only by government seizure, and collective bargaining has almost completely broken down. That is, the parties rarely begin to bargain in earnest until the emergency board has reported.[17] To an increasing degree contract disputes have had to be settled by the direct intervention of the President. The railroads have been especially anxious not to concede anything except under duress as they feel their chances of getting

---

[15] See J. J. Kaufman, *Collective Bargaining in the Railroad Industry,* King's Crown Press, 1954, Chapter V. The following section is based largely on this study and several articles by H. R. Northrup cited therein.

[16] In 1936 the coverage of this Act was extended to include air transportation.

[17] Kaufman, *op. cit.,* pp. 155–157.

rate increases approved by the Interstate Commerce Commission are better if the increases in labor costs are *imposed* upon them by government rather than accepted "voluntarily" in the process of collective bargaining.

The unions, on the other hand, have customarily used the recommendations of Emergency Boards as a springboard for their real bargaining with the President or his deputy. In short, from 1941 to about 1953 railroad wages were, in effect, determined by the government under what is actually compulsory arbitration. The results have not been deemed satisfactory either by participants or students of the process. Since 1953, the existence of an administration with less sympathy for union wage demands has led to somewhat less pressure by the unions for White House intervention. However, the lessons of 1941–1953 are most instructive and must be considered in framing future legislation.

State Strike Curbs in Public Utilities

Not all emergency-creating strikes arise at the national level. Many, perhaps most of them, are of a local nature. These include tieups of streetcar and intracity busses, city-wide truck strikes, strikes in hospitals and, above all, strikes in gas, electricity, and water services. To cope with strikes of this type, fourteen states (including New Jersey, Massachusetts, Pennsylvania, Texas, Virginia) have, since 1934, enacted legislation providing for compulsory arbitration, seizure, or both in labor disputes affecting (broadly) public utilities.[18] The success of these statutes has varied; they have not always prevented strikes, and the penalities for illegal striking have not been enforced consistently.[19] Also, they have encouraged weak bargainers to avoid bargaining in the hope of getting more via arbitration.[20] In short, they have encountered the usual difficulties of compulsory arbitration.

Despite this, it would not be correct to conclude that legislation forbidding strikes in public utilities is valueless.[21] Such laws serve to express the sentiment of the community and, by their very existence, exert pressure

[18] In 1951, the Wisconsin law was declared unconstitutional by the U. S. Supreme Court because it conflicted with Taft-Hartley. As this Act had been a model for many of the others, a number of them have had to be redrawn; in some cases, the acts have not yet been redrafted.

[19] Kaufman, *op. cit.,* p. 167.

[20] See R. R. France and R. A. Lester, *Compulsory Arbitration of Utility Disputes in New Jersey and Pennsylvania,* Industrial Relations Section, Department of Economics and Sociology Princeton University, Princeton, N.J., 1951.

[21] The most authoritative statement of the case for such legislation is that of S. H. Slichter, *The Challenge of Industrial Relations,* Cornell University Press, 1947, pp. 164–170. Professor Slichter was influential in the framing of the Massachusetts law curbing public utility strikes; this statute is certainly one of the best-designed and most successful of the various state laws aimed in this direction.

upon strikers who may well feel uneasy at violating the law. Another virtue of these statutes is, that by compelling (as many do) the elapse of a time period between the notification of the appropriate authority and the outbreak of a legal strike, they give government mediators a chance to function. At the national level where the bargainers are experienced and the process of negotiation is carefully watched by responsible parties in Washington, it is naive to require[22] (by law) that federal mediators be given time to help the disputants reach a settlement. But public utility disputes are often local in character, and the bargainers are often inexperienced. If the locality is small, a state mediation agency may not even learn of a dispute's existence until it erupts in a stoppage; therefore, compelling the bargainers to allow time for mediation may be more than an empty gesture.

SOME INTERESTING IDEAS AND EXPERIMENTS

The principal difficulty with compulsory arbitration, apart from enforcement, is that its presence discourages voluntary collective bargaining. There seems to be a sort of "Gresham's law" of bargaining by which compulsory settlements tend to drive out voluntary ones. To prevent this "law" from operating, various writers have offered proposals for making the use of compulsory machinery unpleasant to the participants, uncertain in its consequences, or both.[23]

The essential thing in these formulas is that the President, Governor, or other official ordering the arbitration should have sufficient latitude of action so that a recalcitrant bargainer can never count on the arbitration machinery working to his advantage, and that both parties should at all times have a strong incentive to reach an agreement.

For example, the executive authority might be given power to impose fines upon unions and management or to order workers and management to continue production until a contract is signed, but at minimal wages and with all profits going to the government.[24] Illegal strikers might be deprived of seniority and possibly pension benefits; unions could be de-

[22] As Taft-Hartley does.

[23] D. E. Cullen, "The Taft-Hartley Act in National Emergency Disputes," *Industrial and Labor Relations Review*, October 1953, pp. 15–39, discusses several of these proposals. Also see R. W. Fleming, "The Search for a Formula," Chapter XI of *Emergency Disputes and National Policy*.

[24] An ingenious proposal of this type has been offered by L. Marceau and R. A. Musgrave, "Strikes in Essential Industries: A Way Out," *Harvard Business Review*, May 1949, pp. 286–292. This proposal envisages compulsory arbitration in lieu of a strike, but with such low wages and profits (if any) that the parties would be under the same pressure as though there were a strike. The trouble, of course, is that output might suffer severely even though the workers reported for work.

certified by NLRB and their officers made ineligible ever again to serve as officers in certified unions, etc.[25]

These proposals are, for the most part, ideas whose practical utility is doubted by many "hard-headed" practitioners in the field of industrial relations. This does not prove that they are useless. However, until they are tried under reasonably favorable conditions, they will serve mainly as interesting topics for intercollegiate debaters.

VOLUNTARY ARBITRATION

The disparaging remarks that we have made about "compulsory arbitration" are aimed at compulsion but not at arbitration. It is highly desirable that bargainers be willing to arbitrate their disputes, and they should be encouraged to do so. A willingness to arbitrate is indicative of the mutual acceptance of certain principles and of confidence that arbitration awards will be kept within the implied limits. A highly favorable set of conditions for reaching a voluntary agreement to arbitrate disputes occurs in connection with the disposition of grievances arising under the terms of specific collective agreements. In 1953, 89 per cent of all collective agreements (in the U. S.) contained provision for arbitration as the final step in the disposition of grievances. That is, if the union and management cannot agree upon the disposition of a grievance, it is then settled through arbitration by an arbitrator or umpire, either appointed in advance or chosen from a panel by some specified method (see p. 161).

The widespread acceptance of "compulsory arbitration of grievances" means that a large number of unions and managements feel that their contracts are sufficiently specific so that their interpretation by a third party will not impose unbearable hardships upon them. (If the interpretations prove to be onerous, they can demand a change in the contract when it comes up for renewal.) Of course, different bargaining partners adopt different viewpoints toward the arbitrator's function; some adopt the "living document" (see p. 170) approach, allowing the arbitrator freedom to act as mediator as well as umpire; others insist that he adopt a narrower and more "legalistic" view of the contract.

The willingness of bargainers to accept arbitration of grievances springs, at bottom, from the well-founded belief that the worst that can befall them, as a result of an arbitrator's decision, cannot be "too bad." Such a belief arises from the development of a body of industrial jurisprudence governing the administration of contracts between the bargainers. Willingness to arbitrate grievances usually arises after some experience of living under a contract with the other party; it is not the bloom of love at first sight.

[25] Chamberlain and Schilling, *op. cit.,* pp. 245–252, make some rather modest but interesting suggestions in this direction.

In a few, but very few, cases the willingness to arbitrate extends even to new contracts. This means that the bargainers delegate the authority to alter their contract, at specified times, to one or more third parties. Such delegation signifies the implicit acceptance of certain "principles" that virtually determine the outcome of negotiations; the arbitrator merely applies these principles to specific cases. If both parties freely accept such an arrangement, well and good. But unfortunately, few bargainers would at present consider such a state of affairs to be tolerable.

CONCILIATION AND MEDIATION

Conciliation and mediation are roughly interchangeable terms designating the process by which a third party assists bargainers either to reach an agreement without a strike, or to terminate a strike. The techniques of mediation vary enormously from one mediator to another, and there are no generally applicable descriptions. These techniques involve, essentially, the effective use of the mediator's skills in inducing agreement among persons with conflicting interests; anything from philosophical discourse to getting "the boys to take a drink together" may prove helpful.

At its best, mediation can greatly facilitate the process of collective bargaining. It sometimes happens, especially between inexperienced bargainers, that personality conflicts arise, and concessions must come through a third party. It may also happen that neither party wishes to be the first to offer a compromise for fear of appearing weak. However, if the mediator has gained the confidence of both parties, each may tell him, in confidence, that he would offer "such and such" if he were sure the other side would accept. The mediator can then propose the terms that he knows are mutually acceptable.

A successful mediator can perform yet another function. Not infrequently union representatives[26] fear the internal political consequences of making certain concessions which the bargaining situation requires. If the mediator, or an arbitrator, can be blamed for the concessions, they can be made far more easily. Finally, because of his greater experience, a mediator can sometimes suggest bases for compromise of which the bargainers themselves would not have thought.

Those various functions can and have been performed by skillful mediators. Of course, not all mediators are appropriately skilled, and even very good ones sometimes fail in special types of situations. As an inept mediator may do more harm than good, it is important that mediators should be professionally skilled.

Most full-time mediators are paid employees of the government although government agencies employ highly skilled and expensive medi-

---

[26] This problem also arises for management representatives, but less frequently.

ators on a part-time basis, also. Mediators are employed largely by state and federal governments; only a few municipalities have made even desultory attempts at mediation work. Many states adopted mediation laws during the 19th century, but, before the 1930's, few of them used full-time personnel to give effect to these laws. However, since 1933, state governments (especially in the big industrial states) have become actively concerned with strike prevention.

Nevertheless, the most important conciliation work is done by the federal government. Between the creation of the Department of Labor in 1913 and the passage of the Taft-Hartley Act, the conciliation work of the United States government was performed by the Department of Labor. In 1917, the United States Conciliation Service was established (as a division of the Department of Labor), and it functioned until 1947 when the Taft-Hartley Act replaced it with the Federal Mediation and Conciliation Service.

This latter agency was established outside of the Department of Labor, to meet employer criticism that federal mediators could not be impartial if they were subject to the Secretary of Labor. Although employer charges that the Conciliation Service was partial to labor have been denied vigorously, the fact that such charges were widely believed reduced the effectiveness of the service. Consequently, removing the service from the Labor Department may, of itself, have helped reduce employer suspicion of it.

In any event, it would hardly be denied that in the past few years the Conciliation Service has performed a valuable function in certain situations, and that it has saved many times its cost in strikes it helped to avert. At present, the service has the confidence of both labor and management groups which is a prerequisite for its effective operation. The fact that the service is now able to operate with the approval of both labor and management is a testimonial to the growing maturity of industrial relations in the United States.

DISCUSSION QUESTIONS

1. Is it possible to reconcile a free enterprise economy with compulsory arbitration?

2. (a) Under what conditions does a compulsory "cooling-off" period contribute to the prevention of emergency strikes?

(b) Are these conditions likely to be met in the "emergency disputes" to which Taft-Hartley refers?

3. What are the principal similarities between the strike prevention clauses of the Railway Labor Act and the Taft-Hartley Law? What are the principal differences?

4. Why is arbitration of grievances accepted so much more frequently (by the parties concerned) than arbitration of new contract terms?

5. Appraise "seizure" as a method for curbing emergency disputes.

Suggested Readings

Braun, Kurt, *Labor Disputes and their Settlement,* Johns Hopkins Press, Baltimore, 1955.

Bernstein, I., Enarson, H. L., and R. W. Fleming, editors, *Emergency Disputes and National Policy,* Harper, New York, 1955.

Chamberlain, N. W. and J. M. Schilling, *The Impact of Strikes,* Harper, New York, 1954.

Kaufman, J. J. *Collective Bargaining in the Railroad Industry,* King's Crown Press, 1954.

Slichter, S. H., *The Challenge of Industrial Relations,* Cornell University Press, 1947.

PART THREE

Employment, Wages, and Income

Much of the material in Part Two is irrelevant to the economic aspect of unionism. This is inevitable; unions are much more than economic institutions. Their inner workings often have little effect upon the operation of the economy or upon the ultimate determination of wages, hours, etc. But, nonetheless, they have to be studied. An organization cannot be partially understood; it must be studied in all of its various contexts or else many of its actions will seem capricious and senseless when, in fact, they reflect its (internal) political and administrative necessities. This is why the reader who would understand unionism must learn both the economics of the labor market, and the institutional structure of union organizations.

However, the reader who comes to this part of the book, fresh from Part Two will find a very abrupt change in subject matter. In Part Two, we were largely concerned with the behavior of unions and the attempts of the government to control it. Now we turn to what is primarily an economic analysis of what determines a wage earner's (hourly) wage rate, his annual income, and the amount and kind of employment he obtains.

To be sure, this discussion is related to the behavior of unions. Indeed, influencing these matters is one of the primary reasons for unions' existence. However, the policies of unions are only one of the forces that influence employment, wages, and income. And, in the first two chapters of Part Three, the union plays a very subordinate roles. This should not disturb the reader; in Chapter 13, and later, unions are given their proper place in the economic system.

Part Three begins with an analysis of the labor market, and the related issues of "who gets which job" and what hourly wage is paid for the job. Chapter 11 deals with the supply side of the labor market and Chapter 12, the demand side. Chapter 13 puts the two sides of the labor market together, and attempts to show how, and the extent to which, labor market forces are both altered and transmitted by unions. Chapters 14 and 15 then apply this analysis to explaining the interrelations of wages in the various industries, regions, and occupations of the United States.

Chapter 16 develops briefly the technique of aggregate analysis, and applies it to explain the *level* of wages in the United States and labor's share in the National Income. Chapter 17, the last of this part, then attempts to show the various ways in which the operation of the economy generates unemployment.

Some Preliminary Definitions

In the following pages, the reader will find a number of concepts with which he is probably already familiar. However, it may be convenient to have the more important of them defined in one place.

The first concept is that of the *straight time hourly wage rate.* This is the pay rate per hour specified in the employment contract (verbal or written) for the standard number of hours worked per week. When we speak of the wage rate without further specification, the reference will be to the straight time hourly rate.

Another concept often used in wage discussions is *"average hourly earnings."* Average hourly earnings are equal to the straight time hourly rate, when the worker is not working overtime (i.e., not working hours in excess of the standard number). "Overtime" typically requires hourly remuneration in excess of straight time rates; in many cases, this is required by law (see below, p. 504), but even in the absence of legal compulsion, union contracts or company policy make similar provisions, as a rule.

"Wages per unit of output" or "per piece" refers to the scale of remuneration operative under a piece rate or incentive system. The characteristics of such systems of remuneration are considered in Chapter 15. Until then, we shall assume (except when the contrary is specified) that the employment contract is based on an hourly rate of pay.

Weekly earnings are a workers average hourly earnings multiplied by the number of hours worked per week; obviously weekly earnings fluctuate with employment as well as with the wage rate. *Weekly "take-home" pay* equals weekly earnings minus deductions for (1) withholding (income) taxes (2) social security taxes (3) contributions to a pension-system, etc. A worker's *"annual wage"* is the sum of his weekly wages throughout the year.

"Real wages," as distinguished from "money wages," refer to any of the above concepts, after adjustments have been made for changes in the worker's cost of living (see below, pp. 404–408). The concept of "real wages" is used principally in connection with questions concerning the relation of changes in the worker's level of economic well-being to changes in his money wages. That is, the real wage measures (or purports to measure) the purchasing power of the corresponding money wage; i.e., a worker's *real* weekly wage would be the "amount" of goods and services that his money weekly wage will purchase.

Measuring the amount of goods and services that a given amount of money will purchase is usually done by comparing the amount that could have been purchased at some specific date (called the base date) and expressing the amount that could be purchased at a given date as a percentage of that amount. Thus we may say that a specific worker's weekly real wage in June 1956 was (for example) 125% of what it was in June 1947, but it makes no sense to speak of real wages except in relation to their level on some other date.

In practice, the real wages of American workers are computed in the following way: the Bureau of Labor Statistics (of the Department of Labor) computes an Index of Consumer Prices (CPI), sometimes loosely called a cost of living index, every month. "Deflating" (i.e., dividing) a worker's money wages (weekly, hourly, etc.) by the percentage change in CPI occurring between any two months equates the purchasing power of a wage dollar in these two months (or years[1]). Then, the percentage change in the deflated wage between these two months is the percentage change in the worker's real wage during this period.

The propriety of this procedure depends upon the accuracy and relevance of the price index used in the "deflating" process. The Bureau of Labor Statistics carefully gathers data (the 15th of every month) on the prices paid for goods and services[2] bought by an "average" urban family (whose income was less than $10,000 in 1952). However, no one family is average and hence, because its desired pattern of expenditures differs from the average, CPI is (at best) only roughly appropriate. For families with unusually low incomes, or over $10,000, CPI is not even roughly accurate; it is also seriously misleading as applied to unusually large families, and it is irrelevant to single persons and rural families.

Furthermore, CPI cannot take account of changes in the quality of

[1] For this purpose, the CPI index for a year is an average of the 12 months in the year.

[2] The goods and services included are taken from a sample of budgets of urban families. The most recent sample was made in 1952.

281

goods or their unavailability (both these factors were serious during World War II). Also, it cannot reflect the changes that steadily occur in the "average" family's desired pattern of expenditure.[3] However, despite these and other difficulties, CPI is the best measure of changes in the prices paid by working class consumers and is almost universally accepted as such. It has a wide currency in collective bargaining negotiations as the measure of changes in the "cost of living" (see pp. 335–336) and is used as the basis for computing wage changes under collective bargaining contracts involving "escalator" clauses (see pp. 413–415).

[3] To some extent this is minimized by recomputing the "average budget" from time to time. However, this is expensive and can only be done once every few years. When changes are slow the errors are not too serious, but in the event of sharp changes important difficulties may arise.

11

The Wage Earner and the
Supply of Labor

This chapter is concerned with the economic and social forces that govern the supply of labor. It discusses the circumstances under which individuals accept and leave jobs, the manner in which they search for jobs, and the job characteristics they find desirable. These individual decisions to accept or refuse certain job offers determine the community's labor supply.

CHOOSING A JOB

The young worker's first job is frequently found in a plant where friends or relatives are working. This is not surprising; a young boy's first job is likely to be a momentous and somewhat frightening experience; therefore, he prefers to meet it in the company of a friend. Another factor of perhaps greater significance is that a young boy (or girl) knows little or nothing of job opportunities and is advised by relatives or acquaintances as to where to look for work. As the opportunities of which these "advisors" know are most likely to be where they (themselves) are working, this strengthens the tendency to find work in the same place as one's friends and relatives. (Employment by a friend or relative is another important source of initial jobs.)

Next to personal advice, the most important source of information concerning job openings appears to be information furnished at a firm's employment office. The choice of the firm at which a neophyte applies is likely to depend upon proximity to his residence, casual information that such a firm is "nice to work for" or "has been hiring recently," or sheer chance. In a great majority of cases, the new labor market entrant takes the first job he comes upon; it is only a small minority of youngsters who compare jobs.

Given this method of finding jobs, it is not surprising that many of them prove unsatisfactory. Fortunately a youngster's first job is usually short-lived; it is taken in ignorance to escape from school or to earn some spending money. If it proves unsatisfactory, he quits and looks for a better one.

These remarks are applicable to youths in urban centers where there are a number of alternative employers. However many youngsters, especially in the South, grow up in or near small towns where one large mill or mine provides the sole or, at least, the major source of gainful employment. For these youngsters, locating their first job presents neither a problem nor an opportunity for choice. And for them, getting a better job implies leaving the area.

The job choices of a mature worker are somewhat more informed than those of a beginner. However, most workers never become expert "job shoppers." Indeed, it is difficult to consider most workers as job shoppers at all. They hardly ever have a list of alternative job openings among which they can compare and choose. Their information concerning job opportunities is limited and, like that of new workers, seems to depend largely on rumor, the "grapevine."[1]

WHAT WORKERS WANT IN A JOB

Typically, a worker is confronted on any given day with a concrete offer, at an employer's hiring office, which he can accept or reject; rarely will a job "wait for him" while he shops around. In deciding whether or not to take a job, an experienced worker is likely to have some roughly defined standards, and usually accepts the first job that meets them.

In general, an (experienced) worker has more or less definite standards of "job acceptability." The nature of these standards varies from person to person, but as a rule they may be discussed under the following heads: (1) wages, (2) psychological characteristics, (3) physical characteristics, and (4) security of employment. Let us briefly consider each of these.

Several labor market studies have found that workers attached considerable importance to wages as a criterion of job satisfactoriness.[2] Lest the reader feel this to be a coy understatement, let it be noted that this finding is a matter of controversy! Various case studies of the determinants of job morale have concluded that wages are not a matter of primary significance in determining job satisfaction.[3] However, exclusion

---

[1] H. S. Parnes, *Research on Labor Mobility,* Social Research Council, New York, 1954, summarizes the findings of a number of labor market studies concerning job-finding techniques.

[2] H. S. Parnes, *op. cit.,* Chapter 6; also L. G. Reynolds, *The Structure of Labor Markets,* Harper and Brothers, New York, 1951, pp. 92–97, especially Table 14.

[3] Reynolds, *op. cit.,* pp. 89 et seq. recognizes this and defends his contrary finding. Also see C. A. Myers and G. P. Shultz, *The Dynamics of a Labor Market,* Prentice-Hall, New York, 1951, pp. 132–134. See, for example, J. S. Duesenberry, *Income,*

of wages from the determinants of "job satisfaction" makes little sense and, having given the reader due warning, we shall assume that (weekly) wages are an important ingredient of job satisfaction.

The satisfactoriness of the wages paid on a job are determined by comparing them with certain criteria. Chief among these are: (1) the cost of maintaining an "adequate living standard," (2) rates paid for similar work in other plants in the same vicinity, (3) the "nature of the work," and (4) the employment security of the job.

(1) What constitutes an "adequate living standard" will obviously vary from one person to another. However, it is reasonable to suppose that it is related to the way in which one's customary associates live. Accordingly, let us suppose that an "adequate living standard" is one that enables a family to "keep up with the Joneses." An adequate living standard is related not only to how one's associates live but also to what one has become accustomed. However, for most workers, these two criteria imply about the same level of income.

(2) and (3) In evaluating the "worth" of a job (i.e., what it ought to pay), workers seem to attach considerable significance to the physical hazards and/or discomfort that it entails and to the degree of skill or training required to perform it. They tend to feel that jobs calling for unusual skill, discomfort, or physical hazard should pay more than jobs less distinguished by these characteristics. The pleasantness of an employee's relations with his fellow workers and with his supervisors, whether he is treated fairly, etc. (the "psychological" characteristics of the job) have also been found to influence worker job satisfaction.

(4) The security of employment that is afforded by his job is usually very important to a worker. This is reflected both in a strong preference for permanent employment connections and for jobs where work is steady, thereby yielding a steady income. (A steady income is necessary in order to "keep up with the Joneses.")[4]

The aforementioned job characteristics are roughly indicative of what is desired in a job by the "typical" American worker who is the chief earner of his family or, if he has no dependents, whose wages are his

---

Saving and the Theory of Consumer Behavior, Harvard University Press, 1949. Also E. Wight Bakke, Adaptive Human Behavior, University of Minnesota, Industrial Relations Center, Bulletin No. 4, p. 44.

[4] A. J. Jaffe and C. D. Stewart, Manpower Resources and Utilization, John Wiley and Sons, Inc., New York, 1951, pp. 396–400, cite several questionnaire surveys which found a very marked reluctance to give up income security in exchange for the chance of substantially higher income accompanied by greater risks of unemployment. It is noteworthy that one such study (by Fortune Survey in 1947) found a substantially greater reluctance to risk income security among factory workers than among other occupational groups.

major source of income.　(Workers in other circumstances are discussed on pp. 289–292.)

Most of the recent labor market studies have found that workers were not concerned with hours of work as a criterion for a good job.　This probably reflects a lack of serious complaint with the *present* length of the work week (and day).　However, in the light of American labor history, it would be very rash to suppose that workers are not concerned with "hours."

LABOR SUPPLY AND JOB MOBILITY

The attitude of wage earners toward changing their jobs varies greatly with their age and family status.　Typically, a man with a family is far less ready to quit his job than one unencumbered by dependents.　And "secondary earners" (wives, children, etc.) display quite different labor market characteristics than "principal earners."　Let us, therefore, consider the behavior of principal and secondary earners separately.

Principal Earners

Principal earners are those persons whose wage earnings are the main source of financial support for themselves and/or their families.　Typically, the principal earner of a family is a man; however, there are many women who are either self-supporting or are the chief breadwinners for a family.

Once they have left school, most men enter the labor force on a permanent basis.　Barring ill-health, they remain available for gainful employment, save for vacations, every week of every year until they retire.　Retirement may, of course, be gradual; men in their late 50's and 60's are more prone to ill-health than younger workers and, therefore, tend to take off more time.　Nonetheless, between the ages of 20 and 65, most men in good health are either working or actively seeking work throughout the year.　Women who are principal earners have much the same labor supply characteristics as men; however, they are a minority of the female population.[5]

The attitude of the principal earner toward his job is likely to be different at different times of his life.　Upon entering the labor force, he begins by taking an unskilled job which he is ready to leave as soon as something better appears on the horizon, or even sooner if he should feel mistreated or restless.　Frequently, this is followed by several jobs which he feels to be unsatisfactory for one reason or another.　Finally, he gets a job which seems reasonably satisfactory and "settles down."　The proc-

[5] The following remarks refer to workers who have neither college nor professional training nor have undergone an apprenticeship for a particular trade.　These latter groups are considered in Chapter 18.

ess of settling down is likely to occur at about the same time as he acquires family responsibilities which make him reluctant to assume the risk of being unemployed, even temporarily.[6] Thereafter, he tends to cling to his current employer, confining his hopes of betterment (if any) to pay raises and promotions. The attachment of the "mature" worker to his employer is not readily severed by the prospect of higher (current) wages. And, when he is laid off, he is usually anxious to return to his old job.

There are good reasons for this attitude: (1) Employers have increasingly tended to discriminate in favor of the long-service employee, i.e., the worker with "seniority." This discrimination encompasses such matters as layoffs, promotions, paid vacations, pensions, shift-preferences, etc. The adoption of such discriminatory policies has been greatly accelerated by union pressure, but employers have frequently adopted such policies of their own volition as a device for reducing labor turnover (pp. 189–192). Discrimination in layoffs tends to give the long-service employee a steadier income. (2) A worker builds a set of personal relations and work routines on a particular job. Changing employers often involves either transportation difficulties in getting to work or moving to another part of town; either alternative is likely to prove unpleasant. As employers tend to be reluctant to hire new workers after age 40 and the fruits of seniority increase with age, workers become increasingly attached to their employer as they grow older.

This picture of principal earners as completely immobile as between employers is, of course, somewhat exaggerated. Not all workers are like this, and probably most workers are, at one time or another, tempted to change jobs. However, at any one time, most "family men" with steady jobs are reluctant to leave them.

Those men who do wish to change jobs do not, as a rule, "up and quit" at just any time. There is a marked tendency for quits, as distinguished from layoffs and discharges, to vary with the state of the labor market. That is, the ratio of voluntary "quits" to layoffs and discharges is very sensitive to, and moves in the same direction as, the volume of employment. The explanation of this fact is very simple; when jobs are hard to get and there are many applicants for them, workers tend to hold on to the jobs they have. Conversely, when alternative jobs are easy to get, workers are more likely to quit a job if dissatisfied. Thus, in the prosperous 1920's, quits exceeded involuntary separations in every year except 1921, a year of marked depression. But in the depressed 1930's,

---

[6] The question of whether the assumption of family responsibilities *causes* the worker to "settle down," or whether the causal relation is reversed, may be avoided. The important point is that the two phenomena are intimately related for most workers.

layoffs plus discharges exceeded voluntary quits in every single year; in the prosperous '40's, the pattern was again reversed, with quits exceeding layoffs plus discharges from March 1941 until December 1948 (with the exception of the "reconversion month" of August 1945). Layoffs tended to exceed quits throughout 1949 and early 1950, but the armament program, inspired by the Korean emergency, immediately reversed the relationship once more.[7]

The remarks we have made concerning the attachment of workers to a single employer refer to workers employed by firms which offer permanent jobs. Most of the larger firms (and many of the smaller ones) in manufacturing, distribution, transportation, public utilities, and government are of this kind. These firms, especially the larger ones, tend to favor "promotion from within" for manual workers; that is, workers must enter at a relatively humble and poorly paid job, and "earn" promotion to a better job, by some combination of merit and seniority.[8]

However, there are types of jobs where workers are hired only for very short periods but where they are (by reason of special skill, aptitude, and/or union organization) protected from the competition of other workers. Skilled construction workers, sailors, musicians, and weavers, are a few examples of workers in this type of situation. Such workers are likely to have a comparatively high degree of movement among *employers*, coupled with a relatively low degree of occupational mobility. Thus, skilled textile workers have been found to be very strongly attached to their occupations and the (one) industry where it may be followed.[9] Similarly, skilled construction workers, garment workers, musicians, sailors, and others follow their "trades" steadily, even though they may change employers frequently.

However, even workers of this type often seem to desire the employment stability and other advantages of a permanent affiliation with a single employer when they are obtainable.[10] Thus, it has been found

---

[7] W. S. Woytinsky, *Three Aspects of Labor Dynamics,* Social Science Research Council, Washington, D.C., 1942, p. 31, Table 3. Also see the reports published currently in the *Monthly Labor Review.*

[8] The extent to which any one firm follows this policy probably varies with the state of the labor market. When workers, with specific qualifications are needed and can't be obtained by promotion, a firm will hire from outside regardless of customary policy. However, the statement in the text applies, as a rule, to a great many firms.

[9] See G. L. Palmer, "Ten Years of Work Experience of Philadelphia Weavers and Loom Fixers," *Report* P-4, WPA National Research Project, July 1938; G. L. Palmer and Constance Williams, "Re-employment of Philadelphia Hosiery Workers After Shutdowns in 1933–1934, *Report* P-6, WPA National Research Project, January 1939; Carrie Glasser and B. N. Freedman, "Work and Wage Experience of Skilled Cotton Textile Workers," *Monthly Labor Review,* July, 1946, pp. 8–15.

[10] Such as company pensions, seniority in layoffs, promotions, health plans, etc.

that, in the interval 1940–1951, there was a very low rate of interfirm movement among highly skilled workers.[11]

Secondary Earners

Although some secondary earners work full time throughout the year, they are the exception. Most secondary earners are in the labor force only part of the year; these would include students who work only during vacations, housewives who work only at the Christmas holidays, part-time workers such as baby-sitters, old men who do "odd-jobs" from time to time, etc. It has been estimated that, in 1950, the population aged 14 and over was distributed, with respect to work status, as shown in Table 11.1.

Table 11.1. Work Status of Adult Population of the United States, 1950.

	Men, millions	Per cent	Women, millions	Per cent
Population over 14	54.6	100.0	55.9	100.0
Normally in labor force	44.0	80.7	16.8	30.1
In labor force throughout year	40.0	73.3	12.8	22.9
Withdraw occasionally	4.0	7.3	4.0	7.2
Normally not in labor force	10.7	19.4	39.1	69.9
Not in labor force at any time	6.7	12.1	31.1	55.6
Work occasionally	4.0	7.3	8.0	14.3

Source: W. S. Woytinsky and associates, *Employment and Wages in the United States*, Twentieth Century Fund, New York, 1953, p. 316.

As Table 11.1 indicates, about four-fifths of all men and three-tenths of all women are "normally" working or seeking work although some of them may drop out of the labor force on occasion. These persons include most of the principal earners and (probably) some of the secondary earners also. But most of the secondary earners are among those "normally not in the labor force."

A distinguishing characteristic of the secondary earner is his emphasis on *immediate* benefits as against long-run considerations. The fact that a job might promise steady employment with a good chance of promotion is not of much concern to him. (The disinterest of most secondary workers in long-run benefits is the obverse side of the fact that these workers feel their employment connection to be a temporary one, see below.) Often (but not always) the benefits sought from employment are mainly pecuniary: for example, a college boy trying to earn money to keep him for the next school year may take an arduous and unpleasant job that pays well, in preference to more pleasant but less remunerative work. He does this because he expects to keep the job for only two or three

[11] See "Patterns of Mobility Among Skilled Workers and Factors Affecting their Occupational Choice, Six Cities, 1940–1951," Massachusetts Institute of Technology (mimeographed), Chapter IV, Table I.

months; but he would not consider such work for a longer period. Conversely, a middle-class housewife seeking "pin-money" may refuse a relatively lucrative job in a factory for more pleasant surroundings and lower wages in a store or office. Housewives, with children, are often very concerned about working only at certain hours, i.e., when the children are at school. This restricts their choice of jobs and sometimes leads them to accept less remunerative employment than they might otherwise obtain. Older workers, or physically handicapped persons, are also available for only a restricted set of jobs.

In other words, secondary workers are likely to vary greatly as to the conditions and times at which they can accept gainful employment. But, with few exceptions, they seek immediate benefits from their job; they are not much interested in long-run prospects. This makes them rather poor union members; i.e., they don't have much interest in prolonged strikes for gains to be reaped over a long period.

From the employer's viewpoint, secondary earners are a kind of "labor reserve," available for handling periods of peak labor demand,[12] but not part of the steady workforce. As the employer sees them, such workers are "unreliable," in the sense that they are far more ready to quit their jobs than are primary earners. This is easy to understand; the job of a secondary earner is not his primary responsibility. A housewife's first concern is attending to her household; if there is serious illness, it is she who must abandon her other pursuits to serve as nurse. If her husband is transferred to another area, she accompanies him. If a schoolboy's studies suffer from inattention, it is usually his job that is abandoned, etc.

As a result of all this, secondary earners are rather more inclined to quit their jobs voluntarily and to exhibit a higher rate of movement between employers, than are primary earners. As we shall see, this is a matter of some significance for the operation of the labor market.

THE LABOR SUPPLY OF A FAMILY

Most families[13] supply at least one worker to the labor force; that is, in most families it is necessary for at least one member to work if the family is not to depend upon charity (public or private) for survival.[14] However, in 1951, 35 per cent of all families supplied more than one earner to the labor force. Usually the second earner was the wife al-

[12] The peak in demand may be seasonal, as with department stores at the Christmas rush, or hourly, as with the lunch counter, or weekly, as with food stores on weekends, etc. The employment pattern of the "extra" workers corresponds to the peak demands.

[13] Including unattached individuals.

[14] This statement refers, of course, to fairly long periods of time, such as a year. Obviously, a family may survive on its own resources for a few weeks or months despite the fact that it has no current income.

though occasionally it would be a child or an adult relative living with the family.

Abstracting from families of complex structure,[15] we may offer the following brief description of the usual characteristics of families that supply more than one earner. Among nonfarm families, the greater the income of the husband the less likely is the wife to enter the labor force.[16] Married women are less likely to work when there are small children (under six years) present than otherwise.[17]

In other words, where the principal earner's wages are relatively low, the wife tends to seek employment in order to bolster the family income. One would suspect that adolescent children would also be more likely to supplement father's paycheck when it is low than otherwise.[18]

Number of Hours

A principal earner has only limited control over the number of hours per week that he works. He usually is required to work the "standard" number of hours as a condition of keeping his job at all. However, he may have the option of accepting or refusing overtime. Where this is the case, his decision will depend upon a large number of factors; obviously, if he is ill or tired he is less likely to work overtime than otherwise. If the family has pressing debts or is saving for a new automobile or appliance, he is more likely to desire overtime than if his savings account is fat. Or, if the house needs repairs, he may prefer to work at home on Saturday rather than go to the shop. Similar remarks apply to an individual's willingness to accept odd jobs during evenings or on weekends.

Intensity of Effort

The amount of labor service supplied by a person per week does not depend merely upon the number of hours worked but also upon how intensively, and effectively, he works. Unfortunately, there is not a great deal that can be said about this matter in a general way although it must be borne in mind in considering labor supply.

LABOR SUPPLY, WAGES, AND UNEMPLOYMENT

The Job Hierarchy

As seen by job seekers, employment opportunities are of various grades; there are very good jobs, pretty good jobs, not so good jobs, etc.

---

[15] That is, families other than unattached individuals and married couples, with or without dependent children.

[16] This is true at least for families where the husband's income is below $10,000 per year. In higher income families, the relation appears to be different.

[17] See Jaffe and Stewart, *op. cit.*, pp. 129–134.

[18] Jaffe and Stewart, *op. cit.*, pp. 138–140.

We have already discussed the things that make a job seem good or poor to a worker. Once a worker decides that he wants to get another job or has been forced onto the labor market by dismissal, he wants to get the best job he can find. As we have seen he is not a very good job shopper; his information is very limited. But even within his limited knowledge, he often knows of better and poorer jobs. The reason he does not always take the better jobs is that he cannot get them.

He may not get them, or even try, because he is manifestly unqualified. The job may require education or specialized training that he does not possess. But it happens not infrequently that he "barely" misses a good job; i.e., it may have been filled half an hour before he applied, by someone no more qualified than he. Failing to obtain a more desired job, he must take one less preferred.

The amount of new hiring that occurs at any given time depends upon employers' needs for additional workers and the number of workers who are quitting (or being laid off). When the demand for labor, the number of job vacancies, is increasing more rapidly than the number of job applicants, vacancies remain unfilled for longer periods and it becomes easier to find a good job. Conversely, when job vacancies decrease more rapidly than applicants, all job vacancies become scarce and good ones almost never appear. This is because there are so many job seekers that a good vacancy is grabbed as soon as it does appear, and it rarely appears because someone already in the firm wants it for himself, or his brother-in-law, and so it is "filled" before its present occupant leaves it. Hence, in a favorable labor market (for workers), job seekers find it relatively easy to move up the "job hierarchy" toward better jobs and vice versa.

Of course, the qualifications required for getting a given job vary with the state of the labor market. When labor is scarce, employers become less insistent upon the various characteristics of the employees they hire. The reverse happens when labor becomes plentiful. Indeed, employers tend, unions and other circumstances permitting, to vary the wages they pay on given jobs with the state of the labor market; but this will be discussed later, pp. 322 et seq.

In the preceding paragraphs we have spoken of "good" and "bad" jobs as though the desirability of a job were an objective fact upon which there was universal agreement. With some qualifications, this is true. Employers that pay well also tend to offer relatively pleasant working conditions, interesting and secure jobs, and vice versa; there are several reasons why this should be so, of which the most important relate to employer "ability to pay" (see pp. 314–318).

Now for some qualifications to this argument. Within a given firm, the unpleasant, hazardous, or ardous jobs are usually paid somewhat more than jobs requiring the same general level of skill but without these attributes. Workers wishing peculiar hours or unusually light exertion will often have to accept lower wages than persons of their skills usually earn. Also, workers hired for only short periods are sometime paid more than similar workers with steady jobs, etc. Obviously, a change from a high wage but arduous job to one paying lower wages but which is less strenuous will be evaluated differently by different persons; i.e., there will be no general agreement as to which job is better. But, nevertheless, there is a hierarchy of employers in a given community, some of whom offer, unambiguously, better jobs than others to persons of roughly comparable skill and training.

Unemployment and the Job Hierarchy

In a general way, the employers that offer the best jobs get the pick of the labor force. Given the imperfections of the labor market, they obviously do not get all the best workers in the community, but they do get more than "their share." They do this by imposing relatively severe hiring requirements for the various jobs they offer. A firm offering very good jobs often insists upon new employees meeting certain age and educational standards, passing certain tests, performing well during a probationary period, etc. When job applicants are numerous, it tends to insist that its new employees meet its standards completely. However, in the face of a labor shortage, it may relax its hiring standards[19] somewhat in order to fill its vacancies.

What is true of the "best" employers is also true of the others although their standards cannot, at any given time, be quite so high as those of the best.[20] In general, the lower an employer ranks in the community job hierarchy, the less selective he can be. However, when the labor market is flooded, even the least desirable employer is able to exercise some power of selection; and the workers he rejects are going to be without jobs, unemployed.

When, for one reason or another, employers find it difficult to find enough job applicants to meet their hiring standards, they tend (among other things) to relax these standards and accept workers whom they would not have hired previously.[21] This means that most workers can get better jobs than they could have obtained previously, and that some workers can get some job who would previously have been unable to find any employment at all.

The role of unemployment in labor supply can be best understood if

[19] A firm's hiring standards are the various conditions, explicit or not, that it insists a job applicant meet as a condition of being hired; see further, pp. 321–324.

[20] Of course, the correlation between a firm's "desirability" as a place of employment and its hiring standards will be, in practice, far from perfect.

[21] This, of course, varies from one firm to another, see pp. 331–332.

we recognize that there is an *employee* hierarchy roughly analogous to the job hierarchy already mentioned. The characteristics that make a worker rank toward the top in this hierarchy are: (1) a suitable age (roughly 20 to 40), (2) a suitable level of education for the job applied for, (3) ability to score well on intelligence tests and/or tests for manual dexterity, (4) experience in the same type of job and favorable references from previous employers, etc. It is also a very substantial advantage to be Caucasian and male. When there is unemployment in a community; it tends to fall most heavily upon those who rank low in these various characteristics.

Thus in April 1940, the percentage distribution of unemployment by age and sex was as shown in Table 11.2. Obviously, the burden of un-

Table 11.2. Percentage Unemployed Among Persons in the Civilian Labor Force, by Sex and Age, 1940–1950

	1940		1950	
	Men	Women	Men	Women
14 years and over	14.3	15.5	4.9	5.3
14–19 years	32.8	27.8	10.8	10.3
20–24 years	18.1	19.9	7.7	6.3
25–44 years	11.1	11.8	3.7	4.7
45–64 years	13.4	13.3	4.2	4.1
65 years and over	10.0	2.1	4.6	3.1

Source: W. S. Woytinsky and associates, *Employment and Wages in the United States,* Twentieth Century Fund, New York, 1953, Table 177, p. 406.

employment fell most heavily on those past 45 who were "too old" and those below 25 who were "too inexperienced." Women were more prone to unemployment than men[22] and, as Table 11.3 shows, negroes more than whites. These general statements still applied in 1950, but the overall reduction in unemployment between 1940 and 1950 clearly gave jobs to many of the erstwhile unemployed.

Table 11.3. Percentage Unemployed Among Persons in the Civilian Labor Force, by Sex and Color, 1950

	Both Sexes	Men	Women
White	4.6	4.5	4.9
Nonwhite	8.5	8.9	7.8

Source: W. S. Woytinsky and associates, *op. cit.,* Table 178, p. 406.

The increased difficulty of getting employees has, since 1940, caused many employers not only to accept previously rejected workers but also to increase the variety of jobs offered. Since World War II employers

[22] The sexual difference in unemployment is understated by these figures because of the tendency for unemployed females to report themselves as not looking for work and, therefore, not appearing in the unemployment statistics.

have been more ready to accept part-time workers than they had been previously. As a result, many housewives have been able to accept employment in the 1950's who could not even have applied for the type of jobs available in the 1930's. This is one reason why the percentage of families with more than one earner has increased from 28 per cent in 1939 to 35 per cent in 1951[23] and also one reason for the sharp rise in the percentage of married women with jobs. This implies that the community's potential labor supply is often somewhat greater than would be inferred from adding to its employed persons only its active work seekers. When employers' hiring standards are rigid, many potential part-time workers simply feel it useless to look for work as do many oldsters, youngsters, negroes, and other unfavored persons who become discouraged by repeated rejections. (There is also some "disguised unemployment," which will be discussed later.)

To summarize: a community's jobs and its job fillers are (roughly) stratified in hierarchies with the most desirable jobs tending to go to the most desirable "job fillers." Employers adjust to abundance or scarcity of labor largely, though not entirely, by becoming more or less insistent upon the "qualifications" of the workers they hire. At the bottom of the employee hierarchy, there is a community "labor reserve" some of whose members actively seek work and some of whom do not. Those members of the labor reserve who actively do seek employment, are the persons recorded as unemployed.

UNEMPLOYMENT AND LABOR MOBILITY

One reason why workers are sometimes unemployed for extended periods of time is that they are available only for a restricted class of jobs. This fact is sometimes referred to as "labor immobility"; reduction of such immobility is often considered (rightly) an important contribution to reducing unemployment (see pp. 441–444). There are a variety of causes for labor immobility, the most important of which we shall discuss briefly.

Occupation

Where a worker has an occupation requiring special skill or training, he is obviously reluctant to abandon it. Employment in this occupation usually gives him pleasure and pride in his work and earnings that he could not otherwise obtain. However, if demand for this occupation has gone into a temporary or permanent decline, he may be very unwise in clinging to the hope of renewed employment in his specialty instead of seeking some other type of work.

[23] H. P. Miller, *Income of the American People,* John Wiley and Sons, Inc., New York, 1955, pp. 121–123.

As might be expected, it is the older workers who adjust less easily and cling most persistently to dying trades.   It also happens that occupational immobility is most pronounced when unemployment is widespread; i.e., when alternative jobs are available, the more enterprising members of an occupation move out and thereby relieve the overcrowding to some extent.   However, even at high levels of employment, there are pools of occupationally immobile workers who remain partially unemployed.

The Industry

Not many workers are attached to an industry, as such, although many are indirectly attached by reason of a particular occupation that can be practiced only in one industry.   Furthermore, certain industries experience unusually large fluctuations in demand, and their workers are, therefore, peculiarly subject to spells of unemployment.   These fluctuations may be seasonal, as in construction, or they may be synchronized with the level of general economic activity, as in heavy industry (iron, steel, machine tools, etc.).   When most of a worker's job experience is in one of these industries, he may resist accepting employment elsewhere, which usually would be at lower wages than he is accustomed to earning, and, hence, remains unemployed for a time.

It is because certain firms and industries are unusually prone to fluctuations in demand, that large numbers of very desirable workers often fall into the pool of unemployed labor while clearly inferior ones remain at work.

The Location

Many people do not like to change their place of residence, especially resisting changes that involve moving to a new city.   Consequently, a decline in employment in a particular locality is likely to be reflected, for some time, in an unusually high rate of unemployment.   It is because of this that even in periods of generally high employment there are usually some localities with labor surpluses.   And, during periods of general unemployment, some areas are hit much harder than others.

People do not change their location quickly in response to unemployment.   It usually takes a prolonged spell of joblessness in a given community to induce many people to leave.   It is not enough that there should be a great deal of unemployment "at home"; before a family will pull up roots and move, it must believe there is a good chance of finding employment where it is headed.   Because of this, geographical movement of labor tends to be lower in depressions than in periods of prosperity. That is, it is the "pull" of attractive employment opportunities elsewhere, rather than the "push" of unemployment at home, that is the most potent cause of labor migration.   Of course, where the "push" and the "pull" are combined, the movement is even greater.[24]

The people who do the moving are not randomly selected.   They are predominantly young persons who are unencumbered by dependents. Some youths would, perhaps, leave their native localities in any event "to see the world," and the effect of unemployment and lack of opportunity is to discourage them from returning.   In other cases, though, young people are induced to leave their native area by its dearth of economic opportunities.

Over the long-run, the secular pattern of geographical migration is from low to high income areas; especially from low income farms where there is disguised unemployment (see pp. 326–330) to cities where jobs are available.   It also is from areas of slower economic growth, such as New England, to those of more rapid development, such as the Pacific Coast.

EMPLOYMENT EXCHANGES AND THE LABOR MARKET

The preceding discussion of the way in which people find jobs (and employers obtain workers) suggests that the process is a disorganized "hit-and-miss" affair.   Indeed, most students of labor markets would accept this as an accurate description.   But why should this be so?   It would seem to the advantage both of workers and employers that knowledge of job applicants and vacancies should be organized and made available to those interested in hiring or being hired.

In other words, why not have employment exchanges that would do for the labor market what security and commodity exchanges do for buyers and sellers of these articles?   There are employment exchanges already in existence, but clearly they do not function as well as we might like.   Let us see what their difficulties are.

Public Employment Exchanges

Every state has a public employment office as part of its machinery for administering unemployment insurance (see pp. 472–473).   However, as presently constituted, the various state employment services are both understaffed and frequently by-passed by employers and workers.[25]   To a considerable extent the shortcomings of the state employment services have resulted from the fact that they are also entrusted with the responsibility of administering the unemployment insurance system.   Be-

---

[24] See H. W. Robinson, "The Response of Labor to Economic Incentives," in Wilson and Andrews, *Oxford Studies in the Price Mechanism,* Oxford University Press, 1951, pp. 204–272, especially pp. 204–243.

[25] See, L. G. Reynolds, *The Structure of Labor Markets,* Harper and Brothers, New York, 1951, pp. 55–75, and C. A. Myers and G. P. Shultz, *The Dynamics of a Labor Market,* Prentice-Hall, New York, 1951, Chapter 5.

cause of this dual responsibility, the state employment services refer many workers to jobs they do not desire but which they must pretend to seek for fear of losing unemployment benefits. When the referred worker appears for an interview with the employer, he soon conveys the impression that he doesn't want the job.[26]   For this and related reasons, employers feel that the state employment agencies are not reliable sources of labor supply.   Furthermore, it is the "good" employers (who are most able to hire easily through other channels) that are most inclined to ignore the state agency, except as a last resort.   This, in turn, causes the better workers to seek jobs through other channels.

As a result of these attitudes, probably not more than one new hiring in four is made through state employment agencies.   And those that are made are primarily for domestic service, unskilled labor, especially in construction and agriculture, and some semiskilled factory jobs of the less desirable sort.   Skilled and white-collar jobs rarely go through the state employment agencies.

The state employment services are handicapped by the fact that they pay low salaries and have a high turnover of personnel.   This, of itself, leads to inefficient placement work.   But, because employers use these services only as sources of last resort, the labor requests they make are inclined to be hard to meet and often require immediate action.   Failures by the service, of course, further deteriorate its reputation.   Despite these many obstacles, the reputation of the state employment agencies has improved since the 1930's, but they are still far from universal good repute.

The defects of our state employment agencies are not inherent in their nature, as some states have much better agencies than others.   Furthermore, public and private *nonprofit* employment agencies have never done a job in the United States that is comparable in scope or quality with that done in many other countries.   The truth of the matter is that in the United States we have never spent the time nor the money necessary to establish adequate public employment services.

In 1918, because of the existing labor shortage, the United States Employment Service was established in the Department of Labor.   But in 1919, the appropriations for it were largely discontinued because of pressure from private employment agencies and the National Association of Manufacturers.[27]   From then until the passage of the Wagner-Peyser Act in 1933, the United States Employment Service (USES) was largely a shadow organization.

---

[26] A worker can lose his unemployment benefits because he rejects a referral but if he accepts the referral and "manages not to get hired" his benefits will continue. See p. 473.

[27] For details, see Commons *et. al., History of Labor in the United States,* The Macmillan Co., New York, 1918, Vol. III, pp. 205–207.

The Wagner-Peyser Act greatly expanded the funds and activity of USES,[28] in 1935 the functions of USES were further enlarged by the requirement (of the Social Security Act) that all claimants to unemployment benefits must be registered with a public employment office. To facilitate this, the employment offices of those states which accepted (as all did) the standards of USES were subsidized by USES to operate its (USES) offices. During World War II, the operation of USES was taken over by the federal government under executive order and managed by the Social Security Board; this was done in order to facilitate the interstate transfer of workers needed in defense industries. Despite many demands for a continuation of federal control of the service, after V-J day Congress returned the system to its prewar status.

Private Employment Agencies

Many workers are placed in their jobs by private employment agencies which charge a fee for their services. Such agencies are especially important in placing clerical, managerial, and professional workers; they are of less significance in the field of manual labor. The private employment agency functions by collecting a placement fee from either the employer or the employee. Traditionally, the fee has been paid by the employee,[29] but in situations of labor shortage employers often pay the agency a fee and the agency, in order to secure job applicants, offers its services (to them) free. In the past, sharp practices and excessive fees[30] (charged employees) brought private employment agencies into disrepute and caused many states to adopt licensing requirements which were intended both to control their activities and to place upper limits upon their fees. The worst "abuses" of private employment agencies are well in the past; this is

---

[28] Ibid., pp. 214–217.

[29] The ability of the agency to collect its fee from the employee (and the correlative tendency to "sell" its services to the employer) reflects the prevalence of a "buyer's market" in labor.

[30] Some of the worst of these practices were: (1) Conspiracy of an agency with an employer to hire persons for a short period in order to collect placement fees. After a brief period of employment, workers would be discharged on some pretext and replaced by others who would also have to pay placement fees, etc. The employer and the employment agency would split the placement fees. (2) Misrepresentation of wages and working conditions by employment agencies. Sometimes an agency would transport workers (often immigrants unable to speak English) long distances to jobs which had been misdescribed and where the workers had to work for some time merely to earn their fare home—or to repay the agency which had advanced their fare. Not infrequently jobs of this kind involved strike-breaking; this fact brought private employment agencies into further ill-repute. See Commons, et. al., op. cit. Vol. III, pp. xi and 185–190 and the literature there cited especially in note 4, p. 187. Also, "Private Employment Agencies," Bulletin No. 57 Division of Labor Standards, U.S. Department of Labor, Washington, D.C., 1943.

partly because of government control but also because of a more sophisticated labor force. However, the best policemen of private employment agencies is a sufficient number of job openings to keep down the scarcity value of a job opportunity.

Private employment agencies play an important role in the hiring process of very small firms. Such agencies often act as a kind of hiring office for employers too small to afford one of their own. That is, these agencies do a good deal of preliminary screening of job applicants for employers who then make the final selection of applicants.[31]

Many unions of skilled craftsmen perform the function of an employment agency. As we have seen, there are some complications because of the Taft-Hartley Act, but in many cities the only simple way to locate a skilled craftsman is to phone the relevant local union. In some cases, the union's entry requirements insure that its members are competent; in others, some selection by the employer may be needed, which may cause difficulties with the union (see p. 187). However, where the union office is the principal (or sole) channel for hiring a certain type of craftsman, knowledge of job openings becomes very much better than in most sectors of the labor market. But, even then, private contacts between workers and employers keep many jobs, particularly good ones, from going through the union office.

The most important method of hiring manual workers, especially for large firms, is at the firm's own employment office. The firm makes known its intention of hiring new workers, either by telling people in the plant or (on occasion) by newspaper advertising, and makes its selections from among the applicants. In short, there are a number of different channels by which workers find jobs. The multiplicity of them and their lack of coordination is the main reason why the job-finding process is so erratic.

DISCUSSION QUESTIONS

1. (a) "If employers were compelled to register all jobs with a centralized public employment service for at least 24 hours before filling them, workers and jobs could be matched much better than at present." Discuss.

(b) What objections can you think of to such a proposal as the above?

2. What contribution does a policy of laying off workers in reverse order of seniority make to reducing labor mobility (of workers) among employers?

3. "To a limited extent, the nation's labor supply expands and contracts with variations in labor demand." What type of worker do you think would be most likely to enter the labor force, when labor demand increases?

4. How could unemployment be confined to secondary earners? In your opinion, is it desirable that it should be so confined?

[31] The relation between employer and private employment agency varies from that of complete dependence by the employer upon the agency's personnel selections, to one where the agency's referrals are treated as mere suggestions.

Suggested Readings

Bogue, D. J., "A Methodological Study of Migration in Michigan and Ohio in 1947," Scripps Foundation Studies in Population, Distribution No. 4, June 1952.

Jaffe, A. J. and C. D. Stewart, *Manpower Resources and Utilization: Principles of Working Force Analysis,* John Wiley & Sons, Inc., New York, 1951.

Lester, R. A., *Hiring Practices and Labor Competition,* Industrial Relations Section, Department of Economics and Sociology, Princeton University, Princeton, N.J.; *Adjustments to Labor Shortage,* Industrial Relations Section, Department of Economics and Sociology, Princeton University, Princeton, N.J.

Long, C. D., "Labor Force, Income, and Unemployment," New York, National Bureau of Economic Research, 1950 (mimeographed).

Miernyk, W. H., assisted by N. P. Rodwin, *Inter-industry Labor Mobility—the Case of the Displaced Worker,* Bureau of Business and Economic Research, Northeastern University, Boston, 1955.

Myers, C. A., and W. R. Maclaurin, *The Movement of Factory Workers,* John Wiley & Sons, Inc., New York, 1943.

Myers, C. A., and G. P. Shultz, *The Dynamics of a Labor Market,* Prentice-Hall, New York, 1951.

Palmer, G. L., *Labor Mobility in Six Cities: A Report on the Survey of Patterns and Factors in Labor Mobility, 1940–1950.* Social Science Research Council, New York, 1954.

Parnes, H. S., *Research on Labor Mobility,* Social Science Research Council, New York, 1954.

Reynolds, L. G., *The Structure of Labor Markets,* Harpers, New York, 1951.

Reynolds, L. G., and J. Shister, *Job Horizons,* Harpers, New York, 1949.

Sobel, I., and R. C. Wilcock, "Secondary Labor Force Mobility in Four Midwestern Shoe Towns," *Industrial and Labor Relations Review,* July 1955, pp. 520–540; also by the same authors, "Labor Market Behavior in Small Towns," *Industrial and Labor Relations Review,* October 1955, pp. 54–76.

Woytinsky, W. S., *Three Aspects of Labor Dynamics,* Social Science Research Council, New York, 1945.

Woytinsky, W. S., and Associates, *Employment and Wages in the United States,* Twentieth Century Fund, New York, 1953.

Yoder, D., *et al., Local Labor Market Research,* University of Minnesota Press, Minneapolis, 1948.

12

The Employer
and the Demand for Labor

In this chapter we shall study the forces that determine an employer's wage policy and his demand for labor. We shall limit the discussion to business firms that are operated primarily for profit.

Basic to any discussion of labor demand is a consideration of the interrelations among a firm's profits, wages, product prices, man-hour physical productivity of labor, raw material costs, etc.; this is covered in the first section of this chapter. However, there are other aspects to labor demand that are integral to any intelligent comprehension of the labor market; these aspects, which are the employer's "specifications" for the labor he hires, are usually relegated to the limbo of "personnel management." We have already discussed these to some extent in Chapter 11, but we shall analyze them further in the sections entitled, *The Peculiarities of Labor as a Productive Instrument* and *Wage Policy and Wage Differentials*.

PROFITS, WAGES, AND THE DEMAND FOR LABOR: SIMPLE CASE

Wages and the Demand for Labor

All businesses must, in the long run, earn profits. A firm may accept losses for a time, but this is only in the hope of eventually reaping profits that will outweigh the current losses; if these profits do not appear, the firm will go out of business.

In the process of earning profits, a firm incurs expenses. The part of its expenses that are incurred on account of labor we shall, for the moment, call wages. Nowadays an employer often incurs sizeable amounts of nonwage expense—contributions to pension funds, social security taxes, insurance payments, etc.—on account of the labor he uses; but we shall ignore this complication for the present (taking it into account later, Chapter 19) and identify employer labor costs with wage payments.

The employer's profits (per year) are the difference between what he receives for selling his output minus what he pays out for the expense of producing it, including depreciation charges and taxes.[1]   What the employer pays out may be divided into two parts: wages and other expenses of production.

Most firms produce a variety of products so that a precise measurement of their physical output involves rather tricky problems of index number construction.   However, one way or another, these can usually be solved well enough for practical purposes, and we shall assume that we can talk sensibly about the firm's annual rate of physical output and its (average) price.   Granting this, we may say that the firm receives so many cents per unit of (physical) output, its average selling price or (for short) price,

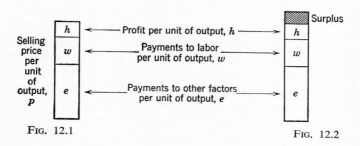

FIG. 12.1   FIG. 12.2

and this is imputed as so many cents to profit, so many to wages, and so many to other expenses of production.   We may say the same thing in an equation:

$$\begin{array}{ccccccc} \text{selling price} & = & \text{wages} & + & \text{profits} & + & \text{other expenses} \\ \text{(per unit of} & & \text{(per unit of} & & \text{(per unit of} & & \text{(per unit of} \\ \text{output)} & & \text{output)} & & \text{output)} & & \text{output)} \\ p & = & w & + & h & + & e \end{array}$$

or in a diagram (Fig. 12.1).

To keep the argument simple, let us suppose that the firm employs only one kind of labor; later it will be necessary to consider more complicated cases.

To focus the discussion, let us ask the following question: What are the channels through which it is possible to increase wages per unit of output?   In order to simplify matters, let us suppose the other expenses of production per unit of output (hereafter called e) remain unchanged. Then, to raise wages per unit of output, w, it is necessary either to raise

[1] There are, of course, all sorts of complications which this statement ignores, e.g., problems of changes in inventories and the valuation thereof and allocation (over time) of capital expenditures.   But these complications are inessential to our limited purpose.

the selling price per unit of output, p, to lower profit per unit of output, h. or both.[2]

Consider increasing p: If this were done, the height of the bar in Fig. 12.1 would be raised, creating a surplus which could (but need not) be used to raise w, as indicated in Fig. 12.2. But if this were done, what would happen to the demand for the output? This would depend, in part, upon the change (if any) in demand conditions that occurred. "Demand conditions" refers to all the forces that determine the quantity of a firm's output that will be purchased (per period of time) at a given price, i.e., in the technical jargon of economists, the forces that determine the demand curve for the firm's product. If demand conditions change so that more will be purchased at a given price than before, we shall say that "demand has increased"; and, if the reverse happens, we shall say that "demand has decreased." If for some reason demand increases, the firm can, if it chooses, sell the same quantity of output as before at a higher price (i.e., move from Fig. 12.1 to Fig. 12.2) and devote some of the resulting "surplus" (extra revenue per unit of product) to increasing w. If demand were to decrease so that a given output could be sold only at a lower price, the sum of $w + e + h$ would have to be reduced.[3]

Now let us consider briefly what will happen if a firm raises its price with *demand conditions given.* The results depend upon the nature of the product market. A priori, the nature of a firm's product market may be anything from the one extreme of a virtual monopoly to the other of pure competition where it cannot charge a penny more than any one of its rivals without losing all of its customers. At the former extreme, competitors are nonexistent, and the only deterrent to price increases is the danger of driving buyers away from the porduct in question. In the latter case, the firm can (without being driven from the market) increase its price only by the same amount as its competitors; if it should try to raise it more, it will make no sales. Most firms lie somewhere between these extremes, and whether it pays to raise selling prices, *with demand conditions unchanged,* depends upon the extent to which its output competes with that of other firms and upon what its relatively close competitors are doing. But in any event, *given the demand conditions for the output of a single firm and of its close competitors* (if any), neither one firm in-

---

[2] The relative sizes of p, e, w, and h vary appreciably from one line of business to another and even from one firm to another within the same general line of business. However, the reader's perspective will be aided if he remembers that h is usually an appreciably smaller part of p than either e or w. That is, $p = e + w + h$ and h/p is (usually) much less than e/p or w/p; even for highly profitable firms, h is usually less than 20 per cent of p.

[3] The reader versed in economic theory will immediately detect that it is implicitly assumed that average costs do not vary with output, i.e., that $e + w$ is independent of the rate of output; see p. 313.

dividually nor the group of firms together will be able to raise selling prices without reducing the physical quantity that can be sold.   In other words, the higher the price charged (demand conditions given) the smaller will be the physical volume of output that will be sold. If the number of hours of labor used varies in the same direction as the amount of output, which is the usual case, then raising the product price (demand conditions given) will cause the number of hours of labor hired (per period of time) to decline, and vice versa.

Therefore, if a firm (or group of firms) attempts to increase w by raising p, *given demand conditions,* it will cause the amount (man-hours) of labor hired to be less than otherwise.   (A similar statement would apply if it were to attempt to increase h or the payment to any other productive agent per unit of product by raising p.)

Wages and Profits

Now let us consider the possibility of raising w by lowering profits per unit.   To some extent this may be possible (see pp. 334–335).   However, there is always a definite limit to how far profits may be reduced because business firms will usually insist, in the long-run, on earning some minimum rate of return on their invested capital as a condition of continuing operations.   The "minimum" rate of return will differ somewhat from one firm to another, depending upon the knowledge, abilities, and attitudes of the enterpreneurs involved, the risks attendant upon the given line of business, etc.   But the important point is that, for every firm, there is some minimum rate which cannot be violated, for long, without causing the firm to disappear, at least from its present line of activity.

Temporarily, a firm may earn *more* than its own (or the general) level of minimum rates because it happens to be in an industry whose output is in great demand and whose prices are correspondingly high.   However, unusually high profits often attract new firms to the line of business where they are being earned (and/or cause firms already there to expand), and the resulting increase in output brings down both profits and prices.[4]   But this does not always happen; it is also possible that a firm should be able *permanently* to earn more than its minimum rate.

A firm's ability to earn profits in excess of its minimum rate may result from several causes.   Of these the two most important are: (1) a firm's management may have more than usual skill and, therefore, have lower expenses of production per unit of output than its close competitors, and

---

[4] There is much dispute among economists as to how effective this process is in bringing profits down to the "minimum rate." It is pointless, for the present purpose, to enter into this debate other than to note that it is not seriously contended either that (1) the process is effective in all sectors of the economy or (2) that it is effective nowhere.

(2) its product may have some distinctive features which enable it to charge a higher price and/or use cheaper production methods.   If, for any reason, a firm should be earning more than its minimum rate of return, it *may* accept the imposition of (by a union), or voluntarily grant, an increase in *w* without either raising *p* or going out of business.   However, there is an upper limit to the amount of such an increase; i.e., the minimum rate of return cannot be violated.   Furthermore, it must be understood that there is no certainty that a firm with an unusually high *h* will choose to share its profits with its workers; i.e., will pay an unusually high *w*.

At this point the reader might well ask how it is possible for *w* ever to rise without reducing profits per unit of output.   There are three principal ways in which this can happen: (1) *p* may rise because of a change in demand conditions; (2) *e* may fall (with production unchanged); and (3) the method of production may change.   We have already discussed the first of these possibilities.   There is not a great deal to say about the second possibility; it arises when declines in raw material or other prices cause a reduction in *e* that (given *p*) produces an increase in the sum, *w* + *h,* which is, (in the short run) available for distribution between wages and profits.

The third possibility, a change in the firm's method of production (e.g., through technical progress), is, and has long been, an important route for increasing *w* without trenching on profits.   Suppose the method of production changes so that fewer hours of labor are used per unit of product. (This type of change is usually referred to as an increase in labor's man-hour physical productivity or, for short, man-hour productivity.)   Then, it would be possible to increase wages *per hour,* in proportion to the decrease in man-hour productivity, without raising *w*.   If wages *per hour* remained unchanged, this would mean (in terms of Fig. 12.1) that *w* would decline as fewer hours of labor would be necessary to produce a given output.   If *p* and *e* remained unchanged, a surplus (see Fig. 12.2) would be created which would be available for distribution between wages and profits.   From such "surpluses," have come a large part of the wage increases discussed in Chapter 16.

However, when considering a single firm or even a small sector of the economy, it is necessary to reckon with the fact that "surpluses" resulting from increases in technical efficiency usually result in temporarily increased profits.   These profits very often lead to expansions in output, either from new or from existing firms, which lead to reductions in price, *p*.   Furthermore, increases in man-hour productivity are sometimes the accompaniment of substantial increases in mechanization.   When this is the case, depreciation charges on the machinery, per unit of ouput, may rise (this would be reflected by an increase in *e*) thereby partially offsetting the initial fall in *w*.   Nonetheless, a very substantial part of the increases in man-hour productivity, during the last century, have been used to increase *real* hourly wages (see pp. 403–404).

WAGES, THE TECHNIQUES OF PRODUCTION AND THE DEMAND FOR LABOR

The amount of labor (in man-hours) that a firm hires in a given time period depends upon the amount of output it wishes to produce; the more output the more labor it needs. It is also true, though by no means so obvious, that the lower the hourly wages paid to labor, given the cost (per unit of output) of the other ingredients of production, the more man-hours of labor will be used per unit of output.

There are certain very important qualifications attached to this latter proposition without which it is completely invalid. The first of these is that the catalog of productive techniques known to the firm must be given. For example, if an entirely new method of producing a particular product is discovered which reduces costs by 50 per cent but uses 1 per cent less labor per unit of output, the fact that wage rates have just fallen by 10 per cent (other factor prices given) will not prevent less labor from being used (per unit of output) than previously. A second qualification refers to the period of time allowed for changes in methods of production; such changes can be made only at certain specific times (e.g., when operations are shut down), and at other times are not made despite the possibility of substantial cost savings.

Some economists are inclined to minimize the importance of wage rates as a determinant of methods of production or to deny that they have any influence at all.[5] However, such arguments are usually directed at the doubtful propositions that wage cuts can prevent mechanization that would otherwise occur, and, conversely, that wage increases may stimulate mechanization that would not be undertaken otherwise.[6] But there are other, and more important, channels through which wage changes affect productive techniques: 1. By influencing the firm's decision as to whether to undertake a particular operation itself or to contract it out to another firm. Such decisions are made largely upon a cost basis and, if a firm is compelled to raise wages, it will reduce its costs more than previously by "contracting out" some of its operations. That is, if a firm pays higher hourly wages than its potential subcontractors, its higher

[5] For good examples of such a position, see R. A. Lester, "Shortcomings of Marginal Analysis for Wage-Employment Problems," *American Economic Review,* March 1946, pp. 63–82; also Joseph Shister, *Economics of the Labor Market,* Lippincott, 1949, pp. 404–411.

[6] S. H. Slichter, *Union Policies and Industrial Management,* Brookings Institution, Washington, D.C., 1941, Chapter VIII, gives a number of examples illustrating the inability of unions to do more than delay the introduction of machinery by accepting wage cuts.

labor costs (per unit of output) may tip the scale in favor of subcontracting. Also, it often happens that a firm, by making minor variations in its product, can alter appreciably the amount of labor and/or materials it uses per unit of output. Hence, an increase in hourly wages may turn the tide in favor of a product change that economizes labor as the alternative to an increase in the product price.

2. The importance of wage rates, relative to other factor prices, as a determinant of the methods of production can be seen quite clearly if we compare methods of heavy construction in "backward" countries such as Egypt with those used in the United States. In the United States, canals, irrigation ditches, etc. are dug by large and expensive dredges, steam shovels, and the like, with labor being used solely for the purpose of tending these mechanical monsters. But in Egypt, a recent improvement in the Suez canal was dug by "native toilers, equipped only with shovels and other hand tools."[7] Pick and shovel labor is rarely used in the United States (in lieu of steam shovels) because of the high wages that would have to be paid laborers relative to the rental cost of equipment. But, in Egypt, the cost advantage is on the side of the "labor intensive" method. Further examples to the same point are provided by the cotton textile industries in Brazil, Chile, and Ecuador. An investigation by the Economic Commission for Latin America (of the United Nations) found the use of substantially more labor per unit of output (and more output per machine) than in the United States. The report attributed this, in part, to the relatively low wage cost, relative to material and machine costs, in the other countries as compared with the United States.[8] The reader will no doubt be able to find many other examples that serve to illustrate this point.

THE MARGINAL PRODUCTIVITY THEORY

Statement of the Theory

The argument of the two preceding sections may be summarized as follows: An increase in the price of an hour of labor (hourly wages) to a given firm will, given the demand conditions for its output, tend to cause an increase in its product price, thereby reducing its rate of output and employment of labor. Such an increase also tends to lead to the use of less labor per unit of output, given (1) sufficient time for the relevant adjustments in productive technique, (2) an absence of changes in other expenses of production per unit of output, and (3) an absence of sharp

[7] *Life,* October 22, 1951, pp. 80–81.

[8] *Labour Productivity of the Cotton Textile Industry in Five Latin-American Countries,* United Nations, New York, 1951, paragraphs 112–115 (p. 18), paragraphs 215–218 (pp. 51–52), paragraphs 251–256 (pp. 67–68).

changes in the available set of productive techniques. (The converse holds for a decrease in hourly wages.) If the change in hourly wages is small, minor variations in profit per unit of output or in the other items in Fig. 12.1 may offset the effect of the change, but if the change is substantial then the statements made will hold.

These two contentions can both be deduced from what is known as the "marginal productivity theory." This theory states that a business firm employs that quantity of labor (in man-hours) that makes the extra receipts resulting from the output of an additional man-hour of labor equal to the extra cost of hiring an additional man-hour.[9] The extra receipts resulting from the output of an additional man-hour are called the marginal value product of labor, hence, the title "marginal productivity theory."[10]

The theory posits the existence of a functional relationship among the marginal value product (marginal physical product $\times$ marginal revenue)[11] of labor, the quantity of labor (in man-hours) and other productive agents the firm uses. This relationship is (partially) exhibited in Fig. 12.3; the marginal value product curve of labor need not be continuous, but its general direction must be downward from left to right. That is, marginal value product must tend to decline as the quantity of labor used increases.

The marginal value product (of labor) curve gives the addition to the firm's receipts from selling the output resulting from hiring an extra man-hour of labor on the assumption that this labor is used in the most effective manner possible, and that the quantities of machinery, other equipment, and plant are unchanged. Because plant and equipment are fixed in quantity, the marginal physical product of labor,[12] and hence its marginal value product also, declines as the quantity of labor used increases.

Since the marginal value product of labor measures the extra receipts derived from using an extra man-hour of labor under the above circumstances and the hourly wage of a firm is the extra cost, a firm will add to

[9] The extra cost of hiring an additional man-hour of labor is equal to the hourly wage rate of labor, except under the rare conditions of "labor monopsony," when the hourly wage rate varies with the quantity of labor hired by the *individual firm*.

[10] As stated the theory applies only to labor. However, the theory is applicable to all agents of production.

[11] Marginal physical product of labor is the extra output (in physical units) from using one extra man-hour of labor with quantities of all other productive agents constant. Marginal revenue is the extra receipts from selling one more unit of output, given demand conditions. Under pure competition this is equal to price; otherwise, it is somewhat less. These concepts are discussed in most good textbooks, e.g., those listed at the end of this chapter.

[12] The reasoning behind this statement is indicated by the "marginal productivity" references at the end of the chapter.

its profit by hiring extra man-hours so long as marginal value product exceeds the wage. Hence, the firm will make the largest possible (maximum) profit by using a quantity of labor that makes the marginal value product equal to the wage rate. This is shown in Fig. 12.3 by the intersection of a wage line w_1, w_2, etc. with the marginal value product curve. If w_1 is the hourly wage, the firm hires *oa* hours of labor; if w_2 is the wage, the firm hires *ob.*, etc. In other words, at each wage rate, the marginal value product curve gives the amount of labor the firm will hire (demand); hence, the marginal value product curve is called the firm's demand curve for labor.

If the amounts of labor demanded by each firm at each wage rate[13] are added together, we get a market demand curve for labor. If we pair this with a labor market supply curve, *S,* as in Fig. 12.4, the intersection of

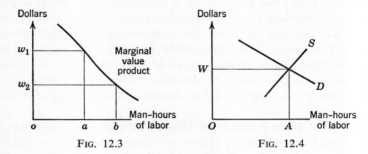

FIG. 12.3   FIG. 12.4

the curves determines the wage rate, *OW,* and the amount of employment, *OA.* Thus, the marginal productivity theory is one in which wages are determined as a market price.

This account of the marginal productivity theory is far from the whole story. In particular, the assumption that the quantities of "other factors" (machinery, raw materials, etc.) are held constant, limits our argument to what is known technically as the "short run." But in its full development, the marginal productivity theory is an elaborate and quite complicated piece of theoretical apparatus with far-reaching implications for the whole of economic theory. Its relevance to labor market analysis is that it provides, or purports to provide, an explanation of the demand for labor, and for this purpose our limited account of it will suffice.

Unfortunately, there is considerable disagreement among economists concerning the validity of the various steps in constructing both individual and market demand curves for labor. (The aforementioned market supply curve creates still further troubles.) Indeed, there is so much disagreement as to the validity of the marginal productivity theory that an

---

[13] This argument implicitly assumes the existence of only one wage rate at a time. The unreality of this assumption disturbs many economists.

argument presuming upon its validity would be unacceptable to many economists, especially those concerned with labor problems.

In deference to this feeling, our subsequent arguments will not presume upon the validity of the marginal productivity theory; this should not, however, be interpreted as a rejection of the theory. We are able to avoid further use of the marginal productivity theory because virtually all of the propositions we shall need can be obtained without it. But many of these propositions could also be obtained, some would say better and easier, by direct use of "conventional" marginal productivity arguments. However, our approach will, it is hoped, minimize the resistance of the "average" reader.

Objections to Marginal Productivity: the "Employment Effect"

There are a number of grounds upon which labor economists have objected to applying the marginal productivity theory to the analysis of wage-employment relations. As we shall not make extensive use of this theory, it is not important that we appraise all the various objections that have been offered. However, one particular argument is noteworthy because it calls attention to an important aspect of the relation between wage rates and labor demand.

This is the contention of certain economists that the effect of wage changes on employment (the "employment effect") is either unimportant or incalculable.[14] Although there are a number of theoretical considerations that may be offered to support, and quite a few to refute, this contention, the most important reason for doubting the importance of the "employment effect" is that "disturbing phenomena" frequently obscure its manifestations so as to make them imperceptible.

Both the marginal productivity theory and the argument in the section entitled *Wages, The Techniques of Production and the Demand for Labor* assert that a rise in hourly wage rates will reduce man-hours of employment offered, *if* demand conditions are given and *if* there is not a "countervailing" change in the catalog of known methods of production. But the American economy, throughout most of its history, has customarily been expanding; business firms have not usually been confronted with given demand conditions, and technology has been steadily improving. Consequently, the amount of employment a firm has been able to offer has seemed to be the result of a tug of war between the expansive effect of increased output and the effect of improved technology which reduces the man-hours of labor used per unit of output.

If the increased output expands the demand for labor more than improved technology reduces it, as often happens, wages and employ-

[14] For example, A. M. Ross, *Trade Union Wage Policy,* University of California Press, Berkeley and Los Angeles, 1948, pp. 80 et seq.

ment increase together. When this happens, marginal productivity defenders are reduced to saying: (1) "this does not contradict our theory as demand conditions and technology were not unchanged, and the theory does not, therefore, apply"; and/or (2) "if wages had fallen, employment would have increased even more than it did." To the first statement, the answer is "then your theory is irrelevant to a large number of cases." The second statement simply invites the question "how do you know?"

The situation is no better if improved technology overbalances increased demand and employment is reduced. In the short-run (at least), firms in this position may be reducing employment while their level of output and profits per unit of output are both increasing. It is often the case that such firms could not be induced to adopt methods of production which would use more labor per unit of output no matter what level of wages (among those practically possible) was attained. Hence, even if wages were reduced, employment would still fall; and to the argument, "the decline in employment would have been even greater if wages had not been cut," there is again the rejoinder, "how do you know?"

Although the "antimarginalists" sometimes neglect the ways in which raising the price of labor may restrict its employment, it must be conceded that, *where* there are sharp changes in either demand conditions for output or in technology, the "employment effect" of wage changes is obscured, and its existence must, at best, be inferred indirectly.[15] However, it is by no means true that all sectors of the American economy have customarily experienced steady increases in demand and/or improvements in technology. For example, the New England textile and shoe industries, important branches of garment and hosiery manufacturing in both the New York and Philadelphia areas, and bituminous coal mining in the older mining areas of Pennsylvania and Ohio have all undergone periods when the product market had stopped growing and/or was being captured by producers in rival areas. In cases such as these, the employment effect of wage cuts[16] was not only visible but fully recognized by "hard-headed" union leaders and businessmen.[17]

Now, it is possible to infer from those cases where the employment effect clearly operates that it is also operative, but "swamped" by the effect of other forces, in the areas where its existence is in dispute. Such in-

[15] That is, it must be inferred from general theoretical considerations and/or from cases where the operation of the employment effect is not obscured. (Antimarginalists tend to deny the validity of such inferences.)

A complete and satisfactory econometric model might make it possible to establish, or disprove, the reality of the "employment effect" in specific sectors of the economy. However, such a model has not yet been constructed.

[16] By enabling employers to reduce prices and thereby gather a larger share of the market.

[17] See G. P. Shultz and C. A. Myers, "Union Wage Decisions and Employment," *American Economic Review,* June 1950, pp. 363–380.

ferences have much to commend them, but economists who doubt that "economic laws operate uniformly throughout the economy" will no doubt persist in being sceptical.

FIXED COSTS AND VARIATIONS IN OUTPUT

In our discussion so far, we have assumed by implication that w and e (in Fig. 12.1) do not change with variations in the firm's level of output. This is unrealistic even in the long-run, and for "short period" analysis it is too drastic a simplification to be tolerated. Within any given year, or in many cases for a longer period, a firm has certain fixed commitments for rent, interest on bonded indebtedness, executive salaries, etc. These expenses are completely independent of output and are usually called "fixed costs." But, although the total amount of fixed cost is independent of output, fixed cost per unit falls as output increases, and vice versa when output decreases. This is because fixed cost *per unit* is a constant dollar sum divided by the number of units of output produced; the numerator is fixed and so the quotient falls as the denominator (output) rises, and vice versa.

When the firm's output is low, its fixed costs (per unit of output) are high, and, unless, selling price is correspondingly high, it will be very difficult with a given level of $w + e$ to keep from suffering losses. That is, in terms of Fig. 12.1, at low outputs e (including fixed costs) becomes very high, and, unless p can be raised or w lowered correspondingly, h must be very small or, more likely, negative (which implies losses). But it is usually not possible to raise p in order to offset a rise in e that results from a decline in output. This is because a decline in output usually occurs as a response to worsened demand conditions for the product, so that the pressure is to reduce rather than to raise prices. Hence, in seeking to reduce his losses, the employer must cut his variable expenses, raw material and labor costs, per unit. As we have seen, this frequently leads to attempts to cut hourly wage rates thereby provoking struggles with unions. The tendency for employers to fight unions particularly hard in depressions (observed in Chapter 3) is, in good part, due to this fact. Conversely, when output expands, profits tend to rise more than proportionately, and generosity, labor market and/or union pressure (or all of them) lead employers to share these profits, to some extent, with their workers.

THE PECULIARITIES OF LABOR AS A PRODUCTIVE INSTRUMENT

So far, in this chapter, we have treated human labor power as though it were merely a source of productive services, like a machine. For certain purposes, this is a useful simplification; but it obscures important differences. One important difference arises in connection with employer policy regarding wages and prices of other instruments of production.

"Good business" implies paying as little as possible for materials, equipment, etc., but not for labor.

There are two reasons for this difference: one of these is that most workers must learn their tasks, and this takes time.[18]   As a worker must be paid (usually more than his current productivity justifies) while he is learning, employers generally prefer to keep an "old hand" on the job rather than hire a newcomer, even though the two workers would otherwise be identical.   Consequently, an employer has good reason for paying his experienced workers a wage higher than the bare minimum necessary to retain their services; otherwise, the workers might leave their jobs too readily for his profit.

The fear of losing employees is not the only "labor supply" consideration which a wise employer takes into account in setting a wage policy. He is also concerned with avoiding low morale, unpleasant employee relations, low man-hour productivity, etc.[19]   The reason for this concern is that when employees approach the "margin of indifference" between keeping their jobs and quitting, they tend to resist supervision, and in other ways lower their value to the employer.   In short, wise buying of labor service does not consist in buying as cheaply as possible; rather it implies keeping wages (and other inducements) sufficiently high to make workers happy in their jobs and anxious to retain them.

A second reason for not paying the lowest wage possible is the strong ethical tradition against "taking advantage" of one's employees, i.e., of paying them as little as the market requires.[20]   Needless to say there is no comparable tradition relevant to the purchase of raw materials, machinery, etc.   Considerable prestige and good-will accrues to firms known as high-wage payers and desirable places to work, but no management is ever commended for paying unnecessarily high prices for its materials.

WAGE POLICY AND WAGE DIFFERENTIALS

Ability to Pay

In recent years, students of labor problems have become keenly aware of the fact that, in a given community at any given time, there is consider-

---

[18] I am referring not to "generalized skill," but to the "know-how" that is peculiar to a particular plant and is of little use elsewhere.

[19] See, for example, L. G. Reynolds, *The Structure of Labor Markets,* Harper Bros., New York, 1951, pp. 160–161; R. A. Lester, *Company Wage Policies; A Survey of Patterns and Experience,* Industrial Relations Section, Department of Economics and Sociology, Princeton University, Princeton, N.J., 1948, pp. 31–32.

[20] See, for example, Reynolds, *op. cit.,* pp. 159–160; Lester, *op. cit.,* p. 32; and W. R. Maclaurin, "Wages and Profits in the Paper Industry, 1929–1939," *Quarterly Journal of Economics,* February 1944, pp. 196–228, especially pp. 206–214 and pp. 224–228.

able variation among the hourly wage rates paid by different firms.   Part of this, of course, reflects differences in the amounts and kinds of skill and training required by different employers.   But quite apart from this, it would seem fairly clear that some employers simply pay more than others for what would seem to be the same kind of labor.

The general pattern of wage differentials, in a given area, would seem to parallel employer's "ability to pay."[21]   That is, the employers whose profit per man-hour of labor used is relatively high tend to pay higher hourly wages than those whose profit per man-hour is less.   In a general way, this means that the larger, better financed, more profitable firms pay better wages (and offer as good or better conditions) than others.

One of the most important manifestations of this is the differences among hourly wages paid in different industries.   These differences are given, for a number of important industries, in Table 12.1.   A great number of different factors affect the ranking of the different industries in this hierarchy.   In general, an industry will rank higher (in Table 12.1) the greater is (1) the percentage of its workers that are skilled and (2) the smaller the percentage of its employees that are women or negroes. High wage industries tend to be those characterized by large, well-financed corporations using a great deal of machinery per worker and operating a number of plants which are located mostly in large cities; low wage industries exhibit the reverse characteristics.

These various factors may, of course, work in opposite directions.   For example, in printing and construction, firms are typically small, but the production processes are such as to require an unusually high percentage of skilled workers and, consequently, they are "high wage industries." Conversely, the technology of cigarette manufacture is such as to permit the use of a great number of very low skilled women in plants located in low wage small towns.   These employees, therefore, receive low wages despite the fact that their employers are large firms.   As a result, tobacco manufacturing is a comparatively low wage industry.

Our knowledge of the empirical relation between a firm's profitability and the wages it pays is still very sketchy.   However, it is widely believed, with some empirical basis, that those firms which are most profitable tend to pay the highest wage rates, and vice versa.[22]   It also seems that "high

[21] "Ability to pay" is a vague term roughly signifying net value product per man-hour.   (Net value product per man-hour is sale value of output per man hour less nonwage costs per man-hour.)   Despite the vagueness of "ability to pay" it is a term widely used in connection with the discussion of this section. Some economists might contend that thus defined, ability to pay and marginal value productivity (of labor) are very similar.   I would suspect that such contentions have considerable merit, but it is not possible to discuss them here.

[22] For example, W. R. Maclaurin ("Wages and Profits in the Paper Industry," *Quarterly Journal of Economics,* February 1944, pp. 196–228) and Jacob Perlman.

Table 12.1   Average Hourly Earnings in Selected Industries
For Selected Years, Cents

	1929	1932	1939	1950
Agricultural labor*	0.24	0.13	0.17	0.56
Bituminous coal mining	0.68	0.52	0.89	2.01
Contract construction			0.93†	1.98
Total manufacturing	0.57	0.45	0.63	1.47
Durable goods manufacturing		0.50	0.70	1.54
Nondurable goods manufacturing		0.42	0.58	1.38
Food and kindred products			0.61	1.35
Tobacco manufactures			0.48	1.08
Textile mill products			0.46	1.24
Apparel, etc.			0.53	1.20
Rubber products			0.75	1.58
Iron and steel‡			0.74	1.65
Machinery (except electrical)			0.75	1.61
Electrical machinery			0.70	1.48
Automobiles		0.68	0.93	1.78
Retail trade (except eating and drinking places)		0.52§	0.54	1.18
Hotels		0.27§	0.32	0.77
Class I railroads	0.63	0.60	0.71	1.55

Sources: Bulletins 694, 916, and 1016 (Handbooks of Labor Statistics, 1941, 1947, and 1950) U. S. Bureau of Labor Statistics, Washington, D.C.

* Composite wage rate per hour, p. 85 of Bulletin 1016, for 1950; earlier dates "extrapolated" from index of United States average wage rate for agriculture, same source.

† Building construction only.

‡ Weighted average of hourly earnings in blast furnaces, steel works and rolling mills, and iron and steel foundries.

§ Figure is for 1934.

wage" employers tend to pay relatively high wages at all skill levels; those that pay high average hourly wages, even when this is partly due to an unusually high percentage of skilled workers, tend also to pay comparatively high wages to their unskilled employees.[23] Furthermore, it

("Hourly Earnings of Employees in Large and Small Enterprises," *Temporary National Economic Committee Monograph* 14, Government Printing Office, Washington, D.C., 1940) found relations of this kind in a number of individual industries. Perlman's findings suggest that this relationship may not be a general one, and it holds only because some industries have a few giant firms which pay well above the others.

S. H. Slichter, "Notes on the Structure of Wages," *Review of Economics and Statistics,* February 1950, pp. 81–92, found that the *industries* that are most profitable tend to pay the highest wage rates. That is, although the highly profitable industries tend to pay relatively high wages, they do not pay such high wages as to eliminate their profit advantage completely. In short, the relatively more profitable industries behave *as though* they shared their profits with their workers.

seems likely that firms tend to "conform," to some extent, to the wage pattern of their industry; i.e., "ability to pay" being equal as between two firms in different industries, the firm in the industry whose "average" employer pays more will tend to pay the higher wage rates. Thus, highly profitable firms in agriculture or food processing tend to pay lower wage rates than unprofitable firms in steel or electronics.

As a result of these various tendencies, we have a situation in which certain industries are characteristically high wage (e.g., durable goods manufacturing, construction, printing, etc.), while other industries (e.g., retail trade, personal services, small scale "soft" goods manufacturing, notably textiles and garment making, and agriculture) are notoriously low wage payers. In the high wage industries, a large part of those employed tend to work for large, profitable firms, and the reverse is true for low wage industries.

Employer Hiring Preferences and Wage Levels

We have already spoken of the "job hierarchy," on pp. 291–294 and noted that the firms offering good jobs tend to get the best workers. This is clearly borne out by a comparison of the kind of workers employed by the typical firms in high and low wage industries. The high wage firms tend to get the cream of the labor market, i.e., young adult males of suitable education and training possessed of "steady" habits. The low wage enterprises tend to get women, schoolboys, part-time workers, drifters, elderly workers, etc.

Because of this, it would be easy to say that high wage firms need or desire a superior type of worker for their kind of business and, in order to attract them, pay more than others. No doubt this is a large part of the explanation of interfirm wage differences. But it may not be all of it. Some students have found that (irrespective of their motives) many employers do not feel that a relatively high wage scale has been of material assistance in attracting superior workers.[24] One leading authority believes that, although the high wage firms do attract a superior type of worker, the resulting increase in productivity is not worth (in pecuniary terms) the extra costs entailed by a "high wage" policy, and that the low wage firms get a better (labor) bargain for their money.[25]

In support of such beliefs as these may be cited the good record of women, oldsters, negroes, and others in jobs from which they had (prior to 1942) been excluded by employer hiring policy. It may well be that, prior to 1940, high wage employers paid a greater premium for their workers than their comparative productivity justified. They may still

[23] Slichter, *op. cit.*
[24] R. A. Lester, *op. cit.*, pp. 31–37 and 44.
[25] Reynolds, *op. cit.*, pp. 158–166.

be doing so, despite the narrowing of interfirm wage differentials since 1940 (see pp. 365–366). However, many economists doubt or deny that there is any very convincing reason to suppose that "high wage" firms pay more than their *own* hiring standards require. Fortunately, our argument does not depend upon which side of this debate is judged victorious.

The emphasis placed upon employer hiring standards, as a determinant of labor demand, is rather unusual. In most treatments of this subject, "labor quality" is assumed to be given. However, doing this makes it impossible to recognize that the employer has some (limited) freedom to choose his hourly wage rates by appropriately selecting his hiring standards. Recognition of this does not "completely overturn" existing labor demand theory; however, it does permit us to understand certain phenomena that are otherwise comprehended only with difficulty.

DISCUSSION QUESTIONS

1. "A man-hour of labor is a commodity, and its price is governed by the same economic laws that govern the price of any other commodity."
   (a) Is this statement compatible with the idea that the wage rates firms pay vary with their "ability to pay"?
   (b) Do you agree or disagree with this statement?
2. (a) What relation does technological progress have to a firm's ability to grant wage increases without reducing profits per unit of output?
   (b) How can the presence of absence of competition affect the answer to (a)?
3. "Only a profitable firm can afford the luxury of paying better than average wages for the grade of labor that it uses." Comment.
4. Some economists believe that the price of an hour of labor relative to the cost of using machines has little or no effect upon the methods of production used. Other economists have the opposite opinion. State the case for each view and give your own opinion.
5. What objections to the marginal productivity theory do you think are most troublesome to students of labor problems?

Suggested Readings

Statements of marginal productivity theory may be found in a number of textbooks on economic theory. Some of the better ones are:
Boulding, K. E., *Economic Analysis*, 3rd edition, Harpers, New York, 1955.
Hicks, J. R., *The Theory of Wages*, The Macmillan Co., London, 1932.
Robinson, J., *Economics of Imperfect Competition*, The Macmillan Co., London, 1933, Book VII.
Rothschild, K. W., *The Theory of Wages*, Basil Blackwell, Oxford, 1955.
Scitovsky, T., *Welfare and Competition*, R. D. Irwin, Chicago, 1951, Chapters VI and VIII.
Weintraub, S., *Price Theory*, Pitman, New York and London, 1949, Chapter 4.
Some of the criticism and debate over marginal productivity and "marginalism" in general are contained in:
Lester, R. A., "Shortcomings of Marginal Analysis for Wage-Employment Problems," *American Economic Review*, March 1946, pp. 62–82.

Machlup, F., "Marginal Analysis and Empirical Research," *American Economic Review,* September 1946, pp. 519–554.

Reder, M. W., "A Reconsideration of the Marginal Productivity Theory," *Journal of Political Economy,* October 1947, pp. 450–458.

A good summary of the debate is:

Gordon, R. A. "Short-Period Prices Determination in Theory and Practice," *American Economic Review,* June 1948, pp. 265–288.

More general discussions of wage determination are:

Lester, R. A. *Company Wage Policies,* Industrial Relations Section, Department of Economics and Sociology, Princeton University, Princeton, N.J., 1948.

Myers, C. A., and G. P. Shultz, *The Dynamics of a Labor Market,* Prentice-Hall, New York, 1951, Part III.

Reynolds, L. G., *The Structure of Labor Markets,* Harpers, New York, 1951, Chapters 6 and 7.

W. S. Woytinsky and associates, *Employment and Wages in United States,* Twentieth Century Fund, New York, 1953, Part IV.

13

The Labor Market
and the Union

In Chapter 11 we discussed labor supply, in Chapter 12, labor demand. In the first three sections of this chapter, we shall put the arguments of these two chapters together and show how "labor markets" operate. The later sections of the chapter analyze the operation of unions in labor markets, and how they affect wage rates.

THE CONCEPT OF A LABOR MARKET

The term "labor market" is an abstraction. When we speak of the "stock market" or the "wheat market" or other organized exchanges, we are speaking of a physical place where buyers and sellers of particular types of objects gather for the purpose of engaging in transactions. The prices of the things bought and sold in such places are determined by the "laws of supply and demand" or the "laws of the market" in a manner described in every elementary textbook of economics. As applied to such organized exchanges, the laws of supply and demand are so obviously valid that no competent person seriously disputes them.

But economics is concerned with far more than organized exchanges. Among other things, it deals with commodities that are sold in different places and whose units differ, more or less, from one another. In such cases, different units of the "same" commodity may have different prices which, to some extent, vary independently of one another. To comprehend the behavior of such prices under the "laws of the market" obviously requires stretching a bit, and in some of these cases the market ceases to be a useful concept. When, where and how the laws of the market should be applied to imperfectly competitive situations is a subject that has greatly concerned economists during the last quarter century, and no general agreement is yet in sight.

Unfortunately for us, the idea of a labor market is about as difficult an application of the market concept as one can find. Indeed, many students of labor problems simply refuse (in effect) to discuss wage determination as though it were a market phenomenon at all. However, we believe that, properly utilized, the idea of a labor market can be used as a partial explanation of wage determination. To relate the market and other forces that bear upon wage rates is the main purpose of this chapter.

THE LABOR MARKET IN THE SHORT-RUN

A Single Locality

As we have already seen, the various employers in a community are usually ranged in some sort of rough hierarchy. There are high wage firms, low wage firms, and those "in between." The high wage firms usually hire the more desired type of worker, i.e., males between 20 and 40 of "steady" habits with appropriate education and training for their jobs. At the other extreme, the low wage firms are more or less compelled to take the "leavings" of the labor force.

To some limited extent, a firm may be able to choose its position in a community's wage hierarchy. However, there are strong social pressures to conform to "expectations." For example, a large wealthy corporation is expected to pay relatively high wages for any given type of labor, just as it is expected to have large, new, and aesthetically pleasing offices, safe factories, etc. These days, most large firms are anxious to conform to the expectations of the communities in which they operate.

The position a firm "chooses" in a community's wage hierarchy also depends upon its industry. Few firms can afford to pay much more for their labor than the great majority of their competitors, and will resist doing so. Sometimes there is a conflict between what a given community would expect, or its unions require, a firm to pay and what its industry customarily pays. This means that the firm is located in a higher wage area than the bulk of its industry and it usually results, sooner or later, in the firm leaving the area. In fact, such conflicts do not occur frequently because firms consider labor costs carefully in deciding where to locate. Thus, one finds very little textile manufacturing (a low wage industry) in high wage, "heavy manufacturing" cities such as Cleveland, Detroit, and Pittsburgh. Such industries tend to congregate in low wage small towns, especially in the south.

The position a firm adopts in the community's wage hierarchy also depends upon the skill of the workers it uses. Whatever a firm's size or other characteristics, if it wants to hire printers, it must (union or no) pay them fairly high wages. (There is usually not so much interfirm variation, in a given locality, among skilled wage rates as among those paid to semiskilled or unskilled workers.[1]) If a firm wishes to hire

[1] See R. L. Raimon, "The Indeterminateness of Wages of Semi-Skilled Workers,"

workers for semiskilled or unskilled jobs, it has a somewhat greater range of possible wage rates. Despite exceptions, there seems to be a general tendency for a firm to be a high wage payer or a low one, "straight across the board"; i.e., firms that pay skilled workers well, do likewise for unskilled, and vice versa.

So much for the community wage hierarchy as its exists at a given moment. Now let us see how it varies with changes in labor demand and/or supply. Let us first consider "labor supply" as given and demand as changing; for concreteness suppose there is an increased demand for the community's output at given selling prices which causes the increase in labor demand.

Some firms which need additional workers will hire job seekers, thereby reducing the community's pool of unemployed workers. Some of the new jobs created may be filled by promoting workers currently employed in the firm at less desirable jobs. Other jobs may be filled by new hirings. As we have already seen, many workers are strongly attached to their employers and will not change because of an improvement in alternative employment opportunities. However, some workers are anxious for improvement and will move, or threaten to, unless they are promoted, given a salary increase, etc. This generates a kind of competitive pressure for promotions and wage increases throughout the locality.

This pressure is highly uneven, being felt far more keenly by some employers than by others. It is reflected in a tendency for workers to get promoted, those who stay with their employers as well as those who change their jobs. Put in another way, the "average" worker tends to rise in the job hierarchy (see pp. 291–294). Of itself, this would raise the average straight-time[2] hourly earnings of the workers, even though the wage rate on every single job remained unchanged. But, in addition, employers will also be compelled to raise the wage rates on some jobs in order to keep good workmen.

Industrial and Labor Relations Review, January 1953, pp. 180–194. Whether the lesser variability of skilled wages is due to stronger unions or to other causes is not easy to determine.

The boundary between skilled and semiskilled workers is not a sharp one; skilled workers are those with a specifically defined occupation for which special training is necessary. Some semiskilled jobs are almost skilled, others less so. Toward the "lower extreme," semiskilled jobs involve simple machine-minding and are hard to distinguish from unskilled work which consists of jobs for which almost no training is required. Unskilled labor was, traditionally, heavy "muscle-work" and some of it still is. However, an increasing number of unskilled jobs involve "light" work, e.g., pushing a hand-truck, janitorial work, etc.

[2] Average hourly earnings fluctuate quite markedly with the amount of "overtime" work (which is paid at premium rates). Straight-time earnings are the earnings computed at the ordinary (i.e., straight-time) hourly wage rates.

Thus, the effect of an increase in demand relative to supply in a local labor market is to increase the average straight-time hourly earnings paid to all manual workers in the area. This is roughly analogous to an increase in the "price"[3] of labor, and its occurrence reflects the operation of the "market-like" forces that affect wage rates.

The reader should note the complex way in which "supply and demand" affect wage rates. Competition for labor operates not only through wage rates on given jobs but also by altering the type of job for which specific workmen will be hired. The extent to which a given employer chooses to raise wages on given jobs, or promote workers into better paying jobs, depends upon a whole variety of considerations that may be summarized as "administrative convenience."

When the demand for labor decreases, the above process is reversed, more or less. The reversal is not perfect, because there are all sorts of emotional resistance to cutting the wage rate on a given job which are not paralleled by resistance to increasing wage rates.[4] In consequence, employers like to avoid the *appearance* of cutting rates; therefore, they tend to accomplish the same thing by adding chores to "given" jobs which disguising a cut in wage rates is to tighten incentive rates (see pp. 394–396) and thereby reduce actual hourly earnings.[5] However it should be noted that, for various reasons (see pp. 400–403), wages rise more in prosperity than they fall in depressions.

Now let us consider the case where labor supply increases with demand given. An increase in a community's labor supply may alter the composition of its labor force in any of a number of ways; e.g., it may disproportionately increase the number of professional persons, of specially skilled workers, or of the unskilled. For concreteness, suppose that the increase in supply occurs mainly among manual workers who can fill a variety of unskilled or semiskilled jobs, but who do not possess the specialized training for any highly skilled craft. One effect of this increase, as soon as it becomes noticeable, is to lead employers to tighten their hiring standards on given jobs. In the view of workers "good" jobs be-

---

[3] J. T. Dunlop, *Wage Determination under Trade Unions*, 2nd edition, Augustus Kelley, New York, 1950, pp. 19–27, points out the difficulties of identifying average straight-time hourly earnings and the "price" of labor. Nonetheless, for our purposes, these difficulties are not serious.

[4] Where there are "oligopsonistic" agreements among employers to avoid wage increases, there may be strong resistance to wage rate increaes.

[5] This is well discussed by C. A. Myers and G. R. Shultz, *The Dynamics of a Labor Market*, Prentice-Hall, New York, 1951, Chapter 9. Myers and Shultz point out that the grievance procedure is a vehicle through which the pressure of the labor market is transmitted to earnings, job content, promotions, etc. This is discussed on pp. 157–163.

come harder to find, promotions become harder to secure, etc.   Workers toward the bottom of the job hierarchy tend to be forced into unemployment and/or out of the labor force.   Those who do not have a steady job, but are employed for only short periods find that the spells of unemployment between engagements become longer, etc.   The general ease of securing workers militates against wage increases and encourages those employers who "need" to reduce labor costs to attempt wage reductions. The reverse of all this applies when labor supply decreases.

In short, the level of hourly wage rates and the number of man-hours of labor used vary in response to changes in labor supply and demand in more or less the manner that one would expect if they were determined by a market.   However, the alteration in hiring standards, and the correlative changes in job opportunities for given individuals, that are the accompaniment (and, in part, the means) of the process of adjustment are not usually thought of as part of market behavior.

Large Areas: the Nation

We have already seen that many workers are reluctant to leave their home areas unless impelled to do so by a very real difference in economic opportunity.   But, as we saw in the previous section, an expansion of labor demand relative to supply (in a given locality) does provide an improvement in the "quality," as well as the number, of jobs in that local area.   If the improvement in a given area's economic opportunities is appreciably greater than elsewhere and especially if there is no improvement at all in other places, workers will tend to migrate to the area.   Of course, the workers who come will not be a random selection; they will tend to be young, without dependents, etc.   But they do make the elasticity of supply of man-hours of labor (to a given area) greater than if such migration were not permitted.

From the viewpoint of the nation as a whole, the labor supply is fixed except insofar as additional persons can be induced to enter the labor force (see pp. 291–297) or immigration occurs.   Prior to 1921, immigration provided a very important element of flexibility in the nation's labor supply.   As the rate of net migration tended to vary in the same direction as labor demand, it is very likely that immigration tended to restrict upward pressure upon wage rates.   Since the 1920's, the role of the immigrant has, to some extent, been filled by southern farm youths and, since 1940, Puerto Ricans have also provided a significant addition to the supply of job candidates.

The Social Minimum Wage Rate

Thus far we have not mentioned one characteristic possessed by almost all labor markets but often overlooked by wage theorists.   This is a minimum hourly rate below which labor may not be hired, at least not by business firms or governments.[6]   In the simplest case, this minimum rate (which we call social minimum) is simply a flat minimum hourly rate applicable to all workers.   However, many minimum wage statutes make special provisions for the physically handicapped, juveniles, learners, etc.

Even in the absence of statutory prescription, there is usually some customary minimum wage rate below which a worker is not expected to accept employment.   This rate is not well-defined, but its level may be inferred (approximately) from the fact that if a worker were offered less, his friends or relatives who help to support him while he is unemployed would not press him to accept the job but would consider such a wage intolerable.   If he is supported by charity, its source adopts a similar attitude toward wage rates below the social minimum; if he is living on savings or credit, he rejects jobs offering less than social minimum.   If a worker can return to a family farm this sets a floor under the minimum weekly earnings and therefore (indirectly) the hourly wage he will accept.

Obviously, social minimum is not an objective quantity except where it is set by statute and enforced.   It varies with a worker's attitudes, expectations and resources, and with those of his family and friends.   Social minimum probably falls as a worker's period of unemployment lengthens and rises with the level of consumer prices.   In short, if one were to estimate social minimum statistically, one would find not a number but a range.   However, the reality of social minimum and the significance of variations in it are hard to deny.   As we shall see, hourly wage rates, especially the relatively low ones, show a great resistance to downward pressure from unemployment.   This resistance is indicative of the effect of social minimum.

Social minimum should not be confused with the minimum income that advanced modern communities guarantee to all their members.   This minimum family income, ultimately backed by public or semipublic charity, is independent of what a family's members earn.   It is quite possible that a family should be partially supported by "outside assistance," while its members accept what employment they can find at whatever wage rates are offered.[7]   To be sure, the effect of "outside assistance," especially unemployment insurance, is to reduce the anxiety of workers to ac-

[6] This is discussed in M. W. Reder, "The Theory of Occupational Wage Differentials," *American Economic Review*, December 1955, pp. 833–852, especially pp. 839–840.   In one form or another, the idea that there is a social minimum wage goes back to classical economics.

[7] For example, under the Speenhamland system of poor relief operating in much of England from 1795 to 1834, workers received support from the parish as a supplement to whatever they were able to earn.   See J. H. Clapham, *An Economic History of Modern Britain, 1820–1850*, 2nd edition, Cambridge University Press, Cambridge, England, 1950, pp. 124 et seq. and pp. 357 et seq.; also Paul Mantoux, *The Industrial Revolution in the Eighteenth Century*, 2nd edition, Jonathan Cape, London, 1928, pp. 447–450.

cept the "first job that comes along" and to encourage waiting for a suitable one. But this does not prevent an unemployed worker from accepting a casual one-day job at less than the minimum rate he would consider on steady work.

Social minimum applies to "regular" business firms and governments. It does not usually have much meaning for households which employ their help on whatever terms they can. Also many "businesses," especially small ones hard pressed to survive, will also skate on the thin edge of law and custom in order to cut labor costs. For example, they may hire commission salesmen who receive no guaranteed hourly wage at all, or subcontractors (e.g., in garment manufacture) may simply hire their workers on a receipt sharing basis. Employers of this sort are either not subject to minimum wage laws or can, because of their fugitive nature, evade them.

An appreciable amount of unemployment in a community usually results in a shift of part of its labor force from "regular employment," at a wage above social minimum, to employment of the above sort. This shift is part of the adjustment of a community's average straight-time hourly earnings to an altered labor market situation.[8] That it occurs so haltingly and erratically is due to the resistance of workers to accepting less than social minimum and of "respectable" employers to offering it.

Wage rates offered in this "subminimum" sector are likely to vary greatly from one job to another, with the vicissitudes of haggling in a market with poor intercommunication. There is little of a general sort that can be said about the wage rates that will be set in such a "market."

THE LABOR MARKET IN THE LONG-RUN

Labor Migration

The economic history of the Western World (since about 1800) is marked by a prolonged migration of people from areas where their incomes were low to those where they were higher. The migration from Europe to the United States was one aspect of this movement. To a very large extent, the European migration to America was part of a world-wide farm-city migration in which (predominantly young) people moved from low income farm areas to urban areas where they could earn more. European immigrants were largely peasants who came to American cities; European cities (at times) were alternative magnets.

Since the early 1920's, European immigrants have not been able to come to the United States in large numbers because of immigration restrictions. However, their places have been taken by rural youths, white

---

[8] This is part, but not all, of what Mrs. Joan Robinson refers to as "disguised unemployment," J. Robinson, *Essays in the Theory of Employment*, 2nd edition, Basil Blackwell, Oxford, 1947, pp. 60–74.

and negro, who move from the low income (rural) south to the higher wage areas of the urbanized north. Upon arrival in urban centers, these southern migrants are not quite the labor market equals of "typical" semi-skilled workers. However, they are sufficiently good substitutes for ac-climated workers so that their median earning power is approximately 90 per cent as high as that of the acclimated group.[9] This results in a sufficient farm-city income differential to induce a continuing flow of rural south, urban-north migration.[10]

The fact that such migration has persisted over a long period of time without eliminating the earning disadvantage of southern workers calls for some explanation. Such explanation involves considering three fac-tors: (1) Rural birth rates, especially in the south, are higher than urban so that people have a tendency to get born in low earning areas from which some must migrate. (2) Migration of labor (and other factors) has led to a relative rise in southern wage rates, but the adjustment proc-ess requires a long time for completion. And (3) an expanding demand for labor outside of the south has kept nonsouthern wages rising and slowed down the "catching-up" process indicated under (2).

However, since 1940, labor migration and other economic develop-ments have reduced the income disadvantage of the south as compared with the rest of the United States.[11] In good part, the migration is re-flected in a change of the industrial composition of the southern labor force. As Table 13.1 shows, since 1920 there has been a more rapid re-duction of the share of agriculture in total employment in the south than elsewhere. This reflects the fact that it is the low income southern farm-er who is disappearing rather than the higher earning southern urban worker.[12] In other words, the movement of low-earning southern farm-ers to higher earning areas and occupations has gradually reduced the growth rate of the south's labor supply, allowing its relative earnings to

---

[9] D. G. Johnson, "Comparability of Labor Capacities of Farm and Nonfarm Labor," *American Economic Review,* June 1953, pp. 296–313, concludes that recent farm migrants to urban areas have earned about 90 per cent of the average income of nonfarm persons of the same age and sex. Also see R. E. Weintraub, "The Productive Capacity of Rural and Urban Labor: A Case Study," *Journal of Political Economy,* October 1955, pp. 412–426.

[10] For a long time, rural emigration came from the nonsouth as well as the south. However, in recent years, emigration has been mainly a southern phenomenon as high earnings on nonsouthern farms have greatly reduced the incentive to move cityward.

[11] C. A. R. Wardwell, *Regional Trends in the United States Economy,* U. S. De-partment of Commerce, Washington, D.C., 1951, especially pp. 63–68. The other economic developments are discussed on pp. 329–330.

[12] This does not mean that the southern farmers, themselves, make all of the northward moves. Often, what happens is that the southern farmers move to south-ern towns, and southern townsmen, in turn, move north. However, the net result is the same.

rise. This is a fairly typical consequence of economic growth, both in the United States and elsewhere.

The effect of economic growth on wages and labor migration might be described roughly as follows: Labor demand increases sharply in large cities leading to high earnings by those residing there. This attracts workers from the lower income rural hinterlands. As rural areas often have a sizeable amount of disguised unemployment,[13] this raises per capita income on the farms the workers leave while decelerating the increase

Table 13.1. Percentage Distribution of Workers Between Agriculture and Other Industries in the South and Elsewhere, 1920–1950

	1920		1930		1940		1950	
Industry	South	Non-south	South	Non-south	South	Non-south	South	Non-south
Agriculture	50.9	17.6	42.8	14.6	34.9	12.8	20.6	9.5
Nonagriculture	49.1	82.4	57.2	85.4	65.1	87.2	79.4	90.5

Sources: Figures for 1920–1940 from C. B. Hoover and B. Y. Ratchford, *Economic Resources and Policies of the South*, The Macmillan Co., New York, 1951, Table XVI, p. 34; for 1950, computed from *1950 Census of Population Preliminary Reports*, Series PC-7, No. 2, Table 8, p. 31.

in wages in the areas they enter. The favorable effect of this process on per capita income in the farm areas may be offset if the farm population grows faster as a result. However, in the 20th century, this last result has not occurred in Western Europe and the United States.[14]

The process of rural-urban migration is very uneven. It is facilitated by prosperity and hampered by depression. In prosperity, when the demand for nonagricultural labor increases relative to supply, the aforementioned process operates with full force. But in depression, when urban labor demand falls relative to supply, some unemployed urban workers return "home" to the farm.[15] Thus, the upward pull of urban labor demand upon farm earnings slackens appreciably when there is substantial unemployment. This, in turn, facilitates the development of low wage pockets (see pp. 360–363) in small towns adjacent to low income farm areas.

[13] This is due largely to the fact that many of such farms in the United States are family enterprises and use (family) labor to the point where its marginal product is well below the wage rate for hired labor. On this point, see E. O. Heady and S. du Toit, "Marginal Resource Productivity for Agriculture in Selected Areas of South Africa and the United States," *Journal of Political Economy,* December 1954, pp. 494–505.

[14] The income-population relation is different, however, in some of the "backward" areas of Asia, Africa, and Latin America.

[15] During depressions the rate of rural-urban migration is well below boom levels, but only rarely is the process actually reversed (resulting in a net exodus from urban areas).

At times it has happened that the growth of rural population has outpaced the increase in urban labor demand. This seems to have happened in England during the first part of the 19th century. As might be expected, per capita farm income was forced down by the increase in farm population[16] and the attempts of the "surplus" rural population to migrate cityward created severe downward pressure on urban wage rates.

Movement of Enterprise and Capital

At any given time, wage rates in some industries and/or areas are well below those in others. However, this does not mean that the firms using low wage labor are unusually profitable; in fact, the reverse is usually the case. The reason why low-wage firms cannot, for long, make unusually high profits is that firms tend to adopt those conditions of production that reduce their costs. Consequently, if a firm is earning unusually high profits while paying relatively low hourly wages, it will soon find a number of new firms beginning to produce a similar output with similar workers; if one firm can hire cheap labor, so can another.

A firm that can use the labor available in low wage small towns, or can operate with boys, oldsters, and other "leavings" of the labor force may, for a time, make unusually high profits. But unless there are some unusual obstacles to entry, other firms will imitate its methods, and competition in the product, if not in the labor market, will eliminate the excess profits. As a result cheap labor will become necessary to the firm's very existence. This is why one finds, at any given moment, that in the low wage industries such as textiles, garment making, etc., firms usually *require* low wage rates. Far from making excess profits, most of these firms are fighting to survive.

Conversely, the industries where profits remain high tend to pay relatively high wages; as we shall see in the following section, this is no accident. There are a number of reasons why profits (as a percentage of invested capital) may be higher in some industries than in others. But, for the moment, all that is argued is that low hourly wages relative to the "productivity"[17] of the labor rarely are, for long, a source of abnormally large profits.

---

[16] Assuming, realistically, that the amount of agricultural capital could not grow proportionately with the labor supply so that the extra workers have a low marginal product (i.e., are in "disguised unemployment").

[17] By productivity, I mean marginal value productivity to the firm. Readers disturbed by this incursion of marginalism may substitute net value product per man-hour =

$$\frac{\text{Value of the firm's output minus all nonlabor expenses of production}}{\text{man-hours of labor hired}}$$

without seriously disturbing the argument in most practical situations.

The movement of capital to areas and industries where hourly wages are low relative to labor's net value product per man-hour is much less slow than the movement of labor out of such situations. Hence there has been a considerable movement of low wage industries to small towns, especially in the south. There, these firms "intercept" rural labor on its emigration from the farm or enable the erstwhile farmhand to maintain his rural contacts on a part-time basis while enjoying some of the advantages of nonfarm employment. The wages paid in these small towns are well below those paid in large cities (see pp. 359–363), but for workers unable or unwilling to migrate (particularly wives and children of farmers) they provide the only source of nonfarm employment.

To put the argument in a slightly different way, the annual earnings that an individual, of the type working on a family farm, could earn in nonagriculture under conditions of "reasonably full" employment[18] are considerably more than the value of his productive contribution to the farm.[19] Therefore, in the long-run, such persons have tended to leave the farm and go where their services are worth more. However, this process has been impeded by all sorts of ties to the family farm. Furthermore, the relatively high rural birthrates have offset, to some extent, the effect of rural-urban migration. As a result, the process of worker movement to better employment opportunities has been insufficiently rapid to prevent countermovement of capital to low wage areas and industries. Thus, there has developed a national wage and job hierarchy, by area and industry, whose characteristics we have already indicated. The wage differentials in this hierarchy have tended to diminish in the "long-run" under pressure of worker mobility (and perhaps other forces). However, in the near future, the broad features of the nation's wage structure will probably persist.

WAGE DISPERSION AND THE LABOR MARKET

High and Low Wage Firms

We have already noted that, within given communities and within given industries, there is a tendency for some firms to pay more than others.[20]

[18] That is, hourly wage rates in urban employment tend to be such that at reasonably full employment, annual income on urban jobs (open to rural emigrants) is substantially greater than the value of their marginal contribution to a family farm. And, at reasonably full employment, there is net rural emigration. However, unemployment reduces the advantage of urban living and when it (unemployment) is great enough, emigration tends to halt.

[19] This may also be stated (in terms familiar to students of economic theory) as follows: the marginal productivity of labor in southern agriculture is materially less than in other sources of employment which such labor can obtain, if it chooses, when the labor market is as it has been since 1945. See the references to the article of Johnson and Weintraub in note 9.

[20] For evidence on this point (in a variety of industries) see G. H. Seltzer, "Pattern

These differences tend to parallel differences in profitability of the various firms, although the association is by no means perfect. One reason why these differences have persisted is the immobility of labor as between employers. Provided a firm was not attempting to increase its labor force in a comparatively tight labor market, it could retain the services of workers able to earn appreciably more within the same city but reluctant to relinquish a job which had presumptions of permanency. This immobility has not been so complete as to prevent market forces from effectively moving the general wage structure among areas, occupations, etc. But it has been sufficient to create all sorts of low wage "pockets" which have defied market forces for long periods of time. Low wage pockets are more easily created in small towns, where a change of jobs is difficult without moving elsewhere, than in large urban areas. Hence, employers desiring low wage scales, and prepared to accept the correlative disadvantages, tend toward small towns.

A given firm often becomes a "substandard" wage payer because it is unable (on account of unprofitability) to match a given wage increase granted by others in its industry or area. The same result emerges if the firm has to demand a special decrease to keep it going. Such events may cause some workers to leave the firm, but others will remain, thereby creating a low wage firm.

It seems likely that in depressions employers who need wage cuts in order to survive obtain them to a greater extent than prosperous firms; this creates or widens the gap between the wage rates paid by different firms in the same industry. Also, industries that are most plagued by product price-reductions are those which reduce wages most, and most promptly, during a depression.[21] This tends to generate interindustrial wage differentials and variations among different regions and cities having different patterns of industrial specialization. Conversely, labor market pressure is more likely to eliminate low wage pockets in a period of full employment, than otherwise.

The most interesting theoretical question about wage dispersion is not why some firms are able to keep workers while paying less than others but why the high wage firms continue to pay more. The frequent failure of the more profitable firms in an industry or area to cut wages propor-

Bargaining and the United Steel Workers," *Journal of Political Economy*, August 1951, pp. 319–331; L. G. Reynolds, *The Structure of Labor Markets*, Harper and Brothers, New York, 1951, pp. 169–176; R. A. Lester, "Wage Diversity and its Theoretical Implications," *Review of Economics and Statistics*, August 1946, pp. 152–159 and "A Range Theory of Wage Differentials," *Industrial and Labor Relations Review*, July 1952, pp. 483–500; W. R. Maclaurin, *op. cit.*, pp. 206–214 and 224–228.

[21] J. T. Dunlop, *Wage Determination Under Trade Unions*, 2nd edition, 1950, Augustus Kelley, New York, Chapter VII.

tionately with other firms signifies a difference between the behavior of labor and other factor markets. The behavior of the high wage firms cannot be attributed entirely to union pressure because it was observed in the depression of 1929–1932 in industries where unionism was not even threatened. Such behavior may be partly due to a desire by the high wage firms to skim the cream off the labor market; but this is not likely to be the whole story. Such an explanation could not account for the fact that the spread between the wages of high and low wage firms tends to vary with the state of the labor market. Furthermore, during depressions, it is quite clear that most firms could satisfactorily find replacements for their present employees at less than current wage rates.

Consequently, it is necessary to invoke "extra-market" factors to facilitate an explanation. One of these is the desire of large firms and their managements to stand well in public opinion. If a large firm that maintained a steady rate of dividends and executive compensation throughout a depression (as many do) should cut wages because "market conditions required it," it would be subject to bitter condemnation. Furthermore, a firm desires the "good-will" of its employees; taking full advantage of a labor market situation is likely to sow seeds of resentment, unless the firm can prove it needs a wage reduction in order to survive.

At this point, it is necessary to refer back to our earlier discussion of the wage-job hierarchy and of social minimum (pp. 324–326). The hourly wage rate that a firm offers for a given job is only one of the "contract terms" for that job. There are also the hiring standards the firm establishes, the precise tasks required of the worker, etc. In a depressed labor market, employers tend to alter all the other terms in the "labor contract" as well as the wage rate. They become more selective about the (few) new applicants they accept; they demand more of the workers who hold given jobs and thereby increase their "productivity"; etc. In these ways employers can reduce labor cost per unit of output without cutting wage rates overtly.

But why not cut wage rates openly? First of all there is social minimum. A respectable firm does not like to have its employees on public charity because their earnings are insufficient; it is obviously embarrassing for a large corporation whose principal officers earn upwards of $100,000 per year to burden a small town's relief rolls with its employees. Then, cutting wage rates gives the workers a common grievance; even in the absence of a union, angry workers may engage in desperation strikes or sabotage. Quietly asking individuals to do a little extra work with no pay increase, especially if attention is called to the fact that other workers are being currently laid off, is much more likely to reduce labor costs without creating trouble.

In short, the adjustments of the labor market occur through variations in employer hiring requirements and job assignments as much, or perhaps more, than via altering wage rates on given jobs.

UNIONS AND THE LABOR MARKET

Individual versus Collective Bargaining

As our argument has proceeded thus far, there is no place in it for unions. Wage rates, promotions, etc. are all decided by the employer under the impetus of his need for workers and their availability; i.e., wages are controlled by the employer subject to the pressure of market forces. But unions are very much interested in all this, and either we must explain why, contrary to appearances, they are unable to affect wages or how they manage to do so.

Our discussion in Chapter 6 portrayed the process of wage setting quite differently than the discussion of this chapter. (In Chapter 6 we described the terms of a collective bargaining contract as being hammered out by the haggling of a union and an employer under threats of work stoppages.) Clearly the two processes look different; the question is whether their consequences are the same, or about the same.

In effect (though not in form) an individual worker bargains with an employer as to the terms on which he will accept a job. What the employer will offer a worker depends upon how badly he needs him; if he needs him "quite badly," he may offer him a better job than ordinarily, even though the wage rate for the job is unchanged. In special cases, an employer may even haggle (over wage rates) with workers on an individual basis. What makes an employer anxious to hire individual workers at a particular time is, of course, strong current demand for output. But this is also what would make him amenable to a union's pressure for wage increases. Conversely, a slack demand for the product makes an employer resistant alike to the demands of unions and of individual workers. Furthermore, the knowledge that alternative employment opportunities are available makes workers both more ready to reject given employment offers (as individuals), and more ready to accept the risks of striking.[22]

In other words, the pressure upon wage rates exerted by unions is, at least to some extent, simply a transmission of the pressure of market forces that would have operated irrespective of collective bargaining. But collective bargaining may also have an effect on wages independent of market forces. The reason why a union can sometimes affect wages where an individual worker cannot is that it confronts an employer with an "all

---

[22] That is, they are more willing both to risk being replaced permanently by a strike-breaker and to risk temporary loss of pay, because they can find temporary employment, than when the reverse is true.

or nothing" offer; i.e., "either you meet our terms, or none of your employees will work." What an employer is prepared to pay to avert such
action depends, given demand conditions for his output, upon how easily
he can replace his strikers.

If his operations are such that an employer is indifferent to whether
he has an entirely new labor force (say) every week, he is not going to
be perturbed about a strike so long as he is physically able to put newly
hired workers in his plant. However, most employers desire a skeleton
force of experienced workers to "break in" new recruits. This fact makes
the services of a firm's experienced workers worth more if offered as a
bloc than if each could be hired separately. The difference between the
value of the services of a firm's present employees offered as a bloc and
their value (to the employer) when he can hire and fire them individually
sets the upper limit to what collective bargaining can get for them, over
and above what they could get through individual negotiation.

Resistance and Yielding to Union Demands: Relative Costs

A specific union demand for (say) a wage increase entails a certain
rise in labor costs per unit of output. But replacing those workers who
are prepared to strike also involves some added labor cost per unit of
output as, for a time at least, the new workers will not be as efficient as
their predecessors. Furthermore, depending upon the "quality" of the
workers and the state of the labor market, it may take considerable time
and the payment of substantial premiums to get satisfactory substitutes
(i.e., strike-breakers); this is to say nothing of the possibilities of mass
picketing to prevent use of strike-breakers. In the event that replacement
of his strikers is too costly or otherwise impracticable the employer may
simply shut down and wait out his workers. As replacement of strikers
has not usually been a practical course of action since 1940, let us disre-
gard it, for the present purpose, and consider the two alternatives of yielding to the union demand or shutting down.

Each course of action has its costs and its benefits; yielding gets continuous production but at a higher unit cost than holding out until the
union reduces its demands. How long it pays to hold out depends, in
good part, upon how costly the settlement is; if competing firms are likely
to experience similar wage increases so that their unit costs and product
prices are likely to rise proportionately, a good part of the wage increase
may be passed along to the customers. But, if the demand is made upon
one employer alone (e.g., if the union is trying to bring him up to the
wage level of most of the industry), his profits will be squeezed. In this
case, it would pay him to endure a longer shutdown in order to avoid
a given wage increase than in the first case.

In general, the more a firm earns from the operation of a particular plant, the more it is worth to that firm to keep it operating. A collective bargaining agreement is a form of "strike insurance"; the more valuable the productive operation it protects the higher the premium the union can charge for it. Thus, a union can force an employer to share with his employees any rents or monopoly gains that he happens to earn. The larger the amount to be shared, other things equal, the larger the "strike premium" the union can collect.

Of course, a highly profitable firm is not helpless; if it decides not to deal with the union at all, it may well be able to endure a longer siege than a less profitable firm. Thus, the larger and highly profitable corporations in durable manufacturing were, prior to the 1930's, better able than most firms to resist unionization.[23] On the other hand, once they decided to live with unions, they have generally paid higher "strike premiums," wages and related benefits, than other firms.

THE DETERMINANTS OF UNION WAGE POLICY: CRITERIA FOR WAGE SETTING

Member Demands

A union leader is not usually free to make the wage objectives of his organization conform to his preconceptions. A union's wage policy is constrained by the expectations of its members, the willingness and ability of employers to grant increases, the policies of the government, and the attitudes of the leaders of other unions.

From one side, the union is pressed to do a good job for its members; this means that it must get them (at least) as much as other unions in comparable circumstances are currently obtaining. Failure to meet this test lessens the prestige of its leaders in the councils of the labor movement and may stimulate internal criticism and encourage political rivals. Another demand made of union leaders is that wage scales should (at least) keep up with the cost of living; failure to satisfy this demand usually provokes bitter criticism and frequently has sparked rebellion against leaders deemed too cautious to protect the living standards of the members of their unions.

At no time will members welcome a worsening of contract terms; a wage cut is always resented.[24] A union leader who accepts a contract embodying a wage cut must tread warily lest he be repudiated. Unions have, of course, accepted wage cuts. But such reductions must be "sold"

---

[23] Of course, it was not the current profitability of these firms that made them such effective foes of unionization; it was their large total assets. However, large corporations usually, though not always, make substantial profits.

[24] Union organizations vary in their willingness to accept wage reductions; see pp. 343–345.

to the membership as being required by the exigencies of the situation and as the smallest possible wage reduction compatible with the continued operation of the firm.   There have been many occasions when the membership, despite the advice of their leaders, rejected worsening of contract terms.   In short, resistance to wage cuts is an essential ingredient of any union's wage policy.

It is impossible to make any simple statement about the upper limit to a union's demands.   When dealing with a prosperous employer, their slogan and policy is to demand "more."   But it is not easy to translate this into any specific set of objectives.[25]   Labor leaders sometimes speak of obtaining a bigger share of the company's profits[26] and sometimes of a larger share of the national income (for labor as a whole), but such statements are not very useful guides to actual union wage demands.

The imperatives of union wage policy set minimal rather than precise targets.   It is necessary to do "as well as some other union" to "keep wages in step with living costs" or to prevent a wage cut; but there are no effective imperatives about making wages rise as fast as the employer's profits.   Even highly aggressive union leaders, such as John L. Lewis, aim only at doing better than their fellow leaders; they do not talk or (apparently) think in terms of raising "labor's share" relative to the employer's.   The hypothetical maximum that might be obtained in a collective bargain does not concern the union leader, provided the various criteria for satisfactory achievement in contract negotiation are met.

Equity and Wage Patterns

The determining criteria of union wage *objectives* are not so much matters of economics as of equity.[27]   Union wage policies, perforce, reflect the operation of economic considerations, but economic considerations usually exert their influence via employer resistance in the bargaining process.[28]   The implications of equity for union wage policy do not lend themselves to easy generalization; in unions, equity has not always meant equality.   However, it is generally correct to say that unions have sought to eliminate wage differences where they could not be "justified" in terms of some ethical or quasi-ethical criterion.

That is, union wage policy has usually sought to eliminate wage dif-

---

[25] For a discussion of the pronouncements of union leaders concerning their objectives see Dunlop, *op. cit.,* Chapter IV.

[26] What is meant is a larger share of wages plus profits, i.e., of "value added."

[27] On this point see A. M. Ross, *Trade Union Wage Policy,* University of California Press, Berkeley and Los Angeles, 1948; also M. W. Reder, "The Theory of Union Wage Policy," *Review of Economics and Statistics,* February 1952, pp. 34–35.

[28] There are exceptions; where strong and farsighted unions (e.g., in garment manufacturing) face weak employers, the union "internalizes" the opposition the employer ought to make (but cannot) and restrain itself.

ferentials, for the same type of job, among firms in a given industry; i.e., unions have tried to eliminate or reduce interregional and intercity wage differentials. In given cities, unions have (usually) tried to eliminate or, at least, reduce wage differentials between allegedly comparable workers in different industries. Within given firms, unions have worked to eliminate differences in wage rates among workers doing the same, or similar, jobs.

Unions have pursued these, and similar, objectives by "levelling upward." They resist attempts to reduce the wage on any given job and, especially, of any given worker. Unions argue that the underpaid workers and jobs should be raised; they resist attempts to worsen the (absolute) wages of the better paid. In short, unionism tends toward equalizing hourly wage rates unless some equitable reason[29] for inequality can be found. However, as we shall see, union pressure for reducing inequality is frequency overborne by "economic considerations."

The equitable tendency of union wage policy is reflected in the phenomenon known as "patterns" of wage settlement. These patterns arise from the tendency of firms and unions in an industry to pattern (imitate) (see pp. 153–154) the contract terms reached by one or another of the major firms in the industry with the union. The initial contract is called the "key" bargain, and it is said to set the "pattern." The union (or unions[30]) then attempts to force other firms into the pattern. Where the other firms can adopt the implied wage scales without great economic discomfort, the pattern tends to be accepted. But where differences in employer "ability to pay" are important, the pattern may be modified or broken; see below, pp. 338–340.

Wage patterns are not one-dimensional affairs. There are industry patterns and local patterns; sometimes conflict between different patterns gives rise to serious difficulties. There is also, at times, something of a "national" wage pattern in which the settlements reached in one industry tend to spread to others. In such situations, what is imitated is not so much the actual level of wage rates, but the amount of the increase, i.e., the size of the "package." Equity has seemed to require that, in the absence of reason to the contrary, the increase in wage rates obtained in one industry should not be less than that obtained in some other. In the United States, a national pattern was most strongly marked in 1946 and 1947[31] but has not been quite so important (except during the Korean

[29] "Equitable reasons" are similar to the considerations that lead workers to feel (see pp. 285–286) certain jobs should receive more than other; e.g., physically unpleasant or dangerous jobs, jobs requiring unusual skill or training or entailing bad hours, etc. should be rewarded more than others.

[30] When there is more than one union in a given industry, pressure for equal treatment becomes intense.

[31] Because in those years the demand for commodities was so great that firms.

affair, 1950–1951) since; however, it may still be discerned from time to time. In foreign countries, such as Sweden, Norway, and Denmark, where collective bargaining is more highly centralized than in the United States, the national pattern is of much greater significance.

The reason why a single pattern can be applied to a large number of firms is that the terms of the settlement are well within the "bargaining range" of the firms accepting them. Recognizing that conformity to pattern is of great importance to the union and that major deviations will not be permitted (except for "cause") without a strike, employers realize that it will not pay to wrangle unless they are determined to obtain a "substantial" deviation from the pattern.

Employer Ability to Pay

A stubborn employer will sometimes reject the union wage demands that are required by considerations of equity and manage either to drive the union from his plant or compel it to take less than it believes proper, despite his ability to meet the relevant pattern. But, since the late 1930's, such stubbornness has become rare because unions have become strong enough to make it very expensive.[32] Usually when an employer seeks exemption from an industry's or an area's wage pattern, he does so on the grounds that he cannot afford to meet it. Unions have generally shown great consideration for firms which cannot afford to meet a pattern. This is not due only to consideration for employers, but it also reflects the union's desire not to jeopardize the jobs of its members by driving employers out of business.[33]

It is sometimes argued that the policy of permitting different employers to pay different wage rates is akin to a policy of discriminating monopoly. However, this is rather misleading as wages varied among employers in more or less the same way prior to unionization. Unions permit interfirm wage variations to continue because they recognize that refusing such permission would, in most cases, force the employees of low wage firms to choose between abandoning the union and compelling their employer either to go out of business or to operate a nonunion establishment. Indeed, some unions have made extensive efforts to help low-wage firms increase their efficiency in order that they might later raise their wage levels.[34]

---

ordinarily unable to grant wage increases equal to those granted by the largest firms in their industries, were willing to do so (temporarily) in order to avoid strikes.

[32] Again exceptions must be recognized: the outstanding examples are in southern textile manufacturing.

[33] Examples of union "wage discrimination" among employers are plentiful; for example, see the references in note 21.

[34] For example, this has occurred in garment manufacturing (S. H. Slichter, *Union Policies and Industrial Management,* Brookings Institution, Washington,

Where product market competition is keen and wages an important element in unit costs (e.g., in coal mining and garment manufacturing), unions sometimes attempt to compel each firm to pay (roughly) equal wages per unit of product, implying that more efficient firms pay higher hourly wages.   Other unions, notably in the service trades, simply classify firms (roughly) in order of ability to pay and vary wages scales accordingly. Still others discriminate without any general formula.   However, despite union-to-union variations, the prevailing reluctance to endanger members' jobs promotes a similar reluctance to exert maximum pressure to reduce interfirm wage differentials.

The limitations imposed upon union wage policy by employer inability to pay are most serious when there is important competition between union and (lower wage) nonunion firms.   At present, this problem is of great importance in textile manufacturing, but in the past it has been a major problem in a large number of other industries.   The existence of a low wage nonunion sector in an industry forces the union to choose between maintaining a sizeable union-nonunion differential, and risking loss of union employment to nonunion firms, and curbing union wage demands which either angers the membership and/or leads it to become indifferent to its "do-nothing" union.   In a number of cases unions have chosen (often under member compulsion) a high wage policy, causing serious losses of employment.[35]   But the more typical policy, as indicated, is to protect member employment, even at the cost of union wage scales.

Cost of Living

In addition to ability to pay and wage patterns, the cost of living provides yet another criterion of wage setting.   However, this criterion is discussed below (pp. 413–415) and therefore need not be considered here.

THE EFFECT OF UNION POLICY UPON WAGES

Surprising as it may seem, the wages paid to union workers are not always higher than those paid in comparable nonunion firms.   In many cases, nonunion employers do not object to union wage scales but to union work rules, and pay wages equal to the union scale or even higher in order to discourage their employees from unionizing.   However, more often than not union workers receive higher wages than nonunion workers. This does not prove that unionism causes the difference; it is fairly clear

---

D.C., 1941, Chapter XVII), in steel production (Golden and Ruttenberg, *The Dynamics of Industrial Democracy*, Harper and Brothers, New York, 1942), and in hosiery manufacture (G. W. Taylor, "Hosiery," Chapter 9 in *How Collective Bargaining Works*, The Twentieth Century Fund, New York, 1945, pp. 504–505).

[35] S. H. Slichter, "Do the Wage-Fixing Agreements in the American Labor Market Have An Inflationary Bias," *American Economic Review*, May 1954. p. 332.

that the better paying establishments are more likely than others to become unionized.   As we shall see, tracing the effect of unions on wages is a very tricky business.

Full Employment

The fact that union wage objectives are somewhat frustrated by employer incapacity to meet the implied wage scales makes it difficult to trace the actual effect of unionism upon wage rates.   This difficulty is greatly increased by the fact that it is only since 1940 that unions have been strong enough, in the United States, to exert a major influence upon the country's wage structure and level; and this has been a period in which objectives of union wage policy have been very similar to what market forces would have led employers to do without prompting from unions. Hence certain economists have argued, in recent years, that union policy is of little, or of exaggerated, significance in determining wages.[36]

As we have already seen, when labor demand in high wage industries and/or areas tends to exceed supply, labor is drawn from lower wage employments.   Reducing the supply of labor available for low wage jobs tends to raise the wages paid for such jobs and tends to raise them more than proportionately to the increase in wages for better paying jobs.[37] This reduces, or eliminates, the wage differentials between high and low wage firms in the same industry and also among different industries and areas.   As we shall see, pp. 365–366, this general narrowing of differentials is precisely what has happened to the national wage structure since 1940. But this is also the result to which the equitable criteria of union wage policy, if followed, would have lead.   Hence, since 1940, union demands for reduction of interfirm and interarea wage differentials have involved, at least to some extent, the forcing of an open door.

The view that union wage policy has not been a major factor in determining wages (since 1940) is supported by the very fact that, during this period, there has been so little unemployment.   If a union, or any-

[36] See, for example, Milton Friedman, "Some Comments on the Significance of Labor Unions for Economic Policy," Chapter X in *The Impact of the Union*, edited by D. Mc. Wright, Harcourt, Brace & Co., New York, 1951; Albert Rees, "Wage Levels under Conditions of Long-Run Full Employment," *American Economic Review*, May 1953, pp. 451–457; also Lloyd Ulman, "Marshall and Friedman on Union Strength," *Review of Economics and Statistics*, November 1955, pp. 384–400 and Friedman's "Comment," in the same issue, pp. 401–406.   Friedman goes so far as to argue that in the postwar boom, unions tended to keep wage rates lower than they would have been in their absence.   For a different position, see S. H. Slichter, "Do the Wage-Fixing Arrangements in the American Labor Market Have an Inflationary Bias," *American Economic Review*, May 1954, pp. 322–346.

[37] This statement is by no means a truism although it is true.   The reasons why the wage rates on low wage jobs rise proportionately more than those on better paid jobs are discussed on pp. 370–372.

thing else, were to push the wage rate of a single firm, or the average wage of an industry, above its "market level," one indication of this fact would be the appearance of more job applicants than jobs, an excess of supply over demand. (That is, demand for labor would be lowered by the high wage rate and/or workers would be attracted by the prospect of high earnings until supply exceeded demand.) But in most countries of the world, since 1940, it has frequently happened that the demand for labor exceeded the supply in most industries throughout the economy and, in particular, in industries that were strongly unionized. In some cases, the unions obviously restrained their wage demands either because of legal provision (see pp. 412–413) or informal agreement; but in other cases they have freely negotiated agreements which left all their members employed, and employers seeking still more workers.

This does not *prove* that the unions concerned failed to make wage rates higher than they otherwise would have been. For example, it is possible that employers may have agreed, informally, not to compete for labor by bidding up wage rates and that union pressure forced the agreed wage levels above what they otherwise would have been, though leaving them below a level that would have caused unemployment.[38] However, when the pressure of market forces drives actual wage rates above union scales, as appears to have happened in Sweden[39] or during World War II in the United States, it is reasonable to conclude that the union scale lay below the rate that would have been set by a competitive market.

Therefore, it is clear that since 1940 unions (with few exceptions) have not wished, or have been unable, to adjust their wage scales high enough to cause their members' unemployment, and frequently there have been labor shortages with actual average hourly (straight-time) earnings rising relative to union rates. Furthermore, large gains in hourly earnings relative to other industries were made by the almost completely non-unionized agricultural workers. Hence, market forces clearly were affecting the nation's wage structure during this period.

However, this does not prove that unions did not also affect wages. Consider the following very real possibility: the very large and prosperous firms (General Motors, U.S. Steel, General Electric, U.S. Rubber, etc.) whose contracts set the key bargains for an important part of the American economy could have been compelled to pay higher wages had the unions

[38] However, if this statement is true, union wage policy kept the demand for labor from becoming even greater than it did. Evidence of employer wage collusion in the form of antipirating agreements is reported by R. A. Lester, "Company Wage Policies," Industrial Relations Section, Department of Economics and Sociology, Princeton University, Princeton, N.J., 1948; and Reynolds, "The Structure of the Labor Market," pp. 51–52.

[39] See Albert Rees, "Wage Levels under Conditions of Long-Run Full Employment," *op. cit.,* pp. 452–453.

with which they dealt been determined to extort them. Their very high current profits strongly suggest this possibility. Conversely, the bitter resistance of these firms to actual union demands suggests that, had they not been under union pressure, they might have offered lower wages. As their wages tend to be the highest in their respective industries, with other firms either matching or keeping a given distance below their levels, their agreements pulled up the wages of many other firms and, hence, the wage level of the whole economy.

This *could* have been happening in the American economy since 1945, but it is not easy to show that it did, or to demonstrate the reverse. The sharp rise in wages in 1937 (see pp. 406–407), led by the newly unionized firms in the face of a great deal of unemployment, provides evidence that this sort of mechanism *can* operate. But more than this is hard to say; at present, students of wage theory are simply not in agreement as to whether unions have or have not added materially to the postwar rise in wage rates or whether they have appreciably affected the structure of relative wage rates.[40]

Underemployment

In an underemployed economy, it is clear that wages are higher than those at which demand would equal supply. As we have seen (pp. 331–333) there are other factors responsible for this, apart from unions. Yet unions certainly are one of the forces making for downward wage rigidity; it is union wage policy to resist wage cuts as much as possible, and it is fairly clear that in unionized industries hourly wages fall less than in nonunion.[41] Furthermore, the difference between union and nonunion wage rates and the attempts to shift production from union to nonunion geographical areas all indicate that, in the 1920's and 1930's, unions did make wages higher in certain industries than they would have been otherwise.

[40] If it is contended that unions exert their influence primarily on the general level of wage rates but do not exert an effect upon the relative wage rates of different groups of workers, it becomes very difficult to test the hypothesis. (Slichter, "Do the Wage-Fixing Agreements in the American Labor Market Have a Inflationary Bias," *op. cit.*, and H. M. Douty, "Union and Non-Union Wages," Chapter 43 in *Employment and Wages in the United States*, Twentieth Century Fund, New York, 1953, both contend that the effect of unions is on the level rather than the structure of wage rates.)

There have also been some studies comparing the wage gains in union and nonunion industries; the most prominent of these are H. M. Levinson, *Unionism, Wage-Trends, and Income Distribution, 1914–1947*, University of Michigan Press, 1951; A. M. Ross and W. Goldner, "Forces Affecting the Inter-Industry Wage Structures," *Quarterly Journal of Economics*, May 1950, pp. 254–281. These also are not conclusive.

[41] Of course, this does not prove that differences in degree of unionization were the "cause" of these phenomena.

It should also be noted that, in the face of unemployment, union job-rationing mechanisms and supply-restricting practices (see pp. 348–355) become operative in the labor market. The existence of such practices indicates that wages are being held above equilibrium levels; the fact they have largely fallen into abeyance in the full employment era of recent years is one important reason why economists have come to doubt that union wage policy has much effect upon wage rates.

UNION WAGE POLICY AND MEMBER EMPLOYMENT

We have already noted that unions frequently restrain their wage demands to preserve the jobs of their members. It has also been remarked that there are exceptions to this statement. Let us now consider this matter a little more carefully.

The conditions under which a union becomes concerned with the employment effect of its wage policies will depend upon (1) the political structure of the union, (2) whether the firms with which it deals are expanding or contracting the volume of employment they offer, (3) the "employment responsiveness" of these firms to wage rate changes.

Let us consider these in order: (1) Union "political structure" affects union policy on wage and other matters in a number of ways. For example, if a union's unemployed members retain their voting rights, they are likely to press the leadership to do everything possible to enhance employment opportunities. But, if, as sometimes happens, the union is controlled by an inner group which issues work permits[42] to others when jobs are available (rescinding them when employment opportunities decline), then the burden of unemployment is borne by workers who have no influence on union policies. Another relevant consideration is the manner in which unemployment is distributed among the membership; if unemployment is shared equally by shortening the work week, all the members are likely to be anxious to do something about the matter. If, however, unemployment is concentrated upon the "junior" members of the union, then the older members whose jobs are relatively secure may be more concerned about preventing "job competition" from the unemployed members, and protecting the wage scale of those employed, than about enhancing employment opportunities.

Political structure influences union policy in yet other ways. Unions which have militant leaders tend to resist wage and other "concessions" to employers, which makes consideration of "employment effects" very difficult.[43] Sometimes, the leadership recognizes the relation between

[42] Work permits are discussed on pp. 188–189.

[43] An interesting example of this type is recounted by G. L. Palmer (*Union Tactics and Economic Change,* University of Pennsylvania Press, 1932, pp. 29–50) involving the Philadelphia Tapestry Carpet Workers.

wages and employment but is thwarted by a recalcitrant membership. This type of situation is promoted by a political structure in which the membership exercises considerable control over the leadership, e.g., when major decisions have to be ratified by the membership through referenda.[44]

(2) Where a union faces a situation in which its policies would, at worst, reduce the growth rate of employment (and membership), it will not usually be concerned with, or even aware of, the adverse effects of its policies on employment. It is the secular increase of total employment in many American industries (which union wage policies would at most slow down) that has been responsible for the lack of concern of many American unions with the relation between wages and member employment.

On the other hand, in industries of declining or of greatly changed employment opportunities[45] unions are often willing to accept sizeable wage reductions to facilitate the survival and growth of the firms which it has organized. This type of behavior has occurred, notably, in interregional competition within various branches of the garment making and textile industries.[46]

Not all unions are greatly concerned with preserving their members' present jobs. For example, where the sales lost by one unionized firm are sure to be captured by another in the same local area, a union may be quite callous about an employer's troubles. Their attitude may be "maintain union conditions or go out of business"; this philosophy seems to have animated union attitudes toward provisions and enforcement of some of the NRA codes[47] and the policy of the Amalgamated Clothing Workers toward "contract shops."[48]   In such instances as these, the union

[44] S. H. Slichter, *Union Policies and Industrial Management,* Brookings Institution, 1941, pp. 374 *et seq.,* points out how the membership prevented the Cigar Makers' and Flint Glass Workers' union leaders from making necessary concessions in the face of technical progress.   Slichter contrasts the behavior of these unions with those of the hosiery workers (see note 45) and the glass blowers where referenda did not operate to prevent unions from making necessary concessions to employers.

[45] For example, when the location of the industry changes (as in textiles) or when the industry adopts mechanized techniques permitting the substitution of unskilled for skilled workers (as in glass making, cigar manufacture).

[46] See, for example, G. W. Taylor, "Hosiery," Chapter 9 in *How Collective Bargaining Works,* Twentieth Century Fund, New York, 1945, pp. 502–507; or G. P. Shultz and C. A. Myers, "Union Wage Decisions and Employment," *American Economic Review,* June 1950, pp. 362–380.

[47] See C. F. Roos, "N. R. A. Economic Planning," *Cowles Commission, Monograph 2,* Bloomington, Indiana, 1937, Chapter XIII, especially General Hugh Johnson's statement to the Senate Finance Committee quoted in note 11, pp. 402–403.

[48] R. J. Myers and J. W. Bloch, "Men's Clothing," Chapter 8 in *How Collective Bargaining Works.*

has apparently felt that it would not lose members and dues by forcing low wage employers out of business.

There are cases where a union has deliberately chosen to pursue a high wage policy even though it recognized that it was purchased at the cost of some members' employment.   John L. Lewis has said: "We decided it was better to have a half-million men working in the industry at good wages and high standards of living, than it is to have a million working in the industry in poverty and degradation."[49]   Another case was that of the Cigar Makers Union which, for many years, refused to admit semiskilled machine operatives and obtained high wages for a diminishing share of the industry's employees.   The market for the union product was protected by the union label, the union's members were unwilling to share the label protected market with the larger number of semiskilled machine tenders who worked at much lower wages.[50]

(3) It is fairly obvious that a union is not likely to restrain itself from demanding higher wage rates to enhance its members' employment opportunities unless its leadership supposes that the foregone hourly earnings are causally related to increased employment.   How strong this relation must be to induce a union to sacrifice wage rates to promote employment gains is impossible to say, except that such "sacrifices" occur only when a wage cut can be plausibly related to an appreciable increase in employment for a membership that has been underemployed for a considerable period of time.

In short, unions will forego wage increases they could obtain (or accept wage cuts they could avoid) only when they believe they can save the jobs of an appreciable number of their *present* members by doing so.   They will do this provided the "political structure" and the distribution of costs and benefits among the membership are such that the leadership does not court internal political disaster by such action and provided there is no other feasible way of saving the members' jobs.

UNIONS AND THE PRODUCT MARKET

Under certain conditions it is possible that a union may be able to compel the employers of its members to grant them hourly wage increases, reduce their profit per unit of output correspondingly, and make no other response.   However, this is likely to happen only when the ratio of wages per unit of output to selling price is very small.   If w/p is at all sizeable and there are no offsetting reductions in nonlabor costs per unit of output, or increases in man-hour productivity, an employer will have to "pass on"

---

[49] Quoted by E. R. Wickersham, *Industrial and Labor Relations Review,* July 1953, p. 601.

[50] S. H. Slichter, "Union Policies and Industrial Management," pp. 216–223; D. J. Saposs, *Left-Wing Unionism,* International Publishers, New York, 1926.

an "ordinary size" increase in wage costs (per unit of output) in the form of higher prices. This will entail making the number of product units sold somewhat less than otherwise: how much less will depend upon "circumstances," i.e., upon what his competitors are doing and the demand for the product.

The responsiveness of customer demand to changes in selling price of the product is summarized by the concept "elasticity of demand." The *relevant* elasticity of demand[51] measures the percentage change in the firm's sales as a function of the percentage change in its price; the higher this elasticity, the greater is the loss of sales and receipts from any given increase. Therefore, the employer's resistance to wage increases grows with elasticity of demand for his product; furthermore, the higher the elasticity of demand for the product the greater will be the loss of employment resulting from any increase in hourly rates the union is able to obtain. As a result, unions have come to realize that there are great advantages in reducing the elasticity of demand for the employer's products.

One important reason why the elasticity of demand for a firm's output is high is that the union in question may have organized only part of an industry and (wage and) price increases in the organized segment are not followed in the unorganized part. Consequently, there would be considerable switching of purchases from union to nonunion employers in the event of a unilateral price advance by the former group. For this reason, among others, unions are very anxious to organize all employers whose products are close substitutes for the output of the employers already unionized. In cases where there is considerable product market competition between unionized and nonunionized employers, "organizing the unorganized" becomes a precondition for raising wages in the organized segment and the first order of union business.[52]

A union may attempt to reduce the elasticity of product demand by extending its organization to encompass the producers of substitutes; it

---

[51] The elasticity of demand for a firm's output obviously depends upon the response its competitors make to its price changes. When competitors tend to match a firm's price changes, the elasticity of demand is less than when they do not; i.e., fewer customers will leave a firm because of a price increase if its competitors raise their prices proportionately than if they do not. The *relevant* elasticity of demand is that elasticity which takes into account the actual responses of the firm's competitors (under given circumstances) to its own price changes. Hereafter, when we speak of elasticity of demand, we shall always mean the relevant elasticity.

[52] For example of pressure upon unions to organize the "unorganized," see *How Collective Bargaining Works*, pp. 263–277 (the case of bituminous coal), pp. 472–483 (the case of hosiery), and pp. 170–171 (the case of book and job printing). Also L. G. Reynolds and C. H. Taft, *The Evolution of Wage Structure*, Yale University Press, New Haven, 1956, Chapter 4 (the case of textiles).

may also attempt to get government orders and contracts for "its" employers and discourage similar contracts for nonunion firms.[53]   Unions have also helped to enhance the demand for their employers' output by lobbying for protective tariffs, by boycotting nonunion firms, by campaigns to purchase only products bearing a union label, and by helping industry-wide marketing campaigns.

Unions in the printing trades have benefited greatly from being able to organize by "selling" the union label to final users.   The union label has also helped to sell beer, garments, cigars, restaurant services, and a variety of other products.   These are all cases where union activities in the product market raise the price at which union employers can sell a given volume of output, and these employers can therefore be forced to bear higher labor costs per unit of output.

Regulated Prices

Where the elasticity of demand for the product is low (i.e., less than one), it would seem that an employer could pass on to the buyer the cost of sizeable wage increases without "greatly" reducing output, employment, and profits.   But if this is possible, it is necessary to explain why the employers do not raise prices, with or without wage increases.[54]   The answer, in part, is that in many of these cases product prices are set by public bodies (e.g., state utility commissions) which limit the earnings of the firms in question; consequently, increases in wage or other cost elements must "justify" a price increase before the regulatory body will permit the increase to occur.   But if this is so, why do public utility companies (e.g., railroad, busses, telephone and telegraph, gas and electric) have wage disputes?   Why don't they simply grant whatever the unions ask and pass on the increased cost to the consumers?   The answer is that, in some cases, competition (e.g., among railroads, busses, and airlines) sets prices at or below the levels prescribed by the regulatory authorities.[55] In others, demand tends to fluctuate in sympathy with general business activity; and out-of-pocket losses (inevitable at low rates of output) increase with the level of wage rates while the regulating commissions will not usually permit price increases to offset lower revenue resulting from reduced volume.   Consequently, the employers, (rightly) fearing that

---

[53] See the discussion of the Walsh-Healey Act in Chapter 20.   The best general discussion of union attempts to affect product markets is J. T. Dunlop, *Wage Determination Under Trade Unions,* 2nd edition, Augustus Kelley, New York, 1950, Chapter VI.

[54] That is, if the elasticity of demand is less than one, employer profits would be greater (at least in the short-run) if they raised their prices.

[55] In these cases, the elasticity of demand exceeds one.

wages will be difficult to cut, are reluctant to grant increases that would (at low rates of output) increase out-of-pocket losses.

Another type of situation in which the employers could, if they acted in concert, raise product prices appreciably without greatly lowering their physical volume of sales (and profits) arises where a group of (oligopolistic) firms adopts a policy of setting prices at levels that keep current profits below the levels that would attract "too many" new rivals to their particular field of endeavor and/or the undesired attentions of governmental agencies, e.g., the Anti-Trust Division of the Justice Department. Spectacular examples of this type of behavior were afforded the large firms in automobile, steel, and other durable goods industries (in the United States) during the post-World War II period when their policy of keeping selling prices below what could have been charged (without loss of sales) produced "grey" markets. Where price policies of this kind are followed, it becomes plausible to suppose that wage rate increases may be passed on without greatly reducing output and employment below what they otherwise would be. (In cases where price ceilings are imposed by the government, this type of situation becomes typical.)

Yet another type of situation in which wage increases may be passed on without greatly reducing output arises where the union bargains with an employers' association or where wage leadership is of such a character that "key bargains" of one or two firms are followed automatically by the others. In such cases as these, the relevant elasticity of demand for any one firm tends to be very low when it passes on wage increases, although it would be much higher if it tried to vary its price independently of cost changes experienced by its competitors. This type of cost situation is fairly common in the service trades of large cities, in the construction industry, and in many branches of manufacturing. In the service trades and construction, it often leads to union-management cooperation to restrict price competition.[56]

Union Wage Policy and Control of Labor Supply

If the wages of union members are appreciably higher than those of nonunion workers (having the same degree of skill), employers will obviously be tempted to use the nonunion workers. Unions take great pains to keep this from happening.

Where a union has a monopoly of all persons possessing the relevant skill, keeping nonunionists from securing jobs within its jurisdiction is easy. But, given the training facilities in the United States and the high general educational level of the workforce, it is difficult, more so now than formerly, to acquire such a monopoly. Hence, it has become increasingly

---

[56] See Dunlop, *op. cit.,* Chapter VI.

important for unions either to restrict entry to the trade and/or to control employer hiring policy.

Methods of Restricting Entry

The unions most actively concerned with restricting entry are the skilled craft unions. (However, let it be noted, professional associations have similarly, and more effectively, done the same thing.) The most obvious devices for restricting entry are (1) requiring that entrants undergo a training program, (2) requiring the passage of examinations, or (3) imposing quantitative restrictions on new entrants. These requirements may be enforced directly by a union or professional association, by a government agency, or by a government agency cooperating with one of the former.

As "voluntary associations," most unions are free within broad limits (see pp. 239–240) to determine their entry rules as they please. This freedom is sometimes used to keep down the number of members. However, The existence of membership qualifications does not necessarily restrict entry (in the economic sense); it is the manner in which they are administered that determines their effect.

APPRENTICE CONTROL. In occupations where apprentices are trained "virtually every union . . . makes some effort to regulate it, but very few of these unions make the serving of an apprenticeship a prerequisite to membership. . . . The reason most apprenticeship regulating unions do not require applicants for admission to have completed an apprenticship is that they control only a small part of the entire trade."[57] Concern with apprentices is a problem confined mainly to craft unions whose members perform jobs requiring considerable skill. Unions in this category are found mainly in the building trades, printing trades, and the highly skilled metal-working trades.[58]

A major reason for union concern with apprenticeship is the desire to prevent employers from using apprentices as cheap substitutes for union labor. This is accomplished by one or all of the following techniques: (1) direct limitations on numbers of apprentices, (2) regulating the term

[57] Sumner H. Slichter, *Union Policies and Industrial Management*, Brookings Institution, 1941, pp. 9–10. The reason given by Slichter for union willingness to admit non-apprentices was more applicable fifteen years ago than at present. One reason why unions are willing (at the present time) to admit non-apprentices is the large number of skilled workers trained on the job, in trade schools, and in the armed services; refusal to admit such workers, or demanding that they undergo apprenticeship, might well create nonunion shops as well as generate enormous public resentment. Another reason is the prevailing condition of full employment which makes such restriction unnecessary.

[58] Slichter, *op. cit.*, Chapter II.

of apprenticeship,[59] and (3) controlling the wages of apprentices.[60] (Union concern with apprenticeship control is more important in some foreign countries, e.g., Denmark, than in the United States.)

SKILL PREREQUISITES. Unions, professional associations, etc. often make skill prerequisites for full membership (e.g., for becoming a "journeyman") highly complex and difficult to satisfy. Sometimes this is done, especially by local unions, with the clear intention of minimizing the number of workers in the field.[61] However, such skill requirements are often connected with sentiments of occupational pride, and a desire to enhance the prestige of the trade or profession by creating a formidable list of skill hurdles that neophytes must overcome. These barriers to entry are often defended as necessary for the protection of the hirer; i.e., it is argued that improperly trained workmen do inferior work and that they, the union or professional associations, are trying to "protect" the public. Once again, it is important to note that such devices have not been so important in the high level employment of recent years, as they were previously.

LICENSE LAWS. In a number of cases, unions have succeeded in securing the aid of the government's licensing power to exclude "inferior" workers; i.e., in consequence of union intervention, or for other reasons, an arm of government has required that, in order to enter certain fields, workers must pass examinations, undergo certain specified training, or both. Licenses have been required for plumbers, stationary engineers, electricians, barbers, taxi drivers, motion picture operators, coal miners, school teachers and others.[62] Often the administration of the licensing requirement is performed (by a state or local government) in close conjunction with a union local, which tends to make the government an enforcement arm of union policy.[63] In some cases, usually where there was some unemployment or where weekly earnings had recently fallen, unions have demanded that public officials refrain from issuing additional

---

[59] This is done to prevent the term of apprenticeship from being made so long that, toward its close, apprentices are as skilled as journeymen, but work for lower wages. It is also done to prevent the trade from being flooded with badly-trained workers (because of an unduly short training period) able to secure work only at rates below the union scale.

[60] To prevent apprentices from being so cheap as to tempt employers to substitute their labor for that of journeymen union members. For details, see Slichter, *Union Policies and Industrial Management,* Chapter II.

[61] Slichter, *Union Policies and Industrial Management,* pp. 63–67. Also C. W. Summers, "Admission Policies of Labor Unions," *Quarterly Journal of Economics,* November 1946, pp. 66–107, especially p. 83.

[62] Slichter, *Union Policies and Industrial Management, op. cit.,* pp. 47–50.

[63] C. L. Christenson, "Chicago Service Trades," Chapter 15 in *How Collective Bargaining Works,* for the notorious case of the Motion Picture Machine Operators of Chicago, pp. 830–847.

licenses (e.g., taxi drivers' licenses) in order not to "overcrowd" a field in which there already is unemployment or in which "earnings are already too low, due to an excess labor supply."[64]

QUOTAS. The aforementioned instances, whatever the motives of the parties involved, restrict entry only as an indirect consequence of pursuing other *avowed* objectives (typically the raising of "standards"). However, acknowledged restriction on entry for the sake of its (anticipated) economic consequences is not unknown. This is sometimes accomplished simply by the refusal of a local union to accept new members (including, on occasion, members from other locals of the same national union) when any of its current members are unemployed. National union officers frequently inveigh against such practices by their locals, but only rarely are they willing and able to prevent them.[65]

Outright restriction on entry varies with the extent of unemployment, becoming more severe as member unemployment increases; as Summers says, "in periods of normal business activity (such practices are) confined mainly to the building trades, food and newspaper delivery, photoengraving, lithography, bill-posting, and diamond cutting. In preiods of depression and mass unemployment it may appear in many other industries, such as the garment trades, mining, printing, and longshore work."[66]

INITIATION FEES AND DUES. High initiation fees may be used to exclude members; such practices are not unknown but they are rare.[67] Even where initiation fees are high, provision is sometimes made for payment by installments, which dilutes their restrictive effects. In general, initiation fees of unions are rarely high enough to be a serious obstacle to entry into a field; nor are their dues much of a deterrent.

SENIORITY. The most common device by which unions restrict entry is by seniority in layoffs and rehiring. (We have already described the operation of Seniority. See pp. 189–192.) Seniority differs from other techniques of entry restriction in that it does not create two classes of workers, "ins" and outs." Rather, it creates a more or less continuous gradation of workers by length of service; those having least service are most likely to become unemployed if unemployment should arise. That

---

[64] Government regulation of entrance into various trades and occupations has had a long history in European countries as an outgrowth of guild practices and traditions. But, in the United States, such practices were unimportant until the 1930's when they received an enormous impetus from the attempts by sellers' associations of all sorts to "restrict entry and maintain price." Such attempts became very frequent and not infrequently received encouragement from the federal or state governments.

[65] Slichter, *Union Policies and Industrial Management*, pp. 63–68; also, C. W. Summers, "Admission Policies of Labor Unions," pp. 77–80.

[66] Summers, "Admission Policies of Labor Unions," p. 79.

[67] *Ibid.*, pp. 80–82.

is, new workers are admitted to a share in the union's job territory on a contingent basis, and with a claim to job opportunities inferior to those with more seniority. If all current union members are employed, new members may secure jobs without hindrance; but if some members have been laid off (and must be rehired before new workers can be hired), then new workers are effectively, if temporarily, denied access to employment and seniority has become identical with entry restriction.

Professional Associations

The restrictive activities of professional associations have, in many respects, been similar to those of labor unions and have often been more successful. These associations usually limit entry via the state's licensing power; the first step is to require that the practice of a profession be legally restricted to those duly licensed; the second is to bring the administrators of the licensing system to accept the standards of the professional association. Thus, in virtually every state of the union it is necessary to get a license in order to practice law, i.e.,"pass the bar." Similarly, a license is a prerequisite to the lawful practice of medicine, dentistry, pharmacy, school teaching, etc. These licensing provisions are (properly) aimed at the preservation and improvement of professional standards, and the protection of the "hiring public."

However, to "protect" the public by licensing professional practitioners requires that licenses be issued only to "competent" persons; to acquire competence requires both training and ability which, in turn, limits the number of persons able to obtain licenses. The professional associations (understandably) try, and often succeed, in getting the licensing boards to accept their own standards of competence. These standards tend to be high in comparison with the attainments of the "average" practitioner currently within the field and have tended to become more severe with the passage of time; this also is understandable and may be socially desirable. But our concern is not with the social desirability of the standards of licensing boards; it is with the effects of these standards (however evaluated) upon relative wages and the distribution of (wage) income.

These consequences can be observed most clearly in the medical profession. "In all but three states, either legal requirements or the rules of the Board of Examiners specify that among individuals studying in this country or Canada, only graduates of medical schools approved by the Council on Medical Education and Hospitals of the American Medical Association may take the examination for admission to practice."[68] Under the leadership of the aforementioned Council, the profession has, since 1910, steadily raised the standards of training given by medical

[68] M. Friedman and S. S. Kuznets, *Income from Independent Professional Practice*, National Bureau of Economic Research, New York, 1945, p. 13.

schools; the Council's role is that it will not *approve* schools that do not meet its standards.   The raising of standards "ushered in a period of rapid rise in premedical requirements and standards of professional training and of rapid decline in the number of medical schools and medical students. . . . The number of medical students declined from a high point of approximately 28,000 in 1904 to under 15,000 in 1915 and under 14,000 in 1920."[69]   The ratio of physicians to the population has decreased since 1910; e.g., in 1920 there were 729 persons to each physician, but in 1940 the ration was 796 to 1.[70]   This was caused by a decline in the number (per annum) of students graduated from medical schools from 5606 in 1905 to a low of 2529 in 1922; the number of graduates, per annum, has now increased to over 5000 per year, but as recently as 1945 it was less than in 1905.[71]

The nongrowth in the graduation rate from medical schools (from 1905 to 1945) is especially marked when compared with the rapid growth in the number of practitioners of almost every other "learned" profession. This nongrowth can hardly be ascribed to a lack of interest in the profession for in each year between 1926 and 1941 (except 1930 and 1931) over one-third of all applicants for admission to "approved" medical schools were rejected.[72]   In late 1934 or early 1935, "the Council on Medical Education issued a warning 'against the admission of larger classes than can properly be accommodated or than can reasonably be expected to satisfy approved scholastic standards.' "   Friedman and Kuznets note that "the warning seems to have had a decided effect (reduction) on the number of students admitted to medical schools."[73]

Although there can be little doubt that the restriction on numbers was intended to raise professional standards (and did), there. is abundant evidence that professional leaders have been aware of the economic consequences of such restriction and (some) have sharply disapproved.[74] Finally, the undoubted prestige and the very high incomes that have been, and still are, characteristic of the medical profession[75] certainly preclude

[69] *Ibid.,* p. 9.

[70] "Post-War Outlook for Physicians," *Bureau of Labor Statistics Bulletin* 863, Government Printing Office, Table 2.

[71] *Ibid.,* Table I.

[72] Friedman and Kuznets, *Income from Independent Professional Practice,* Table 2, p. 14.

[73] *Ibid.,* p. 15.

[74] *Ibid.,* p. 12, especially note 18.

[75] In 1949, the mean *net* income (after deduction of business expenses but before deduction of income taxes) of all physicians in the United States was $11,058.00. This represented an increase of 108 per cent over the corresponding figure for 1929.   During the same period, the mean net income of lawyers and dentists increased from 1929 to 1949 by much less than this.   See William Weinfeld, "Income

the possibility that the relative decline in new entrants has been due to lack of economic incentive.[76]

The dental profession has striven to emulate the medical in raising standards and increasing training requirements.[77]   Nevertheless, the length of training and the other difficulties of entering dentistry are considerably less than in medicine.[78]   The difference in prerequisites is paralleled by a difference in earning power; the average income of all physicians was approximately 32 per cent larger than that of all dentists in the period 1929–1936 (the period covered in the Friedman-Kuznets study).[79]   Friedman and Kuznets (in the most thorough study of the matter yet undertaken) conclude that "about half of the observed difference between the mean incomes of physicians and dentists is attributable to the greater difficulty of entry into medicine.[80]

To turn to somewhat humbler occupations, the barbers (through their union) have been both active and successful in restricting entry into their trade by means of licensing barbers and "stiffening" the prerequisites for entry.[81]   They have also secured government enforced minimum price regulations.   Other service trades (e.g., plumbers, stationary engineers, electricians, and motion picture operators) have made attempts to achieve the same advantages.[82]

Entry Restriction and Wages

Union restriction on entry is not, as a rule, consciously aimed at raising wage rates.   Rather it is intended to insure steady employment (and consequently higher incomes) for an "in" group of members.   This, of course, *permits* the setting of a wage rate so high that it entails unemployment for those not "included"; but, as we have seen, unions do not usually strive to set wage rates so as to achieve this result.   Thus, in times of "strong" demand, they do not attempt to charge all that the traffic will bear for the services of a fixed number of members, but expand the supply

---

of Physicians, 1929–1949," *Survey of Current Business,* July 1951, pp. 9–26, especially p. 10.

[76] Friedman and Kuznets, *Income from Independent Professional Practice,* p. 15 and notes 23 and 23a, estimate that in the period considered (the 1930's) "not more than 55 per cent of all persons who attempt to enter approved United States medical schools gain entry, graduate from an approved school, and pass licensure examination.   This estimate allows for repeated attempts at all stages."

[77] *Ibid.,* pp. 21–30.

[78] *Ibid.,* pp. 124–125.

[79] *Ibid.,* Table 4, p. 104 and p. 122.   Weinfeld, "Income of Physicians" indicates that this advantage has been maintained throughout the 1940's.

[80] *Ibid.,* p. 137.

[81] W. F. Brown and Ralph Cassady, Jr., "Guild Pricing in the Service Trades," *Quarterly Journal Economics,* February 1947, pp. 311–338.

[82] *Ibid.,* pp. 335–338; also Slichter, *Union Policies and Industrial Management* pp. 47–50.

somewhat by issuing work permits[83] and/or accepting new members. In times of "weak" demand they try to reduce supply rather than lower the wage rate[84].

This is not to deny that some unions have used their control over supply to secure differential advantages. But it is to deny the validity of inferring, solely from the presence of entry requirements, that unions are trying to limit supply in order to set "monopoly" wage rates. Indeed, any firm that is not interested in hiring additional workers and which is not itself attempting to lower wages is, automatically, "restricting entry." But here it is the employer who is doing the restricting.

The effect of entry restriction on relative wage and income distribution cannot be judged by looking only at the group being protected. We must also ask what happens to those excluded. Since those excluded from a class of jobs must seek employment somewhere else, they increase the supply of workers for other jobs and thereby tend to lower the wages paid on them.

For example, if unions have been able to raise wages inside the manufacturing segment of the American economy, labor demand therein will have failed to expand as much as it otherwise would have, and the workers who would otherwise have found manufacturing jobs have been forced to work elsewhere; e.g., they may have stayed on southern farms. Hence, if unions have been partly responsible for higher wages in cities, these wage increases will have been secured (in part) at the price of lower per capita incomes in rural areas.

Some Comments on Entry Restriction

It is tempting to condemn all restrictions on entry and demand that they be abolished. However, there are few persons who are really prepared to accept the implications of abolishing *all* restrictions on entry. A world with literally no restriction on entry would be one in which no one's job was secure; one in which everyone needed always to fear a superior competitor (or one willing to work cheap enough). The tradition of free competition with an equal opportunity for all persons at all jobs is in direct conflict with the desire of most people for some form of job security. As we have seen, most employers do not encourage "unlimited competition" in the labor market but instead try to reward competent and industrious employees by giving them job security.

Whether it is socially desirable for unions or individual employers to provide employment security for wage earners, or whether this should be provided only (if at all) by the government, is a large question which we shall touch upon briefly in Chapter 19. Our point here is simply that

---

[83] See pp. 188–189.

[84] Of course, wages tend to fall as well, but the union tries to curb the (inevitable) fluctuations in wage rates by suitable adjustments in supply.

restrictions upon entry (and associated practices) are, from the viewpoint of the benefited groups, simply attempts to gain a measure of economic security by means of "voluntary" collective action. However, it is not usually appreciated that, when sought by exclusive groups, "one man's security is another's lack of opportunity." (Entry restriction is discussed further on pp. 452–461.)

DISCUSSION QUESTIONS

1. "The effect of restricting immigration has been to raise both the hourly wages of all American workers and the incomes of southern farmers." Discuss.

2. "The most difficult thing to understand about a nonunionized labor market is that a worker is not likely to be offered as little as he would be willing to take." Discuss.

3. (a) Name three devices by which unions restrict entry to jobs under their control. Evaluate the social desirability of the consequences of each of these devices.

(b) Explain the sense in which employer hiring standards act as devices to restrict entry to the jobs they offer.

4. If unions do not make wages higher than they otherwise would have been why, then, do employers and unions have such bitter battles on wage issues?

5. What are the principal differences between the functioning of a nonunion labor market in a period of expanding employment and in a period of contracting employment? In answering, take account of (1) the migration of labor, (2) the movement of the level of wage rates, (3) the behavior of interarea and interindustrial wage rates, and (4) the variation of employer hiring standards.

Suggested Readings

Most of the references at the end of Chapters XI and XII are pertinent here, also. Additional suggestions are:

Dunlop, J. T., *Wage Determination Under Trade Unions,* 2nd edition, Augustus Kelly, New York, 1950.

Friedman, M., "Some Comments on the Significance of Labor Unions for Economic Policy"; Chapter X in *The Impact of the Union,* edited by D. McWright, Harcourt, Brace & Company, New York, 1951.

Friedman, M., and S. S. Kuznets, *Incomes from Independent Professional Practice,* National Bureau of Economic Research, New York, 1945.

Johnson, D. G., "Comparability of Labor Capacities of Farm and Nonfarm Labor," *American Economic Review,* June 1953, pp. 296–313.

Rees, A. E., "Postwar Wage Determination in the Basic Steel Industry," *American Economic Review,* June 1951, pp. 389–404; "Wage Levels Under Conditions of Long-Run Full Employment," *American Economic Review,* May 1953, pp. 451–457.

Reynolds, L. G., and C. H. Taft, *The Evolution of Wage Structure,* Yale University Press, New Haven, 1956.

Ross, A. M., *Trade Union Wage Policy,* University of California Press, Berkeley and Los Angeles, 1948.

Slichter, S. H., *Union Policies and Industrial Management,* The Brookings Institution, Washington, D.C., 1941.

Ulman, Lloyd, "Marshall and Friedman on Union Strength," *Review of Economics and Statistics,* November 1955, pp. 384–400; also Friedman's "Comment," same issue, pp. 401–406.

14

Wage Differentials:
The Structure of Wages
in the United States

In the preceding three chapters we have discussed the theory of wage determination. This chapter attempts to apply the theory to the explanation of various aspects of the wage structure of the United States. By the term "wage structure," we mean the interrelation of the wages[1] paid to various groups of workers; wage *structure* is distinguished from wage *level,* which is discussed in Chapter 17. As there are a very large number of ways of distinguishing groups of workers, so there are a number of different, and related, wage structures. There is an industrial structure, a regional or occupational structure, an age structure, etc. In this chapter we shall confine our attention to the first three of the aspects mentioned and discuss some of the others later.

THE INDUSTRIAL WAGE STRUCTURE

General Characteristics

In the course of developing the theory of wages, we had occasion to describe many of the broad characteristics of the industrial wage structure of the United States, pp. 314–333. Therefore, this section will be brief.

As indicated earlier, the nation's high wage industries tend to be those in which durable hard goods are manufactured, in which large firms predominate, and in which a relatively large amount of capital per worker is used. Indicative of the interrelation of the industrial and other aspects of the national wage structure is the fact that the high wage industries tend to be concentrated in relatively large cities outside of the South and New England; they tend to employ disproportionately large numbers of adult males and of skilled workers. Low wage industries have the reverse characteristics.

[1] By "wages" we mean average straight-time hourly earnings, unless otehwise specified.

The position of an industry in the interindustry wage hierarchy tends to be rather stable over time. That is, an industry that is relatively high wage in one year will tend to be high wage in another, even though a considerable period of time may have elapsed between the two years. Thus, among 50 manufacturing industries, it was found that the rank correlation of average hourly earnings in 1939 and 1954 was +0.897.[2] To be sure industries grow and decline, and the declining ones tend to fall in the wage-paying hierarchy and vice versa. But, nonetheless, the position of an industry in the wage-paying hierarchy is subject to a great deal of inertia.

Some attempts have been made to explain the differences in hourly wage changes among industries by associating these changes with changes in various aspects of net value product per man hour.[3] For example, Dunlop found a substantial rank correlation between the percentage changes (occurring between 1923 and 1940) in the man-hour physical productivity of labor in various industries and the changes in average hourly earnings (the coefficient of rank correlation was +0.47). Garbarino made an analysis similar to Dunlop's in which he found a strong rank correlation (+0.67) between the "degree of concentration"[4] in 1935 and the percentage change in average hourly earnings in 1923–1940. Fabricant found a rank correlation between percentage change in wage cost per unit of product and percentage change in selling price (between 1909 and 1937) of +0.49.

Although these studies are all scholarly efforts and worthy of careful attention, the high degree of intercorrelation among the different variables considered and the (admitted) lack of a satisfactory theory make it necessary to consider these findings as very tentative. Probably the most reliable conclusion that emerges is that the percentage change in an industry's average hourly wages is strongly associated with the percentage

[2] L. G. Reynolds and C. H. Taft, The Evolution of Wage Structure, Yale University Press, New Haven, 1956, pp. 332–337. S. H. Slichter, "Notes on the Structure of Wages," Review of Economics and Statistics, Feb. 1950, pp. 80–91, and Carrie Glasser, Wage Differentials, Columbia University Press, New York, 1940, pp. 31–40, come to similar conclusions.

[3] J. T. Dunlop, "Productivity and the Wage Structure," pp. 341–362 in Income, Employment and Public Policy, Essays in Honor of A. H. Hansen, W. W. Norton and Company, Inc., New York, 1948; Ross and Goldner, "Forces Affecting the Inter-Industry Wage Structure," Quarterly Journal of Economics, May 1950, pp. 254–281; J. W. Garbarino, "A Theory of Interindustry Wage Variation," Quarterly Journal of Economics, May 1950, pp. 282–305; A. M. Ross, Trade Union Wage Policy, University of California Press, Berkeley and Los Angeles, 1948, Chapter 6; and Solomon Fabricant, Employment in Manufacturing, 1899–1939, National Bureau of Economic Research, New York, 1942, Chapter 4.

[4] That is, the percentage of output produced by the four largest firms in the industry.

change in *net value product* per man-hour; this result will not cause surprise, but it is empirical information and, as such, must not be ignored.

THE GEOGRAPHICAL WAGE STRUCTURE

Intercity Wage Differentials

In Columns 1 and 2 of Table 14.1 are presented data indicating the percentage variations in the earnings of workers in office and "indirect

Table 14.1. Wage Levels in Various Cities for Office Workers and (Indirect) Manual Workers, 1953–1954 (N.Y.C. = 100)

	Relative Pay Levels	
	Office Workers	Indirect Manual Workers*
Northeast:		
Boston	89	93
Newark-Jersey City	99	106
New York City	100	100
Philadelphia	91	94
South:		
Atlanta	92	77
Dallas	90	78
Memphis	86	74
New Orleans	86	72
Middle West:		
Chicago	106	105
Detroit	108	111
Milwaukee	98	106
Minneapolis-St. Paul	91	100
St. Louis	95	99
Far West:		
Denver	93	90
Los Angeles	107	107
Portland	98	105
San Francisco-Oakland	106	114

Sources: T. P. Kanninen, "Wage Differences Among Labor Markets, 1953–1954," *Monthly Labor Review*, October 1954, pp. 1090–1096.
* Maintenance, custodial, and material movement jobs.

manual"[5] jobs in late 1953 and early 1954. These data indicate that earnings in office jobs were lowest in New Orleans and Memphis (86 per cent of the New York level) and highest in Detroit (109 per cent of New York). Earnings of manual labor varied from 72 per cent (of the New York level) in New Orleans to 114 per cent in San Francisco-Oakland. The rankings of these areas are fairly stable over time. In

[5] "Indirect manual" jobs consist of maintenance, custodial, warehousing, and shipping jobs.

April 1943, in October 1946, and in January–July 1951, data on earnings of factory workers in various urban areas were compiled by the Bureau of Labor Statistics;[6] in these studies, as in that for 1953–1954, Southern cities such as Atlanta, Birmingham, Dallas, Memphis, New Orleans, and San Antonio ranked at the bottom of the city wage hierarchy, while West Coast cities (such as San Francisco, Portland, and Seattle) and Northern industrial centers (such as Detroit, Cleveland, Pittsburgh, Toledo) ranked near or at the top.[7] The general stability (over time) of the rankings of various cities is paralleled by a fairly strong tendency for cities to have similar ranks in different industries and occupations. A "high wage" city will do the reverse. The ranks of cities in various industries do show will pay comparatively high wages in all industries, and a "low wage" city some variation from one industry to another, but these variations are not very large.

The association between the population size of an urban area and the general level of its wage rates has been exhibited in several comparisons of wages in different size communities.[8] These studies show that the community level of wage rates tends, other relevant variables the same,[9] to rise with the population of the community.

Now let us try to explain these facts. First, consider the fact that the Southern cities consistently rank at the bottom of the intercity wage hierarchy. In part, this is because the Southern cities have a small fraction of their labor force employed in the high wage durable goods industries, as compared with the rest of the country; in 1946, for example, only 41 per cent of the persons engaged in manufacturing in the South were employed in the production of durables[10] while 58 per cent of the manu-

[6] See N. B. Belloc, *Wages in California,* University of California Press, 1948, Chapter 5, especially Tables 19 and 20; also L. M. David and Harry Ober, "Intercity Wage Differences, 1945–1946," *Monthly Labor Review,* June 1948, pp. 599–604; "Wage Differences Among 40 Labor Markets," *Monthly Labor Review,* December 1952.

[7] As the individual cities studied varied from one year to another, a rank correlation analysis would present serious (though not insuperable) difficulties.

[8] See J. Perlman, *Hourly Earnings of Employees in Large and Small Enterprises,* TNEC Monograph No. 14, Government Printing Office, Washington, D.C., 1940, pp. 6–7; also S. C. Sufrin, A. W. Swinyard, and F. M. Stephenson, "The North-South Differential—A Different View," *Southern Economic Journal,* October 1948, pp. 184–190; and H. E. Klarman, *A Statistical Study of Income Differences Among Communities,* Studies in Income and Wealth, Volume Six, National Bureau of Economic Research, New York, 1943, pp. 205–226.

[9] Southern cities of given size (i.e., population) tend to pay lower wages than cities elsewhere; conversely, West Coast cities of given size tend to pay higher wages. See references in note 8.

[10] "Factory Workers' Earnings: 1954," Bureau of Labor Statistics, Bulletin 1179 United States Department of Labor, Washington, D.C., Table 3, p. 16.

facturing workers in the United States, as a whole, were so employed.[11] (Similar ratios will be found for other years.)[12]

To a considerable extent, a similar explanation is pertinent to the ranking of non-Southern cities; cities with relatively high percentages of persons employed in the durable goods (especially metal-working) industries have comparatively high general wage levels.   This is a matter of arithmetic; the employment-weighted average wage rates[13] tend to be higher in those places where the relatively high wage paying industries get the heaviest (employment) weights.

The tendency for wage rates to vary with the population of a city is due to a number of factors.   (1) Small urban areas tend to serve as way-points in rural-urban migration.   Young people go from farms to nearby small towns and, thence, to large cities; consequently, the small towns have a steady supply of young workers available at rates that compare favorably with agriculture but are lower than those obtainable in larger cities.   (2) Large cities are the places where the most highly specialized, and hence best paid, work is done.   (3) Large plants tend to be located in large cities, as the workers in a large plant together with their families and the workers (and their families) necessary to provide them with services make a quite substantial city in themselves.   And, as we have noted, big plants tend to pay relatively high wages.

In large manufacturing centers, the wage rates paid in nonmanufacturing industries also tend to be higher than in smaller towns, as a consequence of the labor market competition from the manufacturing plants.   When these plants expand their workforce they attract workers from the lower wage industries in the vicinity, which exerts upward pressure on the low wage rates.   Furthermore, labor unions in the less favored industries (in a given community) tend to set their wage performance standards in terms of the wages paid by the high wage industries in the area, making it difficult for employers to pay as little as they might in areas where high wage industries were less prevalent.   This argument implies that high wages in a city's manufacturing industries are associated with high wages in its nonmanufacturing industries.   That such associations have been found adds credence to the argument.[14]

[11] *Ibid.*

[12] The reader must beware of inferring that the "lines of causation" run one way, i.e. that the South is a low wage area "because" its industries are predominantly low wage.   It is just as true to say that its industries are predominantly low wage "because" it is a low wage area, as the reverse; see pp. 363–365.

[13] It is these employment weighted averages that define a city's wage level.

[14] See Belloc, *Wages in California,* p. 62.   (The correlation coefficient between wage rates in manufacturing and nonmanufacturing industries in selected cities in 1943 was $+0.70$.)   Also see T. P. Kanninen, "Wage Differences Among Labor Markets, 1953–1954," *op. cit.*

The above remarks refer primarily to a situation where a city is in a position of substantially full employment. Where there is local unemployment, wages in the low wage firms and industries of a given city may slump considerably relative to those paid in the high wage industries. However, in a strongly unionized city, unions may prevent employers from instituting wage cuts that they would wish and that the state of the labor market would permit. In a unionized city, therefore, interindustry wage differentials may be *kept* smaller, in a period of unemployment, than they would have been in the absence of unionization.

In general, a city will pay relatively higher wages in an industry of which it is a "leading center" than in others. Thus Detroit and Cleveland paid (in 1945–1946) relatively high wages in the metal-working and chemical industries, while New York paid comparatively low wages in these industries. On the other hand, New York paid the highest wages (of any city) in the apparel industry of which it is the recognized leader.[15] An explanation of this tendency is readily found. In the major centers of an industry (e.g., Detroit for automobiles, New York for apparel, Los Angeles for motion pictures, etc.) are congregated the largest and most successful firms (who are best able to pay) and the most skilled and (well-paid) specialized workers.

Intercity wage differences are sometimes alleged to parallel differences in living costs and, in a general way, they do. However, the intercity variations in hourly wages are considerably greater than those in the cost of living, and the correlation between the rank of a city in terms of living costs with its rank in terms of wage rates is by no means perfect.[16] There are three possible mechanisms which connect a city's relative level of living costs with its relative level of wage rates: (1) workers in cities where the ratio of living costs to wage rates[17] is relatively high tend to move to places where it is lower, thereby tending to equalize real wage rates in different cities, and conversely. This mechanism may be operative, but a great many students of the problem would deny that it has been of any importance. (2) In a high wage city the wage cost and, hence, the prices of locally manufactured products and services will tend to be comparatively high, and conversely.[18] This tends to make the cost of living higher in high wage than in low wage communities, and vice

---

[15] See David and Ober, "Intercity Wage Differences, 1945–1946," pp. 600–602.

[16] *Ibid.*, pp. 603–604.

[17] Workers will, of course, respond to weekly or annual rather than hourly earnings, but the association among these is sufficiently strong in time of "full employment" for the purpose of this argument.

[18] There are two reasons for this: (1) comparatively high wage costs tend to cause higher unit production costs necessitating higher prices to consumers and (2) low wage rates lead to low levels of (local) effective demand which will be unable to support relatively high consumer prices.

versa. (3) Living costs, especially house rents and prices of locally made products and services, will tend to be relatively high in communities whose population has increased rapidly in the recent past. These rapid increases usually result from a sudden sharp expansion in manufacturing, mining, or commercial construction activity which gives rise to a demand for more workers in service, (residential) construction, and other industries catering to local consumption. These (like other) workers move rather slowly with the result that the prices of housing, services, etc. rise sharply in the short-run. And, as wages tend to be high in an area of rapidly increasing employment, there is an association of high wages with high consumer prices. The rather notorious behavior of prices in communities near a "gold rush" affords a pointed, albeit extreme, example of this process.

Interregional Wage Differences

Table 14.2 shows the regional differences in average straight-time hourly earning existing in manufacturing industries as of April 1954. This

Table 14.2. Straight-Time Average Hourly Earnings of Production Workers in Manufacturing Industries, by Durable and Nondurable, United States and Regions, April 1954; also Ratios of Regions to United States

	United States	North East	South	Middle West	Far West
All manufacturing	$1.68	$1.67	$1.36	$1.80	$1.94
Durable goods	1.78	1.76	1.41	1.86	2.00
Nondurable goods	1.54	1.57	1.32	1.66	1.83

	United States = 100				
All manufacturing	100	99	81	107	115
Durable goods	100	99	79	104	112
Nondurable goods	100	102	86	108	119

Source: "The Distribution of Factory Workers' Earnings, April 1954," Monthly Labor Review, April 1955, Table 3, p. 414.

table confirms the well-known fact that wages in the Far West are highest in the nation, with the Middle West being second, the Northeast third, and the South lowest. These figures, which are confined to manufacturing, probably understate the regional differences in wages which are even greater in agriculture, personal service, etc. However, they indicate the general pattern of interregional differentials in hourly wages.

SOUTH.

The lower wages in the South are related to the fact that urban areas in the South are smaller than elsewhere, and wages tend to be higher in large than in small cities. However, even for cities of any given size, there is a tendency for labor incomes to be lower in the South. In part this is due to the disportionately large number of negroes in the South.[19] However, the low income of the negroes is attributable, not to an "inherent lack of earning power," but to the fact that the Southern labor market can offer jobs to its less skilled applicants only at much lower wages than elsewhere, and negroes are placed at the bottom of the list of job-applicants.

The important causal factor at work, in explaining the inferiority of Southern wages is the relative abundance of labor, as compared with the capital stock, plants and equipment, that generates employment opportunities. The reason so many Southerners work for low wages is that there isn't enough capital to employ all who would like (nonagricultural) employment at Northern wages; the "surplus" labor is therefore compelled either to find employment in low wage, underequipped plants, unable to pay Northern wages, or to remain in agriculture.[20]

This does not mean that all Southern workers use less efficient equipment than Northerners; some Southern plants are as well-equipped as non-Southern and their workers about as productive.[21] The workers who are employed in such plants usually get less than those in the North, but the discrepancy is not so great as the general South-non-South differential.

This may be due to a number of factors, but the influence of unionism should be given special mention. High wage Southern plants are frequently branch plants of Northern firms, and the bargaining pressure exerted elsewhere helps both to unionize Southern plants and to raise their relative wage level.[22] Thus, it is suspected that unionism has exerted a significant and independent effect in raising the wages of large Southern plants relative to Northern wages; however, this hypothesis has not been very carefully explored as yet.[23]

As might be surmised from the preceding remarks, there is considerable wage variation within the South. Some writers have concluded that there is greater wage variation within the South than within any other region;[24] this is consistent with the facts that (1) income varies more

[19] For example, among urban *white* males, 25 to 44 years old, median income in 1944 in the South was greater than in the Northeast for given sizes (in population) of urban areas (except for urban areas of less than 10,000 persons).

[20] This is related to the point (see pp. 360–361) that a smaller part of southern manufacturing employment is in durable goods (which use large amounts of capital per head) than is the case for the country as a whole.

[21] See R. A. Lester "Southern Wage Differentials: Developments, Analysis and Implications," *Southern Economic Journal*, April 1947, pp. 386–394.

[22] Of course, larger firms are more inclined, unionized or not, to pay relatively high wages.

[23] It may strike the reader as odd that we should stress the effect of unionism on wage rates in the South, the least unionized area of the country. However, it is precisely *because* the South is so nonunionized that it may be possible clearly to see the effect (on wages) of what unionism does exist.

[24] C. Glasser, *Wage Differentials*, pp. 111–112 and R. A. Lester, "Diversity

(with population) among urban areas in the South than elsewhere[25] and (2) rural farm-urban income differentials are greatest in the South.[26]

FAR WEST.   The labor market in the Far West, particularly the Pacific Coast, is almost the reverse of that in the South.   In the Far West, there is no surplus farm population anxious to move cityward; its strong demand for labor can be satisfied only by pulling workers from other parts of the country.   This keeps the labor market tight; workers do not need to, and do not, enter low wage industries or occupations; hence, the wage level is kept high.

NORTHEAST.   The northeastern region is rather heterogeneous, consisting both of high and low wage industries and occupations.   The New England area has declining industries, notably textiles, which have left pockets of partially unemployed workers available for low wage employment.   Furthermore, the textile industry itself continues to employ relatively large numbers of workers whose wages are kept down by the keen product market competition of the Southern mills.

Also the New York area has large numbers of workers in the relatively low wage garment trades.   These industries employ large numbers of negroes and Puerto Ricans who comprise a substantial fraction of the workers in the lower part of the hourly wage distribution of the Northeastern region.

MIDDLE WEST.   This area includes the bulk of the high wage durable manufacturing industries.   Although this region's demand for labor is rising, it is not increasing so rapidly as in the Far West.   Furthermore, the flow of Southern labor to this area is greater than to the Pacific Coast. This keeps labor more abundant and, hence, more available for lower wage industries and occupations than in the Far West.

WAGE DISPERSION IN THE UNITED STATES

The factors that produce wage differences, or dispersion, within a country are identical with those that give rise to the various industry, regional, occupational, and other wage differences that we have been discussing. To study wage dispersion, as such, is simply to summarize these other findings in a slightly different way.

Most of the data on wage rates (i.e., straight-time hourly earnings) refer to only one sector of the economy, manufacturing.   In manufacturing there has occurred, since 1941, a steady reduction of the dispersion

---

in North-South Wage Differentials and in Wage Rates Within the South," *Southern Economic Journal,* January 1946, 238-262.

[25] H. P. Miller, *Income of the American People,* John Wiley & Sons, Inc., New York, 1955, Table 18, p. 44.

[26] *Ibid.,* Table 17, p. 43.

of wages about the median.[27] This reflects the increase of wages in the relatively low wage industries, a rise of women's earnings relative to men's, a diminution of the North-South differential, etc.

Going outside the manufacturing industries, we find a gain of agricultural earnings relative to manufacturing occurring between 1940 and 1945. Some of this relative gain was lost in the postwar years, but the ratio of farm to manufacturing wages has not declined to anywhere near its 1940 level.[28]

As of 1954, the dispersion[29] of wages was greatest within the South and least in the Far West. The great interregional differences occurred mainly in the percentage of workers at the lower end of the wage distribution; thus, 28 per cent of all Southern (manufacturing workers) earned less than $1 per hour; but only 2 per cent of those in the Far West; 4 per cent in the Middle West and 8 per cent in the Northeast had such low rates of remuneration.[30]

The remarks made in this section refer to hourly wages only. The distribution of annual incomes is discussed later, in Chapter 18.

OCCUPATIONAL WAGE DIFFERENTIALS AND THEIR DETERMINANTS

In the last section we discussed the wage differentials among industries and areas. Now let us consider the very important matter of occupational differentials.

The Concept of Occupation

Within most firms, the distribution of hourly earnings reflects the occupational classification of its employees. The wages paid in the various occupations vary more or less in accordance with the "degree of skill" required for their practice. "Skill" is not easily defined, but, in a general way, we may speak of it as a personal capacity that can be acquired only by a combination of general education and training; this implies that there

---

[27] Thus the interquartile range diminished, as a percentage of the median, from 75 per cent in January 1941 to 45 per cent in July 1947. (The 10–90 percentile range behaved similarly.) See Frederic Meyers, "Notes on Changes in the Distribution of Manufacturing Wage Earners by Straight-Time Hourly Earnings, 1941–1948," *Review of Economics and Statistics,* November 1950, p. 354, Table 2. Computations, based on "Factory Workers' Earnings," *Bureau of Labor Statistics Bulletin* 1179, Washington, D.C., 1955, Table 2, p. 15, shows that the interquartile range was 40 per cent of the median in April 1954, a further decline from July, 1947.

[28] Reynolds and Taft, *op. cit.,* Table 12-4, p. 328.

[29] As measured by either of the following ratios:

$$\frac{\text{3rd quartile minus 1st quartile}}{\text{median}} \quad \text{or} \quad \frac{\text{90th percentile minus 10th percentile}}{\text{median}}$$

[30] "Factory Workers' Earnings," Table 2.

is a *rough* parallel between the degree of education required by an occupation and its rank in the skill, and wage, hierarchy of a firm.

A worker's occupation is defined by the nature of his job; the industry in which he works is determined by the nature of the product he produces.[31] Occupations may be classified in a number of ways; in this chapter, we shall classify workers into one of three broad categories, skilled, semiskilled, and unskilled.[32] Unskilled jobs are primarily those which require no training and which do not involve the operation of machinery. Sometimes a distinction is drawn between "heavy" and "light" unskilled work;[33] heavy unskilled work involves the application of considerable physical strength and effort and/or the undergoing of considerable discomfort because of the unpleasant surroundings in which the work must be done. "Light" unskilled work consists primarily of janitorial, custodial, and related work. Semiskilled work is mainly machine tending; jobs in this category differ from one another in respect of (1) the length of the learning period, (2) the responsibility of the worker for the care of his machine, (3) the amount of judgment (and responsibility) exercised, (4) the amount of initiative required for satisfactory job performance, etc. Skilled jobs characteristically require longer training, involve greater responsibility for the results of certain operations, and require the exercise of more initiative in attaining these results than semiskilled jobs.[34]

The precise boundary lines that define skilled, semiskilled, and unskilled jobs are not the same at all times and places;[35] they depend upon how widespread the requisite skill for performing a particular job happens to be. For example, in the United States the ability to read may be taken for granted, even among unskilled workers; in Egypt, a job requiring this ability would very likely have to be considered as (at least) semiskilled.

As Table 2.4 (p. 22) shows, about 20 per cent of the American workforce is at present (1950) classified as unskilled; in 1910, 36 per cent were in the unskilled category; in 1920, the corresponding figure was 29.4 per cent; in 1930, it was 28.4 per cent; and in 1940, 25.9 per cent. Be-

[31] This fact has not always been clearly recognized. Many of the earlier decennial censuses hopelessly confused the concepts of occupation and industry.

[32] For other purposes, workers might be classified into the more than 19,000 different occupations distinguished in the United States Employment Service's "Dictionary of Occupational Titles." There is no unique set of occupational classifications that is best for all purposes; investigators have chosen different systems of classification depending upon their problem.

[33] See Harry Ober, "Occupational Wage Differentials, 1907–1947," *Monthly Labor Review,* August 1948, pp. 127–134.

[34] Obviously, there are numerous borderline cases where the classification of a particular occupation as skilled or semiskilled (or semiskilled versus unskilled) will be highly arbitrary.

[35] See A. J. Jaffe and C. D. Stewart, *Manpower Resources and Utilization,* John Wiley & Sons, Inc., New York, 1951, pp. 197–199.

cause a substantial part of this decline was due to (1) the fall in the percentage of persons employed as farm laborers and (2) a shift of the workforce from "heavy" manual labor to semiskilled machine operation, it seems plausible to suppose that the decline in the ratio, unskilled workers/all workers, began well before 1910 (when available records commence). The obverse side of the (relative) decline of the unskilled worker has, in part, been the rise of the semiskilled machine operative; Table 2.4 shows they rose from 14.7 per cent of the workforce in 1910 to 19.8 per cent in 1950.[36]

THE MARGIN FOR SKILL

Why Skilled Workers Earn More

It can be seen from Table 14.3 that skilled workers typically receive (appreciably) more than the semiskilled who, in turn, earn substantially more than the unskilled, especially those doing "light" unskilled work.[37] This is true (both with respect to hourly wages and to annual incomes) in a wide variety of countries.[38]

At bottom, the differential between the wages of skilled and unskilled workers rests upon the fact that a skilled worker is worth more to an employer than an unskilled one. As the individual employer sees it, the favorable wage differential commanded by a skilled worker is a fact of the "labor market." Under ordinary circumstances, either he pays the differential or cannot hire workmen with the appropriate skill. Of course, some high wage firms pay more than the "going" wage rate, but there is usually an effective minimum rate for skilled labor, often the union scale.[39] In the presence of a substantial amount of unemployment, skilled workers will sometimes work below the union scale, but the lowest rates they will accept are usually well above those commanded by unskilled labor. This is true because skilled workmen feel that their skill ought to command a certain premium and usually will refuse to exercise it except at

[36] The category of "skilled workers and foremen" has been subject to two forces working in opposite directions: the trend toward mechanization in production work (especially in manufacturing) has led to replacement of skilled workers by semiskilled, but it has simultaneously increased the need for supervisory personnel (e.g., foremen); the net result is that the percentage of this type of workman in the labor force has changed but little since 1910.

[37] In this section our argument is confined to "manual" workers. In Chapter 17 we discuss white collar employees, the self-employed, etc.

[38] Colin Clark, *The Conditions of Economic Progress,* 2nd edition, Macmillan Company, 1951, p. 460, presents indices of the ratios of the earnings of skilled workers (in various occupations) to those of the unskilled for a number of different countries.

[39] Skilled workers are usually more highly organized than others, and usually have been organized longer.

Table 14.3.   Occupational Wage Differentials in the United States

Column 1	Column 2		
Index of Median Hourly Earnings of Different Skill Groups in Manufacturing, 1945–1947 (Average hourly earnings for janitors and hand truckers = 100)	Median Annual Money Income in 1951 for Certain Major Occupational Groups (by Sex)		
		Male	Female
Skilled	155	Craftsmen, foremen, and kindred workers	$3656	*
Semiskilled (Group 1)	135	Operatives and kindred workers	$3108	$1758
Semiskilled (Group 2)	115	Private household service workers	*	$ 492
Unskilled (Group 1)	115	Service workers except private household	$2474	$1106
Unskilled (Group 2)	100	Laborers except farm and mine	$2281	*
		Farm laborers and foremen	$1057	*

Sources: Column 1 is from Table 1 of H. Ober, "Occupational Wage Differentials, 1907–1947, *Monthly Labor Review*, August 1948, pp. 127–134. The entries refer to the median of the ratios of the average hourly earnings of the relevant occupations to the average hourly earnings of janitors and hand truckers. Semiskilled (Group 1) includes jobs closely akin to skilled jobs, whereas semiskilled (Group 2) refers to the more repetitious forms of machine tending that can be learned easily. Unskilled (Group 1) is "heavy" unskilled labor and (Group 2) is "light" unskilled. Column 2, H. P. Miller, *Income of the American People*, John Wiley & Sons, Inc., New York, 1955, Table 23, p. 51.

* Too few in sample for reliable estimate of median.

what they feel to be a "suitable" wage, even though they may accept unskilled work for less.[40]

This attitude of skilled workers is widely shared by employers and the "general public" and it establishes an effective minimum wage rate (for skilled workers) that is appreciably more than that for the unskilled.[41] But, regardless of how the premium for a particular skill is maintained

---

[40] This statement may require amendment in situations where there is a great deal of prolonged unemployment in the skilled trades, and skilled workmen are compelled to eke out a livelihood as best they can; under such conditions there is no guarantee that (say) a painter or a carpenter may not take a household repair job at unskilled rates. (On this point, see the discussion of the cyclical pattern of occupational differentials, pp. 370–373.)

[41] In the long run, this minimum corresponds to what the relevant class of workers is able to earn, but in the short run its acts to maintain the minimum wage rate (that a given type of worker will accept) close to what he has been accustomed to getting.

from day to day, the premium must exist or in the long-run the skill will disappear. For it will not pay prospective trainees for a particular craft to take the time and trouble to acquire the necessary skill unless there is a premium attached to its exercise. Of course, some workers will wish to learn a particular trade, irrespective of the pecuniary rewards it promises. However, when other trades (requiring equal efforts to learn) offer financial inducements, it would be difficult to attract *many* neophytes to any particular one unless its material rewards were roughly equal to those offered by the others and, therefore, considerably in excess of those earned by unskilled labor.

This fact is often misinterpreted to mean that the practitioners of a particular trade or profession *should,* at particular times and places, earn at least a certain minimum to compensate them for the time and money expended in acquiring their skill. But this is not correct; no one gets a reward because of the time, trouble, and money expended in acquiring a particular skill. Generations of hungry artists and scholars provide ample refutation of any naive belief to the contrary. Comparatively high rewards are paid to skilled workmen because of the value of their skill to hirers and its scarcity relative to the demand for it.

The time and cost of training *do* enter the picture, but only indirectly. They enter as forces which restrict the supply of skilled workers. That is, most workers have not been able to afford the time (and/or have not had the opportunity) to acquire the training requisite to the practice of a skilled trade. This has limited the number of skilled workers and kept their wages high in comparison with those of the unskilled. And where increased educational opportunities have made commonplace skills that were once scarce, the reward for their remuneration has diminished relative to the rewards for unskilled labor, see pp. 373–376.

Variations in the Margin for Skill

It is very likely that the annual earnings of workers (of all occupational grades) respond more readily to labor market conditions than their hourly wage rates. Hourly wage rates respond only sluggishly to imbalance between supply and demand, the response mechanism being impeded and/or thwarted by the combined effects of employer (and union) wage and hiring policies, social minimum wage rates, etc. But changes in annual earnings directly reflect changes in the relation of labor demand and supply; i.e., even if the wage rate for each occupation were fixed by statute, the average annual earnings of the workers in that occupation would rise with increases in the number of man-hours hired and diminish with increases in the number of workers among whom these hours were divided.

Of course, when demand exceeds supply (or vice versa) for an appreciable length of time, and none of the other relevant factors prevent, the wage rates concerned will move. As we have seen, most labor market adjustments to a changing balance between supply and demand involve, in varying degrees, alterations both in wage rates and in employer hiring standards. This is true both of the "markets" for skilled and for unskilled workers. The sharp decline in the (percentage) differential between the wages of the skilled and unskilled workers during both World Wars I and II[42] (see Table 14.4) resulted, in good part, from the fact that the increased demand for skilled workers was met to a relatively large extent by lowering employer hiring standards and to a comparatively small extent by boosting their wage rates, while the increased demand

Table 14.4. Median Ratio of Earnings of Skilled to Unskilled Occupations in Manufacturing, Selected Periods, 1907–1947, for the United States

Average Earnings for Representative
Unskilled Occupations = 100

1907	205
1918–1919	175
1931–1932	180
1937–1940	165
1945–1947	155
1953	137*

Source: H. Ober, "Occupational Wage Differentials, 1907 to 1947," op. cit., Table 2, p. 130.

* From T. P. Kanninen, "Occupational Wage Relationships in Manufacturing," 1952–1953, Monthly Labor Review, November 1953, p. 1171.

for the unskilled (and semiskilled) had to be met to a greater extent by increases in wage rates.

During World War II, the up-grading of skilled workers was, in part, accomplished by recalling previously skilled workers who had been down-graded (to less skilled work) during the 1930's. But, in addition, a large number of previously nonskilled workers were up-graded to skilled classifications for the first time.[43] Quite likely the up-graded

[42] The empirical evidence is well summarized by P. W. Bell, "Cyclical Variations and Trend in Occupational Wage Differentials in American Industry since 1914," Review of Economics and Statistics, November 1951, pp. 329–337; also Harry Ober, "Occupational Wage Differentials In Industry," Chapter 40 and Appendices 113–118 in W. S. Woytinsky, and Associates, Employment and Wages in the United States, The Twentieth Century Fund, New York, 1953.

[43] For example, a study ("Patterns of Mobility of Skilled Workers and Factors Affecting Their Occupational Choice: Six Cities, 1940–1951," made by the Industrial Relations Section of the Massachusetts Institute of Technology) found that, of a sample of 185,357 men who held skilled jobs in 1951, 25 per cent held their first job (in the period 1940–1951) as a nonskilled worker performing a task allied to their present skill. On this matter also see Harold Goldstein, "The Changing Occupational Structure," Monthly Labor Review, Dec. 1947, pp. 654–659.

workers were not so fully skilled and, therefore, not so valuable to an employer as the "old hands." The fact that they received a skilled worker's wage therefore involved an implicit wage increase for the quality of work performed and represented a substantial increase in hourly (money) wages for the workers affected. In some cases, there may have been relatively little differentiation, in terms of hourly rewards, between the "old hands" and the up-graded workers; in others, the wages of experienced skilled workers may have risen "substantially,"[44] but this tendency was outweighed by the large numbers of newcomers who received lower pay and thereby held down the average increase.

The tendency to relax hiring standards affected semiskilled as well as skilled jobs. Indeed, in many cases, the new recruits for semiskilled jobs were quite as adept as the "old hands," and had previously been excluded from these jobs only because they had not been "open." But in addition to this, the demand for machine tenders in aircraft plants, munitions factories, etc. was so intense as to cause a considerable degree of job simplification and relaxation of hiring standards so that these jobs became directly competitive with unskilled jobs.

Hiring standards were also lowered for unskilled jobs, as employers accepted women, negroes, oldsters, and youngsters (for unskilled jobs) more freely than before. However, the fact that semiskilled jobs were also opened (in large numbers) to these same classes of workers caused considerable competition for applicants among semiskilled and unskilled jobs, which tended to narrow wage differentials between them. A further factor tending to raise unskilled, relative to other, wage rates during World Wars I and II was the tendency of the social minimum wage rate to rise (in money terms) more or less proportionately to consumer prices; this exercised a much more direct upward pressure upon unskilled than upon skilled rates.[45]

There is no clear cyclical pattern of occupational wage rate differentials.[46] World Wars I and II were periods of unusually great economic

---

[44] It is suggested that the apparent fall in the "margin for skill" *may* have been much less than it seemed and reflected mainly a reclassification of workers coupled with some genuine "on the job" training. It is impossible (on the basis of available data) to verify this conjecture.

[45] The War Labor Board's permission (in World War II) to raise "substandard" wage rates, despite its general policy of "freezing" higher rates, was one manifestation of this policy. See A. L. Gitlow, *Wage Determination Under National Boards,* Prentice-Hall, Inc., 1953, Chapter 8.

[46] It is quite likely that the *annual income* of skilled workers fluctuates less than that of nonskilled over the course of the business cycle because they are less exposed to the risk of unemployment. M. W. Reder, "The Theory of Occupational Wage Differentials," *American Economic Review,* December 1955, pp. 833–852, especially pp. 850–852. The argument of this section is largely drawn from this article.

activity; in "ordinary" periods of prosperity, without acute labor shortage, there is no marked tendency for occupational wage differentials to contract.   Nor is there any systematic tendency for the "skill margin" to increase even in major depressions; for example, the wage advantage of the skilled increased during the 1920–1921 depression but not in that of 1929–1932.

The widening of the margin for skill in 1920–1921 may well have been accompanied by a tightening of job standards and down-grading of workers, which reversed the process that occurred during World War I. It is also possible that the greater unionization of the skilled workers, and the superior stamina of their unions in the face of depression, assisted them in resisting wage cuts.   But in the depression of 1929–1932, the skill margin did not widen greatly, if at all.[47]

One likely explanation of the different behavior of the skill margin in the 1920–1921 and 1929–1932 depressions is that, during the latter depression, employers attempted to keep the *weekly* income of all their employees from falling below a certain minimum, which caused them, in some cases, to cut the *hourly* rates of the relatively well-paid workers more than those of the less well-paid, in order to prevent part-time employment from reducing the weekly wages of any employee below the desired minimum.[48]   To explain such behavior involves speculation about employer attitudes concerning minimum living standards and the changes in these attitudes that allegedly occurred during the 1920's.   However, this raises broad questions that cannot be discussed here.

Secular Trends in Occupational Differentials

If we consider the past forty to fifty years, it seems fairly clear that there has been a narrowing of the differentials between skilled and unskilled workers; the relevant figures (for the United States) are presented in Table 14.4.   As this table indicates, the trend toward narrower wage differentials has been greatly accelerated since 1940.   This trend has been observed not only in the United States but also in Great Britain[49] and

[47] Bell, *op. cit.*, denies that the skill margin widened at all during the 1929–1932 depression.   Other writers assert that it did; however, there is no denial (by anyone) that the increase in the skill margin was much less in 1929–1932 than in 1920–1921.

[48] Of course, there was a great deal of variation of behavior from one employer to another.   Bell, *op. cit.*, suggests that the most common employer practice was to cut skilled and unskilled rates by an equal percentage and that the employers who cut the unskilled rates proportionately more than the skilled about offset those who did the reverse.

[49] See K. G. J. C. Knowles and D. J. Robertson, "Differences between the Wages of Skilled and Unskilled Workers, 1880–1950," *Bulletin of Oxford Institute of Statistics*, April 1951, pp. 109–127.

elsewhere.[50] It would also appear that the ratio of skilled to unskilled wage rates varies from one country to another in (rough) accord with the level of economic development of the country; i.e., in the advanced, industrialized countries, the ratio (of skilled to unskilled hourly rates) tends to be lower than in more "backward countries."[51]

One important element in the explanation of both the long term trend and the intercountry differences is the varying "quality" of labor supply. That is, over the past half century (or longer) there has occurred a steady increase of that fraction of the labor force that is able to perform more than unskilled tasks. In the United States this has been (partly) due to the general growth of literacy and technical education; trade schools, night schools, technical high schools, vocational training programs, and the enormous program of technical training and opportunity for experience given by the Armed Services (during and since World War II) have all served to minimize the share of the population that can offer only untrained services to an employer. The restriction on immigration since the early 1920's has worked in the same direction.

So much for supply factors; now let us consider demand conditions. In the United States, technical progress has tended to reduce the skill difference between more and less skilled jobs. To an increasing degree, all jobs have come to involve cooperating with a highly specialized machine or machines; each job requires some special, but fairly brief, training. Hence, the distinction between workers is no longer one of past training but of aptitude for further training. And in this respect, Americans are becoming increasingly homogeneous due to more equalized educational opportunities. Therefore, the ability to substitute less for more skilled workers has increased, and the labor market advantage of the skilled has correspondingly diminished. Of course, the reduction in skill requirements is not everywhere the same; in some cases, the need for prolonged training is as great as ever; in others, it has completely disappeared. However, the general tendency is as indicated.

This argument does not imply that the relative *hourly* wage rates of skilled, semiskilled, and unskilled workers have responded in any prompt mechanical way to the pressure of slow-acting economic forces. For long stretches of time, employer and/or union wage policy holds traditional wage differentials inviolate. Then, major shifts in labor market condi-

[50] D. W. Oxnam, "The Relation of Unskilled to Skilled Wage Rates in Australia," Economic Record, June 1950, pp. 112–118; A. G. B. Fisher, "Education and Relative Wage Rates," *International Labor Review,* June 1932, pp. 742–764; Colin Clark, *op. cit.,* pp. 458 *et seq.* At present, the ratio of the hourly earnings of skilled to those unskilled workmen seems greater in the United States (of the order of 3 to 2) than in Great Britain, Australia, or Scandinavia (where the differential is of the order of 5 to 4).

[51] Colin Clark, *op. cit.,* pp. 458 et seq. Also M. W. Reder, *op. cit.*

tions (e.g., a war or major depression) cause adjustments whose general effect has been, for reasons already indicated to reduce the skill margin.

It has been argued by a number of writers that union wage policy has been a factor in the secular narrowing of occupational wage differentials, especially that occurring since 1940. For example, it has been argued that the tendency of industrial unions to insist upon equal cents per hour increases for all grades of workers has been a major cause of the reduction of occupational differentials.[52]

There is no reason to doubt that the form of union demands has frequently influenced the relative size of the increases granted to various occupations at given times, and it is likely that union politics may influence the nature of union demands.[53] However, it is doubtful that this could have been a major factor since 1940. For, during this period, employers have frequently raised workers' hourly wages above union scales in order to retain good workmen in a tight labor market. Consequently, had the decline in the margin for skill been inconsistent with the relative values of an hour of the various kinds of labor to employers, relative (straight-time) *hourly-earnings,* though not necessarily wage scales, would have reflected this fact. That relative hourly earnings of skilled workers have declined, *in a period of full employment,* is, therefore, due not to union policy but to pressures of the labor market transmitted through the medium of union demands. Union wage objectives, on the whole, were consistent with this tendency; but even if it had not been consistent, it is doubtful that the unions could have halted this tendency.[54]

This argument is applicable only to situations in which full employment is keeping average (straight-time) hourly earnings of all grades of workers at or above the union scale. It is not relevant to a situation in which there are idle workers at all skill levels and union scales are maintaining floors under the hourly earnings of all groups. In such situations, if union rates determine the straight-time earnings for the various skill groups, i.e., if there are no "serious" violations of union minima, then alterations in union wage policy concerning skill margins will cause changes in them.

[52] For example, Ross and Goldner, "Forces Affecting the Interindustry Wage Structure," *Quarterly Journal of Economics,* May 1950, pp. 263–266, or H. A. Turner, "Trade Unions, Differentials, and the Levelling of Wages," *The Manchester School,* September 1952, pp. 227–282.

Knowles and Robertson, *op. cit.,* argue that (in Great Britain) wage increases, in time of inflation, tend to be granted in the form of absolute additions to wages that are the same for all occupations and hence tend to reduce percentage differentials. (In the United States, cost of living adjustments tend to involve equal *percentage* increases for all occupational grades.)

[53] Turner, *op. cit.*

[54] This argument is stated more fully in Reder, *op. cit.*

Thus, the decline in the skill margin that occurred between 1933 and 1940 may very well have been caused, in part, by union policy. It is also very likely that the increase (during this period) in the social minimum wage rate, promoted by various New Deal measures (see p. 407), forced up the lowest, unskilled, wage rates but did not have any substantial effect upon the higher wages of the more skilled.

DISCUSSION QUESTIONS

1. "Southern workers get less than others because they are less productive and, therefore, deserve less." Consider the pros and cons of this statement.

2. It is generally true that the level of wages in a small town varies with the level of wages in nearby agriculture. Do you think that, because of this, improving income levels in Southern agriculture would raise the wage level in Southern industry?

3. What effect would permitting free immigration of Mexicans to California have upon the interregional pattern of wage differentials?

4. (a) How have changing conditions of labor supply caused a long-run decline in the wage differential between skilled and unskilled workers?

(b) How, if at all, have union wage policies affected this differential?

Suggested Readings

In addition to the references at the end of Chapters 11 to 13, most of which are relevant here, the reader may consult the following:

Belloc, Nedra, *Wages in California,* University of California Press, Berkeley and Los Angeles, 1948.

Glasser, Carrie, *Wage Differentials,* Columbia University Press, New York, 1940.

Gordon, M. S., *Employment Expansion and Population Growth, the California Experience, 1900–1950,* University of California Press, Berkeley, and Los Angeles, 1954.

Lester, R. A., "Southern Wage Differentials: Developments, Analysis, and Implications," *Southern Economic Journal,* April 1947, pp. 386–394. (This source has a good bibliography for further readings.)

Reder, M. W., "The Theory of Occupational Wage Differentials," *American Economic Review,* December 1955, pp. 833–852.

Reynolds, L. G., and C. H. Taft, *The Evolution of Wage Structure,* Yale University Press, New Haven, 1956, Chapters 1, 12 and 13.

Sufrin, S. C., A. W. Swinyard, and F. M. Stephenson, "The North-South Differential —A Different View," *Southern Economic Journal,* October 1948, pp. 184–190.

Woytinsky, W. S. and Associates, "Employment and Wages in the United States." The Twentieth Century Fund, New York, 1953, Chapters 39, 40, 41, and 44.

15

Wage Setting within the Firm: Job Evaluation and Incentive Systems

In this chapter, we shall explain the process by which individual employers set the wage rates on the various jobs within their firms. The process they use seems far removed from the pressures of unions and labor markets that we have been discussing. Therefore, the description of this process is something of a digression. However, as we shall see, the results of a formalized wage setting process must be reasonably consistent with the demands of unions and the requirements of the labor market. Nevertheless, the wage setting procedure is of some economic significance. Later in the chapter, we shall discuss the operation and consequences of systems of incentive payment.

INTRAFIRM WAGE DIFFERENTIALS AND FORMALIZED WAGE SETTING

Nature and Purpose of Formalized Wage Setting

In the previous section, we considered the economic forces that mold occupational wage differentials. But, no matter how powerful these economic forces, they are relatively slow acting and cannot serve as a guide to the day-to-day wage decisions that management (and unions) must make concerning the interrelation among the wage rates on different jobs. Not only are these decisions extremely complicated, but they are of great concern to the workers involved. For the individual worker, these decisions determine his income and status relative to his fellows. Consequently, it is not surprising that they should judge these decisions in terms of "equity and fairness," rather than as a result of impersonal economic forces.[1]

What fairness implies in any specific case may often be debated, but there do seem to be standards of fairness that all parties regard as rele-

[1] The relation between ethical and market criteria in wage-setting is considered on pp. 386–388.

vant, even though they may disagree as to their application in any given instance. "Fairness" usually implies (1) the maintenance of generally accepted wage practices and (2) that similarly situated persons be treated similarly (unless there is "good reason" to the contrary). These two aspects of fairness in wage-setting (and other aspects of labor-management relations) are not always consistent, and their implications for any specific situation are not clear, but one (or both) of them is likely to be cited in any debate over a particular decision concerning relative wage rates within a firm.

In recent years, wage-setting has become greatly formalized;[2] the criteria that are used to determine the wage rates to be paid for particular jobs have been made explicit and reduced to formulas so that they may be more conveniently *justified* to the individual worker or his (union) representative. The progress of unionization has frequently accelerated the adoption of these formal procedures.[3] Prior to unionization (or the threat thereof), management tended to set wages for different jobs in an unsystematic way. Sometimes management attempted to adhere to "rough and ready" criteria of justice; sometimes it permitted the process to be flavored by personal favoritism and nepotism. When shortages of particular kinds of labor required, the wages of scarce grades were (presumably) raised relative to those paid the others. But such shortages were of rather infrequent occurrence and consequently, for long intervals, the "internal" wage structure of most firms was determined by a mixture of unsystematized precedent and sheer caprice.[4]

This type of wage "policy" is now far less frequent than it was (in the United States) prior to 1935. Unionization and associated phenomena

[2] A formalized wage-setting process is one in which specific jobs or occupations are assigned wage rates that are independent of the identity of the person holding the job.

[3] In 1945–1946, about 3 out of 4 manufacturing establishments covered in an extensive survey (of 56 industries, employing almost half of all manufacturing workers in the country, made by the Bureau of Labor Statistics) set wages for *jobs,* as distinguished from setting them for individuals; i.e., they had some form of job evaluation. (The survey did not cover firms with less than 8 employees and is also biased toward large establishments and establishments located in large cities.) The industries where one is most likely to find job evaluation programs in operation are characterized by large firms; they tend to use incentive systems, rather than paying by time (see pp. 388–399) and tend to be unionized. Cf. L. M. David, "Manufacturing Industries: Wage Rate Structure, 1945–1946," *Monthly Labor Review,* March 1948, pp. 281–282. To anticipate the later argument, it is primarily the large, high wage firms that use formal wage-setting procedures; these firms also tend to be somewhat more unionized than most firms.

[4] See, for example, R. A. Lester, *Company Wage Policies,* Industrial Relations Department, Department of Economics and Social Science, Princeton University, Princeton, N.J., 1948, pp. 20–22.

have made it impossible for management to defend its policies (as it once did) by telling its workers that "they have the right to quit if they find arrangements unsatisfactory"; if dissatisfied, unionized workers need not quit. They can strike, and nonunion workers can join a union.[5] The necessity for justifying wage policies to union representatives and/or equity-conscious workers has compelled management to seek appropriate and defensible standards for wage-setting. The search for these standards has caused management critically to examine its own practices and, often for the first time, to adopt coherent wage and personnel policies.

Unionization has been only one of a number of interrelated forces working towards the improvement and codification of management wage policies. For example, the trend toward "scientific management" has also contributed a considerable impetus to the growth of formalized wage-setting. But whatever the cause, in the last quarter century or so, employers have become increasingly concerned with "selling the company" to the employees," developing company loyalty, reducing labor turnover, etc. These objectives have required that the company's policies on wage-setting (and personnel matters) be made defensible to its employees and their unions.[6]

The policies by which management determines the wage rate it sets on each job must be such that they imply wage rates that can be defended as "fair" in comparison with (1) the wage rates paid by other employers and (2) the wage rates paid for other jobs in the same firm. The implications of equity as regards the wage policies of different firms have been considered above (pp. 336–338) and need to be given only incidental consideration here. In this section we shall be solely concerned with questions related to achieving equity within the wage structure of a given firm.

---

[5] The difference between the attitude of unionized and nonunionized workers, in this respect, can be easily exaggerated. However, in a community where workers are mainly nonunionized, the wage earner is likely to be more timid about demanding "justice" than in a community where unionization is widespread. It is the degree of unionization in a community that affects worker attitudes in a given establishment rather than the presence or absence of a union in the establishment itself.

[6] Another factor which has greatly accelerated the adoption of job evaluation plans is the fact that, during World War II, the War Labor Board permitted wage increases in order to correct intraplant inequities that would not otherwise have been permitted under the "wage freeze" then existing (see pp. 412–413). (The Board would usually rule that, if a job rate was below the level implied by a formal job evaluation plan, the job rate was inequitably low.) As the plan could usually be designed to imply numerous increases, employers and unions (both anxious to raise wages although for different reasons) both accepted these plans in a large number of cases. In a number of instances, war-born plans had to be overhauled or scrapped in the postwar period, but there is no doubt that many of the "war-babies" have survived in one form or another.

The Process of "Formalized" Wage-Setting

Consider the situation of a firm that is attempting, for the first time, to establish a "fair" internal wage structure. To do this, it must (1) inventory the various jobs that it offers, describing each one; (2) it must establish a system of evaluating the various jobs relative to one another so that it can rank them in some sort of hierarchy; and (3) it must then decide upon a "wage curve" determining the wage rate (or rates) corresponding to different positions in the job hierarchy. As we shall see, it is very important that these three processes should be closely integrated.

The first of the above tasks is usually referred to as "job description" or "job analysis." A complete job description should specify what the worker does, indicate the degree of skill and training required, the responsibility involved, the physical effort required, etc.

"Job evaluation," as the term suggests, involves ranking jobs for the purpose of deciding the wages that should be paid for each. Many job evaluation plans involve nothing more than ranking the various jobs. Still others set up a number of job classes (like the U.S. Civil Service) and place all jobs in one or another of these classes. However, there are more complicated systems; many job evaluation systems involve the selection of a limited number of job characteristics (called elements or factors) that are required, to a greater or less degree, by all jobs under evaluation. The factors most frequently listed are: education, experience, physical effort required, responsibility for work or safety of others, working conditions, and hazards of work. Each job is given a point score on account of each factor. The factors are then weighted to determine their relative influence in determining the job's final score. Multiplying the score on each factor by the weight of the factor and summing the products gives the job's total score. The company's jobs are then arrayed in order of their scores, with higher ranking jobs being paid more than lower ranking.

From this job array the company constructs its "wage curve"; this curve is constructed by improvising (see below) wage rates for certain jobs, called "key" jobs, thereby establishing certain points on the curve, and then interpolating between the points. Such a "wage curve" is represented by PP_1 in Figure 15.1. On the horizontal axis of this figure is measured the number of points attached to various jobs, and the vertical axis measures the (hourly) wage rate paid for these jobs. The curve is determined by setting the wage rates (AK, BL, and MC) for (say) three key jobs which have OA, OB, and OC points, respectively; other jobs having intermediate numbers of points are assigned rates between those mentioned.[7] Thus a job having OA_1 points (less than OB but more than

---

[7] In practice, the number of key jobs will usually be much larger than three and therefore no simple curve will pass through all of them. The curve must therefore be a statistical "fit" of some kind.

OA) will be paid a rate of A_1R (less than BL but greater than AK). Drawing the curve between the points K, L, and M (and extending it beyond) poses a set of problems that must be solved in the light of "equitable considerations."

The rates on the key jobs are usually set by comparison with rates on similar jobs in other plants in the same community; that is, the jobs used for setting "key" wage rates are usually chosen so as to be (roughly) comparable as between different plants.   A firm can thus relate its wage rates to those of other firms.   This establishes "equitable relations" among different plants.

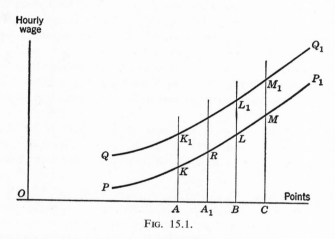

Fig. 15.1.

In practice, there is often a range of rates, rather than a single rate, attached to each job;[8] thus, in Figure 15.1, PP_1 may be thought of as indicating the lower limit to the rate range for each job, and QQ_1 the upper. Between these limits, depending upon merit, seniority, and other factors, the actual rate for each worker will be set (see pp. 385–388.   Contrary to the suggestion of Figure 15.1, there will never, in practice, be a rate (or range of rates) for each number of points; instead those jobs whose point totals lie within certain (point) ranges are grouped into labor "grades," each grade having its own rate (or range of rates) with intragrade point differences ignored.[9]

[8] The Bureau of Labor Statistics survey in 1945–1946 (see note 28) found that about 60 per cent of the firms using formalized wage-setting procedures used single rates, while the others used rate ranges.

[9] The subject of "job evaluation" has developed a whole literature of its own to which the above discussion is at best an introduction.   The interested reader may consult any of the following: *The A.M.A. Handbook of Wage and Salary Administration*, edited by M. J. Dooker and Vivienne Marquis, American Management Association, New York, 1950; J. L. Otis and R. Lenkart, *Job Evaluation*, Prentice-Hall, Inc., 1948; C. W. Lytle, *Job Evaluation Methods*, Ronald Press, 1946;

The Problems of Operating a System of Job Evaluation

UNION ATTITUDES. Union spokesmen usually express a great dislike for "job evaluation."[10] However, their opposition is really directed at the more complicated point or factor comparison systems, than at job evaluation as such. Indeed, one prominent union spokesman,[11] in the midst of a scathing attack upon job evaluation plans, admits (in effect) that collective bargaining procedures (like those of job evaluation) are aimed at establishing job rates so as to eliminate caprice, personal favoritism, and sheer chance in setting the wage rates paid any given person. Unions, almost invariably, desire a *job rate structure,* as distinguished from the employer setting rates for individual workers. However, unions want this rate structure be established by means of a simple ranking of jobs or, at most, by a system of job classification, and not by one of the more complicated, point-factor systems. Naturally, they desire that whatever system is adopted should operate within the process of collective bargaining, and that its results should always be subject to further negotiation.

The hostile attitude of unions toward job evaluation is, in part, simply a mistrust of complicated ideas, especially those originating with management. A basic fear is that complicated job evaluation plans will be

---

R. W. Ells, *Salary and Wage Administration,* McGraw-Hill Book Company, Inc., New York, 1945; J. W. Riegel, *Wage Determination,* University of Michigan, Bureau of Industrial Relations, 1937, William Gomberg, *A Trade Union Analysis of Time Study,* 2nd edition, Prentice-Hall, Inc., 1955. For good brief treatments, see Paul Pigors and C. A. Myers, *Personnel Administration,* McGraw-Hill Book Company, Inc., 1947, pp. 219–230; Dale Yoder, *Personnel Principles and Policies,* Prentice-Hall, Inc., 1952, pp. 433–444; or E. R. Livernash, "Job Evaluation," Chapter 35 in W. S. Woytinsky and Associates, *Employment and Wages in the United States.*

[10] Helen Baker and J. M. True, *The Operation of Job Evaluation Plans,* Princeton University Press, Princeton, N.J., 1947, Chapter VII, obtained opinions from 20 local or international union officers representing nine major unions, serving as bargaining agents with 33 of the companies whose job evaluation plans were surveyed. In all but three cases, the officers expressed dissatisfaction with the operation of the plans. A few international union officers expressed some hope that job evaluation plans might prove helpful in setting wage rates, but the general opinion was one of distrust and hostility. E. R. Livernash in Woytinsky and Associates, *op. cit.,* Table 189, p. 432, cites the results of a survey of union leaders' attitudes toward job evaluation plans in which the overwhelming majority of leaders expressing an opinion (and a slight majority of all leaders asked) opposed such plans. See also S. A. Levitan, "Union Attitudes toward Job Evaluation and In-grade Progression," *Industrial and Labor Relations Review,* January 1951, pp. 268–274.

[11] Solomon Barkin, "Wage Determination: Trick of Technique," *Labor and Nation,* June–July 1946, pp. 25 et seq. Also see Barkin's, "A Rejoinder to William Gomberg," *Labor and Nation,* November-December 1946, pp. 54 et seq.

difficult for local union officers to understand and that, in consequence, the union will be placed at a disadvantage in negotiations concerning them.[12] Another, and related, fear concerns the possibility that a job evaluation plan could be invoked to prevent an adjustment of relative wage rates that the membership might demand or to force an adjustment that the membership might bitterly oppose. Furthermore, unions have sometimes been able to use worker opposition to a job evaluation plan as an effective argument for securing members.[13] Consequently, they are reluctant to commit themselves to accepting the results of a plan (with the implied responsibility of "selling" them to the membership) when it might not be politic to do so; this is especially important where a rival union might make political capital of employee discontent with the job evaluation system. In short, most union leaders are afraid to tie their hands in the matter of intracompany wage structure for fear that this might somehow work to the union's disadvantage.[14] This attitude is especially prevalent among new and insecure unions.

A more specific objection offered by some union leaders is that the re-evaluation of jobs incident to increased mechanization tends to lead to a reduction in the (relative) value of the jobs affected at the same time as their man-hour productivity increases.[15] Such objections might seem ill-founded as (1) the wage rates of the present job holders are not affected and (2) the eventual lowering of the rates on particular jobs releases funds for increasing the general wage level of the firm. However, these arguments do not appear very persuasive to union leaders because the first provision does not prevent those workers (whose jobs have been "devalued") from feeling resentful because the importance of their jobs and their self-esteem has been reduced. Union leaders probably sympathize, subjectively, with this attitude and, in any case, do not wish to be put in the position of having to combat it.

The contention that "job evaluation merely distributes the wage bill without altering its size," has been challenged.[16] For example, when the installation of improved machinery lowers a job's value under a given job evaluation system, this "frees funds" for raising the firm's general wage level, but it does not guarantee that they will be used for this purpose.

---

[12] See Baker and True, *op. cit.,* p. 75.

[13] For an example, see Baker and True, *op. cit.,* pp. 102–107.

[14] Barkin, *op. cit.,* points out that adhering to a job evaluation plan might involve the union in accepting lower wage rates for its members in certain jobs than the "prevailing" rates in the given localities.

[15] Barkin, *op. cit.* Also Clark Kerr and L. H. Fisher, "Effect of Environment and Administration on Job Evaluation," *Harvard Business Review,* May 1950, pp. 77–96. (Reprint No. 21 of the Institute of Industrial Relations, University of California, Berkeley).

[16] Barkin, *op. cit.*

Whether or not they are so used depends upon all the factors that affect the relation of a firm's ability to pay and its average wage rate. It is certainly not clear, a priori, that in the absence of explicit policy and/or union pressure employers will hand back, in the form of general wage increases, all that is saved through job evaluation combined with mechanization.

For one or another of the aforementioned reasons, most unions are unwilling to cooperate in, or assume responsibility for, the operation of job evaluation plans. Usually a union will tolerate such plans as a device which management is free to use if it wishes but whose implications are not binding and which they may resist whenever they see fit.

However, there are a few cases in which unions have cooperated with management in establishing a system of job evaluation or classification. The most famous of these is the job classification plan jointly sponsored by the U. S. Steel Corporation and the United Steelworkers; the union has encouraged the adoption of similar plans throughout the steel industry and, according to the research director of the union, the plan has eliminated many current and prospective rate grievances.[17] Another example of joint union-management sponsorship (of job evaluation) is found in the West Coast paper and pulp industry;[18] the New York local of the American Newspaper Guild has also participated in a job evaluation plan.[19] The Commercial Telegraphers Union took the initiative of urging a job evaluation plan upon the Western Union Co. (which the company has adopted) in order to eliminate wage inequities among different localities.

The advantages of a system of job evaluation to a *secure* union are considerable. Like management, unions must sometimes defend relative wage rates on different jobs to their members, some of whom may feel keenly that they are being wronged. The existence of a job evaluation plan, especially if it has been agreed to by the union and the membership, can be very useful in preparing such defenses. A job evaluation plan can also be useful to a union in deciding which member complaints to resist and which to support in negotiation with the employer.

But these remarks apply only to secure, well-entrenched unions. The leaders of new unions or unions subject to external rivalry or internal wrangling are not free to do as they see fit but are subject to the pressures engendered by the conflicting demands of their membership, and the need to maintain the allegiance of as many members as possible. These pressures become most acute in the face of overt competition from rival unions. For example, in the Southern California aircraft industry, there was

[17] See Levitan, *op. cit.*, p. 270.
[18] Baker and True, *op. cit.*, p. 103.
[19] Levitan, *op. cit.*, p. 270.

keen rivalry, between the International Association of Machinists and the United Auto Workers, for additional membership. As Kerr and Fisher put it, "The unions were fighting for members all the time. One method of attracting them was evidence of ability to make individual gains for them under the plan, as against nonmembers. Over 4,000 wage-rate grievances were filed at Lockheed in a single year. That this reflected the struggle for members is indicated by the fact that at Boeing, where the union shop guaranteed members, the plan was not subject to the same assault."[20]

One major purpose of job evaluation is to make the wage rates paid individual workers wholly dependent upon the jobs they hold, thus eliminating the possibility of personal favoritism. But to the extent that the worker's reward is made to depend solely upon the job he holds, his incentive to perform well at the job is minimized. In order to retain some of its former freedom to reward good performance, many firms use the latitude permitted by rate ranges to grant "merit" increases. However, the principle of increases for merit only is resisted (or sabotaged) by unions who demand that promotion through rate ranges should be more or less automatic and (in effect) be rewards for length of service. In the event of disagreement between worker and supervisor concerning the satisfactoriness of worker performance, the dispute becomes subject to the grievance procedure with the result that worker progress through rate ranges often becomes more or less automatic, registering length of service rather than unusual merit.

Indeed, the wider the range of wage rates applicable to a single job, and the more discretion management has in deciding which rate to pay in individual cases, the less important is the role played by job evaluation. For then the possibility of favortism that job evaluation purports to eliminate from the wage-setting process, re-enters via "merit raises." This is not to deny the need for rewarding merit but to indicate the problems involved in doing it under a system of job evaluation.

At bottom the antagonism of unions toward job evaluation systems is due to their "mechanical" character. A union must always be able to fight for the demands of politically important segments of its membership; otherwise it courts internal rebellion. But there is no guarantee that the dictates of job evaluation will be compatible with the balance of political power within the union. Therefore, a union must be in a position to resist, at least through the grievance machinery, unpopular consequences of job evaluation.

Because of this, it is necessary to recognize that the equitable imperatives (see pp. 336–338) to which union leaders must bow act as external constraints upon a system of job evaluation. Few managements are pre-

<hr>

[20] Kerr and Fisher, *op. cit.*, p. 86.

pared to undergo prolonged strikes *solely* to preserve inviolate a system of job evaluation.

JOB EVALUATION VERSUS LABOR MARKET. It should be clear that a labor market may yield evaluations of the worth of particular jobs quite divergent from those produced by a job evaluation system.

That conflicts between labor market valuations of jobs, and those produced by systems of job evaluation are not more frequent is (partly) due to the fact that market considerations indirectly enter the job evaluation process. They do this in two ways: (1) Those qualities that add to the value of a job (under a job evaluation system) tend to be similar to those that give a job relatively high market value. Jobs requiring time-consuming training, unusual dexterity, strength, or intelligence tend to acquire both high point values under job evaluation and wage premiums in a labor market. (2) The weights attached to particular job factors in the evaluation process tend to be chosen so as to yield comparatively high point values for those types of workers to whom the firm must pay relatively high wages, as a condition of securing and retaining their services.

However, the reader must not suppose that job evaluation plans are aimed at producing results identical with those of a market, and that failure to do so implies inadequacy in the plan. In the first place, filling certain "high wage" jobs on the basis of some combination of merit and seniority, and "overpaying" them (relative to a market valuation), may be a device useful in reducing labor turnover.[21] Even more important is the fact that job evaluation is an administrative device designed to dispense equity rather than minimize costs; in principle, the purpose of job evaluation is to distribute a given wage bill "properly," i.e., equitably, but not to reduce it. (The gains to the employer are expected to be by-products of improved employee morale rather than a lower wage bill.)

When inconsistency between job evaluation and the demands of the labor market arises, employers use various expedients to conform to job evaluation criteria while getting the labor they need. One such expedient is to subcontract certain kinds of work; another is to shift "factor weights"; re-evaluation of jobs is a third device; etc. When all else fails, "exceptions" are made; i.e., the plan is violated because of the requirements of the labor market.[22]

When job evaluation plans are initiated, they are usually so constructed as to be more or less compatible with the "realities" of labor market and union wage pressures, as they exist at the time. Conflicts arise when there is a change in the wage structure required to satisfy these pressures.

---

[21] Unions often prefer such a method of recruitment for "good" jobs, as it tends to favor older and permanent workers who tend to be more union-conscious, and influential (in the union) than others.

[22] The classic discussion of this is Kerr and Fisher, *op. cit.*

It is a truism to note that successful operation of a system of job evaluation requires constant adjustment of relative job rates. Changes in the nature of products and/or methods of production create new jobs (which must be fitted into the evaluation system) and alter the nature and importance of old ones, necessitating rate revisions.[23]

In other words, the requirements of the labor market make it necessary that a system of job evaluation contain important elements of flexibility. But, the more flexible the plan, the less precise are its implications and the more opportunity there is for the exercise of judgment, discretion, and favoritism (and/or accusations thereof) by wage setters. Consequently, flexibility tends to defeat the main advantage of job evaluation, the mechanical dispensation of equity.[24] Permitting too many exceptional rates to exist clearly destroys the value of the plan; for arguments concerning specific job rates then degenerate into disputes as to whether or not the plan is applicable. But to permit no exceptions may create impossible difficulties in recruiting labor. Analogous questions arise concerning the number and variety of job titles, job grades, etc. Successful navigation among these shoals requires both wise administration and good luck.

Because the requirements of successful labor recruitment can be so disturbing to the operation of a system of job evaluation, it will obviously operate more successfully when these requirements are not effective constraints upon a firm's wage policy. Thus it seems likely that high wage firms (all of those whose wage rates are more than adequate to attract the needed quantities and kinds of labor) will be less troubled than others by conflict between the pressures of the labor market and the requirements of job evaluation. It is also true that conflict between job evaluation and market criteria are less likely to emerge in conditions of substantial unemployment[25] when alternative job opportunities are scarce, than when there is a strong demand for the relevant types of labor.

The reader should not conclude from this discussion that job evaluation systems are either valueless or unworkable. The limitations imposed upon such plans by external pressures (of labor markets and unions) are important and must be taken into account. Yet, within a given firm that

[23] It is worth noting that, customarily, downward rate revisions do not apply to the current job holders and affect only new workers on a given job; this is to minimize opposition to rate reductions. But even so, down-grading the job rates can cause great resentment among the holders of "devalued" jobs who feel that their status has been lowered by depreciating the value of their jobs. Cf. Baker and True, *op. cit.*, pp. 103–104.

[24] This is not to deny that job evaluation facilities standardization and central control over hiring and personnel.

[25] When the wage rates paid by most firms in the business sector of the economy exceed the minimum necessary for recruitment.

is insulated from immediate external pressures, such a plan is often a useful administrative device.   However, the primary concern of this book is with the "external pressures" that affect evaluation plans, not with the plans themselves.

Economics and Ethics in Wage Setting

Most people feel that ethical considerations should play an important role in determining relative wages.   Our analysis has, in large part, aimed at showing how limited is the role that ethics can play.   However, this role is not nonexistent; to an increasing degree, mature and older workers are becoming bound to their present employers because their accumulated seniority and pension rights make job changing extremely costly.   Therefore, so long as the wage rates of such workers are placed above some lower limit, the employer may set them where he chooses without fear that they (these workers) will quit.   (The employer can, if he chooses, take advantage of this situation by reducing the wage premium placed upon jobs requiring experience within the firm.)   However, it is manifestly unfair that he should take advantage of this situation; most employers do not wish to take such advantage and, even if they did, unions would prevent them from doing so.

But once jobs are removed from the "test of the market," determination of their appropriate relative wage rates becomes a matter of equity and here, formalized wage setting techniques acquire a genuine economic function.

INCENTIVE SYSTEMS

One aspect of formalized wage-setting is job evaluation; another, and important one, is the establishment of incentive systems.   The purpose of job evaluation is to relate the wages paid for various jobs to the places occupied by those jobs in some hierarchy of "worthiness."   The purpose of an incentive system is to relate the hourly or weekly wage paid to a worker on a given job, to his performance, measured by his output, on that job.   As we shall see, an incentive system and a job evaluation plan can come into conflict.

The Rationale of Incentive Systems

Giving wage earners an incentive to work diligently has always been a major problem for employers.   Historically, employers have attempted to solve this problem both by close supervision and by use of incentive methods of payment; some employers chose one method and some the other.   However, in the past two or three decades, there has been a strong trend toward adoption of the techniques of "scientific management"[26]

---

[26] "Scientific management" refers to the whole panoply of procedures by means of which costs are minimized through the analysis and improvement of techniques of

which include a whole array of systems of "incentive payments." It is no accident that firms having job evaluation also tend to employ incentive systems; both techniques (in their modern forms) are the fruit of "scientific management."

In its most rudimentary form, a system of incentive payments involves nothing more than setting a payment per unit of output and letting a worker's weekly wage equal the number of units produced (per week) multiplied by the payment per unit. This is payment by the "piece" and the wage per unit of output is called the "piece rate." The piece rate has had a long history; it has been used in a number of industries but, in the 19th century, was most famous in textile and clothing manufacturing.[27]

There is, however, at least one important difference between the operation of the old "piece rate" system, and modern incentive systems. The latter involve a study of the time necessary to produce a unit of output; that is, the payment per unit of output is not established until an estimate has been made of the time needed for an "average worker" under "average conditions" to produce an output unit. Under the old piece rate system, rates were set in an arbitrary manner, based on crude and untested assumptions of worker productivity.

There are a large number of different incentive systems in current use, but most of them are similar to one another (or some combination) of those we shall now describe. The most common incentive systems are modified and elaborated piece work systems, combined with a guarantee of minimum earnings. The differences among them refer to the method by which the piece rate is determined, and its relation to output; thus, under one plan (the Halsey Plan), a product is assigned a "normal" time for production and the worker is guaranteed a certain minimum hourly wage. If the worker produces more units (per week) than the "normal" amount, he is paid a "bonus" of 50 per cent of his guaranteed time rate for time saved. Thus, if a worker's guaranteed wage were $2.00 per hour and the "normal" time for one unit of output were an hour, his guaranteed wage for a 40 hour week would be $80.00. But, if he produced 50 units in a 40 hour week, then he would have produced 1¼ pieces per hour, implying that he worked at a rate of ⅘ hours per unit, thereby "saving" ⅕ of an hour per piece. Thus he would have saved 10 hours of work per week (50 units per week times ⅕ hours per piece). As his hourly rate is $2.00, the total savings would be $20.00, of which he would

---

production.   "Scientific management," in the United States, stems from the teachings of F. W. Taylor whose principal work was *The Principles of Scientific Management*, Harper and Brothers, New York, 1911.   Scientific management emphasizes the importance of incentive methods.

[27] It is worth noting that the famous "putting out" system, under which a manufacturer would consign cloth or material to be worked upon at home, required payment by the piece as workers worked only in their spare time and, since they worked at home, could not be supervised or otherwise placed under employer discipline.

get ½ or $10.00; this is added to his minimum wage, bringing his weekly earnings to $90.00.[28] There are other and more complicated systems which we shall not attempt to discuss here.[29]

The straight piece rate system is described by line A in Fig. 15.2; it yields the same wage rate per unit of output irrespective of how much is produced. The slope of OA is the piece rate. The effect of a minimum daily guarantee is indicated by the "curve," WDB; that is, there is a guaranteed daily wage of OW and the daily "standard" output is OR. For daily output in excess of OR, incentive pay is earned at a piece rate, given by the slope of BD. Yet another incentive system might be represented by curve C, where the piece rate diminishes at high levels of output.

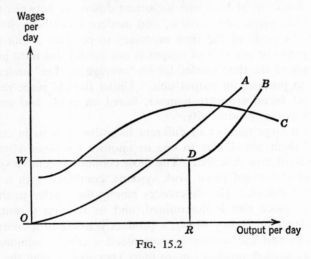

Fig. 15.2

In principle, an incentive system could be designed to yield any desired relation between the piece rate and the level of daily output.

The principal advantage that is claimed for incentive systems is that they induce workers to produce as much as they are able in order to earn as great a weekly wage as possible. This, it is argued, also serves to minimize the need for supervision, and provides an "automatic" method of payment in accordance with at least one aspect of "merit." Incentive systems encourage the worker to strive (by increasing production) to aid his employer to earn greater profits by guaranteeing that he will share in them. These arguments are strongly persuasive to Americans, reared in a

[28] The division of the "savings" need not be "50-50"; some plans divide the savings on other bases.

[29] For a discussion of these plans and the problems related to them see J. K. Louden, *Wage Incentives,* John Wiley & Sons, Inc., New York, 1944; C. W. Lytle, *Wage Incentive Methods,* Ronald Press, New York, 1942; or Philip Arnow, "The Forms of Wages," Chapter 34 in *Employment and Wages in the United States.*

tradition sympathetic to making reward dependent upon performance. In fact, the force of this tradition sometimes leads beginning students to overlook the very real difficulties to which incentive systems are often subject.

The Importance of Incentive Plans in American Industry

Unfortunately, there is no complete survey of American employers that would enable us to say with reasonable precision just how many workers in each industry work under incentive plans. The most complete study thus far was made by the Bureau of Labor Statistics in 1945–1946.[30] This study found that 30 per cent of the workers in the manufacturing industries studied received incentive pay of some sort. However, the percentage of workers under incentive plans varied greatly from industry to industry; the largest percentage (65 per cent) was in apparel; in textiles, 39 per cent of the workers were on incentive pay as were 25 per cent of the employees in metal-working; but in chemicals only 7 per cent were so paid.[31] In the apparel and textile industries about 19 out of 20 plans used (simple) individual piece rates, but in metal-working, where an individual's output is more difficult to identify, group piece rate systems were found almost as frequently as individual rates.

In general, incentive workers receive higher hourly wages than time workers in similar jobs, but the size of the differential varies from one industry to another. However, as incentive pay is more common in large (than small) establishments, it would be difficult to say (without more research than has yet been done) whether the higher earnings of incentive workers are related to their methods of pay or is simply one aspect of the tendency for large employers to pay higher wages than small ones.

Difficulties of Incentive Systems

Some of the more important difficulties found in applying systems of incentive payments are as follows:

[30] J. M. Sherman, "Incentive Pay in American Industry, 1945–1946," in *Bureau of Labor Statistics, Bulletin* 939, Government Printing Office, Washington, D.C., 1948. In 1953–1954, a survey of 17 major labor markets found that the percentage of workers in manufacturing employed under some sort of incentive plan varied from 10 to 40 per cent among the various (city) labor markets. Cf. "Wage Differences and Establishment Practices; 17 Labor Markets, 1953–1954," *Bureau of Labor Statistics Bulletin,* 1173, Government Printing Office, Washington, D.C., 1955, Appendix Table 10, p. 33.

[31] The percentages of workers under incentive plans in nonmanufacturing is known in only a very limited number of industries: automobile repair shops (where 37 per cent of the workers get incentive pay), bituminous coal where 22 per cent of the underground workers got incentive rates (but the surface miners were all paid on a time basis), clothing stores (34 per cent), department stores (28 per cent), limited price variety stores (3 per cent), and power laundries (14 per cent).

1. It is by no means a simple matter to determine the appropriate piece
rate. The piece rate (or, inversely, the standard time) is presumably
set after careful empirical study by one or more management representatives. Often this study is made by one or more industrial engineers,
armed with stop watches and other paraphernalia of precise measurement, who analyze the operations performed on a particular job into a
set of component motions and periods of rest. From these studies, the
piece rate for a particular job is derived. The piece rate does not, of
itself, determine a worker's weekly earnings; almost always he is guaranteed
some hourly minimum wage (irrespective of output) called the "base rate";
failure to earn the base rate is sometimes cause for dismissal. "It has
always been incentive practice . . . to figure on a 15%, 20%, 25% or
similar differential between base rates and actual earnings."[32]

In a modern factory, the piece rate is set with reference to the "average"
worker, working under "average" conditions at his "average" pace. But
workers differ from one another in strength, ability, etc. Even an individual worker's proficiency and pace will differ from one day to the
next, depending upon a multitude of complex physiological and psychological factors. Finally, working conditions vary (even from hour to
hour) depending upon the nature of the product, the flow of materials, etc.
These variations compel the rate setter or setters to use their judgment
in deciding which worker on which day and under which conditions is
"average." Taking statistical "averages" of worker time spent on various
operations will not obviate the need for judgment; judgment must still be
used to decide which "average" should be used and whether the sample
of worker performance is appropriately drawn.[33]

Furthermore, it is necessary to decide how many units of output
should be a "standard performance" for an hour or a week; the question
is not merely a matter of fact, but is partly a matter of how much incentive pay a worker is to be permitted to earn per week. If the output
rate that must be attained before incentive earnings begin to accrue is set
so high that the ordinary worker cannot exceed it, he is likely to become
discouraged and cease striving for incentive earnings. If, on the other
hand, it is set "too low," incentive earnings on a given job *may* become
extremely high and cause jealousy among workers; e.g., highly skilled
workers paid on an hourly basis often become very upset because of the
fact that they earn little more (or even less) than semiskilled workers
under incentive pay. Furthermore, if the task of earning incentive pay on
some particular job in a factory happens to be appreciably more difficult

[32] See V. D. Kennedy, *Union Policy and Incentive Wage Methods,* Columbia University Press, New York, 1945, p. 221.
[33] These and related matters are well discussed in William Gomberg, *A Trade
Union Analysis of Time Study,* 2nd edition, Prentice-Hall, Inc., New York, 1955.

than that on other jobs, workers may (properly) resent being assigned to the job in question, and may even strike to prevent such assignment.

These considerations make it very important that incentive rates be set properly; but, in the nature of the case, this is not easy. Consequently, experimentation, retiming of jobs, and resetting of rates are often necessary before "satisfactory" adjustment of incentive rates can be achieved. Where a particular job is well defined and continuously performed over a long period of time, it will usually be possible by continued study eventually to arrive at a satisfactory incentive rate. But, where the job to be performed by a given worker (or group of workers) varies from one day to the next or the conditions under which it is performed vary, it becomes very difficult to establish incentive rates on a firm basis.

The problem of setting appropriate incentive rates is complicated by the inevitable struggle between workers who wish incentive rates to be as favorable as possible and management time study men who are striving to determine the maximum speed at which it is feasible to perform a given job. Workers will obviously not minimize the difficulty of their job while being timed, although crude attempts to slow down during the timing process will not fool an experienced time study man or a foreman. Nevertheless workers may successfully hide some of the "tricks" they have discovered (on the job) from the time study man.

The obvious remedy for this is to time workers without their being aware of it; however, such tactics cause great resentment and can easily backfire, as workers will often respond to the threat of secret timing by maintaining a uniformly slow pace whenever a stranger appears in the shop. Management has used other devices to time jobs; they sometimes study "pace-setters" (who are often unusually strong and adept workers) to find out how fast a job can be done and attempt to set rates on the basis of the pace-setter's output. Needless to say, workers furiously resent such practices and they are often forbidden under union contracts.

2. A second difficulty concerns the quality of the work performed. Incentive systems place a premium upon output quantity, but in some cases additional output may be "purchased" by reducing the quality of the product. To prevent this, it is necessary to establish quality standards and adequate inspection systems to enforce them. The nature of the standards and their administration then become focal points of worker complaint; where the standards are precise and satisfying them a matter of mechanical performance, there is obviously less opportunity for complaints of favoritism (by inspectors), than when an inspector's judgment determines whether a particular unit is to be accepted or rejected.

3. An effective incentive system for individual workers usually requires that the output of the worker be readily identified. But, where the individual worker produces only one part of an output unit (or is merely

one participant in a production process), the most he can do is to keep up with the team; he cannot respond effectively to pecuniary incentives even if he wishes to do so. Under these circumstances, managements have devised group incentive systems under which a whole group of workers participate (on some predetermined basis) in incentive rewards. The social pressure of the other persons involved is supposed to spur on the individual to his best efforts in the interest of the group. Under some circumstances such an incentive plan can produce group solidarity and high rates of output. However, it can also create cliques among workers, leading to bad feeling between different groups, resistance to transfer of individuals from one group to another, and other undesirable consequences.

There also are workers whose "product" is so vague as to defy definition and who are, therefore, not usually considered as suitable for incentive pay. These include janitors, maintenance men, "indirect" labor, (e.g., supervisors, inspectors, etc.). This is not to say that these types of workers cannot be paid on an incentive basis, but they rarely are.

4. A further difficulty in applying incentive systems is due to the fact that the worker's output is affected by the flow of materials to the machine he is tending, the condition of the machine, and power failures and other phenomena causing delays in the process of production. In other words, a worker's incentive earnings are determined not only by his own skill and effort but by the whole complex of forces that affect a firm's output. In the event of a marked decline in a worker's output for reasons beyond his control, there arises the question of how the worker is to be remunerated; i.e., is he to be paid his guaranteed base rate or his average hourly earnings (over some period) or whichever is higher? Sometimes one basis is chosen and sometimes another; often the issue is hotly disputed among workers, unions, and management as the problem is a difficult one.

5. Perhaps the most serious difficulty encountered by incentive systems is that of "rate-cutting" and worker suspicion thereof. Workers fear that if their earnings under an incentive system become "too high" the piece rate will be reduced. This fear which is very widespread (and, historically, well-founded)[34] leads workers to ask themselves, "Why produce your utmost, when this leads merely to a cut in the piece rate?" This, in turn, leads to a tendency to keep output below levels that will induce rate-cutting; that is, there is a tendency for workers to "hold back" instead of striving for the high output which incentive systems are designed to encourage.[35] Output restriction stems not only from fear of rate-cutting but also from the fear of "working yourself out of a job"; i.e., workers try not to finish the job "too fast" so that there will be work the next day.

[34] See Kennedy, *op. cit.*, pp. 81 et seq.
[35] Kennedy, *op. cit.*, Chapter IV.

Unions are often blamed for output restriction, but there is considerable evidence that restrictive practices are deeply rooted in worker mores that antedate unionization.[36]   Although unions sometimes introduce restrictive practices, often they merely formalize existing customs and enforce them against violaters; in their role of "enforcers" of output limitations, unions acquire a good deal of unfavorable publicity.[37]

It has sometimes been thought that the tendency toward output restriction might be overcome if management would guarantee that incentive rates would not be cut, i.e., that workers need not fear that increasing their output would cause a reduction in their piece rates.   However, this does not always "work," although such guarantees may help to curb rate-cutting or allay fears thereof.[38]   Worker fears of rate-cutting in the face guarantees to the contrary are by no means irrational.   Management is usually able (under a collective bargaining agreement) to "retime" or "restudy" jobs where there has been a change in the method of production;[39] and the presence of high incentive earnings acts as an invitation to management to institute minor changes in job specifications so as to be able to claim that there has been a change in methods, thereby permitting a retiming of the job.   Thus, making out "too well" under an incentive system is usually considered an incitement to (piece) rate-cutting; and "rugged individualists" who violate shop conventions concerning output rates are dealt with harshly by fellow workers, union officers, and sometimes even by foremen.

The reader should not leap to the conclusion that rate cutting is simply a manifestation of management's avarice.   The truth of the matter is that workers require time (on a particular task) to become proficient; the time required to do a job when a worker is first introduced to it is usually considerably (and often far) longer than what is needed after he "gets into the groove" and/or discovers various short cuts.   Often these short cuts are not so much the result of management know-how as of worker ingenuity.   And the workers (and their union spokesmen) argue that be-

[36] The most famous studies of output restriction among unorganized workers are S. B. Mathewson, *Restriction of Output Among Unorganized Employees,* Viking Press, Inc., New York, 1931 and F. J. Roethlisberger and W. J. Dickson, *Management and the Worker,* Harvard University Press, Cambridge, Mass., 1939. An excellent recent case study of worker attitudes toward restriction is Donald Roy, "Quota Restriction and Goldbricking in a Machine Shop," *American Journal of Sociology,* March 1952, pp. 427–452.

[37] See Kennedy, *op. cit.,* Chapter IV.

[38] *Ibid.*   Kennedy cites cases where a guarantee of piece rates has served to stimulate increased output, and others where it has not.

[39] Collective bargaining contracts very frequently contain clauses restricting (or prohibiting outright) management's right to "retime" jobs or otherwise reduce incentive earnings.

cause these increases in productivity are the fruit of worker inventiveness, workers should reap the full reward (in incentive pay) of their skill. However, allowing incentive pay on different jobs to vary without limit would make the wage structure in any given plant utterly chaotic and introduce grave inequities; for example, one worker might earn several times as much as another in the same job classification.

The consequences of these inequities can be readily imagined; the workers who are earning relatively little will protest that their rates are "too tight"[40] and that they are, therefore, the victims of injustice.[41] Such complaints, if they become widespread, can easily provoke a great deal of unrest and lead to strikes. Indeed, the very purpose of a job evaluation system is to prevent this type of inequity from arising; thus, the maintenance of a satisfactory job evaluation system requires the limitation of differentials in incentive pay among workers in the same job grade or class. Consequently, management must strive to keep incentive earnings within some sort of "reasonable" limits. Unions, for the most part, implicitly recognize this necessity but must, nevertheless, resist attempts to tighten rates; it is not surprising, therefore, that union officers are not "too unhappy" when workers curb output in order to prevent retiming.

The problems of inequity arising from differing incentive earnings on different jobs can, in principle, be overcome by applying the incentive systems not to individual or small groups of workers but to all the workers in a plant or company. This, however, would create still other problems which cannot be considered here; in any case, it is rarely done.

Union Attitudes toward Incentive Systems

The various difficulties found in operating incentive systems, especially rate-cutting, serve to explain why many unions bitterly oppose them. However, union opposition to incentive systems is by no means universal. Many unions accept such systems, some with enthusiasm.

In many cases, unions and management agree as to whether time or incentive wage systems are preferable; their joint attitude being determined by the technical conditions of production.[42] Where supervision is difficult to maintain, where the unit of output is easily defined, where jobs

---

[40] Piece rates are said to be "tight" when the worker finds it difficult to earn the expected amount of incentive earnings. In the converse case, piece rates are said to be "loose."

[41] It is neither fair nor effective to tell the complainants that they should be more ingenious if they wish the high incentive earnings of others. Jobs vary greatly in terms of their susceptibility to short cuts and chance plays an important role in determining the extent to which ingenuity can reduce the time necessary for performing a given job.

[42] See Sumner Slichter, *Union Policies and Industrial Management,* The Brookings Institution, Washington, D.C., 1941, Chapters X and XI.

and job conditions change infrequently, and where the worker (or group of workers) has substantial control over the rate of output, incentive systems tend to be favored. The further conditions depart from the above, the more likely is a system of time wages to be preferred by both unions and management. However, some of the large industrial unions have had sharp differences with management concerning the desirability of incentive plans. Where there is disagreement on this issue, it has usually been management that desired an incentive system.[43]

The willingness of a union to accept an incentive plan will, in general, depend upon its past experience with such plans as well as upon the technical conditions of production. However, a union's experiences with incentive systems are not independent of the technical conditions in which they have been tried; experience is much more likely to be satisfactory in an environment where technical conditions are appropriate than otherwise. A further factor that has tended to induce certain unions to accept incentive plans it that such plans greatly assist in "standardizing" wage costs per unit of output among the firms in an industry, thereby inhibiting price-wage competition within their area of application.

That a union's attitude toward incentive systems will depend upon its members' past experiences with them is obvious; e.g., if a union has used worker opposition to an incentive plan as an organizing argument, it is likely to be opposed (at least in that plant) to incentive plans. In other cases, favorable experience may give the union officers a different attitude. Thus, certain international unions (e.g., United Auto Workers and the International Association of Machinists) have gone on record as opposing incentive plans, but some of their locals accept them willingly; conversely, the United Electrical Workers has not taken an official stand on the issue, but some of its locals have recorded opposition. Among the larger industrial unions, the United Steel Workers' leadership has expressed tolerance of, if not sympathy for, incentive systems.[44]

Unions are especially likely to endorse incentive plans when they strongly desire to minimize interfirm differences in unit labor costs.

---

[43] A survey of union leaders made in the late 1940's indicates that the majority of union officers oppose incentive systems. Arnow, *op. cit.*, Tables 187 and 188, pp. 423–424.

[44] See the views expressed by the United Steel Workers' late president, Philip Murray (in Murray and Cooke, *Organized Labor and Production*, Harper and Brothers, Inc., 1940. As is said on p. 116, "Fundamental principles of fair remuneration have been obscured by over-emphasis on "wage systems" as such. As a matter of fact, the method of payment matters little as compared with the method of determining the standards upon which the wage is based." See also Clinton Golden and Harold S. Ruttenberg, *The Dynamics of Industrial Democracy,"* Harper and Brothers, Inc., 1942, which expresses the same view; the authors were (at the time of writing) officers of the United Steel Workers of America.

Consider the following situation: (1) A union is dealing with a group of employers who differ appreciably from one another in terms of the man-hour productivity of their workers (usually because of differences in machinery and other equipment); (2) wage cost is a substantial part of total cost; and (3) the employers in question are faced with sufficiently keen price competition in the the product market so that appreciable differences in unit cost will entail losses for the disadvantaged firms. In this situation the union will be obliged either to equalize (approximately) unit labor costs or to let the high cost firms be driven out of business (or try to operate on a nonunion basis). As neither of the latter two alternatives is desired by the union, the above conditions would require that different *hourly* wage rates be set for different employers. But this would be administratively difficult; the union's key problem is, therefore, how to determine the relative rates for different employers?

Adopting a system of uniform piece rates settles this question more or less automatically. The labor cost per unit of output for every firm becomes the same, irrespective of capital used per worker, relative employe efficiency, etc. (However, workers in the more efficient firms have higher hourly earnings.)

The Amalgamated Clothing Workers, who are in a situation where it is imperative to equalize unit wage costs among competing firms, have for many years sought (successfully) to establish piece rate systems even (in some cases) over the opposition of their members.[45] The International Ladies Garment Workers Union, which must also equalize wage costs among competing firms, for many years resisted "piecework" but later was forced to accept it.[46] The United Mine Workers has also permitted payment by the ton (piece) because of the difficulty of supervising workers in mines, and because it wished to equalize wage costs (per ton) between mines.

However, union acceptance of incentive systems is never unconditional. Few, if any, unions will accept a system which reduces piece rates as output increases; that is, they will not accept a plan which could be represented by curve C in Fig. 15.2. Unions also have strong preferences for "simple" plans, such as straight piece rates (with a guarantee of an hourly minimum), as distinguished from complicated ones under which many workers find it difficult to compute their own earnings.

Incentive methods give the worker and his union an intimate concern with the management of the business. Poorly maintained equipment, badly organized shop layouts, etc. reduce worker output and earnings and become matters for union concern and intervention.[47] Indeed, union concern about methods of production can lead it to intervene in the firm's in-

---

[45] Slichter, *op. cit.,* p. 290.

[46] *Ibid.,* pp. 298–300.

[47] *Ibid.,* pp. 135 et seq.; also Chapters XIV, XVII, and XVIII.

vestment policy, product design, etc.[48]   Thus, incentive plans raise important questions concerning "management prerogatives" (see pp. 180–183).

In short, our discussion of incentive plans adds up to the following: incentive plans are intended to relate a worker's earnings to his output. This is believed to stimulate worker effort to increase output and earnings and to reduce the cost of supervision.   Under favorable conditions, this is the actual effect of incentive systems.   However, difficulties of measuring output, controlling its quality, fear of rate-cutting, etc. limit both the applicability and effectiveness of incentive techniques.   Furthermore unions are, more often than not, suspicious of incentive pay systems. Usually the firms that make incentive payments pay higher hourly wages than other firms in the same industry, but it is not known whether this is due to the use of incentive pay or to other factors (e.g., size of firm) associated with a tendency to adopt such systems.

DISCUSSION QUESTIONS

1. The annual salaries of *positions* in the Civil Service are set by law.   Despite this fact, the forces of the labor market do affect the salary that can be earned by any person in the Civil Service.   How do these labor market forces manifest themselves?

2. Under what conditions can a system of job evaluation set different relative valuations upon the wages paid in different jobs than would be set by the labor market without thereby creating difficulties in attracting and keeping the underpriced labor?

3. It is sometimes alleged that when an incentive system is effective it has the same effect upon wage rates as an increase in the supply of labor.   In what sense, if any, is this correct?

4. Explain the reasons for the usual attitude of unions toward job evaluation. What factors have encouraged the spread of job evaluation techniques?

Suggested Readings

Baker, Helen, and J. M. True, *The Operation of Job Evaluation Plans,* Princeton University Press, Princeton, 1947.

Gomberg, William, *A Trade Union Analysis of Time Study:* 2nd edition, Prentice-Hall, Inc., New York, 1955.

Kennedy, V. D., *Union Policy and Incentive Wage Methods,* Columbia University Press, New York, 1945.

Kerr, Clark and L. H. Fisher, "Effect of Environment and Administration on Job Evaluation," *Harvard Business Review,* May 1950, pp. 77–96.

Livernash, E. R., "Job Evaluation," Chapter 35 in W. S. Woytinsky and associates, *Employment and Wages in the United States,* The Twentieth Century Fund, New York, 1953.

Lytle, C. W., *Job Evaluation Methods,* Ronald Press, New York, 1946.

Presgrave, Ralph, *The Dynamics of Time Study,* 2nd edition, McGraw-Hill Book Company, Inc., New York, 1945.

[48] See, for example, Golden and Ruttenberg, *op. cit.;* Slichter, *op. cit.,* pp. 517 et seq.; and G. W. Taylor, "Hosiery," Chapter 9 in *How Collective Bargaining Works,* Twentieth Century Fund, New York, 1945, pp. 502–507.

16

Wages, Employment, and Labor's Share

In this chapter we study the broad movements in the general level of wages. That is, we shall discuss the events to which people refer when they say that "wages" have gone up or down. To focus our attention better in discussing the *level* of wages, we shall abstract from those changes in the *structure* of wages upon which we have centered our attention in previous chapters. In other words, except when the contrary is specified, we shall argue as though all wage rates varied proportionately.

REAL AND MONEY WAGES: THE RECORD

Money Wages

As the argument on p. 313 indicates, abrupt fluctuations in output cause sharp fluctuations in overhead costs (per unit of output) which rise as output declines and vice versa. The fluctuations in unit overhead costs are reflected in marked fluctuations in profits (per unit of output) which vary in the same direction as movements in output. Output fluctuations also cause variations in demand for labor and raw materials which are likely to produce changes in labor and raw material costs per unit of output. These movements in wage and material costs per unit of output are in the same direction as, but less violent than, those in unit profits. (Unit wage costs usually move less than unit raw material costs.)

These statements describe the general pattern of variation in wages, profits, and other costs per unit of output that occurs in *manufacturing industries* during the course of a business cycle.[1] It is very likely that this pattern also applies to transportation, public utilities (insofar as they are subject to cyclical fluctuations in demand), mining, and trade. The

---

[1] For a rather similar view, see J. T. Dunlop, "The Demand and Supply Functions for Labor," *American Economic Review*, May 1948, pp. 340–350. See also the criticism of this paper by R. A. Gordon, in same issue, pp. 354–356.

"pattern" is applicable wherever firms have sizable fixed charges which reflect a permanent organization and/or a large amount of plant and equipment. But the pattern does not fit well in construction and service, where myriads of small firms, with virtually no fixed charges, appear and disappear with fluctuations in demand; nor does it apply in agriculture or government.

The cyclical pattern of money (hourly) wage rates is fairly simple; in general, money wage rates rise in prosperity and rise less, or decline, in depression. In the United States, during the period 1860–1913, the level of money wages rose in 16 out of 21 years in which "general business activity" was increasing; in 12 years when business activity was roughly unchanged, the level of wage rates rose 7 times, fell 3 times, and was constant twice; in 17 years of declining business activity, wages rose 9 times, fell 7, and were constant once.[2]

From 1914 to 1920, money wage rates rose steadily and sharply; they broke in the big depression of 1920–1921 and continued down through 1922.[3] From 1923 through 1929 money wage rates rose (being about 8 per cent higher in the terminal year than in the initial) although from 1926 on the increase was negligible. The level of wages broke violently in the major depression of 1929–1933, but since 1933 has risen steadily. This rise continued through 1937–1938, despite the sharp cyclical downturn, and has continued throughout the period from 1939 to 1956. The broad outlines of this record are shown clearly in Fig. 16.1.

The cyclical pattern of money wage rates described for the United States applies, more or less well, to other industrialized countries although in details the record varies from one country to another.[4] The general level of money wages (like individual wage rates) is rather insensitive[5] to cyclical forces, and declines appreciably only in response to rather major depressions.

[2] E. H. Phelps-Brown with S. V. Hopkins, "The Course of Wage-Rates in Five Countries, 1860–1939," *Oxford Economic Papers*, June 1950, Table III, p. 233.

[3] *Ibid.*, p. 282; also P. H. Douglas, *Real Wages in the United States, 1890–1926*, Houghton, Mifflin and Co., Boston, 1930, p. 205, Table 73.

[4] See Phelps-Brown, *op. cit.*, pp. 229–235. The other countries studied are the United Kingdom, France, Germany, and Sweden. The intercountry similarity of wage patterns has become decidedly less marked since World War I, and especially since 1929, than it was before 1913.

[5] D. C. Creamer (with the assistance of Martin Bernstein), "Behavior of Wage Rates during Business Cycles," *Occasional Paper* 34, National Bureau of Economic Research, 1950, found that the cyclical turning point in manufacturing wage rates lagged behind turning points in general business activity (in the United States between 1919 and 1938) by an average period of about 8½ to 9½ months (Table I, p. 7). Similar figures for seven British industries during the same period show an average lag of wages behind business activity of about eleven months (*op. cit.*, pp. 25–32).

Thus, the level of money wages (in the United States) fell 19 per cent during the great depression of the 1870's, about 12 per cent in the depression of 1920–1921, and 23 per cent in 1929–1933.[6] These major depressions also made themselves felt in the wage levels of other advanced countries. But minor cyclical downturns have not regularly caused money wage declines. To a considerable extent this is because of a persistent long-term upward trend in the level of money wages; this trend has been world-wide. The forces mirrored in this trend (see pp. 15–24) have at

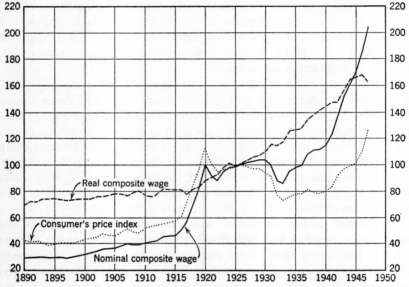

[1] "Nominal composite wage" is (roughly) what is called the level of money wages in the text.

FIG. 16.1. Composite indexes of nominal and real wages, 1890–1947 (1926 = 100).
Source: W. S. Woytinsky and Associates, *Employment and Wages in the United States,* 20th Century Fund, New York, 1953, p. 51.

times caused the level of money wages to rise in the face of a decline in general business activity but rarely to fall in a period of rising activity. However, as might be expected, wage rises in depression years were less, and declines more frequent, than in prosperity, and what increases did occur in depressions were, percentage-wise, smaller than in periods of business expansion.[7]

The sluggishness of the level of money wage rates is reflected in prosperity as well as in depression. Sharp increases in the level of money

[6] Phelps-Brown, *op. cit.,* p. 282.
[7] *Ibid.*

wage rates have occurred only during periods of violent upward price movements coupled with labor shortages. Such periods are characteristic of and, with rare exceptions, occur only during wartime or immediate postwar inflations.[8] Thus, money wages (in the United States) rose 84 per cent in the period 1860–1869, 132 per cent in 1914–1920, and 112 per cent in 1940–1949;[9] apart from these periods of war inflation the per annum rate of increase in the level of money wage rates was about 1.4 per cent during the interval 1860–1939.[10] In fine, apart from wars and their aftermath, the level of money wage rates, in the period 1860–1939, climbed slowly but steadily upward. (The period since 1939 will be considered separately, pp. 412–417).

Real Wages

In any discussion of wage levels, it is necessary to distinguish sharply between money and real wages. *Money wages* (per hour, day, or year) refer to the amount of money paid for the hire of the corresponding amount of labor time. *Real wages* refer to the amount of goods and services that can be purchased with a given amount of labor time.[11]

For the United States, over the period of the last century or so, there is no argument but that *real* wage rates have increased, although by not so great a percentage as *money* wage rates. One estimate placed the increase in the level of *real* wage rates to be 160 per cent, between 1860 and 1939;[12] another estimate found the increase (between 1890 and 1939) to have been 103 per cent and, between 1890 and 1947, 132 per cent.[13] From either of these estimates, it is apparent that the increase in real (hourly) wages has been very considerable. This increase has not been accomplished primarily by reducing the nonwage share in national output, and no one pretends that it has. It has been due (see pp. 16–18) mainly to the enormous secular increase that has occurred in output per man-hour.[14]

[8] Two notable exceptions were the "NRA period" in the United States (in 1933) and the "Blum Experience" in France, 1936–1938; see p. 407.

[9] The figures for the first two periods are from Phelps-Brown, *op. cit.* p. 282; the figure for 1940–1949 is computed from the Bureau of Labor Statistics data on average hourly earnings in (all) manufacturing industries.

[10] Computed from Phelps-Brown, *op. cit.*, Table I, p. 229.

[11] See above, pp. 281–282.

[12] Phelps-Brown, *op. cit.*, Table V, p. 236.

[13] Witt Bowden, "Trends in Wages and Hours," Chapter 5, in *Employment and Wages in the United States, op. cit.*, Table 21, p. 51.

[14] This mirrors the net effect of changes in worker skills, capital equipment, and *all other forces* bearing upon the ratio of output to labor input for the economy as a whole; i.e., changes in output per man hour are not indicative of changes in labor's productive "contribution." The increase in output per man-hour is given by column 3 of Table 2.1.

Although there have been periods of sharp *year to year* changes in the index of real wages, there have also been appreciable time intervals when these changes have been quite small. For example, from 1895 till 1903 in the United States, the index of real wage rates lay between 99 and 104 (with the exception of 1890 when the index hit 96); in 1903–1914, this index climbed from 104 to 110, but in only one year did it move by more than two points; in 1922–1929, the index climbed from 96 to 103, but never by more than three points in any one year.[15]

In contrast to these long intervals of torpor, there have been short periods of violent movement; in the United States, real wage rates rose 23 per cent between 1917 and 1921; they also rose 10 per cent in 1933–1934, 15 per cent between 1936 and 1939, and 14.4 per cent between 1939 and 1947.[16]

MONEY WAGES AND THE PRICE LEVEL

Usually, year to year changes in money and real wages tend to be in the same direction.[17] The exceptions to this statement, where real wages have declined while money wages were increasing, have occurred where either (1) the cost of living first rose again after a decline or (2) there had been a big and prolonged rise in living costs.[18] That is, real and money wages tend to move in the same direction except that money wages sometimes tend to lag behind movements in consumer prices which (when the latter are rising) causes them to rise proportionately more than money wages. However, when this happens, money wages have tended soon to "catch up."

A significant characteristic of the index of real wage rates is that for long stretches its year to year movements have been small, but during a few short intervals it has undergone abrupt and relatively large movements.[19] These movements have occurred, as a rule, simultaneously with sharp movements in money wages and have been the by-product of major wars (and their aftermaths) or of major depressions. The mechanism producing these movements has been vividly described, in capsule form, by Dunlop: "The cost of living may be viewed as a push, and the profits influence a pull, upon wage rates.[20]

---

[15] Phelps-Brown, *op. cit.*, pp. 277–282.

[16] Phelps-Brown, *op. cit.*, pp. 277 and 282; data for 1939–1947 from Bowden, *op. cit.*, p. 51, Table 21.

[17] Phelps-Brown and Hopkins, "The Course of Wage-rates," pp. 243–246.

[18] *Ibid.*, p. 245.

[19] The "cyclical" pattern of real wage rates is not very distinct and, as the data are not easily adjusted for trend, the pronounced upward trend in both real and money wage rates may be responsible for much of the similarity (of direction) in their year-to-year movements.

[20] J. T. Dunlop, "The Demand and Supply Functions for Labor," p. 350.

Spelled out, what this means is that a rise in living costs, especially a sharp one, will cause unions to demand money wage increases sufficient to maintain real wage rates; unorganized workers may also have their wages "pushed up" because the money value of the social minimum wage rate rises. This is the "push" of living costs.

But the "pull" must come from the side of demand; i.e., employers must be willing to pay more in order for money wage rates to rise. Such willingness springs either from an anxiety to fill orders that is sufficient to induce them to yield to union demands rather than permit a strike and/or a belief that customers are sufficiently anxious for goods to accept price increases sufficient to cover the higher wages. Furthermore, if the relatively high wage firms desire to expand their work forces, they may attract workers from lower wages enterprises, up-grade workers occupationally, etc., generally stimulating labor market competition and raising the level of wage rates. This is the "pull" of profits.

In wartime and postwar booms, both the push of living costs and the pull of profits act to make *money* wage rates rise. However, it is difficult, without overt control, to synchronize movements in the indices of living costs and of money wage rates. To appreciate the forces at work, imagine the economy to be divided into two sectors: a "wage-goods" sector and the remainder. The wage-goods sector produces foodstuffs, provides housing services, and all other goods and services purchased by wage earners for consumption.[21] Food and housing are produced in the wage-goods sector, in which their prices are far more important than in the economy as a whole. In wartime, housing construction is virtually halted and the supply of food to domestic, nonmilitary consumers cannot be much increased because of the needs of the armed forces and foreign allies. At the same time the increased incomes of urban workers, resulting from fuller employment and a longer work week, increase demand for food and housing sharply, driving up their prices. The attempt of wage earners to make their money (hourly) wages rise proportionately with the cost of living is the "push" of living costs.

It may well be asked how living costs can affect money wage rates. If the pull of labor demand is not present, how can the "needs" of workers affect money wages? The answer is that the government may, directly or indirectly, respond to the push of living costs by adding to the "pull." That is, the government may induce employers to grant wage increases by indicating its own willingness to pay higher prices (e.g., via "cost plus" contracts) to offset higher "living costs"; this is especially important in wartime. Also, when price controls are in operation, government willing-

---

[21] Of course, "wage goods" are bought by many nonwage earners. The list of the goods entering into this category is essentially the same as those entering into the index of consumer prices (cost of living index) of the Bureau of Labor Statistics.

ness to grant price increases to offset wage increases (made "necessary" by cost of living increases) generates "pull" (on wages) from the side of demand.[22] (More subtle long-run influences of government on wage rates are discussed below.)

When living costs fall drastically, as in a major depression, real wage rates at first tend to rise as money wages do not fall so rapidly as retail prices; however, towards the latter part of the depression, money wage rates have often tended to fall more sharply than living costs. This was the general experience of the United States, Great Britain, and Sweden in the depressions of 1920–1922 and 1929–1932. The reason for the stickness of money wage rates has been explained above (pp. 331–333); the eventual fall of money wage rates (after a year or two of depression) is readily explained by increased anxiety for work in the face of continued unemployment, coupled with employer financial difficulties induced by successive years of losses. Such losses are due to rises in overhead cost per unit of output consequent upon a fall in the level of output. In other words, in *major* depressions rises in overheads *per unit of output* tend to depress profits per unit (often making them negative) leading to a "downward pull" on money wage rates, i.e., the reverse of the upward pull discussed above. However, this factor produces actual money wage declines only in very marked and prolonged depressions.

The above remarks would suggest that whenever the ratio money wage rates/living costs has risen or fallen sharply, the variable which has moved less has later tended to catch up. In general this has been true, although there have been instances where a prolonged slump in output per head has forced a fall in real wage rates for a relatively long period. For example, German real wage rates did not reach 1913 levels until 1928, although there were several cycles of money wage rates between these two dates.[23]

Although most of the sharp year-to-year movements in real wage rates have been associated with war or postwar booms, there have been (at least) two interesting exceptions: the rise (in the United States) in real wage rates of 9 per cent in 1933–1934, of about 8 per cent in 1936–1937, and of 11 per cent (in France) during 1935–1940.[24] These increases were caused by sharp increases in money wage rates, induced by a combination of union and government pressure on the "push" side.

[22] This also applies when firms act voluntarily to hold down prices as many (large) firms did (in the United States) during 1947–1949. Such firms would raise their prices only when cost increases "justified" them. Cf. A. E. Rees, "Postwar Wage Determination in the Basic Steel Industry," *American Economic Review,* June 1951, pp. 384–404.

[23] See J. W. Angell, *The Recovery of Germany,* Yale University Press, New Haven, 1929, p. 256, note 1.

[24] Phelps-Brown, "The Course of Wage Rates," p. 278 and p. 282.

In the United States, the 1933–1934 increase was primarily the result of the NRA codes[25] which forced up the money wage rates of the lowest paying firms by government order and also encouraged unionization (which worked in the same direction). The 1936–1937 rise was caused mainly by the money wage increases that were granted by the newly unionized manufacturing firms. In both 1933–1934 and 1936–1937, unemployment was quite high and wage increases can hardly be explained in terms of labor shortage. To be sure, in both years, business activity increased and interest rates fell so that overheads per unit of output declined and profits per unit of output increased (or losses fell). But profits (both per unit of output and as a rate of return on net worth) had been far higher in 1923–1929 without provoking an upward movement of money wage rates of more than about 3 per cent, whereas in 1933–1934 the index of money wages climbed by about 14 per cent and in 1936–1937 by about 11 per cent.[26] The difference in money (and real) wage rate behavior between the 1920's and 1930's must be explained in terms of government-union upward pressure on the social minimum wage rate.

The French experience of 1935–1937 also reflects a process of government-union raising of the social minimum wage rate under the "Popular Front" regime. In the French case, however, living costs rose much more rapidly than in the American.

Apart from these short intervals of sharp changes in real and money wage rates the year-to-year movements in both variables have been quite small. But over the long pull, there has been a tendency for real wage rates to rise a little each year. This has occurred through the movement of workers from low to higher wage industries, occupations, and areas. It has also occurred through upward adjustments of wage rates on given jobs. There is no *a priori* reason why this movement should, for long periods, have proceeded slowly but steadily; it could have occurred through a series of violent year-to-year fluctuations. The fact that it has not done so is due, I think, to (1) the operation of monetary and/or fiscal policy, which has usually prevented violent short-period fluctuations in finished prices,[27] and (2) the fact that the process of increasing man-hour productivity has, for the economy as a whole, usually proceeded more or less slowly. Given a slowly changing price level, the slow rate of increase in man-hour productivity inhibited sharp movements in money wage rates.[28]

[25] See pp. 65–66.

[26] To be sure, product prices rose in the 1930's while they didn't in the 1920's. Nevertheless, the rise of real wages was so much sharper in the latter period than in the former as to preclude any denial of the "significance" of this difference.

[27] This does not mean that this has always been an explicit objective of monetary-fiscal policy.

[28] This implies that entrepreneurial behavior is such as to resist appreciable short-period fluctuations in the ratio of product prices to unit direct costs. This is also

But beyond considerations such as these, economics does not, at present, have an explanation of why real wage rates do not oscillate more (than they have) from one year to the next.

WAGES, PRICES, AND INCOME DISTRIBUTION

The Fixed and the Variable Shares of National Income

In the short-run, a considerable part of the payments that compose the national income are fixed by contract.   That is, people rent buildings, lend money, agree to work,[29] etc. in exchange for payments which are fixed, for a number of years, in money terms.   These payments constitute the "fixed income" share of the national income.

Sudden sharp increases in the price level, usually called inflationary, are accompanied by temporary reductions in the share of income going to receivers of contractually fixed money payments.[30] Not only does the fixed income *share* (temporarily) decline with rises in the price-level, but the purchasing power of the income received by individuals dependent upon fixed incomes declines.   Hence, sharp price increases work a hardship upon such persons.   These persons include individuals retired upon the income from interest-bearing bonds, annuity and pension receivers, persons who have rented their property for a fixed money rental for a long time period, persons with a long-term commitment to work for a fixed salary, etc.

The obverse side of this picture is the effect of price increases upon the incomes of those who are committed to make fixed payments.   Such firms and individuals experience a gain in their incomes (other things equal) after making their contractual payments.   This is one important source of the profits that usually accrue to business firms during an inflation.[31]

However, in the "long run" fixed commitments expire, and new contracts must be renegotiated.   Then the increased value of the resources (in dollars) resulting from the inflation causes their prices to rise and the new contracts tend (roughly) to restore the pre-inflation ratio of "fixed"

---

the inference of Phelps-Brown and Hart, "The Share of Wages in National Income," *Economic Journal,* June 1952, pp. 253–277, especially pp. 267–268.

[29] This is common among executives and professional employees but not among manual workers.

[30] That is, the ratio, total "fixed" income/national income, varies in the opposite direction from the denominator, the numerator being a constant during short intervals.

[31] There are, in addition, "inventory profits" and other capital gains resulting from a rise in the replacement costs of assets.

incomes to other incomes. But it must be emphasized that this restoration is imperfect, as well as delayed.

Inflation and the Demand for Labor

As we have already seen, sharp increases in the prices of goods tend to induce increases in money wages. This occurs partly because of the upward push on the social minimum wage rate caused by rising prices but also through the pull of increased labor demand. Inflation, in modern times,[32] tends to result from abrupt increases in demand which lead to competition for labor and raw materials thereby driving up their prices.[33]

This comes about, in its most dramatic form, during the booms created by wars and near wars. In these situations, the government demand for goods is increased and taxes are not usually increased sufficiently to keep total spending, government plus nongovernment, from increasing. That is, part of the government spending is financed by borrowing from banks which increases the money supply. The result is that the demand for goods of all kinds becomes greater than the amount supplied at the going price level; the result is to drive up the price level.

The combination of rising goods prices and expanding output (which implies lower overheads costs per unit of output) expands business firms' profits and induces an increase in output. This, in turn, leads to competition for labor and raw materials, bidding up their prices. Thus profits and money wages both tend to rise during an inflation, at the expense of fixed income.

Money Supply and the Aggregate Demand for Labor

When we discussed the role of labor demand in wage determination, *in a single firm or industry,* we assumed that demand conditions for output were given; this limits the "ability to pay" of the firm or industry and sets the upper limit to the wage rate. But this assumption is meaningless when we deal with the economy as a whole; for the demand for the output of one sector of the economy is derived from the incomes earned in the other sectors, and it increases as their output expands. What then, if anything, limits the demand for labor and the money wage rate for the entire economy?

The answer is, at bottom, the quantity of money. With a given quantity of money in existence there is always some upper limit to the volume

---

[32] Historically, crop failures and other natural catastrophes have also caused price inflations. However, in modern times in "advanced" countries, this has not been a very important factor in inflationary phenomena, except as a repercussion of a war.

[33] This argument assumes, by implication, that the increase in output brings the economy to, and beyond, the point of "full employment." In an economy with less than full employment, these remarks are inapplicable.

of output (in dollar terms)[34] the economy will produce. To be sure, by more efficient use of a given quantity of money,[35] the economy can expand its volume of output somewhat without any increase in the quantity of money. But after some level of dollar output is reached, the need of firms, households and governments for cash becomes so pressing that they simply will not undertake to handle a greater dollar volume of sales unless they can increase their cash balances.[36] This "tightness" of cash is manifested in increased difficulties in borrowing and in high interest rates, which cause firms to attempt to reduce their inventories of goods in order to increase their holdings of cash. To accomplish this they must sell goods and not replace them, which reduces the demand for labor.[37]

Assuming as we do (for the moment) that the economy's level of physical production is given, the quantity of money sets an upper limit to the price level.[38] This, in turn, sets an upper limit to the money wage level employers will pay. Sharp inflations, therefore, require increases in the quantity of money; refusal (by the monetary authorities) to permit such increases would prevent, or limit, inflation. Why, then, isn't the money supply limited? Usually it is, but, during war or near war, the demand of the armed forces for material is so imperative as to require paying whatever price is necessary to obtain the output demanded by the military establishment on given delivery dates. It is conceivable that economic mobilization could be accomplished in a noninflationary manner, but it would not be easy to do, and, in fact, the production required by a major 20th century war has never been accomplished without serious price inflation.[39]

The imperative need for speedy production creates competitive pressure on the markets for labor and raw materials, causing their prices to be bid up. The usual limits upon this process, the need for selling price to cover production costs, cease to be effective because the government, one way or another, guarantees producers against loss; output, not econ-

---

[34] This is usually called the gross national product.

[35] That is, an increase in the (income) velocity of circulation.

[36] This means that businesses and other "transactors" need to hold a certain amount of cash to conduct their activities, and that this amount increases with the volume of transactions.

[37] The reader experienced in economic theory will recognize this as a highly abbreviated account of the (generally accepted) theory of the interrelation among the level of (money) gross national product, supply of money, and the interest rate.

[38] There may be some variations depending upon the distribution of cash balances in the community, etc., but there is always a fairly definite *upper* limit to the price level, given the amount of money.

[39] The difficulties involved in "economic mobilization" without inflation are well discussed in Scitovsky, Shaw, and Tarshis, *Mobilizing Resources for War*, McGraw-Hill Book Company, Inc., New York, 1951.

omy, is the objective. Ultimately the government pays for the higher price of labor and materials through higher taxes and inflationary borrowing.

Unions and the "Cost Push"

So far this argument makes the inflationary pressure come entirely from the side of demand. But what about prices being "pushed up" through higher costs; how does that enter into the picture? It enters in the following way: foodstuffs and housing which bulk large in the wage earner's cost of living have a relatively low short-run elasticity of supply. Furthermore, as their production, beyond essential minima, contributes nothing to the war effort, the government tries to limit it. But rising worker money incomes swell the demand for these items and, hence, their prices tend to rise. This implies a rise in the cost of living which leads workers to demand increases in wage rates "to keep up with living costs."

The "cost push" is felt by employers in those sectors of the economy where the demand for output does not increase promptly. Here, the economic impact of the war is brought home through the increased difficulty of retaining labor, especially low wage labor. A rise in living costs makes workers restive and prone to demand wage increases on pain of quitting and/or striking. To be sure, some of these workers would have left for high wage war plants anyway, but many workers who are loath to change jobs are made restive by a rise in living costs.

The wage increases that are granted to satisfy these demands may be said to "push up" the prices of affected firms. Probably this process would occur in the absence of unions. But unionism accelerates the process and is, itself, fostered by it. By voicing complaints about rising living costs, unions call them to the attention of workers before some of them might otherwise have become aware of the situation. Unions make the individual aware that there are others in the same position as he, and they make clear that circumstances favor demands for wage increases. In short, unions serve to make timid or naive workers, especially those reluctant to change their jobs, aware of what a strike threat can accomplish.

In war plants and other sectors of the economy directly exposed to the pressure of increased demand, unions may also have some tendency to boost wages. However, this is disputed, and it is difficult to bring evidence to bear on the matter (see pp. 339–342). In any event, it would be generally agreed that the dominant force in this part of the economy is the almost limitless demand for output at any price. But this does not end the matter; for the relation of unions to wages during (recent) inflations cannot be understood without taking into account the fact that these inflations are partially suppressed; i.e., there is some kind of direct price control.

WAGES AND PRICE CONTROLS

World War II

It is debatable as to whether, over the last 15 years, unions have made wages (much) higher than they would have been anyway. But it is undoubtedly true that, if unions had gone "for all they could get" during World War II, wages would have risen in 1942–1945 much more than they did.[40] The need for continuous output was such that very substantial wage increases could have been obtained as "ransom" for continuing to work; the success of Lewis and the coal miners (in gaining wartime wage concessions through strike action) is indicative of the possibilities in this direction.

But, instead of pursuing this policy, during World War II most labor leaders chose to cooperate with a program of "inflation control." This program involved (1) reducing inflationary demand for goods through taxation and semicompulsory purchase of government bonds, (2) controlling prices and allocation of scarce items through price ordinances (price "ceilings") and rationing, and (3) controlling wages by ordinances of the War Labor Board.

The leaders of AFL and CIO both agreed to forego strikes for the duration of the war and to abide by the orders of the War Labor Board. This meant, in effect, that they agreed not to push wages as high as a "free market" would have bid them; as we have seen (pp. 74–75), they carried out their part of this agreement. Insofar as responsible labor leadership implies restraint of money wage demands to restrain inflation, American[41] labor leaders were highly responsible during World War II.

But the no-strike pledge was conditional upon effective control of living costs. Labor leaders would not have undertaken (and probably could not have succeeded if they had) to curb wage increases in the face of rapid price increases. During World War II, consumer prices were curbed rather effectively, as compared with the postwar inflation. Prior to President Roosevelt's "general freeze" order of October 3, 1942, the index of consumer prices (cost of living index) rose 18.1 per cent above its January 1941 level. But, from October 1942 to August 1945, the index climbed only 8.7 per cent further. However, from August 1945 to November 1946, consumer prices climbed 17.7 per cent, and in the six hectic months after price controls broke down completely (June–

---

[40] A qualification to this must be noted; if unions had pursued such an objective, it is quite likely that very severe antiunion legislation would have been enacted. The probable consequences of this can only be imagined.

[41] With the exception of John L. Lewis. Similar statements would apply to British, Australian, and Scandinavian labor leaders.

November 1946) consumer prices rose 14.2 per cent.[42]   The contrast between the slow climb of October 1942 to August 1945 and the rapid ascent of June–November 1946 is striking.

The "Little Steel" formula of June 1942 made it War Labor Board policy to permit wage rates to be increased up to 15 per cent above their January 1941 levels (15 per cent being the increase in living costs between January 1941 and May 1942), but no further increases, on account of cost of living rises were permitted.

The reader should not suppose, because of this, that during World War II all wages were held under a rigid ceiling.   The labor market (see pp. 375–376) operated with considerable effect,[43] and the War Labor Board (WLB) made a variety of exceptions to its wage freeze policy.   WLB permitted wage adjustments for workers receiving less than 50 cents per hour,[44] adjustments to correct "gross inequities," adjustments for the cost of living rise from January 1941 to May 1942,[45] and other adjustments where needed to recruit labor.[46]   In short, wages were not completely frozen during World War II, but they were made a good deal less fluid than they became in the years following 1945.

Cost of Living Adjustments

The experience of the years 1946–1948 has made union leaders and members very conscious of the distinction between real and money wages. During this period they saw several "rounds" of wage increases dissipated by rises in living costs; from 1945 to 1948, average hourly earnings in manufacturing rose by 32 per cent in money terms but *declined* a little less than 1 per cent in real terms.[47]

Partly as a result of these experiences, in 1948 the United Auto Workers

[42] These data are from H. M. Douty, "The Development of Wage-Price Policies," Chapter 3 in "Problems and Policies of Dispute Settlement and Wage Stabilization," *U. S. Bureau of Labor Statistics Bulletin* 1009, Government Printing Office, Washington, D.C., 1951.

[43] Prior to October 1942, the War Labor Board had no control over "voluntary" wage adjustments as distinguished from collective bargaining agreements.   Labor market competition became so intense between mid-1941 and October 1942, that WLB chairman William H. Davis remarked in June 1942, "It is a fact that this voluntary wage increase business is going to kick the bottom out of the bucket. There is no doubt about that."   Quoted in A. L. Gitlow, *Wage Determination Under National Boards,* Prentice-Hall, Inc., New York, 1953, p. 148.

[44] These were the cases of "substandard" wages.   Originally the minimum level was set at 40 cents per hour; later it was raised to 50 cents and, in 1945, to 55 cents.

[45] This was the "little steel" formula.

[46] Exceptions for this purpose were made only very infrequently, mainly in cases where the plant was geographically isolated or the work extremely unpleasant.

[47] From L. G. Reynolds and C. H. Taft, *The Evolution of Wage Structure,* Yale University Press, New Haven, 1955, Table 12-1, p. 319.

signed a two year agreement with General Motors which provided for automatic cost of living adjustments every three months.   These adjustments guaranteed that the hourly wages of General Motors' workers would vary proportionately with the cost of living, with a time lag of no more than three months, but provided that during the life of the agreement wages would not decline more than five cents per hour.   There were other important clauses in this contract (see pp. 427–429), but for the moment let us concentrate attention upon cost of living adjustments.   The provision for automatic cost of living adjustments is sometimes called an "escalator clause"; i.e., wages "ride up the cost of living escalator."

General Motors offered automatic cost of living adjustments in exchange for a long-term contract; it wanted the agreement to run for five years but accepted two years as the best it could obtain.   In effect, General Motors conceded that it would match all increases in the cost of living during the life of the contract, and more, in exchange for a promise of continuous production.   The union, by accepting the contract, relinquished its right to strike for better terms for two years in exchange for a ride on the escalator plus the annual "improvement factor."   In 1950, General Motors and the United Auto Workers signed a new agreement for five years; this new agreement also contained provision for automatic cost of living adjustments as did the three year contract signed in 1955.

The 1950 agreement was of major importance in that it came in the midst of the inflation prompted by the outbreak of hostilities in Korea. The automatic escalator increases achieved by General Motors workers became very attractive to other unions, especially after the Wage Stabilization Board approved wage increases granted in accordance with escalator clauses (see below).   Consequently, in 1950–1951, there was a rapid growth in the number of workers covered by agreements including such clauses.   These clauses are most common in large manufacturing plants, especially automobile manufacturing, and in railroading.

Automatic cost of living adjustments have not spread very rapidly since 1951.   This is due partly to the fact that, with the cost of living more or less stabilized since 1952, there has been no great pressure from unions for such clauses.   And in the absence of pressure, employers have not been anxious to offer such provisions.   After all, once union members take cost of living adjustments for granted, the leaders feel the need to deliver "something extra" in a new contract.   Thus, in the absence of escalation, the employer can "sell" a cost of living adjustment to a union; but with escalation he may have to offer more to get a contract.[48]

---

[48] In the absence of escalation, contractual provision for frequent wage reopenings, with full freedom to strike, accomplishes much the same result.   Provision for wage reopenings during the life of a collective bargaining contract have become quite frequent.

But, irrespective of contractual arrangements, American workers have become very sensitive to changes in the cost of living. Any renewal of inflation will bring instant demands for proportional wage increases. If the inflation occurs, as is most likely, with full employment and high profits, employers will not be likely to resist such demands. Thus, in a very real sense, most or all union members are likely to have their wages escalated, irrespective of contractual provisions, in the event of renewed inflation; the implications of this are discussed on pp. 421–422.

Wage Stabilization during the Korean Episode

On June 24, 1950, we became engaged in a shooting war in Korea. As a result, we were soon on the path toward economic mobilization with the attendant inflationary pressure. To ward off inflation an attempt was made at both "wage and price stabilization"; however, neither attempt was more than half-hearted.

During the Korean episode wage stabilization was entrusted to the Wage Stabilization Board (WSB). This board, like its predecessor the War Labor Board, was a tripartite body whose members represented labor, management, and the public. However, WSB could never seriously attempt to "hold the line" as WLB did. Initially, WSB was not given any power to settle disputes because of management objections. Later it was given limited dispute settlement powers, but these were (by Congressional action in 1952) again taken from it.[49]

Furthermore, neither labor nor management was prepared to make sacrifices to halt inflation during this partial war, as they had been during World War II. Consequently, major agreements were signed which violated WSB rules, and both union and management would jointly request WSB approval. And WSB was constrained to grant approval; both labor and management had taken a lesson from John L. Lewis' book, and they met unsatisfactory rulings with defiance. Thus, early in 1951, the labor representatives[50] left the Board in protest over one of its rulings and its lack of dispute-settlement powers. And they did not return until the Board was reconstituted with (limited) powers of dispute-settlement and the offensive ruling had been (in practice) over-ruled. In 1952, the steel companies refused to accept a recommendation of WSB for settling a steel strike until the Office of Price Stabilization granted a price increase that they considered acceptable.[51]

[49] Gitlow, *op. cit.*, pp. 180–189.

[50] At this time the labor members of WSB were directed by the United Labor Policy Committee, a group representing AFL, CIO, Railroad Brotherhoods, and the Machinists' Union (then independent) on matters dealing with economic stabilization.

[51] The steel companies finally got their way after a 90 day strike.

WSB operated by establishing a set of conditions under which increases could be granted without Board approval. Increases larger than the prescribed maximum required specific authorization. Once authorization was granted, a precedent was set, and a new and higher maximum was in effect. The history of WSB was a history of retreat to ever higher maximums. At its inception, WSB avoided a challenge from the coal miners, who had just obtained a large wage increase, by ruling that contracts negotiated prior to the wage and price freeze order of January 25, 1951, did not require board approval. In February they ruled that increases of more than 10 per cent above those of a base date required board approval; it was this ruling that caused the labor members to "walk out." Soon after, the Economic Stabilization Administrator[52] approved violation of the 10 per cent provision where this was required by escalator clauses. In the summer of 1951, WSB permitted cost of living increases to meat packing workers although there was no provision for them in their contracts; they also permitted a 10 per cent increase in textiles because of "interplant inequities." Then WSB approved "productivity increases" of the kind in the General Motors-United Auto Workers agreement (see pp. 427–429).

By this time (autumn 1951) it was clear that WSB was not restraining wage rates but simply converting "key bargains" into national wage policy. It has been persuasively argued[53] that this policy tended to accelerate the rate of increase in the general wage level by making union leaders and members aware of a target, the maximum permitted, and reluctant to settle for less. At any rate, WSB made little contribution to wage control during its brief and not too happy career.

Suppressed Inflation and the "Cost Push"

Effective control of wages in an inflationary situation means keeping wages below what they would have been in the absence of regulation. In the presence of strong unions and an urgent need for output, this implies that the unions refrain from exerting their full power to raise wages. It is very likely that, in this sense, there was (reasonably) effective wage control during World War II and that there was not such control in 1950–1952 (during the Korean episode).

Effective control requires cooperation both of employers and unions. The cooperation of union leaders in *restraining* wage increases cannot be

---

[52] WSB's rulings could be, and were occasionally, overruled by the Economic Stabilization Administrator, who was under heavy pressure to get continuous production.

[53] See Clark Kerr, "Governmental Wage Restraints: Their Limits and Uses in a Mobilized Economy," *Proceedings of the Fourth Annual Meeting of the Industrial Relations Research Association,* 1951.

forthcoming except in exchange for a fairly effective program of price controls. Indeed, it is very doubtful if union leaders could prevent their members from demanding that wage rates keep pace with living costs (even if they wanted to) when it was obvious that labor was scarce and profits high.

Consequently, under suppressed inflation, living costs affect wages in a simple and direct fashion; rises in living costs lead unions to relax their curbs upon wage demands (roughly) to the extent necessary to keep real hourly wages from falling. Since product prices are "controlled," i.e., kept below market levels, the higher wages can be passed on to buyers without loss of sales if the price regulating agency permits. Political pressures being what they are, price increases have usually been allowed to offset increases in unit costs. Hence the "cost push" upon prices.

Under a system of direct controls upon wages and prices, unions serve as the spokesmen for the interests of the wage earner. They attempt to have the relation among money wages, living costs, and profits per unit of output made as favorable to the wage earner as possible. Lobbyists for business and agriculture attempt to do the same for their groups. In the multiparty bargain, labor leaders have been no more grasping, or successful, than others; indeed, they have been conspicuously less successful than agriculture.

It is quite true that (under suppressed inflation), if unions were willing, *and able,* to permit living costs to rise relative to hourly wages, increases in money wages could be reduced. The money cost of the war and the correlated increase in the money supply would then be less, and the subsequent postwar inflation milder. But there is no reason to single out union leaders or members as responsible for the inflation; it might be equally, or more, appropriate to blame agriculture for preventing effective control of food prices.

In short, under suppressed inflation any unified group receiving an appreciable share of the national income can probably promote inflation or make its avoidance easier by the terms on which it will agree to participate in the national productive effort. Unions are merely one such group, though a very important one.

UNEMPLOYMENT AND WAGE CUTS

In recent years, there has been much concern about whether or not union demands will, or will not, make inflation more likely. Such concern was far less frequent before World War II than it has been since 1945. The reason is that it is only recently that such a possibility became a serious one.

Before World War II, the idea that money wage increases might cause an inflation did not seem plausible because the monetary authority could always stop an inflation by refusing to increase or, if necessary, by reducing the money supply. It is not questioned that this will stop an inflation; however, it may also start a depression. And the long depression of the 1930's has stimulated, in almost all western countries, such fear of a repetition that it is doubtful that a "tight money" policy could be long pursued once unemployment began to arise.

But were economists before 1939, or before 1929, completely indifferent to unemployment? The answer is that they were not indifferent to it but felt that it could be kept within "tolerable" limits by making the level of money wages sufficiently flexible in a downward direction. That is, many (though not all) economists believed that a sufficient cure for unemployment lay in wage cuts.

In its crude form, their reasoning was roughly as follows: In any one firm or industry, wage reductions will lead to lowered costs and, hence, to lower prices and increased sales, output, and employment. And what is true of each sector of the economy taken separately must be true of all sectors taken together.[54] But this, of course, is not true; demand for the output of any one sector comes, to a sizeable extent, from the wage incomes earned in other sectors. A general wage cut, by reducing these incomes, will reduce the demand for the output of all sectors, in total.[55] The net effect of the wage cut upon output and employment thus becomes very uncertain. Moreover, wage reductions often lead to expectations of still further reductions, and this causes prospective buyers of durable goods to delay purchases, thereby tending to reduce current demand for output and employment still further.

This line of reasoning was put in a most striking form by J. M. (later Lord) Keynes,[56] who argued that the only sure effect of wage cuts was upon the rate of interest (by reducing the demand for cash balances).[57] Reducing the rate of interest would, other things equal, increase employment, but Keynes argued that it was foolish to put an economy through the wringer of wage cuts, deflation, and unemployment when the same result (i.e., a reduction in the rate of interest) could be accomplished by expanding the supply of cash balances through banking policy.

[54] This particular minor premise was rarely made explicit. If it had been, this argument could never have had the currency that it did.

[55] Of course, if the effect of the wage cut is to increase the spending of profit receivers or to stimulate investment, this need not be true. But these "secondary repercussions" of a wage cut are highly uncertain and may go in either direction.

[56] J. M. Keynes, *The General Theory of Employment, Interest and Money,* Harcourt, Brace & Company, Inc., New York and London, 1936. For simplified expositions the reader may consult Dudley Dillard, *The Economics of John Maynard Keynes,* Prentice-Hall, Inc., New York, 1948, or A. H. Hansen, *A Guide to Keynes,* McGraw-Hill Book Company, Inc., New York, 1953.

[57] This is the converse of the argument advanced on p. 410, that a shortage of cash balances forces up the rate of interest.

But reducing the rate of interest, however it is accomplished, is not always sufficient to increase employment. Keynes argued that there was a minimum below which the rate of interest could not be reduced and that, when this rate was reached, further expansions of the money supply and/or wage cuts could not increase effective demand.[58]

When this minimum is reached, the only way to increase aggregate demand and employment is direct stimulation of expenditures, and the most practical method of accomplishing this is by increasing government expenditure.[59] Keynes maintained that major depressions in general, and the "great depression" of the 1930's in particular, were characterized by such declines in the inducement to invest that full employment could not be restored solely by reducing the rate of interest and that increased government expenditures were therefore needed.

The Keynesian theoretical model is still debated in professional circles, but its practical implications are widely accepted, even in circles which view them with evident misgivings. Today few economists seriously argue that general wage cuts are either a (politically) possible or an economically efficacious method of ending unemployment. Few men in public life would be prepared to assume responsibility for permitting more than (about) 3.5 to 4.0 million persons to remain unemployed for more than a month or two.[60] Hence, unemployment is likely to be countered, by either major political party, through tax cuts and/or increased government expenditure. But, this creates a danger of secular inflation.

FULL EMPLOYMENT, AND INFLATION

Fear that maintaining full employment promotes inflation arises from the following considerations.[61] Suppose that, in a given year, union demands implied an increase in cost per unit of output of 4 per cent.

[58] This is sometimes called the "liquidity trap." On this point there is still considerable professional disagreement; some economists still insist that, in principle, if wages are cut enough, expenditure in real terms will increase and full employment be restored. (On this point, see M. W. Reder, "The General Level of Money Wages," *Proceedings of Third Annual Meeting, Industrial Relations Research Association,* 1950, pp. 186–202.)

[59] There are, of course, all sorts of other devices that might stimulate total expenditure.

[60] This figure would represent an hypothetical average for the entire economy.

[61] The following writers differ from one another in the extent to which they have expressed concern over this possibility, but all have been concerned over it: Henry Simons, *Economic Policy for a Free Society,* University of Chicago Press, Chicago, 1948; Sir W. H. Beveridge, *Full Employment in a Free Society,* George Allen & Unwin, Ltd., London, 1944, especially pp. 198 ff.; H. W. Singer, "Wage Policy and Full Employment," *Economic Journal,* December 1947, pp. 438–455; M. W. Reder, "The Theoretical Problems of a National Wage-Price Policy," *Canadian Journal of Economics and Political Science,* February 1948, pp. 46–61; Martin Bronfenbrenner, "Postwar Political Economy: the President's Reports," *Journal Political Economy,*

And suppose that employers would not continue to produce the current (full employment) level of output if their profits (per unit of output) were reduced by more than (say) 2 per cent; i.e., if profits per unit of output fell by more than this, they would reduce output and employment. Then, if the unions will not yield on their wage demands, either employment will decline or product prices must rise so that union wage demands may be satisfied without reducing profit margins by more than 2 per cent.

If the government is determined to maintain full employment under all circumstances, then it will, if necessary, increase public expenditure and/or the supply of money so that the price level rises sufficiently to settle the conflict between employers and unions without sacrifice of full employment. And, once it is understood that the government will behave in this way, employers lose the incentive to resist union demands because they know that monetary-fiscal policy will provide the effective demand to purchase the full employment output at prices inflated by (at least) the cost increase resulting from the wage bargain. Some economists believe this opens up the prospect of an unending inflation.

Others disagree, on various grounds:

1. Some economists stress the fact that in the United States, individual or, at most, industrial groups of employers make collective bargaining decisions. These employers retain the incentive to resist union demands whatever the state of monetary-fiscal policy; for, although the government may provide effective demand in general, it will not do so for any one firm or industry.[62] This argument is reinforced by the consideration that maintaining "full employment" need not imply keeping the number of unemployed job seekers at zero but may imply only that unemployment is kept below a tolerable maximum. This may permit considerable losses to employers who yield "too much, too easily" to union wage demands. Hence, these economists argue that unless maintenance of full employ-

---

October 1948, pp. 373–391; C. E. Lindblom, *Unions and Capitalism,* Yale University Press, New Haven, 1949; J. M. Clark, "Criteria of Sound Wage Adjustment, with Emphasis on the Question of Inflationary Effects," Chapter I of *The Impact of the Union,* edited by D. Mc. Wright, Harcourt, Brace & Company, Inc., New York, 1951; Gottfried Haberler, "Wage Policy, Employment and Economic Stability," Chapter II of *The Impact of the Union, op. cit.;* S. H. Slichter, "Do the Wage-fixing Agreements in the American Labor Market Have an Inflationary Bias," *American Economic Review,* May 1954, pp. 322–346.

[62] This line of argument has been espoused by G. L. Bach, "Monetary-Fiscal Policy Reconsidered," *Journal of Political Economy,* October 1949, pp. 383–394; W. A. Morton, "Trade Unionism, Full Employment and Inflation," *American Economic Review,* March 1950, pp. 13–39, M. Friedman, "Some Comments on the Significance of Labor Unions for Economic Policy," *op. cit.,* Albert Rees, "Wage Levels under Conditions of Long-Run Full Employment," *American Economic Review,* May 1953, pp. 451–457; and C. L. Christenson, "Variations in the Inflationary Force of Bargaining," *American Economic Review,* pp. 347–362.

ment is interpreted to mean guaranteeing that every person shall have a job in his present industry, occupation, and location, unions will not be able to exploit a commitment to maintain full employment in such a way as to generate a steady long-run inflation.

2. A second line of reasoning is that even where bargaining is sufficiently centralized so that employers might be tempted to concur in inflationary wage demands, union leaders are sufficiently responsive to considerations of community interest (in avoiding inflation) to restrain themselves and their followers.[63] Some outstanding examples of this are provided by the self-restraint of the British unions during the postwar readjustment, 1945–1951, and by the voluntary adoption of a "wage stop" by the Swedish unions, in 1949–1951, in order to help avoid a further inflation.

3. A third consideration to be taken into account is the fact that technical progress provides, every year, a "cushion" for absorbing the cost-increasing impact of union wage demands. That is, every year the man-hours used per unit of output decline somewhat; over the last 50 to 100 years, this decline has averaged about 2 to 2½ per cent per year. Hence, wages per unit of output can rise at (roughly) this rate without reducing profits per unit of output or increasing the level of prices.[64] This does not, of itself, prevent inflationary wage demands from arising, but it does provide something of a "shock-absorber" to relieve whatever inflationary pressure might develop.

4. Finally some economists, notably S. H. Slichter, argue that, although under continuous full employment strong unions probably cause some inflationary pressure, this can be borne without too much damage to the economy.

The fear that unions would make it impossible to combine full employment with a stable price level was considerably more acute during the hectic days of postwar inflation, 1946–1951, than it is now. However, the dilemma is not permanently resolved, nor can it be. We have now developed an economic philosophy which considers major depressions intolerable; this precludes (in practice) any major downward adjustments in the level of money wages. Along with this view, we have, under political pressure, come to consider major downward adjustments of agricultural prices as impossible of attainment. As a result, we have

[63] See R. Meidner, "The Dilemma of Wages Policy under Full Employment," and Gösta Rehn, "The Problem of Stability: an Analysis and Some Policy Proposals," in *Wages Policy under Full Employment*, edited by Ralph Turvey; William Hodge and Company, London, 1952; also M. W. Reder, "The General Level of Money Wages."

[64] That is, if components of cost, other than wages, are constant, then, with product prices constant, variations in labor cost per unit exactly offset variations in profits per unit.

created an economy in which major inflations are possible, under pressure of war, crop failures, etc., but not deflations. Relative prices must adjust upward to a higher price level and not downwards. This creates an upward bias in prospective yields from investments which would not otherwise exist. Other things equal, this has an inflationary impact upon the economy.

The inflationary potentialities of a full employment policy are greatly increased by the fact that they are becoming recognized, and long-run economic decisions are being made to protect *individuals* or groups from their consequences. Thus, escalator clauses protect union members from loss of real income because of inflation; in a number of countries (though not in the United States), government bonds have had to carry "escalator clauses" in order to find buyers at "reasonable" rates of interest; etc. It is entirely sensible that individuals or groups of individuals should take such steps to protect themselves against inflation. But the effect of such action is to accelerate the rise of costs brought about by an incipient inflation and make it that much more difficult to supress such an inflation, even temporarily. In other words, escalator clauses, "parity" prices for farmers, etc. may not, of themselves, start an inflation, but they make it spread faster once it has commenced.

The reader should not interpret these remarks as implying that the "good old days," when serious depressions were viewed as unavoidable, were preferable to the present state of affairs. The "old" type of monetary-fiscal policy was more effectively insulated against risks of inflation than present-day policy, but it was far more vulnerable to depressive influences. Neither inflation nor depression is pleasant; debate over their relative demerits is akin to discussing the gas chamber versus the firing squad.

WAGES, PRICES AND THE DISTRIBUTION OF THE GAINS OF ECONOMIC PROGRESS

It has frequently been argued that a constant price level is a desirable state of affairs and that increases in the money wage level "should" be limited to what is compatible with a constant price level. This view is often expressed, somewhat elliptically, by saying that the level of money wages should vary proportionately with man-hour productivity;[65] such

[65] Among the more prominent spokesmen for this viewpoint are A. H. Hansen, *Monetary Theory and Fiscal Policy,* McGraw-Hill Book Company, Inc., New York, 1949, Chapter 8; Sir W. H. Beveridge, *Full Employment in a Free Society,* p. 200; S. H. Slichter, *The Challenge of Industrial Relations,* Cornell University Press, New York, 1947, p. 89; J. C. Davis and T. K. Hitch, "Wages and Productivity," *Review of Economics and Statistics,* November 1949, pp. 242–248; J. M. Keynes, *General Theory,* p. 272; Henry Simons, *Economic Policy for a Free Society,* and G. L. Bach, "Monetary-Fiscal Policy Reconsidered."

proposals are usually made on the assumption that (approximately) full employment will be maintained.[66]

The reason for setting a constant price level as a desirable target for monetary-fiscal policy is, in part, a matter of equity. For example, if the price level is constant over time, debt contracts calling for specific money payments at far distant times can be enforced without injustice as the "value" of the money that is repaid will be the same as that which is loaned. Stabilizing the "value" of the currency thus tends to avoid "inflationary injustice" to the numerous pensioners, widows and orphans, college professors, etc. whose income is wholly or in part derived from interest payments on debts (e.g., bonds). Similarly, a constant price-level protects those persons (e.g., civil servants and white collar workers) whose money wages move only slowly.

Conversely, a constant price level protects debtors from the ravages of deflation. It must not be forgotten that sharp price declines have, in the past, caused large numbers of farmers and home owners to lose their property, via foreclosure, in order to satisfy the mortgage holder's or tax collector's claims. However, there have been reputable economists who have advocated, or would tolerate, a secularly rising price level, and others who would desire a falling one.[67]

The desire for a constant price level has other roots besides those of equity. Many economists believe that it is essential to avoid a secularly declining price level in order to avoid discouraging investment and employment. These economists are greatly concerned with avoiding unem-

[66] If there are sharp fluctuations in the level of employment, man-hour productivity will also oscillate markedly and there are few economists who would advocate that money wages should follow the course of man-hour productivity over the course of business cycles.

Before going further, it should be made clear that a wage-price policy aimed at keeping the level of money wages varying proportionately with man-hour productivity is appealing only as a guide to *long-run* policy. Year-to-year variations in man-hour productivity are sometimes quite sharp, but no one would (or ought to) expect that money wages would be varied to keep pace with them. For example, crop failures or a sudden increase in output requiring the use of untrained workers may result in a sharp decrease in over-all man-hour productivity; to reduce money wages under these conditions would imply reducing money wages in the face of rising prices. The impracticability of doing this need hardly be labored to even the most casual reader of a newspaper. Cf. Clark Kerr, "The Short-Run Behavior of Physical Productivity and Average Hourly Earnings," *Review of Economics and Statistics,* November 1949, pp. 299–309.

[67] E. C. Nourse, *Price-Making in a Democracy,* The Brookings Institution, Washington, D.C., 1944, argues for the distribution of productivity gains via a secularly falling price level; this is one implication of his "low price" policy. F. C. Mills, *Prices in Recession and Recovery,* National Bureau of Economic Research, New York, 1936, also argues in favor of disbursing the gains of increased productivity by lowering prices rather than by increasing money incomes.

ployment and are therefore anxious to avoid expectations of falling prices as these would lead prospective buyers of durable assets to defer their purchases until prices were lower, which would lead to lower current output and employment. Thus an economy in which the price level was steadily falling would be one in which there was always an incentive to defer buying durable goods. Conversely, an economy with a steadily rising price level would be one in which there was always an incentive to acquire durables in anticipation of need, in order to "buy before the price goes up." This fact sometimes leads to a desire for a rising price level in order to make it easier to attain full employment. And some economists who feel that there is great danger of a recurrence of mass unemployment, are probably willing to accept the risks of a secularly rising price level in order to avoid those of unemployment. However, most economists are as much concerned with the Scylla of inflation as with the Charybdis of unemployment and announce as their goal "high level employment without inflation."

Reconciling these two objectives is, unfortunately, harder than espousing them. Maintaining a constant price level implies that wages and prices in some industries must fall (when demand for the product falls) and rise in others. Obviously unions and employers in declining industries and areas will resist deflation; if their resistance is successful, relative price adjustments will imply a rise in the general price level. Also, a constant price level implies that industries which experience unusually rapid increases in man-hour productivity would be supposed to pass on these gains via lower product prices rather than as higher wages (to their own workers). These price declines would be needed to offset the rise in product prices resulting from the increase in unit labor costs on account of wage increases in industries experiencing "less than average" increases in man-hour productivity.

Achieving these relative price adjustments would not be easy; unions dealing with firms experiencing rapid increases in man-hour productivity might be (understandably) reluctant to relinquish possible wage gains in order to benefit consumers. And employers in technologically stagnant industries might be very hesitant about raising wages as part of a "national policy." In fact, there is very little that can be done, without fixing individual wages and prices, to implement a policy of relative wage and price adjustments aimed at maintaining "high level employment without inflation." Some economists believe that competitive forces are strong enough in product markets, and unions weak enough in labor markets, so that competitive forces will achieve this result automatically, albeit slowly. Such economists believe that all that is necessary for reasonably close attainment of this objective would be "sound" monetary-fiscal policy.

Other economists, more impressed with the power of unions and monopolies, are inclined to feel the problem less simple.

Relative Shares: Wages versus Profits

The discussion concerning the distribution of the gains of economic progress has thus far proceeded on the implicit assumption that the share of wages in the national income was to remain constant.   But many spokesmen for labor would object and insist that labor's share of the national income ought to increase.   As a matter of ethics, this contention seems more valid to some people than it does to others.   And, because it would take us far afield and ultimately lead nowhere, we shall resist the temptation to join this debate.

However, there is also an important though extremely difficult economic problem involved in this contention.   That is, it is a very real question as to whether it is possible to raise labor's share in national income, relative to the share of profits, by union and/or government policy.   Unfortunately, economists do not agree on an answer to this question, or even upon what would be an effective approach to investigating it.

It is fairly clear that whatever success unions have had in pushing up the level of money wage rates, they have not done so, to any appreciable degree, by causing a reduction in profits (as a share of the national income).   It is possible that in the absence of unionism, the level of profits would have *risen* relative to the level of money wages, and that unionism has merely served to prevent this.   But there is no agreement among economists as to what would have happened to the level of profits if there had been no unions; and there is no hope, at present, of bringing their hypotheses to test and choosing among them.[68]

The basic difficulty in analyzing the relation between wages and profits is that the level of profits depends upon so many important variables, in addition to union or government wage policy.   Most important are the expectations of business men regarding future profits and the prevailing "degree of competition."   In general, high profits tend to attract new investment which, ultimately, tends to lower profits per dollar invested. However, the relation between current profits and the rate of investment depends upon what entrepreneurs expect profits to be in the future.   A

---

[68] See, for example, Clark Kerr, "Trade Unionism and Distribution of Shares," *American Economic Review,* May 1954, pp. 279–292; Martin Bronfenbrenner, "The Incidence of Collective Bargaining," *American Economic Review,* May 1954, pp. 293–307; H. M. Levinson, "Collective Bargaining and Income Distribution," *American Economic Review,* May 1954, pp. 308–318 and *Unionism, Wage Trends and Income Distribution,* Ann Arbor, University of Michigan Press, 1951; and P. E. Sultan, "Unionism and Wage-Income Ratios," *Review of Economics and Statistics,* February 1954, pp. 67–73.

generally pessimistic attitude will permit a relatively high level of current profits to persist for a long time without stimulating the new investment necessary to bring it down; conversely, optimism may prompt substantial new investment at relatively low levels of current profits.

The "degree of competition" affects the level of profit margins in that it determines the extent to which firms will slash profit margins in order to utilize their capital more fully and get larger markets. Obviously the more willing firms are to scramble for larger market shares, the more (other things equal) they will need to add to their productive capacity. And the more they cut prices in their struggle for markets, the lower will be the ratio of profits to costs (and to wages). It might be surmised that entrepreneurs have become more optimistic since World War II than they were in the 1930's, and that in some industries (notably automobiles) they seem to have become more aggressively competitive for markets than they were previously. However, not enough is known about these matters to justify more than the most casual speculation.

Variations in labor's share in the national income[69] depend upon more than changes in the ratio of the "level of profits" to the "level of wages." For the relative importance of wage and nonwage income differs greatly from one industry to another, and shifts in the relative importance of these various industries have caused important changes in labor's share of the national income. Thus the relative decline of agriculture (as a contributor to the national income) has tended to raise labor's share because agriculture has an unusually low ratio of wages to total income. Also, the relative growth of government service and finance (which have relatively high ratios of wages to income) have helped to produce the rise in labor's share for the economy as a whole that is indicated in Table 16-1. These relative shifts in the importance of different industries have been especially important in the period since 1941.[70]

A further factor that affects labor's share of national income is the behavior of the shares of interest and rent. Over short intervals, these shares (especially interest) are determined largely by contract and therefore vary markedly with the price level and the level of economic activity.

---

[69] Labor's share of national income is best measured (as in Table 16-1) by the ratio of Employee Compensation to National Income. Employee Compensation includes not only Wages and Salaries but also Supplements thereto (see pp. 192–194). In 1955, 5.7% of Employee Compensation consisted of Supplements.

[70] See E. F. Denison, "Income Types and the Size Distribution," *American Economic Review*, May 1954, pp. 254–269; Jesse Burkhead, "Changes in the Functional Distribution of Income," *Journal of the American Statistical Association*, June 1953, pp. 192–219; G. J. Schuller, "The Secular Trend in Income Distribution by Type, 1869–1948," *Review of Economics and Statistics*, November 1953, pp. 302–324, and S. S. Kuznets, "Long Term Changes," *op. cit.*, and *National Income: A Summary of Findings*, National Bureau of Economic Research, New York, pp. 49–52.

Thus these shares rose sharply during the great depression of 1929–1933, helping to put a tremendous "squeeze" on profits[71] which impaired ability to pay and probably compelled wage cuts.

Conversely, since 1941 inflation and economic expansion have drastically reduced these shares to the benefit of profit receivers and perhaps (via increased ability to pay) wage earners. But the relation of interest to profits is a most involved matter which depends in good part upon monetary-fiscal policy.

These remarks only scratch the surface of the deep-seated economic forces that determine labor's share in the national income. But this is as far as it is possible to go at present without expounding a whole theory about this subject which is, and has been for some time, the center of extensive and unresolved debates among a number of earnest and highly competent researchers.[72]

Table 16.1. Share of Employee Compensation in National Income in Selected Years, 1929–1952

	Per Cent
1929	58.1
1933*	73.4
1941	61.9
1948	62.7
1949	64.7
1950	63.8
1951	64.3
1952	66.3
1955*	68.9

Source: E. F. Denison, "Income Types and the Size Distribution," American Economic Review, May 1954, pp. 254–269: Table 1, p. 257.

* Computed from Department of Commerce data.

PRODUCTIVITY INCREASES IN COLLECTIVE BARGAINING CONTRACTS

A significant recent experiment in wage-price policy at the single-firm level is the United Auto Workers-General Motors arrangement which, since 1948, has provided for an annual "improvement factor." This "improvement factor" provides for an annual wage increase of 2 to 2½ per cent[73] in hourly wage rates and is supposed to represent the claim of General Motors' workers to their share of the annual increase in labor productivity.

[71] This is the obverse side of the rise of overhead cost per unit of output as a result of a decrease in output (see above, p. 313).

[72] Some of the pertinent analytical refinements are discussed in E. H. Phelps-Brown and P. E. Hart, "The Share of Wages in National Income," Economic Journal, June 1951, pp. 253–277.

[73] Originally the improvement factor amounted to about 2 per cent per year. Later it was increased and is now closer to 2½ per cent.

In 1951, the Wage Stabilization Board (see p. 416) approved wage increases granted in accordance with contractual "improvement factors." This prompted some imitation of such arrangements, but, even so, the "improvement factor" is not very common in collective bargaining contracts outside the automobile industry where the General Motors "pattern" has spread to other major producers. In early 1956, somewhere between 1.5 to 2.0 million workers, most of whom were in automobile production, were subject to an "improvement" factor.

The annual improvement provision is intimately connected with the growth of long-term contracts in the automobile industry. It represents an advance concession, by the manufacturers, of the wage increase which the union could (presumably) secure were it free to renegotiate wages (say) every year. Automobile firms have felt able to offer these terms in exchange for long-term contracts because the increases in productivity that they anticipate (and have experienced) are well in excess of the national average, which was about what they conceded. Indeed, in some union circles, the United Auto Workers has been adversely criticized for accepting too small an improvement factor.

In discussing the annual improvement factor, it is important to distinguish between the viewpoint of the economy as a whole and that of the individual employer.

For a long period of time, the economy as a whole has averaged a growth rate in man-hour productivity of 2 to $2\frac{1}{2}$ per cent. If the objective of monetary-fiscal policy is to maintain labor cost per unit of output constant,[74] it would then be wise for the Federal Reserve System to arrange its operations so as to provide for an appropriate increase in the money supply. The tax and expenditure programs of the Treasury should also be coordinated with banking policy and the over-all economic objectives.

But this does not imply that any individual employer can be expected to commit himself, in advance, to granting the national average wage increase. And, outside of the automobile industry, few employers have been willing to make such commitments. It is proper that monetary and fiscal policy should be designed so as to provide (if possible) the economic climate in which (say) a $2\frac{1}{2}$ per cent per annum increase in average hourly wages will emerge from the operation of labor markets and collective bargaining. It is quite another matter to attempt to direct individual bargainers to grant such increases to conform to a national policy.

It is well to remember that a considerable part of the increase in worker productivity arises from the up-grading of workers from unskilled to semi-

[74] This means increases in wages per hour are proportional to increases in man-hour productivity.

skilled jobs, from the shift of workers from agriculture to industry, and the like. These increases in productivity involve increases in average hourly wages without any change in the wage rates of any specific job. This must be taken into account in calculating the amount "available" for wage rate increases through collective bargaining.

As these remarks would indicate, it is the author's opinion that it is unsound "to attempt to settle individual contracts by referring to targets of monetary-fiscal policy.[75] However, bargainers and arbitrators will, no doubt, continue to talk about "inflationary" and "noninflationary" wage demands without worrying overmuch about whether their remarks make much sense economically. It is probably fortunate that the behavior of bargainers is determined far more by the practical exigencies of their situations than by the "theories" they offer in defense of their actions. (Bargainers' rationalizations and economic realities are discussed further on pp. 155–157.)

DISCUSSION QUESTIONS

1. "Rises in living costs cause increases in the level of money wages." Comment, indicating the elements of truth and falsity in such a statement.

2. Some economists claim that union wage demands cause increases in the price level; others insist that it is increases in the money supply that cause this effect. Are these two contentions incompatible? Under what conditions, if any, can they be reconciled?

3. (a) How does a transfer of workers from agriculture to manufacturing affect the ratio of employee compensation to national income?

(b) What effect does a more favorable outlook for profits have on the share of employee compensation in national income?

4. (a) Discuss the pros and cons of the proposition that a reduction in the general level of money wages will increase the level of employment.

(b) What is the relation among the price level, the level of money wages, and the quantity of money.

(c) How, if at all, do the levels of employment and man-hour productivity affect this relation.

Suggested Readings

Douglas, P. H., "Are There Laws of Production?" *American Economic Review*, March 1948, pp. 1–41.

Dunlop, J. T., *Wage Determination Under Trade Unions*, 2nd edition, Augustus Kelley, New York, 1950.

Friedman, M., "Some Comments on the Significance of Labor Unions for Economic Policy," Chapter X of *The Impact of the Union*, edited by D. McWright, Harcourt, Brace & Co., Inc., New York, 1951.

Hicks, J. R., *The Theory of Wages*, The Macmillan Company, New York and London, 1932.

Kalecki, M., *Theory of Economic Dynamics*, Rinehart & Company, Inc., New York, 1954.

[75] Except when overt wage controls, e.g., under suppressed inflation, are undertaken.

Lindblom, C. E., *Unions and Capitalism,* Yale University Press, New Haven, 1949.

Morton, W. A., "Trade Unionism, Full Employment and Inflation," *American Economic Review,* March 1950, pp. 13–39.

Phelps-Brown, E. H. with S. V. Hopkins, "The Course of Wage-Rates in Five Countries, 1860–1939," *Oxford Economic Papers,* June 1950, pp. 226–296.

Phelps-Brown, E. H. and P. E. Hart, "The Share of Wages in National Income," *Economic Journal,* June 1952, pp. 253–277.

Reder, M. W., "The Theoretical Problems of a National Wage-Price Policy," *Canadian Journal of Economics and Political Science,* February 1948, pp. 46–61; "The General Level of Money Wages," Industrial Relations Research Association, Proceedings of Third Annual Meeting, 1950, pp. 186–202.

Rees, A. E., "Wage Levels under Conditions of Long-Run Full Employment," *American Economic Review,* May 1953, pp. 451–457.

Slichter, S. H., "Do the Wage-Fixing Arrangements in the American Labor Market Have an Inflationary Bias," *American Economic Review,* May 1954, pp. 322–346.

Turvey, Ralph, editor, *Wage Policy Under Full Employment,* William Hodge and Company, London, 1952.

Woytinsky, W. S., and Associates, *Employment and Wages in the United States,* Twentieth Century Fund, New York, 1953, Chapters 4, 5, and 7.

17 The Problem of Unemployment

When laymen and, I fear, many economists think of unemployment they often have in mind something like the following concept: the "unemployed" worker is a male family head, always available for work, whose nonemployment is the result of a decline in aggregate demand for output, and who will be re-employed when "business picks up." Such a simplified notion is, for certain purposes, quite useful, but it can also be very misleading.

Unemployment is the result not only of declines in labor demand but also of increases in supply, and the forces of supply and demand interact in a very complicated fashion. Because the demand for labor in many industries fluctuates from one time of the year to another, we have seasonal fluctuations in employment. These fluctuations are not always paralleled by opposite movements in unemployment because part of the labor supply is also seasonal. This is discussed under Seasonal Unemployment. Then, there is the unemployment that results from the "structural maladjustment" of labor demand and labor supply; this is considered under Structural Unemployment. In General Unemployment we consider the unemployment that results from insufficient effective demand.

SEASONAL UNEMPLOYMENT

The Industrial Pattern

In 1950, the number of persons in the labor force *averaged* about 60 million throughout the year. But this figure considerably understates the total number of persons in the labor force at *some time* during the year, for there is usually considerable seasonal fluctuation in labor force membership.

In the period 1946–1950, the month of highest average employment was July and of lowest, January; the estimated average difference (in employment) between these months was 3.8 million workers.[1] But not all "seasonal workers" enter the labor force at the same time, and, hence, the number of workers in the labor force at *some time* during the year would exceed considerably, perhaps by 5 to 10 per cent, the number of persons "normally" in the labor force during the year.

AGRICULTURE. The most important source of seasonal employment is agriculture. The annual employment cycle in this industry results from its need of many laborers to tend and harvest crops in the summer and early autumn (i.e., from June through October), combined with a need for relatively few workers from November through April. The farm labor force is quite complex in structure and its seasonal fluctuations vary considerably from one region to another. For the country as a whole, in 1950, the monthly average employment on farms was 10.4 million persons; in the low month of December there were 6.8 million persons employed, and in the high month of September, 13.7 million. (The seasonal range was thus about two-thirds of the average level.)[2] About 58 per cent of all farm workers are self-employed farm operators; the majority of these are full-time farmers although it has been estimated that about two-fifths of them devote part of their time to work outside their own farm, and over 25 per cent do some nonfarm work.[3]

The seasonal pattern of agricultural production impresses itself upon employment in the food processing industries which also reach sharp peaks in employment in August and September and hit low points in February-to May. Between 200,000 and 300,000 more workers are employed in the August peak than in the April trough.[4]

CONSTRUCTION. Climatic conditions produce sharp seasonal fluctuations in construction employment.[5] Contractors set plans so that the bulk of the outdoor work is performed in April through October, thereby avoiding the lowered labor efficiency and material spoilage that comes from working out of doors in winter months. In 1946–1950 the difference between the high point of employment in August and the low point in February averaged about 400,000 workers. Prior to World War II, the seasonal fluctuations in construction employment were greater,

[1] W. S. Woytinsky and Associates, *Employment and Wages in the United States,* Twentieth Century Fund, New York, 1953, pp. 315–316.

[2] L. J. Ducoff, "Employment in Agriculture," Chapter 30 in Woytinsky, *op. cit.,* pp. 368–369.

[3] *Ibid.,* pp. 368–370. It should be noted that these farm operators contribute to the seasonal fluctuations in the nonfarm labor supply.

[4] Woytinsky, *op. cit.,* p. 340.

[5] Woytinsky, *op. cit.,* pp. 337–340.

ranging from 675,000 to 1,125,000, and varying with the level of construction activity.[6]

OTHER INDUSTRIES. Coal mining also has a fairly marked seasonal pattern induced by climatic conditions; both anthracite and bituminous mines have higher employment in winter months than in spring and summer. Trade, especially retail, has a marked pattern of seasonal fluctuations. In the autumn months it offers decidedly more jobs than in July and August, and employment reaches a sharp seasonal peak in December during the Christmas rush. Trade employment is lower from January through June than in the fall but not so low as in the summer months; also, February and March employment is typically less than that of April through June. In 1946–1950, trade's seasonal pattern produced an employment fluctuation from the December peak to the February trough of 700,000 to 1 million workers.[7]

The Level of Employment

The significance of seasonal employment fluctuations depends upon the general level of employment. In a fully employed economy, the fact that employment declines in certain industries at certain times of the year need not imply the existence of many idle men looking for work. Ideally, there would be none; seasonal fluctuations in labor demand would merely reflect a transfer of men from one line of work to another. However, the dovetailing of seasonal demands (for labor) of different industries is by no means perfect and (even in the most fully employed economies) a certain amount of wasted time is involved in transferring workers from one employer to another. But in situations of full employment the loss is appreciably smaller than otherwise.

This is partly due to the fact that when labor is scarce it becomes increasingly difficult to secure regular, full-time, male wage earners for seasonal jobs. Such workers find it comparatively easy to get the steady jobs they desire and, therefore, either leave the seasonal industries or compel the "seasonal" employers to make such arrangements that they can offer steady, year-round work.[8] The extra workers taken on for seasonal peaks in employment tend to be "casuals," or part-time workers who enter the labor force just to handle "peak" labor demand.

These part-time workers are, for example, students who take jobs as waiters, athletic instructors, etc. at resorts and hotels during summer vaca-

[6] See W. S. Woytinsky, *Seasonal Variations in Employment in the United States,* Committee on Social Security, Social Science Research Council, Washington, D.C., 1939, pp. 82–85.

[7] Woytinsky, *Employment and Wages in the United States,* p. 340, Table

[8] By using regular workers overtime, spreading out work by producing for inventory, carrying regular workers during slack season when there is relatively little to do (see discussion of guaranteed annual wage, pp. 480–483).

tions, or accept summer jobs as farm hands, in (food) canneries, or in construction gangs. They may also accept clerical or delivery jobs during the Christmas rush. Similarly, housewives take sales jobs in department stores during the Christmas season. The inexperience of such workers and their lack of incentive to be "kept on" combine to make them less desirable employees than family heads.

The comparatively poor quality of the extra workers available in a fully employed economy encourages employers to minimize the number of "extra workers" hired. Another reason for this policy is the fact that, in a fully employed economy, demand is likely to be sufficiently urgent to require some work (ordinarily seasonal in nature) to be done out of season, either to speed completion or to get it done at all. These pressures would suggest that a period of full employment, especially a prolonged one, would see a reduction in the amplitude of seasonal fluctuations in employment. Such reductions seem to have occurred if we compare post-World War II seasonal fluctuations with those existing prior to 1941; however, it is necessary to be very cautious in interpreting data for such a short and atypical period as 1946–1950.[9]

In an economy with a substantial amount of unemployment, seasonal fluctuations in labor demand have an entirely different significance. Under these conditions, it is only at seasonal peaks (if at all) that many family heads can find work. In months of low seasonal demand, many of these workers are simply looking for work. The quality of the extra workers available is, of course, far superior to that available in a "tight" labor market and employers are, correspondingly, not so averse to keeping down the number of steady employees and taking on extras when needed. The wasted labor power of these unemployed is one aspect of the economic loss involved in a depression.

The strong desire of workers for steady jobs with a single employer has, in recent years, led to a proliferation of plans for eliminating seasonal fluctuations in employment within the individual firm. These plans may reduce the loss of man-hours that occurs when individuals are seeking jobs. On the other hand, they may prevent the more efficient interfirm specialization that might arise were firms better able to get satisfactory seasonal workers. It is difficult to guess whether the tendency toward reducing seasonality of work represents a net loss or gain of real gross national product.

Casual Employment

Casual employment is the reverse of steady employment. The casual worker is engaged only for short intervals, by the day, or at most for a week at a time. At present, casual workers are found mainly in agri-

[9] Woytinsky, *Employment and Wages*, p. 340.

culture, longshore work, and in domestic and personal service. The technological basis for casual unemployment is a noncontinuous demand for labor. For example, when ships arrive in port, there is an immediate demand for longshoremen to unload them but, when there are no ships to load or unload, there is no demand at all. Similarly, the need of farmers for harvest workers, of housewives for domestics to help with spring cleaning, of an employer for a substitute stenographer arise only on particular occasions.[10]

The number and quality of casual workers available depends upon the general level of unemployment. In a depression, workers who cannot find work elsewhere tend to invade the casual (and seasonal) industries. The reason for this is obvious; it is in these industries that *new* hirings are made, and a job seeker has his best chance of success. In a depression, openings for steady work become very scarce. Indeed, casual trades such as longshoring have (in the past) tended to have a chronic oversupply of labor except during periods of (over-all) labor shortage. This is because they were the "pools" in which unskilled immigrant labor tended to congregate when other work was not available.

The number of workers in these pools of casual labor depends principally upon the difference between the rate of increase of "steady" urban jobs and the rate at which new workers enter the urban labor force. When the former rate exceeds the latter, the pools of casual labor dry up, and vice versa.

STRUCTURAL UNEMPLOYMENT

Unemployment is called "structural" when it results from a reduction in the demand for labor caused either by a decline in the demand for a particular product, by a change in the method or location of producing a particular commodity, or both. Unemployment is called structural only if the aforementioned reduction in demand is expected to be permanent (i.e., not seasonal or cyclical) and if it cannot be eliminated by *practicable* reductions in wage rates. That is, structural unemployment can be eliminated only by movement of the unemployed workers from their previous industry, occupation, or locality (as the case may be) to some other.

Structural unemployment may result from one or a combination of circumstances: (1) Technological change may reduce the number of man-hours of labor needed for producing a given product and the expan-

---

[10] The perceptive reader will note the overlap of the categories of seasonal and casual employment. A great deal of seasonal employment is simply a seasonally recurring demand for (casual) laborers who are hired for short periods. More or less sharp distinctions between seasonal and casual labor can be drawn on the basis of either the length of the period for which the worker is engaged, or upon the degree of specialized skill required, or both.

sion in output (if any) may not be sufficient to prevent a decline in employment offered by the industry producing this product.   This particular type of structural unemployment is often called "technological unemployment."[11]   (2) A decline in the demand for a particular type of product may cause some of the workers employed in its production to become idle.   (3) A change in the relative advantage of a region for the production of certain commodities, in which it has hitherto specialized, may cause a decline in the volume of employment that it offers.   In practice, it is usually the combination of two or more of these circumstances, working together, that (together with the slow response of labor to unemployment) produce the phenomena we term "structural unemployment."

A few examples may serve to illustrate what we have in mind.   In the 1920's there was a relative shift in demand from high to low priced men's suits.[12]   The Chicago producers who had hitherto tended to specialize in the production of high priced garments were compelled to shift a substantial part of their output to lower priced items.   The lower priced garments used substantially less labor per suit (and output of suits did not increase proportionately with the decline in labor time per suit) so that total employment declined.

The effect of this change in product upon the workers involved may be seen from the following: In a study of 370 of the workers who had been dismissed from tailoring (cutting) jobs because of firms dissolving or leaving the area during the period 1921–1926, it was found that only about one-fourth were, by the summer of 1928, "engaged in any trade at all similar to cutting."   Of the workers who had left "cutting" 61.0 per cent wished to return.[13]   Almost half of the workers studied had found no regular employment for at least three months after their last cutting job, and 32.9 per cent had had no regular employment for six months after being dismissed.[14]

A similar pattern of work histories (in the late 1920's) was found by Isador Lubin[15] who interviewed 754 workers (in three cities) who had lost their jobs due to technological changes.   Of these, 45 per cent had not (at the time of interview) found new jobs, and 65 per cent of these unemployed had already been idle for more than three months.   Of those

---

[11] This is one way of defining technological unemployment; however, it is not the only way. See H. P. Neisser, " 'Permanent' Technological Unemployment," *American Economic Review,* March 1942, pp. 50–71.

[12] R. J. Myers, "Occupational Readjustment of Displaced Skilled Workmen," *Journal of Political Economy,* August 1929, pp. 473–489, especially pp. 473–475.

[13] *Ibid.,* Table VI, p. 480.

[14] *Ibid.,* Table III, p. 479.

[15] I. Lubin, *The Absorption of the Unemployed by American Industry,* The Brookings Institution, Washington, D.C., 1929.

finding jobs, 56 per cent had gone three months or more without work. Forty-eight per cent of the workers displaced received lower wages in their new jobs, and only 19 per cent received higher wages than before.

A more recent study (1948–1949) of workers laid off (because of a mill shutdown) has been done by Myers and Shultz.[16] The city studied had an appreciably greater percentage of unemployment than the country as a whole, although unemployment was low in comparison to what it had been in the 1930's. In general, the workers experienced considerably less difficulty in finding jobs than those reporting in the earlier studies; only 29 per cent of the workers laid off were out of work more than three months. However, over 40 per cent accepted lower earnings in their new jobs, whereas only 14 per cent earned more; furthermore, 17 per cent moved down the occupational hierarchy whereas only 4 per cent moved up.[17]

Still more recently in the early 1950's, it was found that among New England textile workers (who had been laid off as a result of mill shutdowns) almost half of the men were idle for over five weeks before finding other jobs; two-thirds of the women were idle for over ten weeks. The new jobs tended to have lower earnings and to be less skilled than the jobs from which workers were displaced.[18]

In all of these studies and in a study in Great Britain as well,[19] it is made clear that it is the older workers (those past 45) who find it most difficult to get new jobs. In some of the studies, the very young workers seem to find it a little harder to get re-employed than those in the 25 to 40 age group, but this tendency is not clear. However, there is no doubt but that an appreciable reduction in the employment offered in a given occupation in a given locality creates a serious adjustment problem for the workers involved, even during a period of general prosperity.

The problem of re-employing displaced labor is especially serious in areas and industries in which the rate of output growth is comparatively slow, or even negative. Increases in man-hour productivity do not *necessarily* cause unemployment in the firm or industry where they occur; they do this only when the percentage reduction in man-hours per unit of output is greater than the percentage increase in the rate of output. For example, employment increased substantially during the 1920's (1923–1929) in the rapidly growing industries such as automobiles, rubber tires, agricultural implements, electrical goods, etc., despite enormous increases in

[16] C. A. Myers and G. P. Shultz, *The Dynamics of a Labor Market*, Prentice-Hall, New York, 1951.

[17] *Ibid.*, Chapter 3.

[18] W. H. Miernyk, *Inter-Industry Labor Mobility*, Northeastern University, Boston, 1955, Chapter 2, especially pp. 16–25.

[19] *Men Without Work*, Cambridge University Press, Cambridge, England, 1938, pp. 20–23.

output per man hour.[20] But, in the industries where output climbed more slowly or declined (e.g., cigars, cordage and twine, cotton goods, leather shoes, soap, coke oven products, cement, lead), employment fell,[21] despite lower rates of increase in man-hour productivity. (Industry employment figures may, of course, obscure the structural unemployment resulting from regional shifts of production within industries or changes in the type of employee hired.)

It is fairly obvious that increases in man-hour productivity will create more serious adjustment problems in depression than in prosperity. In prosperity, the output of any given industry is more likely to be rising, and increases in man-hour productivity are more likely to be reflected in increased output (and not in lowered employment). Furthermore, in prosperity, the voluntary quit rate is relatively high, and the reductions in workforce that a firm must make can, to a greater extent than in depression, be made by nonreplacement of job quitters (instead of by layoffs). Also, in a period of prosperity, workers who have been thrown out of their occupation can more easily find a new one. In general, the distressing type of prolonged idleness (described below) that is conjured up by the phrase "structural unemployment" is usually a mixture of "structural maladjustment" and depression rather than of the former alone. This is because workers do move, albeit slowly, to new trades if jobs are available (even though the jobs are not so good as those formerly held).

"Structural maladjustments" that produce serious unemployment problems are likely to involve a decline in the volume of employment offered by one or more dominant industries in a *given area*. Where the decline of one industry in an area is offset by the rise of another, the transfer of workers can usually be accomplished[22] although the transfer will not be painless to those in the declining industry. It is where employment opportunities decline in an area as a whole that one usually finds the phenomena indicative of structural unemployment.

Examples of structural unemployment could be found in the 1920's and 1930's in many New England mill towns where the decline in cotton spinning (due to a shift of the industry to the South) caused a reduction in employment opportunities.[23] This decline was interrupted during

---

[20] See S. Fabricant, *Employment in Manufacturing: 1899–1939,* National Bureau of Economic Research, 1942, Appendix F.

[21] *Ibid.*

[22] The transfer may, and often does, involve several steps; e.g., young workers enter the expanding industry leaving openings in (say) local service industries for older workers being discharged from the declining industry.

[23] See H. J. Lahne, *The Cotton Mill Worker,* Farrar & Rinehart, 1944, pp. 90–91. Lahne points out that there were (according to the Census of Manufactures) 203,008 New England workers employed in textiles in 1919 and only 66,000 in 1939.

World War II and the period immediately following, but it began again in 1951. As a result one can again find pockets of "structurally unemployed" workers in New England mill towns, though they are not so numerous as in the 1930's.[24] Other examples could be found in coal mining towns in Ohio, Pennsylvania, and West Virginia in the late 1920's and 1930's where declining coal production combined with mechanization reduced employment from 1,356 million man-hours in 1923 to 1,168 million in 1929 and to 678 million in 1939.[25]

However, the United States has been subject to relatively little structural unemployment because of the relatively rapid growth of output (especially in heavy industry). "Structural adjustments," i.e., changes in occupation and location of workers, have been accomplished without the creation of many pockets of prolonged regional unemployment. However, in Great Britain in the 1920's and 1930's, over-all growth in output and employment was insufficient to permit such (comparatively) easy adjustments. Consequently, the stagnation in such industries as shipbuilding and repairing, coal mining, and textile products created pockets of industry-wide unemployment which "beautifully" exemplify the phenomena characteristic of structural unemployment.

For example, in the summer of 1936, the unemployed constituted but 6.2 per cent, 7.6 per cent, and 8.9 per cent of the insured workers in the Southeast, London, and Southwest regions (of England) respectively; but the corresponding percentages were 21.2 per cent in the Northeast and 32.2 per cent in Wales.[26] This uneven distribution of unemployment was, to a considerable extent, the obverse side of the relative decline in employment offered by the aforementioned industries which were concentrated in the regions hardest hit by unemployment.[27]

One manifestation of structural unemployment is a tendency for continuous joblessness to become prolonged (even to periods in excess of a year). Long stretches of unemployment, unrelieved even by temporary work, reflect a dearth of new job openings, a phenomenon characteristic of a "depressed" area.[28] In such areas, new firms do not spring up, old ones do not expand, and, in consequence, workers hold on for dear life

[24] Miernyk, *op. cit.*

[25] See "Historical Statistics of the United States," *op. cit.*, Table G-158, p. 153.

[26] *Men Without Work*, Table IV, p. 16. See also D. G. Champernowne, "The Uneven Distribution of Unemployment in the United Kingdom, I," *Review of Economic Studies*, 1937–1938, pp. 93–106, especially Table II, p. 95.

[27] In these depressed areas there were important secondary effects, especially on construction activity, which intensified the unequal distribution of unemployment among regions.

[28] The strong positive association between the percentage of workers unemployed and the ratio of "long unemployed" (without a job for one year or more) to all unemployed is made very clear in *Men Without Work*, pp. 9–17.

to whatever jobs they have. As might be expected, the incidence of prolonged unemployment is far heavier among the older workers than among the younger ones. The "propensity to lose one's job" may increase with age but not by so much as the "propensity not to get a new job."[29] This is partly due to the fact that the young (see pp. 295–297) are more ready to move in order to get a job; i.e., unemployed young people tend to leave the depressed areas, leaving behind the old who thus become an increasing fraction of the unemployed in the areas where new jobs are least likely to develop.

Older workers tend to "hang on" to a declining industry or area (or both) in the hope of once again getting steady employment rather than to make the painful adjustment involved in finding a new type of job in a new place. If it were made clear, once and for all, that a particular area or industry would not again furnish workers with steady employment, it might be easier to induce them to look for a new kind of job (if necessary) in a new place. But the issue is rarely so clear; industries or areas "die slowly" and unevenly. A worker whose situation implies declining employment opportunities is not, as a rule, continuously unemployed for years at a stretch;[30] rather, he finds work only intermittently, frequently at (temporary) odd jobs. These intermittent jobs plus relief or unemployment benefits enable him to stay alive while clinging to the declining industry or region.

The reason for clinging to a declining employment opportunity is that the good permanent jobs in an industry or area do not all disappear at once; some workers who lose their jobs are able to secure new (steady) ones, and their example keeps hope alive in others. Coupled with hope is fear of the adjustments involved in changing occupations; if a worker has a specialized skill, this skill will (very likely) be useless in a new occupation and he will be compelled to accept a job as an unskilled laborer. And even if a worker's job does not involve any special skill, the seniority factor in layoffs, promotions, and other matters makes him anxious to preserve his seniority with a given company rather than start over again somewhere else.

The problem of reducing resistance to changes in employer, area, etc. is thus interrelated with that of compensating "structurally unemployed" workers for loss of opportunity to use valuable skill, for loss of seniority rights, etc.; this is discussed on pp. 479–480. It might be noted that union attempts to protect members' jobs through make-work rules,

---

[29] See *Men Without Work*, pp. 20–24.

[30] Even in the extreme situations found in Britain during the 1930's, continuous unemployment for more than a year was the exception rather than the rule. See H. W. Singer, "The Process of Unemployment in the Depressed Areas (1935–1938)," *Review of Economic Studies*, 1938–1939, pp. 177–188.

etc. (see pp. 197–200) are part of the resistance to adjustment that is a by-product of structural unemployment.

GENERAL UNEMPLOYMENT

Cyclical Unemployment

It is not easy either to distinguish the cyclically unemployed individual from one who is structurally unemployed or even to allocate a community's unemployed, on any given day, among the categories cyclical, structural, seasonal, etc. Fortunately, it is not necessary that we should do so; it is enough that we should be able, conceptually, to distinguish among these different causes of unemployment. The reason for distinguishing between different kinds of unemployment is that their economic significance differs and so do their appropriate remedies.

"Cyclical" unemployment may be thought of as the unemployment that results from declines in the community's demand for output. An initial decline in output, for any reason, causes a decline in employment which reduces the total income of wage earners, thereby reducing their expenditure, which in turn reduces demand for output and employment still further, etc.[31] The reduction in employment resulting from this process is roughly equal to cyclical unemployment, as the cyclical fluctuation in labor supply is small.

From the viewpoint of economic policy, "pure" cyclical unemployment is remediable by expanding effective demand through monetary policy, fiscal policy, or both. It does not require special efforts in particular industries or areas.[32] The "cyclically" unemployed will get their old jobs back, or similar ones, when the course of the business cycle heads toward expansion.

Not so the structurally unemployed. Prosperity lightens and depression adds to their job-getting difficulties, but they are, in all phases of the business cycle, less fully employed than the labor force as a whole. To attempt to give them more employment, through over-all expansion of the economy, would create labor shortage and inflation in the other parts of the economic system before the structurally unemployed found steady work.[33]

[31] This is the famous "multiplier effect."

[32] This is, in practice, an exaggeration. Unemployment never hits the labor force in a random manner; cyclical declines are usually concentrated in durable goods manufacturing and the middle-western cities (e.g., Detroit, Chicago, Pittsburgh) that specialize therein. Furthermore, there are some fairly well known "cycles," which generate unemployment that is both structural and cyclical. The moral of these remarks is that "pure" cyclical unemployment is an intellectual construction with no exact counterpart in the "real world." Actual situations of unemployment involve cyclical and other causes in varying degrees.

[33] Of course, if the total demand for labor, and the resulting inflationary pressure,

A more fruitful approach toward this type of unemployment is to encourage movement of the structurally unemployed toward new areas, industries, or both.   One technique, now being tried in New England, is to encourage new industry to move to areas where there are large numbers of "structurally" unemployed workers.   Favoring such areas in awarding government contracts can help to encourage such movements.   Another method is to encourage people to leave localities of structural unemployment.   This approach, though often a sound one,[34] meets with bitter resistance from those having economic or sentimental ties to the depopulated area.

As we have already seen, seasonal and cyclical unemployment are so related that maintaining full employment substantially reduces employment fluctuations in "seasonal" industries, as well as facilitating the securing of "fill-in" jobs for those workers who remain seasonally unemployed.

PERMANENT SECULAR UNEMPLOYMENT

There has never been any doubt but that the levels of employment and unemployment fluctuated with the general level of business activity.   However, it was only in the 1930's that economists[35] began seriously to consider the possibility that even in prosperity there might be general, as distinguished from a "little" structural, unemployment.   The events that prompted these unhappy speculations are well indicated by Table 17.1.   As this table shows, for most of the 1930's the average annual level of unemployment was 9 to 10 million or higher; even in the "boom year" of 1937, unemployment was 7,700,000.

Given these facts and Keynes' explanation of them,[36] a number of economists devised theories of secular stagnation.   These theories have not been so popular in the fully employed 1950's as in the depressed 1930's; however, convinced "stagnationists" will argue that the difference between the 1930's and the 1950's is due to expenditure by the govern-

---

becomes great enough, the structurally unemployed will be floated into jobs on the flood of a general inflation.   For example, the structural unemployment in New England was eliminated during, and immediately after, World War II.   The issue is not whether structural unemployment *can* be cured in this manner but whether it is desirable to do it.

[34] However, there are hidden costs in abandoning an area.   "Developed" areas have schools, roads, and other public facilities which must be built afresh in new areas.   Relative local tax rates do not always reflect these cost differences.

[35] I am referring to the "respectable" section of the fraternity.   "Heretics" like Marx, Hobson, and Veblen had long discussed such possibilities.

[36] J. M. Keynes, *The General Theory of Employment, Interest and Money,* Harcourt, Brace and Co., New York, 1936.

Table 17.1.   Estimated Unemployment, 1929–1954

Year	Average Annual Number Unemployed, in Thousands	Percentage of Civilian Labor Force
1929	1,550	3.2
1930	4,340	8.7
1931	8,020	15.9
1932	12,060	23.6
1933	12,830	24.9
1934	11,340	21.7
1935	10,610	20.1
1936	9,030	16.9
1937	7,700	14.3
1938	10,390	19.0
1939	9,480	17.2
1940	8,120	14.6
1941	5,560	9.9
1942	2,660	4.7
1943	1,070	1.9
1944	670	1.2
1945	1,040	1.9
1946	2,270	3.9
1947	2,140	3.6
1948	2,060	3.4
1949	3,395	5.5
1950	3,142	5.0
1951	1,879	3.0
1952	1,673	2.7
1953	1,602	2.5
1954	3,230	5.0

Source: 1929–1949, from Woytinsky et al., *Employment and Wages in the United States,* Twentieth Century Fund, New York, 1953, Tables 169 and 170, pp. 398–399; 1950–1954 from Bureau of the Census.

ment for military purposes, and that ending the "Cold War" would start a prolonged depression.

Most economists would strongly disagree with this contention, and it is not necessary to consider its merits here.   We mention the stagnation thesis only for the purpose of pointing out that "general" unemployment can exist (and, at times, has) at all phases of the business cycle.

How Full Should Employment Be?

It is generally accepted, both among economists and politicians, that "full employment" is a primary desideratum of government policy.   However, the goal of full employment is by no means unambiguous.   One can posit that everyone should always have a job available to him at not less than his current weekly wage.   But attaining such a goal would imply either creating special jobs (by government action) for workers in declining industries and areas and/or generating considerable inflationary pressure on the economic system.   Any approximation to full employment which might be consistent with a tolerably constant price level would probably leave some unemployment in textile towns in New England, in coal mining towns, etc.

Suggesting that we tolerate some unemployment to prevent inflation and to permit relative expansion and contraction of employment in different industries may seem heartless and wanting in sympathy for the unemployed.   And, if the full cost of unemployment must be borne by the hapless workers whom it befalls, there is much to be said for "a job for every man every day."   However, a well designed Social Security system, better than what we now have by a considerable margin, should relieve us of this dilemma.   This problem will be discussed later, in Chapter 19.

DISCUSSION QUESTIONS

1. Why has seasonal unemployment been less since World War II than in the 1930's?

2. What objections can be offered to a full employment policy aimed at providing job security for all by always having more job openings than job applicants?

3. What effect would the restoration of free immigration have upon the number of seasonal and casual workers?   Why?

Suggested Readings

The references at the end of Chapter 4 are also applicable here.

P A R T   F O U R

The War on Poverty

18 | The Causes of Income Inequality

To a considerable extent, the analysis of wages is, of itself, an explanation of income differences. A major reason why some people have higher incomes than others is that they are able to work more hours per year, earn more per hour, or both. However, there is another reason; some people have acquired or inherited more income-yielding property than others. In practice, it is the high earners who inherit or accumulate property rather than the low ones, and therefore the unequal distribution of property income tends to reinforce rather than offset the inequality of income from wage earnings.

There are two main reasons why people are concerned with inequality of income:[1] one is the purely ethical question of fairness; the other is the question of whether the incomes of the less fortunate members of the community are high enough to enable them to maintain a standard of living assuring "health and decency."

These two reasons are interrelated but not identical. Many people feel that incomes in the United States are distributed unfairly even among those who are well above minimum "health and decency" standards and would like to remedy this by increasing the personal income taxes paid by the more well-to-do. Others feel that only extreme physical discomfort of the poor, if that, can justify income equalizing activity by the state.[2] However, historically, the effective limitation upon ability to raise minimum income standards has not been ethical reluctance but simple (economic) incapacity; this is still the case in all but a very few "advanced" countries. Until recently, we could not have given everyone, or almost everyone,

[1] Another reason for concern with income distribution is that the more equal the distribution of income, other things being equal, the higher the level of consumption expenditure. However, we shall not discuss this aspect of the matter here.

[2] This statement applies only to activity directly and avowedly aimed at income equalization. The "side effects" of war financing, etc. also have tended to equalize (post-tax) income distribution.

an income sufficient to maintain him in accordance with even the then current notions of health and decency. Now, however, in the United States at least, we are (or are close to being) economically able to provide everyone with a decent minimum income. Furthermore, the government, through social security and other measures to be discussed, has made a substantial beginning toward providing such incomes to all, though there is still need for improvement.

There remain, of course, important questions of how high the social minimum income[3] shall be and how it shall be guaranteed. That is, we must decide the combination of devices, e.g., minimum wage legislation, family allowances, unemployment insurance, etc., to use in guaranteeing the social minimum.

Reducing income inequality, in general, and raising the social minimum, in particular, has always been of great concern to the labor movement. This is partly because of the fact that most wage earners are low income receivers and are benefited by whatever benefits low income groups. Hence a large part of the political efforts of the labor movement have been expended on behalf of low income groups as such.[4] Furthermore, raising and defending the social minimum is of the utmost importance to organized labor as a method of curbing low wage competition.

Raising the incomes of low earners may be approached in two ways: (1) We may attempt to increase their earning power in the labor market, and (2) we may attempt to supplement their income so as to enable them to attain the social minimum income whatever their earnings. In Chapter 19 we consider "income supplementation" and in Chapter 20 we discuss measures to increase earnings and achieve related objectives. But first, it is necessary that we analyze the economic forces that place certain persons and families in the position of low earners or income receivers. That is the task of the present chapter.

THE SIZE DISTRIBUTION OF INCOME

Family Income

The significance of figures on income is very limited unless income receivers are grouped as families. If large families tended to have higher

[3] We posit that in a given community there is some minimum income, either in cash or goods and services, that will be given to anyone so long as he is accepted as a member of the group. This income we call the "social minimum income" or, for short, the "social minimum." The social minimum is not easily measured, but its "height" is reflected in such things as the amount of unemployment benefit paid, the size of old age pension, etc. This is related to the social minimum *hourly* wage rate that we have already discussed (pp. 324–326), but they are not the same. For brevity, we refer to both of them as the "social minimum," but will distinguish explicitly whenever there is danger of confusion.

[4] The only outstanding exception to this statement would be the behavior of the AFL in its "voluntristic" period, see pp. 94–96.

incomes than small ones, income inequality among families would, in fact, reflect a tendency for per capita income among individuals to be distributed more equally than income among families.

As Table 18.1 shows there is a good deal of variation of income among families of the same size. And (median) family income is related to family size, but not in such a way as to give more income to families with

Table 18.1.   Distribution of Families by Total Money Income (in per cent), 1954; also Median Income of Families by Number of Children under 18, 1954

Total Money Income	Per Cent 100.0
Under $500	4.6
$500– 999	4.2
1,000– 1,499	5.6
1,500– 1,999	5.4
2,000– 2,499	5.5
2,500– 2,999	6.4
3,000– 3,499	7.5
3,500– 3,999	7.9
4,000– 4,499	8.4
4,500– 4,999	7.2
5,000– 5,999	11.9
6,000– 6,999	8.5
7,000– 9,999	11.1
10,000–14,999	4.4
15,000–24,999	1.0
25,000 and over	0.4

Families with Specified Number of Children under 18 Years

	All Families	0	1	2	3	4	5	6 or over
Median Income	$4,173	$3,929	$4,335	$4,506	$4,335	$3,949	$3,155	$3,252

Source: "Family Income in the United States: 1953 and 1954," *Current Population Reports*, Bureau of the Census, Series P. 60, No. 20, December 1955, Table 5, p. 14.

more members and therefore (presumably) more need.   Median income increases with number of children only up to two and diminishes with the number of children when there are more than two; this is true both of urban and rural families.   However we explain this fact, it implies that families with more children do not have higher median incomes than those with fewer.[5]

[5] Put succinctly, when children are classified by the income level of their parents, the income of the median child (in 1954) was $10 less than the income of the median family.   From "Family Income in the United States; 1954 and 1953," *Current Population Reports*, Bureau of the Census, Series P-60, No. 20, December 1955, Table 5, p. 14.

However, there is a greater tendency for wives to work when the husband's earnings are low than when they are higher.[6] That is, the working habits of wives tend to equalize the distribution of income among families. In effect, the typical American family behaves as though freedom from gainful employment for the wife was one of the "luxuries" purchased by relatively high earning husbands.

It is quite likely that the substantial increase, since 1939, in the percentage of married women engaged in gainful employment[7] has been a factor in the reduction in inequality of family income that has occurred since that date.[8] That is, it is likely that it was the wives of relatively low earning (rather than those of higher earning) spouses who accepted the jobs newly created in the 1940's. Other factors in this equalization (since 1939) have been the reduction in occupational wage differentials (discussed in Chapter 15) and the relative increase in farm incomes which were (and are) among the lowest in the nation.

But although families whose chief breadwinner is a relatively low earner can partially remedy their deficiency in income by furnishing extra labor services, large families still tend to be at an income disadvantage and constitute a major part of the subminimal income group. This is especially true when the presence of small children prevents the wife from working. Furthermore, the incomes of such families are particularly sensitive to depression as secondary earners are more likely to become and/or remain unemployed than primary earners.[9]

Age and Incomes: Life Income Patterns

Another important group of subminimal families are those whose chief earner is relatively old. As Table 18.2 shows, after age 45 to 54, median income tends to decline with age. This is partly, but not wholly, offset by the fact that older persons have few dependents.[10] The decline in income with age is due largely to a decline in earning power; older persons cannot work so steadily or effectively as younger ones and, hence, they tend both to earn lower hourly rates of pay and to work fewer hours per year.

Older workers are peculiarly sensitive to depressions, for, as we have

[6] See H. P. Miller, *Income of the American People*, John Wiley and Sons, Inc., NewYork, 1955, pp. 121–122.

[7] See Miller, *op. cit.*, pp. 86–91.

[8] This change in the distribution of income is discussed in Miller, *op. cit.*, pp. 109–112; see also Selma Goldsmith et al., "Size Distribution of Income Since the Mid-Thirties," *Review of Economics and Statistics*, Vol. 36, February 1954; S. S. Kuznets, *Shares of Upper Income Groups in Income and Savings*, National Bureau of Economic Research, New York, 1953, Chapters 2–4.

[9] This is indicated by the higher incidence of unemployment among females.

[10] See M. W. Reder, "Age and Income," *American Economic Review*, Vol. XLIV, May 1954, pp. 661–670.

seen (pp. 293–295), once they lose a job they find it unusually difficult to get another.   In addition, those older workers who find it most difficult to work steadily are the manual laborers whose previous low earnings have made it difficult for them to save.   And, most serious of all is the plight of the very numerous aged widows who have never worked, or not for a very long time, and are incapable of beginning at an advanced age.[11]

For these reasons, providing for the aged presents an important problem to the community.   And, the attempts of workers to solve this problem for themselves, through collective bargaining, has had considerable repercussions on labor-management relations in the past decade.

Table 18.2.   Median Total Money Income, for the United States in 1954, for Families, by Age of Head and for Unrelated Individuals

	Families Age of Head, Years							Unrelated Individuals
	14 to 24	25 to 34	35 to 49	45 to 54	55 to 64	65 & over	Total	
Median Income	$3136	4255	4657	4811	4052	2294	4173	↓

Age of Person, Years

	14 to 24	25 to 34	35 to 44	45 to 54	55 to 64	65 & over	Total
Median Income	$1108	$2570	$2094	$1936	$1288	$796	$1224

Source: "Family Income in the United States: 1954–1953," *Current Population Reports,* Bureau of the Census, Series P. 60, No. 20, December 1955, Table 4, p. 10.

As Table 18.2 shows, it is the very young workers, many of whom are still in school and working only part-time, and the elderly who are the low earners (and their families the low income recipients).   This fact should be taken into account in interpreting data on income distribution such as those presented in Table 18.1.   For such figures refer only to one given year and are not indicative of the *life* earnings of the various families in the nation.   To *some extent,* each family takes a turn in the relatively high income brackets, when its earners are in the prime of life, but at the beginning and end of the life earning cycle[12] are in comparatively low income classes.   In any one year, the family income distribution includes families in all stages of their life income cycle.

However, some people, because they have more property, or are in a more lucrative occupation, have higher incomes than the average at all

[11] See P. O. Steiner, "The Size, Nature and Adequacy of the Resources of the Aged," *American Economic Review,* Vol. XLIV, May 1954, pp. 645–660.

[12] Different occupations have different "typical" life earning cycles.

stages of their lives. In the following sections of this chapter we shall consider the various factors that cause some persons to *earn* more than others, irrrespective of age. We shall not consider that part of income inequality that results from unequal ownership of property.

INCOME AND OPPORTUNITY: RESTRICTION ON ENTRY

In this section we shall study the differentials in earnings that are associated with differences in "economic opportunity." That is, we shall study those economic and social forces that operate to secure higher incomes for doctors, lawyers, and corporate executives than for common laborers; we shall also consider the forces that give an income advantage to the members of certain social and racial groups.

It is obvious that certain occupations typically pay more than others and are pleasanter and more prestigious as well. Why then, don't people in the less favored occupations change to the more favored? In some few cases, it may be that people in the less favored occupations would not want to change, but usually their wishes are irrelevant because they are unable to change. This is not merely a matter of persons who are "too old to change," for most young people enter lines of work which they recognize are less promising than certain others but "choose" as they do because the superior opportunities are, somehow, closed to them.

The superior earning power of the professions, of corporate executives, and the like is related to the fact that "qualified" personnel is scarce, and the services of such persons are highly valuable to a person or firm in need of them. "Qualified" personnel is relatively scarce because, wisely or not, employers of this type of "labor" insist, as evidence of qualification, upon training and credentials that imply both college education and/or a great deal of successful experience. College education is becoming increasingly widespread, but it is still not possessed by the bulk of the labor force. Hence, the rapid increase in demand for this type of "skilled labor" has not been offset by an up-grading of manual or clerical workers analogous to the up-grading of the unskilled to fill vacancies in skilled jobs. (For example, without entering the merits of the question, it may be noted that we do not attempt to relieve shortages of (medical) doctors by promoting veterinarians.)

In other words, the continuing high wages of members of the professions and of management are due both to the need for their services and the exacting requirements of their employers. The combination of these factors results in a short supply of acceptable job candidates relative to a demand that is expanding rapidly, at least in the United States. These two groups of "workers" are, therefore, "noncompetitive" with the rest of the labor force.

THE VALUE OF A COLLEGE EDUCATION

The obvious income advantage of corporate managers, professional, and technical personnel is well known to be somehow associated with the fact that persons in these occupations possess college training. The association of college training with relatively high income is clearly indicated by Table 18.3 and the relation of occupation to education is shown in Table 18.4.[13]

Table 18.3.   Median Incomes of Heads of Spending Units, Classified by Age and Education* of Heads of Units, 1954

Median Income of Unit by Education of Head of Unit

Age of Head of Unit (1)	Elementary Grades Amount (2)	High School Grades Amount (3)	High School Grades Amount in Excess of Elementary (4)	College Amount (5)	College Amount in Excess of High School (6)
18 to 24...	†	$2,630	†	$2,860	$230
25 to 34...	$3,110	4,970	$1,860	5,690	720
35 to 44...	3,490	4,910	1,420	6,910	2,000
45 to 54...	3,530	4,590	1,060	6,980	2,390
55 to 64...	2,810	4,190	1,380	5,440	1,250
65 and over	1,260	1,770	510	†	

Source: Testimony of James McCaskill before Joint Committee on the Economic Report, 84th Congress; "Low Income Families." *Hearings before Subcommittee on Low Income Families of the Joint Committee on the Economic Report; 84th Congress*, Government Printing Office, Washington, D.C., 1955, p. 247.

* Education signifies attendance but not necessarily graduation.
† Not reported.

The tendency for members of the high earning occupations to possess college training is due to the fact that, in practice, entry into the higher ranks of management is restricted mainly (though not entirely) to those with college degrees. A college degree, therefore, is almost a ticket of admission to the race for the better paying and more prestigious jobs offered in business. There are, of course, other characteristics that help or hinder a career in management; but a college diploma is a major asset —and lack of one, a serious handicap.

[13] It should be noted that Table 18.4 understates seriously the true occupational advantage of the college trained, for most of the 13 per cent of nongraduates in the class of proprietors, managers, and executives are self-employed small businessmen or farmers. Few, indeed, would be hired as executives.

Table 18.4. Percent Distribution by Major Occupation Group, for Employed Males 22 to 74 Years Old, by Years of School Completed, for the United States, 1950

Years of School Completed

Major occupational group	Total Employed Males, 22 to 74 Years Old		Elementary School		High School		College		Median School Years Completed
	Num-ber*	Per Cent	Less than 5 Years	5 to 8 Years	1 to 3 Years	4 Years	1 to 3 Years	4 Years or More	
	Thou-sands								
Total	35,644		3,429	12,825	6,618	7,341	2,658	2,774	11.2
Per cent		100.0	100.0	100.0	100.0	100.0	100.0	100.0	
Nonfarm white collar workers:									
Clerical and sales workers	4,463	12.5	3.2	6.5	12.7	21.0	26.9	15.1	12.3
Managers and pro-prietors	4,055	11.4	5.0	7.4	10.8	15.4	22.2	17.9	12.2
Professional workers	2,774	7.8	0.8	1.2	2.5	6.1	17.3	55.0	16+
Nonfarm manual workers:									
Operatives	7,111	19.9	21.3	24.5	25.3	17.3	8.3	2.3	8.8
Craftsmen and foremen	7,044	19.8	12.6	22.1	25.2	22.3	13.1	4.5	9.5
Laborers	2,733	7.7	17.9	10.2	6.8	3.9	1.9	.7	8.1
Service Workers	2,122	6.0	8.0	7.2	6.2	5.1	3.9	1.4	8.7
Farm workers:									
Laborers	1,157	3.2	9.9	4.2	2.1	1.6	0.8	0.4	7.6
Farmers	3,894	10.9	20.2	15.8	7.7	6.6	4.7	2.0	8.3
Not reported	291	0.8	1.0	0.9	0.8	0.7	0.8	0.7	8.9

Source: Paul C. Glick, "Educational Attainment and Occupational Advancement," Table 1, Paper presented at the Second World Congress of the International Sociological Association held in Liege, August 24 to September 1, 1953.

* The small number of males with school years not reported is excluded.

It is also clear that college training is necessary in order to pursue a career in the professions. A career in the higher ranks of civil service, in the ranks of commissioned officers in the armed services, in the managerial ranks of business, and in the various professions (law, medicine, engineering, etc.) is confined mainly to those with college training.

The income advantage of the college graduate does not always[14] appear immediately upon graduation, but it becomes quite marked for persons in

[14] The incomes of skilled workers hit their peaks relatively early in their lives and for a short part of their careers (corresponding to the years immediately after college graduation) may exceed those of college graduates.

their 30's and it increases thereafter with age (until retirement).[15] Estimates of the size of the differential in earning power accruing to the typical college graduate may differ, but the existence of an appreciable differential is scarcely open to question.

Who Gets a College Education?

The continued existence of this differential in earning power is the net result of differences in the financial ability and willingness of the various families in the community to provide for the education of their offspring and in the ability of the offspring to benefit from such education. The cost of a college education in terms of tuition, board and room, etc., is quite high. How high depends on the college, whether or not the student lives at home, etc. But the effect of cost as a restriction upon college entry is very appreciable, as is evidenced by the fact that a very much larger percentage of the children of high income recipients (than of other income groups) attend college;[16] this also holds true, although to a lesser degree, for high school training.[17]

In view of the facts, it will cause no surprise to learn that among children of the same level of ability, there is a strong association of the level of parental income with the percentage of children who (eventually) go to college.[18]

But can't poor boys work their way through college? Yes, but it is not easy. It is not hard for a student to defray part of the expenses of a college education by working, but it is difficult to earn all of them. In a recent study[19] it was found that only 38 per cent of the male and 17 per cent of the female graduates earned as much as half of their college expenses, though only 17 per cent of the male and 45 per cent of the female

[15] See J. O. Kamm, "Investment-In-Self," *Review of Economics and Statistics*, May 1952, pp. 179–188, especially Table 4, p. 183. The median annual wage income (in 1939) of college graduates as compared with that of all white males at various ages between 25 and 64 was as follows (source: Kamm, *loc. cit.*):

	Age				
	25–29	30–34	35–44	45–54	55–64
Persons in college (4 years or more)	1567	1998	2465	2679	2395
All persons	1017	1221	1320	1349	1090

[16] See S. E. Harris, "How Shall We Pay for Education," Harper and Brothers, New York 1948, pp. 9–13, 53–58, and Chapter 12. Also P. E. Davidson and H. D. Anderson, *Occupational Mobility in an American Community*, Stanford University Press, Stanford, Calif., 1937, pp. 35–38 and 172–175.

[17] See Table 18.3.

[18] Harris, *op. cit.*, pp. 9–11 and 55–58.

[19] Havemann and West, *They Went to College*, Harcourt, Brace & Company, Inc., New York, 1952, p. 19.

graduates were entirely supported by their parents. In short, it is possible, although not easy, for a determined and energetic person to put himself through college without financial assistance.

The reason why more do not do so is to be found in the background of the children of low income families. The parents of these children are themselves uneducated for the most part; they are likely neither to appreciate the advantages of education nor to be able to furnish guidance to their children as to the method for securing them. Furthermore, such parents are not likely to furnish the type of home environment in which concern with intellectual attainments is encouraged; this makes it more difficult to succeed in school, which tends to discourage ambition to go further. And lack of parental encouragement is not the only hurdle for the children of manual workers in pursuit of a college education; their school and neighborhood friends will also be uneducated. For a child reared in such an environment, going to college represents a rejection of family and neighborhood customs and a breaking of social ties. It is not surprising that relatively few children manage to surmount these interrelated barriers to a college degree.

The direction of social pressure on the offspring of a college graduate is the reverse of that described above. He is reared to be a "college man" and often accepts schooling with resignation rather than alacrity. But any scholarly tendencies that he does possess are likely to be encouraged and developed rather than crushed or neglected. Under the circumstances, it is not surprising that the children of college graduates should exhibit a much greater propensity to attend college than the population as a whole. As a recent study concluded, "only about 6 per cent of all Americans old enough to have a college degree actually do have one . . . of the men graduates in our sample, a full 32 per cent came from families in which at least one parent had gone to college . . . of the women . . . a total of 44 per cent (came) from college families.[20]

And the children of noncollege graduates who do go to college come mainly from families of successful independent businessmen or farmers, who are likely to be on friendly terms with numerous college graduates (who are their economic equals) and thus create an atmosphere in which college trained people are familiar and respected. (The "self-made" man may sneer at "college boys" but nevertheless insists, as a matter of personal pride, that his sons have degrees from prestigious universities.)

Thus parental economic advantage and parental educational advantage combine to favor one group of the population as compared with others. Unfortunately, this advantage is not usually overcome by those who work their way through college; among the graduates over 40 years old, 42

[20] *Ibid.*, p. 14.

per cent of those who earned none of their college expenses were earning over $7500 per year, but only 38 per cent of those who earned up to half of their expenses and 31 per cent of those who earned more than half of their expenses received incomes as large as $7500.[21] A similar statement holds for graduates between 30 and 39.[22]

Environment and Heredity

The strong association between parental socioeconomic status and the education of offspring makes it quite likely that there should be a strong tendency for children to "inherit" the occupation (or a similar one) of their parents. Several studies have found evidence of a distinct relation between the "occupational grades" of fathers and sons.[23] For example, one study found that 67 per cent of the fathers in manual labor or farm tenant occupations had sons in the same occupational classes, whereas sons of 80 per cent of the fathers in nonmanual occupations also held nonmanual jobs.[24] These sample studies might not, of themselves, be sufficient to convince us of this association were it not for its consistency with everyday observation and with certain other findings. For example, there is a strong association between a father's occupational grade and the amount of schooling given his children;[25] there is also a strong association between the number of years of school completed by an individual and his occupational grade.[26] Hence, a strong association between a father's occupational grade and his son's is not surprising; indeed, this association is merely an extension of the well known immobility of given individuals between manual and nonmanual occupations. That is, most people are either manual workers or nonmanual, and which class they fall into is strongly related to their parents' socioeconomic characteristics.

At this point, the reader might well inquire what roles, if any, are played by "native ability" and "hard work" in determining an individual's occupational grade and income. Might it not be that advantaged parents gained their advantages because of superior industry and intelligence and transmitted, genetically, these qualities to their children? If so, it might

[21] *Ibid.*, Chapter 14, especially p. 171.

[22] *Ibid.* This difference is not apparent in the incomes of graduates under 30 years of age.

[23] Richard Centers, "Occupational Mobility of Urban Occupational Strata," *American Sociological Review*, April 1948, pp. 197–203; Davidson and Anderson, *op. cit.*, Chapter II and pp. 162–167; L. G. Reynolds, *The Structure of Labor Markets.* Harper and Brothers, New York, 1951, Chapter V, especially pp. 114–117; Natalie Rogoff, *Occupational Mobility*, Free Press, Glencoe, Ill., 1953.

[24] Centers, *op. cit.*, p. 200.

[25] See Reynolds, *op. cit.*, pp. 117–122 and Davidson and Anderson, *op. cit.*, pp. 35–38.

[26] Davidson and Anderson, *op. cit.*, Chapter IV.

be that these qualities, as well as (or rather than) socioeconomic advantage, are responsible for the greater economic success of the children of relatively successful parents.

Opinions on both sides of this question are very strongly held, but relevant evidence is both scanty and difficult to interpret. (Because of the notorious difficulties of defining and measuring intelligence, the matter is much too complicated to be discussed in any detail here.)   However, in an interesting recent study[27] the authors found clear evidence that the level of "intelligence"[28] possessed by persons in the "professional," "manager and proprietor," and "office clerical" occupational strata was appreciably higher than that in the manual labor strata.[29]   It was further found that there were very few low-scoring individuals in the former three occupational strata, but a considerable number of high scores among manual workers.   This would suggest an asymmetry in the interrelations among socioeconomic status of parents, intelligence of children, and occupational status of children.   That is, parents of high socioeconomic status find it difficult to transmit "high" occupational status to offspring who do not possess a certain minimum of intelligence; such children tend to fall below their parents' occupational stratum.   But the converse is not so likely to be true; it is not so easy for unusually bright children of low status parents to rise as it is for the dull children of high status parents to fall.   This is an interesting speculation, but, until further evidence is accumulated, it is a hazardous one.

To summarize, native ability may be presumed to have some association (of unknown degree) with occupational status and probably even more with success in any given occupation; however, the difficulties of acquiring higher education greatly influence any such association and confine many highly intelligent individuals to humble occupations.   The reader is further warned that there is very likely some interaction between a child's home environment and his performance on any "intelligence test" so that inferences concerning "native ability" can be drawn from such tests only with the greatest of difficulty.[30]

[27] C. A. Anderson, J. C. Brown, and M. J. Bowman, "Intelligence and Occupational Mobility," *Journal of Political Economy*, June 1952, pp. 218–239.

[28] Level of intelligence is here indicated by the score achieved on the Army General Classification Test.

[29] Anderson, et al., *op cit.*, pp. 219–222.

[30] For what it is worth, it appears that there is a clear association between a student's grades and his later income.   This is partly the result of the fact that high grade students tend to enter the professions, but the association holds (with varying degrees of strength) in all occupations.   Cf. Havemann and West, *op. cit.*, Chapter 13; also Walter Gifford, "Does Business Want Scholars?" *Harpers Magazine*, May 1928, and D. S. Bridgman, "Success in College and Business," *Personnel Journal*, June 1930, pp. 1–19.

THE VANISHING ADVANTAGE OF THE WHITE COLLAR

The role of scarcity (of satisfactory applicants) in preserving the income advantage of managerial and professional occupations can, perhaps, be better appreciated if we examine the economic fate of an occupational class that once had the protection of an educational barrier but has so no longer, the clerical worker.

Throughout most of world history, the possession of literacy was an aspect of social class. Those who possessed it were in a higher class than those who did not, and occupations that required its use paid far more than others. In the last century, however, the growth of popular education has, in western countries, made literacy and related skills virtually universal. As a result, there has been a decline in the earning advantage of clerical over manual workers.[31] This advantage was, to a considerable extent, associated with the rapid growth of female employment in clerical jobs; however, it also can be found, to a lesser degree, if we consider males exclusively. This decline has been in progress for a long time although it has been intensified since 1939.

The upsurge of labor demand since 1939 has completely eliminated the advantage of the white collar among men as is indicated by Table 18.5. As this table shows, in 1939, the median income of clerical workers was $1421 as compared with $1309 for craftsmen, foremen, and kindred workers; in 1954, clerical workers received a median of $3856, but craftsmen, etc. received $4290. In other words, the effect of the substantial elimination of unemployment (and some adjustments in relative rates of hourly pay) was to make the median male clerical worker economically inferior to the median male skilled manual worker. The economic advantage of the white collar wearer over the semiskilled operative was greatly reduced during this period, though not obliterated.

These statements apply only to males and, therefore, do not (directly) reflect the drag upon clerical wages resulting from the increased proportion of female workers. However, one important reason for the relative decline in male clerical earnings is the ease with which women can be substituted for them.

SMALL BUSINESS AND OCCUPATIONAL MOBILITY

The argument of the previous section might well be disconcerting to the common belief that America is a land of opportunity for all, including the economically underprivileged. However, we have not yet considered the

[31] P. H. Douglas, "Real Wages in the United States, 1890–1926," Houghton, Mifflin Company, Boston, 1930, pp. 246, 361–362. Also K. M. McCaffree, "The Earnings Differential Between White Collar and Manual Occupations," *Review of Economics and Statistics,* February, 1953 pp. 20–30.

Table 18.5.   Median Income by Occupation for Males and Females:
1939 and 1954

	Male		Female	
Occupation	1954	1939	1954	1939
Professional, technical, and kindred workers	$5225	$1809	$2991	$1023
Farmers and farm managers	1309	373	*	348
Managers, officials, and proprietors, excluding farm	4927	2136	2300	1107
Clerical and kindred workers	3856	1421	2512	966
Sales workers	3862	1277	1429	636
Craftsmen, foremen, and kindred workers	4290	1309	*	827
Operatives and kindred workers	3450	1007	1914	582
Private household workers	*	429	581	296
Service workers, except private household	3006	833	1329	493
Farm laborers and foremen	990	309	*	176
Laborers, except farm and mine	2570	673	*	538

Sources: 1939, from H. P. Miller, *Income of the American People*, John Wiley & Sons, Inc., New York, 1955, Table 55, p. 105; 1954, from "Income of Persons in the United States; 1954," *Current Population Reports*, Series P-60, No. 19, October 1955, Table 5.
* Too few cases reporting for sampling reliability.

main avenue of social and economic ascent of the manual worker, going into business.   Education is an important route for intergeneration occupational mobility but not for the man who wants to climb out of a manual labor job.

It must be realized that people, even in the United States, do not usually "climb" out of their general occupational class.   Thus it has been found that there is an appreciably greater likelihood (in the United States) of a person moving from one manual job to another (or one nonmanual job to another) than from a manual to a nonmanual job (or vice versa).[32]

What movement has occurred from manual to nonmanual jobs has been mainly through the channel of self-employment.   Thus, 41.3 per cent of all persons owning their own business had been (in their previous job) manual workers; but only 27.7 per cent of all sales persons and 10.2%

[32] S. M. Lipset and R. Bendix, "Social Mobility and Occupational Career Patterns," *American Journal of Sociology*, January and March 1952, pp. 366–374 and 494–504. The data in this reference are taken from a sample of the job histories of 935 working family heads (of 30 years of age or over) in Oakland, California, during 1949–1950.   Lipset and Bendix found that among persons currently employed as manual laborers, 79.7 per cent had been manual (urban) laborers in their previous jobs; 4.2 per cent had held jobs as farm laborers and 16.1 per cent had been nonmanual workers.

of the professional and semiprofessional workers had previously been manual workers. In other words, the principal way in which manual workers "rise" occupationally is by acquiring their own business. Sales jobs and "lower" white collar jobs are somewhat less frequently used as a path to "higher" occupational status, and professional, semiprofessional, and upper white collar jobs are rarely filled (see pp. 452–455) from the ranks of manual workers. These figures indicate the importance of the role of small business in providing a vehicle for social and occupational mobility and, by implication, the significance of obstacles to entering it.

The movement from manual labor to self-employment typically occurs via a small retail establishment or a small shop engaged in repairing and servicing mechanical equipment; e.g., a garage, service station, radio or television repair shop, where the mechanical skills of American workers can be used effectively. In the case of salesmen, the obvious direction of movement is toward establishment of an independent sales agency.

The mortality of such small enterprises as these is notoriously high.[33] Hence, the variation among incomes from such self-employment is quite large, considerably larger than among wage earners. Consequently, when a wage earner goes into business for himself, he relinquishes a more secure income for the chance of independence and a higher income.

The freedom to choose between accepting the risks of independent enterprise and the relative security of wage earning is a good part of what is meant by "freedom of enterprise." Of course, the freedom to try entails the freedom to fail, and many do fail. Whether the chance of success is worth the stakes (i.e., capital) that must be hazarded is a question that can be answered only by the individual undertaking the venture. However, for manual workers, it provides the major road toward economic self-improvement. This statement refers primarily to workers with steady jobs. Unemployed workers obviously risk less in embarking upon their own businesses.

RACIAL DIFFERENCES IN EARNINGS

Negroes

It is well known that there is a tendency toward labor market discrimination against certain persons because of their ethnic or racial origins. Notoriously, the group that suffers most from this is the negroes, of whom there were about 16 million in the United States (in 1952). Fifty years

[33] A study by the Department of Commerce (Betty C. Churchill, "Survival Patterns of the Postwar Business Population," *Survey of Current Business,* December 1952, pp. 12–19) showed that in the period 1944–1950 about 30 per per cent of all firms failed to survive their first year, about 50 per cent failed to survive the first two years, and only about 25 per cent survived the first five years. The firms failing to survive were predominantly small.

ago negroes were predominantly employed in agriculture, but very few were landowners.[34] For the most part, they were share-croppers, tenants, or hired workers. Their lack of land ownership resulted in weak ties to the land which, together with their extremely low incomes, led them to migrate toward urban centers in large numbers. There, their low educational attainments combined with employment discrimination forced them either into the least desirable jobs or unemployment.[35]

The nature of job discrimination against negroes is more severe in the South than elsewhere in the United States, although it varies considerably from one part of the South to another. Of course, racial discrimination in hiring exists in other parts of the United States, but the pattern is more rigid and formal in the South than elsewhere.[36] Race relations in the South are such that, *at any given time,* jobs are more or less divided into those "fit" for whites and those available only to "negroes."[37] But this occupational color line can and has varied over time, depending upon the state of the labor market. In the past, scarcity of suitable employment opportunities for whites has caused them to move into what had hitherto been colored occupations;[38] once this movement began, the mores governing race relations compelled the rapid exclusion of negroes from these occupations. Conversely, shortages of white labor (e.g., during World War II) have caused employers to resort to negroes for certain types of jobs previously reserved for whites.

That the employment opportunities of negroes are much more severely restricted in the South than elsewhere is due not only to the greater intensity of racial feeling but also to the fact that interracial labor market

[34] See Gunnar Myrdal, "An American Dilemma," Harper and Brothers, New York, 1944, Chapter 11; also Richard Sterner, *The Negro's Share,* Harper and Brothers, New York, 1943, pp. 12 et seq.

[35] In March 1940, 26.3 per cent of all nonwhite, urban, male labor force members were either seeking work or employed on public emergency work, but only 15.0 per cent of the (similarly described) whites were in either of these situations. Corresponding figures for nonwhite and white females were 18.1 per cent and 12.7 per cent (see Sterner, *op. cit.,* p. 42).

Negro income is substantially lower than white income, even in given city sizes, regions and occupations; see H. P. Miller, *op. cit.* Chapter 4. However, the negro-white income differential has been reduced substantially (in percentage terms) since 1939, largely because of the decline in unemployment which has benefited negroes even more than whites. In 1939, median income for white males was $1100 and in 1951 it was $3300; but median income for negro males climbed from $500 to $2100 during the same period (Miller, *op. cit.,* p. 100).

[36] See the penetrating discussion of Donald Dewey, "Negro Employment in Southern Industry," *Journal of Political Economy,* August 1952, pp. 279–293, especially pp. 280–282; also Myrdal, *op. cit.,* pp. 388–396.

[37] Dewey, *op. cit.,* pp. 283–286.

[38] Spero and Harris, *The Black Worker,* Columbia University Press, New York, 1930, Part I.

competition is keener (in the South) than elsewhere. This competition stems from the fact that rural-urban migration (which has been, in the South, far greater than elsewhere) has sent migrants cityward at a greater rate than Southern industrial development was able to absorb (as evidenced by the fact that there has been a steady northward and westward migration of both Southern whites and negroes). This has created a situation in which *white* labor has been available, in the South, for a greater percentage of all production jobs (both in manufacturing and in other urban industries) than elsewhere.

At this point, the reader may well ask why substitution of relatively low wage negro for (high wage) white labor has not previously occurred, or is not now occurring more rapidly, in the South. That is, why do not employers, bent on getting low wage labor,[39] hire more negro and less (higher wage) white labor than they do? The answer (which must, of necessity, be speculative) would seem to be that the educational disadvantages, lack of appropriate work experience, and alleged work habits make negroes seem undesirable "employment risks," despite their lower wage rates. Furthermore, an entirely negro labor force is likely to be lacking in essential skilled personnel whereas a (racially) mixed crew creates problems of racial conflict which Southern employers are anxious to avoid, unless labor shortages provide an overriding reason for experimentation in this direction. Individual negro workers who are fully qualified for jobs find it hard to establish this fact to an employer's satisfaction and, in addition, there would be great difficulty in fitting individual (superior) negro workers into predominantly white work groups as occupational equals. Hence, the better negro workers tend to move north, which reinforces the tendency of Southern employers to continue existing employment policies as regards negroes.[40]

Northern employers have also discriminated against negroes in hiring. However, their determination to do so is generally far less than that of Southern employers. In general, the attitude of Northern employers has reflected "administrative convenience" as much as anti-Negro sentiments, although undoubtedly both factors have been involved. To the Northern employer, a black skin has long served as a convenient "rule of thumb" to indicate workers who were less well-educated than the average white job applicant, who were also less healthy, had a record of less steady employment, etc. There was unfortunately a factual basis for the assumed inferiority of the *average* negro worker; he was the victim of the inferior status of his parents. However, such "rules of thumb" worked grave injustice upon the superior negro, and often demoralized him.

---

[39] Southern employers are, generally, more inclined than others to use low wage labor. This is, in good part, due to the industrial composition of Southern industry.
[40] This argument draws heavily on Dewey, *op. cit.*

As already indicated, the strong demand for labor since 1940 has forced employers to abandon many of their traditional prejudices against negroes, and they have made substantial advances up the community job ladder. This advance has been aided by federal government policy during World War II, which officially (and actually) discouraged job discrimination against negroes. This was done by the Fair Employment Practices Committee established by a Presidential executive order in 1941. This Committee ceased to function at the end of the war.

Since 1946, a number of northern states and municipalities have enacted "Fair Employment Practices" laws, which "forbid" discrimination in employment because of race, color, or creed.

The effect of such laws is uncertain; they are extremely difficult to enforce because of the problems of proving the existence of discrimination. Enforcement consists mainly in attempts to persuade employers of the evils of discrimination and, sometimes, in publicizing recalcitrants. An employer determined not to hire negroes, Jews, Catholics, etc. can probably evade such laws. But evasion is a nuisance, and some employers who had discriminated merely out of habit, or who feared adverse publicity, have altered their personnel policies because of pressure from local Fair Employment Practice Boards. However, these laws have thus far operated on a "rising labor market"; how well they would function during a depression is an open question. Furthermore, in a fully employed economy, the problem of job discrimination does not so much concern hiring, as promotion. In this connection, it is not feasible to use governmental pressure.

Government hiring policies have probably done more to assist the negro in obtaining good jobs, especially white collar jobs, than antidiscrimination measures. The federal government and most state and local governments (at least in large cities outside the South) rigidly refrain from discriminating against negroes and, as a result, hire relatively large numbers of them. Government employment serves to give negroes the necessary initial employment experience which enables them later to obtain and hold good jobs in private industry. It also serves to accustom the public to seeing negroes in responsible white collar positions.

Immigrants and Ethnic Minorities

Employer hiring preferences have resulted in ethnic as well as racial discrimination. Before immigration was restricted in the 1920's, employer hiring preferences confined the members of each new wave of immigrants[41] to the humblest and least remunerative jobs. These hiring preferences were, to be sure, often intended as devices for choosing superior workers; however, they had the effect (intended or not) of dis-

[41] Herman Feldman, "Racial Factors in American Industry," Harper and Brothers, New York, 1931, Chapter V.

criminating among workers on the basis of national or ethnic origin.   In the states bordering on Mexico, Mexicans (who possess many of the occupational characteristics of negroes) are subjected to much of the same kind of discrimination.   Orientals have also been subjected to such discrimination (especially in California) although restriction on their entry to the United States has kept down the number of workers affected. More recently, the growing number of Puerto Ricans (whose entry is not limited by quota) entering the United States have shouldered the traditional labor force role of the "new immigrant."

There is also evidence of overt discrimination, based on ethnic antipathy and relatively unalloyed with concern about ability, against Catholics (especially Italians) and, more often and severely, against Jews. However, there is not space for full consideration of all facets of the economics of discrimination.[42]

For the most part, discrimination against immigrants and negroes has been discrimination aimed at socially and economically inferior groups, with the consequence and (in the case of negroes) often the intention, of impeding their occupational rise.   However, the secular growth in the demand for labor has been such that the children of each succeeding wave of immigrants has, thus far, been able to ride up on the "occupational escalator."   There is evidence that the younger and more educated negroes are now striving to follow in the footsteps of previous "immigrant" groups.

However, at present, only a small part of the negro labor force is sufficiently educated to qualify for nonmanual jobs.   Consequently, they (and their labor market competitors) have decidedly benefited from the restriction of immigration.   This restriction has undoubtedly reduced the supply of unskilled workers far more than of any other type and has, therefore, raised the earnings of unskilled native-born workers relative both to other members of the American labor force and to those foreign workers who would have been immigrants had they been permitted to enter.   It is quite likely that immigration restriction has been one of the important forces in promoting the growth of income equality that we have experienced in the United States during the past twenty years.

SEX DIFFERENCES IN EARNINGS

Women in the Labor Market

From the very beginning of the industrial revolution, women have been an important source of low wage labor.   There are several interrelated reasons why a woman should be, typically, a low wage earner.   On the side of demand, she is clearly of less value than a man for jobs requiring

---

[42] Discrimination against these minorities is discussed in Feldman, *op. cit.,* Chapters III–V.

physical strength. Furthermore, as she is not expected to be a wage earner, she is usually not as well educated, or trained for skilled labor, as a man. Yet another factor limiting her desirability as an employee (relative to a man's) is the fact that earning a living is not usually her primary concern and her working life is controlled by her family's needs. Thus, she will often change residence with the job movements of father or husband and will quit jobs or be absent because a member of the family is ill and in need of care.[43]

These "basic" demand factors have begotten several "secondary" labor market disadvantages for women. Because women have not been employed in better paying jobs, they have not had much experience at them and are likely, for this reason alone, to be less qualified for them than the "representative" male. Furthermore, long traditions of not employing women in certain establishments, or parts thereof, create certain masculine social patterns among workers which make difficult the entry of women.[44] Related to this is the fact that the initial hiring of women involves the employer in additional expenditure on lavatory facilities, etc.

But all of these more or less good reasons for preferring men to women workers have been, in a wide variety of occupations, outweighed by a shortage of male job applicants. For example, during World War II, the percentage of women employed in durable manufacturing rose from 340,-000 (8.6 per cent of the total) in October 1939 to 2,939,000 in July 1944; in October 1944, women comprised 24.8 per cent of all production workers in durable manufacturing.[45] These women did welding and riveting, operated lathes, presses, and other jobs that had formerly been held exclusively by men. It is not necessary to argue (or deny) that women were as good (at these jobs) as men; the point is that they could be, and were, used as male substitutes for a wide variety of jobs when needed. (After the termination of hostilities, the share of women in the employment offered by durable manufacturing fell to 12.6 per cent in April 1947.)[46]

On the supply side, many women are secondary earners; i.e., the major earner in the family is the husband or father and the woman's earnings are merely supplementary. Consequently, the social minimum wage rate

---

[43] This in addition to the fact that childbirth and rearing usually interrupt her employment history for a number of years.

[44] For example, the camaraderie of men (especially manual workers) on the job simply cannot include women. In addition, attractive women can create rivalry among male workers which plays hob with work discipline. These problems make it difficult to *introduce* women into a masculine environment, but do not impose permanent and insurmountable barriers to sexually mixed work forces.

[45] M. E. Pidgeon, "Women Workers and Recent Economic Change," *Monthly Labor Review*, December 1947, pp. 666–671, especially Table 1.

[46] *Ibid.*

for them is less than that for a male who is presumed to be a primary earner.[47] For this reason, they are often available at (hourly) wage rates a man need not and will not accept.

Because they are available at low wage rates and because there was not, prior to 1940, any demand for their services in more lucrative occupations, women have been usually confined to low wage occupations and industries; domestic service, food processing, garment and textile manufacturing are outstanding examples of areas characterized by large scale employment of women.

It is clear that employers have rarely employed as many women as might have been induced to enter the labor market. For, as female employment opportunities have increased in the past sixteen years, many women previously not in the labor force have accepted jobs on a more or less permanent basis. The competition of high wage industries has pulled up the relative wages of the low wage female-employing industries and has caused movement out of the less favored of these industries, notably domestic service.

There has also been a steady relative improvement of education and job training for girls, which has improved women's qualifications for non-manual jobs. This, when accompanied by an expansion of employment opportunities, has placed them, as it has other unfavored labor groups, on the occupational escalator. Indeed, we would not be far amiss if we thought of women (in their capacity as wage earners) as a particular group of immigrants whose labor market characteristics are similar to those of other victims of entry restriction.[48]

Equal Pay for Equal Work

Our discussion of the labor market position of women has not mentioned the oft-denounced cases of "pure" sex discrimination; i.e., cases where men and women perform identical jobs but the men are paid more. This overt discrimination is not as pervasive as the indirect kinds we have been discussing; however, where found it provokes violent protest and the demand of "equal pay for equal work."

In response both to union and feminist pressure, several states have passed laws requiring "equal pay for equal work"[49] as between the sexes.

[47] That is, they cannot get economic assistance from outside the family on any terms as they are supported by the primary earner. But they are effective substitutes for women who are self-supporting (or even have dependents) and, hence, (in the absence of regulation) force down the wage rates these women can earn. For further discussion see pp. 289–290.

[48] Indeed, Dewey, op. cit., stresses the supply of Southern (white) female labor as one reason for the failure of Southern employers to use more negroes in urban jobs.

[49] The most detailed investigation of this matter was by the British Royal Com-

It is by no means clear what "equal pay for equal work" means,[50] but it implies, at least, that in the event of a formal job evaluation plan there should not be different rates for men's and women's jobs in the same job classification.   However, it is likely that, given an employer's desire to discriminate against women wage-wise, he could usually arrange his job classification system so that jobs commonly held by women would receive low ratings.[51]   Indeed, the fact that women workers (of any degree of education) are available at lower wage rates than men makes it economical for a firm seeking to minimize labor costs to use men only in jobs where women are appreciably less satisfactory.   Of course, the sexual division of labor, at any given time, is intimately related to social conventions, and complete economic rationality is impossible.   Nevertheless, firms seeking low wage labor often tend both to arrange their jobs so that as many as possible can be filled by women and to "price" these jobs so that "women's work is compensated by women's wages."[52]

When labor shortages require a shift in the demarcation line between male and female jobs, the move is often accomplished by a change in job content rather than job title.   That is, the functions of women's jobs are sometimes expanded so as to include additional duties previously handled by men, but they keep their old job titles.[53]   Consequently, formal distinctions can usually preserve the fiction of "unequal work," even when economic realities belie it.   Therefore, legislation aimed at securing "equal pay for equal work" is likely to be frustrated by juggling of job titles and duties, unless and until employer hiring preferences alter or some mixture of labor market and union pressure alters them.   For the most part, unions cooperate in maintaining sex differentials and whatever facade is necessary to rationalize them.

The above remarks should not be interpreted as implying that, typically, sexual wage differentials are not rooted in work differences.   Usually these differentials are so rooted; the *major* element of discrimination arises from

---

mission on Equal Pay, 1944–1946. Its report (*Command Paper,* 6937) and the appendices (especially Appendix IX) cover the ground thoroughly. There is an excellent summary of the report in E. H. Phelps-Brown, "Equal Pay for Equal Work," *Economic Journal,* September 1949, pp. 384–398.

[50] See Phelps-Brown, *op. cit.*

[51] However, Lester, *Company Wage Policies,* Industrial Relations Section, Department of Economics and Sociology, Princeton University, Princeton, N.J., 1948, p. 17, reports that "A number of companies with job-evaluation programs explained that they followed the market in the matter of sex differentials, which were traditional but were not justified according to job-evaluation results."

[52] Phelps-Brown, *op. cit.* notes that different time rates for similar jobs are frequently found in Britain.

[53] For example, a secretary with long service often assumes many of the functions of her current boss who may know less about certain aspects of the job than she does. Yet she remains a "secretary" albeit at a small increase in salary.

the fact that the sexual division of labor often prevents women from securing the better paying jobs. But a secondary type of discrimination enters when a job is retitled, or has its duties altered in an unessential way, when filled by a woman in order to justify reducing its wage. It is this type of discrimination at which "equal pay" legislation is aimed. Unfortunately, the problems of enforcing such legislation raise some very difficult questions of job evaluation.

DISCUSSION QUESTIONS

1. There is no doubt but that the children of high income parents tend to earn more than those of low income parents. Some people believe this is due to the biological inheritance of superior talent by the children of the affluent; others believe it is primarily the result of the social transmission of economically valuable skills and attitudes. What is your opinion? What factors make it difficult to "prove" your case?

2. Some economists believe that "equal pay for equal work" laws restrict the employment opportunities of women and are, therefore, not in their interest. Construct an argument in support of this position. Do you, personally, agree with this argument? Why?

3. In what ways is a fully employed economy more conducive to income inequality than one with an appreciable amount of unemployed labor?

4. "Equality of opportunity implies that every child possessing a specified minimum of ability, measured (say) by scores on an examination, should be financed to go through college, and no one scoring below this minimum should (irrespective of private means) be permitted to attend." What is your opinion of this proposition?

5. "The greatest economic boon conferred upon the American negro since the Emancipation Proclamation was limiting immigration." Is this true? If so, why?

Suggested Readings

Anderson, C. A., J. C. Brown, and M. J. Bowman, "Intelligence and Occupational Mobility," *Journal of Political Economy,* June, 1952, pp. 218–239.

Davidson, P. E., and H. D. Anderson, *Occupational Mobility in an American Community,* Stanford University Press, Stanford, Calif., 1937.

Feldman, Herman, *Racial Factors in American Industry,* Harper and Brothers, New York, 1931.

Harris, S. E., *How Shall We Pay for Education,* Harper and Brothers, 1948.

Havemann, Ernest, and Patricia West, *They Went to College,* Harcourt, Brace & Company, Inc., New York, 1952.

Lipset, S. M., and R. Bendix, "Social Mobility and Occupational Career Patterns," *American Journal of Sociology,* January 1952, pp. 366–374 and March 1952, pp. 494–504.

Myrdal, Gunnmar, *An American Dilemma,* Harper and Brothers, New York, 1944.

Phelps-Brown, E. H., "Equal Pay for Equal Work," *Economic Journal,* September 1949, pp. 384–398.

Spero, H., and A. Harris, *The Black Worker,* Columbia University Press, New York, 1930.

Sterner, Richard, *The Negro's Share,* Harper and Brothers, New York, 1943.

Thomas, L. G., *The Occupational Structure and Educational,* Prentice-Hall, Inc., New York, 1956.

19 | Social Security

In most societies of which we have knowledge the community assumes some responsibility for the individual in time of misfortune. It was only in the heyday of 19th century individualism that a few countries, among which England and the United States were the most prominent, rejected responsibility for their indigent citizens. Even in these countries, the indigent were never completely without governmental assistance, but it was rendered (as public charity) on such onerous terms as to discourage reliance upon it.

The spirit of 19th century "poor relief" was dominated by the fear that such relief would be abused. A major fear of legislatures was that if public assistance was made available too easily, many persons would abandon efforts to support themselves and go on the bounty of the government, to the cost of the taxpayers. The overwhelming concern with the taxpayers' pocketbook and apparent indifference to the health and comfort of the candidates for assistance strikes a later generation, as it did many contemporaries, as cruel.

But, whatever the merits of "Social Darwinism," they need not concern us for such attitudes and beliefs no longer have wide currency. As early as 1883, Germany adopted a system of sickness insurance, and in the next few years broadened its coverage to provide old age pensions and invalidity insurance. The "Bismarckian" system of social insurance was widely studied and imitated in other European countries in the period 1890–1910. The Australian states (in the 1890's) also began to provide social insurance. In 1897, Great Britain adopted a workmen's compensation law and in the years 1906–1911 adopted a system of unemployment assistance and began to provide old age pensions and other measures of social security.[1]

[1] Readers interested in the earlier history of social insurance may consult B. N. Armstrong, *Insuring the Essentials*, The Macmillan Company, New York, 1932.

The world-wide drive of labor and middle-class reformers for social legislation had its American counterpart in the 15 years before World War I. The fruit of the American drive for social security was the adoption of Workmen's Compensation laws by a number of states (see pp. 491–492). However, prior to the 1930's no public provision was made for unemployment or old age insurance.[2]

The mass unemployment of the 1930's swept aside prejudices against government action (and the resulting inertia) that had prevented the adoption of social insurance. The Townsend Plan for old age pensions attracted millions of adherents, and the demands of the unemployed for more than mere relief became overwhelming. The result was the Social Security Act of 1935, which provided both for unemployment insurance and old age pensions. First, let us discuss unemployment insurance.

UNEMPLOYMENT INSURANCE

Philosophy and Purpose

The idea underlying the term "unemployment *insurance*" is that unemployment is an economic risk against which workmen should be insured. The unemployment insurance "policy" pays off to the worker when he is unemployed, partially offsetting the decline in his income. This has the advantages of saving unemployed workers the humiliation of applying for public assistance and, thereby, relieving general tax funds. In this connection it should be noted that, under the American system of unemployment insurance, benefit payment are a matter of right, not of need. To collect benefits a worker must be "available" for work and not have any; under these conditions, he is *entitled* to unemployment compensation, irrespective of need. Conversely, persons not qualifying for benefits cannot obtain them no matter how great their need. In short, in the United States unemployment compensation is a kind of insurance benefit.

However, the idea of *insuring* workers against unemployment presents some peculiar actuarial problems. For the operation of the economy is such as to make unemployment a peculiarly contagious "disease" and to render the entire country subject to epidemics. Hence, there are times when an unemployment insurance fund is paying out far more than it is receiving, and vice versa.

If the unemployment insurance fund is viewed as a private account, as it is under the present law, this presents a difficulty. For then the fund may become bankrupt, requiring either that payments be stopped or that they be financed from general tax funds. But, from the viewpoint of

[2] A few states, in the 1920's, did begin old age pension programs but on a very small scale.

compensatory fiscal policy, this is no disadvantage. From this viewpoint, the unemployment fund has the very desirable characteristic of tending to run surpluses during prosperity, when unemployment is low, and deficits during depressions, when unemployment is high. As an adjunct to fiscal policy, unemployment insurance get very high marks.

Incentive Effects: Eligibility and Benefits

However, unemployment insurance has certain difficulties. The most important of these are connected with the incentives to work. Obviously, there are some persons who would prefer idleness with a smaller income to working for a larger one; and despite precautions against it, such persons can exploit a system of unemployment insurance.[3] Fear that unemployment insurance would encourage malingering was a major argument against its initial adoption. And, from time to time, newspapers and magazines run big "exposés" of abuses. But, after almost 20 years experience, it is clear that it is only a very few workers who prefer idleness and unemployment benefits to work and a higher income. Of course, weekly benefits are small relative to weekly wages; in 1954 average weekly benefits were only 34 per cent of average weekly wages of covered workers;[4] were the ratio (say) 90 per cent, the problem of malingering might become more serious.

Abuse of unemployment insurance is most serious among marginal members of the labor force, i.e., part-time workers, students, oldsters on the verge of retiring, etc. Such persons may be able to qualify for unemployment benefits while they have actually left the labor force.[5] To be sure, in order to qualify for unemployment benefits a worker must prove he is "able and available" for work. Although this requirement is more than a mere formality, it has not been feasible to administer unemployment benefits so as to confine them to those actually seeking work.

However, the availability of unemployment benefits to unqualified persons is often exaggerated. Under our system of unemployment insurance, each state establishes its own rules for eligibility, and there are considerable variations from one state to another. All states restrict benefits to those who are presently unemployed and "able and available" for work, but the tests for "ability and availability" exhibit substantial interstate differences. As a minimum, all states require that benefit claimants

[3] For a full discussion of this see J. M. Becker, *The Problem of Abuse in Unemployment Benefits: a Study in Limits,* Columbia University Press, New York, 1953.

[4] "Twenty Years of Unemployment Insurance in the United States, 1935–1955," *Employment Security Review,* Vol. 22, No. 8 (August 1955), p. 37.

[5] These people are not necessarily social undesirables; many of them are respectable citizens who simply take all to which they are legally entitled. On this point, see C. A. Myers and G. P. Shultz, *The dynamics of Labor Market,* Prentice-Hall, New York, 1951, pp. 86–91.

be registered at a state employment office. But, in addition, some states require that benefit receivers show evidence that they are applying to employers for work; others require merely that beneficiaries accept job referrals from the state employment agency.[6] In most states, (voluntary) job quitters find it difficult to get unemployment benefits unless they can show that there was "good reason" for quitting the job; the interpretation of "good reason" varies greatly from one state to another, and is obviously subject to administrative discretion. Workers discharged for "misconduct" are ineligible for benefits in all states, although the meaning of misconduct clearly is subject to interpretation. Strikers are always ineligible for benefits.

Over the years there has been a general tendency for the states to tighten eligibility requirements. There are several reasons for this: (1) The ending of widespread unemployment has created a suspicion that a worker unemployed for any long period is likely to be "responsible" for his idleness. (2) Experience with abuses has indicated the need for stricter eligibility requirements. And (3) the adoption of "experience rating" (see below) has given employer organizations an incentive to lobby for more restrictive concepts of eligibility in order to keep down their pay-roll tax.[7] Appeals from administrative rulings (that disqualify a person for benefits) are possible, and machinery exists, in all states, for handling such appeals.

In addition to the above requirements for eligibility (for unemployment benefits), most states require a waiting period between filing a claim for benefits and the initial payment. Originally, these waiting periods tended to be for two or three weeks; but at present almost all states require one week and a few require no waiting period. Finally, it is necessary, in order to qualify for benefits, that a worker have had some minimum amount of earnings and/or employment in a covered industry during a base period.[8] The majority of states require that base period earnings be some multiple (usually 30 times) of his weekly benefit; some states add to this a minimum earnings requirement for that quarter of employment

[6] Obviously, a person not wishing to be hired can usually manage to avoid doing so without actually refusing the job.

[7] Disqualification for benefits may be for varying lengths of time; this, too, varies from state to state. Since 1945, disqualifications have run 1½ to 2 per cent of claims filed; "Twenty Years of Unemployment Insurance," *op. cit.*, Table 7, p. 46.

[8] The base period is defined as follows: a worker's benefit year is a period of 52 weeks (with minor variations in a few states) usually beginning with the first week in which he files a valid claim. The maximum benefits a worker may receive are defined with reference to a benefit year. The base period (usually a year) is a period preceding the benefit year by some specified time period, usually 13 weeks. The benefits a worker receives during his benefit year are related to his earnings and/or employment in his base period.

(in the base period) in which earnings were highest.[9]   The purpose of
these earnings requirements is two-fold: (1) to restrict benefits to persons
normally in the labor market and (2) to prevent benefits from becoming
so high relative to a person's past earnings as to impair his incentive to
work.   As wages and benefits have increased during the past 15 years,
minimum earning requirements have also risen, more or less in proportion.

As can be seen, unemployment insurance is administered with an eye
to preventing fraudulent claims.   And, for the vast majority of workers,
unemployment insurance is simply a financial backstop in time of involuntary idleness and not a substitute for employment.

As already noted, average weekly benefits are about one third of
average weekly wages of covered workers.   This ratio has tended to fall
since 1939, despite a very appreciable increase in benefits, as wages have
risen even faster.[10]   As of June 1955, 38 states computed benefits as a
fraction (usually $\frac{1}{20}$) of a claimant's earnings in the highest quarter of his
base period.   The benefit formulas themselves permit benefits to rise with
earnings, but every state imposes a weekly maximum benefit; these weekly
maximums have risen steadily from their level of around $15 in the late
1930's to $30 or more in 1955.   (In June 1955, 14 states had maximums
between $30 and $36; 18 others had minimums of $30 and those of 13
states were between $26 and $28.)   And the maximums have not kept up
with earning levels; as a result of 1939, about one-fourth of all payments
were at the maximum legal rate, but the corresponding percentage in
1954 was 61 per cent.[11]

The length of the period for which an unemployed worker may draw
benefits has also increased since the late 1930's.   All states prescribe a
maximum number of weeks of benefit (in any one benefit year).   In
1937, this maximum was 16 weeks or less in 42 states; in 1955, it was
20 weeks or more in all but 4 states and 26 weeks or more in 27 states.
However, the actual number of benefit weeks to which a given worker is
entitled varies with his earnings in his base period.

In 11 states, qualified claimants are entitled to some extra benefits on
account of dependents.   This is, perhaps, a halting first step toward
family allowances (see below); however, there has been no general movement toward this type of provision.

[9] For details see E. M. Burns, "The American Social Security System," Houghton
Mifflin Company, Boston, 1949, pp. 130–132, and for more recent material, "Twenty
Years of Unemployment Insurance in the U.S.A.," *op. cit.,* pp. 34–36.

[10] In 1939, the ratio of average weekly benefits to average weekly wages was 41
per cent.   In the Economic Reports of 1954 and 1955, President Eisenhower
recommended that weekly benefits should be raised to one-half weekly earnings for
the majority of covered workers; this goal has not yet been approximated in any
state.

[11] "Twenty Years of Unemployment Insurance," *op. cit.,* p. 33.

Unemployment Insurance and Wage Levels

The effect of unemployment insurance is probably to put a floor under wage levels, so far as regular full-time jobs are concerned. It seems fairly clear that workers will not accept a *regular* job unless it pays them somewhat more than they could get from their unemployment insurance.[12] But, because benefits are small relative to actual weekly earnings, it is doubtful that this affects any but the lowest wages.

It would seem reasonable to suppose that because unemployment insurance softens the financial blow of unemployment, it serves to keep older children in school, housewives with young children out of the job market, etc. To the extent that this is true, it tends to reduce the labor supply of secondary earners and, thereby, to raise wages in the (largely non-skilled) labor markets in which they sell their services.

The effect of unemployment insurance is to set a social minimum *income* for (covered) workers. This probably sets a minimum weekly wage on full-time jobs, but it need not set minimum hourly wage rates on part-time, intermittent work. There is nothing to stop a person from accepting part-time jobs while receiving unemployment benefits, and some persons do.[13] It is possible, though by no means certain, that, if unemployment insurance, by setting a floor under the weekly wage of steady jobs, reduces the number of such jobs that can be filled, it increases the number of applicants for "odd jobs" and drives down their wage rates; however, this is mere speculation.

Financing Unemployment Insurance

Unemployment insurance is financed by a payroll tax, which, in all but four states, is paid by the employer.[14] Before 1939, the payroll tax was 2.7 per cent of total payrolls; however, in that year the law was amended so that only the first $3000 paid to each worker was taxable. Also, "experience rating" permitted reductions in rates to employers having "favorable employment" records; as a result, in 1954, the payroll tax rate was about 1.2 per cent of taxable payroll for the average employer.[15]

---

[12] Myers and Shultz, *op. cit.,* pp. 92–94.

[13] In all states except Montana, benefits are paid for weeks of partial unemployment. To encourage workers to accept partial employment, when offered, benefits plus partial earnings are allowed to exceed (somewhat) benefits for the completely unemployed. Furthermore, it is obviously difficult to ascertain whether earnings are no larger than reported.

[14] The tax is *nominally* paid by the employer; its actual incidence is another matter; see below.

[15] There has been a steady decline in this ratio since 1939 when it stood at 2.7 per cent. See *Employment Security Review,* August 1955, p. 28.

The tendency of the payroll tax is, other things equal, to reduce the demand for labor. This effect has been outweighed since 1940 by the increase in labor demand for other reasons. However, in the event of a serious depression, the payroll tax could be an aggravating factor in reducing employment. Furthermore, under a system of "experience rating" (see below), the payroll tax would rise during a period of unemployment.

These remarks are subject to an important qualification, i.e., that the payroll tax is paid by the employer and not shifted back to the wage earner. It is quite possible, that the payroll tax diminishes the package that a union can obtain for its members and/or reduces labor demand thereby reducing market wages. To the extent that this is true, the tax is shifted to the wage earner and is, in effect (wholly or partly), paid by him in that he receives lower wages than could otherwise be obtained. Unfortunately, little is known about the actual pattern of shifting and incidence of a payroll tax.

Experience Rating

The payroll tax rate of an employer is set by the various state governments and varies from state to state. The state law provide for a certain maximum rate, usually 2.7 per cent, but all states (since 1948) have provided for reductions in an employer's tax rate depending upon his unemployment "experience." That is, the smaller the number of claims for unemployment benefits made by (previous) employees of a firm, the better its experience, the higher its "experience rating," and the lower its payroll tax.[16]

The supporters of experience rating have contended that it gives employers an incentive to regularize employment in order to minimize their payroll tax. The incentive is of course present, but so many other and more powerful forces determine a firm's hiring and layoff patterns that the importance of this factor is doubtful. Furthermore, the effect of incentive rating is to lower the taxes of firms in lines of production where employment regularization is easy and to raise it where the reverse applies; this is a form of tax discrimination that is of debatable equity and wisdom. At bottom, the case for experience rating rests on the proposition that unemployment can be reduced (materially) by proper output planning by individual firms. This is a proposition that most economists would deny.

The widespread adoption of experience rating since 1939 has not been due to the persuasiveness of its supporters, but to the fact that it was the most effective way of reducing payroll taxes. In each state, legislators were besieged by employer representatives pointing out that other states had lowered taxes through experience rating and that employers in their

[16] For a description of the various systems of experience rating see E. M. Burns, *op. cit.*, pp. 156 ff.

state would, in consequence, be placed at a cost disadvantage unless they were also given the benefits of experience rating.

The high level of employment prevailing since 1940 has made it seem that reducing payroll taxes has been "costless." However, the effect has been to hold down the reserves of the unemployment insurance funds. These reserves would, in most states, probably be adequate to sustain the present level of benefits in a small or "middle-sized" recession, but they would not be sufficient for a major depression. In some states, particularly in New England where unemployment has been higher than in the nation as a whole, there is danger that the unemployment reserves would not sustain current benefit levels during even an "ordinary" recession. Therefore, the effect of lowered employer contributions *may* have been to reduce their savings for a specific, though contingent, liability. Whether this has been wise will depend upon the course of future unemployment.

The peculiar structure of our unemployment insurance system gives each state its own reserves. Thus one state's reserve fund might be bankrupted while another's reserves were growing. To prevent this from happening, in 1954 Congress renewed earlier legislation establishing a $200 million fund for interest free loans to states with depleted reserves. Whether $200 million is an adequate fund for this purpose remains to be seen, but it is a start.

The Roles of State and Federal Governments in Unemployment Insurance

It has truly been said that the United States has not one system of unemployment insurance, but 48. The Social Security Act of 1935 provided that a payroll tax be levied on all employers in commerce and industry hiring 8 or more workers in at least 20 weeks of the year; this tax was scheduled (from 1938 on) to be 3 per cent. However, the Act provided that in those states where approved unemployment insurance laws were adopted, 90 per cent of the taxes (or 2.7 per cent of the taxable payroll) paid to the state could be credited to the payment of the federal payroll tax. (As already noted, the state governments could, once certain reserve requirements were satisfied, allow additional credits against the federal tax on account of favorable experience rating.) The remaining $\frac{3}{10}$ per cent was retained by the federal government to finance administrative costs; this has usually been considerably in excess of actual costs of administration.

The individual states were left free not to adopt unemployment insurance, but this would not reduce the tax bill of employers within their boundaries. As a result, within a year, all states adopted legislation conforming to federal law in order that their citizens might get unemployment benefits. The federal law had the effect of preventing the various states from attempting to compete with one another in minimizing costs and benefits, and it accelerated enormously the nation-wide adoption of unemployment insurance. But, it might be asked, why didn't the federal government simply establish a federal system of unemployment insurance without reference to the states?

There were two main reasons: (1) fear that a plan for unemployment insurance operated solely by the federal government would be held unconstitutional and (2) desire by many supporters of social security legislation that the individual states be given opportunity to "experiment" with different types of insurance schemes. Supporters of the "Wisconsin idea," which embodied experience rating, were especially anxious that it should be given a place in the federal system.

For a state unemployment insurance system to qualify (for tax offset purposes) under federal law, it must satisfy certain minimum standards. The principal ones are: (1) All funds collected must be used for paying unemployment benefits through public employment offices (or other agencies) approved by the Social Security Administrator. (2) Immediately upon receipt all funds must be deposited in the Unemployment Trust Fund (invested in U.S. government bonds) and administered by the Secretary of the Treasury. (3) No benefits would be paid until two years after collection of contributions began. And (4) no state law might refuse benefits to a person because he refused to accept (a) a position which was vacant as a result of a labor dispute; (b) a job where wages, hours, or other conditions of work were substantially less favorable than those prevailing in the area; or (c) a job where he would be required either to join a company union or resign or refrain from joining a bonafide union. The first two of these requirements were designed to insure that the funds collected were used for unemployment insurance and not some other purpose, the third was intended to give the various state systems time to build up working reserves, while the fourth requirement was for the purpose of preventing state employment agencies from encouraging strike-breaking and helping antiunion employers secure workers or attempt to beat down local wage scales.

The Social Security Act of 1935 required coverage of firms employing 8 or more workers for 20 weeks per year or more. However, it permitted states to cover workers in smaller firms as well; as a result there was a gradual increase in the coverage of small employers until, by 1953, 17 states covered employers of 1 person or more and 27 states covered employers of 4 or more. In 1954, the Social Security Act was amended so that, as of January 1, 1956, all firms employing 4 persons for 20 weeks or more per year, not otherwise exempted, are covered by unemployment insurance. (Many states require even less than 20 weeks employment per worker in order to qualify for coverage.)

In addition to the size of firm limitation, the 1935 Act excluded agricultural labor, domestic servants, merchant marine, the self-employed, family workers, employees of federal, state, and local governments, and employees of nonprofit organizations of a religious, charitable, or educational nature.   In 1939, railroad employees were covered by a separate system of insurance and withdrawn from this general system,[17] and some food processors were "uncovered" by broadening the definition of agricultural labor.   In 1946, most of the merchant marine was accepted into the system and (in 1954) certain borderline government employees were covered.   It should be emphasized that the coverage specified by federal law is minimal coverage, and the individual states may broaden the categories of covered employers if they choose.   Some states do provide broader employer coverage in various respects than federal law requires.

The percentage of the labor force covered by unemployment insurance has risen over the years from 36 per cent in 1938 to (about) 61 per cent in 1956.   In large part, this has been due to the relative shift of workers from noncovered to covered employment;[18] but broadened coverage (especially the 1954 amendments) has also contributed to this trend. However, the coverage of old age insurance (see pp. 485–487), which was similar to that of unemployment insurance in 1935, has grown much faster in the last 20 years (than that of unemployment insurance).

INADEQUACIES OF THE UNEMPLOYMENT INSURANCE SYSTEM

Long-Period Unemployment: the Dismissal Wage

As previously noted, most states limit the number of weeks of unemployment benefits a worker can receive (in one benefit year) to 26.   This is adequate for ordinary spells of short-period idleness, but it does not help workers in declining firms and/or areas.   For example, older workers in New England textile mills may experience considerably more unemployment than 26 weeks per year as a result of a mill shutdown.   The present unemployment insurance system is not designed to cope with this type of problem; i.e., it is not designed to handle "structural unemployment."

One possible approach to alleviating the plight of the structurally unemployed is the "dismissal wage."   The dismissal wage is usually a lump sum cash payment made by a firm to long-service employees who are being permanently dismissed because of a shift in the plant's location, a permanent reduction in workforce due to technological progress, etc.   The dismissal wage is, in effect, (partial) compensation for the advantages of seniority that long-service workers lose when they are discharged.

[17] See Burns, *op. cit.*, Chapter IX, on railroad workers.

[18] In good part this reflects the shift of the labor force away from agriculture.

For many years, some progressive companies have paid dismissal wages to long-service employees voluntarily.   However, most companies have undertaken it only under union pressure; the American Newspaper Guild has been the union most active in this field, but the Railroad Brotherhoods, Textile Workers Union, and the unions in the garment trades have also negotiated dismissal wages for (some) of their members.

These unions have all been faced with serious problems of permanent job losses by their members and have, naturally, been more concerned with this problem than unions in industries where employment is expanding.   This suggests some difficulties in achieving dismissal pay through collective bargaining: (1) the unions most concerned are operating in relatively unprosperous industries where the ability to pay of employers is limited; (2) whatever unions can obtain in dismissal pay must be "purchased" by foregone wage increases.   Those workers who do not fear dismissal, resent trades of wage increases for dismissal pay, which creates intraunion friction.

If we accept that it is desirable to secure workers against the risk of long-term unemployment, it would clearly be better to have this risk born by all sectors of the economy rather than concentrated upon those sectors where the problem already exists and the financial capacity for meeting it is, therefore, very limited.   That is, if dismissal wages are desirable, they should be incorporated into the unemployment insurance system.

Spreading the risk of structural unemployment would, however, lose one advantage often claimed for the dismissal wage.   Proponents of the dismissal wage (through collective bargaining) argue that a firm faced with the obligation of a dismissal wage will have an incentive to retain long-service employees whose dismissal compensation would be large.[19]   This is true, but there would be wide disagreement as to the importance of this as compared with the considerations mentioned above.

Inadequate Benefits: the Guaranteed Annual Wage

As we have seen, maximum weekly benefits fall far short of many workers' weekly earnings.   Hence, unemployment insurance does not prevent layoffs from causing serious economic hardship to those affected. As a result, a number of unions (especially the Steel Workers, Auto Workers, and Packing House Workers) began, during World War II, to demand "guaranteed (weekly) wages," 52 weeks a year.   The demand for a guaranteed annual wage has been advanced by all of these unions, in collective bargaining, since 1945.   But it was always sacrificed to other objectives until 1955 when the United Auto Workers made a "start" to-

---

[19] Most dismissal wage formulas involve a schedule of payments which increase with the employee's term of service.

ward the guaranteed annual wage in their contracts with Ford and General Motors.

Guaranteed annual wage is not a new idea; it was tried by a number of firms in the 1920's. Three famous plans (those of Hormel, Nunn-Busch, and Proctor and Gamble) have appeared to please both workers and management over a long period, but other plans failed and were abandoned. As guaranteed annual wage plans have attracted so much attention in the last few years, it will be well to analyze them briefly.

The Cost of a Guaranteed Annual Wage. If an employer knew in advance that he would hire a worker 50 or 52 weeks a year, it would re-quire only slight pressure to induce him to guarantee him that much em-ployment. And, in some lines of business (e.g., telephone and electric utilities), employers could probably offer a full year of guaranteed employ-ment (and wages) to most of their employees with little risk of paying workers whose services would not be needed. But, for precisely this reason, such guarantees are not sought avidly by workers in these indus-tries. It is precisely in industries subject to marked fluctuations in output and employment (like steel and automobiles) that guaranteed employment is worth most, and costs most.

The value of guaranteed employment is clearly not the same to all workers in a given firm. Very senior employees, or those whose special skills are needed continuously, have relatively little fear of being laid off and are not nearly so eager for an employment guarantee as the junior workers who bear the brunt of layoffs. Conversely, management would be far more willing to guarantee annual wages to 50 or 75 per cent of their employees than to 90 or 100 per cent; it is the "first to be fired" who most want a guarantee of work and wages.

A company undertaking any form of guaranteed wage plan is accepting a risk of hiring labor it may not wish to use. If it should happen that it can use all the man hours it has agreed to hire, it will (very likely) have profited by trading the guarantee of wages for (at least part of) a wage increase it would have had to pay otherwise. But, if the firm should ex-perience an unexpected slump in demand, its guarantee will cost it dearly.

In discussing the cost of a guaranteed annual wage plan it is important to specify very carefully just what is guaranteed. The "businessman's nightmare" of a guaranteed annual wage envisages a guarantee of 52 weeks employment to a specific number of employees, which guarantee would be legally binding, like a debt. Such a guarantee to all of a firm's employees could put the firm in peril of bankruptcy. Recognizing this, employers would simply not offer it, and unions could strike "till doomsday" and not get it; furthermore, since they do not wish to bankrupt their employers, in the final analysis most unions will not (seriously) demand it.

However, it might come to pass in a few years that an employer's obligations to a permanent employee (though limited to preserve solvency) would be sufficiently heavy that he would become very reluctant to add to his permanent workforce.   This would lead him either to hire only temporary workers, not subject to a guaranteed annual wage, to give his permanent workers a great deal of overtime, or to subcontract extra work. The result would be to create two classes of workers; those with guaranteed annual wages, and the others who would find it more difficult (than at present) to get a permanent job with a firm covered by a guaranteed annual wage plan.[20]   Furthermore, resort to temporary workers or extensive overtime would tend to raise (marginal) costs and hold down output, employment and profits.

THE GAINS FROM A GUARANTEED ANNUAL WAGE AND ITS COSTS.   A guaranteed annual wage would yield its beneficiaries a steady (or steadier than present) flow of income.   Undoubtedly, this would tend to help maintain effective demand in time of depression.   (Of course, if the guarantee is only an *annual* one, this would not help in those big depressions which last over a year.)

Another possible gain from a guaranteed annual wage is that it might induce firms to plan their production so as to avoid sharp month to month fluctuations.   Union spokesmen allege that great gains in employment stabilization can be made in this direction.   The contention is that firms with known patterns of seasonal demand would be able to produce for inventory or, possibly, go into new products which require a complementary seasonal pattern of production (so that the firm could produce these new products during present seasonal lulls).   However, there is, at present, much debate as to the feasibility of this type of action on a large scale.   Furthermore, the large producers of durable goods, with irregular fluctuations in demand, may find output regularization extremely difficult.   However, union spokesmen are probably right when they contend that only few firms have really tried to stabilize output and employment, and that a guaranteed annual wage may act as a real spur in this direction.

However, it is not likely that a firm's total demand for labor during a given year will be much affected by adopting a guaranteed annual wage; at most, it will be spread out more evenly week by week and will be concentrated upon a smaller number of workers (i.e. those receiving the

[20] In general, these firms would be the most desirable employers.

When there is full employment, this means that work is kept from intermittent members of the labor force to the benefit of regular workers.   This may be deemed "proper."   But, in the event of serious unemployment, the excluded workers may well be family heads in need of earnings.   The resulting inequality in employment opportunities would be difficult to justify.

guarantee). This will, of course, contribute to the psychological security of the protected workers which is all to the good.

But what of the workers not protected by a guarantee? They will find it more difficult than before to secure steady employment because employers will tend to avoid letting new workers work steadily enough, for a long enough period, to acquire the right to guaranteed employment. The more valuable this guarantee is to a prospective worker (and hence the more costly to the employer), the more reluctant the employer will be to permit the worker to qualify for the guarantee. Also, insofar as guaranteed employment leads firms to regularize production, it will reduce the amount of seasonal and/or casual employment it offers, i.e. it will tend to concentrate its employment on fewer persons than in the absence of a guarantee.[21] In short, a guaranteed annual wage tends to create a restriction on entry (for new workers) into the "class" of regular employees.

Furthermore, a union that can induce a firm to assume the cost of a guaranteed annual wage could have used the same economic pressure to compel the company to offer a larger wage increase than it did. Hence a union "purchases" a guaranteed annual wage, of benefit mainly to junior workers, by relinquishing some wage gains for all.

Because we have stressed the costs of a guaranteed annual wage, the reader should not infer that we are, therefore, opposed to it. There are, obviously, benefits for the protected workers which must be compared with the burden imposed on the unprotected. However, improving the system of unemployment insurance and extending it to cover all workers would accomplish most of the things now sought through a guaranteed annual wage, and without creating privileges for some workers at the expense of others.

SUPPLEMENTARY UNEMPLOYMENT PAYMENTS. In June 1955, the United Auto Workers signed contracts with Ford and General Motors which embodied what the union hailed as a first step toward a guaranteed annual wage. These contracts have been imitated by a number of other large companies so that by October 1955 over 1½ million workers were covered by plans more or less like those of Ford and General Motors.

These contracts provide that workers laid off, and subject to reemployment should receive weekly cash payments as a supplement to their unemployment benefits; hence the term, "supplementary unemployment payments."

In general, to receive supplementary unemployment payments a worker must be eligible for state unemployment benefits and these are supplemented up to a maximum of $25 per week for a maximum of 26 weeks in

[21] E. J. Eberling, "Supplementary Unemployed Payments: a New Development in Collective Bargaining," *Employment Security Review*, Vol. 23, No. 1 (1956), pp. 25–30.

any one year.[22]   The object of the Ford plan (which is more or less typical) is to give a worker 65 per cent of his weekly straight-time pay (after taxes) for the first four weeks of benefits and 60 per cent for the next 22 weeks.   The duration, though not the rate, of benefits varies with a worker's seniority.

The plan is financed by contributions of the company of 5 cents per hour for every man-hour of (covered) labor hired.   The "maximum funding" of the company's obligation is set at $55 million.   If the amount in the fund should fall below 13 per cent of this figure, weekly benefits will be reduced by 20 per cent; if the fund falls below 4 per cent, no payments will be made at all.

In effect, the employer has committed himself to saving 5 cents per hour to be paid the worker in the event of a layoff.   As it was perfectly clear that this 5 cents could have been obtained as a straight wage increase, the company has merely undertaken to save the worker's money for him. The company is not committed to paying a cent that it has not accumulated in this fashion.

Payment of supplementary unemployment benefits requires amendment of unemployment insurance eligibility requirements, as in many states such receipts would be considered as wages and would disqualify the recipient for unemployment insurance.   Many states have already made the appropriate administrative rulings or legal changes to permit supplementary unemployment payments to be made.   However, Ohio (as a result of a referendum) has refused to do so.

Some employer groups are waging a bitter-end battle against supplementary unemployment payments, but it would seem that ultimately they will lose.   Supplementary unemployment payments are relatively harmless and constitute a step toward raising the benefit levels of unemployment compensation.   However, in the near future, the benefits of supplementary unemployment payments will probably be confined to the employees of the wealthier firms in the economy.

OLD AGE INSURANCE

Economic support of the aged has become, in recent years, an increasingly pressing problem.   The aged (persons over 65) are a growing part of the population; in 1900, the aged were 4.1 per cent of all Americans, but in 1950 they were 8.2 per cent.   Increased longevity, due to medical discoveries, and the choking off of mass immigration have been the two basic factors responsible for this development, and it is not likely that the trend toward a relative increase of the aged in our population will soon be reversed.

[22] These remarks refer to the Ford plan; others differ from it in minor respects. For details, see Eberling, *op. cit.*

To a very substantial degree these older persons are not able to support themselves by their earnings (see pp. 450–452) and must, therefore, maintain themselves on their past savings or be supported by others. It is quite clear that most aged persons do not have assets nearly adequate for self-support, and are, therefore, in a position of dependency.[23] Understandably, neither they nor their children (upon whom the burden of their support usually falls) are happy about this situation, a fact which has contributed to the enormous political pressure for public assistance to the aged.

Old age pensions had been demanded by social reformers since the 1890's, but it was only in the 1930's that the depression born "Townsend movement" became an important political force. Probably old age pension legislation would have been adopted in any case, but the vocal demand for such measures no doubt hurried their enactment and probably helped to make their provisions more generous than they would have been otherwise. The Social Security Act of 1935 was passed in the midst of this agitation and was, in part, a response to the demand for old age pensions.

Old Age and Survivor's Insurance (OASI)

The Social Security Act of 1935 established not only our system of unemployment insurance but also our system of old age insurance. However, the administration of the two systems is entirely different: unemployment insurance is essentially a state matter, subject to certain broad conditions imposed by the federal government; old age insurance is entirely a federal program with which the states have no connection.

Old age insurance is financed (like unemployment insurance) by a payroll tax. However, the payroll taxes differ (in the two systems) in that the old age tax is paid (incidence questions aside[24]) half by the employer and half by the employee. At present, this tax is 2 per cent for both employer and employee[25] and is levied on the first $4200 per year earned by a covered employee. (Earnings in excess of $4200 are not taxable for this purpose.) The tax is scheduled to rise to $2\frac{1}{2}$ per cent in 1960, and further scheduled increases will bring it to a maximum of 4 per cent for both employer and employee (8 per cent in all) beginning in 1975. However, in the past, Congress has frequently (though not always) deferred scheduled increases, so that planned increases are not certain to go into effect.

COVERAGE. At its inception, OASI covered roughly the same groups

---

[23] P. O. Steiner, "The Size, Nature and Adequacy of the Resources of the Aged," *American Economic Review,* May, 1954, pp. 645–666.

[24] See p. 476.

[25] Self-employed persons pay 3.0 per cent.

as unemployment insurance. However, amendments to the law in 1950 extended coverage to employees of nonprofit organizations, agricultural wage earners, household workers, many persons in public employment, and the urban self-employed.[26] Further amendment, in 1954, extended coverage to (self-employed) farm operators and slightly broadened the coverage of domestic workers, farm workers, ministers, and certain other groups.[27] As of January 1, 1955, about 90 per cent of all paid jobs were covered by OASI; the bulk of those uncovered being federal workers covered by Civil Service Pensions, self-employed professionals, domestic, farm, and self-employed workers with earnings below a certain minimum.[28] Subject to these exceptions, American workers (including the self-employed) are covered by OASI.

BENEFITS. The benefits of OASI lagged far behind the rising cost of living during and after World War II, and the value of the pensions was seriously reduced. However in 1950, and again in 1954, benefits were raised appreciably, the increased cost being financed by increasing the amount of worker income subject to the payroll tax.[29]

The various benefits a family may derive from OASI are all based on the insured worker's "primary monthly benefit" which is the benefit he would receive were he a single man over 65 and retired. The "primary monthly benefit" is computed (since January 1, 1955) by taking 55 per cent of the first $110 of "average" monthly earnings ($60.50) and adding to that 20 per cent of the next $240 ($48). The maximum primary benefit for a single worker would be $108.50 ($60.50 + $48) per month. Of course, not all workers will have earned enough to receive the maximum benefit; the minimum monthly payment (irrespective of earnings) to anyone eligible for benefits is $30. (The computation of the "average" monthly earnings is complicated by permitting certain quarters of low earnings to be excluded in order that extended disability should not, by lowering a worker's earnings for a time, also lower his retirement benefits; there are also various technical matters concerning starting dates into which we need not enter here.)

In addition to the primary benefit (which accrues to the insured worker himself), there are other benefits for his dependents. For example, the spouse of a retired worker is entitled to one-half of his primary benefit if she (or he) is past 65; the widow (or widower) of a deceased worker is

[26] Coverage of employees of state and local government units and nonprofit organizations was on an elective rather than a compulsory basis.

[27] See Cohen, Ball, and Myers, "Social Security Act Amendments of 1954; a Summary and Legislative History," *Social Security Bulletin,* Vol. 17, No. 9 (September 1954), pp. 3–18.

[28] Victor Christgau, "Old Age and Survivor's Insurance After Twenty Years," *Social Security Bulletin,* Vol. 18, No. 8 (August 1955), p. 13.

[29] For details, the reader may consult Cohen, Ball, and Myers, *op. cit.,* p. 6.

entitled to three-fourths of his primary benefit if she is past 65. In addition, the child of a retired worker, if under 18, is entitled to one-half the
primary benefit; if the worker is deceased, the child receives three-quarters
of the primary benefit.[30] The mother of the child of a deceased worker
receives three-quarters of the primary benefit; however, the maximum
payments to a widow and children may not exceed either 80 per cent of
the average monthly earnings on which they are based or $200 per month,
nor may they fall below the larger of $50 or $1\frac{1}{2}$ times the primary benefit.
The dependent parent of a deceased worker (with no widow, widower, or
child eligible for benefits) is entitled, if past 65, to three-quarters of the
primary benefit. Finally, there is a lump sum payment, three times the
primary benefit, but in no case to exceed $255, payable on the death of an
insured worker.

ELIGIBILITY. To be eligible for benefits, a worker must have been
covered for six quarters; coverage in a quarter requires receipt of either
$50 in wages, or $100 of self-employment income in employment subject
to OASI. If these six quarters fell within the preceding three years, the
worker is *currently insured*. To be *fully insured at* death or age 65, a
worker must have been either (1) in covered employment (at any time)
for 40 quarters, (2) in covered employment in half the calendar quarters
since 1950, or (3) in covered employment in all quarters since 1954, provided there are at least six covered quarters. In addition, survivor benefits have been made payable (retroactively) to dependents of deceased
workers (with six quarters of coverage) who died between December
1939 and September 1950. Special provision has also been made to
preserve the benefit rights of disabled workers.[31]

In order to qualify for total retirement benefits, a person under age 72
may not earn more than $1200 in a year. If he earns (from wages or
self-employment) more than this amount, one month's benefit will be
withheld for each $80 (or fraction thereof) in excess of $1200.[32] Individuals may earn freely without impairment of benefit rights, after they
have passed their seventy-second birthday.

Old Age Assistance (OAA)

Although OASI benefits are not altogether "adequate" as a sole source
of income, they were considerably more than most aged persons were

---

[30] In the event of there being more than one child, each one gets one-half the
primary benefit, and an additional one-fourth of the primary benefit is divided
equally among them.

[31] On eligibility, see Cohen, Ball, and Myers, *op. cit.,* pp. 10–12.

[32] Except that benefits will not be withheld for any month in which an individual
earned less than $80 in wages and did not render "substantial services" as a self-
employed person.

(prior to 1951) able to obtain because they lacked sufficient covered employment. Anticipating this, the Social Security Act of 1935 provided not only for Old Age Insurance but also for Old Age Assistance.

OAA involves grants of federal funds to the states to assist them in providing for their needy aged. The grants are conditional upon the recipient state accepting certain conditions governing minimum qualifications of (successful) individual applicants for assistance. Stated negatively, these conditions are: (1) The age requirement for assistance may not exceed 65 years. (2) No citizenship requirements may exclude any citizen of the United States. And (3) no residence requirement shall require that the applicant shall have resided in the state for more than five out of the last nine years or for more than one year continuously immediately prior to application for aid. The purpose of these requirements was to induce the states to increase the number of aged persons eligible for assistance, and in this they succeeded.[33]

The Social Security Act stated that OAA grants were to be used for aid to needy persons, but the definition of need was left to the individual states.[34] As there are wide interstate variations in the concept of "need," persons eligible for assistance in some states would not be eligible in others. OAA grants are on a "matching basis" currently; the federal government pays up to $35 per month per recipient, four-fifths of the first $25 of his assistance and one-half of the remainder up to $55. A number of states pay more than the maximum ($55) for which they receive federal assistance, but many pay less; in 1955 the average monthly OAA payment was $51.89.[35]

Prior to the 1950 amendments to the social security laws, more people received OAA than OASI. Thus in June 1948, there were 2,367,547 persons receiving OAA as compared with 1,465,092 aged beneficiaries of OASI.[36] However, the liberalization of eligibility requirements in 1950 caused a large jump in the number of persons receiving OASI, many of whom thereupon became ineligible for OAA. By June 1955, 5,900,000 aged persons were receiving OASI benefits, but only 2,500,000 were getting support from OAA.[37] However, inadequate OASI benefits caused about 500,000 recipients to obtain OAA as well. Eventually OASI will replace OAA almost completely. However, this is still some time away. Despite the increase in benefits in 1954, the *average* primary benefit to an insured male worker was $79.64 per month, and to a married couple

[33] Burns, *op. cit.,* pp. 298 ff.

[34] Subject to the conditions that the income and resources of the individual be considered in determining need and that there be an annual review of eligibility.

[35] J. L. Rosey, "Twenty Years of Public Assistance," *Social Security Bulletin,* Vol. 18, No. 8 (August 1955), p. 20.

[36] Burns, *op. cit.,* p. 296.

[37] *Social Security Bulletin,* December 1955, p. 22, Table 1.

(both over 65) was $125.16 per month.[38] (This is well below the maximum benefits available under the 1954 amendments.)

Pensions and Collective Bargaining

The shrinkage in the real value of OASI pension rights in the postwar inflation caused considerable uneasiness among aging workers. As a result, a number of major unions demanded, in the years 1946–1950, the establishment of company financed pension plans to supplement OASI. The first big success in the pension drive was achieved by John L. Lewis (in 1946) when he obtained a widely publicized health and welfare fund for miners. In 1949, the steel workers won a strike for company-financed pensions which set a pattern. The following year the auto companies adopted pension plans, and the Korean inflation combined with the activities of the Wage Stabilization Board spread pension plans throughout the economy.

The contagious nature of the pension movement is indicated by the following figures: In 1945, about 500,000 workers were covered by collectively bargained health, insurance, and pension plans; in 1948, about 3 million were so covered; in 1950, about 7½ million, and, in early 1954, about 11,300,000.[39] In early 1954, about 7 million workers had some sort of collectively bargained pension plan.[40]

Of the workers covered by pension plans in early 1954, about 85 per cent were under plans financed entirely by the employer. This fact sometimes disturbs those who feel that "people should make at least some contribution to their own pensions." However, such "feelings" ignore the realities of the situation; the employer's burden of paying the whole pension is largely offset by smaller wage increases than he would otherwise have to pay. Furthermore, payments into a pension fund by an employer are deductible as a business expense for income tax purposes;[41] therefore, the pension dollar paid by the employer will usually cost him (after taxes) far less than it would cost the worker who is in a lower tax bracket. Hence, worker and employer have a "dividend" to split by foregoing a wage increase in exchange for the employer bearing the full cost of the pension.[42]

---

[38] *Social Security Bulletin*, September 1955, Table 28, p. 42.

[39] E. K. Rowe, "Health, Insurance and Pension Plans in Pension Contracts," Monthly Labor Review, September 1955, pp. 993–1000.

[40] *Ibid*. Only 7 million workers had (collectively bargained) pension plans, but 4,300,000 others had health and/or insurance benefits (but no pension), adding up to a total of 11,300,000 workers with one or more of the aforementioned benefits.

[41] This was not the case prior to 1942. The change in the Internal Revenue Code at that time has, no doubt, smoothed the path for bargained pensions.

[42] The cost of this dividend is born ultimately by other taxpayers.

The collectively bargained pension plans typically provide for a guaranteed minimum pension composed of OASI and company payments, with the actual pension for any given worker depending upon his earnings and length of service.   Under these plans, the company contribution tends to fall as OASI benefits increase, unless otherwise specified.

Company pension plans are usually not "vested" in the worker.   That is, when he leaves his job he leaves some or all of his accumulated pension rights.   Failure to vest pension rights in the worker creates yet another obstacle to voluntary labor mobility.[43]   It also gives the union and/or the management an enormous club over the aging worker; for, by causing his discharge, they can obliterate thousands of dollars worth of accumulated pension rights.   Some unions have begun to demand full vesting of pension rights in the worker.   Thus far management has resisted this demand because it raises the cost of the pension plan by eliminating the savings due to workers being separated from their jobs before retirement.

The Economic Consequences of Pensions

FISCAL POLICY.   Old Age Insurance does not merit the same approval as Unemployment Insurance as an economic stabilizer.   The outpayments do not tend to increase with reductions in employment, and the payroll tax, especially with the scheduled increases, could easily become a depressive influence at an awkward time.   Fortunately, Congress has felt free to defer increases in the payroll tax in the past and may do so again, if needed.

The demand that a special OASI fund be accumulated, irrespective of business conditions, has not commended itself to modern economists. During an inflationary period such accumulation may be all to the good; but during a depression, it will have adverse effects on aggregate expenditure and should, therefore, be avoided.

LABOR SUPPLY.   OASI was depression's child. The denial of benefits because of earnings (see above) clearly discourages oldsters from working, and was so intended.   In the 1930's, one of the major arguments in favor of old age pensions was that they would take old folks out of the labor market and make jobs for younger persons.   In the 1950's, this objective does not seem quite so attractive.   Yet, in a somewhat weakened form,[44] the eligibility conditions for OASI still include a species of "work tax." This is not to argue that the "retirement test" should be summarily abolished; there would be considerable complications from any such drastic

---

[43] The effect of seniority with respect to layoffs and other matters is so big an obstacle to labor mobility that the additional effect of nonvested pension rights may be quite small.

[44] The 1954 amendments to the act permitted greater earnings than before without loss of benefits.

change.[45]   However, the effect of the "retirement test" on labor supply is clear.

For the future, both in private and public pension plans, there is much to be said for giving the worker a choice among retirement dates (with corresponding variations in benefits) and some opportunity for partial retirement.

OTHER FORMS OF SOCIAL INSURANCE

Workmen's Compensation

The adoption of legislation requiring that employers insure their workers against injury was the first type of social insurance to be adopted widely in the United States.   The initial Workmen's Compensation law was enacted by New York in 1910; in 1948, Mississippi became the 48th state to adopt some provision for workmen's compensation.   However, although all states now have some kind of workmen's compensation law, their contents vary enormously.

Some states require that workers be protected against certain types of disability but not others; variations in duration, kind, and amount of benefits are great.   In general, compensation benefits are small, maximum weekly payments during disability rarely exceed $50, and their maximum duration is often shorter than the disability.   Administration of workmen's compensation is often poor; claims are processed slowly; workers are not informed of their rights; etc.   In addition, administrative costs often run quite high, absorbing as much as 40 per cent of the costs of workmen's compensation.[46]   Furthermore, in many states the employer may elect to remain uncovered by insurance (i.e., "self-insured"), requiring the worker to sue for damages if injured.   The costs and trouble involved are a severe deterrent to such suits.

It is widely agreed that the entire program of workmen's compensation is badly in need of overhauling.   However, because it is entirely a state responsibility this will be done, at best, only very gradually.   Wholesale reform will be resisted by the insurance companies, doctors, and lawyers who have vested interests in present arrangements.   There is a growing tendency to remedy the inadequacies of statutory provisions by collective bargaining arrangements.[47]   However, this will help only certain parts of the labor force.[48]

[45] On this point see R. J. Myers, "Basis and Background for Retirement Test," *Social Security Bulletin*, Vol. 17, No. 3 (March 1954), pp. 14–17.

[46] See H. M. Somers and A. R. Somers, "Workmen's Compensation, Unfulfilled Promise," *Industrial and Labor Relations Review*, October, 1953, pp. 32–42.

[47] Rowe, *op. cit.,* p. 994.

[48] The reader interested in the current situation in workmen's compensation law and administration should consult: H. M. Somers and A. R. Somers, *Workmen's*

Despite the justified criticism of current workmen's compensation arrangements, it is important to remember what they *did* accomplish. Until the passage of these laws, the common law applied, and an injured workmen could collect no damages from his employer unless he could prove (in court) the injury was the fault of the employer and not that of a fellow-worker or (even partially) of himself. Under this common law doctrine, injured workers were, in practice, left to the mercies of private and public charity.

Workmen's compensation laws cut through the legal knot by ignoring the question of blame and requiring that workmen be insured against occupational hazard, irrespective of responsibility. These laws also gave, and continue to give, employers an incentive to take all possible safety measures in order to keep down accident rates and insurance costs; an employer's premium for Workmen's Compensation Insurance varies inversely with the number and severity of accidents in his plants.[49]

Disability Insurance

The purpose of disability insurance is to compensate workers for disability *not* arising from occupational hazards (which is the province of workmen's compensation). As unemployment benefits are (usually) available only to workers currently able and available for work, disabled workers cannot collect unemployment benefits. A few states will continue unemployment benefits to workers who become disabled while unemployed, but only four states (California, Rhode Island, New York, and New Jersey) provide specific disability insurance.

In 1946, the Social Security Act was amended to permit states that levied taxes upon *employees* for unemployment insurance to use the funds thereby accumulated for making disability payments. The systems of California, Rhode Island, and New Jersey are more or less integrated with state unemployment insurance; New York's system is not.

The failure of most states to provide disability insurance has been partly offset by collective bargaining. In early 1954, 73 per cent of the 11.3 million workers covered by health, insurance, and pension plans had some form of disability insurance.[50] Certain other groups, such as railroad workers, also have disability protection, but the earnings of the vast majority of the nation's workers are completely exposed to hazard from ill-health or accident.

Compensation: Prevention, Insurance, and Rehabilitation of Occupational Disability, John Wiley & Sons, Inc., New York, 1954; A. H. Reede, *Adequacy of Workmen's Compensation,* Harvard University Press, Cambridge, Mass., 1948; and the series of six articles in the *Monthly Labor Review,* April to October (except July) 1953.

[49] However, safety programs are much more common in large than in small plants, and there is much that yet needs to be accomplished in this area.

[50] Rowe, *op. cit.*

Health Insurance.

At the present time, there is no health insurance program sponsored by either the federal or any state government.[51] In some other countries, however, notably Great Britain and New Zealand, there are broad programs of prepaid medical care sponsored and financed by the government. Demands for such care have been made here, and a number of bills embodying such legislation have been presented to Congress. The most famous of these was the Wagner-Murray-Dingell Bill which, in modified form, was recommended by President Truman in 1949. However, owing to the strong opposition of the American Medical Association and other groups who felt this was a step toward "socialism," these bills were rejected. These groups also defeated a proposal by President Eisenhower in (1954) that the federal government establish a fund of $250 million to reinsure private health insurance plans, thereby enabling such plans to broaden coverage and extend benefits.

To some extent, the inaction of public authorities has been offset by individual and group initiative. In early 1954, through collective bargaining provisions, about 9 to 10 million workers were provided with prepaid hospital care, 8.5 to 9.0 million with prepaid surgical benefits, and about 4.5 to 5.0 million with prepaid medical care.[52] Over 90 per cent of the workers receiving hospital or surgical benefits had these benefits for their dependents also, but "somewhat less than half had their families protected by some kind of medical care."[53]

In addition to benefits achieved through collective bargaining, many individuals and employers, fraternal and other groups have bought prepaid hospitalization, (through Blue Cross). A much smaller number of persons are covered for medical and surgical care through such organizations as Permanente (operating in California) or Health Insurance Plan (HIP) in New York.

Family Allowances

In the United States, no provision is made for extending aid to family heads based on the number in the family, except where the family is in need, i.e., through public assistance. However, in many countries, family allowances are regularly extended to all families, irrespective of need. In France, for example, family allowances are a very substantial fraction of unskilled wages; thus, in Paris (circa 1952) the weekly family allowance for a wife and two children would have been over 50 per cent of the

[51] The New York City government is involved in HIP (Health Insurance Plan) for its own employees and certain other groups.

[52] Data are adapted from Rowe, *op. cit.*

[53] *Ibid.*

weekly wage of an unskilled worker.[54]   As the French family allowances
are financed by taxes which are borne largely by the working class, much
bitterness has been engendered among childless workers.   French workers
have remarked "We are getting paid less and less from our work, and
more and more for being 'Father-Rabbit'."[55]

The French system of family allowances actually covers the marginal
cost of a child (at working class living standards) so that a family of 5 or
6 can live as comfortably as a family of 1 or 2.[56]   The English, Australian, and other systems do not go so far as the French, but they do make
an (halting) attempt to relate income to "need."   However, such plans
have not been well received in the United States and are not likely to be
seriously considered (here) in the near future.

THE AMERICAN SOCIAL SECURITY SYSTEM AS A WHOLE

The United States does not have, like Great Britain, a "womb to tomb"
system of social security.   There are serious uncovered risks to income
from accident and injury; medical costs of serious illness are high, and
most workers are uninsured against them although hospitalization insurance is becoming quite widespread.

Virtually the whole labor force is now covered by OASI, and the benefits, if not large, will eventually become "adequate."   Meanwhile, many
oldsters must accept the scanty offerings of OAA.   Unemployment insurance is unavailable to a sizeable part of the labor force, and benefit
levels are well below the target (set by President Eisenhower) of 50 per
cent of regular weekly earnings.

To a very considerable degree, the initiative in broadening and improving social security benefits has passed from the government to the
unions, especially the large ones.   The Miners, Steel Workers, Auto
Workers, etc. have pioneered in obtaining larger pensions, supplementary
unemployment pay, health and disability insurance, etc.   As a result,
other workers have been in the position of trying to catch up.

Because of our federal system, all social security programs not controlled entirely by the federal government exhibit considerable state to
state variation.   The low benefits of the "backward" states entail lower
costs to employers and act as a brake (via competition) upon the programs of the more advanced states.   However, to get any federal legislation at all, it has often been necessary to extend substantial latitude to
state administration.

[54] L. G. Reynolds and C. H. Taft, *The Evolution of Wage Structure,* Yale University Press, New Haven, 1956, pp. 223–224.

[55] Quoted by Val Lorwin in Chapter 5 of "Comparative Labor Movements," edited
by Walter Galenson, Prentice-Hall, New York, 1952, p. 362, n. 71.

[56] Reynolds and Taft, *op. cit.,* p. 224.

The effect of the American social security system has been to raise the incomes of the lowest *urban*[57] income recipients, the aged, the disabled, and/or the unemployed relative to the rest of the community. This was as intended. But thus far, it has accomplished less in this direction than was originally hoped.

In short, social security programs have had a significant effect in alleviating the distress of low income receivers. But their influence has been far overshadowed, since 1940, by the transformation of our economy from one of large scale unemployment to one of substantially full employment. Fortunately for the aims of social security, this transformation also worked in the direction of equalizing the distribution of family incomes.

DISCUSSION QUESTIONS

1. It is often contended that company financed pension plans lead companies to discriminate against older workers in hiring. Under what conditions is this likely to be true? What measures would you advise, if any, where it is true?

2. Do you think it is desirable that workers past 65 should lose some OASI benefits if their earnings exceed a specified annual amount? Do you think that appropriate variations in this rule according to the level of unemployment, might promote desirable fluctuations in labor supply?

3. What is the case for "vesting" pension rights in the individual worker? Why are employers usually opposed to vesting?

4. What arguments do you think would be offered against a system of family allowances, were one proposed in Congress?

5. What effect, if any, has unemployment insurance had upon labor supply? Do you think that raising the level of benefits appreciably, relative to average weekly earnings, might affect this relationship?

Suggested Readings

Armstrong, B. N., *Insuring the Essentials,* The Macmillan Company, New York, 1932.

Beveridge, Sir William H., *Social Insurance and Allied Services,* His Majesty's Stationery Office, London, 1942.

Burns, E. M., *The American Social Security System,* Houghton Mifflin Company, Boston, 1949.

Douglas, P. H., *Social Security in the United States,* The Macmillan Company, New York, 1936.

Hansen, A. H., and P. A. Samuelson, "Economic Analysis of Guaranteed Wages," *Bureau of Labor Statistics Bulletin* 907, Washington, D.C., 1947.

Kaplan, A. D. H., *The Guarantee of Annual Wages,* The Brookings Institution, Washington, 1947.

Somers, H. M., and A. R. Somers, *Workmen's Compensation: Prevention, Insurance, and Rehabilitation,* John Wiley & Sons, Inc., New York, 1954.

"Twenty Years of Unemployment Insurance in the U.S.A., 1935–1955." *Employment Security Review,* Vol. 22, No. 8 (August 1955), p. 37.

[57] The government has also done much to aid low income farmers but not through what are usually thought of as social security measures.

20   The Government as Wage Setter

In this chapter we shall study the legislative enactments and administrative procedures aimed at establishing and maintaining social minimum standards concerning wages and hours. The history of statutory enactments governing minimum standards for wages and hours has been long and varied. In the United States, the earliest state legislation dates well back into the 19th century, but it is only since 1938 that such legislation has covered a substantial part of the American labor force. Initially, legislative concern was more with hours than wages[1] and more with women and children than with men.

It was not inappropriate that the earliest attempts to give legislative sanction to social minimums should have been concerned with women and children; these were (and are) the lowest paid workers in the community. In the United States there was a fairly typical pattern by which "protective legislation" (especially that concerning women and children) came to be adopted;[2] first, there was a recognition of "abuses" by a small number of earnest, middle-class citizens who agitated for remedial legislation. The relevant legislative body would respond slowly, partly because of laissez-faire preconceptions and partly because of political pressure from employer interests that would be adversely affected by such legislation.[3]

[1] Some advocates of hour restriction believed that restricting hours would, indirectly, raise (hourly) wage rates. This belief is expressed in the old union jingle, "Whether you work by the piece or work by the day, the longer the hours the shorter the pay.

[2] See E. Brandeis, *History of Labor in the United States, 1896–1932*, Vol. III, The Macmillan Company, New York, 1935, pp. 405–409, 461–466, and 506–508.

[3] After the collapse of the Knights of Labor in the late 1880's, union pressure for protective legislation was not strong, as the American Federation of Labor was not much interested. The Federation supported legislation curbing child labor, and favored limiting daily hours (of women and children) to eight. However, for many years it opposed wage and hour legislation for men. (Brandeis, *op. cit.*, pp. 555–559.)

Finally, a law would be passed prohibiting some of the "worst abuses" which (usually) had already been ended by the larger and more efficient employers. But in the 19th and early years of the 20th century, regulatory legislation often had no provision for enforcement; and in other cases, the administrative provisions were meager or inadequate (see pp. 500–502).

STATE "PROTECTIVE" LEGISLATION

In this section, we shall present a brief summary of legislation by the various state governments to "protect" workers from undesirable conditions of unemployment.

Child Labor Legislation

Child labor legislation has traditionally aimed at (1) establishing a minimum age at which children might work, (2) insuring that children had a minimum of education, (3) restricting the number of hours of work that children might perform, and (4) excluding children from certain types of work that would tend to undermine their health and/or morals.

MINIMUM AGE LAWS. Child labor legislation was enacted (in Massachusetts) as early as 1842, but it was not until the first years of this century that such legislation became common. There was great legislative concern with conditions of child (and other) labor during the first fifteen years of this century. Between 1902 and 1916 "the volume of legislative achievement in the states . . . was tremendous. . . . In the one year of 1903, 11 states passed comprehensive child labor laws. . . . From 1902 to 1909, 43 states enacted significant child labor legislation. . . . In 1900 there were still 24 states and the District of Columbia in which there was no minimum age for employment in factories. In 1909 there were only six states without such a standard."[4]

SCHOOL ATTENDANCE LAWS. School attendance requirements work in the same direction as minimum age requirements in that they make it difficult or impossible for children below a designated age to accept gainful employment. Soon after 1900, there developed a widespread drive for laws requiring attendance for the full school year, and by 1919 laws requiring this were in effect in all but ten states (seven of them in the South). During this period, there was also a gradual increase in the legal school-leaving age; in 1900, only seven states required children to attend school until they were sixteen; but in 1932, forty-two states plus the District of Columbia had this requirement.[5]

MAXIMUM HOUR LAWS. By the end of 1916, nineteen states and the District of Columbia had enacted an eight hour law for children under

[4] Brandeis, *op. cit.*, p. 409.
[5] *Ibid.*, pp. 410–413.

sixteen employed in manufacturing and mercantile establishments. But some of the states (especially those in the South) most in need of child labor legislation were reluctant to pass it, thereby giving their manufacturing firms a competitive advantage over those in states possessing such laws. This gave rise to a demand for federal legislation which resulted, in 1916, in a law establishing (among other things) a minimum age of sixteen years for mine workers and of fourteen years for others engaged in producing goods entering interstate commerce. This law was declared unconstitutional by the Supreme Court in June 1918.[6] Thereupon, another federal statute with the same objective was enacted (in 1919). But this law also was declared unconstitutional (in 1922).[7] Following this, Congress passed (in June 1924) a constitutional amendment giving the federal government the power to regulate child labor. The proposed amendment was submitted to the states for ratification, but a bitter (and successful) campaign was waged against it; as a result many state legislatures refused to ratify it, and it has never been ratified.[8]

After 1933, considerable progress was made in strengthening state laws governing child labor. This legislation was both stimulated and supplemented by the "codes of fair competition" of the National Recovery Administration (established in 1933) which prohibited "child labor" (most industry codes specified a minimum age of sixteen years) on goods entering into interstate commerce.[9] As a result of this state legislation, by 1940 thirteen states had established a minimum age of sixteen years for the employment of children, and thirty others had established minimums of fourteen years for factory work.[10] However, numerous exemptions (varying from state to state) made it possible legally to employ persons below these minimum ages, even in factories. Laws governing nonfactory employment of children embodied lower and more varied standards of protection; in agriculture and domestic service child labor was hardly regulated at all.

The shortcomings of state legislation have, to some extent, been remedied by federal legislation. By far the most important federal statute

[6] Hammer vs. Dagenhart, 47 U. S. 251 (1918); see Brandeis, *op. cit.,* pp. 437–443 and 694–695.

[7] Bailey vs. Drexel Furniture Co. 259 U. S. 20 (1922); see Brandeis, *op. cit.,* pp. 437–443 and 694–695.

[8] Brandeis, *op. cit.,* pp. 446–450.

[9] Although the National Industrial Recovery Act was declared unconstitutional by the Supreme Court (in 1935), the provisions of its codes concerning labor policies left a permanent imprint upon employer practices in many industries. See Judith Grunfel, "Regulation of Child Labor," Chapter 11 in W. S. Woytinsky and associates, *Employment and Wages in the United States,* Twentieth Century Fund, New York, 1953.

[10] *Ibid.,* p. 123.

dealing with child labor is the Fair Labor Standards Act of 1938 (see pp. 504–512); this act forbids the shipment in interstate or foreign commerce of goods on which "oppressive child labor" has been employed within thirty days of shipment. "Oppressive child labor" is defined as the employment of any minor under sixteen in any industry covered by the act, or under eighteen in occupations found to be especially hazardous by the Secretary of Labor. The Secretary of Labor is empowered to permit children between fourteen and sixteen to work (outside of manufacturing and mining) provided it does not interfere with their schooling, health, or well-being. Exemptions granted have permitted children to work in agriculture, as actors, and for their parents (except in manufacturing or mining). In the 1949 amendment to the Act, "oppressive child labor" was broadened so as to plug certain "loopholes" that had appeared.

The combination of legislative pressure and widespread unemployment caused a very substantial reduction in the number of gainfully employed children during the decade of the 1930's (see Table 2.2). However, the labor shortage of the war years reversed this trend with the result that in the spring of 1945 there were three times as many gainfully employed persons between the ages of fourteen and seventeen as there had been in 1940. This number has declined since 1945; but in 1948 there were still 2 million children gainfully employed. Since the end of World War II, there has been a renewed drive to curb child labor which has met with some success. Child labor, especially in the rural South, is still a social problem, but it is no longer the major social evil that it was a generation ago. In large urban areas, children have simply ceased to be an important factor in the labor market.

Protective Legislation for Women

The history of wage and hour legislation for women has paralleled that for children. In the reform wave of 1900–1916, a number of states passed legislation limiting women's hours of work; little further was done in the 1920's, but a renewed wave of regulatory laws were enacted in the 1930's. The first minimum wage legislation (applying to women and minors) was passed in 1912 (in Massachusetts); in the following year, 1913, eight other states passed minimum wage legislation, but not much further progress was made until the 1930's. To some extent this was due to a decision by the U. S. Supreme Court (in 1923) which held the minimum wage law of the District of Columbia unconstitutional.[11] Thereafter, until 1933, only one minimum wage law was passed, a number of laws were repealed, and those that remained were unenforced because of their presumed unconstitutionality.

[11] Adkins vs. Children's Hospital, 261 U. S. 525 (1923).

However, in 1933, stimulated by President Roosevelt[12] and the generally reformist sentiment then prevailing, seven states passed minimum wage laws. After further legal vicissitudes, these and earlier laws were finally declared constitutional by the Supreme Court in 1937.[13] Subsequently, other states passed minimum wage statutes with the result that, by 1950, twenty-six states and the District of Columbia had minimum wage laws. Most of these minimum wage statutes applied to women and children only; in only five states did they apply to men. (The first state minimum wage law applying to men was that of Oklahoma passed in 1937.)

Most state minimum wage laws involve the appointment of a wage board whose function it is to determine the minimum income necessary to maintain "suitably" a woman and her dependents and to set wages accordingly. (Only a few states set statutory minimum wage rates.) In addition to the foregoing protective legislation, several states have passed laws requiring "equal pay for equal work" as between the sexes, see pp. 467–469.

THE OBSTACLES TO THE ENACTMENT AND ENFORCEMENT OF PROTECTIVE LEGISLATION

As indicated at the beginning of the chapter, a major objective of protective legislation is to set minimum standards for living and working conditions. However, there has not always been widespread agreement upon the role of government (state or federal) in establishing and maintaining this minimum. The early attempts to get state legislatures to enact protective legislation were bitterly resisted by persons with a deeply rooted philosophy of laissez-faire. These persons believed that, however unfortunate the circumstances of certain individuals, it either was not, or ought not to be, within the power of government to remedy their distress by restricting "freedom of contract." They further contended that regulating hours, wages, and working conditions would force many less efficient employers out of business, thereby reducing employment and worsening the circumstances of the workers affected.

To attribute an articulate laissez-faire philosophy to those resisting protective legislation is, perhaps, to give too much credit to their intellectual powers (and knowledge) and too little to their feelings of human

[12] "Early in 1933, President Roosevelt communicated with the governors of thirteen industrial states, urging the enactment of minimum wage laws 'for the protection of the public interest,' and pointing out that 'the continual lowering of wages is a form of unfair competition against other employers, reduces the purchasing power of the workers, and threatens the stability of industry.'" H. A. Millis and R. E. Montgomery, *Labor's Progress and Problems,* McGraw-Hill Book Company, Inc., New York, 1938, p. 319.

[13] Millis and Montgomery, *op. cit.,* pp. 342–356.

sympathy. The big task of "reformers" seeking protective legislation was to get the "facts" before the legislature and the public; once the facts concerning the working and living conditions of women and children were made clear, some (though by no means all) of the opposition to protective legislation evaporated. To understand some of the more bitter opposition to protective legislation, it is necessary to remember that, prior to World War I, a large fraction of the workers in need of protection were newly arrived immigrants who were felt to have "lower standards of living" than native Americans and whose plight did not, therefore, excite the sympathy aroused a quarter century later by their native-born successors.

However, the major source of opposition to protective legislation was (obviously) the employers affected. Their opposition was overt and articulate,[14] and their arguments were far less important than the political pressure they were able to place upon lawmakers. This pressure has always been a strong brake upon the rate at which minimum standards of wages and working conditions could be raised.

But, despite this opposition, feelings of sympathy and fear of the voting strength of urban workers have, from time to time, been sufficiently strong to cause enactment of minimum standards. The stream of protective legislation has not flowed steadily; in periods of "reform" (such as 1910–1916 and 1933–1938) protective laws have been passed in rather large numbers, but in times of complacency (such as the 1920's) few have been enacted.

However, enactment of protective legislation was only the first step in establishing minimum standards. The Act had then to be enforced; the opposition to protective legislation, once it recognized its inability to defeat the legislation outright (and sometimes as a strategic move from the outset), shifted its fire to the more obscure questions of enforcement. At first, they were able to restrict legislation to mere declarations of public policy with no provision for enforcement;[15] at other times, they have been able to restrict enforcement to publication of the names of violators. Another tactic has been to hamper the enforcement agency with an inadequate budget and staff. "Exemptions and exceptions" have also weakened the force of protective legislation. But by far the most potent obstacle to enforcement of protective legislation has been the courts.

Before the 1930's, the American judiciary generally shared the social outlook of the conservatives of the time. Their decisions seemed, to many acute observers,[16] to be strongly influenced by laissez-faire precon-

---

[14] See Brandeis, *op. cit.,* Vol. III, pp. 445–448, 468–491, 506–522.

[15] *Ibid.,* pp. 457–461.

[16] Such as Justice Oliver Wendell Holmes who said (in dissenting from the majority of the U. S. Supreme Court in Lochner vs. New York, 1905, a decision which invalidated a maximum hour law for male bakers), "This case is decided upon an

ceptions.   Whether these preconceptions led the U. S. Supreme Court to misinterpret the Constitution is not for laymen to say.   However, the Court certainly interpreted the Constitution differently (with regard to protective legislation) in the 1920's than it has since 1937.   Their earlier doctrines[17] led them to declare unconstitutional among other things: (1) a New York statute regulating the hours of men in baking establishments,[18] (2) a District of Columbia statute regulating women's wages,[19] and (3) two federal statutes curbing child labor.[20]   Until the late 1930's the constitutional question hung like a "Sword of Damocles" over every piece of protective legislation.   As already remarked, fear of court invalidation caused the virtual cessation of attempts to enforce minimum wage laws in 1923–1933.

THE CASE FOR PROTECTIVE LEGISLATION

The advocates of protective legislation were, to a considerable extent, earnest middle-class citizens who had no economic stake[21] in the issue. They were variously moved by an ethical or religious desire to "do good," by a desire for prominence, and, perhaps, by political ambition.   They found political allies in agrarian reformers seeking to "bust trusts," curb railroads and other "monopolies," and in urban politicians anxious to strengthen their hold on low income voters.   As already noted, the strength of organized labor was not heavily committed in these struggles.

The case that was made for protective legislation was, at bottom, based on humanitarian grounds.   However, it was buttressed by various other considerations, depending upon the law in question.   For example, arguments for child labor legislation (rightly) made a great issue of the fact that in a political democracy it is necessary that future citizens have some minimum of education and that the need for such education was incompatible with (very much) gainful employment of any individual child. It was also argued that, unless working hours of children were restricted, their health would be impaired, and their usefulness as citizens diminished. Similarly, it was argued in support of hour legislation for women that such legislation was necessary to protect their health, and that such protection was necessary in order to safeguard the health of future mothers. Hour legislation for men in hazardous occupations (e.g., mining) was

---

economic theory which a large part of the country does not entertain. . . . The Fourteenth Amendment does not enact Mr. Herbert Spencer's Social Statics."

[17] These doctrines were by no means consistent with one another; see Millis and Montgomery, *op. cit.,* pp. 523–527.

[18] Lochner vs. New York, 198, U. S. 45 (1905).

[19] Adkins vs. Children's Hospital, 261 U. S. 525 (1923).

[20] Hammer vs. Dagenhart and Bailey vs. Drexel Furniture Co., *op. cit.,* notes 6 and 7.

[21] Some of them stood to be injured economically by the legislation they sought.

defended on the ground that working "too long" at such occupations created unusual hazards to health and safety.

The case for minimum wage laws usually involved an argument in terms of minimum income standards and the hourly wages necessary to attain them. Indeed, these state minimums are usually set so that they enable the wage earner to earn a designated minimum income. However, we have not gone so far as several other "advanced countries" in assuring that our minimum wage legislation provides an adequate income for the recipient.

THE NEW DEAL AND THE FAIR LABOR STANDARDS ACT OF 1938

The New Deal period (1933–1938) saw the accomplishment of more, and more basic, economic reforms than any other five year period in American history. Among these reforms was a tremendous extension of wage and hour legislation, partly at the state but mainly at the federal level.

The first piece of federal legislation affecting wages and hours was the National Industrial Recovery Act of 1933 under which codes of "fair competition" were established (under the aegis of the National Recovery Administration) regulating wages and hours within individual industries. However, the National Industrial Recovery Act was declared unconstitutional by the U. S. Supreme Court in 1935.[22] This decision left in grave doubt the regulatory powers of the federal government in the general "wage hour price" field. A further decision of the Supreme Court, in 1936, invalidated a New York state minimum wage law passed in 1933, which further reduced the regulatory powers of government.[23]

However, in 1937 the Supreme Court abruptly changed its policies,[24] holding a Washington (state) minimum wage law constitutional. In so doing, it specifically reversed the Adkins' doctrine[25] which, by implication, left the states free to set minimum wages. The Supreme Court's reversal of position was further manifested in its upholding of the (federal) Fair Labor Standards Act of 1938,[26] which left the federal government

[22] Schechter Poultry Corporation vs. United States 295 U. S. 495.

[23] Morehead vs. People ex rel. Tipaldo, 298 U. S. 587, 56 Sup. Ct. 918.

[24] The Supreme Court had invalidated several New Deal measures in 1935 and 1936 by 5 to 4 majorities. This led President Roosevelt to ask for legislation enabling him to appoint additional justices under certain conditions; this request provoked the famous "court-packing" fight which led to the rejection of the proposed legislation. However, in 1937 one justice "switched sides" and the court began upholding New Deal legislation by 5 to 4 margins. Soon after, death and resignation changed the composition (and philosophy) of the Supreme Court.

[25] West Coast Hotel Co. vs. Parrish and Parrish, 300 U. S. 379. See Millis and Montgomery, op. cit., pp. 351–356.

[26] U. S. vs. F. W. Darby Lumber Co., 312 U. S. 100 (1941). In validating the act's provisions concerning child labor, the court explicity overruled Hammer vs. Dagenhart (op. cit., note 6).

free to regulate wages and hours in interstate commerce and, incidentally, gave a very broad definition of interstate commerce.

In 1938, the federal government enacted, for the first time in its history, a wage and hour law applying broadly to a substantial part of the nation's labor force; this act is known as the Fair Labor Standards Act of 1938, or more briefly, as the Federal Wage and Hour Law. It provided (1) that covered employees[27] should receive not less than twenty-five cents per hour after October 24, 1938; thirty cents an hour after October 24, 1939; and forty cents after October 24, 1945;[28] (2) that after October 24, 1940,[29] all time over forty hours per week shall be remunerated at $1\frac{1}{2}$ times the standard rate; and (3) that "oppressive child labor"[30] shall not be employed in the range of industries covered by the act.

These broad provisions are subject to a number of exceptions; thus, workers in agriculture or in agricultural processing operations carried on "in the area of production" are exempted from the act, so are workers in fishing, in air or interurban transport, in retail and service establishments which are predominantly intrastate, weekly newspapers with less than 3000 subscribers or telephone switchboard operations in small exchanges, and certain executive, administrative, and professional occupations.

About half the workers in private industry are covered by the Act; the uncovered workers are mainly in agriculture, trade, services, and government. However, a disproportionately large part of the low wage employees in the nation are employed in the private industries not covered by the Act.

THE ECONOMICS OF WAGE-HOUR REGULATION WITH SPECIAL REFERENCE TO THE FEDERAL LABOR STANDARDS ACT (FLSA)

The Case for FLSA[31]

The principal economic arguments offered in support of wage-hour legislation are as follows: 1. Reducing the length of the work week serves to reduce the number of unemployed persons because any given number

---

[27] Covered employees include all employees who are "engaged in interstate commerce, or in the production of goods for (interstate) commerce." The term "production of goods for commerce" has been interpreted very broadly.

[28] Section 8e of the act empowered the administrator to continue wage rulings (of less than forty cents per hour) beyond October 24, 1945, if he and the appropriate industry committee both believed it necessary to prevent a "substantial curtailment of employment." This power was never used.

[29] After October 24, 1938, the time and a half for overtime applied only after forty-four hours per week; after October 24, 1939, it applied after forty-two hours; and after October 24, 1940, after forty hours.

[30] See p. 499.

[31] Hereafter, for brevity, we shall refer to the Fair Labor Standards Act as FLSA.

of hours of work will be spread over a larger number of workers. This was a major argument urged in support of the "time and a half" requirement for hours in excess of forty per week. The purpose of imposing penalty rates on overtime was not primarily to raise worker income by compelling the payment of overtime but to shorten the work week, thereby causing more persons to be employed (even though this need not involve the employment of additional man-hours of labor.)[32] It was not always appreciated that penalty rates on overtime raise marginal costs and thereby tend both to raise selling prices and lower the demand for man hours of labor. However, the number of *persons* would (probably) be increased by reducing overtime work, even though the number of *hours* of employment were lowered. This argument was of major importance in the depression year of 1938. It would not be so persuasive at present (1956).

2. Another argument for limiting the work week is the effect of long hours upon worker efficiency. It has long been recognized that increasing the work week beyond a certain length will yield (under a given productive "set-up") reduced physical output per worker *per week*.[33] However, the length of the "optimum" work day or week will depend greatly upon (a) the nature of the productive process, (b) the psychological attitude of the workers toward their work, (c) the number of consecutive days in which the workers are to work a specified number of hours,[34] (d) the age and health of the workers involved, etc.

In general, it is agreed that the work week can be too long for maximum sustained weekly output per worker. However, it is rarely the case that (say) 44 hours per week would be "too long" by this standard; considerations of physical health and efficiency were rightly urged against the length of the work day and week prevalent in many industries (see pp. 195–197) as recently as the 1920's, but they have not been considered of much importance in connection with FLSA.

3. Perhaps the major ground for public support of FLSA was concern with establishing a social minimum income. This view was well expressed by the Senate Committee on Education and Labor:

The Committee feels that a minimum wage of 40 cents per hour, which will yield no more than an annual income of $800 a year to a small percentage of workers fortunate enough to find 50 weeks employment in a year, does not give a wage

[32] See the testimony of Leon Henderson at the Joint Senate and Congressional Hearings on the Fair Labor Standards Act of 1937 (75th Congress, 1st session, on S. 2475 and H.R. 7200) pp. 155–172.

[33] See H. M. Vernon, *Industrial Fatigue and Efficiency*, E. P. Dutton & Co., Inc., New York, 1921; P. Sargant Florence, *The Economics of Fatigue and Unrest*, Henry Holt & Company, Inc., New York, 1924; and "Hours of Work and Output," *U.S. Bureau of Labor Statistics Bulletin* 917, Washington, D.C., 1947.

[34] That is, occasional long "stints" do not have the adverse effect on output that would be produced by a frequent repetition of such "stints."

sufficient to maintain that we would like to regard as the minimum American standard of living. But 40 cents per hour is far more than millions of American workers are receiving today. . . . [35]

But, if the Senate Committee felt that a minimum income of $800 per year was inadequate, why did it not recommend a higher minimum wage? And why did it permit a delay of seven years before making a minimum wage of 40 cents an hour mandatory? The answer lies mainly in their fear that the proposed minimum, especially if imposed too suddenly, would cause unemployment; this fear is manifested in their policy injunction to the administrator of the act to "set the highest minimum wage . . . that will not substantially curb employment. Let us consider some of the consequences (for the framing of the Act) of this fear of causing unemployment.

Minimum Wages under FLSA

The most important thing to remember about the minimum wage provisions of FLSA is their narrow applicability. The large block of low wage earners in retail trade and agriculture are not covered by the Act. And not many of the covered workers earn less than the minimum established by the act. About 10 per cent of the covered workers were earning less than the minimum rates set by administrative committees in the early days of the Act (i.e., before 1940).[36] When the minimum wage rate was increased to 75 cents per hour in 1949 (effective January 1950), only about 1.5 million workers, 6 per cent of those covered, needed hourly pay raises to comply with the law. Prior to March 1, 1956 (when the 1955 amendment to FLSA raised the minimum wage rate to $1 per hour), only about 2.1 million workers (8.7 per cent of the 24 million workers covered by FLSA) had been earning less than $1 per hour.[37]

In other words, the role of the minimum wage provisions of FLSA has been to raise the wage floor for the lowest 5 to 10 per cent of the nation's low wage payers in *covered* industries. In practice this means raising wages in low wage manufacturing firms, mostly in the South, and heavily

[35] Fair Labor Standards Act of 1937, S. Dept. 884, 75 Congress 1st session, p. 4.
[36] Testimony of L. Metcalfe Walling, Administrator FLSA and Public Contracts Act, Dept. of Labor, in Hearings on S. 1349, 79th Congress, 1st session, p. 263.
   The aforementioned "administrative committees" were established by the Administrator of the act to designate intra-industry classifications within which separate hourly wage minimums could be set. The object of these committees was to bring as many workers as possible, to a 40-cent hourly minimum as rapidly as possible, but without creating unemployment. Therefore, the intra-industry classifications were supposed to distinguish groups of firms with differing "abilities to pay"; within each classification the highest hourly minimum was established that could be paid without causing unemployment (but not exceeding 40 cents.)
[37] *Business Week*, March 3, 1956, pp. 130–131.

concentrated in textiles, garment making, (southern) lumber mills, etc. The big low wage areas in agriculture and retail trade are not affected by the law.

The reason for not establishing a higher wage floor was, in 1955 as it had been in 1938, fear of driving "marginal" firms out of business and causing their workers to become unemployed. Let us consider the basis for this concern.

Minimum Wage Laws and Employment

There has been much controversy between economists who feared that FLSA would have an adverse effect upon the level (and allocation) of employment and those who believed that it would not reduce (and might even increase) employment. In good part the controversy was misplaced as it is very unlikely that FLSA ever raised enough wages sufficiently to have had an appreciable effect on the economy as a whole. However, the issue involved is important; i.e., if a minimum wage law that "seriously affected" wages were imposed, what effect would it have on the level and distribution of employment? Unfortunately, the answer to this question is entirely speculative and one can get a wide variety of answers, depending upon the model used.

If one argues from the "macroeconomic" viewpoint and it is assumed (1) that other things the same, consumption expenditure increases as the distribution of income becomes more equal; (2) raising the hourly wages of low income earners, by law, will make the distribution of income more equal (because of a presumed shift of income from profit makers to wage earners); (3) that the level of investment is not reduced sufficiently (if at all) by the imposition of the wage minimum and the resulting repercussions, and (4) that there is unemployed labor, then it follows that imposing a minimum wage rate will tend to increase employment.[38] (This argument also implies that, if there were full employment, an increase of the minimum wage rate would cause an increase in the general price level.) However, if one chose to reverse any one of the above assumptions,[39] it would no longer follow that a minimum wage law would tend to increase employment.

[38] An argument of this type underlies the testimony of Leon Henderson, op. cit., in the Congressional hearings on the Fair Labor Standards Act of 1937. Weir M. Brown, "Some Effects of a Minimum Wage Level Upon the Economy as a Whole," American Economic Review, March 1940, pp. 98–107, expresses a carefully qualified argument pointing in the same direction.

[39] For example, one might argue plausibly that an increase in minimum wage rates might lead to an increase in selling prices so that there was no redistribution of income between wage and profit earners and (perhaps) no shift in the consumption function.

However, some economists contend that a minimum wage law tends to reduce employment.[40]   These economists usually do not argue in "macroeconomic" terms; instead they assume, in effect, the existence of a wage structure (in each community) similar to that discussed in Chapter 12, pp. 314–318.   They argue that the effect of a minimum wage is to preclude the employment of many of those workers who would otherwise earn less than the statutory minimum.   It is, of course, possible that the expenditure previously directed at the goods produced by the (previous) subminimal wage earners will be directed elsewhere, thereby creating new jobs.   What ultimate effect this will have on total employment is anybody's guess.   The effect of a minimum wage law on *total* employment is, in practice, incalculable.   Let us therefore consider its effect upon the firms directly affected by the law.

"Conventional" economic theory argues that imposing a higher wage upon a firm than it is currently paying for (at least some of) its labor, will cause it to use less of this labor than otherwise.   It argues that many low wage firms cannot (or will not) absorb higher wage costs per unit of output and must, therefore, either raise their prices (and curtail output and employment) or go out of business.   Therefore, in situations where the product market is keenly competitive and rival firms have previously been paying hourly wages higher than the newly imposed minimum and getting greater man-hour output, there is grave danger that the (low wage) employers affected by the wage minimum will cut output and employment.

A striking example of this possibility appears to have occurred in Puerto Rico immediately after FLSA went into operation in 1938.   The twenty-five cent hourly minimum which was imposed, appreciably exceeded the earnings of Puerto Rican needleworkers;[41] as a result, needlework exports declined from $15.6 million in 1939–1940 to $4.8 million in 1940–1941 (a decline of 63 per cent in one year).   Thereupon, the Puerto Rican delegate to Congress, at the urging of union labor (as well as other interested parties), appealed for the establishment of minimum wage rates for Puerto Rico at lower levels than those set for the United States;[42] this appeal was heeded, and an appropriate amendment to FLSA was passed in June 1940.

The heavy impact of the minimum wage law on the Puerto Rican needlework industry was due to the fact that the industry's task consisted mainly

[40] The outstanding examples of this view in recent years is G. J. Stigler, "The Economics of Minimum Wage Legislation," *American Economic Review,* June 1946, pp. 358–365. An important example of the earlier literature is A. C. Pigou, *The Economics of Welfare,* The Macmillan Company, London, 4th edition, 1932, Part III, especially Chapter XIX.

[41] The average hourly earning in "Apparel and other finished products made from fabrics" was (in 1939–1940) 18.3 cents; H. S. Perloff, *Puerto Rico's Economic Future,* University of Chicago Press, Chicago, 1950, Table 46, p. 154.

[42] *Congressional Record,* Vol. 84, Part II, Appendix, pp. 1129–1130.

of performing various sewing operations on imported materials which implied a high ratio of labor to total cost (per unit of output). Furthermore, almost all the labor used was affected by the minimum wage regulation. It is worth noting that even prior to 1938, a considerable part of the work was done at home, and that the minimum wage law caused a considerable (further) shift of (the reduced) output from home to factory.[43] Other instances where FLSA apparently reduced employment occurred in tobacco stemming, pecan shelling, lumbering, and bagging.[44]

However, there are economists who argue that a minimum wage law may have the effect of "shocking employers into action," getting them to adopt labor saving techniques, or save on other items of cost, so as to raise net man-hour productivity.[45] This may make it possible for the employer to employ as many (or more) man-hours of labor per week as before, providing he manages to sell the increased output profitably.[46]

One instance where this tendency seems to have been set in motion by FLSA was in the seamless hosiery industry where there was "an increase of some magnitude" (between September 1938 and September 1940) in the use of automatic machines that had been substituted for machines involving more hand labor per stocking.[47] The increase was especially marked in those plants where average hourly earnings were (in 1938) below the minimum wage (of 32.5 cents per hour) that became effective in September 1939.[48] However, in the opinion of one authority,[49] the substi-

---

[43] See Judd Polk, "The Plight of Puerto Rico," *Political Science Quarterly,* December 1942, pp. 481–503, especially pp. 496–497.

[44] P. H. Douglas and J. Hackman, "Fair Labor Standards Act of 1938, II," *Political Science Quarterly,* March 1939, pp. 29–55 (note 107, p. 44), quotes Administrator Andrews as reporting to the President that "between 30,000 and 50,000 persons, or less than one half of one per cent of the workers affected by the law, lost their employment for reasons probably traceable to the act. Of these, about 90 per cent were concentrated in a few industries in the south such as pecan shelling, tobacco stemming, lumbering and bagging."

[45] The same result may be accomplished by compelling existing managers to turn over a firm's assets to more efficient employers, or those bettter able to secure financing. For example, see the testimony of R. W. Johnson, President of Johnson & Johnson, before the Textile Industry Committee (under FLSA) as quoted in *Wage Theories Before Certain Industry Committees of the Wage and Hour Administration,* (by Sister Mary Yolande Schulte, Catholic University Press, Washington, D.C., 1946), p. 109.

[46] However, this is likely to cause unemployment elsewhere.

[47] See H. M. Douty, "Minimum Wage Regulation in the Seamless Hosiery Industry," *Southern Economic Journal,* October 1941, pp. 176–190; also A. F. Hinrichs, "Effects of the 25-cent Minimum Wage on Employment in the Seamless Hosiery Industry," *Journal of the American Statistical Association,* March 1940.

[48] See the testimony of Claudius T. Murchison before Textile Industry Committee, as quoted by Sister M. Y. Schulte, *op. cit.,* pp. 107–108.

[49] Douty, *op. cit.*

tution would have occurred without the imposition of the minimum wage, and he concludes, "Perhaps the most that can be said is that the establishment of these standards lent some impetus to the further use of automatic machines and converted transfer machines."

In short, the effect of a compulsory wage increase upon the output and employment offered by a *given* firm will depend upon the ability and willingness of its management to adopt plans for raising (net value) productivity per man-hour. Where management can be shocked into measures that increase man-hour productivity, it is possible, but by no means certain, that a minimum wage law will lead a firm to increase man hours of employment.[50] However, if the demand for the firm's output is insufficiently elastic and/or the management cannot increase man-hour productivity appreciably, the reverse will presumably occur.[51] It is impossible, at present, to make any very general statements about the conditions under which the employment stimulating or retarding effects of an imposed wage increase will predominate.[52]

The reader should bear in mind that all the remarks in this section refer to employment measured in terms of *man-hours;* i.e., even if it should be judged that the effect of a minimum wage law is to reduce man-hours of employment, this *may* be considered unimportant (or tolerable) *if* suitable provision is made for shortening the average work week, and redistributing the burden of the resulting unemployment.

There is some reason for doubt as to the efficacy of minimum wage laws in accomplishing their avowed objective, i.e., raising minimum annual earnings for all persons who desire employment. It is *possible* that a given law will achieve this objective; but it is also possible that it will, as in Puerto Rico, force many inefficient enterprises to cease operations in industries subject to the act, causing a fall in their workers' employment and income. Even if these workers are not forced to become completely unemployed, they may be forced to return to "self-support" in agriculture, or to work in occupations not covered by the act, where they will presumably earn less than otherwise. This involves an alteration in the allocation of the labor force which is usually unintended, and may be undesirable.

[50] The result will turn upon the elasticity of derived demand for labor; "other things equal," the higher this elasticity the greater will be the amount of employment offered.

[51] An exception should be noted where the percentage increase in a firm's wage bill (resulting from a minimum wage law) is small (e.g., the scrub women in the office building of a manufacturing corporation may be its only employees affected by the law). In such a case, the firm may absorb the increase in labor cost by a negligible decrease in profits, and not bother to react.

[52] We neglect the possibility that a minimum wage law might, by eliminating monopsony, oligopsony, etc. succeed both in raising hourly wage rates and incerasing employment. This will not frequently be a factor of major importance.

Furthermore, the imposition of a minimum wage may force unemployment upon certain groups of workers (e.g., women and negroes) who can secure employment only at lower wage rates than others if there are other workers available for all job openings.[53]

It is sometimes argued that one effect of minimum wage laws is to cause increases in the wages of the higher paid workers as their unions will fight to preserve their traditional differentials. The reader should appraise such contentions in the light of the arguments of Chapter 13; in the author's opinion they are of doubtful validity.

The Actual Consequences of FLSA

The effects upon employment that *might* have flowed from FLSA were completely swamped by the general wage and price increases consequent upon our preparation for, and entry into, World War II. By 1943, the forty cent hourly minimum was enforced virtually everywhere but by labor market competition rather than by law. This is not to say that FLSA had no serious effect upon earnings during World War II; it did have such an effect, but it came from the requirements for overtime pay rather than from the wage floor.

It was not intended that the requirement of time and a half for weekly hours over forty should raise weekly earnings; this provision was intended as a deterrent to employing workers more than forty hours per week. And this was its effect, until the labor shortages which developed in 1941–1942 caused overtime work and pay to soar; in 1941, overtime pay in "all manufacturing" was 3.8 per cent of average hourly earnings; in 1943 and 1944, the corresponding percentages were 7.6 per cent (in both years).[54] This rise in overtime pay gave rise to many (unsuccessful) demands for the abolition (or at least suspension for the "duration") of the penalty rates on overtime.

The steady rise of prices during and after World War II materially reduced the real value of any given (money) wage and, therefore, the real income implied by FLSA; furthermore, the steady rise of wage rates re-

---

[53] For example, the minimum wage provisions of the NRA codes (which did not provide for negro-white differentials) caused the administrator to believe that their operation was causing a substitution of white for negro workers (who had previously worked for less than whites). Cf. C. F. Roos, *NRA Economic Planning,* Cowles Commission Monograph, No. 2, Principia Press, Bloomington, Ind., 1937, pp. 172–173. It is also alleged that FLSA caused a substitution of white for negro labor. (G. Myrdal, "An American Dilemma," Harper and Bros., New York, 1944, pp. 397–399, and note 4, pp. 1295–1296

[54] These figures are computed from the difference between "gross" and "adjusted" average hourly earnings; cf. "Handbook of Labor Statistics, 1947," *Bureau of Labor Statistics Bulletin* 916, Table C-2, p. 89. The data understate slightly the actual overtime earned.

duced the number of workers receiving less than 40 cents per hour from 17 per cent of all production workers in manufacturing[55] in January 1941 to 2 per cent in June 1943, and less than 1 per cent by the summer of 1945.[56]   There were Congressional hearings on a revision of the minimum wage provisions of FLSA as early as 1945, but the act was not amended (in this respect) until 1949, when the minimum wage (under FLSA) was set at 75 cents an hour.   It was estimated (in 1949) that 1,500,000 workers (of whom more than 800,000 resided in the South or Southwest) covered by the Act were currently receiving less than this amount.   However, the sharp increase both in wages and prices that has taken place since 1949 has again prevented the act from having any very important effects on wage rates; i.e., the increases that have occurred would probably have taken place irrespective of the act.[57]   On March 1, 1956, the minimum wage under FLSA was increased to $1 per hour.   This may, for the first time, raise minimum wages without an accompanying increase in effective demand; if so, its consequences will be watched with deep interest.

STATE MINIMUM WAGE LAWS

We have already discussed briefly the background and coverage (pp. 499–502) of the various state minimum wage laws.   These laws usually do not provide for statutory wage minimums as does FLSA but instead call for the establishment of wage boards[58] for various industries or occupations whose function it is to set wage minimums for the indicated groups of workers.   These boards, which are usually tripartite in character (with equal representation for employers, employees, and the "public"), set wages on the basis of a mixture of considerations with the need for wages to cover a minimum "living standard" usually receiving great attention.[59]

[55] It is certain that the hourly earnings of a far larger percentage of nonmanufacturing (than manufacturing) wage earners would lie below any specified minimum.

[56] See Table C-3, p. 90, in *Bulletin* 916 of the U. S. Bureau of Labor Statistics (Handbook of Labor Statistics, 1947).

[57] The 1949 amendments to FLSA not only raised the minimum wage rate but also (1) extended the coverage of the prohibition on child labor (see p. 499) and (2) otherwise narrowed the coverage of the act (eliminating from coverage 350,000 to 1,000,000 workers previously covered).   These newly "uncovered" workers were mainly employed in enterprises on the "fringe" of entering into interstate commerce.

[58] The use of wage boards in setting minimum wage rates has been more extensive in foreign countries than in the United States, but we cannot enter into a discussion of their policies and practices.   The interested reader should consult Millis and Montgomery, *op. cit.,* pp. 278–300 and the literature there cited; also Reynolds and Taft, *op. cit.*

[59] For details, see Brandeis, Vol. III, *op. cit.,* Chapter IV and Florence P. Smith, "State Minimum Wage Laws and Orders—an Analysis," *Department of Labor, Bulletin,* 167, Women's Bureau, Washington, D.C., 1939 and subsequent supplements thereto; also Millis and Montgomery, *op. cit.,* pp. 301–324.

In many of the states it is also required that "due consideration" be given to the "value of the service rendered"[60] or, in some cases, the wages paid by "fair" employers, or determined by collective bargaining. Very often several of these conflicting prescriptions are included in the law with the result that the wage boards are left without effective guidance and the resulting wage minimums have to be (more or less) "bargained out."

The minimums that emerge as "wage orders" from such board deliberations are usually higher than the wage rates prescribed by FLSA and, although lagging behind, have tended to rise with living costs. However, employer objection to rising wage minimums has been a potent source of resistance to attempts to accelerate this rise.

GOVERNMENT AS EMPLOYER: WAGE POLICY

In a nutshell, government wage policy (federal, state, and local) has been, at least in recent years, to pay comparatively high wages (in given communities) for manual labor, and relatively low wages in the higher ranks of civil service. Wage policies for clerical employees vary from one local government to another although the federal government is generally "high wage." One reason governments tend to pay relatively high wages to manual labor is that such labor is customarily paid the applicable union scale (by the federal government and by most state and larger city governments) because of the political pressure of unions.

The effect of political pressure by unions and their sympathizers on government wage policy has been manifested, at the federal level, by several pieces of legislation. In 1916, Congress passed the Adamson Act which made eight hours the basic work day for men employed in (interstate) operation of trains and required overtime pay for hours in excess of eight per day. Two other pieces of federal legislation, the Davis-Bacon Act of 1931, and the Walsh-Healey Act of 1936 required the payment of "prevailing wages" on government contracts.

The Davis-Bacon Act (as later amended) requires that contractors on construction work for the federal government pay at least the "prevailing" wage rates to laborers and mechanics. The Walsh-Healey Act prescribes that *"prevailing minimum wages"* (or higher) be paid on all government contracts in excess of $10,000; it also prescribes that work should not exceed eight hours per day (or forty per week), except by permission of the Secretary of Labor, and that such (overtime) work must be compensated at one and one half times the basic rate; child and convict labor is prohibited on government contracts, and work on such contracts must be under "safe and sanitary" conditions. The "prevailing wage" under Davis-Bacon or "prevailing minimum wage" (under Walsh-

[60] This means considering the employer's ability to pay and in crucial cases is likely to conflict directly with the "living standards" principle.

Healey) is determined by the Secretary of Labor, after suitable hearings and investigations. Under the Davis-Bacon Act, the relevant wage is that prevailing in the locality; under Walsh-Healey, the range of firms to be considered in determining the "prevailing minimum" is not clear, but, in practice, the basis for determination is usually the "industry."[61] The prevailing wage, for Davis-Bacon purposes, has tended to be the union scale in the locality, Walsh-Healey minimums tend to be set so that something under 10 per cent of all workers in the industry were receiving less than this minimum at the time of the determination (of the "prevailing minimum").[62]

The philosophy underlying both of these acts (Davis-Bacon and Walsh-Healey) was that the low wage employer should not be given an advantage over his higher wage ("fair") competitors in seeking government contracts. (The Walsh-Healey Act was originally intended to replace, so far as possible, the NRA codes which had been invalidated by the Supreme Court in 1935.)[63] The economic effects of the legislation are not easy to determine; however, it seems quite possible that, prior to 1940, the Davis-Bacon act increased the percentage of jobs in contract construction performed at high wages. Since 1940, the demand for construction has been sufficient to keep construction wages at or above the Davis-Bacon minimums without the assistance of the Act.

The consequences of Walsh-Healey are more intricate than those of Davis-Bacon; Denison showed that in fiscal years 1938 and 1939 government procurement took only a negligible percentage of the output of virtually all industries except shipbuilding and aircraft. He also pointed out that the $10,000 limit exempted the great bulk (both in number and value) of government contracts (prior to World War II) and presented instances where avoidance of the terms of the Act had been accomplished by "splitting bids" (among competitors) so that no one firm was forced to accept a contract of more than $10,000. He further showed how selling to the government from "stock" has permitted avoidance of the Act[64] and cited examples of companies who have divided their labor force

[61] The difficulties of defining "industry" are pointed out by Reilly, Haslam, and Modley, "Threat of the Walsh-Healey Act," *Harvard Business Review,* January 1951, pp. 86–98 especially p. 88.

[62] See Exhibit II in Reilly, Haslam, and Modley, *op. cit.,* p. 94. The procedures that have led to this result are described on pp. 91–93 of the reference. The fact that Walsh-Healey requires the determination of prevailing *minimum* wages and not merely prevailing wages (as Davis-Bacon requires) complicates the problem.

[63] See E. F. Denison, "The Influence of the Walsh-Healey Public Contracts Act Upon Labor Conditions," *Journal of Political Economy,* April 1941, pp. 225–246, especially p. 227.

[64] A contractor's obligation to comply with the act does not begin until notification of the award of the contract has reached him. See Denison, *op. cit.,* pp. 229–230.

so that their higher piece rate earners (whose earnings satisfied the requirements of the Act) concentrated upon government work while low wage earners did nongovernment work.[65]

Denison's discussion refers to the pre-World War II situation; since then, the growth of the government as a purchaser might be supposed to have increased the "leverage" of the Act.   Indeed some writers have expressed great concern that (in recent years) the effect of Walsh-Healey has been to handicap firms and workers in low wage areas.[66]

However, even if these writers are correct, which many economists would deny, they tend to overlook the fact that in a period of great business activity many firms are likely to be operating at capacity and, hence, the effect of barring low wage firms from government contracts is to force them to take the nongovernment "leavings" from the high wage firms (who can choose between government and nongovernment business). But this need not alter either the wage policies, or the share of industry output, of the low wage firms.   That is, the Walsh-Healey might not affect any wage rates, but merely alter the allocation of government and nongovernment work among high and low wage firms.

THE GOVERNMENT AND SOCIAL MINIMUM: A SUMMARY

In Chapter 19 we discussed the various attempts of the government to raise social minimum incomes through social insurance or direct assistance. In this chapter, we have surveyed the principal ways in which governments set statutory minimums for wages and maximums for hours.

The history of government attempts at regulating wages and hours is one of slow advance against great opposition from employers and the courts.   Until well into this century, the economic impact of the laws regulating the working conditions of women and children must have been very slight, as so little effort was put into their enforcement.[67]   However, as these laws became better enforced, they undoubtedly began to reduce the supply of some of the least skilled grades of labor.   This tended to make the wages of this type of labor higher than otherwise and probably assisted the other forces at work, during the 1930's, in reducing the margin for skill.

[65] If this can be done completely, the effect of the act upon wages is eliminated; low wage earners are simply shifted to private production and high wage earners to government work.

[66] Reilly, Haslam, and Modley, *op. cit.*   Also J. V. Van Sickle, *The Walsh-Healey Public Contracts,* American Enterprise Association, New York, 1952.

[67] In recent years, the enforcement of FLSA and other government measures aimed at raising wage floors has been greatly aided by union activity.   Unions have provided legal assistance for complaining workers and have, in general, sought to compel employers to live up to the letter of the law.

Legislation regulating the wages and working conditions of men was very scanty prior to 1933, except on railroads, government jobs, and on especially hazardous work in mines, factories, etc. The effect of the hour limitations of the NRA codes and FLSA was to distribute employment and income more equally among the labor force and to reduce labor supply (by shortening hours). The minimum wage provisions of these laws (directly) affected only the lowest paid earners, and the effect on employment was varied. In some cases, minimum wage statutes may have "shocked" employers into increased efficiency and higher wages, but in others (e.g., in Puerto Rico) it simply caused unemployment. Fear of this possibility has impeded attempts to raise wage floors by statute and continues to do so. (Congressional concern, however, is at least as great for the employer of the low wage earner as for the worker himself.)

The effect of FLSA on employment (if any) was swamped by inflation during World War II and the effect of the 1949 amendment was similarly obscured by the Korean inflation. However, the penalty rates for overtime probably caused average hourly wages to rise somewhat more during World War II than they otherwise would have.

DISCUSSION QUESTIONS

1. What effect would a relatively high minimum hourly wage law (not applicable to agriculture) have upon rural-urban migration?

2. Exclusive of the effect on overtime pay, how could a reduction in hours affect the general wage level in a community?

3. "A community that refuses family allowances to parents has no right to restrict the labor of the children." What is your opinion of the economics and social philosophy underlying this statement?

Suggested Readings

Douglas, P. H., and J. Hackman, "Fair Labor Standards Act of 1938," *Political Science Quarterly,* December 1938 and March 1939.

Douty, H. M., "Minimum Wage Regulation in the Seamless Hosiery Industry," *Southern Economic Journal,* October 1941, pp. 176–190.

Florence, P. S., *The Economics of Fatigue and Unrest,* Henry Holt & Company, Inc., New York, 1924.

Lescohier, D. D., and E. Brandeis, *History of Labor in the United States,* Vol. III, The Macmillan Company, New York, 1935.

Millis, H. A., and R. E. Montgomery, *Labor's Progress and Problems,* McGraw-Hill Book Company, Inc., New York, 1938.

Stigler, G. J., "The Economics of Minimum Wage Legislation," *American Economic Review,* June 1946, pp. 358–365.

Woytinsky, W. S., and associates, *Employment and Wages in the United States,* Twentieth Century Fund, New York, 1953.

"Hours of Work and Output," *U. S. Bureau of Labor Statistics Bulletin* 917, Washington, D.C., 1947.

The Role of the Union in Modern Society: An Appraisal

There are few economic or social activities in which an organization can engage that one union or another has not tried. Historically, unions have been service organizations, ministering to whatever needs their members felt. In Europe this meant agitating for political equality; however, this was never an (unfilled) need of the American wage earner. On the other hand, American unions had, a generation or two ago, the peculiar problem of helping immigrants adjust to American life, in terms of language, folkways, education, etc. The unions that filled this need (e.g., the garment unions) survived and prospered while many unions that ignored it fell by the wayside. In many countries, including the United States, unions found that workers needed social insurance of various kinds, and, for a long time, some unions (mainly of skilled workers) were a major provider of social security for their members. Finally, in many countries unions have been the rallying point for member political activity.

The evolution of society in the past 50 years has transferred many union functions elsewhere. Social security and educational functions have been largely taken over by the state. The many diversions of urban society have robbed the union of the position it once had as a focus of member social activity. What is left to the union primarily is collective bargaining, and the political activity ancillary to it. The pattern of union evolution (or, as some view it, retrogression) differs from one country to another and among unions within the same country. But the general trend toward the strong, well-financed, respectable union with a large apathetic membership has been observed in many countries having well-developed labor movements.

In the United States, the "heroic period" of union founding is over. There is, of course, room for further organization, but the basic industries of the country are now substantially unionized. American unions are primarily (in many cases, solely), bargaining organizations. Therefore, to judge the contribution of unions to the well-being of American workers, it is necessary to see what gains they have made through bargaining.

One very important change brought about by unionism is in the worker's status in the "factory community." The union ends, forever, the possibility of arbitrary discharge. In a unionized establishment, no member of management may tell a workman, arbitrarily, "You're fired." The union member is a "citizen," and, if he protests discharge or any other kind of treatment, he has a chance for redress via the grievance system. In short, unionism ends arbitrary rule in the factory.

The obverse side of this is a reduction in management authority to impose discipline, which many management spokesmen insist reduces worker efficiency. This may be true in individual cases, but the continuing rapid rise in man-hour productivity in the United States suggests that its over-all effect has probably been slight. One reason why it has been slight is that mature unions tend to be cooperative in promoting or, at least, not impeding worker efficiency.

There are, of course, famous instances where unions have tried to hold down worker productivity through make-work rules. However, these instances have occurred largely in stagnant or declining industries where labor demand was falling. As the American economy has, with the exception of the 1930's, been expanding in most sectors, its labor unions have not been impelled to attempt to curb its increasing man-hour productivity. It is also well to remember that informal work rules, which serve to restrict worker productivity, often exist prior to unionization. Unions are frequently blamed for initiating practices restrictive of output when, in fact, they have merely formalized and enforced (at the demand of their members) pre-existing patterns of behavior.

By abolishing the right of arbitrary discharge and establishing the correlative freedom to present grievances, unions have compelled management to create orderly processes of layoff and discharge which would be acceptable to the union. The fruit of this is the present-day seniority system. The over-all effect of formal seniority on company personnel policy is debatable, as many firms would tend to favor senior workers anyway. However, there is a big difference in the security and independence of a worker whose job rights are protected by a collective bargaining agreement and one whose job security is subject to the discretion of management. Furthermore, some firms have tended to discriminate against aging workers who were becoming less efficient.[1] Union protected seniority rules prevent this.

Another change caused by unionism is in the attention paid to personnel problems. Before the arrival of the union, management decisions were often made in ignorance of, and without concern for, the feelings of the workers involved. Intraplant inequities in wage rates, discriminatory treatment of workers by foremen, etc. were widespread. Often the situation was not known to top management, and senior executives were not sufficiently concerned to find out. But when workers' dissatisfaction is voiced by a strong union, it behooves management to pay attention. As a result, management decisions are now made with full consideration for worker reaction.

In short, the union has made the worker a full-fledged "citizen of industry." But has it given him a "larger share of industry's product," as it sometimes promises? As we have seen, this is difficult to determine. First, consider the case of depressions; during depressions, union wages clearly do not fall sufficiently to eliminate unemployment, but, then, neither do nonunion wages. During depression, union wage rates fall less than nonunion, but it cannot be said with confidence that unionization is the "cause" of this difference. In view of the increased spread between union and nonunion wage rates (on comparable jobs), and the frequent "chiseling" on the union scale by individual employers, it is probable that the union tends to maintain wage rates on those jobs that it can control. However, the fact that it does this induces the employers who can operate on a nonunion basis to do so. The shortage of jobs for union members (as for others) during a depression compels the union both to allocate employment opportunities among existing members and to discourage new members. This is responsible for the common view of the union as an economic agent; i.e. it is a monopolistic price (i.e., wage) fixer compelled to ration the jobs made scarce by its own high prices.[2]

But this view is entirely inconsistent with the behavior of unions under full employment.[3] Here we find unions, all of whose members are employed and who are accepting new members constantly, negotiating wage

---

[1] This often arises in connection with changes in productive processes that involve learning new tasks. Such learning is difficult for older workers, and, without the protection of seniority, they have often been discharged for incapacity.

[2] This is the view offered by Selig Perlman in his famous book: *A Theory of the Labor Movement,* Augustus Kelley, New York, 1949, especially Part II.

[3] For brevity, we speak of "depression" and "full employment." What we mean to contrast are situations in which all the "regular" members of the union are employed with those ("depression") cases where this does not hold.

contracts which do not reduce employment and are not intended to do so.   Under these circumstances economists may well ask, "In what sense have unions made wages higher than they otherwise would have been?"

There are several answers to this question, each appropriate to different circumstances:

1. Where the union materially helps to raise product prices and/or to stimulate product demand, it may raise the demand curve for labor.

2. If the employers have been holding down product prices, either for fear of public resentment and/or of attracting new competition through high profits, the union may be able to raise wages (and product prices) materially through bargaining.

3. Where firms, especially large multiplant firms, are earning rents or monopoly profits, the union may be able to compel that they be shared with the workers.[4]

These "answers," together, leave plenty of room for unions to have increased (their members') wages, despite continuing full employment. However, if one does not choose to believe that these (and similar) arguments are very widely applicable, there is little evidence that can be brought to bear.   Similar skepticism may be offered concerning the alleged effects of unionism on the margin for skill.

The sharp rise of wages during the depressed 1930's is a case where unionism, in conjunction with governmental pressure on the very low wage rates, may well have "pushed up" the general level of wages.   However, sharp money wage increases and large scale unemployment have coexisted only very rarely.

It is quite likely that governmental action has restricted labor supply via labor laws for children and women, FLSA, and, above all, restricting immigration.   Unions, as instruments for (helping in) the retention and enforcement of such laws, have thereby tended to assist in raising wages through this channel.   Furthermore, union pressure for a full employment policy has probably helped to create the political conditions conducive to a monetary-fiscal policy aimed at maintaining high level employment.

In short, unions in the United States have cooperated with "middle-class" reformers who have espoused political and economic reforms that benefitted the wage earner.   That is, the unions have been part of the political support for both the New Deal and the Fair Deal whose legislative programs both encouraged unionism and promoted independent economic reforms on behalf of wage earners.   In this way the unions have, by their political efforts, contributed to raising the incomes of wage earners.   But

---

[4] This is most likely to occur where a modern efficient firm locates in a low wage area and the plant is then unionized.   If the firm has other (unionized) plants, union pressure can be brought to bear more easily, at these other plants, than if the firm has only one plant.

the precise contribution of unionism to these legislative developments will never be known.

Apart from its economic effects, unionism is the vehicle through which the working classes, in all advanced countries, have expressed their aspirations for political and social equality with other members of the community. The change in the wage earner's status in the factory is the fruit of unionism, even though many non-union managements have come to conduct personnel policy in a far different manner than they once did. In society at large, the political influence of unions, though often exaggerated, gains a respect for the viewpoint and interests of the wage earner that was formerly lacking. We may never reach what Sumner Slichter has termed a "laboristic society," but in a nation of competing pressure groups, the demands of unions reflect in an imperfect but nonetheless recognizable way the interests and desires of their membership.

Index

Adamson Act (of 1916), 94, 96n
AFL-CIO, 77, 82, 83, 85, 112–116, 236,
    241–242
    Committee on Political Education
        (COPE) of, 106
    Committee on Racial Discrimination
        of, 115
    Departments of, 114
    Ethical Practices Committee of, 115
    Executive Committee of, 113
    finance of, 113
    formal structure of, 113–116
    officers of, 113–114
    power to expel affiliates of, 113
    state and local organizations of, 113–
        114
Aged persons, and hiring preference,
    317
    and income, 450–452
    and occupational mobility, 296
    and pensions, 485–491
    and seniority, 189–191
    and unemployment, 294–295, 440–441,
        450–451
    in labor force, 20
    Old Age Assistance (OAA), 487–489
    see also Pensions,
Agency Shop, 179
Agriculture,
    and distribution of employment, 328–
        330
    employment in, 20, 432
    wages in, 328–330
Alinsky, Saul, 69n, 70n, 105n
Amalgamated Association of Tin, Iron
    And Steel Workers, 47, 67, 68, 69
Amalgamated Clothing Workers, 52, 57,
    58, 62, 66, 68, 69, 129, 183, 344,
    398

Amalgamated Textile Workers, 57
American Arbitration Association, 161
American Federation of Labor (AFL),
    43ff, 71–3, 77, 79, 80, 82, 83, 84–5,
    99, 101, 103, 110, 112, 137, 214–
    215, 218, 220, 234, 236, 412, 415
    Executive Council of, 64, 71, 80, 141
    finances of, 71
    Labor's League for Political Education
        (LLPE), 105–106
    philosophy of, 91–96
    political affiliations of leaders, 109
    political attitude of, 93–96
    opposition to social legislation of, 94–
        6, 98
    and "no-raiding" pact, 77, 79, 113
American Federation of Musicians, 75,
    184, 198, 224–225
American Medical Association, 352–354
American Plan, see Open shop
American Railway Union, 53, 213–214
Anderson, C. A. 458n, 469
Anderson, H. D., 455n, 457n, 469
Andrews, P. W. S., 297n
Angell, J. W., 406n
Apprenticeship, 33, 35, 38, 39, 184
    control of, 349–350
Arbitration, 56
    compulsory, 43, 259 et seq.
    of grievances, 161–162
    voluntary, 274–275
Arbitrators, umpires, impartial chairmen,
    conciliators, mediators, etc., 161,
    261–262, 275–276
Armstrong, B. N., 470n, 495
Arnow, P., 390n
Arrow, K. J., 237n

Bach, G. L., 420n, 422n
Baker, H., 382n, 383n, 384n, 386n, 398n, 399
Bakke, E. W., 202, 285n
Ball, R. A., 486n, 487n
Barkin, S., 382n, 383n
Beck, Dave, 115, 138n
Becker, J. M., 472n
Bell, Daniel, 84n, 88n, 96n, 99n, 100n, 110, 140n, 141n, 142
Bernstein, Martin, 401n
Berry, George L., 140
Beveridge, Sir W. H., 419n, 422n, 495
Birthrates, 327
Blacklist, 33
Bloch, J. W., 344n
Bogue, D. J., 301
Bott, George J., 232n
Boulding, K. E., ix, 318
Bowden, Witt, 403n
Bowman, D. O., 223n, 233n, 234n
Bowman, M. J., 458n, 469
Boycotts, 33, 41, 206, 213–215
  and hot cargo, 231
  secondary, 166, 245, 249–251, 255;
    (see also Taft-Hartley Act)
Brandeis, E., 496n, 497n, 498n, 501n, 512n, 516
Brandeis, Justice Louis D., 208
Braun, K., 277
Brewery Workers, 41, 47, 48, 62, 64, 68
Bridgman, D. S., 458n
Brissenden, P. F., 55, 85
Bronfenbrenner, M., 419n, 425n
Brooks, G. W., 189n
Brooks, R. R. R., 68n, 69n, 70n, 169n
Brown, E. C., 221n, 224n, 225n, 226, 231n, 232n, 233n, 234n, 235n, 237n, 244n, 247n, 251n, 254n, 255n
Brown, J. C., 458n, 469
Brown, W. F., 354n
Brown, W. M., 507n
Bryan, William Jennings, 94, 109
Budish, J. M., 57n
Building Service unions, 75n, 139–141
Building Trades union, 44, 65, 76, 82, 198; see also Carpenters
  corruption in, 139–141
  department of, 114
  jurisdictional disputes in, 79, 246–247
Burkhead, Jesse, 426n
Burns, E. M., 474n, 476n, 479n, 488n, 495
Byrnes Act, 206

Capital, movement of, 329–330
Capital goods, 16, 17
Cassady, Ralph Jr., 354n

Case Bill, 75
Catholic Church, 40
Catholic Trade Unionists, 100n
Centers, R., 457n
Chamberlain, N. W., 173, 175n, 183n, 202, 263n, 264n, 274n, 277
Champernowne, D. G., 439n
Chaplin, Ralph, 55n
Checkoff, 179–180; see also Union security
Chicago Federation of Labor, 57
Child Labor, 19, 20
  regulation of, 497, 499
Christenson, C. L., 350n, 420n
Christgau, V., 486n
Churchill, B. C., 461n
Cigar Makers union, 38, 39, 40, 62, 344–345
Clapham, J. H., 325n
Clark, Colin, 368n, 374n
Clark, J. M., 420n
Class struggle, 90–93
Clayton Act, 94, 213, 215–217
Clegg, H. A., 151n
Closed shop 33, 73, 177–178, 184–188;
  see also Compulsory unionism;
  union shop
Cohen, W. J., 486n, 487n
Cole, G. D. H., 11n
Coleman, J. R., 173
Coleman, J. S., 132n, 142
Collective bargaining, 143–202
  and contracts, 174–175
  and mutual problem solving, 157–158
  and strikes, 156–157, 163 et seq.
  benefits of, 262
  employer attitudes toward, 144–148
  in "good faith," 244–245
  key bargains, 153–154, 157; see also
    Wages, patterns of
  multi-employer bargaining, see Em-
    ployer associations
  negotiations, see Contracts, negotiation
Common Law, conspiracy, 32, 33, 203–205, 249
Commons, J. R., 31n, 32n, 33n, 36n, 38n, 39n, 42n, 43n, 45n, 48n, 85, 87n, 88n, 111, 197n, 204n, 298n, 299n
Communism, and racial discrimination, 103
  Anti-Fascist stand, 101–102
  Communist International, 55, 101
  Communists in unions, 54, 64, 69, 78–84, 102–104, 110, 133n, 135–136
Communist Party, 57, 100–104
  "fellow travelers," 102

Compulsory unionism, pros and cons, 175–178; *see also* Closed shop; Union shop; Maintenance of Membership
Congress of Industrial Organizations, Committee of Industrial Organizations (CIO), 65ff, 77, 80–82, 84–85, 99–103, 110, 112, 146, 147n, 220, 234, 243, 412, 415
and Communists, 80–82, 101
and "no-raiding" pact, 77, 79
Political Action Committee of, 76, 105–106
political affiliations of leaders, 109
Contracts (union-management), 174–175; *see also* Collective bargaining
administration of, 158–163, 170–171; *see also* Grievance procedure
and employer representatives, 148–150; *see also* Employer associations
legal enforcement of, 254–256; *see also* Damage suits
"living document," interpretation of, 163, 170
negotiation of, 148–158
ratification of, 155
strategic considerations in, 155–158, 163 et seq.
union representatives 154–155
union security clauses 175–180; *see also* Managerial prerogatives
Cooke, M. L., 202, 397n
Cooperatives, producer, 36, 88–9
Cost of living, 7, 24n, 33, 57, 58, 74, 281–282, 404–407; *see also* Price level
adjustments in, 413–415, 422; *see also* "escalator" clauses
Council of Industrial Organizations, 114–115; *see also* CIO
Courts, 32, 50, 65; *see also* Supreme Court
and wage-hour legislation, 501–504
Cox, A., 266n
Creamer, D. C., 401n
Cullen, D. E., 273n
Curran, Joe, 81

Damage suits, 214–215, 254–255
David, L. M., 360n, 362n, 378n
Davidson, P. E., 455n, 457n, 469
Davis, J. C., 422n
Davis, John W., 109
Davis, W. H., 413n
Davis-Bacon Act, 513–515
Debs, Eugene, 53n, 209

DeLeon, Daniel, 53–54
Democratic Party, 93–94, 99, 100, 105, 106, 108–110
Denham, Robert N., 231–232, 250
Denis, H., 165n
Denison, E. F., 426n, 427, 514n
Denmark, 270
Dewey, Donald, 462n, 463n, 467n
Dewhurst, J. F., 17
Diamond Workers Protective Union, 116, 119n
Dickson, W. J., 199n, 202, 395n
Dillard, D., 418n
Disability Insurance, 492
Discharge, 6–7
employer right of, 180–181
Discrimination, *see* Restriction on entry; Wage differentials
Dismissal wage, severance pay, dismissal compensation, 479–480
Dooker, M. J., 381n
Dorfman, Joseph, 87n
Douglas, P. H., 429, 459n, 495, 509n, 516
Douty, H. M., 342n, 413n, 509n, 516
Dubin, R., 172n
Dubinsky, David, 138n
Ducoff, L. J., 432n
Duesenberry, J. S., 284n
Dunlop, J. T., 46n, 79n, 173, 323n, 331n, 336n, 347n, 348n, 356, 400n, 404n, 429

Earners (of wages), principal, 286–289
secondary, 289–290, 466–467
Eberling, E. J., 483n, 484n
Education, 22
and child labor, 502–503
and income, 453–457
and margin for skill, 368–370
years of, 19–20
Edwards, A. M., 22
Effort (work), 4–6, 195–200, 291, 397
Egbert, D. D., 90n
Eight hour day, 37, 43
Eisenhower, President Dwight D., 110, 230, 238, 256–257
Electrical Workers, International Union of (IUE), 81–82, 114n; *see also* United Electrical Workers (UE)
Ells, R. W., 382n
Employee hierarchy 295; *see also* Hiring preferences
Employee representation plans, 63; *see also* Company unions
Employer, associations, 150–154, 166
and price fixing, 152–154

Employer, attitudes toward collective
    bargaining, see Collective bargaining
    attitudes toward labor problems, 149–
    150
    government as an, 513–515
    hiring preferences and wage policies
        of, 317–318, 321–324
    methods of handling grievances, 162–
        163
Employment exchanges (United States
    Employment Service), 297–300
Employment opportunities, see also Jobs;
    Unemployment, and economic
    progress, 438–441
    of Negroes, 461–464
    of Women, 465–469
    union control of, 183–192
Enarson, H. L., 263n, 277
"Escalator" clauses, see Cost of living
    adjustments

Fabricant, S., 358n, 438n
Fact-finding Boards, 269
Fair Employment Practices Committee,
    464
Fair Labor Standards Act, 99n, 195–197,
    503–512, 516; see also Wages and
    Hours Law
Family Allowances, 493–494
Family, farms, 8–10
    labor supply of, 290–291
    producing units, 8–10
Farmer-Labor Party, 109
Fay, Joe, 140n
Featherbedding, see "Make work" rules
Federal Mediation and Conciliation
    Service, 161
Federation of Organized Trades and
    Labor Unions (American Federa-
    tion of Labor), 43n–44n
Feldman, H., 464n, 465n, 469
Fichandler, T. C., 191n, 192n
Fisher, A. G. B., 374n
Fisher, L. A., ix, 150, 151n, 190n, 227n,
    383n, 385n, 386n, 399
Fiscal Policy, 407, 422, 424–425, 428,
    491
Fitzpatrick, John, 57, 58
Fixed costs, 313
Flanders, Allan, 151n
Fleming, R. W., 263n, 273n, 277
Florence, P. S., 196n, 202, 505n, 516
Ford Motor Co., 70, 481
Foremen, 159–160, 162, 180–181, 186–
    187, 235
Foster, William Z., 57, 58, 101

France, R. R., 272n
Frankfurter, Justice Felix, 216n, 225
Free land, 87–88
Freedman, B. N., 288n
Friedman, M., 340n, 352n, 353n, 356,
    420n, 429
Fringe benefits, 175, 192–194, 200–201
Full Employment, 443–444
    and inflation, 419–422
    and the margin for skill, 375

Galenson, Walter, ix, 71n, 151n, 260n,
    270n, 494n
Gamm, Sara, 189n
Garbarino, J. W., 358
General Motors, 69, 413–414, 428, 481
Gifford, W., 458n
Ginger, Ray, 53n
Gitlow, A. L., 372n, 413n, 415n
Glasser, Carrie, 288n, 364n, 376
Glick, P. C., 454
Golden, C. S., 173, 339n, 397n
Goldner, W., 342n, 358n, 375n
Goldsmith, S., 450n
Goldstein, H., 371n
Gomberg, W., 382n, 392n, 399
Gompers, Samuel, 39, 44–45, 48–51,
    57, 64, 91–99, 110, 141, 214–215
Gordon, M. S., 376
Gordon, R. A., 319, 400n
Government employees, 94, 464
Gould, Jay, 42
Green, William, 64, 68, 80n, 83
Greene, Nathaniel, 216n, 225
Grievance procedure, 6–7, 74, 159–163,
    170, 186
Gregory, C. O., 32n, 204n, 205n, 207n,
    208n, 210n, 211n, 213n, 215n,
    216n, 217n, 226, 244n, 249n
Griffen, J. I., 172n
Gross national product, see National
    Income
Grunfel, J., 498n
Grossman, Jonathan, 36n
Guaranteed annual wage, 77, 201, 480–
    484

Haber, William, 140n
Haberler, G., 420n
Hackman, J., 509n, 516
Hanna, Mark, 92, 93
Hansen, A. H., 418n, 422n, 495
Harbison, F. H., 70n, 173
Hardman, J. B. S., 118n, 122n, 142
Harris, A., 51n, 462n, 469
Harris, S. E., 455n, 469
Hart, P. E., 408n, 427n, 430

Haslam, R. S., 514n, 515n
Hatch Act (of 1940), 105
Havemann, Ernest, 455n, 458n, 469
Hayes, A. J., 115
Haymarket bombing, 43
Haywood, William D., 53, 55
Heady, E. O., 328n
Health insurance, 493; see also Health and welfare funds
Health and welfare funds, 115, 140n, 141, 200–201, 244, 248–249
Healy, J. J., 173
Henderson, Leon, 505n, 507n
Herberg, Will, 96n, 130n, 142
Hicks, J. R., 165n, 429
Higgins, Father G. G., 95n, 96n, 98n, 111
Hildebrand, G. H., 263n
Hillman, Sidney, 52n
Hinrichs, A. F., 509n
Hiring, see also Jobs,
    of government, 464
    preferences (of Employers), 317
    standards, 293, 323–324, 370–376, 462–464
    union control of, 184–189
Hiring hall, 185–186, 188
Hitch, T. K., 422n
Hobbs Act, 225
Hobson, J. B., 442n
Holmes, Justice O. W., 501n
Hopkins, S. V., 401n, 404n, 430
Hoover, C. B., 328
Hours of work, 17, 18, 59, 88, 195–197, 291, 306, 502–505
Hoxie, R. F., 111
Hughes, Chief Justice Charles E., 217
Hutcheson, Maurice, 129
Hutcheson, William L., 109, 216–217

Immigrants (Immigration), 23, 24, 34, 35, 37, 50, 51, 55, 97, 326–327, 464–465
    Chinese coolies, 37
    East European Jews, 50
    Effect on labor market of, 324, 326, 465
    Irish, 34
    Italian, 50
    Slums, 50
Imprisonment for debt, 88
Incentive system, 388–399; see also Output restriction
    difficulties of, 391–396
    Halsey Plan, 389–390
    and rate cutting, 394–396
    and union attitudes, 396–399

Income distribution, among families, 448–452
    and age, 450–452
    and education, 453–457
    and environment and heredity, 457–458
    and entry restriction, 452–461
    and inflation, 422–425
    and negroes, 461–464
    and Social Security System, 494–495
    and the price level, 422–425
    fixed share of national income, 408–409
    labor's share in 425–427
    variable share of national income, 408–409
Industrial relations, see Collective bargaining
    experts in, 149
Inflation, 408–418
    and structural unemployment, 441–444
Injunctions, 53, 61, 62, 65, 94, 96, 209–217, 253–255, 267–269
Insurance,
    accident and health, 8
Intellectuals, 48; see also Social reformers
Interest, rate of, 418–419
International Ladies Garment Workers (ILGWU), 52, 64, 66, 68, 69, 70, 97, 101, 103n, 135n, 138n, 398;
International Workers of the World; "Wobblies" (IWW), 51, 52, 71, 85, 97–98, 100, 137
    Chicago, 54
    Detroit, 53
    Ideology of, 54–55
Iron Molders Union, 35–38
Irwin, Donald, 172n

Jaffe, A. J., 18n, 19, 21, 285n, 301, 367n
Jensen, V. H., 53n
Jobs, see also Employment; Labor Force; Occupation
    characteristics of, 285–286, 289–293
    choice of, 283–286
    satisfaction in, 285
    security of, 285, 288–289, 355–356
    manual, 20–24
    professional, 84, 452–453
    semiskilled, 22, 23, 38, 366–376
    skilled, 22, 23, 38, 288–289, 366–376
    unskilled, 22, 23, 38, 366–376
    white collar, 20–24, 84, 459
Job evaluation, 376–388
    and the labor market, 386–388
    union attitude toward, 382–386

Job hierarchy, 291–293, 332–333; *see also* Hiring standards; Employee hierarchy
  and local labor market, 321–324
  movement within, 322–324
  and unemployment, 293–295
Job rationing, 175, 185–189, 354–356; *see also* Hiring, union control of
Johnson, D. G., 327n, 330n, 356
Johnson, General Hugh S., 219, 344n
Johnson, R. W., 509n
Josephson, Matthew, 52n, 57n
Jurisdiction (Jurisdictional Conflict), 67–68, 71–72, 78–79, 112–113, 223–224, 245–247

Kalecki, M., 429
Kamm, J. O., 455n
Kanninen, T. P., 359, 361n, 371
Kaplan, A. D. H., 495
Kaufman, J. J., 271n, 272n, 277
Kennedy, V. D., 392n, 394n, 395n, 399
Kerr, Clark, ix, 150, 151n, 172n, 190n, 383n, 385n, 386n, 399, 416n, 423n, 425n
Keynes, Lord J. M., 418–419, 422n, 442
Killingsworth, C. C., 224n, 226
Kipnis, Ira, 90n
Klarman, H. E., 360n
Knight, Governor Goodwin J., 109
Knights of Labor, 40–47, 54, 71, 85, 88
Knights of St. Crispin, 35, 36
Knowles, K. G. J. C., 172n, 262n, 373n, 375n
Kornhauser, A., 172n
Krislow, J., 78n
Kuznets, S. S., 17, 25, 352n, 353n, 356, 426n, 450n

Labor (worker), definition of, 3–4
  demand for, 302–319
    and inflation, 409
    and money supply, 409–411
    discipline of, 158–159
  indentured, 37
  indirect manual, 359
  markets for, 320–356
    local, 321–324
  movement of, 287–289, 326–329
  shortages of, 56
  supply of, 283–301
  white collar (clerical), 459–461
Labor force (working force), 18, 19, 289–290
  composition of, industrial, 21, 327–329, 431–432
    occupational, 22, 366–368
    socioeconomic, 22, 366–368

Labor Party, 108–109
Labor Statistics, Bureau of, 281–282, 381
Labor unions, 7, 8, 24, 517–521
  attitude of workers toward, 123–125
  city centrals (also city federations), 33–34, 40, 48–49, 57–59
  company, 62, 63, 66, 70, 78, 218
  constitutions of, 116–117, 130
  conventions of, 116–117
  corruption in, 80, 115–116, 135–136, 138–142, 185, 188n
  craft organizations, 39, 45–46, 48, 50, 64–65, 68, 97, 104
  disciplinary procedures, 133–136, 239–242
  district organizations, 117–118
  economic effects of, *see* Collective bargaining; Strikes; Wages; Wage differentials
  elections, 130–132
  finances, 33–35, 39, 58, 71, 84, 88, 120, 167, 179–180
    benefits, 35, 39
    dues, 35, 50, 57–58, 97, 120, 122, 134, 167, 180
    initiation fees, 33–35, 39, 58, 71, 84, 88, 120, 167, 179–180
  independent, 78; *see also* company
  industrial organizations, 47, 52–55, 64–65, 68, 78, 97
  international organizations, 116–117
  Joint boards (joint councils, district councils), 118
  judicial procedures, 133–136, 239–242
  legal status of, 203–277
  membership, 60–61, 63, 65–66, 70–73, 76, 82, 84–85, 112, 116
    active members, 125–126
    passive members, 103, 121–123
  national organizations, 33–34, 39–40, 83, 116–117
  officers, business agents, 119–120
    compensation of, 119–120, 136–138
    local, 126–127
    national, 127–130
    shop stewards (grievance committeemen), 127, 160
  opposition of employers to, 49, 75, 84–85, 145–146, 218–223
  organizing campaigns of, 42–43, 56–58, 64, 66, 69, 71–73, 75, 112
  policies, *see* Collective bargaining; Contracts (union-management); Wages
  political influence of, 104–110
La Follette, Senator Robert M., 109

Lahne, H. J., 438n
Larrowe, C. P., 140n, 185n, 186n, 188n
Law and unions, 203–277
  state laws, 223–224
  unlawful means, 206–209
  unlawful objectives, 204–206
Layoff (involuntary separation), 6–7,
  180, 189–192, 287–289
Leiserson, W. M., 51n
Lenkart, R., 381n
Lescohier, D. D., 516
Lester, R. A., 46n, 272n, 301, 307n,
  314n, 317n, 318, 319, 331n, 341n,
  364–365n, 376, 378n, 468n
Levinson, Edward, 67n, 68n, 69n
Levinson, H. M., 342n, 425n
Levitan, S. A., 382n, 384n
Lewis, John L., 64, 68, 69n, 71, 74, 75,
  79, 80, 81, 104, 105n, 109, 112,
  193, 225, 243, 268, 345, 412, 415
License laws, 350–351
Lieberman, Elias, 70n, 204n, 207n, 208n,
  211n, 213n, 214n, 215n, 216n, 226
Lindblom, C. E., 165n, 420n, 430
Lipset, S. M., 130n, 132n, 142, 460n,
  469
"Little Steel" formula, 413
"Little Steel" companies, 70, 72
Livernash, E. R., 382n, 399
Livingston, John W., 114
Lockouts, 156, 163–164; see also Strikes
Loewe vs. Lawlor (Danbury Hatters'
  case), 214
Long, C. D., 301
Longshoremen, 185–187
Longshoremen and Warehousemen, In-
  ternational Union of (ILWU), 82,
  139–141
Longshoremen's Association, Interna-
  tional (ILA), 80
Lorwin, L. L., 64n, 85, 95n, 218n, 219n
Lorwin, Val, 494n
Louden, J. K., 390n
Lubin, I., 436n
Lytle, C. W., 381n, 390n, 399

Machinists, International Brotherhood
  of, 78, 216, 385, 397, 415
Maine, Sir Henry, 11
Maintenance of membership, 73, 179;
  see also Compulsory unionism
Machlup, F., 319
Maclaurin, W. R., 301, 314n, 315n, 331n
MacDonald, David, 82, 115, 129
McKinley, President William, 93
McCaffree, K. M., 459n
McCaskill, James, 453

"Make work" rules (featherbedding),
  198–200, 248; see also Output re-
  striction
Managerial prerogatives, 146, 174–175,
  180–183
Mann, J. K., 265n
Mantoux, Paul, 325n
Manufacturing, employment in, 20
Marceau, L., 273n
Marginal productivity theory, 308–313
Marquis, V., 381n
Marx, Karl, 90, 92, 442n
Marxism, 89–93, 97, 101
Master and Servant Act, 11
Mathewson, S. B., 199n, 202, 395n
Meany, George, 80, 83, 115
Mechanics' liens, 88
Mechanization, see Technological prog-
  ress
Mediation (Conciliation), 270–271, 275–
  276; see also Arbitration
Meidner, R., 421n
Melman, Seymour, 21n
Meyers, F., 366n
Michels, Robert, 130n, 142
Miernyk, W. H., 301, 437n, 439n
Migration, rural–urban, 328–330; see
  also Immigrants
Miller, H. P., 295n, 365n, 369, 450, 460,
  462n
Millis, H. A., 63n, 66n, 221n, 224n,
  225n, 226, 231n, 232n, 233n, 234n,
  235n, 237n, 244n, 247n, 251n, 254n,
  255n, 500n, 503n, 512n, 516
Mills, C. W., 109n, 141n, 142
Mills, F. C., 423n
Mine, Mill and Smelter Workers, 53, 68,
  82; see also Western Federation of
  Miners
Miners, coal, 47, 48, 74–75
  demands for safety legislation, 96n
  metal, 53
Minorities, ethnic, 464–465; see also
  Negroes
Mobility of labor, and knowledge of
  alternative job opportunities, 283–
  289, 292
  between industries, 296
  between jobs, 286–290
  between locations, 296–297
  between occupations, 20–24, 295–296,
  459–461
  between social classes, 12–14
Modley, R., 514n, 515n
Money supply, 37, 88, 409–411, 420
  and demand for cash balances, 418
  and wage cuts, 418–419

Monetary policy 407, 418, 422, 428; *see also* Money Supply
Montgomery, R. F., 63n, 66n, 500n, 503n, 512n, 516
Morgan, C. A., 252n
Morton, W. A., 420n, 430
Murchison, C. T., 509n
Murray, Philip, 71, 72, 81, 82, 129, 202, 243, 397n
Musgrave, R. A., 273n
Mutual benefit associations (societies), 8
Myers, C. A., 284n, 297n, 301, 312n, 319, 323n, 344n, 382n, 437n, 472n, 475n
Myers, R. J., 344n, 436n, 486n, 487n, 491n
Myrdal, G., 462n, 469, 511n

Nash, J. F., Jr., 165n
National Association of Manufacturers, 49, 59
National Civic Federation, 49, 92
National income, 15; *see also* Income distribution
  per capita, 17, 18, 23
National Industrial Recovery Act of 1933, 65, 66, 195–197, 217–219, 222, 503
National Labor Board, 218–219
National Labor Relations Board, 70–72, 78, 110, 121, 145–146, 168, 175, 219–226, 230–239, 241, 244–247, 249–258
  and union jurisdiction, 233–236
  bargaining units, 152, 175n, 232–236
  decertification elections, 146, 238–239
  General Counsel, 230–232, 253
  representation (certification) elections, 78–80, 236–238
  union shop elections, 121
National Labor Union, 37, 38, 41
National Recovery Administration, 66
  codes of, 344, 407, 503, 515–516
Negroes, 23, 24, 51, 317
  and Communist Party, 103
  and racial discrimination, 115, 461–464
  and unemployment, 294–295
  economic opportunities of, 461–464
Neisser, H. P., 436n
Neufeld, M. F., 122n, 126n, 142
Norgren, P. H., 151n
Norris-LaGuardia Act, 65, 209, 212–213, 216–217, 221, 255
Northrup, H. R., 271n
Nourse, E. C., 423n

Ober, H., 360n, 362n, 367n, 369, 371
Occupation (occupational), and education, 453–457
  and income, 453–457, 459–461
  definition of, 366–368
  mobility, 295–296, 459–461
  wage differentials, 366–376
Oil, Gas and Refinery Workers 68
Open shop (American plan), 59, 60, 63, 179; *see also* Compulsory unionism
Otis, J. L., 381n
Output restriction, 198–200
  and fear of incentive rate cutting, 394–396
Overhead costs, 313, 406
Oxnam, D. W., 374n

Padway, Joseph A., 223n
Palmer, G. L., 202, 288n, 301, 343n
Parker, V. D., 173
Parnes, H. S., 284n, 301
Paschell, William, 30n, 117n
Pen, J., 165n
Pensions, 77, 485–491; *see also* Aged persons
  and collective bargaining, 489–491
  economic consequences of, 490–491
  Old Age and Survivors Insurance (OASI), 485–487
Perlman, J., 315–316n
Perlman, Selig, 49n, 54n, 55n, 58n, 60n, 63n, 86, 92n, 111, 151n, 519n
Perloff, H. S., 508n
Permit cards, 187–189, 343, 355
Persons, Stow, 90n
Petrillo, James, 75
Phelps-Brown, E. H., 401n, 402n, 403n, 404n, 406n, 408n, 427n, 430, 468n, 469
Picketing, 166, 168, 206–209, 224
Pidgeon, M. E., 466n
Pierson, F. C., 269n
Pigors, P., 382n
Pigou, A. C., 165n, 508n
Polk, J., 509n
Porter, A. R., Jr., 186n, 188n, 191n
Potofsky, Jacob, 129
Powderly, T. V., 41, 45
Preferential shop, 178–179
Prices (of products), and competition, 144
  and union policy, 345–347
  and wages, 302–319
  price-fixing of, 152–154
  regulated, 347–348
Price level, and income distribution, 422–425

Price level, and money wages, 404–408, 420

Index of Consumer Prices, 281–282, 412–417

Productivity, and unemployment, 435–441

and wages, 144, 306–308, 358–359; see also Wages; Annual Improvement factor, 407, 427–429

per man-hour, 15, 16, 20, 424

per worker (output per capita), 18

Professional associations, 352–354

Profits, 4–5, 7, 143–144, 302–319

and demand for labor, 302–319

and movement of capital, 329–330

and strikes, 166

per unit of output and overhead costs per unit, 313, 406

rate of (rate of return on capital), 143–144, 406–407

as a share of national income, 425–427

Promotion, 192

Protective legislation, see Wage and hour legislation; Child Labor

Puerto Ricans, 324, 465

Quill, Michael, 81

Quint, H. H., 90n

Quit rate, 287, 292; see also Mobility of labor

Railroad Brotherhoods, 46, 47, 75n, 96n, 109, 113, 198, 415, 480

Locomotive Fireman, Brotherhood of, 53, 116

Railway Carmen, Brotherhood of, 57

Railway Labor Act, 271–272

Raimon, R. L., 321–322n

Randolph, A. Philip, 116

Raskin, A. H., 140n

Ratchford, B. U., 328

Reading formula, 218

Reder, M. W., 319, 325n, 336n, 372n, 374n, 375n, 376, 419n, 430, 450n

Reede, A. H., 492n

Rees, Albert E., 172n, 340n, 341n, 356, 406n, 420n, 430

Rehmus, C. M., 269n

Rehn, G., 421n

Reilly, G. D., 514n, 515n

Relief (poor), 470

Republican Party, 93–94, 106, 109–110

Restriction on entry, 349–356, 452–469, 483; see also Job Rationing

Reuther, Walter, 80–83, 112, 115

Reynolds, L. G., 284n, 297n, 307n, 314n, 317n, 319, 331n, 341n, 346n, 356, 358n, 366n, 376, 413n, 457n, 494n

Riegel, J. W., 382n

"Right to work" laws, 79, 84, 107, 109, 177–178

Roberts, H. S., 67n, 68n

Roberts, Justice Owen D., 217

Robertson, D. J., 373n, 375n

Robinson, H. W., 297n

Robinson, J., 318, 326n

Roethlisberger, F. J., 199n, 202, 395n

Rogoff, N., 25, 457n

Roos, C. F., 344n, 511n

Roosevelt, President Franklin D., 69, 71–72, 80, 104, 219, 224, 500n, 503n

Roosevelt, President Theodore, 93

Rosenfarb, Joseph, 223n

Rosey, J. L., 488n

Ross, A. M., 172n, 311n, 336n, 342n, 356, 358n, 375n

Rothschild, K. W., 318

Rowe, E. K., 200n, 489n, 491n

Roy, Donald, 199n, 395n

Run-away shops, 65

Ruttenberg, H. S., 339n, 397n, 399

Safety, 197-198

Samuelson, P. A., 495

Sanders, B. S., 197n

Saposs, D. J., 111, 345n

Savage, M. D., 57n

Sayles, L. R., 123n, 142

Schilling, J. M., 263n, 274n, 277

Schulte, Sister M. Y., 509n

Schuller, G. J., 426n

Scientific management, 62

Scitovsky, T., 318, 410n

Sedgwick, R. C., 226, 248n

Seidman, Harold, 95n, 140n, 141n, 142

Seidman, Joel, 52n, 65n, 142, 240n

Seizure (emergency strikes), 266–268

Seltzer, G. H., 330–331n

Seniority (priority), 186–187, 189–192, 289, 351–352

Shackle, G. L. S., 165n

Shape-up, see Hiring hall

Shaw, Chief Justice (of Massachusetts), 204

Shaw, E. S., 410n

Sherman, J. M., 319n

Sherman Antitrust Law, 50, 94–95, 213–217, 248

Shift-preference, 192

Shister, Joseph, 46n, 117n, 142, 301, 307n

Shop Stewards, *see* Labor unions, officers
Shultz, G. P., 284n, 297n, 301, 312n, 319, 323n, 344n, 437n, 472n, 475n
Siegel, Abraham, 172n
Simon, H. A., 158n
Simons, Henry, 419n, 422n
Singer, H. W., 419n, 440n
Skill, margin for 368–376
  and education, 374
  and technological progress, 374
  see also Wage differential, occupational
Slichter, S. H., 136n, 187n, 188n, 191n, 198n, 202, 252, 254, 272n, 277, 307n, 316n, 317n, 338–339n, 340n, 342n, 344n, 345n, 349n, 350n, 356, 396n, 398n, 399n, 420n, 421, 422n, 430
Small business, 459–461
Smith, E. S., 233n
Smith, F. P., 512n
Smith-Connally Act (of 1943) (War Labor Disputes Act), 105, 225, 269
Social Darwinism, 470
Socialism (Socialists), 51, 88–93, 96–97, 99–100, 104, 109
Socialist-Labor Party, 48, 53, 96
Social insurance, 95, 98, 99n; *see also* Social Security
Social minimum wage rate (social minimum income), 324–326, 332, 376, 409, 448, 505–506, 515–516
Social reformers, 87, 471
Social Security, 470–495
  Act of 1935, 471 et seq.
  and Unemployment, 444
  Taxes, 475–477
Sole bargaining rights, 175–176, 179
Sorel, George, 98n
Soule, George, 57n
Spencer, Sir Herbert, 502n
Somers, A. R., 491n, 495
Somers, H. M., 491n, 495
Spero, H., 51n, 462n, 469
Stagecraft unions, 75n, 198
Status (and contract), 10–12
Steiner, P. O., 451n
Stephenson, F. M., 360n, 376
Sterner, R., 462n, 469
Stevenson, Adlai E., 110, 112
Steward, Ira, 37
Stewart, C. D., 18n, 19, 21, 285n, 291n, 367n
Stigler, G. J., 508n, 516
Stockyard Labor Council, 57, 58
Stolberg, Benjamin, 52n, 65n, 138n
Strasser, Adolph, 39
Strauss, G., 123n, 142

Strikes, 32, 33, 50–52, 55, 58, 60, 63, 74, 84–5; *see also* Picketing
  cost of, 171–173
  cyclical patterns in, 172–173
  emergency, 262 et seq.
  emotional factors in, 169–171
  for eight hour day, 43
  general, 59, 98
  Homestead, 47
  jurisdictional, 71–2, 78, 79, 223–224, 245–247
  man days lost in, 73
  no-strike pledge, 72, 74
  organization strikes, 168–169
  outlaw (unauthorized or unofficial), 58, 74, 161, 163, 169–171
  on public utilities, 262 et seq.
  politically-required strikes, 169
  quickie strikes, 74, 169–171
  right of government employees, to, 94
  role in collective bargaining, 156–157, 163 et seq.
  sitdown, 69, 224
  strike benefits (strike pay), 167–168
  strike power, 164–168
  statistics of, 171–173
  survival strikes, 168
  sympathetic, 48, 54, 59
  and wages, 333–335
Strike-breakers (also "Scabs"), 35, 41, 46, 54, 76, 166, 207
Suffrage (right to vote), 11, 88
Sufrin, S. C., 226, 248n, 360n, 376
Sultan, P. E., 425n
Summers, C. W., 134n, 350n, 351n
Supervision of labor, 5–7, 314
Supreme Court of the United States, 70, 71, 175, 207–217, 220, 243, 251, 502–503, 514
Swinyard, A. W., 360n, 376
Sylvis, William, 36, 37
Syndicalism, 55, 98

Taft, C. H., 346n, 356, 358n, 366n, 376, 413n, 494n
Taft, Philip, 49n, 54n, 55n, 58n, 60n, 63n, 100n, 111, 121n, 126n, 130n, 132n, 134n, 136n, 137n, 142, 151n
Taft, Senator Robert A., 232
Taft, President (later Chief Justice, U.S. Supreme Court) William Howard, 93
Taft-Hartley (Labor Management Relations Act of 1947) 75, 76, 79, 80, 84, 105, 107, 110, 145–146, 156, 162–163, 166, 175, 178–180, 198, 205–206, 208, 221, 223–226, 227–258, 265–269, 271, 276, 300

Tannenhaus, J., 208n
Tarshis, L., 410n
Taylor, F. W., 389n
Taylor, G. W., 339n, 343n, 399n
Teamsters, International Brotherhood of, 67n, 77, 80. 82, 83, 114n, 115, 116, 139, 153, 183, 225, 244
Technological progress, and margin for skill, 374
and productivity, 16–18
and unemployment, 195, 435–441
and wages, 306–308
effect on skill, 20-21, 38–39, 61-62
Ten hour day, 33
Theodore, Rose, 76n, 122n, 177n, 178n, 180n
Thomas, Brinley, 25
Thomas, L. G., 469
Tighe, Michael, 68n
Tobin, Daniel, 67n, 138n
Townsend Plan, 471
du Toit, S., 328n
Toner, Rev. J. T., 202
Trade Union Educational League (TUEL), 101
Trade Union Unity League (TUUL), 101, 102
Trotskyites, 101
Trow, Martin, 132n, 142
True, J. M., 382n, 383n, 384n, 386n, 398n, 399
Truman, President Harry S., 75, 76, 225, 230, 232, 256–257, 267
Turner, H. A., 375n
Turvey, Ralph, 421n, 430
Typographical Union, International (Printers), 36, 47, 130, 132, 185–189, 244

Ulman, Lloyd, 86, 340n, 356
Unemployment, 7, 8, 23, 293–297, 431–444
casual, 434–435
cyclical, 441–442
seasonal, 431–435
secular, 442–443
structural, 435–441
disguised, 326
and wages, 342–343, 417–419
Unemployment insurance, 471–484
and strikes, 168
benefit payments, 298, 474–475
effect on incentive to work, 472–475
eligibility, 472–474
experience rating, 476–477
financing of, 475–477
federal system of, 477–479
coverage, 478–479

Unemployment insurance, federal system of, inadequacies in, 479–484
supplementary unemployment payments, 483–484
Unfair labor practices, 219–223, 245–256
Union label, 47, 347; see also Boycott
Union Label Department of AFL-CIO, 114
Union security clauses (in collective bargaining contracts), 73, 175–180
and checkoff, 179–180
Union shop, 73, 77, 121, 177–178, 241–242
United Auto Workers, 67, 68, 69, 81–83, 112, 114, 116, 118, 135n, 183, 385, 397, 413–414, 428, 480
United Electrical Workers (UE) (see also Electrical Workers, International Union of), 81–82, 397
United Garment Workers, 52, 57
United Hatters, 214
United Labor Policy Committee, 415n
United Mine Workers, 41, 47, 61, 64–66, 68, 69, 74, 80–83, 112–113, 118
United Rubber Workers, 67, 68
United Steelworkers (Steel Workers Organization Committee, SWOC), 66, 69, 72, 82–83, 115, 116, 118, 129, 183, 383, 397, 480
United Textile Workers, 57, 68
U.S. Steel Corporation, 47, 58, 66, 69, 161, 383
U. S. Conciliation and Mediation Service, 268, 276

van Sickle, J. V., 515n
Veblen, T., 442n
Vernon, H. M., 505n
Voluntarism, 94–96, 98

Wage Differentials (wage dispersion and wage structure), 357–376
among cities, 359–363
among firms, 317–318, 330–333
among industries, 314–317, 357–359, 363–365
and ability to pay, 314–317, 337–348
and job evaluation, 377–388
and union policy, 336–348
ethnic, 464–465
intrafirm, 377–388
interregional, 363–365
north-south, 327–328
occupational, 366–367, 452–461
racial, 461–464
sexual, 465–469
"equal pay for equal work," 467–469

Wage and hour legislation, 95, 98, 280, 496–513; *see also* Fair Labor Standards Act
State laws, 497–503, 512–513
and Courts, 501–504
effect of (on employment), 507–511
effect of (on wages), 506–507
and overtime payment, 511
Wages, 194–195, 279–430; *see also* Labor Markets; Wage differentials
and ability to pay, 314–317, 329–330
and collective bargaining, 333–335
and effort, 5–6, 399
and employment, 343–345, 417–419
and "employment effect," 311–313
and ethical (equitable) considerations, 313–314, 336–338, 376–380, 386–388
and inflation, 408–417
and marginal productivity of labor, 308–313
and price controls, 412–413
and technique of production, 307–308
and union member demands, 335–337
annual, 281; *see also* Guaranteed Annual Wage
annual improvement factor (productivity increases), 416, 427–429
"freeze," 75
general level of, Chapter 16
hourly (hourly earnings), 24, 77, 280, 315–316
incentive (piece) rates, 5, 323; *see also* incentive systems)
in France, 406–407
in Germany, 406
money (wages), 281, 400–403
cyclical pattern in, 401–403
overtime, 74, 196–197, 280
patterns of, 153–154, 337–338
per unit of product, 302–308
real (wages), 24, 281, 403–404
straight time hourly earnings, 280, 332, 413
system of, 8
Wage Stabilization Board, 414–416, 428
Wagner Act (National Labor Relations Act of 1935), 7, 70, 75, 85, 145–146, 156, 162, 168, 175, 206, 219–226, 228–239, 244, 247, 251–253
Wagner, Senator Robert F., 219
Walker, K. F., 260n
Walling, L. M., 506n
Walsh-Healey Act, 347, 513–515
Wardwell, C. A. R., 327n
Ware, N. J., 34n, 35, 38n, 41n, 86, 87n

War Labor Board (WLB), 56
World War I, 72, 74, 266–268, 270, 379
World War II, 412–413
Webb, Sidney and Beatrice, 11n
Weinfeld, W., 353n, 354n
Weintraub, R. E., 327n, 330n
Weintraub, S., 318
West, P., 455n, 458n, 469
Welfare Capitalism, 62
Western Federation of Miners (also see Mine, Mill and Smelter Workers), 53–4
Wickersham, E. R., 345n
Willkie, Wendell, 80, 104
Wilson, T., 297n
Wilson, President Woodrow, 94, 109, 215
Wirtz, W. W., 252n
Witney, Fred, 208n, 213n, 226, 231n, 235n, 243n, 250n
Witte, E. E., 209n, 210n, 212n, 226
Wolfe, F. E., 51n
Woll, Matthew, 64, 141n
Wolman, Leo, 45, 56, 66
Women
earnings of, 465–469
employment status, 18, 19
legislation controlling employment, 499–500
and unemployment, 294–295
and unions, 84
Workers (see Labor)
Working Class
in Marxian Theory, 89–91
solidarity of, 54
Working Conditions, 175
Work Sharing (also see Layoff), 191–192
Work Stoppages (see Strikes and Lockouts)
Workmen's Compensation, 471, 491–492
Woytinsky, W. S. 24n, 25, 288n, 289, 294, 301, 319, 371n, 376, 382n, 402, 430, 432n, 433n, 434n, 443, 498n, 516
Wright, D. Mc., 420n
Wubnig, Arthur, 218n, 219n
Wunderlich, Frieda, 162

Yellow-dog contract (Ironclad Oath and Document, 65, 211–213
Yoder, D. 301, 382n

Zeuthen, F., 165n
Ziskind, David, 224n